The Growth of

SCANDINAVIAN LAW

BY

LESTER BERNHARDT ORFIELD

FOREWORD BY

BENJAMIN F. BOYER

THE LAWBOOK EXCHANGE, LTD.
Clark, New Jersey

ISBN 978-1-58477-180-7

Lawbook Exchange edition 2002, 2018

The quality of this reprint is equivalent to the quality of the original work.

THE LAWBOOK EXCHANGE, LTD.

33 Terminal Avenue
Clark, New Jersey 07066-1321

*Please see our website for a selection of our other publications
and fine facsimile reprints of classic works of legal history:*
www.lawbookexchange.com

Library of Congress Cataloging-in-Publication Data

Orfield, Lester B.
    The growth of Scandinavian law / by Lester Bernhardt Orfield ;
forword by Benjamin F. Boyer.
        p. cm.
    Originally published: Philadelphia: University of Pennsylvania
Press for Temple University Publications, 1953.
    Includes bibliographical references and index.
    ISBN 1-58477-180-1 (cloth: acid-free paper)
    1. Law—Scandinavia—History. I. Title.

KJ690 .074 2001
349.48—dc21

                    2001023454

Printed in the United States of America on acid-free paper

The Growth of

SCANDINAVIAN LAW

BY

LESTER BERNHARDT ORFIELD

FOREWORD BY

BENJAMIN F. BOYER

Philadelphia

UNIVERSITY OF PENNSYLVANIA PRESS FOR
TEMPLE UNIVERSITY PUBLICATIONS

1953

FOR MY
BROTHERS and SISTERS

FOREWORD

The Growth of Scandinavian Law is a unique and pioneer contribution to American legal literature. For writing it, Professor Lester B. Orfield has earned well-merited thanks.

Until the publication of this volume, one who was interested in learning of and studying the development of law and legal institutions in Denmark, Iceland, Norway, and Sweden could do so only by gathering materials through careful searching in numerous books and periodicals. Many of these publications are not found in typical American libraries. Unfortunately, too, an effective employment of many of these requires multi-lingual translating skills not customarily found among our legal scholars. As a consequence of these difficulties, Scandinavian law has been a neglected field of study.

Professor Orfield has employed his own linguistic and legal talents to provide in one handy volume the basic materials on the development of legal institutions in Scandinavia. He thus provides real orientation for a comparison of those legal institutions with our own. And he effectively supplies information not heretofore readily available in our language. As he does so, he discusses legal developments in each of the countries considered separately. Naturally he also presents a wealth of material dealing with their history, politics, and economics.

Providing, as he does, an understanding of Scandinavia for the student of comparative law, Professor Orfield also supplies materials of value to the economist, political scientist, sociologist, and historian. His extensive bibliographies will make easier the task of those who follow his lead and develop the field which he has opened up in *The Growth of Scandinavian Law*.

BENJAMIN F. BOYER

Temple University School of Law

CONTENTS

INTRODUCTION

FOLLOWING World War II there has been a rapidly growing and continuing interest among American lawyers in comparative law.[1] In 1950 the first American case book on comparative law was published by Professor Rudolf B. Schlesinger of Cornell University.[2] This casebook takes its materials largely from the law of France, Germany and Switzerland. Italian law has received some attention. Russian law, in view of the role played by Soviet Russia in world affairs since World War II, is now coming in for its share of attention. In 1950, Phanor J. Eder published a valuable survey of Latin-American law, comparing it with the law of the United States.[3]

Unhappily the law of the Scandinavian states has attracted but little attention.[4] A plausible reason may be that their populations are small, Sweden having about seven millions, Denmark four millions, Norway three millions and Iceland 140,000. But their total population is over fourteen millions. Since much of their law is similar, account may well be taken of the latter figure rather than the population of each separate country. But there are additional considerations of the highest importance which should not be overlooked. There are no states more democratic in outlook than the Scandinavian states. There are no states having a higher rate of literacy. There are no states with more comprehensive and progressive social legislation. There are no states which have cooperated for so long a time and so continously and so comprehensively in the adoption of uniform laws. There are few if any states which afford such excellent examples of law based largely on custom and usage as distinguished from Anglo-American case-law and continental codes. There are few if any states which have such full and accurate statements of the written law going back so many centuries. A writer has recently pointed out that "there is no single volume presentation of the most important features of the social, political, and economic systems of Scandinavia."[5] Likewise there has been no presentation in English, whether in one or more volumes, of the growth of Scandinavian law. A distinguished authority on comparative law has stated: "A course in comparative law to be really worth while should give the student above all an insight into the great historical, political, social, and economic forces which have shaped and still shape the laws of the western civilization and have molded and still mold their common and divergent characteristics."[6] The author has endeavored to bear this suggestion in mind.

The Scandinavians have been in the United States long enough so that they are commencing to make an impact on higher education. There are at the present time a considerable number of them teaching in the American law schools. Most of such teachers have made their very respectable contributions in the field of local American law. Many of them as second and third generation Americans are not familiar with the Scandinavian languages. The author of this book therefore feels that he has a real opportunity to serve as a pioneer in introducing Scandinavian law to the United States. Three of his grandparents came from Norway and one from Denmark. He spoke almost only Norwegian until he entered the public schools, studied Norwegian at Minneapolis, Central High School where he received in 1921 the Dr. Ivar Sivertsen prize annually awarded to the best student of Norwegian, and has been a regular reader of the *Nordisk Tidende,* the leading Norwegian American newspaper, during the last decade. He has therefore been able to read the Scandinavian law and legal literature in the original untranslated form. He has assisted an American appellate court in finding and translating the applicable Danish law in two cases.[7] He has made use of the very full collections of Scandinavian laws and legal literature in the Congressional Library. He has also had access to the excellent Scandinavian materials in the Library of the University of Pennsylvania Law School. Mr. Axel Teisen, a leading American writer on Scandinavian law, presented a considerable collection of Scandinavian legal materials to the latter library.

At the present time it is quite frequently stated that there are five Scandinavian states: Denmark, Finland, Iceland, Norway, and Sweden. This volume does not treat Finland as a Scandinavian state.[8] From some points of view, it is true, Finland is a Scandinavian state. It has participated to some extent in the drafting and adoption of uniform Scandinavian laws. As in the other four Scandinavian states the Lutheran Church is the state church and 96 per cent of the Finns are Lutherans. Finland was under Swedish rule for almost six centuries prior to 1809. But racially and perhaps culturally the Finns are quite different from the other Scandinavians. Only ten per cent of its population is Swedish. Its language is entirely dissimilar, whereas Danes, Norwegians and Swedes have no difficulty in understanding each other. The *American-Scandinavian Review* does not treat Finland as a Scandinavian state, nor does Arneson[9] or Friis[10] or Hovde.[11] Scott,[12] in treating Finland as Scandinavian, seems to depart from the more usual practice. The author would add, with the greatest emphasis, that the exclusion of Finland from the Scandinavian category is not intended as implying that its law, history, government and culture are not equally significant.

Much space has been devoted to the international relations of each Scandinavian state. It is impossible to understand the present legal system of the Scandinavian states without some knowledge as to how they emerged into their present positions. Students of international law and diplomacy are of course vitally interested in how the present states of the world came to attain their status as states. Yet the literature on the subject is meager and scattered in many books and articles. It therefore seemed desirable to bring all these materials into one single volume. The international relations of each Scandinavian state has been considered separately and in such a manner that one interested in the international relations of only one state need not read the chapters dealing with the other Scandinavian states. This has inevitably involved a certain amount of overlapping, yet has made for clarity and saving the time of those interested in studying single Scandinavian states rather than all or several of them.

The survey of the international relations of the Scandinavian states reveals that their relations have been chiefly with each other. Prior to the Viking period and even during such period, one cannot always be sure that a given king or chieftain is Danish, Norwegian, or Swedish. King Gorm, the first king of all Denmark, seems to have been the son of a Norwegian chieftain. King Harold Fairhair, the first king of all Norway, was a descendant of Swedish kings, the son of a Danish princess, and married a Danish princess. Iceland was settled by Norwegians. Finland was a part of Sweden from 1249 to 1809. Denmark and Norway were ruled by a common king from 1028 to 1035, and from 1042 to 1047. Iceland became a part of Norway in 1262. There was a union between Norway and Sweden from 1319 to 1371. The Kalmar Union between all five Scandinavian states existed from 1397 to 1521. Denmark and Norway were united from 1380 to 1814. Norway and Sweden had a union between 1814 and 1905. The last union was that between Iceland and Denmark from 1918 to 1944; Iceland had been ruled as a Danish province from 1536 to 1918, following Norwegian rule from 1262 to 1536. Much of what is now Swedish territory was formerly held by Denmark and Norway. Prior to 1645 Gotland and Ösel had been Danish, and Härjedalen and Jämtland had been Norwegian. Prior to 1658 Blekinge, Halland and Skåne had been Danish, and Bohuslän had been Norwegian. Bornholm, now Danish, was Swedish between 1658 and 1660. Trondheim, now Norwegian, was Swedish between 1658 and 1660.

But the Scandinavian states have for more than a thousand years had numerous and important contacts with the other European states.

Missionaries from England had a great deal to do with the Christianization of Norway and Sweden. Prior to 1300, trade with England was of very great proportions. King Canute with headquarters in England, ruled over a large empire including Denmark and Norway. Shortly before the Norman Conquest, King Harald the Hard of Norway lost the historic battle of Stamford Bridge in England. From 1250 to 1550 the Hanseatic League dominated Scandinavian commerce. The Protestant Reformation in the sixteenth century meant that religious ties with the Germans would henceforth be strong. The Thirty Years' War of the seventeenth century resulted in close ties between France and Sweden who were the guarantors of the peace. The victory of the Russians over the Swedes at Poltava in 1709 meant that Russia had emerged as a dangerous neighbor, which a century later took Finland from Sweden. Denmark became involved on the French side in the Napoleonic wars with the result that she lost Norway. From this time the Scandinavians remained neutral and at peace until 1940 except that in 1864 Denmark lost Schleswig-Holstein to Germany. The Scandinavian states now face the menace of Soviet Russia. Denmark, Iceland and Norway are now aligned with the western powers in the Atlantic Pact. Sweden is endeavoring to remain neutral. The Scandinavian states have been members of the League of Nations and the United Nations. Events since the end of World War I have brought the Scandinavian states into wider world contacts. They have brought them into closer relations with the United States. As Bryn J. Hovde has said so well: "The peoples of Scandinavia pass the middle of the twentieth century bound together by almost every tie that is possible between sovereign states. They are very near in their cultures and eagerly exchange their material goods and have the same interest in those of the whole wide world. They represent to a paramount degree the same rights of person and of civic action, even though upon the American escutcheon there is still the blot of racial prejudice. They have the same desire for peace, though not at any price."[13]

Lawyers in the United States with some familiarity with Continental law are accustomed to thinking of the world's legal systems as divided into two major types: common law based on judicial decisions and codes. They overlook the fact that there may be a third possible type, namely, customary law, based on the customs, usages and practices of the community rather than of the courts of the community. The Scandinavian states have such a legal basis. Despite much legislation by the parliaments and despite numerous uniform Scandinavian laws adopted during the past eighty years, much of the law, particularly private law, remains customary. Students of comparative law, legal history, and legal philosophy may with profit examine the Scandinavian customary law.

The Scandinavian states have had national codes some of which go back more than seven centuries. The first of these is the Danish Code of 1240, known as the Jutland Code, promulgated by King Valdemar Victorious. Next is the Norwegian Code of 1275 promulgated by King Magnus Lawmender. This was shortly followed by the Icelandic Code of 1281, known as the *Jonsbok*. Last of the early codes was the Swedish Code of 1347 promulgated by King Magnus Eriksson. These were followed by the codes of modern times. Denmark was the first to adopt its modern code, in 1683, known as King Christian V's Danish Law. This code was shortly followed by the Norwegian Code of 1688, closely modeled on the Danish Code, and known as King Christian V's Norwegian Law. The last modern code was the Swedish Code of 1734. While there was much talk about a modern code for Iceland, none was ever approved by the King of Denmark-Norway. Each of the modern Scandinavian codes has some of its provisions surviving in the law of today. A student of Scandinavian law should have some acquaintance with these codes.

Though the Scandinavian states have no such tremendous masses of case-law as the United States and England, it should be pointed out that during the past century they have developed a sizable and significant body of judicial precedents. Doubtless they feel less bound by the doctrine of *stare decisis* than American courts, though some of them seem to be moving towards the Anglo-American approach. They are less prone to draw sharp distinctions between *obiter dicta* and the *ratio decidendi*.

Each of the Scandinavian states has a written constitution. The oldest is the Swedish constitution of 1809, second in age only to the American Constitution. Next is the Norwegian constitution of 1814, drafted after a careful study of the American Constitution. Third is the Danish constitution of 1849, later supplanted by the constitution of 1915. Iceland has the newest constitution, that of 1944. Of particular interest are the constitutional provisions concerning civil liberties, the legislative bodies, the courts, and amendment of the constitution. In general, save in Norway, the Scandinavian courts do not pass on the the constitutionality of statutes. The Norwegian constitution is unique in providing that constitutional amendments shall not violate the spirit of the existing constitution.

Students of the legislative process may well examine the legislative process in the Scandinavian states. Since each state is thoroughly democratic each has a parliament independent of the executive. The Icelandic parliament is the oldest in the world going back to 930. Next oldest is the Swedish parliament going back to 1435. The Norwegian parliament was established in 1814 and the Danish in 1849. Parliamentary government, in the sense of a responsible ministry chosen from the majority party in the lower chamber, was established in Norway in 1884, in Denmark in 1901 and in Sweden in 1917. Norway has in effect a unicameral legislature as the voters select but a single body which subsequently divides itself into two divisions. Iceland has followed the Norwegian example. There is a strong movement in Denmark to eliminate the upper chamber. The Scandinavian parliaments are unique in having but a small handful of communist members. At the same time from 1932 to 1951 the labor parties have been in control in Denmark, Norway, and Sweden for all but brief periods. The year 1951 may mark a trend towards a more conservative attitude. In Denmark the labor party government was replaced by a coalition of Liberals and Conservatives. In Sweden the labor party government formed a coalition with the Farmers' party and the latter party received four of the sixteen seats in the new cabinet. At the 1949 elections in Iceland the Labor party elected the least members of the parliament of the four parties and the Conservatives elected the most.

Each of the Scandinavian states has well developed and independent courts. Judges are appointed for life, subject to retirement after reaching a certain age. Each has a supreme court at the head of its judicial system. Sweden has six intermediate courts of appeal, Norway five and Denmark two. At the bottom of the judicial hierarchy are the local judges and the city courts. Sweden is unique in having a supreme administrative court. Juries have been introduced in the more serious criminal cases in Denmark and Norway. Lay judges sit in the local courts with the professional judges and sometimes sit in the intermediate appellate courts. Denmark and Norway have pioneered in the established of conciliation tribunals.

The Scandinavian states have developed effective systems of local government beginning in the nineteenth century. The largest local unit corresponds to the American county. The lowest unit is the rural parish or district. The national government exercises close control and supervision over the local units, through the ministry and the county governors who are appointed by the ministry. There is wide public ownership of water, gas and electric utilities and even of movie theaters.

It is interesting to compare the relation of church and state in the Scandinavian states prior to the Protestant Reformation with the relation in other European states. On the whole the Scandinavian states seem to have enjoyed greater independence than most other states. The

Protestant Reformation may well be compared with that in England and Germany. For a considerable time there was little tolerance of Protestants who did not belong to the Lutheran State Church. A little over a century ago there was even little tolerance of Lutherans who did not belong to the Lutheran State Church. During the past century there has been virtually no discrimination against Protestant dissenters. By about 1850 legal discriminations against Jews had been eliminated. During the nineteenth century most of the serious discriminations against Roman Catholics were abolished. For the past century they have been able to hold regular church services. Denmark has long permitted the establishment of monasteries and convents. A Swedish statute of 1951 permits religious orders to found monasteries and convents. The Norwegian Constitution still provides that Jesuits shall not be tolerated, but there is a strong movement to repeal this provision. The state church is largely supervised by a member of the ministry. Recently there has been a movement to give the state church more autonomy.

In view of the high literacy rate and the democratic attitude of the Scandinavian states their laws as to education deserve close scrutiny. For a century there has been compulsory elementary school education. High schools have been established and technical training has been incorporated in their curricula. American promoters of adult education have pointed to the Scandinavian folk schools.

The Scandinavian law concerning agriculture has been such as to promote ownership by the farmer of the farm which he operates. By this time more than ninety per cent of Scandinavian farmers own their farms. In the United States in 1932 about 58 per cent of the farmers owned their farms. By 1952 this percentage had increased to seventy-five. The Scandinavian farm cooperatives have been outstandingly successful.

A study of the growth of criminal law in the Scandinavian states indicates that there are many close parallels with the growth of the criminal law in England. Concepts of private vengeance existed contemporaneously in both groups. There was outlawry, ordeals, and the use of compurgators and oath helpers in both groups. Movements to eliminate the wide use of the death penalty occurred side by side in both groups. A century ago the Scandinavians became interested in American methods of prison administration. During the past century all the Scandinavian states have developed modern codes of substantive and of procedural criminal law, which deserve study in other states when modernization of the criminal law is being attempted. The Scandinavian states have developed a unique alternative for the juvenile courts, namely, the use of committees and boards instead of courts. Criminal penalties are light, yet the Scandinavian states have a much lower percentage of crime than the United States. Scandinavian criminal procedure has moved away from the inquisitorial principle to the accusatorial.

The Scandinavian codes of civil procedure deserve attention. The influence of German ideas on early Swedish procedure, and indirectly that of Italian ideas must interest students of legal history and comparative law. Many abortive efforts were made in the nineteenth century to secure the preparation and adoption of modern codes. In 1915 a Norwegian code emerged, in 1916 a Danish, and in 1942 a Swedish. Great care was exercised in their formulation. Committees of outstanding experts worked continuously over long periods of time before the codes were presented to the parliaments for adoption, and the codes were not placed into operation until some time after their approval by the parliaments. The Norwegian code of 1915 went into effect in 1927, and the Swedish of 1942 went into effect in 1948. The codes were made familiar to the bar by numerous meetings held throughout the states with addresses and lectures and discussions by judges, professors and leading practitioners.

Possibly there is no branch of Scandinavian law of such interest for Americans as their social legislation. There is an ever growing literature in English concerning Scandinavian labor and labor unions, workmen's compensation, unemployment insurance, general assistance, child and family welfare, old age insurance and pensions, disability insurance, health insurance, medical care, housing and liquor control. The Scandinavian states were among the first to attack and outlaw negro slavery. Legal equality was conferred on women either simultaneously or before it was done in the United States and England. The Scandinavian divorce laws go further in permitting divorce on the basis of tempermental incompatibility of the parties, mutual consent of the parties, or living apart than any other states in the world. Their laws on illegitimacy offer models for the rest of the world. The labor courts and labor laws of Denmark, Norway and Sweden have attracted the attention of several American writers. A recent survey under the auspices of the United Nations reveals that the Scandinavian states are among the leaders in making numerous types of family allowances. When the problem of health insurance is considered in the United States, its outstanding and unqualified success in the Scandinavian states should not be overlooked. Students of housing may learn much from the Scandinavian states with respect to housing cooperatives, planning and house design, housing of the elderly, aid to large families, and anticipatory acquisition of land sites for housing. The Swedish system of liquor control offers one of the finest models. American students of social legislation may learn much from the excellent and comprehensive *Social Denmark* published in English in 1947.

The first meeting of the National Conference of Commissioners on Uniform State Laws in the United States was held in 1892. The Canadian Conference on Uniformity of Legislation was organized in 1918. The Scandinavian states commenced the drafting of uniform Scandinavian laws in 1872. By the present time much of the old customary Scandinavian private law has been replaced by uniform Scandinavian statutes. Notable are the monetary convention of 1872, the Bank Drafts Act of 1880, the Navigation Act of 1892, the Bank Check Act of 1897, the Act on Purchase and Selling of 1905-1907, the 1917 Acts on contracts, commissions, commercial agencies, commercial travelling and Hire and Purchase, the Marriage and Divorce Acts of 1918-1925, the Insurance Act of 1931, the Bankruptcy Act of 1935 and acts regulating trade marks, trade registers, air traffic and various aspects of property. There has also been much cooperation in social legislation. Common rules of conflict of laws looking to domicile rather than nationality have been adopted for marriage, adoption, guardianship, succession, wills and administration. Recently there has been interest in the drafting of uniform acts concerning purchases on credit and responsibility for the torts of government employees. Later on there is likely to be consideration of prescription, sales, arbitration agreements and the law of names. It seems fair to conclude that the laws of the Scandinavian states resemble each other more closely than the laws of the forty-eight American states and that no other states have had a finer record of continous cooperation.

In recent years American legal scholars have become interested in legal education in the major continental countries such as France and Germany. It is likely that much of value may be learned from the history and experience of the Scandinavian university law schools. The University of Uppsala in Sweden was founded in 1477 and that of Copenhagen in 1479. In 1668 the University of Lund in Sweden was founded. The University of Oslo was established in 1811, and the University of Iceland in 1911. Law is taught at the University of Stockholm. The most recent Scandinavian university offering courses in law is that of Aarhus in Denmark founded in 1928. Matters of interest are the courses offered, the methods of instruction, the emphasis on theory, the qualifications of professors, the use of lectures in preference to the case method, the offering of socio-economic subjects in the law schools, the preparation of treatises and law journal articles by the faculty members and the participation of faculty members on commissions preparing statutes and in general governmental affairs.

There have been virtually no studies in English of the legal profession and its organization in the Scandinavian states. One may inquire whether or not the bar associations are purely private and voluntary in character. What are the requisites for admission to the bar? Under whose auspices is one admitted to the bar? What are the methods of disciplining lawyers?

The Scandinavian states go very far in providing legal service for low income groups. American lawyers may with profit examine the Swedish system. In some of the Scandinavian states the courts may exempt a party from all the costs of litigation in both civil and criminal cases and even the attorney's fees may be paid by the state. In Denmark and Norway persons accused of crime are given free legal services and incidental expenses irrespective of financial status. In Sweden the groups corresponding to American legal aid societies are governmental undertakings. Moreover, unlike the American legal aid societies they are not limited to indigents. They represent plaintiffs as well as defendants, handle appeals and render service outside the immediate area. The Swedish system combines care of the indigent with care of low income groups, all within one single system.

The study of jurisprudence and legal philosophy may be enriched by comparison with the Scandinavian literature of legal philosophy. The writings of Vilhelm Lundstedt of the University of Uppsala and Karl Olivecrona of the University of Lund have frequently appeared in English both by way of general treatise and law review articles. The same may be said of Alf Ross of the University of Copenhagen. Unfortunately not available in English are the writings of Anders Örsted, the nineteenth century Dane who is often referred to as the founder of modern Danish and Norwegian jurisprudence. Also not available in English are the writings of Anton Schweigaard who was second only to Örsted in his influence on Norwegian legal philosophy. The author has attempted to introduce the names of some of the key figures in legal philosophy of each of the Scandinavian states. Legal historians may also profit by examining Scandinavian legal history. The author has therefore made some references to outstanding authors and treatises in that field.

The author would make it crystal clear that he is not proposing any wholesale copying of Scandinavian law in the United States. The Scandinavian states have no problems of homogeneity as to race and religion. Aside from a small number of Lapps in Norway and Sweden there are no sharp racial differences. Ninety-seven per cent of the people are Lutherans. Illiteracy has been virtually wiped out, as have great differences in wealth. An attitude somewhere between the two extremes of wholesale copying and wholesale rejection seems the sanest one to adopt. In the words of Phanor J. Eder: "In fine, foreign law can serve principally as a stimulus to provoke new currents of ideas. It should never be slavishly copied. The marrow of it should be extracted and then mixed with our home-grown products; only then is it a dish fit to eat, and it must be thoroughly digested."[14]

This volume is not a study made principally from original sources. Primary sources have been tapped at a good many points. But the general objective is to interpret already available, but generally scattered, materials. Obviously one could spend a lifetime studying the law of any one of the four Scandinavian states. It is the hope of the author that others will be stimulated to make more detailed and comprehensive studies of single states, or to select certain specific topics such as Contracts, Torts, or Sales. It is to be hoped that the new *American Journal of Comparative Law* will point the way to continued study of Scandinavian law.[15]

The writing of this book was commenced in January, 1950. Bernhard Gomard, a graduate of the University of Copenhagen Law School and a graduate student in the Harvard Law School from 1951 to 1952, has offered some suggestions as to Danish law. Godtfred Holmvang, a graduate of the University of Oslo Law School, and a graduate student in the Harvard Law School from 1950 to 1951, has offered some suggestions as to Norwegian law.

Two of the chapters were published in 1950 and 1951 in law reviews. The Chapter on Danish law appeared in the *Miami Law Quarterly* and that on Icelandic law in the *Dickinson Law Review*. These reviews have graciously consented to the reprinting. The chapters on Norwegian and Swedish law have been added. They have not been previously published.

Gratitude is due to the Congressional Library and to the University of Pennsylvania Law School for the use of their libraries. The author is deeply indebted to Temple University for its making possible the achievement of a long cherished dream. Grateful acknowledgment is made to Dean Benjamin F. Boyer for encouragement in the publication of this book and for writing the Foreword.

LESTER BERNHARDT ORFIELD

Philadelphia, Pennsylvania
June 5, 1952

[1] See the list of 26 American law schools offering instruction in comparative law in 1950 in John R. Stevenson, "Comparative and Foreign Law in American Law Schools," 50 *Col. L. Rev.* 613, 623 (1950).

[2] *Comparative Law Cases and Materials*, Foundation Press (1950).

[3] *A Comparative Survey of Anglo-American and Latin-American Law*, New York: New York University Press (1950).

[4] As "late as 1932 the Committee of the American Historical Association on the

Planning and Research pointed to Scandinavian history as a neglected field." B. J. Hovde, *The Scandinavian Countries, 1720-1865,* p. 7 (1948). In 1858 a writer had pointed out that the "history of no part of Europe is less familiar to the general mind." Paul Sinding, *History of Scandinavia,* p. XI (1858).

[5] Henning Friis, *Scandinavia Between East and West,* p. IX (1950).

[6] Stefan A. Riesenfeld, Book Review, 3 *J. Leg. Ed.* 620, 622 (1951).

[7] Callwood v. Kean, 189 F. 2d 565, 574-582 (3rd Cir. 1951); Burch v. Burch, 195 F. 2d 799, 805-808 (3rd Cir. 1952).

[8] All the juridical literature concerning Finland during the period 1809-1948, with the titles of some 20,000 books and articles, is listed in *Litterature Juridique de la Finlande,* Helsinki. The book is in French, Finnish and Swedish, and was prepared under the direction of Dean V. Merikoski of the Faculty of Law of Helsinki University.

[9] Ben A. Arneson, *The Democratic Monarchies of Scandinavia* (2d ed. 1949).

[10] Henning Friis, *Scandinavia Between East and West* (1950).

[11] Bryn J. Hovde, *The Scandinavian Countries, 1720-1865* (1948).

[12] Franklin D. Scott, *The United States and Scandinavia* (1950). See in accord with Scott, S. M. Toyne, *The Scandinavians in History* (1948).

[13] Henning Friis, *Scandinavia Between East and West,* pp. 349-50 (1950).

[14] Phanor J. Eder, *A Comparative Survey of Anglo-American and Latin-American Law,* p. 159 (1950).

[15] See Hessel E. Yntema, "The American Journal of Comparative Law," 46 Am. J. Int. L. 343 (1952).

CHAPTER I

DANISH LAW

THE Danes were the first Scandinavians to settle in America, the earliest authenticated arrival occurring in 1611. In 1639 Jonas Bronck and others settled along the Harlem River, later called "Bronx." Danes joined the Dutch in New York and the Swedish colony in Maryland and Pennsylvania, while still others joined the Moravian colonies in North Carolina and Pennsylvania. From 1820 to June 30, 1948, a total of 338,085 Danes came to the United States.[1]

Of the 443,815 Danes in the United States in 1940, 305,640 were native-born and 138,175 foreign-born. Of the foreign-born Danes, 19,726 were in California, 14,304 in New York, 13,869 in Illinois, and over 10,000 each in Iowa and Minnesota. A larger proportion of Danes have become naturalized than any other group, the percentage being 78.1 compared with 64.6 for all foreign-born.[2]

About one-half of the Danes in the United States own farms, and nearly 60 per cent are in agricultural pursuits. The first permanent farm settlement was in 1845 in Waukesha County near Milwaukee. Later, Danish farmers came to Minnesota, Iowa, Nebraska, Kansas and the Dakotas.

International Relations

It has frequently been pointed out that Denmark is the oldest state in Europe. While the "Merovingians were still fragmenting the ruins of the Western Roman Empire along evanescent and uncertain lines—while Germany was still a seething mass of half-civilized tribal states—while England was a kaleidoscope of petty monarchies, Denmark was already a united nation, with a body of common traditions and experience."[3] Until about three thousand years ago the Teutonic races were found only in the Old-Danish countries.[4] The separation of the Scandinavian tribes from the Germanic tribes occurred about seventeen hundred to two thousand years ago.[5] The poem "Beowulf" dating from 700 refers to Denmark as an existing kingdom. By 800 most of Scandinavia had been colonized from Denmark.

In 449 Hengest, a Dane, at the head of a group of Jutes, Angles, other Danes, Saxons, Frisians and Franks, came to England.[6] With his landing on the Isle of Thanet the historian Green states, "English history begins." The Jutes, who came from Jutland, conquered Kent. The Angles

1

who came from Angel in Slesvig, conquered northeast Britain including East Anglia, Mercia and Northumberland, and gave England its name. The Saxons from Holstein conquered southern England.

Shortly before 810, Godfrey, the strong Danish king in Slesvig, fought Charlemagne in Frisian territory and later along the Elbe River.[7] His successor, Hemming, made peace in 811. The Eider River was made the boundary line. Charlemagne was forced to grant Walcheren in fief to the Danes, who thus secured control of the mouth of the Rhine. Danish rule extended into southern Norway and into Skåne and other areas in southern Sweden. In 826 King Harold I secured the Weser territory, south of the Eider River, thus gaining a foothold in the Empire. In 845 Godfrey's son, Erik, sacked and burned Hamburg.

Later Danish invasions of England following those of 449 A.D. came over three centuries later.[8] In 790 they came to Wessex and in 793 to Northumbria. From 840 to 854 they raided the east and south coasts.[9] In 851 they captured London and Canterbury, and a period of settlement lasting from 851 to 897 began. The Danes dominated in southern and eastern England and vied with the Norwegians in northern England, the other settlers being predominantly Norwegian.[10] It should be noted that the invasions before 900 were not by the Danish or Norwegian governments as there were no truly central governments for the entire nations in Denmark and Norway before 900.

In 845 Ragnar Lodbrog, ancestor of Danish and Swedish kings, took Rouen and conquered Paris. About 860 his sons made an eventful expedition to Spain, North Africa, Italy, and Greece. In 866 a Viking fleet sailed from France to Kent. It soon conquered York and the Danish "five-boroughs," Lincoln, Derby, Nottingham, Stamford, and Leicester. The Danes later conquered East Anglia and Mercia and in 872 London. Most of England except Wessex was for a time in Danish hands and in 886 a large area was placed under the Danish rule known as the Dane-law,[11] following a treaty made with King Alfred the Great.[12] The Dane-law became one of the three great divisions of English law so recognized by the laws of Henry I.

In 891 the Danish Vikings were defeated after attacking Paris in 886 by the German king, Arnulf, at Louvain. From 892 to 896 the same Danish army sought to conquer England but was held in check by Alfred the Great. No further Danish attacks on England were made until 982. The Danes now turned their attention to France, and in 911 Rollo received Normandy as a fief from Charles the Simple.

Between 900 and 940 King Gorm the Old built the rampart of Dannevirke in Slesvig to protect Denmark from the Germans. He completed the unification of Denmark though each province retained its own law.[13] He pressed a claim to Vestfold in Norway.[14] About 920 he was defeated by the German Emperor and forced to permit Christianity in Denmark. In 941 his son Canute was killed on a viking expedition to England. The first Norwegian king, Harold the Fairhaired (872-930) married a Danish Princess, but the Danish claims to southern Norway were not surrendered. Eirik (930-934), the second Norwegian king, also married a Danish princess, Gunhild. After Eirik's death, the Danish king, Harold Bluetooth (950-985), tried to place Gunhild's son on the Norwegian throne, but succeeded only in 961.[15] But when the latter assumed control over Viken claimed by the Danish king, Harold contrived to have him ousted in 970.[16] Harold now entered Norway and retained eastern Norway, the Uplands and Viken, ruling through local Norwegian chiefs. The remainder of Norway was ruled by Haakon of Lade, as the jarl of the Danish king. Haakon eventually revolted and was able to defeat a Danish fleet in 994.

In 974 King Harold was compelled to reaffirm his vassalship to the Holy Roman Empire and to promise to introduce Christianity. In 983 he gave aid to an ousted Swedish king. He built a fortress at Jomsburg on the island of Rügen near Pomerania, which later became the starting point for viking raids.

King Harold, having consolidated Denmark and secured an overlordship in Norway, began an attack on England in 982. His successor, Sweyn (985-1014), attacked England and in 991 the first tribute or Dane-geld was paid.[17] In 994 he joined Olaf Tryggvason of Norway in attacking London and the second Dane-geld was paid. In 1000 the Danes supported by the sons of the prior Norwegian ruler, Haakon, and the Swedish king, defeated Olaf, who had refused to recognize Danish claims to Norway. As a result the Danes retained the Vik region to Bohuslän and the personal obligation of the two jarls of Lade. In 1002 the English paid a third Dane-geld to Denmark. Sweyn attempted to conquer England, was for many years its virtual ruler, and was recognized as king in 1014.

Following Sweyn's death his son Canute the Great (1018-1035) reasserted Danish rule over England and in 1024 threatened to enforce a claim to Norway. Olaf, king of Norway, allied himself with Sweden and attacked Denmark. In 1028 Canute was recognized as king of Norway.[18] Canute sent his son Sweyn to rule there until 1035 when the Danes were expelled. Canute considered England the principal realm and resided there. He conquered much of the Baltic from the Wends, a Slavic race. Ruling over England, Denmark, Norway, southern Sweden, southern Scotland and the Baltic as far as Esthonia, he was probably the most powerful ruler in Europe. His sons Harold and Harthacanut ruled over

England from 1035 to 1042, the last period of Danish rule in England.

The Danes made several important contributions to English law.[19] First was the concept of personal freedom. Second was the concept of central taxation through the Dane-geld. Thirdly it supplied one of the three main bodies of English customary law—the Dane-law, the Mercian law, and the West Saxon law. The way was made easy for the establishment of the grand jury, as the Danes had a somewhat similar accusatorial group.[20] The very word "law" is itself of Danish origin, the Danish word being *lov*.[21]

On the death of Harthacanut, King Magnus the Good, of Norway, succeeded under a treaty as King of Denmark in 1042 and reigned there until 1047.[22] On Magnus' death his successor to the Norwegian throne, Harold the Hard, also claimed Denmark and waged war to that end for seventeen years. But Canute's nephew, Sweyn Esthrithson (1047-1074), kept the Danish throne which Magnus had bequeathed to him. In 1066 Sweyn claimed the throne of England, and in 1067 attacked Norway. In 1085 the Danes sent a fleet to England which returned after merely taking some booty. This was the last viking attack on England.[23] The Wends made many successful attacks on Denmark, continuing to do so for the next century and a half.

Denmark early became a transit-country.[24] Denmark was the junction between the northern route from western Europe to the Baltic and the route starting in Central Europe on the Danube and proceeding via the Elbe, the Rhone and the Oder as far as Scandinavia. It was long the Danish external policy to command the foreign banks of these trade routes, their markets and seaports. On the North Sea this brought Denmark into conflict with England and the Netherlands. On the Skagerrack it brought her into conflict with Norway. On the Baltic it brought her into conflict with the Germans and the Swedes.

In 1101 following a war between Norway and Sweden a peace meeting was held at Konghelle. King Erik the Evergood (1095-1103) of Denmark participated as mediator. A treaty was signed constituting the first peace treaty of the three Scandinavian kings.[25]

About the year 900 Henry the Fowler, Emperor of Germany, founded the margraviate of Slesvig. In 1026 Canute the Great induced the Emperor to renounce his claims to the margraviate, and his daughter married the son of the Emperor.[26] About 1125 Canute Lavard secured Slesvig for the Danish crown, and became its duke or earl.[27]

Following the murder of Canute Lavard in 1131 his friend, the German emperor, compelled the murderer who was heir to the Danish throne to do homage to the emperor as liege lord of Denmark, and a papal bull brought the Scandinavian countries under the archbishopric of Hamburg-Bremen. In 1134 King Erik Emune successfully aided a rival king of Norway.[28] Something close to anarchy prevailed in Denmark just before Valdemar the Great (1157-1182) became king.[29]

In 1162 Valdemar assisted a successful revolt against the king of Norway on a promise of receiving the Vik area, which was confirmed in 1171.[30] He fought the Wends and in 1169 conquered Rügen, an island north of Germany, and founded Danzig.[31] Under Canute (1182-1202) Danish forces invaded nearly all of Pomerania and Mecklenburg and conquered territory in Esthonia.[32] Holstein, Lübeck, Hamburg and Lauenburg had to submit to Denmark, and Schwerin acknowledged its vassalage.

Valdemar Victorious (1202-1241) seized the cities of Hamburg and Lübeck. In 1214 Emperor Frederick II ceded to Denmark all land north of the Elbe and the Elde, and France sought a marriage with the widowed king. In 1219 in a crusade for Christianity Esthonia was conquered and inroads made on Livonia.[33] The Mongols were thus prevented from breaking beyond the Baltic. Denmark in 1219 included Holstein, Ditmarsch, Lauenburg, Schwerin, Mecklenburg, Rügen, Pomerania, Ösel, and parts of Prussia and Curland. Denmark was thus again an empire, to retain which a four-century struggle ensued. But in 1227, following a capture of the king while he was hunting, Denmark lost her north German conquests except Rügen and Esthonia, and the Eider River was again the boundary line.[34]

Erik IV (1241-1250) gave Slesvig to his brother Abel. In 1252 when King Christopher I succeeded his brother Abel, Slesvig was lost to the Danish crown, as the dukedom passed to the descendants of Abel.[35]

A military expedition was sent to Esthonia in 1249, and the Frisians were attacked in 1252. A brief war with Norway was fought in 1256 and 1257. The Norwegian fleet was so large as to inspire Denmark to make peace on Norway's terms without venturing a battle.[36] The son of the Norwegian king married the daughter of the Danish king. As the Danish king failed to pay the dowry, the Norwegian fleet attacked in Skåne in 1274. It was defeated, but Norwegian attacks continued for four decades.[37] In 1275 Denmark intervened in a civil war in Sweden. In 1289 following the assassination of the Danish king, the assassins received refuge in Norway, and Norway declared war on Denmark.[38] An armistice was signed in 1295. In 1309 the long war was ended by the Treaty of Copenhagen, Halland being ceded by Denmark to Norway. In 1310 Denmark aided the Swedish king against his rebellious brothers.

In the first half of the fourteenth century the Count of Holstein took over the Danish border province of Slesvig.[39] Slesvig was now no longer under Danish administration. This was the first time Slesvig was given

to the German Holstein. In 1315 there began the practice of mortgaging
Danish provinces to north German princes. In 1319 Christopher II, to
pay his accession debts, mortgaged Halland to Knud Porse, and in 1326
it was ceded to him.[40] In 1326 King Valdemar of Slesvig ceded away
much of Denmark,[41] and in 1330 much the same occurred. In 1332
Count Johann of Ploen mortgaged Skåne and Blekinge to Sweden.[42]

From 1332 to 1340 there was no king or regent or government in
Denmark. The nobles who held most of Denmark were foreigners, chiefly
German from Holstein and Mecklenburg who were under feudal obliga-
tions to the Emperor of the Holy Roman Empire.[43] The Hanseatic
League was growing dangerously strong.

Valdemar Atterdag (1340-1375) came to the throne with only north-
ern Jutland under him.[44] He had signed away Esthonia to Brandenburg
in lieu of his sister's dower. In 1342-1344 he defeated King Magnus of
Norway and Sweden. He regained Jutland and the islands. In 1346
Esthonia was sold to the Teutonic Order.[45] In 1360 he secured Skåne,
Halland and Blekinge by cession from Sweden. In 1361 he conquered
Gotland including Visby, a member of the Hanseatic League. At the
beginning of his reign Sweden had been more powerful than Denmark.
Despite loss of a war with the Hanseatic League in 1370, Denmark lost
no territory but had to grant liberty to trade with Denmark, protection
by the courts, and reparations. An alliance made in 1356 with France
contemplated a Danish invasion of England and assertion of claim to
the English throne.[46] While the English invasion never came off, Welsh
and Scottish leaders made promises to help Valdemar, as did the old
Viking states of Sodor and Man.

Valdemar's daughter Margaret was married in 1363 to the king of
Norway.[47] When Valdemar died in 1375 Margaret's son Olav became
King of Denmark. In 1380 he became King of Norway upon the death
of his father. A dynastic union between Denmark and Norway was thus
established which lasted until 1814. In 1385 Margaret had Olav proclaimed King of Sweden as the last descendant of the Swedish royal line,
and prepared to attack the new German King Albert of Sweden. To
achieve this she sacrificed Slesvig by granting it in 1386 to the Duke of
Holstein as a hereditary fief. He had previously held it as conquered
territory. Thus for a second time Slesvig was given to the German princes
in Holstein, the traditional foes of Denmark.

In 1387 Margaret succeeded as ruling queen, and conquered Sweden,
and also regained Skåne. In 1388 she was the recognized ruler of Denmark, Norway and Sweden. In 1392 she allied herself with Richard II
of England.

At a conference held in Kalmar, Sweden, in 1397 Margaret proposed the passage of a federative law aimed to insure the union of the three nations under an elective king with the same lineage and allied in a common defense.[48] The Kalmar charter never became law, but often served as a basis for discussion later. The Danish policy of centralization was incompatible with the wishes of Norway and Sweden to manage their own affairs. But Denmark, Norway and Sweden had the same king from 1388 to 1523, except for brief periods.

King Erik of Pomerania (1412-1439) carried on a twenty-year war with the Holstein dukes for possession of Slesvig, but the treaty of 1435 left the question unsettled.[49] He also carried on an unsuccessful war when attacked by the Hanseatic cities in 1426. Revolts occurred in Norway and Sweden. In 1443 King Christopher of Bavaria (1439-1448) to secure military support granted Slesvig to the Holstein Duke Adolph as a hereditary fief.[50] It has been pointed out that except Hans (1483-1513) and Christian II (1513-1523) "all the kings of the fifteenth and sixteenth centuries were Germans, not so much as able to speak Danish with their subjects."[51]

From 1429 on, the Danish king levied a toll at Elsinore on every ship passing through the Sound.[52] This was the Sound-toll, which ships of most nations paid until 1857. The Hanseatic League was forced to agree to the toll in the reign of Frederick II (1559-1588).[53] During his reign the Sound-toll was no longer levied at a fixed rate per ship, but as a duty on the cargo, thus bringing in three times as much revenue. Following an unsuccessful war in 1645 Denmark had to exempt Swedes from the toll, and reduce the toll paid by Netherlands ships.[54] The Sound-tolls were discontinued in 1857 under foreign pressure.[55]

In 1448 the present Oldenburg dynasty came to the throne in Denmark.[56] Christian I (1448-1481) was a nephew of Adolph, Count of Holstein. When the Count of Holstein died in 1460 the nobles of Slesvig and Holstein chose Christian as their prince as they desired the preservation of the union. Slesvig was a part of the Danish kingdom and Holstein was German and held as a fief under the German emperor. Christian had to promise to keep Slesvig and Holstein united forever instead of incorporating Slesvig as a forfeited fief, thus creating difficulties four hundred years later. Each province was to have its own law and administration. Christian "succeeded in bringing under his rule a larger realm than any king in the North had held since the days of Canute the Great."[57] In 1468 he mortgaged the Orkney and Shetland Islands to the Scottish king to provide a dowry for the marriage of his daughter Margaret to the Scottish king.[58] To destroy the influence of the Hanseatic League, Denmark allied itself with England, Scotland,[59] France and Burgundy. The Swedes were unwilling to accept the new dynasty and instead elected a Swedish lord as ruler.[60] Christian was defeated in 1471 at Stockholm and did not press his claim further. Hans (1483-1513) invaded Sweden and was elected king of Sweden in 1497, but a successful revolt soon broke out. He was unsuccessful in 1500 in enforcing a claim to Ditmarsch, which the German emperor had given to Denmark in 1474. In 1512 he secured the first favorable peace treaty with the Hanseatic cities, and granted equal privileges to the Dutch and English cities. Denmark was so powerful as the key to the Baltic that Christian II (1513-1523) was able to marry Elizabeth, a sister of Emperor Charles V. Sweden revolted, Charles invaded in 1517 and in 1520 a blood bath ensued in Stockholm. In 1523 Gustaf Vasa was proclaimed king of Sweden, and thereafter no Danish king ever ruled in Sweden.

Because Norway had supported the deposed Christian II, and to secure estates for Danish nobles, Christian III signed a charter in 1536 under which Norway ceased to be a separate kingdom and was incorporated into Denmark.[61] While this was not literally carried out, nevertheless the Norwegian Council of State disappeared, the only national office left was that of Chancellor, and the Norwegian dependencies such as Iceland and Greenland were brought directly under the Crown.[62] A dispute with Sweden over the possession of the Island of Gotland was ended, and an alliance made in 1541. In 1544 Christian III provided for his three brothers by sharing Slesvig and Holstein with them, thus causing many later difficulties.[63]

In 1559 the Danes conquered Ditmarsch and added it to Holstein.[64] About the same time they purchased Curland and Ösel, an island southwest of Esthonia, but declined Reval to avoid offense to the Russian Czar.[65] There was a war between Denmark and Sweden between 1563 and 1570.[66] It was the most disastrous war that had ever been fought in the North. The war left Denmark still holding Ösel and the area near Reval. But soon after the Russians captured most of the Danish bases in that area. Frederick II (1559-1588) continued the fatal division of Slesvig and Holstein made under Christian III.[67]

The Danish period of expansion was over about 1600.[68] Her policy now was to defend her former status as the key to the Baltic against the Swedish menace to Skåne and the German menace to Slesvig and Holstein.

It was in the reign of Christian IV (1588-1648) that Denmark acquired her first overseas colony, Tranquebar in India.[69] An East India Company, like the English, was founded to whose shares officials and wealthy citizens were compelled to subscribe. The Danish West India-Guinea Company, founded in 1672, acquired St. Thomas, St. Jean and

St. Croix, selling them to the state in 1755.[70] In 1916 Denmark sold her West Indies Islands to the United States.[71]

Early in the seventeenth century Sweden fought Poland and tried to prohibit all trade with Riga. The Swedish king assumed the title of "King of the Norwegian Laplanders" and levied taxes in Finmark. Denmark protested and soon was at war with Sweden.[72] This was known as the Kalmar War (1611-1613) and was won by Denmark. Sweden gave up all claim to Finmark, Denmark gained Elfsborg in northern Sweden, and retained Gothenburg to secure Swedish indemnities. During the war Denmark forbade all shipping into Swedish ports. Holland and Lübeck agreed to defend their commerce by force of arms. Sweden joined in this agreement in 1614, but it never came into force. If it had, it would have been the first modern "armed neutrality."[73]

During the Thirty Years' War which began in 1618 both Denmark and Sweden issued general interdictions of commerce. As they declined in relative power the interests of trade grew stronger than those of military advantage.[74] In 1625 Denmark intervened unsuccessfully against the Emperor to defend the Protestant cause. Consequently by the Treaty of Lübeck in 1629 Denmark ceded Bremen, Verden and Schwerin to the Emperor.[75] The strength of Sweden had been increasing, and in 1643 assisted by Holland, she began a war on Denmark. By the Treaty of Brömsebro of 1645 Denmark had to cede to Sweden the Norwegian provinces of Jämtland and Härjedalen, and also Gotland and Ösel, mortgage Halland for thirty years, and exempt Sweden from the Sound-toll.[76]

In 1657 Denmark declared war on Sweden. The Swedes won and by the Treaty of Roskilde in 1658 Denmark had to cede Bornholm, Skåne, Halland, Blekinge, and the Norwegian provinces of Bohuslän and Trondhjem.[77] After another war commenced by Sweden, Denmark with the aid of Holland was more successful and in 1660 by the Treaty of Copenhagen regained Bornholm and Trondhjem.[78] The heroism of the Danish king in this war facilitated the establishment of absolute monarchy. Following a brief war with England peace was concluded in 1667.[79] In 1675 the Scanian war was fought to regain the lost Swedish provinces. Due to French interference the Peace of Lund restored the status quo as of the date the war commenced.[80]

A new war of the great powers began in 1689.[81] Great Britain and Holland sought to defeat France by a total blockade. French privateers retaliated against the Dutch and English from Danish territorial waters. The Danes and Swedes finally took action to defend their trade. When the Dutch seized Danish ships sailing to France, the Danes confiscated Dutch ships in Denmark, and established joint Danish-Swedish con-

voys. The Dutch were forced to relent, and in 1691 Denmark and
Sweden made an agreement for the first active armed neutrality. Holland
and England persuaded Denmark to modify her demands, but the armed
neutrality treaty was reinstated in 1693.

In 1699 Denmark made an alliance with Poland, Russia and Saxony
against Sweden. In 1700 the Swedes landed in Zealand, and their fleet
together with Dutch and English ships bombarded Copenhagen. Denmark sought to recapture the part of Slesvig held by the Duke of Gottorp,
who was allied with Sweden. The war went against Denmark, and the
Treaty of Travendal was made in 1700.[82] In 1709, allied with Hanover,
Poland, Prussia and Russia, Denmark again fought Sweden, this time
successfully. By the Treaty of Frederiksborg of 1720 Sweden had to pay a
Sound-toll, and the ducal port of Slesvig was incorporated under the
Danish crown.[83] The treaty ended the longest, bloodiest and last war
between the Scandinavian countries. By this time German legal procedure had been introduced into North Slesvig, and the German language prevailed in South Slesvig.[84] Denmark remained at peace for the
balance of the century. Swedish dominance in the Baltic was now ended.
To augment the revenues Denmark furnished 20,000 soldiers to Austria,
England and Holstein in the War of the Spanish succession. In 1721 the
second colonization of Greenland began with the founding of Godthaab
on the western coast.[85] In 1742 a new settlement was made at Fredericks-
haab. Greenland traffic now went out from Copenhagen instead of from
Norway.

The marriage of the Duke of Gottorp to a daughter of Peter the
Great of Russia made Russia a potential menace to Slesvig-Holstein from
about 1725.[86] In 1762 Czar Peter III, of Gottorp descent, came to the
Russian throne, allied himself at once with Prussia and marched on
Denmark.[87] In 1763 Denmark renounced all future aggression against
Sweden, and was promised a settlement of the Gottorp question under
which the Gottorp part of Holstein was also to be included in Denmark.
In 1773 a land exchange treaty was made with Russia under which the
Gottorps relinquished all Slesvig and Holstein in exchange for Oldenburg
and Delmenhorst in Germany.[88] For the next century it was Danish
policy to be on good terms with Russia, without causing too much
offense to England.

Denmark cooperated with Sweden in maintaining an armed neutral-
ity during the Seven Years' War.[89] During the American Revolutionary
War which developed into a world war, Denmark made a treaty with
England to protect her trade in 1780.[90] A few days later she signed the
Armed Neutrality with Sweden, Holland and Russia. In October 1780,
the United States Congress passed a resolution agreeing to the principles

of the Armed Neutrality. In 1783 the United States negotiated its first commercial treaty with Denmark, a treaty serving as a model for later American treaties.[91] Denmark was the first Scandinavian country to display interest in the United States. In 1780 John Quincy Adams wrote: "The north of Europe (excepting Denmark) think very little about us."[92]

In 1788 Denmark invaded Sweden successfully, but the war was ended after England interfered.[93] Sweden had attacked Russia, and Denmark, under the terms of an earlier alliance, had come to her assistance. Following the French Revolution in 1794 Sweden and Denmark made an agreement providing for armed support of their shipping and the closing of the Baltic to belligerent vessels.[94] The Swedes approached the United States about acceding to the agreement, but the Danes thought this would not be helpful. Russia sided with Great Britain against France. The armed neutrality came to naught. In 1797 the Danish fleet defeated the Tripolitan fleet, and thus secured freedom to trade with Africa.

Shortly before 1800 the Scandinavian nations resumed their struggle for free trade. For them it was principally a conflict with Great Britain. The Russian Czar proposed a new armed neutrality which Denmark, Sweden and Russia accepted in 1800.[95] The British bombarded Copenhagen, and a compromise arrangement was worked out. In 1807 the British again bombarded Copenhagen after the Danes had placed their fleet at Napoleon's disposal for the purpose of a Continental blockade.[96] Denmark now joined the war on Napoleon's side, and fought Sweden from 1808 to 1809. In 1813 Russia offered Sweden its aid in depriving Denmark of Norway. Swedish, Russian, and Prussian troops invaded Denmark. Under the Treaty of Kiel in 1814 Denmark ceded Norway to Sweden and received in return Swedish Pomerania, later exchanged for the Duchy of Lauenburg. In 1815 the Congress of Vienna provided that Holstein be incorporated into the Germanic Confederation. In 1806 Denmark had incorporated Holstein into Denmark.

The Treaty of Kiel had stipulated that Norway take over a fair share of the Danish-Norwegian state debt.[97] The Norwegians were reluctant to pay and the Swedish king supported them. The great powers backed the Danish claim, which was extremely fair to Norway, and in 1821 the Norwegian Storthing finally agreed to pay. As Denmark had joined France in depredations on American commerce she finally agreed in 1830 to pay $650,000 to the United States.[98]

Beginning about 1830 the problem of Slesvig-Holstein was uppermost in Denmark. The Slesvig area had held a special position as a duchy since early times.[99] In the late Middle Ages it had been united with the

German Holstein under the nobles of Holstein, who bought estates in Slesvig. Neither Valdemar Atterdag nor Margaret were strong enough to bring it back. After the departure of Eric of Pomerania the cause was lost. German culture became stronger not only as to nobles and landowners, but also as to the clergy and the townspeople. In 1460 the Holstein nobility acknowledged the Danish king as their overlord so long as Slesvig and Holstein remained undivided. Christian III, however, shared them with his brothers in 1544 and inaugurated the period of divisions which lasted until 1720. The Protestant reformation accelerated the use of German in church services. There were long quarrels between the Danish kings and the Gottorp dukes. The Gottorp dukes supported the German culture while the Danish kings made no clear distinction. In 1720 the entire province of Slesvig was united under Danish administration.[100] However, the officials were mostly German. In 1773 Gottorp-Holstein was also incorporated. As a result for the first time since 1544 both provinces were again united under the king of Denmark, who was their duke. But this in turn created a movement away from the kingdom, assisted by the nobility and the University of Kiel in Holstein.

In 1830 a Slesvig official published a pamphlet demanding a free constitution in Slesvig and Holstein and a joint government of the two duchies with only a personal union with the kingdom.[101] In 1842 Orla Lehmann, a National Liberal, proposed that Slesvig be incorporated into the Kingdom, and German Holstein be separated from the Danish State, the Eider River to be the border. But the Danish Conservatives with the king and the government sought to preserve the tripartite unitary state. The National Liberals came to advocate a military alliance of the three Scandinavian countries against German aggression. In 1848 Denmark fought a war with the duchies, lasting three years. Prussian and Hanoverian troops aided the duchies.

The German claim was that Slesvig and Holstein were independently connected with Denmark only in personal union; that Slesvig and Holstein were inseparably united in a real union; and that the succession in the duchies followed the Salic Law. The Danish claim was that Slesvig was rightfully a province of Denmark since its incorporation in 1721; that neither law nor history justified an inseparable union between Slesvig and Holstein; and that in Slesvig, the succession was the same as in Denmark proper, where the Lex Regia of 1665 permitted it to pass through females.[102]

War with Prussia and Austria finally came in 1864, and Denmark received no support from any other nations. As a result of the war Denmark lost a third of its territory and a million inhabitants out of a total of two and one-half millions, including 200,000 Danes.[103] Following

World War I Denmark was the sole Scandinavian state represented at the peace conference. Provision was made for a plebiscite which resulted in the return of Northern Slesvig by a vote of 75,000 to 25,000.[104] Central Slesvig voted to remain German.

Following World War II 300,000 German refugees crowded into South Slesvig.[105] In 1947 the Danish prime minister lost the confidence of the Liberal party because of his activist line in the South Slesvig question.[106] Today the Danish government does not demand frontier revision or a plebiscite. There is a feeling that many of the Germans in South Slesvig seek annexation to avoid the burdens of having lost the war.[107] The present German state of Slesvig-Holstein has a sizeable political party made up of refugees dangerously Nazistic in character.[108] It is Denmark's present policy to safeguard the status of the Danes in South Slesvig and to seek some relief from the pressure of displaced Germans in the province.[109]

In 1905 when Norway ended her union with Sweden her most outspoken friends were Denmark and England.[110] Norway selected as her king Prince Carl of Denmark, brother of Christian X (1912-1947). In 1914 Denmark joined a neutrality entente with Norway and Sweden under which the war should not lead to hostilities between them.[111] Norway, the chief beneficiary, was strongly backed up by Denmark and Sweden.

In 1918 Iceland became a free sovereign state in personal union with Denmark.[112] The act of Parliament on this was valid until 1940, when Iceland severed all connections with Denmark and became a republic in 1944.

Denmark was invited to become a charter member of the League of Nations. It hesitated the least of the Scandinavian countries, entering the League on March 3, 1920, by a unanimous vote of its parliament.[113] It also supported the Permanent Court of International Justice and immediately recognized unconditionally the competence of the court in certain legal disputes, that is to say its compulsory jurisdiction. D. G. Nyholm, a Dane, was elected a member of the Court and served from 1922 to 1930. Born in 1858 he had previously served for 28 years as a member of the Superior Court at Copenhagen and a judge of the Mixed Court at Cairo.[114]

A conflict between Denmark and Norway over Greenland was referred to the Permanent Court of International Justice which decided in 1933 that the Norwegian occupation of certain coastal tracts was invalid and that Denmark had sovereignty over the entire island.[115]

The Danish ambassador to the United States, Henrik de Kauffmann, declared himself not bound to the coerced government in Denmark and in 1941 he made a treaty with the United States allowing the use of temporary bases in Greenland.[116] Since the war negotiations between the United States and Denmark over a new agreement permitting the United States to retain its bases have been going on intermittently. During World War II Great Britain took the Faroe Islands and Iceland under temporary protection. The United States landed forces in Iceland in 1941.

Denmark like Norway became a charter member of the United Nations on its formation in June 1945. Denmark was chosen to have a representative in the Economic and Social Council. In March 1950, the Danish Parliament voted to join the Atlantic Pact.

In 1948 the Faroe Islands were given self-government in home affairs. They are represented in the Danish Rigsdag. The same year a commission was appointed for the economic opening of Greenland, Denmark's only colonial possession, and for the development of self-government within the framework of the Kingdom.[117] The state monopoly of trade was ended in 1948.

Custom, Case-Law and Codes

Denmark resembles Norway and Sweden in never having developed a case-law like that of England and the United States nor comprehensive codes like those of France and Germany. Much of its law is customary.[118] Danish law gives more weight to custom than Swedish, but less than Norwegian law.[119]

Danish law has evolved independently of Roman law, and is essentially national in character.[120] The other Scandinavian nations have been the chief outside influence, with Germany and England next. Danish law resembles German law only in the respect that both of them give much weight to the "theory of law," that is to say, scientific discussions of the law which suggest solutions when positive legislation fails.[121] To some extent Roman law has affected the Danish law of contracts and torts.[122] That Danish law has not been submerged by the Germanic influence "is above all due to the prominent work of a single man—the Danish Blackstone, I might call him—Anders Sandoe Örsted, who in the beginning of the 19th century founded the entire Danish law on a national and quite realistic base."[123] The Code Napoleon has had considerable influence.

As in other nations the Danish courts tend to follow earlier judicial decisions.[124] The tendency to follow precedent is said to be stronger in Denmark than in Sweden.[125]

The earliest written forms of law in Denmark appeared in the twelfth century.[126] The vigorous role of the Valdemars caused the Landsthings to fix and preserve the existing law in writing.[127] The great provincial laws were now recorded. The laws of Skåne and of Zealand were drafted by private individuals. But the Jutland Code, the greatest of them all, was drafted by a royal committee, then passed by the Landsthing at Viborg and finally issued by King Valdemar Victorious about 1240 at a meeting of the nobles.¹²⁸ It is the oldest Danish civil code and remained in effect until 1683.¹²⁹ The Jutland Code, together with "The Articles of Thord" containing a gloss of explanations, decisions, customs, and new rules, was ratified by the King and the Council of State in 1326 as official law.¹³⁰ It was made applicable to all Denmark. Chancellor Nils Kaas instituted a revision made effective in 1590.

The Jutland Code is in the tradition of national legislation. That is to say there is no Imperial Law nor Roman law in it.¹³¹ There is, however, canon law in it. It has a famous preamble borrowed from the Church:

By law shall the land be built. Were every man content with what is his and granted to other men the same right, no law would be needed. Were the land without law he would have the most who could take the most; therefore law shall be made to meet the needs of all. It is the office of the King and chiefs who are in this country to guard the law and to do justice and save whosoever shall be put to duress, such as widows and children, without a guardian and pilgrims and foreigners and poor men who are most encroached upon.

Elsewhere in Europe the principle of status prevailed under which a man's duty to his fellows was regulated by his position in the state. There is no trace of status in the Laws of Valdemar. Everywhere else there were provisions for serfdom. The Danish laws did not provide for it. The Jutland Law declared: "No man may meddle with the law, and the king may not set it aside without the will of the land."

It is an interesting fact that the establishment of absolute monarchy which made the king independent of the Council of State and the *things* made it possible for the king to establish a uniform system of law for Denmark. In 1661 the king directed a commission to prepare a modern code. Commissions were also appointed in 1662 and 1666, but little progress was made. The king then commanded each member of the last commission to prepare his own synopsis for a code. Peder Lassen of the Supreme Court and Rasmus Vinding, Professor of History at the University of Copenhagen and a Supreme Court Justice, complied. Vinding's draft served as a basis for later drafts. Chancellor Peder Griffenfeld assisted in the work as did Peder Scavenius, Professor of Law and a member of the Supreme Court. There were revisions in 1672, 1675, 1680 and 1681. On January 3, 1682, it was adopted and ordered printed by the king. On April 15, 1683, "King Christian V's Danish Law" was proclaimed as the law of the land and ordered announced at the *things*, to become effective three months later.[132]

It contained six books: (1) Courts and Practice, (2) Ecclesiastical Regulations, (3) City, Rural and Family Relations, (4) Marine Law, (5) Obligations and Inheritances, and (6) Penal Code. The sources were the Danish legislation of the sixteenth and seventeenth centuries. There was but little resort to canonical, Roman and German law except such as had already been incorporated into Danish law. The law of evidence was radically changed. The Danish Code is the earliest of the modern Scandinavian codes, the Norwegian Code being adopted in 1688 and the Swedish in 1734. Parts of the Code are still the law of Denmark. The Code is simple, liberal and humane in spirit. In form, however, it is unsystematic, casuistic and omits important subjects, hence a wide scope for judicial interpretation was left.[133] The Norwegian Code of 1688 is largely based upon it. In 1701 and 1710 vain attempts were made to introduce a code governing political affairs. Subsequent statutes and codes covering specialized phases of the law are discussed in other parts of this chapter.[134]

The King

The institution of kingship deserves full attention because it was the major centralizing influence in Denmark. Moreover it was largely through the king that the common people won relief from the nobility. The changing character of the kings has affected foreign policy and domestic prosperity. The Danish kingship has gone through three stages: (1) the period prior to the commencement of the absolute monarchy in 1660; (2) the period of absolute monarchy from 1660 to 1849, the date of the Danish Constitution; and (3) from 1849 to the present, as a constitutional and limited monarchy.

The Danish king was at first simply one of the great landowners, who led the army in war and officiated at sacrifices to the deities.[135] His bodyguard, the hired *hird*, consisting of sons of prominent families, were paid out of his estates. The important kings at the beginning of the Viking Age around 800 were those of South Jutland. Harold I, by being baptized in 826, secured areas in Germany. Harold II (950-985) also permitted himself to be baptized, and more effectively, made the Danes Christians. He moved the capital from Leire to Roskilde, where it remained until Copenhagen became capital in 1440. The powers of the king were consolidated by the Viking armies; fortified camps were established for garrisoning of armies and new small political units—townships—were created which in league with the king broke the power of the clans.[136]

The kings took advantage of the church to build up their powers among the nobles.[137] To offset the influence of Hamburg and Bremen, Canute the Great appointed English bishops at Odense, Roskilde, and Lund. King Sweyn Estrithson (1047-1074) secured additional bishops for Denmark, and then won the bishops over to himself.[138]

King Canute the Saint (1080-1086) sought to enforce the royal prerogatives.[139] He levied a special tax on the farmers, asserted the royal rights of forest and waters and entertainment and conveyance. He was very harsh in collecting the fines that fell to the king for enforcing the judgments of the moots. Such enforcement involved the seizure of land. A revolt occurred in Jutland. Canute fled to Odense, the Landsthing refused to protect him, and he was killed in a church. His successor had him canonized and proclaimed that it was sacrilege to rebel against the king, the deputy of the Lord. This was the first time that such an idea had been voiced in Denmark, and the idea never became very popular, though it strengthened the alliance between the king and the Church.

King Niels (1104-1134) by negotiation acquired the judicial fines imposed by the courts, the rights to ship-wrecks and treasure trove.[140] In return he secured to the Church both tithes and ecclesiastical jurisdiction in matters concerning the clergy. This represented a weakening of the Landsthing.

In 1170 Archbishop Eskil anointed the son of Valdemar the Great as king.[141] This was an attempt to introduce the concept of hereditary kingship in Denmark. About this time the nobility emerged as a separate upper class.[142] At first personal, eventually it became hereditary.

The aim of the Valdemars was the same as that of Henry II in England. It was attained through the administration of justice and the organization of the army.[143] Justice in the courts was to be administered by the king.

During the reign of Valdemar the Great (1157-1182) the royal administration was increased so as to include a chancery, a great royal household, and several provincial officials.[144] Denmark had thus advanced to the status of a medieval European state. The writing of history flourished. Saxo, secretary of Absalon, wrote a great history of Denmark from the Mythical Age to the 1180's.

The wars in the thirteenth century resulted in a raising of taxes, which from then on were imposed on all cultivated lands by way of personal assessments.[145] The only persons exempted were the clergy and the members of the royal *hird* who served the king in person. The cities paid regular taxes.

After 1260 there were gathered around the king the large landowners, the king's officials, and the heads of the clergy. At first known as the *Rigsmöde (curia regis)* they were later known as the Danehof.[146] It accepted the king's suggestion about royal jurisdiction in certain cases, entirely dispensing with the Landsthings and the law. It did this with a view to restoring order after the civil wars. At the same time it safe-guarded itself against new tariffs and arbitrary embargoes on exports, and obtained liberty for Lübeck, Rostock, and Wismar to trade freely with Denmark.

In 1282 during the reign of Erik Klipping (1259-1286) the Danehof assembled and the king for the first time was forced to sign a charter, called the Danish Magna Carta, defining his duties to the lords.[147] The Danehof was to meet once a year as the supreme legislative body together with the king. Nobody could be held under arrest unless he had made a confession and judgment had been pronounced. Nobody could be judged more severely by the royal court than he would have been before the Landsthing courts. Thus Denmark got her first constitution recog-nizing a legislative assembly of lords beside the king. Sweden shortly afterwards set up a similar arrangement.

The Danehof was the first national parliament in Denmark. It took over many of the powers once exercised by the *Landstinger* (the regional assemblies).[148] There grew out of the Danehof a smaller body known as the *Rigsraad* (council of the kingdom) consisting of about thirty mem-bers. They served as close advisers to the king and also on the highest Danish court.[149] They enforced the king's compact. They controlled the succession to the throne, and the making of a new compact with an incoming king.

In 1319 before becoming king, Christopher II was bound by a strict charter.[150] He promised not to go to war without the consent of the nobles and clergy, not to give German officers any authority, and to govern together with a council which met annually. The latter, as the Council of State, was to be the Danish legislative assembly for the next 350 years. No priest might be brought before a secular court unless the church courts had released him. No taxes might be levied on church property. Nobles need not render services outside of Denmark. The right to tax was severely limited. Royal courts were deprived of appellate jurisdiction, and appeals from them could be taken to a general court of the nation. The income from fines passed to local nobles instead of to the king. The power of the nobility and the clergy was never greater in Denmark.

Perhaps the greatest Danish king is Valdemar Atterdag (1340-1375). A well-known American writer has said that Valdemar "made Denmark into the first modern state."[151] The only charter to which he consented on ascending the throne was one to obey the Danish law.[152] He had previously known Marsilio of Padua who advocated a government subject to law. Denmark had just had a period of eight years without a king or regent. Valdemar labored incessantly for a revival of the *thing* courts and restoration of the laws of Valdemar Victorious.[153] The title of *foged* began to replace the older one for law officers.[154] The *foged* presided over the *herred* courts. In addition the *fogeds* collected taxes, acted as commanders of the garrisons and superintendents of the local militia. They were the backbone of the King's Council. Nearly half of them were Germans. At the meeting of the Danehof in 1354 at Nyborg, Fünen, it was decided to hold an annual meeting there each year. Appeals lay from the *thing* of the *herred* to the Landsthing, and then to the king's drost or the king himself, and finally to the Danehof. In 1355 Valdemar called a conference at Roskilde "on how to improve the realm," the first economic conference in western history.[155] The main result was a national plan for water regulation. Grist mills and dams were constructed. Stone roads were built throughout the nation. In 1360 a charter defined and punished treason to the nation as distinguished from disloyalty to an individual.[156] Valdemar's council was called *Rigets Raad* (nation's advisers) instead of *Kongens Raad* (King's advisers). It took the place of the Danehof which met only on extraordinary occasions, as in 1354, 1356, 1360, and 1375. Though it had no legal authority Valdemar relied heavily on it. In 1370 it was the council rather than the king which made a treaty of peace with the Hanseatic League. From this time on the council was increasingly important.

The position of the Danish nobility in the time of Valdemar Atterdag is of interest.[157] While in all Europe except Scandinavia one became an earl, count or baron through heredity and had territorial ownership, the right to lead armies into battle, to decide cases at law, and to legislate, in Denmark the nobility had no title, hereditary or otherwise. Not all of them had wealth. Legislation was through the *things* and the King. In the *thing* a noble's vote carried no more weight than anyone else's. Members of the leading families simply had some training in military and political leadership and the opportunity to demonstrate ability in those fields. Even the crown was elective. In only four out of twenty-four reigns from 900 to 1340 had the eldest son succeeded the father.

Queen Margaret (1387-1412), the only ruling Danish queen, laid down the law that every Dane should have six securities for any violation of which he could claim the help of the royal *fogeds*—church-security, wife-security, house-security, plow-security, the security of his stead, and the security of his *thing*.[158]

By the time of Christian II (1513-1523) the Landsthings were no longer of importance.[159] Many landowners had judicial power over the peasants who lived on their land. Aside from this, judicial authority was exercised by the royal officials. The Landsthings came to an end because the free peasantry, on whom they had depended for their existence, no longer existed. The peasants were stripped of their rights to use the forests, villeinage changed from free copyhold to a form of adscription, and the villeins had to do labor services. The lords of the manors bound their tenants to the farms. Enclosure of common land took place on a large scale so that there might be more corn and cattle.

King Christian I (1448-1481), the first of the Oldenburg dynasty, gave to the Norwegian people their first charter guaranteeing the rights of the people and making the kingship elective rather than hereditary.[160] As to Denmark he simply gave a communication in writing to the Council of State declaring the kingship elective, and binding himself not to impose taxes nor declare war without the consent of the Council.[161] In 1468 he called the first national assembly of all classes in Danish history. As he assumed broad powers his son Hans (1481-1513) was bound by a very strict charter virtually placing the government in the hands of the Council.[162] The king agreed not to buy up any estates held by the nobles; and only the nobles could buy land exempted from taxation. If the king violated the charter, the people were authorized to use violent means against him. His son, Christian II (1513-1523), exercised broad powers and weakened the nobility and increased the power of the lower classes. He was supplanted by his uncle, Frederick I (1523-1533), who signed a charter repudiating the absolutist claims and strengthening the nobles.[163] The Council was to consist of nobles and clergy. No burgess could hold public office.

At the time of Christian II most provincial officials, the *lords-lieutenant*, were owners of estates.[164] Their offices, however, were not hereditary as in most other countries. They received the profits. The king tried in vain to reduce their fiefs to areas of administration with the officer receiving a fixed sum and the remainder falling to the king. In the reign of Christian III (1534-1559), following the Reformation, the king was successful as to three-fourths of such fiefs.[165]

In 1521 there was much law-making activity.[166] Former mercantile laws were consolidated. Provisions were made for royal and local government in the towns; social relief, and the administration of justice in the country. The copyholders in Zealand were granted liberty to move. The clergy were prohibited from purchasing land. The religious organizations and the schools which had been exclusively operated by the Church were reformed.

In 1536 Christian III called together an assembly of twelve hundred nobles, burghers and peasants to destroy the powers of the Catholic clergy.[167] Subsequently the *Rigsraad* continued as a check upon the king.

But it no longer represented the clergy, was made up entirely of nobles, and was reduced in size to twenty members. A new compact with Christian III did not contain a prohibition against the king's seeking to make his son his successor nor any clause permitting popular revolt if the king violated his compact. This compact fixed the form of the Danish government for many years. The king could not be a despot, yet he had more powers than the nobles wished him to have. Denmark was now ruled by the king and the nobles.

In 1660 the king was proclaimed hereditary monarch and in 1661 absolute monarch.[168] A war had just ended in which the king played an heroic role and the nobles were blamed for the defeat. Certain German and Danish court officials, help from the Netherlands, the support of the Bishop of Zealand and the burghers of Copenhagen—all were factors in bringing about the absolute monarchy. The king's secretary, Peder Schumacher, a German, drew up the King's Law (1665) setting up an absolute monarchy. The king was to be a Lutheran and keep the kingdom undivided. He was to be the supreme head and judge of the people, and independent of all laws except the King's Law itself and respect for rights of property. For any one to suggest a change in the law was made treason. The document itself expressly forbade any amendment. The king ruled under this law from 1660 to 1848 without a parliament or Estates Assembly as in Sweden. In theory, the Danish-Norwegian absolutism was the most logically developed and complete divine-right absolutism in all Europe.[169] But it "was for the most part patriarchal and benevolent in practice, and administration was in the hands of a bourgeois bureaucracy."[170]

Following the establishment of an absolute monarchy in 1661, a new system of administration was set up by Hannibal Sehested.[171] Administrative boards or departments (*Kollegier*) were established, and burghers were appointed to administrative posts side by side with the nobles. The colleges were: (1) the college of state to administer foreign affairs, maintain the new constitution, and interests of the crown; (2) the sacred college to make ecclesiastical appointments; (3) the college of justice to deal with the courts and the police; (4) the college of the treasury to administer financial and tax affairs; (5) the college of war to administer the army; and (6) the admiralty college to administer the navy. The signature of the king was necessary to put their decisions into effect. The Supreme Court as highest judicial tribunal was instituted with the king at the head.

Extremely important changes occurred in the period from 1770 to 1772 as the result of a coup d'etat by the mad king's German physician, Johann Struensee.[172] Administration was now reorganized after the Prussian model. Political and judicial authority was closely centralized, and Copenhagen lost its autonomy. A single consolidated municipal court was set up in Copenhagen. The religious sects outside of the Lutheran State Church were given greater freedom. The criminal law was made more humane and the death penalty restricted.[173] Police were not freely to enter private homes or places of business. Torture to obtain confessions was abolished. Illegitimate children were given protection. Permanent pauper commissions were established. Tariffs were reduced. Censorship of the press was abolished.[174] A second coup d'etat in 1772 put an end to the Struensee Government and many of its reforms.

In 1776 a Citizenship Law was passed by the government and the nobility reserving state posts for people born in Denmark, Norway, and Holstein.[175] However, the German influence was not ended until 1848.

There was another era of liberal reform from 1784-1797.[176] The criminal law made more humane. Imprisonment was substituted for the death penalty as to many crimes. Torture in executions was abolished. There was more freedom of speech and press than in any other country. No such sweeping reforms were accomplished in any other country prior to the French Revolution.[177]

The reaction after the Napoleonic Wars was not so extreme in Denmark as in Norway or Sweden.[178] Absolutism continued, but the king delegated more powers than formerly. There was an effort to reorganize the system of administration to secure greater honesty and efficiency. The chief grievances were against the narrowly legalistic and subservient bureaucracy which the king had developed after 1800. In 1820 the king permitted the Danish students who had volunteered in his campaigns to form the Student Association. It gradually became the center of a liberal movement. Between 1815 and 1830 there was little change.

From 1830 on the Danish nobility performed no special function, and its interests were identical with those of other landlords.[179] In 1830 the king began preparation to establish consultative assemblies of estates. The king felt compelled by the necessity of according to his Danish subjects privileges equal to those he knew must be extended to his German subjects. But he followed the Prussian system established in 1823 instead of the Norwegian Constitution. The formal provisions issued in 1834 provided for four assemblies: one for the islands to meet at Roskilde, one for Northern Jutland at Viborg, one for Slesvig to meet at the city of Slesvig, and one for Holstein at Itzehoe.[180] There were to be three groups of voters: owners of city property, owners of rural estates, and owners of smaller rural properties. The assemblies could not legislate. The king pledged himself to consult them on all projects for ordinary laws, and granted them extensive powers to suggest changes in existing laws. Danish liberalism became articulate in this period. A group of university professors assumed the leadership: the jurist, P. G. Bang; the economist, C. H. David; the theologian, H. N. Clausen; and the botanist, J. Fr. Schouw. The first issue was over freedom of the press. In 1834 the king forbade his subjects to subscribe to the Norwegian newspaper *Morgenbladet* which favored the radicals and the peasants. A. S. Örsted, the attorney general, did his utmost to urge the king not to curb the press. In 1837 an ordinance curbing the press was issued supplementing that of 1799. The king met the demands of the Roskilde and Viborg assemblies for a published financial statement and a project for tariff reform tending towards free trade. In 1838 the Estates of Roskilde and Viborg requested that they be united into a national assembly, but the king refused. Steen Blicher wrote favorably of the Norwegian Storthing. In 1839 when Christian VIII, who had been king of Norway in 1814, ascended the Danish throne, numerous petitions asked him to give Denmark a constitution similar to the one he helped to write for Norway.[181] But the king refused, and merely stated his intent to undertake administrative and fiscal reforms. In 1847, the last year of his reign, he delegated to P. G. Bang, a moderate liberal, the assignment of preparing a first draft of a constitution. His death on January 20, 1848, prevented its consideration by him. In March 1848 King Frederick VII declared that he would regard himself henceforth as a constitutional monarch and would hold the ministry responsible for the formulation of policy.

The Constitution

The movement for a constitution was produced in a large degree by the Slesvig-Holstein question.[182] The revolutionary wave in Europe also played a role. A constitutional national assembly was elected in 1848 by equal and universal suffrage for males of independent means.[183] Largely on the basis of the Declaration of the Rights of Man in 1789 and the Belgian Constitution, D. G. Monrad, a famous Danish theologian often called the father of the Danish Constitution, proposed the creation of a bicameral Rigsdag, a Folkething (lower house) and a Landsthing (upper house) with universal suffrage for both chambers. The desire of the Left for a unicameral parliament was ignored. Six months discussion resulted in a compromise. The Folkething was to be chosen for a three-year term by direct election by all males over thirty with their own household, the Landsthing for an eight-year term by the same body of electors, but by indirect election. The Constitution was signed on June 5, 1849, which the Danes now celebrate as their Constitution Day. American institutions had been carefully studied. A constitutional

monarchy was set up. Executive power is vested in the Crown and the
ministers, legislative power in the Crown and Parliament, and judicial
power in the courts. The ministers are chosen by the king. All men over
thirty except domestic servants and apprentices could vote. Political
and religious censorship are abolished. Anyone taken into custody must
be placed before a judge within twenty-four hours. The police may not
search a house except with a warrant. All privileges of nobility, title and
rank are abolished.[184] There is to be liberty to trade, free local government, separation of the courts from the administration, public and oral
judicial procedure, juries in important cases, a Constitution for the
Lutheran National Church, and transition to free ownership as to en-
tailed estates and feoffments. The 1849 constitution "was a very radical
one for its time."[185]

From 1849 to the present time Denmark has had six constitutions.
Five of them were drafted between 1849 and 1866.[186] The second, third,
and fourth. arose out of the Slesvig-Holstein conflict. The Danish king
was *monarch* over Denmark, Slesvig and Holstein. The Danish *realm*
or *state* included Denmark and Slesvig. The *kingdom* of Denmark did
not include Slesvig or Holstein. Holstein was already a member of the
German federation in 1849. The 1849 constitution was intended to apply
to Slesvig, and served as the constitution for Denmark without the
duchies until 1866. This constitution co-existed with the 1854, 1855,
and 1863 constitutions. The 1854 constitution for the *monarchy* included
Slesvig and Holstein, but did not affect the structure of the government
for Denmark proper.[187] The Constitution of 1855 also covered the *monarchy*. The *monarchy* was to be governed by a unicameral council, three-
fourths of its members elected by the people and one-fourth chosen by
the king. Proportional representation was to be used.[188] The election in
1856 was the first in the world to use this system. In 1858 the constitution
was declared not to apply to Holstein. The 1863 constitution endeavored
to unite Slesvig more closely with Denmark.[189] It set up a bicameral
council alongside the bicameral Rigsdag for the kingdom proper. Its
adoption was the immediate cause of the war with Prussia and Austria.

The Constitution of 1866, which was in effect up to 1915, represented a compromise between the 1849 and 1863 constitutions.[190] The
Council ceased to exist. The Bill of Rights resembled that in the 1849
constitution. But the provisions as to the election of the Landsthing
were very conservative. The Landsthing was to be elected by the wealthy
people in the cities and by the large farmers, and 12 members out of
66 were to be appointed by the Crown.

In 1870 the Liberal Left party was formed, advocating return to the
1849 constitution. In 1905 the new Radical Left party took the same

position. It was only in 1914 that the Landsthing, after its first dissolution alone under the 1866 constitution, was ready to adopt a new constitution.[191] The 1915 constitution provided universal suffrage for all men and women over 25 for the lower house, but a voting age of 35 for the upper house. Members of the Landsthing nominated by the Crown were replaced by 19 members or one-fourth elected by the outgoing Landsthing.[192] The Constitution was amended in 1920 to provide for the incorporation of Northern Slesvig following a plebescite. To be elected to the lower house one must be at least 25 and for the upper house at least 35. The lower house is elected for a four-year term and the upper house for eight. Proportional representation is used in electing the lower house and for choosing the electoral college which in turn elects members for the upper house. The cabinet is responsible to the lower house alone.[193] The leader of the strongest party in the lower house is chosen prime minister.

Section Two of the Danish Constitution provides that the judicial power is in the courts (*den dommende Magt er hos Domstolene*). Other provisions as to the judiciary appear in articles 66 through 72. The structure and organization of the courts is left for the Rigsdag to deal with through legislation. The only tribunal specifically mentioned is the *Rigsretten* (Court for State Trials). It is a tribunal to hear charges against the cabinet ministers, and is almost never resorted to. The Constitution provides that its membership shall include all the judges who sit in the "highest court of the land." This would seem to imply that at the head of the judiciary shall be a Supreme Court and that the *Rigsretten* is not a part of the regular judicial organization.

The organization and structure of the courts is fixed by legislation. The Constitution seems clearly to make the courts subject to legislation. The Rigsdag appears to have vast discretion to set up special tribunals. There is no doctrine of separation of powers as in the United States. The judiciary is hemmed in by legislation prescribing almost every detail of its functioning and structure. However, no judge may be removed from office until after proper notice and hearing. No judge may be transferred from one court to another except when there is a statutory reorganization. Under the Constitution any judge may be retired on full pay at the age of sixty-five.

If the Danish courts have the power to declare statutes unconstitutional, thus far they have never exercised it.[194] The Constitution provides that there shall be no expropriation of private property except for a public purpose and after the payment of fair compensation. A statute of this kind has been attacked only once (in 1919) and the statute was upheld. Protection of constitutional rights thus hinges on the attitude of the

Rigsdag. Thus far the Rigsdag has shown no disposition to violate the civil and political liberties of the individual. Judicial review of constitutionality in actual practice is even more nonexistent in Denmark than it is in Norway.

Mention has been made of the constitutional guaranty against expropriation of private property. Other constitutional rights are: (1) religious liberty, (2) freedom of the press, (3) freedom of assembly, (4) the right to form associations, (5) the right to engage in economic activity, (6) freedom from unreasonable searches and seizures, (7) the right of a criminal defendant to a speedy trial, and (8) the right to appeal to a higher court.

The amending process of the Danish Constitution is rather a difficult one. The proposed amendment must pass both houses of the Rigsdag. This must be followed by a dissolution of the Rigsdag and a general election. The amendment must be passed by the new Rigsdag. Finally it must be submitted to a popular referendum. It passes only if it receives a majority of those participating in the referendum and at least 45 per cent of all those eligible to vote. A new proposed constitutional law was passed by the Rigsdag in March 1939, but failed to receive approval by the required referendum of May 23, 1939. The proposed new constitution would have lowered the franchise age and granted suffrage to all Danes domiciled in the country who are twenty-three years of age or over. The Landsthing was to be abolished and the use of the referendum increased. The Rigsdag was to consist of the Folkething and Rigsthing and would comprise together 210 members, a majority to be elected from among candidates nominated in the various constituencies and a minority to be taken from a national list to be made public prior to the general election. A public meeting in 1945 demanded constitutional amendments abolishing the upper chamber and lowering the voting age to twenty-one.

The Rigsdag

The Constitution provides that the size of the lower house (the Folkething) is to be fixed by law, but that it shall not exceed 152. The present elective laws fix the size at 151.[195] For this purpose the nation is divided into 105 constituencies, and these are grouped together into 24 electoral districts. From each electoral district as many members are chosen as there are constituencies within the district. This provides for 105 members. In addition there are 44 supplementary mandates apportioned among the various parties and electoral districts. The list system of proportional representation is used.

Under the Constitution there may be as many as 78 members in the upper house (the Landsthing). By statute the present number is seventy-six.[196] All are chosen indirectly for an eight-year term. One-fourth are elected every eighth year by proportional representation by the outgoing Landsthing. Of the remaining seats one-half are filled every four years by the electoral colleges chosen in each of the seven Landsthing districts by proportional representation. The electoral colleges in turn choose the Landsthing members to which each district is entitled by proportional representation.

Interest in election to the Rigsdag is keen. In the last Danish elections prior to 1950, 86 per cent of the electorate voted.[197]

For many years there was a sharp conflict between the Right and the Left as to which house of the Rigsdag should prevail in case of conflict and from which house should the ministry be chosen.[198] The Constitution was silent. Until 1901 the king chose his cabinet according to the majority in the upper house. The Left advocated the English system under which the ministry must be in harmony with the lower house. The Left had a majority as early as 1875. In 1884 it had 69 seats to the Right's nineteen. But the Right government did not resign until 1901 when the Left had 76 seats, the Social Democrats 14, and the Right only eight. For the first time a cabinet was chosen because it represented the majority in the lower house. Full parliamentary government is thus only a half-century old in Denmark. The first resignation of a prime minister because of a vote of lack of confidence occurred in 1909.

The abolition of the upper house is favored by the Social Democrats and the Radical Left parties.[199] Its retention is favored by the Conservative and Liberal Left parties.

The first Social Democrat government came into power in 1924 under the leadership of Thorvald Stauning.[200] After a short period for the Conservative party (1926-1929), the Social Democrats again came into power in 1929, and kept control until 1943 when martial law was declared by the Germans. The Liberal Lefts, a conservative party, were in power from 1945 to 1947. In 1947 the Social Democrats again came into power under the premiership of Hans Hedtoft.[201] At the same time the number of Communist members in the lower house dropped from eighteen to nine. The Social Democrats, unlike those in Norway and Sweden, have never had a majority, although they have been the largest single party, excluding coalitions, since 1924. Socialist ideas play a less important role in the Danish Social Democratic party than they do in Norway. Following World War I the Norwegian Labor party had a strong revolutionary tendency and was for a short time a member of the Communist International. There were no such deviations in Denmark. The Danish government is less involved in economic enterprise than the other Scandinavian governments. In 1948 the government use of re-sources was only ten per cent of the disposable product compared with over twenty-five in Norway.[202] Denmark has not adopted the complete controls of Soviet Russia, nor direct nationalization of industry as in Great Britain. She has, however, shifted from short-term to long-term government planning.[203] Freedom of religion, speech and press, protec-tion of civil liberties and property rights all indicate that Denmark is a thoroughly democratic country although the "Danes worry openly . . . that foreigners will confuse their highly organized social-democratic government with totalitarianism."[204] The September 1950 election in-creased the strength of the conservative parties, left the Social Demo-cratic party as it was, weakened the Agrarian party and reduced the Com-munist party from nine to seven members in the lower chamber.[205] The Social Democrats have 59 out of 151 members in the lower chamber or 39 per cent of the members, whereas in Norway's single chamber parliament they have 57 per cent, and in Sweden they have 56 per cent of the first chamber and 49 per cent of the second and larger chamber. On October 28, 1951 a new coalition government of Conservatives and Liberals replaced the Social Democrats.

Political leadership in Denmark is very stable, especially in the Social Democratic party. Thorvald Stauning was undisputed leader of that party from 1910 to 1942. Since that time it has been headed by Hans Hedtoft. No parliamentary regime in Europe, except that of England, has been as stable as that of Denmark, where the average government tenure during the period between the two World Wars was five years.[206] In Norway and Sweden such period was about two years.

No legislation may be enacted in Denmark without favorable and separate action by both houses of the Rigsdag. Action on finance bills must originate in the lower house. All other bills may originate in either house. Members of the lower house may be elected irrespective of where they live in Denmark. Members of the upper house, except those chosen by the upper house itself, must live in the election districts from which they are chosen. Members of both chambers are paid at the rate of 6,000 to 9,000 kroner a year depending on how far they live from Copen-hagen.[207] Under the Constitution they are inviolate. They may not be arrested during a session without the consent of the house, nor be held accountable for what they say as part of their duties. Each house is the determiner of qualifications and elections of its members, and sets up rules of legislative procedure. Annual sessions are held commencing the first Tuesday in October. The cabinet may call a special session at any time. At the beginning of the session each house chooses a speaker and one or more vice-speakers. The speaker may vote and participate in debate. Each house has an ample secretarial staff.

The Constitution makes provisions for joint sessions in two cases. The first is the opening session to hear a speech from the throne or the prime minister. The second is that arising in the event of the death of the king without heirs, in which event the joint session selects a king and prescribes the rules of succession.

Each house has several standing committees, five in the lower house and four in the upper.[208] There is also a single joint standing committee to select the officers who represent the entire Rigsdag. In both houses there are standing committees on: (1) Rules and Procedure, (2) Petitions and Memorials, (3) Elections, and (4) Finance. The lower house has in addition a standing committee on salaries and compensation in the public service. Special committees are set up to consider certain legislative topics. All committees are chosen by proportional representation. The speaker is usually a member of the Committee on Rules and Procedure.

Mention should also be made of government committees whose work precedes the introduction of bills.[209] These committees are normally appointed by the government at the request of the Rigsdag or on its own initiative. They are made up of experts, representatives of political parties and of organizations specially concerned. As the Danish committee has a broader representation of interested groups and government authorities than the Swedish, its report is not sent out for criticism before the cabinet acts, as is the case in Sweden.

The two houses jointly choose the Board of State Auditors (*Statsrevisorer*) and the Council on Compensation in the Public Service (*Lonningsraadet*). The former, four in number, check the income and expenditures of the treasury at the close of the fiscal year. The latter, consisting of eight members, two appointed by the cabinet, two by the minister of finance, and four by the two houses, investigates the salaries and working conditions of government employees.

The Rigsdag, in addition to engaging in the constitutional amending process, deals with ordinary, finance, and provisional laws.[210] The enactment of ordinary laws will be discussed first. Under the Constitution no law may be enacted unless it is dealt with (*behandlet*) three separate times in each house. It does not, however, specify as to the amount of time which must elapse between each reading. But the rules of each house provide for three distinct and separate readings. There is no such requirement in Norway and Sweden. Although a bill may be introduced by a private member, most bills are introduced by cabinet ministers.

Upon first reading a bill is discussed usually as to its general purpose.[211] In the lower house no one except ministers may speak more than twice except with the consent of the house. In the upper house there is no limit on debate. When the debate is over a vote is taken on whether the bill should pass to second reading and if so whether it should be sent to a committee. Usually a bill is sent to a special committee between first and second reading. Though each house meets in public, the committee meets in secret.

Second reading usually occurs only after at least two days have elapsed since the first reading. If the bill was sent to a committee even more time will elapse. On second reading the bill is taken up paragraph by paragraph. Germane amendments are permitted. On third reading only the ministry and members of the committee handling the bill may propose amendments. When the third reading is over, the bill is now ready for passage. A majority of the membership of the house is required.

After passage in its original form by the other house, the bill goes to the king for approval. But if it is amended it must go back to the house of origin for approval. If the two houses disagree, the bill may be sent to a special committee at the request of either house. If both houses accept the final form, the bill is then transmitted by the prime minister to the king. The king has not exercised the power of veto since 1865. Thus it is a fixed custom for the king to sign all laws enacted by the Rigsdag. The statutes are published in the *Lovtidende* (Law Journal) issued by the government.

The procedure as to finance laws is similar, except as required by two constitutional provisions. A finance bill can be passed in the first instance only by the lower house. The annual finance bill must be introduced at the beginning of a session. Thus there can be full discussion before March 31, the end of the fiscal year. In case of disagreement between the two houses, temporary appropriations may be made. The budget must be passed annually.

Under Section 25 of the Constitution in cases of necessity and when the Rigsdag is not in session, provisional (*forelobige*) laws may be promulgated by the government. A provisional act must not be in violation of the Constitution. But it may even repeal ordinary laws already enacted. Finance laws may be passed only by the Rigsdag, hence may not be the subject of provisional laws. As soon as the Rigsdag convenes provisional laws must be presented to it. If either house disapproves it ceases to be operative. If it is not passed by both houses it ceases to operate when the Rigsdag adjourns, Denmark employs the system of provisional legislation more than Norway and Sweden.

The most important treaties, such as treaties of peace, alliance, cession of territory, and commercial treaties require ratification by the Rigsdag. Only the Rigsdag may approve a declaration of war. In 1923 a law established a joint Commission (*Navn*) on foreign affairs consisting of sixteen members chosen annually from the two houses. It may make recommendations to the Rigsdag and the ministry. It meets at the request of the ministry or of six of its own members. It operates even when the Rigsdag is not in session.

The members of the ministry or cabinet need not be members of either house.[212] Usually they are members of the lower house from the controlling party or coalition of parties. A minister may speak in either house but may vote only in his own house. Every member of the Rigsdag has the right of interpellation as to any minister. An interpellation does not lead to the fall of the ministry.

The ministry may call and adjourn special sessions at any time. It may adjourn a regular session but not for more than two months and not more than once in the session except with the consent of the Rigsdag. The king, acting through his ministers, may dissolve the lower house, and then decide when the next election shall be held, provided that this be done within the four-year term. It is much more difficult, however, to dissolve the upper house. It may be dissolved only if the lower house passes a bill which the upper house fails to pass and if after a regular lower house election, the new lower house passes the same measure again and the upper house again fails to pass it. Furthermore, the intervening election to the lower house must be the regular one at the end of the four-year period. Thus the upper house may be dissolved only once in four years for failure to agree with the lower house. A constitutional amendment abolishing the upper house was proposed in the 1930's, but failed to receive the support of 45 per cent of the eligible voters.

Lobbying in the objectionable sense does not appear to exist in Denmark.[213] In this respect she resembles Norway and Sweden.

Under the Constitution the Court for State Trials (*Rigsretten*) may try cases involving official conduct of members of the ministry. It is made up of the Supreme Court and of an equal number of members of the upper house chosen by the upper house for a four-year term. The king or the lower house may make accusations. There is no appeal. One convicted may not be pardoned unless the lower house gives its consent. It has seldom been used, and never since 1909.

The Courts

The organization of government and a judicial system seems to have proceeded as follows.[214] The districts from which a group rode out in a body to carry on a war soon united into *herreder* (*hundreds and wapentakes*). The freemen of the *herred* assembled to pass on matters of common concern at the *herredsting* (folk moot). The *herreder* gathered together into larger districts known as *lands* or shires.[215] Each *land* held a *landsthing* (shire moot). The five most important *landsthings* were held at Viborg in northern Jutland, Urnehoved in southern Jutland, Odense on the island of Fünen, Ringsted on the island of Zealand, and Lund in Skåne (now a part of Sweden).[216] The Landsthing decided on what should be law, passed judgment on law suits, decided on campaigns, and elected their leader, the king. Though Denmark was unified about 900, each province had its own law. As one writer has stated:

> In Scandinavia the development of law precedes the establishment of the state. Farther back in time than we can know, the chieftains and freemen met in periodic 'Law things' to decide cases and to formulate rules of conduct. The things were district meetings of the farmer-freemen who brought the force of public opinion to bear upon criminals, and which slowly built up bodies of law which were carefully phrased and just as carefully preserved. In ordinary civil disputes the thing often acted as a court of conciliation or arbitration, getting the opposing parties to agree on a reasonable settlement.[217]

The position of lawman which existed in Norway and Sweden did not so clearly exist in Denmark.[218] If it did it had no official character, and resembled the early Norwegian and Icelandic lawman.

In the age of the Valdemars from the twelfth through the fourteenth centuries authority tended to pass from the Landsthings to the king or the bishops.[219] Much the same occurred in Sweden, whereas in Norway the things persisted longer. The development of the Danehof and the Council of State following 1284 involved assumption of legislative functions; the Council of State also became the supreme judicial tribunal in the fourteenth century.[220] The Landsthings continued to exercise the most important judicial functions and declared the customary law of their areas. The inferior courts were the *things* of the *herred* and *syssel* of the *by* (village) and the *birke* (market). The actual judicial authority gradually passed to the *Foged*, a royal official who presided over the *herred* and village courts. In the fourteenth century the Landsthing was presided over by a judge appointed by the king (*Landsdommer*) who soon in effect exercised the judicial authority.

The Supreme Court of Denmark was set up in 1660 in the same year as the absolute monarchy was created. In 1690 an instruction to the Court ordered that the Court should always ask the king for his opinion in doubtful and difficult cases, as he nominally was the supreme judge himself.[221] This ordinance was repealed in 1753 to secure the independence of the court. A prohibition of 1690 against the quotation of precedents by lawyers was not abolished until 1771. There were reorganizations of the court in 1771, 1774, and 1854. During the reign of Christian VI (1730-1746) legal procedure was improved by a new regulation of the Supreme Court.[222]

The highest court in Denmark today is the Supreme Court (*Höjesteretten*).[223] It consists of a president and fifteen judges. At least nine judges must sit, and superior court judges may be called if less are present. Its members, as well as lower court judges, are appointed for life by the cabinet.[224] The Supreme Court holds three regular sessions annually. The first and shortest session begins after New Year's Day and continues for six weeks; the second and longest begins in March and runs into June; the third begins in October and runs until Christmas. Special sessions during the summer and early fall are frequent. While in session it sits daily except Saturday and Sunday from nine in the morning until two in the afternoon. Opinions are brief, seldom exceeding two printed pages.[225] It is not the practice to cite earlier decisions or legal treatises, nor to discuss any points except those at issue. The statement of facts is made as brief as possible.

Next below the Supreme Court are the two intermediate appellate courts, called *Landsretter* (the provincial courts).[226] These courts replaced the Landsthings which were abolished in 1805.[227] The Western Superior Court sitting at Viborg acts for Jutland. The Eastern Superior Court sitting at Copenhagen acts for the islands. Non-jury cases are tried at Viborg and Copenhagen. Each court holds sessions in other cities to hear jury cases. The Western District Court consists of a president and fourteen other members. The Eastern District Court consists of a president and twenty-three other members.

The Superior Courts (*Landsrettene*) hear both criminal and civil appeals from the lower courts. In addition they have original jurisdiction over important civil cases and all criminal cases requiring a jury trial. At least three judges must sit on all cases. The superior court is the only court in which a jury is employed, as is the situation in Norway. The jury is never used in civil cases. The jury consists of twelve members as compared with ten in Norway. They are chosen by lot from a carefully selected list of names drawn up annually in each of the areas in which the court sits. The prosecution and the criminal defendant may each object to not more than four names as the jurors are drawn. The law requires a jury for all serious offenses, including political crimes. For a conviction eight or more jurors must concur, compared with seven out of ten in Norway. In case of conviction the court may order a new trial if it feels that the jury has based its verdict on insufficient evidence. But at the new trial there must be another set of judges and jurors. The most severe sentence is life imprisonment, capital punishment having been abolished in 1933. In many criminal cases coming up on appeal from the lower courts, three lay judges without legal training participate on an equal basis with the regular district judges both as to determination of guilt and fixing the penalty.[228]

Double appeals are not usually allowed.[229] When the appeal is from the lower court to the superior court, the decision of the latter is final. But on the initiative of the Supreme Court or upon a motion of the Minister of Justice, a case begun in the lower court and appealed to the superior court may be taken up to the Supreme Court. Such procedure is rare. Almost all the cases in the Supreme Court originate in the district courts.

There are about one hundred lower courts (*Underrettene*). Each has jurisdiction over a circuit (*Kreds*). Usually there is a single judge, but in a few districts two or three. When there is more than one judge, cases are distributed by subject-matter; for example, criminal cases will go to one judge, civil to another. These courts have both criminal and civil jurisdiction. The criminal jurisdiction is as to cases of a minor nature not requiring trial by jury. The civil jurisdiction is as to cases involving small amounts of money, domestic relations, illegitimacy, and the like. As there is an ample number of judges the use of masters, examiners, etc., is unknown.

Although Copenhagen contains almost a fourth of the population of Denmark, there is only one lower court organization, *Byretten*, (the town court) established in 1771.[230] This court consists of a president and twenty-two other judges. It is divided into about twenty sections according to types of cases; about half the sections handle criminal cases.

The law sets up a procedure for reconciliation between the parties so as to make formal court procedure unnecessary.[231] This procedure may be in charge of the regular judge himself, as it usually is in the cities, or may be handled by a conciliation commission as it usually is in the rural areas. In 1922 more than 75,000 law suits were disposed of by conciliation. The American experiments have been inspired by the Danish and Norwegian precedents. Conciliation procedure was first set up by an edict of Christian VII in 1795 which was finally supplanted by the 1916 Code. It has been thought that the new use of lay judges will make the conciliation procedure less essential.[232]

In addition to the regular courts thus far discussed there are a number of special courts. The most important one is the Maritime and Commercial Court (*Sö-og Handelsretten*), sitting in Copenhagen. It has jurisdiction over maritime and commercial controversies arising in Copenhagen; cases arising elsewhere in Denmark may be tried by it if the parties consent. It is made up of two lawyers and a panel of persons engaged in maritime affairs. An appeal from it may be taken directly to the Supreme Court. A second important special tribunal is the Permanent Arbitration Court for settling disputes involving collective agreements between employers and workers. Matters involving the clergy are handled by the ecclesiastical courts. There is no separate set of administrative courts as in some Continental nations, including Sweden.

Local Government

In 1841 local government was reformed by introducing parish councils to which the peasants elected some representatives.[233] In turn the parish councils elected members of the county councils. The pastors were no longer to be chairmen of the parish councils, but continued to be members ex officio. The right to vote was extended to owners of but 1.4 acres. The councils were created to deal with school matters and poor relief; but road maintenance, public health, business and industrial licenses, and liquor licenses were also within their province.

The right to vote in local elections was long narrowly restricted. Under legislation of 1837 the six largest cities other than Copenhagen chose councilmen on a property basis permitting only seven per cent of the population to vote. Early in the nineteenth century rural communities began to vote for poor law and school officials. Following the 1849 Constitution municipal powers and local suffrage slowly broadened out. But as late as 1900, only twelve per cent of the people in Copenhagen, sixteen per cent in the larger cities, and eighteen per cent in the rural areas could vote. After 1900 municipal suffrage was greatly broadened, though not as broad as parliamentary suffrage. Municipal voters must have had residence in the city since January first of the preceding year, and must be taxpayers in the community. The local units have increasingly become administrative districts for carrying out national policies and for administering national laws. Section 89 of the Constitution provides that "the right of municipalities to manage their own affairs independently under control of the State shall be laid down by law."

Excluding the larger cities and towns Denmark is divided into 22 areas called *Amter.*[234] In turn each *Amt* is made up of parishes (*Sogne communer*), about thirteen hundred in all. In addition there are about eighteen hundred ecclesiastical parishes (*sogner*). The Danish cities, which are outside of the jurisdiction of the *Amt*, are of two classes: (1) the capital, Copenhagen; and (2) *Kobstäderne* (the provincial towns) about eighty in number.

The chief official of the *Amt* is the *Amtmand* (governor). He is appointed for an indefinite term by the cabinet upon the recommendation of the Minister of the Interior. He presides over the *Amtsraad* (county council) and acts as the chief executive in all local administration. He also represents the national government in the administration of the general laws. He need not have been a resident of the *Amt.*

The county council is popularly elected by the list system of proportional representation. It meets regularly four times a year. It consists of from nine to fifteen members, always an odd number. Its members are elected for a four-year term at the same time as members of the parish council are chosen. It prepares a budget, levies taxes, makes appropriations, and supervises a small number of administrative officials. Members of the council serve without pay. It has much to do with the local police, but recently the national government has taken closer charge. It controls matters of public health, including the operation of hospitals. It handles the public roads. It supervises the parishes. It selects a county school board which has charge of educational funds.

The chief governmental agency of the parish is the parish council (*Sogneraadet*). Its members are chosen for a four-year term by proportional representation. It varies in size from five to nineteen members. The council selects a chairman (*Formand*) who is the chief parish official, and also selects a treasurer. Members of the council receive no pay, but the chairman and treasurer usually do. The council meets once a month.

The parish assesses the value of property for taxation purposes. It collects information as to the liability of its inhabitants to pay income taxes both national and local. It administers relief and social legislation. It participates with the national government in paying the costs of social insurance. It administers public education, which is in the hands of a five-member school commission appointed by the parish council. It builds and maintains local highways. It prepares the official list of those entitled to vote in all elections. It gathers population and vital statistics. It deals with fire prevention.

There are about eighty provincial towns outside the jurisdiction of the *Amter* and the county councils. They vary in population from one thousand to eighty thousand. Each town has a town council (*Byraadet*) of from seven to twenty-five members elected by proportional representation. The town council elects a chairman from its members who then becomes mayor (*Borgmester*). Up to 1919 the cabinet appointed the mayor. The town council selects a school board of from five to nine members to administer the local school system. They have much to do with administration of social welfare. Many cities own and operate hospitals, and help the poorer classes to build homes. Water, gas and electric utilities are publicly owned. Some have municipal heating plants.

The chief officer of the city government of Copenhagen is the *Over-*

präsident appointed by the cabinet.[235] The legislative department is made up of two parts: (1) the *Borger repräsentation* (municipal council), made up of 55 members chosen for four years and presided over by the *Overborgmester* (chief mayor); and (2) the *Magistrat* (executive council) made up of five *Borgmestere* and five *Raad-maend* (councilors) chosen by the municipal council for eight-year terms, and the chief mayor. All are paid salaries. An ordinance must pass both groups, so that Copenhagen really has a bicameral city council.[236] If a measure passed by the municipal council is twice rejected by the executive council, the former may appeal to the Minister of the Interior who can validate the measure. No measure can be passed without the approval of the municipal council. Conflict seldom occurs as ten of the eleven members of the executive council are chosen by the municipal council. The *Over-präsident* has the power of suspensive veto. The veto stands only if upheld on appeal to the Minister of the Interior. The members of the executive council also have important administrative duties. The chief mayor and the five mayors are each in charge of one of the six sections into which the city administration is divided. The various municipal activities are: (1) education, (2) regulation of industry, (3) legacies and foundations, (4) police, (5) hospitals, (6) social welfare, (7) highways, (8) public health, and (9) publicly owned utilities.

In 1764 a municipal sanitation office was set up in Copenhagen to regulate the disposition of garbage and rubbish. Paving was made a public function in 1777. In 1863 Copenhagen reorganized her police force after the English model. By 1865 all the larger cities had made fire protection a municipal function. In 1867 Copenhagen set up a municipally owned gas plant. From 1860 to 1880 almost every city set up a public water supply system.[237]

Religion

Christianity came into Denmark during the Viking period. King Harold I was baptized in 826, though largely as a diplomatic gesture to secure German territory. King Harold II was baptized in 974 and a much more sweeping Christianization ensued.[238] The complete introduction is generally ascribed to Canute the Great (1018-1035).[239] He appointed English bishops to counteract the influence of Hamburg and Bremen. Pope Gregory VII (1073-1085) suggested without success that the Danish king make his kingdom a papal fief.[240]

It was not until the twelfth century that the church really became incorporated into the Danish community. Shortly after 1100 a Danish archbishopric was created at Lund independent of Hamburg-Bremen, as the supreme authority over all the Scandinavian churches including the Norwegian and Swedish.[241] The first archbishop, Asser, organized the Danish church, and by the introduction of tithing made the church economically secure. King Niels (1104-1134) secured for the Church both tithes and ecclesiastical jurisdiction in matters concerning the clergy. It was through the Christian church that Denmark became culturally integrated with Europe.

In the reign of Valdemar the Great (1157-1182) there arose the first great conflict between the royal power and the Church.[242] Archbishop Eskil adhered to the ideas of Pope Gregory VII that the spiritual should be independent of the temporal power. Eskil strove for independence not only from the Hamburg-Bremen see but also from the Danish king. Consequently he was exiled for several years. On his return he came to an agreement with Valdemar and in 1170 anointed his son as king, thus helping to introduce the idea of hereditary kingship in Denmark. In turn Valdemar recognized a modified independence of the Church. Eskil prepared the first ecclesiastical code for Skåne.[243] In 1177 Eskil was again exiled, and Valdemar forced the clergy of Lund to recognize his foster-brother Absalon[244] as his successor. Following Valdemar's death Absalon was virtually a joint ruler over Denmark with Canute (1182-1202), even leading armies.[245] It was Absalon who wrote the first church law for all Denmark, and founded Copenhagen.

Although in most European nations the Church handled its own penal problems involving clergy, Valdemar Atterdag (1340-1375) prosecuted before a *thing* court clergymen alleged to have swindled a Copenhagen merchant.[246] About 1365 Valdemar secured from the Pope an arrangement making the Danish church a national self-contained church.[247] From now on there was a prescriptive right of the crown to nominate to church offices in some cases. There was also a power to remove from office. The Danish church was the only one in Europe not containing a single foreigner.

Next to Switzerland the Scandinavian nations were the first to embrace Lutheranism. An edict of 1527 permitted a choice between Catholicism and Lutheranism.[248] In 1536 a great assembly of Danish nobles abolished the offices of the Catholic bishops, handed their lands over to the king and the nobles, and set up the Lutheran State Church after the pattern of the North German Churches.[249] The clergy lost its political power, and the king and the nobles were supreme. The revenue of the king was increased threefold.

For long witchcraft was tried by an ecclesiastical tribunal. The burning alive of sorceresses was forbidden by Christian II (1513-1523), yet as late as 1675 two were thus punished.[250]

The Lutheran Church at first showed little tolerance of other Protestant sects. Christian III (1534-1559) banished Calvinist refugees from Denmark.[251] Aliens could not settle in Denmark unless they passed an examination on the Creed. In 1698 Christian V refused permission to the French Huguenots to settle in Denmark though later his queen induced him to permit settlement in Copenhagen.[252]

A pietistic movement in conflict with orthodox Lutheranism sprang up about 1700.[253] The members met in small groups called conventicles. The orthodox church induced Frederick IV to forbid conventicles in 1706. Another conventicle Act was enacted in 1741. This act was used, though less rigorously than in Norway and Sweden, far into the nineteenth century to suppress religious dissent.[254] Sabbath ordinances of 1730 and 1735 forbade innocent pleasures. A decree provided for fining of pastors who preached longer than one hour. In 1736 the king decreed the rite of confirmation.[255] This had a great influence on education, as ability to read religious texts was a prerequisite.

About 1350 the Black Death came to all of Europe including Denmark. This was made a ground of persecution of Jews in many countries. In Denmark, however, a convocation of bishops called by the king "proclaimed that the Black Death could hardly be the work of the Jews in Denmark, since there were none; that it was not the work of the devil, but an ordinary virulent sickness, for which the remedy lay in fortitude and prayer."[256] About 1675 concessions were made to Jewish capitalists and manufacturers.[257] In 1788 the Danish government placed native Jews on almost the same plane of civil equality as other persons.[258] A law of 1814 seems to have given equal rights.[259] In 1832 when the royal commission on the establishment of consultative estates for Denmark reported, it recommended that Jews be accorded the same franchise and eligibility as other citizens. In 1943 the Danes assisted the six thousand Jews who remained in Denmark to escape to Sweden. A pastoral letter of the Danish bishops protested the persecution "because Christ was a Jew, because the persecution violates Christian ideals and love of mankind and because it violates the Danish sense of justice."[260]

The Constitution of 1849 established full religious freedom. A provision for the drawing up of a comprehensive church constitution remained a dead letter, and the Rigsdag passed legislation from time to time.[261] An 1862 statute permitted the layman to go to church wherever he might please; he could cross parish lines. In 1903 congregational councils for the election of parsons were established, and assistance was given to the free congregations.[262]

In Denmark today 98 per cent of the population is Lutheran in religion. Denmark has, however, a larger proportion of non-Protestants than either Norway or Sweden.[263] There are 23,000 Roman Catholics compared with 3,500 to 6,500 in Sweden and 3,000 in Norway. There are 6,000 Jews compared with 6,000 to 6,500 in Sweden and 1,400 in Norway. The State Lutheran Church is the most broadly inclusive organization outside the state itself.

Education

From about 1721 the government under the influence of pietism opened about 240 elementary schools on crown property on which the teachers could live and instruct the peasant children in Scriptures and reading.[264] In 1739 every young person was required to learn to read under a decree commanding the Danish landlords to follow the example set upon the royal estates; later decrees left the matter to the judgment of the landlords, hence no national system was established. A movement beginning in 1789 resulted in the Educational Reform of 1814.[265] Every child must be given instruction from his sixth to his fourteenth year. Rural schools were to be so close together that no child had more than a mile to go. Instruction was to comprise Scripture, reading, writing, arithmetic, gymnastics and some practical gardening.

The Great School Commission, operating from 1789 to 1814, had worked out the above mentioned reforms. It also abolished the Latin disputation at the University of Copenhagen. Between 1797 and 1802 a new plan requiring more attention to the vernacular and to utilitarian subjects was introduced experimentally in Copenhagen, Odense, and Oslo for the preparatory schools. A law of 1809 made the plan applicable in both Denmark and Norway. Denmark in 1791 was the first Scandinavian nation to establish a teachers' college. By 1814 Denmark had a comprehensive national school system, followed by Norway in 1827 and Sweden in 1842.

In 1844 the 1814 laws were revised for stricter enforcement; and Copenhagen appointed its first superintendent of schools. In 1848 the Danish statistician Bergsoe announced that all children of legal school age were actually in school, "a result which both England and France, not to mention all the south European countries, must view with envy."[266] In 1854 a Bureau of Education was established in the Ministry of Culture. In 1856 a new general school law was adopted. It embodied the latest ideas on pedagogy and sanitation of school buildings, and increased teachers' salaries and pensions. The problem of elementary public education was now solved, except that pauper children were segregated in pauper schools.

In 1850 a bill was introduced in the Rigsdag which recognized the Latin schools and the practical schools (*realskoler*) as equally valid, and terminated the reactionary influence exercised by the university through its entrance examination. In 1851 the preparatory schools were required to establish practical courses leading to the bachelor of arts degree. Denmark has carried out adult education farther than any other country. Between 1844 and 1864 about twenty folk schools were founded under the leadership of Grundtvig and Kristen Kold to instruct persons preferably from eighteen to twenty-five.[267] History, political science, and literature were the subjects emphasized, but there were no classes, recitation, examinations, grades or accreditation. The folk schools were privately owned, but later received public support.

In 1903 secondary schools were changed in the direction of a unified school with three senior branches, classical, modern, and mathematics and natural science.[268]

The present basic law on education is the National Education Act of 1937.[269] Compulsory instruction begins at seven and ends at fourteen. Elementary schools are of two types: urban and rural. The town school consists of a junior department for children between seven and eleven and a middle school for children between eleven and fifteen. The middle school is bifurcated: one branch giving a cultural education and the other a practical. The elementary public schools are supervised by local committees of education approved by the local councils. Schools are locally financed but receive aid from the national government. Ninety per cent of the children between seven and fourteen attend public schools, though private schools are permitted.

The national subsidy per pupil is the same as in the private school; but in the private school the remainder is privately paid, whereas in the case of the public school the locality pays.[270] The secondary schools consist of the middle school and the senior high school, the former covering a four-year course and the latter a three-year course. Upon graduation from the latter the student may enter college. Elementary education is free. A small charge may be made at the middle and senior high schools if the parents have a high income. There are universities at Copenhagen since 1479 and Aarhus since 1933 where instruction is free.

Agriculture

During the period from 1241 to 1340 the new manorial lords gradually regained their powers in Denmark.[271] They were exempt from taxation, and to be certain of their military support the government had to exempt their tenants too. This caused grave inadequacy in royal finance. There was a strong incentive for freeholders to give up their estates and become tenants under the nobility. By the time of Christian II (1513-1523) the temporal and spiritual lords owned nearly three-fourths of all the land in Denmark; and only twenty per cent of the farmers were freeholders.[272] They monopolized the great offices of state, and limited admission to their class by patents slowing their lineage and exemption from taxation. In the reign of Christian II there were about 250 such families.

In 1702 the Danish monarchy abolished serfdom in the islands where alone in Denmark proper it existed.[273] But in 1701 there was established a militia system which bound the peasant to the place of his birth. The cultivators of the soil on the estates were tenants who occupied their land under varied regulations. Their position was only a little better than that of the German serfs and with respect to tenure often more precarious. Tenure for a term of years was common, at the end of which the owner might not renew if he did not so desire. Between 1660 and 1720 the estates had encroached increasingly until only a small fraction of the soil was freehold. As the king needed money, estate property was sold, but the land went to creditors and nobles even after 1764 when the Crown planned to sell in small parcels.

The most severe restrictions on the peasants occurred in 1733 when the system of a national militia was combined with the *Stavnsbaand*, providing that between the ages of fourteen and thirty-six the peasants' sons should be bound as villeins to the estates on which they were born.[274] A few years later this was extended so as to cover the peasant from his fourth to his fortieth year. The medieval system of common tillage still survived. To make matters worse the number of estates increased. It was not until 1740 that a law freed the peasants from their obligation to assist their lords in hunting. The increase of rural population was facilitated by laws of 1769 and 1781 removing restrictions on parcellization of land.[275]

Largely through the efforts of Christian Colbjornsen (1749-1814) a Norwegian lawyer in the service of the Crown, the landlords were deprived in 1787 of their judicial authority over their tenants.[276] In 1788 the *Stavnsbaand* was abolished. At the same time the State started a Credit Bank to enable the peasants to free their land and move out from the villages. As a result most Danish farms had been separated by 1807. In 1837 cattle owners were made responsible for damage done on others' property. Only the crofters remained to be freed. About 1916 legislation confiscated about a third of the large landowners' estates for parcelling out into smaller holdings, which were allotted in a form of State copyhold.[277]

When at the close of the eighteenth century the land was being divided up into individual holdings, the government attempted to provide land for the crofters but only with small success.[278] The tendency was to give them little or no land and to increase labor obligations. In many places they were systematically peonized. As of 1843 and 1844 their status was somewhat better than that of the Norwegian and Swedish crofters. But proposals to improve their lot were not as yet enacted into law.

In 1835 the government submitted projects for further land reform to the Roskilde and Viborg assemblies.[279] Tenantry was still common and personal tenure obligations attached to much of the land so held. The government proposed to give the landlords greater freedom in dealing with their tenants, as larger enterprises were more efficient. The assemblies were opposed. At Viborg the peasants suggested the establishment of a public loan fund to assist tenants to purchase their holdings. There were discussions as to the hunting rights of landlords, the problem of the rural proletariat (*Husmaend*), and the redemption of personal service obligations by money payments.

In 1844 a decree was issued limiting the free hauling required as to public officials, and to some extent substituting money payments for the hauling required.[280] In 1850 the distinction between privileged and unprivileged lands in their obligation to bear the costs of maintaining roads, schools, churches, cemeteries, and the livery service was abolished. Compulsory service obligations were commuted into cash payments. In 1863 legislation abolished payment of tithes in kind. A decree of 1818 consolidated rural taxes and converted their payment from kind to silver. In 1850 land was equally taxed and tax privileges taken away. In 1854 a statute gave strong inducements to landlords to sell their lands to their hereditary tenants, though they were not required to do so. By 1850 fifty-eight per cent of Danish farms were held as freeholds. Denmark was the pioneer in Scandinavian agricultural legislation.

The status of farmers was greatly improved by the farmers' cooperatives first established in Denmark in 1882, after which the Norwegian and Swedish were later patterned.[281] In general, the rules of a dairy cooperative are as follows: (1) Membership is open to all farmers in the neighborhood. (2) The farmers are jointly liable. (3) Profits are to be distributed in proportion to the quantity of milk delivered. (4) Each farmer is to have one vote. (5) Each farmer is to deliver all his milk to the dairy, except that used on the farm.

In 1903 the old taxes on land were changed to modern property taxes and combined with general income and capital taxes, and the tithes were gradually commuted.[282]

At the turn of the nineteenth century the holders of the large estates were willing to let their workers have five-acre plots of their own in return for part-time work on the estates. In 1899 the Rigsdag passed an act offering state loans of ninety per cent of the cost of such small holdings.[283] In

1919 the program was broadened.[284] It was realized that larger farms of
fifteen to thirty-five acres were desirable. The government therefore
bought private lands for redivision, and used the old glebe lands also.
A heavy tax was laid on landed estates unless they would surrender one-
third of their land for compensation to the state. In 1919 following the
ideas of Henry George, the holder paid no purchase price for his land,
but rather an annual "ground-rent" of four per cent of the value of
the lands as reappraised at periodic intervals. At first rents were made
to fluctuate with farm commodity prices. Later a sliding scale was calculated each year based on the earning capacity of small farms. Detailed
controls were embodied in legislation of 1933, 1938 and 1943.[285] It should
be noted that three-fourths of the small holdings, averaging twenty-five
acres in size, were established without state aids.

Today about ninety-five per cent of the Danish farmers own their
land. Legislation aids the farm laborer to become a land holder, and
at the same time prevents the large estates from buying up smaller holdings.[286] Seventy-five per cent of the land is used for agriculture compared
with eleven per cent in Sweden and three in Norway. The average Danish
farm is larger than that in Sweden and Norway, being 38 acres in size.
Steps are being taken to reclaim the heath of Jutland. In 1938 seventy-
two per cent of Denmark's exports consisted of farm produce; her foreign
trade per person was the highest in Europe.

Criminal Law

In the reign of Harold Hein (1074-1080) there was a great alteration
in criminal procedure.[287] Previously criminal defendants had to prove
their innocence by duel, or ordeal by fire. Under the new law a criminal
defendant, where positive evidence was wanting, might clear himself
by an oath, when certain impartial parties swore that they believed him
innocent.

The criminal law of the thirteenth century is to be found in the Laws
of King Valdemar Victorious (1202-1240).[288] The police power was
weak. The state did not intervene except where it was a party directly
in interest as in cases of murder, kidnapping and repeated theft. Whereas
the law of other countries abolished private revenge by making the state
the sole avenger, the Danish law sought to bring the victim and the
wrongdoer into agreement, thus securing the peace. Hence penalties were
mild, consisting chiefly of fines, most of which went to the victim. Introduction of Roman law was changing this approach in other European
nations. Murder, treason and theft resulted in the penalty of hanging.
Mayhem and kidnapping carried the penalty of imprisonment but the
defendant could buy his freedom from the king provided he could obtain

a pardon from the victim. The more serious criminal cases were prosecuted by the king's *embedsmand* or local sheriff, one for each *herred*. In
other cases he could act only at the request of the plaintiff. In such cases
the royal treasury received part of the fine if it were over three marks
of silver. This was one of the main sources of royal income. The proceeding was in the *thing* courts, the primary assembly of each *herred*. When
a case came up, they elected three, six or twelve of their fellows, depending on the gravity of the crime, to pronounce judgment. Thus a system
of jury trial was introduced. The jurors were called *Naevninger* or "named
men". If the jury were evenly divided six more were elected to it, until
one side had a majority. In Jutland and Fünen there was a special class
of professional jurors and inquirers, eight to a *herred*, appointed by the
king, known as *Saendemaend*. They constituted the juries in cases of
murder, mayhem, kidnapping of women, boundary disputes, ownership
of land and slander. Their judgment could be set aside by the assembled
thing. The *embedsmand* could not make any decisions, but could only
enforce them. If he had to levy on household goods, he must do it without public display. There was no ordeal by battle. While ordeal by the
hot iron had existed in the old codes, Valdemar abolished it. As in England, compurgators, known men of the district could swear a man free
from a charge. But in Danish law they were merely character witnesses.
The accused still had to stand trial before the juries if the *embedsmand*
thought there was a prima facie case against him, or in civil cases if there
were compurgators on both sides.

The substantive criminal law of the thirteenth century was broad
in scope, much as the modern.[289] In some cases vengeance by the victim
was allowed. In others the defendant could buy off the victim. In still
others the defendant was punished by a fine going to the king or by loss
of his life. Outlawry was employed. The English law of the same period
was much further advanced, the Danish resembling the earlier Anglo-
Saxon. The law of negligence had not yet arisen. But Danish criminal
procedure was ahead of the English. A presenting jury was in operation.
The ordeal had been abolished, though wager of law was not. The *royal*
justice in England was stronger.

Danish legislation from 1500 to 1550 reveals an increasing progress
towards the conception that the end to be sought is the maintenance of
public order and safety rather than private redress.[290] More severe penalties were provided for violent crimes such as murder, as there were wars
and internal strife. The laws of Christian II (1513-1523) penalized with
death all cases of deliberate homicide. Following the Reformation
ecclesiastical jurisdiction was taken over by the state; this involved crimes
such as adultery and seduction. Legislation in the seventeenth century

provided for public prosecution of murderers.[291] Capital punishment was the penalty for deliberate murder (except by the nobility), rape and adultery. Accidental acts were no longer regarded as criminal. Witchcraft, vagrancy, incest and concealment of child-birth were now prosecuted by the State.

John Howard, a leading English penologist, found the Danish prisons dirty and offensive in 1781.[292] Because windows were kept shut, trials were carried on under unpleasant conditions. An article published in the Danish journal *Minerva* in 1796 described the Philadelphia system, and from that time forward American as well as English developments were closely followed.[293] In 1797 there was founded in Odense the Society for the Rescue of Fallen Citizens. It favored prisons stressing social rehabilitation rather than retribution.

The reforming activities of the government set up in 1784 under Crown Prince Frederick extended to criminal law and the penal system.[294] Its legal expert, the Norwegian lawyer, Christian Colbjornsen, held advanced ideas. In 1789 two principles were enunciated: punishment as mild as compatible with public safety, and the object of punishment to be redemption of the offender. The last vestiges of torture were abolished. The Supreme Court declared mutilation and branding to be unseemly "in our times."

In 1790 the government separated the younger and first-time offenders in the "children's house" in Copenhagen from the more hardened offenders. In 1793 the first national prison law was promulgated. It prescribed minimum standards of sanitation and comfort, and made it obligatory upon officers to enforce them. The same year an ordinance on debtor prisoners ordered that they be accorded special consideration and must not be placed on the same basis as criminals. In 1836 a reform school for boys was established. Following a visit of Elizabeth Fry of England in 1841 a Prison Society was formed, and in 1842 the king appointed a commission to study the problem. The Danish leader was Professor C. N. David, who journeyed abroad to investigate prison conditions and in 1848 was appointed inspector-general of the prison system.

In 1800 police systems were inadequate and obsolete. In the reign of Christian VIII (1839-1848) the police did not confine itself to maintenance of good order, but sided with the reactionary authorities. In 1863 Copenhagen reorganized her police force after the British system, setting up a professional corps, including a detective squad, well equipped and paid.[295]

Scientific investigation of the theory of punishment for crime led to a series of modern codes of substantive criminal law on the initiative of A. S. Örsted in 1833, 1840 and 1841.[296] In 1850 a commission was appointed to prepare a draft of a complete criminal code. This draft served as the basis for the work of a new commission appointed in 1859. A new code thus prepared went into effect in 1866.

With respect to criminal procedure a code of 1819 more effectively established the inquisitorial process.[297] The Danish constitutions of 1849 and 1866 provided for the introduction of the jury. During the nineteenth century the most important legislation occurred in 1845.[298]

The inquisitorial system of criminal procedure was not abolished until 1916. But that system was never practiced in its purest form and existed for less than a century and a half and even then a lawyer was appointed for the criminal defendant and paid for by the state unless he chose to select his own counsel.[299]

From 1916 to 1919 important changes, based in part on the law of England, France, Germany, Austria and Norway, were made in the entire judiciary system. The public was admitted, oral procedure replaced documentary or written proof, and in important criminal cases juries were provided.[300] In 1936 the courts were further democratized. The jury institution was supplanted with lay judges sitting on the bench together with the professional judges in the first and second instances.[301] Justice is speedy. "In Denmark the whole disposal of a case from its first beginning to the end generally does not take more than one or two months."[302]

The Penal Code of 1930-1933 was introduced by the Minister of Justice, C. T. Zahle. Taking account of the new concepts as to a treatment of criminals, it gives weight to the offender's mentality, environment and motives and provides punishment in proportion to its educative effect.[303] The age of responsibility was raised to fifteen. Juvenile prisons, planned to operate through the mediums of education and training, were introduced for offenders between fifteen and twenty-one. Capital punishment was abolished. The state was given authority to confine for an indefinite period dangerous criminals not amenable to correction.

On June 1, 1945, two laws were passed to deal with the Danish quislings.[304] One law was a supplement to the Civil Penal Law of 1930. This law introduced the doctrines of retroactivity and reestablished the death penalty. The Danish Constitution, unlike the Norwegian, does not provide against retroactive penal laws, though in practice previously no such laws had been passed. The 1945 law penalized acts from April 9, 1940, to June 1, 1946. The other law was a supplement to the Law of Procedure of 1919. To secure speed the lowest court judges could try cases, the tribunal to consist of a judge and two jurors. The right of appeal was restricted. On arrest the defendant is to be kept in custody until final decision. A law of August 28, 1945, penalized offensive collaboration in work and trade. A law of June 19, 1946, made the earlier laws less severe.

Persons accused of crime are given free legal services and incidental expenses irrespective of financial status.[305] Free representation by counsel is also provided, under certain circumstances in matrimonial matters. In 1885 the Danish bar association instituted legal aid (*Retshjaelp*) to provide legal advice.[306]

In the lowest courts the prosecution is represented by the chief of police or his deputy. In the superior courts and Supreme Court prosecution is by the State prosecutor, an appointive official, and his assistants.

The Department of Justice has existed since 1848 when Denmark set up a constitutional monarchy. It is in charge of law enforcement. It acts as legal adviser to the government and represents the government in all cases both criminal and civil.[307] Judges are appointed by the king acting through the cabinet, but obviously the minister of justice is very influential. One of the key officials is the director of prisons, who has control of penal and correctional institutions and matters relating to parole and pardon. The system of state police is administered by the Department of Justice. Local police are supervised by the department. Within the department is the Council on Medical Jurisprudence (*Retslageraadet*), which gives attention to the legal rights and duties of physicians and pharmacists. There is a similar agency (*Teaterraadet*) with regard to the theater industry. The office of film censor is in the department.

In 1888 Denmark passed a law providing compensation to the victims of erroneous criminal prosecutions. It was the most liberal European law on the subject.[308]

Social Legislation

During the period from 1891 to 1933 Denmark developed its present social legislation. In 1933, under the leadership of K. K. Steincke, present Minister of Justice, Denmark codified its legislation by enacting the so-called "Social Reform." This contains the National Insurance Act, which includes regulations governing health insurance, disability insurance, and old-age pensions; the Industrial Accidents Act; the Labor Exchanges and Unemployment Insurance Act; and the Public Assistance Act, including regulations for child welfare, the care of the insane, the crippled, the blind, the deaf, and other special groups, and ordinary public assistance.[309] Eighty-two per cent of social welfare expenditures are paid for by the national government and the municipalities. Large proportions of the expenditures of the plans traditionally regarded as insurance rather than assistance schemes are financed by the government. It seems fair to say of Danish social legislation "that the Danes are seldom satisfied with anything for long, because of a national instinct to improve what already exists and to forestall every possible future difficulty."[310]

Mr. Justice Brandeis expressed to the author a keen admiration of Danish social legislation.

Slavery. In 1792 Denmark was the first European country to stop the slave trade in African negroes, which supplied her West Indian islands.[311] This was done at the instigation of Ernst Schimmelmann, the Minister of Finance. In 1840 a Danish law on the status of slaves in the Virgin Islands made provision for humane treatment, established their right to purchase their freedom, and permitted them one free day per week to earn purchase money. The actual emancipation of slaves occurred in 1848.

Freedom of Occupation. With the establishment of absolutism in 1660 the gild system was encouraged by the government. Eventually there was a reaction against the gild monopolies, and a rescript of 1761 sharply limited their privileges, as did also a decree of 1800.[312] In 1857 the Rigsdag established freedom of occupation.[313]

Tariff. Mercantilistic protectionism reached its climax in Denmark with the tariffs of 1762 and 1768. The former carried import prohibitions against over 150 commodities.[314] In 1797 it enacted the most liberal tariff law in all Europe.[315] The rates were reduced, most export duties abolished, and 750 items removed from the list of articles which could not be imported. The tariff of 1838 simplified schedules and lowered duties.[316] It subordinated protection to revenue, and launched Denmark on the way to free trade. The tariff of 1863 marked the triumph of free trade sentiment, and was the basis of Danish tariff legislation until 1908.

Women. The right of women to equality of education, work, and political activity was defended in the eighteenth century by Ludvig Holberg, Christian Falster, Frederik Eilschow, and the Sneedorffs.[317] The Danish feminist movement dates from 1850 when Mathilde Fibiger published *Tolv breve* (Twelve Letters), asserting the right of women to be individuals. In 1857 Pauline Worm published a novel of feminine revolt, *De fornuftige, en dansk roman* (Sensible People, a Danish Novel). Unmarried women were made independent of guardians in 1851.[318] Equal rights of inheritance were given to women the same year. A proposal in 1810 to combat prostitution by giving women opportunities to engage in trade and crafts was defeated by the gilds. Finally in 1857 a law established the right of an unmarried woman to earn her living in any craft or trade. Minor civil service posts were opened to them in the 1860's. After 1825 women of the upper social stratum were admitted more freely to university lecture courses, without, however, the privilege of taking examinations. The first intermediate school for girls was established in Copenhagen in 1851. In 1859 the Danish government established an examination for certifying women school teachers, but it was not until 1867 that women were placed on the same basis as men. In 1880 married women were given control of their earnings. In 1948 three women pastors were ordained in Denmark, the first in Scandinavia.

In 1907 women were given the right to vote for town and parish councils.[319] In 1915 they were given the right to vote for members of the Rigsdag.[320] Through liberal laws on marriage and divorce Danish women enjoy a maximum degree of personal freedom.[321] Absolute divorce may be obtained where there is mutual consent after a period of separation. Denmark was the first Scandinavian nation in which a woman served in the ministry. Miss Nina Bang was Minister of Education in 1924.

Labor. In 1835 royal decrees forbade Danish journeymen to reside in countries where labor was permitted to organize.[322] Gilds were abolished in 1862. The modern trade union movement dates back to about 1875.[323] The Danish Federation of Labor was established about fifty years ago. Until recently the Danish federation embraced a greater proportion of the eligible workers than the Norwegian and Swedish. The Danish federation differs from the Norwegian and Swedish in that they are federations of industrial unions. The Danish federation is less centralized than were the Norwegian and Swedish. While in the United States, acceptance of contract terms by union negotiations is equivalent to union ratification, in Denmark the requirements of a secret ballot on proposed agreements is the crucial stage in collective bargaining. But legislation has been enacted to prevent the rejection of agreements by compact minorities in the event of majority indifference. Section 10 of the Conciliation Act provides that a draft agreement is deemed rejected if more than fifty per cent of the votes are cast against it, provided that seventy-five per cent of those eligible to vote do so. The percentage necessary for rejection increases by one-half of one per cent for every percentage by which the recorded vote is below seventy-five per cent.

Denmark goes further in government regulation of labor than Sweden and less than Norway. Danish legislation, however, has usually been enacted on the basis of joint agreement between the central organizations of labor and employers. There is a well developed system of government mediation. If the employer and trade union fail to reach agreement in bargaining over new contracts, a mediator comes into the picture. There are three principal mediators, one designated as chairman, and twelve associate mediators. Mediation proceedings are conducted by a single mediator. Both factions must attend mediation proceedings, and postpone direct economic action for a maximum period of one week at the request of the mediator. The mediator may frame a mediation proposal, which both sides are required to submit to their constituents. While the proposal is not binding, it is usually accepted; as to the public it represents a reasonable settlement. If the mediation fails, the parties are ordinarily free to resort to economic weapons.

In 1896 there was a centralization of employers' associations through the formation of the Employers' Association. In 1898 the workers followed suit by forming the Amalgamated Trade Unions. These two groups drew up the constitution of Danish labor law by the September Agreement of 1899.[324] This agreement, still in force today, defines the relations between employers and employees. Each party may decree labor stoppages. A strike or lockout must be voted by at least three-fourths of a competent assembly. Two notices must be given, fourteen and seven days before a stoppage; and a three-month notice for cancellation of a labor agreement. A right to organize is recognized, but also the right of an individual to refrain from joining. The employer is to have the right to allocate work. Foremen need not join a trade union.

At various times emergency legislation has provided that certain existing wage scales should continue for certain periods unless the parties agreed to changes. In 1936 a special arbitration board was given full powers by a special act to settle strikes of national importance. In view of the general satisfaction with the labor courts and mediation boards, Denmark is not moving toward general compulsory arbitration. But during the Second World War the employers and workers asked for legislation to some extent resembling compulsory arbitration. In September 1940 the Danish government created the Labor and Conciliation Board to hear disputes over issues not covered by trade agreements and which could not be settled by negotiations between the employers and workers even with the help of the government conciliation service.[325] The employers, the workers and the government each have three representatives on the board, which may make a final decision in such disputes and also make recommendations to the government for further legislation or administrative provisions for maintaining industrial peace. Denmark has had less strikes than either Norway or Sweden.[326]

There are certain types of disputes which must be submitted to a public tribunal for a decision enforceable by the nation. These disputes have to do with rights arising under existing agreements between employers and workers. There may be no strike or lockout over disputed interpretations of collective agreements. Such disputes are tried by a permanently established labor court at the request of either party. A failure to accept the decision results in a liability for damages. In 1910 Denmark set up the Permanent Arbitration Court (*Den Faste Voldgiftsret*) made up of three members chosen by the employers and three by the workers.[327] One of each group of three must have legal training. The chairman of the court, who is selected by the six appointees, must also have legal training. No appeal lies from its decisions. From 1910 to 1943 it handled over three thousand cases.[328]

When disputes arise over matters not covered in the collective agreements or over renewal of such agreements, the labor court has no jurisdiction, and strikes may legally occur. Such disputes are handled by a mediation board which, however, can make no decision nor enforce any suggestion. The Danish mediating agency consists of three *Forligsmaend* (conciliators) who hear cases individually or collectively. Few cases have come to this board.

Workmen's Compensation. Workmen's compensation was introduced by an act of 1898.[329] Under the law of 1933, Denmark has one of the most comprehensive systems in the world. Fishermen were included in 1900, seamen in 1905, and agricultural laborers and woodsmen in 1908. The present law covers virtually every one working for another, including domestic servants. State and local employees are covered. Employers are compelled to carry liability insurance for all workers in a company approved by the Department of Social Affairs. If an employer fails to take out insurance, he is personally liable, and if he is unable to pay, all the approved accident insurance companies of the country are jointly liable. Since 1933 workers are also protected against occupational disease. During the first weeks the worker is taken care of through his sick club, in which all workers are compulsorily insured. If he dies, funeral expenses are paid and his family receive a cash payment. In case of permanent disability the worker receives a pension based on his usual earnings and the degree of incapacity. The pension may never be more than sixty per cent of his regular earnings. If the disability is less than fifty per cent he may be paid a lump sum, thus permitting him to start some enterprise for himself. The administration of the law is by a directorate of accident insurance (*direktoratet for ulykkeforsikringen*) in the Ministry of Social Affairs. The directorate is made up of representatives of employers and workers. Its decisions may be appealed to the Accident Insurance Council (*Ulykkeforsikringsraadet*). Its decision is final.

Unemployment Insurance. In 1907 the government began to make contributions to the unemployment benefit societies which were largely sponsored by the trade unions.[330] Today the basic feature of the Danish unemployment insurance system is these approved and state-aided societies. The funds of the societies come from contributions by members, the national treasury, and the municipality.[331] Employers do not contribute as this would be added to selling prices and therefore borne by the population as a whole. When a worker has difficulty in contributing, the municipality may assist him by paying half of his contribution. Ninety-five per cent of all workers in industry and transport are members of the societies.

After a short period of unemployment, usually six days, the worker is paid a cash allowance for a certain number of days, varying from ninety to two hundred days in any one fiscal year. The length of the waiting period and the amount of the allowance varies with different societies.[332] But no worker receives more than two-thirds of the average earnings of his trade. No benefits are paid to strikers, recipients of sick benefits or similar allowance, or those who unreasonably refuse to accept other work.

To cope with periods of extreme unemployment a State Unemployment Fund was set up. Employers contributed a fixed number of kroner per worker. Grants were made to the societies with the result that payments could be extended over much more of a fiscal year.

Administration and supervision is in the hands of the director of labor and other agencies in the Department of Labor. Representatives of the Societies and of the Rigsdag advise the director. Employment exchanges are set up to aid in bringing prospective employers and the unemployed together.

Public Assistance—General Relief. Prior to the Reformation much church property was devoted to poor relief.[333] Thereafter such property was diverted to other purposes. Legalized beggary became the most extensive form of relief. In 1755 the Danish government ordered city beggars placed in workhouses. In rural districts resident paupers incapable of work were taken care of by members of the parish in rotation. In Denmark parcellization of land spread the means of subsistence more evenly, hence conditions were better than in Norway and Sweden. In 1820 N. F. S. Grundtvig remarked that food was still found in the homes of the poor despite a financial crisis, and added that a country might be accounted rich "when few have too much and fewer too little."[334] In 1799 and 1803 Denmark revised her poor laws and established commissions for rural parishes and municipalities.[335] There was no change until 1867 at which time the poor commissioners were made elective instead of appointive. The poor laws of 1799 and 1803 established the duty of the local authorities to provide necessary assistance in cases of distress, as did the 1849 constitution. Modern social legislation began in Denmark in the 1890's.[336] The poor law of 1891 provided that when distress arose out of specified diseases or disability, relief could be given without the imposition of legal disability and without loss of the right to vote.[337] A law of the same year removed the care of the aged from the operation of the poor law.

In 1918 preparatory work for a radical revision of the poor laws was commenced. In 1933 the Public Assistance Act, a part of the Social Reform legislation, was enacted.[338] In 1900 fifty-two per cent of the costs resulting from social legislation involved public assistance, in 1930 thirty-four per cent, and in 1942 only twenty-five per cent. Public assistance is granted to those not aided by social insurance. It is administered through the Social Committee, a popularly elected local authority. Appeal lies to the county governor and then to the Minister of Social Affairs. Aid is of three kinds: Special Relief, Communal Relief, and Poor Relief. Special relief is granted to persons suffering transitory and unpredictable distress, and does not affect the legal status of the recipient.[339] Communal relief is extended in ordinary cases of need for maintenance, house rent, etc., and involves only an obligation to repay; but if the distress is a result of laziness or extravagance, or is over a long period, the recipient loses the right to vote and to hold public office.[340] Poor relief is assistance to work-shy, neglectful persons, drunkards, vagabonds, etc., and entails the same loss as well as certain others, as denial of right to marry.[341] In some such cases the aid consists of institutional board and lodging. The amount of the assistance must be enough to maintain life, and to provide medical and nursing care in case of illness. Beginning in 1933 food rebate coupons have been issued to the needy.[342]

Work Relief. The Danes prefer work relief to direct or cash relief.[343] The public works program has not been as comprehensive as in Norway and Sweden. But there are provisions by law for both national and municipal projects. The wages paid must be lower than the prevailing wages in the open market but higher than unemployment benefits. Public subsidies may be given to private projects undertaken primarily to make new jobs. Local camps for men from eighteen to twenty-five may be subsidized by the national government, and several municipalities have set them up. Non-competitive work is done in such camps and there are educational and recreational advantages.

Other Public Assistance. Denmark was the first European country to provide aid to dependent children. In 1913 such aid was given to widows with low incomes.[344] Since 1933 it has been extended to widowers.

The laws as to child welfare were codified in the Public Assistance Act of 1933, which also covers other types of public assistance.[345] Following the earlier Norwegian model, child welfare work is handled locally by the child welfare committees of the municipalities. It includes supervision of orphans, illegitimates, and children whose parents receive public aid. The committees also supervise and guide parents and guardians where this appears necessary, and send children to public institutions when necessary. In some cases school children are provided with free meals. Maternity assistance may be provided. Public assistance costs are met one-third from the municipalities and two-thirds from an inter-municipal fund to which all municipalities contribute.

A final category of public assistance is known as special care. This is the relief given to lunatics, feeble-minded, epileptic, the crippled or deformed, the blind, and deaf-mutes.[346] These are provided for in the Public Assistance Act of 1933. Legislation of 1929, 1934 and 1935 provides for sterilization in certain cases.[347]

Family Welfare. In 1935 an executive order was issued appointing the Danish Government Population Committee, to deal with the problem of a lowered birth rate, though the birth rate was higher than in Norway and Sweden.[348] In 1948 the Danish Government Youth Committee submitted proposals for marriage loans. It recommended the lending of amounts up to 3,000 kroner, fixed in relation to the amount of savings and the income of the couple during the previous two years. The couples would pay one per cent interest, and the government would pay the rest of the interest and guarantee repayment of the loans.

Abortion is legal for medical reasons, that is to say, when indicated by considerations of heredity such as insanity or imbecility or when there is danger to the mother's life and health due to exhaustion, chronic malnutrition, attempted suicide, or other acts of despair.[349] It may be performed if the child was conceived under violence or threat of violence. In 1939 a semi-official case-work agency, the Maternity Aid Association was established to give free personal advice to pregnant women and mothers.[350] All pregnant women are entitled to three free health examinations by a doctor and seven by a midwife. Two-thirds of all confinements take place in the home.

Legislation of 1888 provides that when the father of an illegitimate child fails to support it, the mother may draw advances from the public, which may then collect from the father.[351] The 1888 act is the earliest of the modern Danish social legislation, though the Poor Law and the Old Age Relief Act of 1891 because of their greater importance are normally so regarded. The present Danish law stresses the right to proper support and education rather than the right to inherit.

Since 1937 Denmark has made grants to municipalities that appoint public nurses. Without charge the nurse examines all children at regular intervals during the first year. Under a 1945 law parents are entitled to have all children under seven examined free by a physician three times during the child's first year and later once a year. Free school lunches in elementary schools are provided. Since 1948 all children whose parents so desire are entitled to meals. Danish farmers offer free vacations to school children of city families with small incomes, and the state pays transportation costs. Since 1949 home help services have been provided free to mothers of small children with small means. Preschool institutions have been set up to care for at small fees the children of parents both of whom are employed outside of the home. The most important device for equalizing the cost of children is the tax rebate. Children's allowances are now under discussion. At the present time grants of 370 to 600 kroner per year are given to children of widows and widowers having limited incomes. Unmarried, separated or divorced mothers are entitled to payment by the government of the father's contribution when the father is slow in paying.

No child under fourteen may be employed except in agriculture, forestry, on ships, or in the fishing industry.[352] No one under eighteen, except under exceptional circumstances, may be employed at night or for longer hours than adults in the same trade.

Old Age Pensions. In 1891 Denmark established an old age pension system under which the localities decided as to the individual needs of the aged.[353] Denmark was the first European nation to do this. The Act of 1922 provided that all persons past sixty-five had the right to such a pension, varying according to the income of the recipient. But the most important act is the National Insurance Act of 1933. It fixed an annual basic pension for persons past sixty-five, with variations according to marital status, geographical location, and amount of private income. The pension is paid only to persons of limited means, hence half of those 65 or more receive no pensions. In 1937 the age limit was lowered to sixty.[354] Payments may be increased if the cost of living increases. If the recipient delays in applying the amount is proportionately increased. The individual makes no contribution to the system. But he is required to take out sickness and permanent disability insurance, or if ineligible for them, to show that he has applied. The funds for pensions are paid four-sevenths by the national treasury and three-sevenths by the locality. In 1942 one-fourth of the total expenditures for social services was for such pensions. Administration is in the hands of the social welfare committees appointed by municipal councils. Up to 1942 about five hundred old peoples' homes were erected for aged persons unable to live alone.[355] Since 1937 the government has erected homes for old age pensioners able to live without special care.[356]

Medical Care. Copenhagen was provided with a public physician in 1531, but the office was not in full function before 1630.[357] By 1750 a few provincial towns had public physicians. By 1800 there was one such physician for each province and each city. A Danish decree of 1740 placed affairs of medicine and public health under the *Collegium Medi-*

cum. In 1803 all such functions were centralized in a Royal Bureau of Health. The bureau drew up instructions for the public physicians and midwives, recommended certain regulations, recommended candidates for state medical offices, and conducted examinations for licenses. The duties of public physicians were well-established by 1750. The first census was taken in 1769. Although laissez faire ultimately became dominant in economic affairs almost no one favored abolition of public physicians. By 1865 Denmark had developed its system of public health administration farther than almost any other nation. Samuel Laing, a Scotchman, wrote in 1852: "Our sanitary-condition politicians may envy Denmark such a complete medical arrangement for the health of the people."[358]

Freedom of trade in drugs was not permitted after 1700. Druggists had to take a state examination and licenses to sell drugs were monopolistic. Druggists were subject to the supervision of the public physicians. In 1842 Denmark forbade the sale of licenses to sell drugs by possessors of licenses.

The confiscation of church properties during the Protestant Reformation resulted in a great decline of the hospitals. The Danish king erected the first public hospital in 1755. Lying-in hospitals for illegitimately pregnant women grew up from 1775 to 1800. In 1806 the Danish king placed the duties of providing general hospitals on the county and city councils.[359] After 1830 several new hospitals were founded, almost always by private enterprise. Examinations for licenses to practice dentistry were not decreed until 1873. Denmark in 1810 made vaccination against smallpox legally mandatory, being one of the first countries to do so. Denmark was a pioneer in combatting venereal diseases; after 1788 hospitalization and medicine might be had at public expense. Beginning in 1853 decisive steps were taken to eliminate Asiatic cholera. From 1801 to 1869 the Danish death rate diminished, being lower even than the Swedish rate. Denmark had developed a system "so extensive as to justify the appellation of state medicine."[360] Epidemic legislation proper dates from 1882. From 1921 to 1940 there was not a single death from Asiatic cholera and only three from smallpox. The present legislation covers typhoid, diphtheria, scarlet fever, infantile paralysis and meningitis. All Danes are entitled to free hospital treatment of infectious diseases.[361] In 1937 Denmark and Sweden had the lowest typhoid mortality in the world. Venereal diseases have been virtually eliminated. Denmark ranks second only to New Zealand in tuberculosis mortality. In Copenhagen school children receive free dental inspection and treatment twice a year.[362]

Health Insurance. Denmark has had private and voluntary health insurance through group health associations or sick clubs (*Sygekasser*) for several decades.[363] The national treasury began to subsidize them in 1892. In such clubs only those with the income of a skilled worker or less are eligible. Ninety per cent of the population over fourteen are members. In 1933 the National Insurance Act in effect made health insurance compulsory. Every person between twenty-one and sixty must contribute to one of the 1600 approved sick clubs. The clubs are operated locally through leaders chosen by the insured, subject to some state supervision. Persons with higher incomes are provided for by special sections of the clubs, or may join a benefit society controlled by the state. The state subsidies are given only to persons in the workers' income class. No one has a right to old age or disability pensions unless he belongs to a sick club. Ill persons are furnished medical attendance by general practitioners and specialists and hospital treatment and an allowance during illness up to six months. The total fee of the doctor is paid directly by the insurance system. Maternity benefits are paid, and since 1940 funeral assistance.[364] The national treasury contributes for all this to the sick clubs a small amount per member. But most of the income is derived from premiums paid by the members.[365] The municipalities provide certain subsidies. Almost all hospitals are operated by the local or national governments, hence the rates are very low. In many cases the municipality furnishes free transportation of the ill person to the physician or hospital.

The societies enter into contracts with physicians. In urban areas they are paid fixed annual fees, per member; in rural areas they are paid fixed fees per consultation. Doctors may also retain their private practices.[366] Unlike the Norwegian and Swedish systems, the Danish involves the choice of a family doctor for long periods. He may refer the patient to a specialist who later gives an account of the treatment to the family doctor. This secures a double advantage: there is no excessive resort to specialists; and the general doctor gets a more thorough knowledge of his patients. Denmark has a higher percentage of doctors to population than Norway and Sweden. In hospitals the work is done by full-time staff physicians. Medicines are sold below cost. The societies pay three-fourths of the cost of medicines. In 97 per cent of the cases dental treatment is provided, though artificial teeth are not provided.[367] Today free hospitalization and free or below-cost medical attention are unquestioned. "It is the general consensus, in the medical profession as well as among the public, that these services are abused to only a very small degree."[368] Next to Holland, Denmark has the lowest mortality rate in Europe.[369]

Disability Insurance. Since 1922 all citizens in good health must carry disability insurance.[370] Chronic invalids are cared for under the

Public Assistance Act. The annual premium for disability insurance is a little over seven kroner. The employer also contributes six kroner a year for each worker. About one-half of the cost is paid by the national government and one-seventh by the municipality. The amount of disability benefits is determined on the same basis as old age pensions, except in case of severe disability. In 1946 about one per cent of the population received such pensions. The system is administered by the Disability Insurance Court (*Invalid forsikringsretten*) in the Department of Social Affairs. Its decision as to the degree of disability is final. No benefit is paid until the capacity to work has been reduced at least one-third.

Public health laws are administered by the National Health Service (*Sundhetstyrelsen*) in the Department of the Interior. Every *Amt* has a trained publicly paid physician, as has Copenhagen, under the National Health Service. Sanitation, child health, prevention of epidemics, and public hospitals are all embraced in a nation-wide program. Socialized medicine is advancing rapidly in Denmark, particularly in conjunction with social insurance. But there is still much private practice and there are many private clinics.

Housing. In 1887 and 1898 the Rigsdag stimulated the organizing of many building associations which took advantage of government loans to builders.[371] Subsequently the government gave subsidies to municipal and private building projects as well as to the cooperative associations founded as early as 1865. The subsidies consisted of grants and loans at low interest rates. Legislation of 1933 made a large sum available for building loans. Loans may be made to municipalities and cooperative societies up to 97 per cent of the total cost and to private owners up to seventy per cent. The municipal governments also furnish aid. Copenhagen has not only recognized housing cooperatives, but has developed a building program of its own. In the 1920's about one-half of housing was being constructed by the city and the cooperatives. Today one-fifth of the population of Copenhagen lives in such buildings. Spacing standards are better than in Norway and Sweden. Beginning in 1938 rent subsidies have been granted to less well-to-do families having three or more children under sixteen. The subsidy varies from thirty per cent of the cost for families with three children to sixty per cent for families with six or more children. Slum clearance is carried on by local authorities, but the national government furnishes subsidies in the form of grants and loans. Danish cities have in some instances encouraged "garden cities," a form of suburban resettlement, by furnishing the ground rent free of charge, or laying out and subsidizing model suburban units. In 1949 a commission of United States Senators visited Denmark, and returned convinced that the Danish approach held the answer to the housing problem of America's middle income group. The most notable aspects are: (1) housing cooperatives, (2) planning and house design, (3) housing for the elderly, (4) aid to large families, and (5) land policies.[372] In 1937 government grants were made for the housing of old age pensioners able to care for themselves. Danish cities systematically increase their landholdings both within and without their city limits. Copenhagen owns more than one-third of the total area available for building within its city limits. Copenhagen's building law of 1939 allows for more freedom in planning, and facilitated the building of balconies.[373]

Liquor Control. There was a temperance movement in the Scandinavian countries beginning about 1830. Prior thereto a royal ordinance forbade households to distill brandy, thus reducing the use of liquor among the peasantry. There was, however, no prohibition against purchase. The use of liquor was not as extensive as in Norway and Sweden.[374] This may explain the fact that the temperance movement was weakest in Denmark. However, in 1882 "the consumption of spirits was greater than in any other country."[375]

The control of intoxicants is approached by heavy taxes on alcoholic drinks.[376] There are also regulations concerning their sale. The number of places of sale is limited by law. Denmark's per capita alcohol consumption is one of the lowest in the world. From 1891 to 1940 it fell from 8.70 litres of pure alcohol per capita to 2.20.

Uniform Scandinavian Laws

There has long been cooperation between the Scandinavian nations in law-making just as there has between the States of the United States and the members of the British Commonwealth of Nations. Indeed the Danish Ambassador to the United States has recently pointed out that in some aspects the laws of the Scandinavian nations are closer to each other than the laws of American states.[377] When the three Scandinavian nations emerged more than a thousand years ago, they conceived of their vernacular as one single language, the "Danish tongue," spoken as late as 700 A.D.[378] The old Icelandic code accorded to "heirs of Danish tongue" a privileged position in comparison to that of other aliens. A Swedish provincial code of 1200 provided for a higher penalty for the manslaughter of a Dane or Norwegian than for the killing of an Englishman or German. Denmark and Norway were united from 1380 to 1814, and all three Scandinavian nations from 1388 to 1523. There were unions between Norway and Sweden from 1814 to 1905, and Denmark and Iceland from 1918 to 1944. Iceland was once a part of Norway and later until 1918 a part of Denmark.

Many Inter-Scandinavian conventions have been adopted.[379] In 1874 a Scandinavian monetary connection was adopted, making Scandinavian coins and notes legal tender in all three countries. In 1880 the Inter-Scandinavian Bank Draft Act was enacted after study by a joint committee of the three parliaments. Other common codifications are the Maritime Act of 1892, the Check Act of 1897, the Sale of Goods Act of 1907, the Contracts Act of 1917, the Act of 1922 as to Minors and Guardians, Marriage Law of 1922 to 1925 and many laws with respect to trademarks, insurance, trade registers, commercial agents, selling on the installment plan, promissory notes, adoption, property, and air traffic. Finland and Iceland have participated in the past three decades.

All five nations have coordinated their family law concerning marriage and divorce and the legal effects of marriage and adoption. There has been partial coordination as to minority and tutelage and legacy. Basic principles of criminal law have been worked out as to juvenile delinquency, alcoholism, and abortion. Denmark and Sweden have almost identical laws of citizenship. The common law of the countries is much alike due to the close political relations for centuries. Danish law affected Norwegian and Icelandic law, while Swedish law affected Finnish law. The uniform codes are not treaties, hence each nation is free to change. Forums for negotiations are the periodical joint sessions of the ministers of Justice, the Scandinavian Inter-Parliamentary Union and the Scandinavian Jurists Conventions which have met since 1872.

With respect to social security legislation the aim is reciprocity rather than coordination. Nationals of one Scandinavian country residing in another should receive the same benefits as the local citizens even if the recipient had paid part of his contribution in his own country. Reciprocity has been attained as to industrial accident insurance and health and unemployment insurance, but not before 1950 as to old age and disability insurance. In 1919 the three Scandinavian nations signed a reciprocity convention concerning industrial accident insurance. In 1937 all five nations concluded a new convention extending its scope to workers not resident in the nation where injured. In 1926 Denmark signed a health insurance convention with Norway, enabling members of a health insurance society in one country to transfer to a similar society in the other regardless of age or health. Denmark concluded similar conventions with Sweden in 1939 and 1947. Denmark signed a similar convention with Iceland in 1939, revised in 1948. In Denmark resident foreigners are eligible for membership in unemployment insurance societies. In 1946 representatives of Danish and Swedish societies made an agreement permitting transfer of members of the societies of one nation to those of the other, and similar arrangements are being prepared with Norway.

Since World War II a convention ratified by Denmark and Sweden concerning exchange of labor did away with the rule that foreigners could accept employment only with the consent of the government.[880] Conferences on workmen's safety were held in 1928, 1937 and 1948, and a commission is now outlining regulations for safety devices for machinery and tools.

Major criminals are subject to extradition. A bill is now in preparation making it possible to recover fines and execute short-term prison sentences imposed by a court of one nation in all the other nations. Special arrangements were made as to quislings. In civil procedure, judgments of one nation may be executed in another. A Danish convention with Sweden, concluded in 1861, was later adhered to by Norway. A convention on bankruptcy became effective in 1935.[881]

Legal Education and Admission to the Bar

King Eric of Pomerania (1412-1439) obtained the consent of the Pope to found a university, but the University of Copenhagen was not established until 1479.[382] Previously Danish students attended the University of Paris where a special college for Danes was founded about 1200. The University had a law faculty from the very beginning, but only a single law professor until 1657. For lack of funds the University did not really become active until 1539 at which time church funds acquired through the Protestant Reformation were made available. In 1539 it was made compulsory to give lectures on the Institutes of Justinian.[383] The new University Charter of 1732 made comprehensive provision for the study of law, which, under the influence of the Dutch and German schools of natural law, was receiving more attention. Law was now regarded as second only to theology. For the first time Danish law itself was taught. Andreas Höjer (1690-1739), a German historian and physician, assumed one of the newly created law professorships and "achieved results that entitled him to be called the father of modern Danish jurisprudence."[384]

A royal order of 1735 set up the bar under official sanction. One of 1736 for the first time required examinations of judges and attorneys.[385] To be a judge, government employee or practitioner (except in the lowest courts) one must pass a civil service examination in law (*Den juridiske Embedseksamen*). Before taking this examination the applicant must have a Bachelor of Arts degree and pass an examination in philosophy at the University. The University studies are entirely theoretical except that a course in accounting must be taken.[386] The civil service examinations are given by University professors, with practitioners and judges as assistant examiners. There are two parts to the examination. The first is oral and comes after two years of study and covers: (1) the main features of Danish private law, (2) Danish constitutional and public international law, (3) history of Danish law, and (4) political economy and statistics. The second part of the examination comes three or four years later and is both oral and written. It covers (1) Danish private law as to persons, family, inheritance, general principles of law, commercial law and conflict of laws, (2) Danish private law as to property, contracts, torts and admiralty law, (3) Danish criminal law, (4) Danish procedural law, and (5) the main features of Roman law.

There is no requirement that the applicant attend the law school. The curriculum includes lectures, case discussion,[387] and seminars. Practitioners teach a course covering legal documents, and other practical problems arising in practice.[388] The library includes statutes, judicial decisions, textbooks and foreign legal literature. The doctor's degree in law is rarely given and is more difficult to obtain than in Germany. A candidate must write a satisfactory thesis and defend it publicly, and gets a right to teach. During 1946 to 1947 there were 2,079 law students at the University of Copenhagen and 210 at the University of Aarhus.[389]

Attorneys are commissioned by the Minister of Justice.[390] There is admission to the lowest courts, to the Superior Courts, and to the Supreme Court.[391] All attorneys belong to the Society of Attorneys which is governed by a Lawyers Council with wide disciplinary powers.[392] Attorneys, like the judges, occupy an independent position, as they are not admitted by the courts, and cannot be suspended or disbarred except following a criminal prosecution. The high qualifications demanded of both judges and attorneys result in excellent decorum on the part of both. There is no division of the bar into barristers and solicitors as in England.

Jurisprudence and Legal History

A leading student of the Scandinavian countries has pointed out that "the Danes are more inclined by national character to cold, intellectual criticism than the two sister nations. The country is small and compact; business and agriculture require prudence for success; headlong adventures imitating spectacular foreign successes cannot safely be risked; and in all Danish thought there is a strong strain of peasant skepticism and conservatism. The Dane is therefore, even more than the Swede or the Norwegian, an ingrained individualist, who shies away from every extravagance of claim and expression."[393]

Niels Hemmingsen, professor of theology at the University of Copenhagen about 1560-1580, produced a pandect on natural law, which was read all over the continent. This was an investigation of law based on natural principles to find out "how far reason will reach without the prophetic and apostolic word." This was before the time of Grotius. "Hemmingsen thus became one of the founders of modern *jurisprudence*."[394]

The Danish code of 1683 expressly refers to the Decalogue and the "Law of God." Beginning in 1539 Roman law was taught at the University of Copenhagen Law School. Natural law as distinguished from divine law was taught early in the eighteenth century by Professors Reitzer and Andreas Höjer.[395] Ludvig Holberg (1684-1754), a native of Bergen, Norway, father of modern Danish and Norwegian literature and the first thoroughly modern Scandinavian philosopher, had studied at Oxford and learned natural law in Germany. He presented a system of natural law similar to Pufendorff and Thomasius.[396] He was a defender of absolute monarchy based on the rationalistic theory of Hobbes. It was the aim of J. B. Dons,[397] L. Norregaard,[398] and J. F. W. Schlegel[399] to bring the basic truths of the Law of Nature into actual operation in the life of the law. Norregaard would apply natural law even where it conflicted with positive law, but Schlegel would use it only where the law was silent and uncertain.[400] It was not until the time of Örsted that natural law was abandoned.

Tyge Rothe (1731-1795) wrote *Nordens Statsforfatning* (Scandinavian Constitutional Law) in 1782, pointing to Norway as the true home of freedom and independence.[401] The Norwegian peasant, unlike the Danish, had preserved his social integrity. He proclaimed agricultural reform as the sole means of national regeneration.

Professor Martin Hubner of the University of Copenhagen developed significant concepts of international law during the American Revolutionary War.[402] His position with respect to the English blockade policy was that the oceans were free and that the flag covered the cargo. That is to say, neutrals were free to carry cargo except war contraband, and neutral trade could be prevented only in harbors effectively blockaded. In 1856 these rules became established international law through the Declaration of Paris.

The abandonment of natural law as authoritative and basic in the development of positive law was affected by Anders Sandoe Örsted.[403] A Danish historian refers to his work as "the finest Denmark has known in the domains of justice and legal philosophy."[404] He understood natural law as including merely such general ideas as have arisen from time to time within the field of law, especially customary law.[405] He developed an historical approach to the law similar to that of Savigny and assisted the Norwegian scholar, Anton Schweigaard, in developing an historical approach to Norwegian law.[406]

Örsted engaged in an interesting philosophical controversy with Franz Howitz (1789-1826) who attacked punishment of insane criminals.[407] Howitz criticized the tendency of lawyers to refuse to distinguish between degrees of insanity, and attributed it to their acceptance of Kant's doctrine of the freedom of the will. Instead he stressed the physiological causes of insanity and advocated that physicians be called in regularly by the courts to make psychiatric examinations of offenders.[408] Örsted assailed Howitz as a rank materialist. Howitz ranks with Niels Treschow[409] (1751-1833), professor at the University of Copenhagen in Scandinavian philosophy, in denouncing speculation and defending the scientific method. The punitive system of treating the insane disappeared in the 1830's.

Örsted, following Treschow, applied the idea of evolution to legal theory.[410] Since the process of evolution continually creates variations, no classification can be wholly accurate or permanent, particularly in ethics. Humaneness and tolerance are therefore necessary.

One of the leading Danish legal scholars of today is Professor Alf Ross of the University of Copenhagen. His views "bear a close relationship to American legal realism."[411] He is the author of a leading general treatise on international law.[412] Together with Hal Koch he has made the most comprehensive survey of Scandinavian democracy.[413] Other recent outstanding Danish legal scholars, whose publications are listed in the bibliography at the end of this book are: Poul Andersen, Knud K. Berlin, H. Holm-Nielsen, Stephan Hurwitz, Vinding Kruse and H. Munch-Petersen.

The first Danish printing office was established in 1482.[414] In 1514 there was published the great history of Denmark up to 1180 which had been written by Saxo.[415] During the reign of Christian IV (1588-1648) Arild Huitfeld, the Danish chancellor, wrote a modern history of Denmark as seen through the eyes of the nobility. This history was a quarto edition of four thousand pages and contained a large number of documents from the National Archives. In 1652 Christian O. Weylle published a glossary or short review of early Danish legal history.[416] Christian Stubaeus, who had access to manuscripts destroyed in the fire of 1728, preserved much of value.[417] Ludvig Holberg presented a fairly complete account of early legal history a half a century later.[418]

One of the best Danish legal histories is by Peder Kofod-Ancher.[419] Another is by J. F. W. Schlegel.[420] A useful compendium was prepared in 1822 and 1823 by J. L. A. Kolderup-Rosenvinge.[421] Important criticisms were made by J. E. Larsen.[422] In 1871 Christian L. E. Stemann published a history of Danish law up to 1683.[423] In 1878 Konrad Von Maurer, a German scholar, published a general survey.[424] In 1896

H. Matzen published a study.[425] S. Wiskinge published a history of the Danish Constitution in 1928.[426] In 1947 Paul J. Jorgensen published a history of Danish law up to 1650.[427]

NOTES—CHAPTER I—DANISH LAW

1. *The Immigration and Naturalization Systems of the United States.* Report of the Committee on Judiciary pursuant to Sen. Res. 137, Sen. Rep. No. 1515, 81st Cong., 2d Sess. 91-94 (1950).

2. How one Danish immigrant reacted to this country may be seen in Jacob A. Riis, *The Making of an American* (1908).

3. Fletcher Pratt, *The Third King*, p. 31 (1950).

4. Viggo Starcke, *The Viking Danes*, p. 6 (1949).

5. Sigrid Undset, *Return to the Future*, p. 246 (1942); Fletcher Pratt, op. cit., p. 29 (1950). The oldest history of Denmark written just before 1176 by Svend Aggesson contains an interesting account of a prehistoric conflict between Danes and Germans. It is quoted in Sigrid Undset, op. cit., pp. 226-27 (1942).

6. Viggo Starcke, op. cit., pp. 8-14 (1949).

7. John Danstrup, *A History of Denmark*, p. 15 (1949); Karen Larsen, *A History of Norway*, p. 38 (1948); Hjalmar H. Boyesen, *A History of Norway*, p. 31 (1900). Danish kings prior to 800 A.D. are briefly discussed by Paul Sinding, *History of Scandinavia*, pp. 44-49 (1858); J. H. S. Birch, *Denmark in History*, pp. 14-22 (1938).

8. J. E. G. DeMontmorency, "Danish Influence on English Law and Character," 40 L. Q. Rev. 324, 326-31 (1924); Viggo Starcke, op. cit., pp. 14-34 (1949).

9. In 852 Danish vikings held possession of Dublin, but the Norwegians were more successful in Ireland. Karen Larsen, op. cit., pp. 40, 45 (1948).

10. *Ibid.*, p. 51 (1948).

11. See J. Steenstrup, *Normannerne*, IV, (1882) for a full discussion of the Dane-law.

12. See White and Notestein, *Source Problems in English History*, pp. 3-32 (1915).

13. Paul Sinding, op. cit., pp. 81-82 (1858). Denmark's status as a nation dates from about 925 according to Amos J. Peaslee, *Constitutions of Nations*, I, 641 (1950).

14. Karen Larsen, op. cit., pp. 81-82 (1948). Denmark at this date consisted of Zealand and adjacent islands, Jutland including Slesvig to the Eider River, and Skåne, Halland and Blekinge in Sweden. Paul Sinding, op. cit., p. 56 (1858).

15. Karen Larsen, op. cit., p. 91 (1948); J. H. S. Birch, op. cit., p. 32 (1938).

16. Viken was the area near the Oslo fjord, and was divided into Vestfold, Vingulmark, and Bohuslän.

17. Paul Sinding, op. cit., pp. 62-67 (1858); J. E. G. DeMontmorency, op. cit., pp. 329-31 (1924).

18. Hjalmar H. Boyesen, op. cit., pp. 214, 225 (1900); Karen Larsen, op. cit., pp. 103-05 (1948); J. H. S. Birch, op. cit., pp. 39-40 (1938).

19. J. E. G. DeMontmorency, op. cit., pp. 324-43 (1924); Viggo Starcke, op. cit., p. 24 (1949).

20. Pollock and Maitland, *History of English Law*, I, 121-22 (1895).

21. Hartley Shawcross, "Administration of Justice in England," 10 Mod. L. Rev. 1 (1947); Viggo Starcke, op. cit., p. 24 (1949).

22. Karen Larsen, op. cit., p. 113 (1948); Hjalmar H. Boyesen, op. cit., pp. 231, 234 (1900); Paul Sinding, op. cit., p. 75 (1858).

23. A national meeting of leaders of the Danish farmers in 1074 favored the end of foreign raids and simple preservation of national independence. John Danstrup, op. cit., p. 20 (1949).

24. *Ibid.*, pp. 6-7, 11-12 (1949); Franklin D. Scott, *The United States and Scandinavia*, pp. 31-32 (1950).

25. J. H. S. Birch, *op. cit.*, p. 48 (1938).

26. Paul Sinding, *op. cit.*, p. 70 (1858).

27. *Ibid.*, p. 89 (1858).

28. *Ibid.*, p. 93 (1858).

29. John Danstrup, *op. cit.*, p. 23 (1949); Fletcher Pratt, *op. cit.*, pp. 50-53 (1950).

30. Karen Larsen, *op. cit.*, p. 137 (1948); for the next century the Norwegians sought Swedish friendship to offset the Danish strength.

31. Paul Sinding, *op. cit.*, p. 97 (1858); John Danstrup, *op. cit.*, p. 193 (1949).

32. Paul Sinding, *op. cit.*, pp. 102-03 (1858).

33. Fletcher Pratt, *op. cit.*, pp. 42, 150-51 (1950).

34. *Ibid.*, pp. 287-89 (1950).

35. *Ibid.*, p. 270 (1950).

36. J. H. S. Birch, *op. cit.*, p. 80 (1938).

37. Paul Sinding, *op. cit.*, p. 119 (1858).

38. J. H. S. Birch, *op. cit.*, p. 86 (1938); Karen Larsen, *op. cit.*, p. 173 (1948).

39. Paul Sinding, *op. cit.*, pp. 130, 138 (1858); John Danstrup, *op. cit.*, p. 35 (1949); Fletcher Pratt, *op. cit.*, pp. 43, 53-64, 74-80, 270, 292 (1950).

40. Fletcher Pratt, *op. cit.*, p. 56 (1950).

41. Paul Sinding, *op. cit.*, pp. 130-31 (1858).

42. Fletcher Pratt, *op. cit.*, pp. 43, 152, 156 (1950).

43. *Ibid.*, pp. 19-21 (1950). Prior to the arrival of these foreigners, feudalism had not existed in Denmark.

44. John Danstrup, *op. cit.*, pp. 36-37 (1949). Holberg regarded him as the greatest Danish king. For an account of the lives of Valdemar I the Great (1157-1182), Valdemar II the Victorious (1202-1240) and Valdemar Atterdag see Fletcher Pratt, *The Third King* (1950). How Denmark had been split up is described in Fletcher Pratt, *op. cit.*, pp. 43-44 (1950); and see the map on p. 49. North Halland had passed to Norway, and South Halland, Blekinge, and Skåne to Sweden. Other parts were held by German and Danish nobles, and Copenhagen flew the flag of the Hanseatic League.

45. Fletcher Pratt, *op. cit.*, pp. 140-43 (1950).

46. *Ibid.*, pp. 212-15, 226-29, 263 (1950).

47. *Ibid.*, pp. 295-97 (1950).

48. John Danstrup, *op. cit.*, p. 39 (1949); Hjalmar H. Boyesen, *op. cit.*, p. 469 (1900).

49. Karen Larsen, *op. cit.*, p. 213 (1948); Paul Sinding, *op. cit.*, pp. 150-54 (1858).

50. Paul Sinding, *op. cit.*, p. 160 (1858).

51. *Ibid.*, p. 214 (1858).

52. John Danstrup, *op. cit.*, p. 45 (1949).

53. *Ibid.*, p. 54 (1949).

54. *Ibid.*, p. 57 (1949).

55. Charles C. Hyde, *International Law*, I, 520 (2d ed. 1945); Bryn J. Hovde, *The Scandinavian Countries, 1720-1865*, p. 233 (1948); Charles E. Hill, *Danish Sound Dues* (1926).

56. John Danstrup, *op. cit.*, p. 41 (1949); Paul Sinding, *op. cit.*, p. 165 (1858).

57. Karen Larsen, *op. cit.*, p. 219 (1948).

58. Paul Sinding, *op. cit.*, p. 171 (1858); Karen Larsen, *op. cit.*, p. 220 (1948).

59. W. S. Reid, "The Place of Denmark in Scottish Foreign Policy, 1470-1540," 58 *Jurid. Rev.* 183 (1946).

60. John Danstrup, *op. cit.*, p. 41 (1949).

61. J. H. S. Birch, *op. cit.*, p. 166 (1938); Paul Sinding, *op. cit.*, p. 220 (1858).

62. Karen Larsen, *op. cit.*, pp. 232, 243 (1948).

63. John Danstrup, *op. cit.*, pp. 53, 191 (1949); Paul Sinding, *op. cit.*, p. 227 (1858).

64. Paul Sinding, *op. cit.*, p. 231 (1858). For a map of Scandinavia in 1560 see John Danstrup, *op. cit.*, p. 52 (1949).

65. John Danstrup, *op. cit.*, p. 54 (1949); Paul Sinding, *op. cit.*, p. 227 (1858).

66. J. H. S. Birch, *op. cit.*, pp. 175-79 (1938); Paul Sinding, *op. cit.*, pp. 233-37 (1858).

67. Paul Sinding, *op. cit.*, pp. 227, 239-40 (1858).

68. John Danstrup, *op. cit.*, p. 7 (1949). Denmark occupied the central position first in Scandinavia, being succeeded by Sweden by the eighteenth century. On Danish neutrality policy from 1600 to 1814 see Franklin D. Scott, *op. cit.*, pp. 205-11 (1950).

69. John Danstrup, *op. cit.*, p. 56 (1949); Paul Sinding, *op. cit.*, p. 266 (1858). A number of Danes settled in Bergen, New Jersey in 1624, as the first settlers of New Jersey. Paul Sinding, *op. cit.*, p. 268 (1858).

70. Bryn J. Hovde, *op. cit.*, pp. 38, 43 (1948).

71. See Charles C. Hyde, *op. cit.*, pp. 359, 364-65, 382, 405, 432-33, 436, (2d ed., 1945); Green Hackworth, *Digest of International Law*, I., 422-26, 477-82, 556-57 (1940). For a recent case involving the application of Danish law concerning the scope of appellate review of the facts in criminal cases see People of Virgin Islands v. Price, 181 F. 2d 394 (3rd Cir. 1950). This case is discussed by Lester B. Orfield, "Appellate Review of the Facts in Criminal Cases," 12 *F.R.D.* 311 (1952).

72. Paul Sinding, *op. cit.*, pp. 249-51 (1858); John Danstrup, *op. cit.*, pp. 56, 191 (1949).

73. Franklin D. Scott, *op. cit.*, p. 205 (1950).

74. *Ibid.*, p. 206 (1950).

75. Paul Sinding, *op. cit.*, pp. 251-53 (1858); John Danstrup, *op. cit.*, pp. 57, 191 (1949).

76. Paul Sinding, *op. cit.*, pp. 255-61 (1858); Karen Larsen, *op. cit.*, pp. 284-85 (1948); John Danstrup, *op. cit.*, pp. 57, 191 (1949); J. H. S. Birch, *op. cit.*, pp. 214-17 (1938).

77. John Danstrup, *op. cit.*, pp. 63-66 (1949); Paul Sinding, *op. cit.*, pp. 272-75 (1858); J. H. S. Birch, *op. cit.*, pp. 226-30 (1938).

78. Karen Larsen, *op. cit.*, p. 290 (1948); J. H. S. Birch, *op. cit.*, pp. 230-34 (1938).

79. John Danstrup, *op. cit.*, p. 70 (1949); Paul Sinding, *op. cit.*, pp. 297-300 (1858).

80. Karen Larsen, *op. cit.*, pp. 292-93 (1948).

81. Franklin D. Scott, *op. cit.*, p. 206 (1950).

82. Paul Sinding, *op. cit.*, pp. 310-12 (1858); John Danstrup, *op. cit.*, p. 71 (1949).

83. Paul Sinding, *op. cit.*, pp. 314-21, 323-34 (1858). For a map of Scandinavia as of 1721, see John Danstrup, *op. cit.*, p. 76 (1949).

84. Paul Sinding, *op. cit.*, p. 323 (1858).

85. Karen Larsen, *op. cit.*, p. 325 (1948). Christian IV (1588-1648) had tried to reopen the old Norwegian colony which was found to have disappeared. *Ibid.*, p. 281 (1948).

86. Paul Sinding, *op. cit.*, pp. 324, 344, 348, 350 (1858).

87. *Ibid.*, pp. 350-52 (1858); John Danstrup, *op. cit.*, pp. 74-75 (1949).

88. Paul Sinding, *op. cit.*, p. 375 (1858); John Danstrup, *op. cit.*, p. 82 (1949).

89. Franklin D. Scott, *op. cit.*, pp. 206-07 (1950).

90. *Ibid.*, pp. 207-09 (1950).

91. Henning Friis, *Scandinavia between East and West*, p. 341 (1950).

92. Quoted by Franklin D. Scott, *op. cit.*, p. 76 (1950).

93. Paul Sinding, *op. cit.*, p. 381 (1858).

94. Franklin D. Scott, *op. cit.*, p. 209 (1950).

95. *Ibid.*, p. 210 (1950); John Danstrup, *op. cit.*, pp. 85-88 (1949); Karen Larsen, *op. cit.*, pp. 365-69 (1948); Paul Sinding, *op. cit.*, pp. 384-89 (1858).

96. C. J. Kulsrud, "Seizure of the Danish Fleet, 1807," 32 *Am. J. Int'l. L.* 280 (1938).

97. Karen Larsen, *op. cit.*, pp. 405, 409-10 (1948); Bryn J. Hovde, *op. cit.*, p. 53 (1948).

98. Franklin D. Scott, *op. cit.*, p. 77 (1950).

99. It was Danish at the beginning of its history. The Germans first entered in the Middle Ages. In the late Middle Ages its rulers and great landowners were Germans. Danish was spoken as far south as Angel until about 1825. L. D. Steefel, *The Schleswig-Holstein Question*, p. 4 (1932).

100. As to the legal effects of this incorporation see Kristian S. A. Erslev, *Frederik IV og Slesvig, En Historisk Fortolkning af Arvehyldnings Akterne af 1721* (1901).

101. John Danstrup, *op. cit.*, p. 92 (1949).

102. L. D. Steefel, *op. cit.*, pp. 6-7 (1932). The standard volume of documents bearing on the legal aspects is Nils N. Falck, *Sammlung der wichtigsten Urkunden, welche auf das Staatsrecht der Herzogthumer Schleswig und Holstein Bezug haben* (1847).

103. John Danstrup, *op. cit.*, p. 120 (1949). For a full treatment of the subject with special reference to the years 1863 and 1864 see L. D. Steefel, *op. cit.*

104. John Danstrup, *op. cit.*, p. 136 (1949).

105. There was also a problem as to refugees in Denmark proper. H. S. Kemble, "Refugee Camps—A Special Dilemma in Denmark," 111 *Just. P.* 624 (1947).

106. Henning Friis, *op. cit.*, p. 17, 286-90 (1950).

107. Knud Fabricius, "The South Slesvig Problem," 36 *Am. Scand. Rev.* 207 (1948).

108. *New York Times*, July 9, 1950. It was the first west German state to choose a former Nazi party member as its Minister-President. *New York Times*, September 6, 1950.

109. *New York Times*, September 14, 1950; S. M. Toyne, *The Scandinavians in History*, pp. 328-31 (1948).

110. Karen Larsen, *op. cit.*, p. 493 (1948); John Danstrup, *op. cit.*, p. 131 (1949).

111. Franklin D. Scott, *op. cit.*, pp. 215-24 (1950).

112. John Danstrup, *op. cit.*, p. 137 (1949); Green Hackworth, *op. cit.*, I, 59, 213 (1940). Some writers regarded the union as a real rather than a personal union. Oppenheim, *International Law*, I, 158, n. 2 (5th ed., Lauterpacht, 1937).

113. Henning Friis, *op. cit.*, p. 262 (1950).

114. Manley O. Hudson, *The Permanent Court of International Justice*, p. 248 (1934).

115. Green Hackworth, *op. cit.*, I, 405, 443, 471-74; V, 32-33, 157, 160-61, 230; Charles C. Hyde, "The Case Concerning the Legal Status of Eastern Greenland," 27 *Am. J. Int. L.* 732 (1933); L. Preuss, "Dispute between Denmark and Norway on the Sovereignty of East Greenland," 26 *Am. J. Int. L.* 469 (1932).

116. Green Hackworth, *op. cit.*, V, 467-70 (1943). On the legal status of Denmark during World War II, see Franklin D. Scott, *op. cit.*, 248-58 (1950); Outze, *Denmark During the German Occupation* (1946); M. Satz, "Enemy Legislation and Judgments in Denmark," 31 *J. Comp. Leg. Int. L.* (3d ser.) pp. 1-3 (1949).

117. John Danstrup, *op. cit.*, p. 161 (1949). On the history of Greenland see Franklin D. Scott, *op. cit.*, pp. 22-26 (1950). In October, 1950 it was announced that for the first time a council, courts and prisons would be established in Greenland. *New York Times*, October 5, 1950.

118. *Den Lille Salmonsen*, X, p. 33 (*Retssaedvane*); Vinding Kruse, *Retslaeren*; T. Leivestad, "Custom as a Type of Law in Norway," 54 *L. Q. Rev.* 95 (1938).

119. Ebbe Hertzberg, in *A General Survey of Continental Legal History*, pp. 531, 568 (1912).

120. Nils Skavang, "History and Development of Scandinavian Law—Some Salient Traits," 6 *Seminar* 60 (1948).

121. H. Munch-Petersen, "Main Features of Scandinavian Law," 43 *L. Q. Rev.* 367 (1927).

122. On Danish tort law, see H. Holm-Nielsen, "The Law of Torts in Denmark," 15 *J. Comp. Leg. & Int. L.* 176-79 (1933).

123. H. Munch-Petersen, *op. cit.*, p. 167 (1927).

124. Vinding Kruse, *Retslaeren; Den Lille Salmonsen*, X, 33 (*Retspraksis*).

125. Ebbe Hertzberg, *op. cit.*, p. 569 (1912).

126. *Ibid.*, pp. 533, 545 (1912).

127. John Danstrup, *op. cit.*, pp. 29-30 (1949).

128. The three laws are known as the Laws of King Valdemar Victorious (1202-1240). They were reduced to writing in the twelfth century. Fletcher Pratt, *op. cit.*, pp. 65-66 (1950). See also Holberg, *Kong Valdemars Lov* (1886); Thorsen, *Danmarks Gamle provindsial Love* (1852-1853). The Jutland Code applied at first only to Jutland, "was adopted later as the law for Zealand and Scania." J. H. S. Birch, *op. cit.*, p. 68 (1938). The seven hundredth anniversary of the Jutland Law is discussed in Elias Wessen, "Jydske lov.Et 700—arsminne," 26 *Svensk Juristtidning* 494-96 (1941).

129. Ebbe Hertzberg, *op. cit.*, pp. 545, 547 (1912).

130. *Ibid.*, p. 548 (1912).

131. Fletcher Pratt, *op. cit.*, p. 65 (1950). In Holstein just south of Slesvig there was going on a codification of tribal customs and a simultaneous reception of the Roman law on a limited basis.

132. Paul Sinding, *op. cit.*, pp. 286, 293-95, 304 (1858); Secher, *Kong Kristian Vs Danske Lov;* J. L. A. Kolderup-Rosenvinge, *Kristian Vs Lov;* Ebbe Hertzberg, *op. cit.*, pp. 557-59, 562 (1912).

133. H. Munch-Petersen, *op. cit.*, p. 366 (1927); T. Leivestad, *op. cit.*, p. 98, (1938).

134. As to revision in the eighteenth and nineteenth centuries see Ebbe Hertzberg, *op. cit.*, p. 567 (1912).

135. John Danstrup, *op. cit.*, pp. 14-15 (1949). The Danish kings are listed in John Danstrup, *op. cit.*, p. 193 (1949).

136. *Ibid.*, p. 18 (1949).

137. *Ibid.*, p. 19 (1949).

138. *Ibid.*, p. 20 (1949).

139. *Ibid.*, p. 21 (1949).

140. *Ibid.*, p. 22 (1949).

141. *Ibid.*, p. 24 (1949).

142. Paul Sinding, *op. cit.*, p. 105 (1858). The three other classes were the clergy, burghers and peasants.

143. John Danstrup, *op. cit.*, pp. 28-29 (1949).

144. *Ibid.*, p. 30 (1949).

145. *Ibid.*, p. 26, 29 (1949).

146. *Ibid.*, p. 32 (1949). The weakness of the burgher class and the cities during the Middle Ages has been ascribed to the existence of the privileged Hanseatic League. Paul Sinding, *op. cit.*, pp. 126-27 (1858).

147. John Danstrup, *op. cit.*, p. 34 (1949). Later kings likewise made such compacts (*Haandfaestninger*). They constitute a series of constitutions for Denmark up to 1660. Up to 1536 these compacts provided that no important action be taken by the king without the consent of the nobility and the clergy and that the king should call an annual meeting of the best men of the kingdom.

148. Ben A. Arneson, *op. cit.*, p. 21 (1949). It has been pointed out that while the Landsthings were not needed in the fourteenth century, as late as 1400 they approved general and local laws. Ebbe Hertzberg, *op. cit.*, pp. 548, 562 (1912). They were abolished in 1805 and town courts created.

149. Ebbe Hertzberg, *op. cit.*, p. 548 (1912).

150. Fletcher Pratt, *op. cit.*, p. 55 (1950); Paul Sinding, *op. cit.*, p. 128 (1858).

151. Fletcher Pratt, *op. cit.*, p. 299 (1950).

152. For an interesting case in which the king appeared at the *thing* court and pleaded a case as an ordinary subject see *ibid.*, pp. 84, 112 (1950). While previous kings had their documents written in Latin, Valdemar employed Danish.

153. The clash between Danish and German concepts is described in Fletcher Pratt, *op. cit.*, pp. 65-73 (1950).

154. *Ibid.*, pp. 199, 216, 270-72 (1950).

155. *Ibid.*, p. 206 (1950).

156. *Ibid.*, pp. 236-37 (1950).

157. *Ibid.*, p. 129 (1950).

158. *Ibid.*, p. 295 (1950).

159. John Danstrup, *op. cit.*, p. 43 (1949). From about 1300 the Landsthing was presided over by a judge appointed by the king. (*Landsdommer*). Ebbe Hertzberg, *op. cit.*, p. 548 (1912).

160. Karen Larsen, *op. cit.*, p. 218 (1948).

161. Paul Sinding, *op. cit.*, p. 166 (1858).

162. John Danstrup, *op. cit.*, p. 42 (1949).

163. Paul Sinding, *op. cit.*, p. 196 (1858); Karen Larsen, *op. cit.*, p. 228 (1948).

164. John Danstrup, *op. cit.*, p. 44 (1949).

165. *Ibid.*, p. 53 (1949).

166. *Ibid.*, p. 46 (1949); J. H. S. Birch, *op. cit.*, pp. 152-53 (1938).

167. Ben A. Arneson, *op. cit*, p. 22 (1949); Paul Sinding, *op. cit.*, p. 220 (1858).

168. John Danstrup, *op. cit.*, pp. 67-69 (1949); Paul Sinding, *op. cit.*, pp. 283-85 (1858); Carl O. B. Andersen, *Statsomvaelteningen i 1660. Kritiske studier over kilder og tradition* (1936).

169. Karen Larsen, *op. cit.*, p. 289 (1948).

170. Franklin D. Scott, *op. cit.*, p. 50 (1950).

171. John Danstrup, *op. cit.*, p. 68 (1949); Paul Sinding, *op. cit.*, p. 285-86 (1858).

172. John Danstrup, *op. cit.*, p. 80 (1949); Karen Larsen, *op. cit.*, pp. 343-45 (1948).

173. Bryn J. Hovde, *op. cit.*, p. 699 (1948).

174. Censorship as to discussion of economic conditions was dropped in 1755. *Ibid.*, pp. 18, 130 (1948). There had been strict regulation of the press through censors under Christian V (1670-1699). Paul Sinding, *op. cit.*, p. 307 (1858). Strict censorship was restored in 1773. *Ibid.*, p. 378 (1858).

175. John Danstrup, *op. cit.*, p. 82 (1949); Paul Sinding, *op. cit.*, p. 378 (1858).

176. Karen Larsen, *op. cit.*, pp. 350-51 (1948); John Danstrup, *op. cit.*, pp. 84-85 (1949).

177. Bryn J. Hovde, *op. cit.*, p. 206 (1948).

178. *Ibid.*, p. 510 (1948).

179. *Ibid.*, p. 519 (1948).

180. *Ibid.*, p. 540 (1948); John Danstrup, *op. cit.*, p. 94 (1949).

181. Bryn J. Hovde, *op. cit.*, p. 544 (1948).

182. John Danstrup, *op. cit.*, p. 98 (1949); L. D. Steefel, *op. cit.*, p. 7 (1932).

183. Bryn J. Hovde, *op. cit.*, p. 550 (1948).

184. In 1580 there were 250 noble families and in 1660 less than 125. J. H. S. Birch, *op. cit.*, p. 133 (1938). Today about 220 families are listed in the various ranks of the titled nobility. No special privileges go with the titles, which are of social importance only. Ben A. Arneson, *op. cit.*, p. 51 (1949).

185. Henning Friis, *op. cit.*, p. 4 (1950).

186. See Niels Neergaard, *Under Junigrundloven. En Fremstilling af det danske Folks politiske Historie fra 1848 til 1866* (1890, 1916).

187. Ben A. Arneson, *op. cit.*, p. 25 (1949); John Danstrup, *op. cit.*, p. 104 (1949); L. D. Steefel, *op. cit.*, p. 15 (1932).

188. C. G. Andrae invented it in the process of preparing the composition of the *Rigsraad*. S. Wiskinge, *Vor Forfatnings Historie*, pp. 113-14 (1928).

189. Ben A. Arneson, *op. cit.*, pp. 25-26 (1949); John Danstrup, *op. cit.*, pp. 108-09 (1949); L. D. Steefel, *op. cit.*, pp. 70-78 (1932).

190. Ben A. Arneson, *op. cit.*, p. 26 (1949); John Danstrup, *op. cit.*, p. 121 (1949); Bryn J. Hovde, *op. cit.*, pp. 554-55 (1948).

191. The constitution is set forth in Amos J. Peaslee, *Constitutions of Nations*, pp. 644-53 (1950). The outstanding treatise on the Danish Constitutional Law is Knud K. Berlin, *Den danske Forfatningsret* (1943).

192. The political parties have now reached a preliminary agreement to revise the constitution to lower the age limits. Henning Friis, *op. cit.*, p. 5 (1950).

193. However, all legislation must be approved by the upper house. Though the Social Democrats gained control as early as 1924 in the lower house it was not until 1936 that they gained control in the upper house, and then by only one vote. Ben A. Arneson, *op. cit.*, p. 55 (1949).

194. *Ibid.*, p. 153 (1949). Compare Axel Teisen, "Power to Declare Legislation Unconstitutional in Denmark," 10 *A.B.A.J.* 792 (1924).

195. Ben A. Arneson, *op. cit.*, p. 74 (1949).

196. *Ibid.*, p. 77 (1949).

197. Henning Friis, *op. cit.*, p. 10 (1950).

198. *Ibid.*, p. 4 (1950); Ben A. Arneson, *op. cit.*, p. 54 (1949); John Danstrup, *op. cit.*, pp. 127-28 (1949).

199. Ben A. Arneson, *op. cit.*, p. 56 (1949).

200. John Danstrup, *op. cit.*, pp. 151, 154 (1949).

201. Ben A. Arneson, *op. cit.*, p. 57 (1949).

202. Franklin D. Scott, *op. cit.*, p. 195 (1950).

203. *Ibid.*, pp. 194-96 (1950). None of the Scandinavian socialist parties is as doctrinaire and Marxian as in France and Italy. *New York Times*, June 25, 1950.

204. "Denmark," *Atlantic Monthly*, p. 8 (July, 1950).

205. *New York Times*, p. 21, September 8, 1950.

206. Henning Friis, *op. cit.*, p. 11 (1950).

207. Ben A. Arneson, *op. cit.*, p. 83 (1949). On Danish legislative organization and procedure see Knud K. Berlin, *Den danske Statsforfatningsret* (1943).

208. Ben A. Arneson, *op. cit.*, p. 85 (1949).

209. Henning Friis, *op. cit.*, pp. 11-12 (1950).

210. Ben A. Arneson, *op. cit.*, p. 86 (1949).

211. The *Rigsdagtidende* published daily during sessions contains verbatim reports of proceedings in each house.

212. Ben A. Arneson, *op. cit.*, p. 89 (1949).

213. *Ibid.*, p. 111 (1949).

214. John Danstrup, *op. cit.*, p. 14 (1949); Paul Sinding, *op. cit.*, pp. 37-40 (1858). For the history of Danish law see an article by Stig Juul in *Den lille Salmonsen*, III, 77; Paul J. Jorgensen, *Dansk Retshistorie* (1947); Ebbe Hertzberg, *op. cit.*, pp. 531-76 (1912).

215. There was a court intervening between that of the *herred* and of the *land*, termed the *syssel-ting*. Ebbe Hertzberg, *op. cit.*, p. 540 (1912).

216. The *Länder* were said originally to be Jutland, Fünen, Zealand, Laaland, Skåne, Halland, Blekinge and Bornholm. Ebbe Hertzberg, *op. cit.*, p. 545 (1912).

217. Franklin D. Scott, *op. cit.*, p. 47 (1950). The Danish kings exercised greater authority at the Landsthings than did the Swedish. Ebbe Hertzberg, *op. cit.*, p. 541 (1912); John Danstrup, *op. cit.*, p. 29 (1949).

218. Ebbe Hertzberg, *op. cit.*, pp. 533-37 (1912).

219. John Danstrup, *op. cit.*, pp. 28, 32 (1949).

220. Ebbe Hertzberg, *op. cit.*, pp. 542, 548 (1912). But proposed statutes long continued to be submitted to the Landsthing for adoption.

221. T. Leivestad, *op. cit.*, p. 112 (1938).

222. Paul Sinding, *op. cit.*, p. 337 (1858).

223. As to the qualifications required of judges see Axel Teisen, "The Danish Judicial Code," 65 *U. Pa. L. Rev.* 543, 551-53 (1917).

224. The Social Democratic party as well as other Danish parties does not favor popular election of judges or limitation on their tenure of office. Evan Haynes, *Selection and Tenure of Judges*, p. 182 (1944).

225. Axel Teisen, "How They Decide Cases on Appeal in Denmark," 76 *Cent. L. J.* 185 (1913).

226. The various Danish courts are described by Axel Teisen, "The Danish Judicial Code," 65 *U. Pa. L. Rev.* 543, 546-48 (1917); Ben A. Arneson, *op. cit.*, pp. 152-59 (1949); *Den Lille Salmonsen*, III, 343-44 (*Domsmaend-Domstol*).

227. Ebbe Hertzberg, *op. cit.*, p. 564 (1912).

228. The Danish legal profession rather disfavors the use of lay judges. Evan Haynes, *op. cit.*, p. 183 (1944). "A court consisting of lay judges would be considered in Denmark a retrograde step in legal culture, and the possibility of using lay judges to do more than assist our judges is out of the question." H. Munch-Petersen, "The Social Aspect of Procedure From a European Point of View," 11 *Minn. L. Rev.* 624, 633 (1927).

229. Axel Teisen, *op. cit.*, pp. 566-67 (1917).

230. Ebbe Hertzberg, *op. cit.*, p. 564 (1912).

231. Reginald H. Smith, "The Danish Conciliation System," 11 *J. Am. Jud. Soc.* 85 (1927); George H. Ostenfeld, "Danish Courts of Conciliation," 9 *A.B.A., A.J.* 747 (1923). Report of the Committee on Legal Aid Work, 48 *A.B.A. Rep.* 374, 375 (1923).

232. H. Munch-Petersen, *op. cit.*, p. 634 (1927).

233. John Danstrup, *op. cit.*, p. 96 (1949); Bryn J. Hovde, *op. cit.*, pp. 545, 549 (1948).

234. Ben A. Arneson, *op. cit.*, pp. 178-90 (1949).

235. For a discussion of the government of Copenhagen under the 1840 and 1857 charters see Bryn J. Hovde, *op. cit.*, pp. 569-71 (1948).

236. In 1856 there was an official proposal for a unicameral city council. *Ibid.*, p. 570 (1948).

237. On municipal functions before 1865 see *ibid.*, pp. 718-36 (1948).

238. John A. Danstrup, *op. cit.*, p. 19 (1949); Paul Sinding, *op. cit.*, p. 60 (1858).

239. Paul Sinding, *op. cit.*, p. 69 (1858).

240. Rene Wormser, *The Law*, p. 186 (1949).

241. John Danstrup, *op. cit.*, pp. 21-22 (1949).

242. *Ibid.*, pp. 23-24 (1949); Paul Sinding, *op. cit.*, 93-96 (1858).

243. Ebbe Hertzberg, *op. cit.*, p. 545 (1912).

244. Absalon has been called the greatest Scandinavian of the Middle Ages. Paul Sinding, *op. cit.*, p. 104 (1858).

245. On Absalon see Fletcher Pratt, *op. cit.*, pp. 80-82, 108-10, 130-31 (1950).

246. *Ibid.*, p. 112 (1950).

247. *Ibid.*, pp. 265-66 (1950).

248. Paul Sinding, *op. cit.*, p. 202 (1858).

249. John Danstrup, *op. cit.*, p. 52 (1949).

250. Paul Sinding, *op. cit.*, pp. 216, 268 (1858).

251. *Ibid.*, pp. 222, 244 (1858).

252. *Ibid.*, pp. 308-09 (1858).

253. *Ibid.*, pp. 334-36 (1858). Bryn J. Hovde, *op. cit.*, pp. 97-100 (1948).

254. Bryn J. Hovde, *op. cit.*, p. 312 (1948). From 1842 to 1849 there was compulsory baptism of infants, directed against Baptists. *Ibid.*, 6. 314 (1948).

255. *Ibid.*, p. 592 (1948).
256. Fletcher Pratt, *op. cit.*, p. 174 (1950).
257. John Danstrup, *op. cit.*, p. 70 (1949).
258. Bryn J. Hovde, *op. cit.*, p. 696 (1948); Paul Sinding, *op. cit.*, p. 403 (1858).
259. J. H. S. Birch, *op. cit.*, p. 297 (1938); Solomon and Fisher, *Memorial of the Centennial Law of March 29, 1814* (1914).
260. John Danstrup, *op. cit.*, p. 186 (1949).
261. Bryn J. Hovde, *op. cit.*, p. 345 (1948).
262. John Danstrup, *op. cit.*, p. 128 (1949).
263. Ben A. Arneson, *op. cit.*, p. 5 (1949); Henning Friis, *op. cit.*, p. 18 (1950); Franklin D. Scott, *op. cit.*, p. 10 (1950).
264. John Danstrup, *op. cit.*, p. 73 (1949); Bryn J. Hovde, *op. cit.*, p. 591 (1948).
265. John Danstrup, *op. cit.*, p. 91 (1949); Bryn J. Hovde, *op. cit.*, p. 596 (1948); *Social Denmark*, p. 345, (1947).
266. Quoted by Bryn J. Hovde, *op. cit.*, p. 603 (1948).
267. In Chapter VIII on "Adult Education" Per Stensland states in Henning Friis, *op. cit.*, p. 227 (1950) that the "folk schools in Denmark may be 'a way out' offered to modern community educators." He also states at p. 229 that if any Northerner be selected as the father of modern adult education, it is Denmark's Grundtvig. See also MacKaye, "Grundtvig and Kold," 30 *Am. Scand. Rev.* 229-39 (Sept. 1942); Hal Koch, *Grundtvig* (1952).
268. John Danstrup, *op. cit.*, p. 128 (1949).
269. *Social Denmark*, pp. 345-99 (1947).
270. *Ibid.*, p. 356 (1947).
271. John Danstrup, *op. cit.*, pp. 32-34 (1949); Fletcher Pratt, *op. cit.*, pp. 69-73 (1950); J. H. S. Birch, *op. cit.*, p. 131 (1938).
272. John Danstrup, *op. cit.*, p. 43 (1949). Christian II had to grant a charter permitting the nobles to sentence and punish their peasants at their own discretion without the intercession of the courts. Hjalmar H. Boyesen, *op. cit.*, p. 483 (1900).
273. Bryn J. Hovde, *op. cit.*, p. 61 (1948); Paul Sinding, *op. cit.*, p. 324 (1858).
274. John Danstrup, *op. cit.*, pp. 75-76 (1949); Bryn J. Hovde, *op. cit.*, p. 66 (1948); Paul Sinding, *op. cit.*, pp. 332, 356 (1858).
275. Bryn J. Hovde, *op. cit.*, p. 286 (1948); Paul Sinding, *op. cit.*, pp. 379, 400 (1858).
276. John Danstrup, *op. cit.*, p. 84 (1949); Bryn J. Hovde, *op. cit.*, pp. 276-82 (1948); Paul Sinding, *op. cit.*, pp. 400-03 (1858); J. Steenstrup, *Den Danske Bonde og Friheden* (1888).
277. John Danstrup, *op. cit.*, p. 135 (1949).
278. Bryn J. Hovde, *op. cit.*, pp. 620, 622, 643 (1948).
279. *Ibid.*, pp. 543-56, 643-44 (1948).
280. *Ibid.*, pp. 282, 552 (1948).
281. Henning Friis, *op. cit.*, p. 204 (1950); *Social Denmark*, pp. 454-62 (1947).
282. John Danstrup, *op. cit.*, p. 128 (1949).
283. Franklin D. Scott, *op. cit.*, pp. 178-81 (1950); *Social Denmark*, pp. 328-30 (1947).
284. *Social Denmark*, pp. 331-34 (1947); H. Munch-Petersen, "Main Features of Scandinavian Law," 43 *L. Q. Rev.* 366, 377 (1927).
285. *Social Denmark*, pp. 332-36 (1947).
286. *Ibid.*, pp. 327-44 (1947); Ben A. Arneson, *op. cit.*, p. 256 (1949).
287. Paul Sinding, *op. cit.*, p. 80 (1858). See also Esmein, *A History of Continental Criminal Procedure*, pp. 34-36 (1913) as to early Danish procedure.
288. Fletcher Pratt, *op. cit.*, pp. 67-69 (1950).
289. A. W. G. Kean, "Early Danish Criminal Law," 19 *J. Comp. Leg. & Int. L.* 253 (1937); Von Bar, *A History of Continental Criminal Law*, pp. 119-41 (1916),

based largely on Stemann, *Den danske Retshistorie indtil Kristian V's Love* (1871).
290 Von Bar, *op. cit.*, pp. 291-97 (1916).
291. A seventeenth century murder prosecution is the subject of a novel by Janet Lewis, *The Trial of Sören Qvist* (1947).
292. John Howard, *The State of Prisons in England and Wales, with Preliminary Observations and an Account of Some Foreign Prisons*, p. 82 (1784).
293. Bryn J. Hovde, *op. cit.*, p. 699 (1948).
294. *Ibid.*, p. 700 (1948).
295. *Ibid.*, p. 721 (1948).
296. Ebbe Hertzberg, *op. cit.*, p. 563 (1912); Von Bar, *op. cit.*, pp. 367-68 (1916).
297. Ebbe Hertzberg, *op. cit.*, p. 563 (1912). For discussion of the difference between the accusatory and inquisitorial systems see Esmein, *op. cit.*, pp. 3-12 (1913).
298. Esmein, *op. cit.*, pp. 592, 604, 606; C. Goos, *Den Danske strafes proces* (1880).
299. Axel Teisen, "The Danish Judicial Code," 65 *U. Pa. L. Rev.* 543 (1917). For a description of Danish criminal law prior to 1875, see C. Goos, *Den Danske Strafferet*, 1875; Esmein, *op. cit.*, pp. 592-93, 604; Von Bar, *op. cit.*, pp. 119-41, 291-301, 367-68 (1916).
300. John Danstrup, *op. cit.*, p. 135 (1949); Axel Teisen, *op. cit.*, p. 543 (1917). With respect to civil procedure see Axel Teisen, *op. cit.*, pp. 558-70 (1917); *Den Lille Salmonsen*, II, 597 (*Civil processen*); Stephen Hurwitz, *Tvistemaal*; H. Munch-Petersen, "The Social Aspect of Procedure from a European Point of View," 11 *Minn. L. Rev.* 624 (1927); H. Munch-Petersen, *Den danske Retspleje*, (2d ed., 1923).
301. John Danstrup, *op. cit.*, p. 160 (1949).
302. H. Munch-Petersen, *op. cit.*, 624, 626 (1927).
303. John Danstrup, *op. cit.*, p. 160 (1949); E. Kampmann, "Prisons and Punishment in Denmark," 25 *J. Crim. L.* 115 (1934). On present Danish criminal procedure, see Stephen Hurwitz, *Den danske Strafferets Pleje*; *Den lille Salmonsen*, XI, 229.
304. Carl G. Givskov, "The Danish 'Purge-Laws'," 38 *J. Crim. L.* 447 (1948).
305. Eric Schweinburg, "Legal Assistance Abroad," 17 *U. Chi. L. Rev.* 270, 291, n. 30 (1950).
306. Albert H. Jessel, "A Poor Man's Lawyer in Denmark," 7 *L. Q. Rev.* 176 (1891).
307. Ben A. Arneson, *op. cit.*, p. 117 (1949).
308. Edwin M. Borchard, "European Systems of State Indemnity for Errors of Criminal Justice," 3 *J. Crim. L.* 684, 693, 711-12 (1913); Edwin M. Borchard, *Convicting the Innocent*, pp. 384-404 (1932).
309. Cash benefits paid in the way of health insurance, unemployment insurance, old age pensions, disability pensions, and industrial accident insurance as of 1949 are listed for Denmark, Norway and Sweden in Henning Friis, *op. cit.*, pp. 150-51 (1950). Danish benefits are adjusted annually according to changes in the cost-of-living index.
310. "Denmark," *Atlantic Monthly*, p. 4 (July, 1950).
311. Jens Larsen, *Virgin Islands Story* (1950); Bryn J. Hovde, *op. cit.*, p. 695 (1948). On slavery in ancient and medieval times, see Paul Sinding, *op. cit.*, pp. 39-40 (1858); Karen Larsen, *op. cit.*, pp. 28, 78, 120, 131 (1948); Gjessing, *En Fremstilling af Traeldommens sandsynlige Oprindelse hos Normaendene* (1862); Ericksen, "Om traeldom i Norden," *Nordisk Universitets-Tidskrift* VII, nos. 3 and 4 (Copenhagen, 1861).
312. Bryn J. Hovde, *op. cit.*, p. 22 (1948).
313. *Ibid.*, pp. 237-40 (1948).
314. *Ibid.*, p. 23 (1948).
315. *Ibid.*, pp. 43-46 (1948).
316. *Ibid.*, pp. 232-33 (1948).
317. *Ibid.*, p. 684 (1948).

318. Ebbe Hertzberg, *op. cit.*, p. 565 (1912).
319. John Danstrup, *op. cit.*, p. 130 (1949).
320. *Ibid.*, p. 132 (1949).
321. Bryn J. Hovde, *op. cit.*, p. 693 (1948). See also H. Munch-Petersen, "Main Features of Scandinavian Law," 43 L. Q. Rev. 366, 369, 373-77 (1927); Walton, "Scandinavian Law of Husband and Wife," 9 J. Comp. Leg. & Int. L. 263-64 (1927).
322. Bryn J. Hovde, *op. cit.*, p. 625 (1948).
323. Ben A. Arneson, *op. cit.*, p. 219 (1949). See Walter Galenson, *The Danish System of Labor Relations* (1952); Walter Galenson in Henning Friis, *op. cit.*, Chap. IV; *Social Denmark*, pp. 251-301 (1947).
324. *Social Denmark*, pp. 245-56 (1947).
325. *Ibid.*, pp. 266-68 (1947).
326. Henning Friis, *op. cit.*, p. 134 (1950).
327. *Social Denmark*, pp. 256-60 (1947).
328. The principles developed by the court are set forth in Knud Illum, *Den Kollektive Arbejdsret* (1939) and Knud V. Jensen, *Arbejdsretten i Danmark* (1942).
329. Ben A. Arneson, *op. cit.*, p. 219 (1949); *Social Denmark*, pp. 76-89 (1947). On factory legislation see *Social Denmark*, pp. 283-301 (1947). The Holiday Act of 1938 gives a vacation with pay of one day for each month worked, payable at the beginning of the vacation. *Ibid.*, pp. 400-05 (1947).
330. Ben A. Arneson, *op. cit.*, p. 223 (1949); Henning Friis, *op. cit.*, p. 115 (1950); *Social Denmark*, pp. 95-112 (1947).
331. *Social Denmark*, pp. 108-12 (1947).
332. *Ibid.*, pp. 105-08 (1947).
333. *Ibid.*, pp. 14-16 (1947); Bryn J. Hovde, *op. cit.*, p. 623 (1948).
334. Quoted by Bryn J. Hovde, *op. cit.*, p. 625 (1948).
335. *Social Denmark*, pp. 16-17 (1947).
336. *Ibid.*, pp. 14-21 (1947); Henning Friis, *op. cit.*, Chapter V, "Social Welfare."
337. *Social Denmark*, p. 18 (1947).
338. *Ibid.*, pp. 113-16 (1947).
339. *Ibid.*, pp. 124-27 (1947).
340. *Ibid.*, pp. 127-28 (1947).
341. *Ibid.*, pp. 128-30 (1947). Prior to 1933 about one-third of those receiving general relief were penalized. In 1942 only six per cent were penalized.
342. *Ibid.*, pp. 133-36 (1947).
343. *Ibid.*, pp. 301-27 (1947); Ben A. Arneson, *op. cit.*, p. 235 (1949). The number of unemployed from 1940 to 1944 are listed in *Social Denmark*, p. 320 (1947).
344. *Social Denmark*, pp. 184-88 (1947).
345. *Ibid.*, pp. 136-88 (1947); Ben A. Arneson, *op. cit.*, p. 253 (1949).
346. *Social Denmark*, pp. 188-214 (1947).
347. *Ibid.*, pp. 194-95, 202 (1947).
348. *Ibid.*, pp. 437-39 (1947); Henning Friis, *op. cit.*, p. 159 (1950).
349. *Social Denmark*, pp. 165-68 (1947); Henning Friis, *op. cit.*, p. 162 (1950).
350. *Social Denmark*, pp. 170-78 (1947).
351. *Ibid.*, pp. 179-84; H. Munch-Petersen, "Main Features of Scandinavian Law," 43 L. Q. Rev. 366, 376-77 (1927).
352. *Social Denmark*, pp. 298-99 (1947); Ben A. Arneson, *op. cit.*, p. 218 (1949).
353. *Social Denmark*, pp. 52-76 (1947); Ben A. Arneson, *op. cit.*, p. 241 (1949); Henning Friis, *op. cit.*, p. 146 (1950).
354. As to the amounts paid see *Social Denmark*, pp. 64-67 (1947).
355. *Ibid.*, pp. 70-72 (1947).

356. *Ibid.*, pp. 72-74 (1947).
357. Bryn J. Hovde, *op. cit.*, p. 576 (1948).
358. Quoted in Bryn J. Hovde, *op. cit.*, p. 580 (1948).
359. *Social Denmark*, pp. 241-50 (1947).
360. *Ibid.*, pp. 215-50 (1947); Bryn J. Hovde, *op. cit.*, p. 588 (1948).
361. *Social Denmark*, pp. 215-16 (1947).
362. *Ibid.*, p. 230 (1947).
363. *Ibid.*, pp. 33-52 (1947); Ben A. Arneson, *op. cit.*, p. 245 (1949); Henning Friis, *op. cit.*, pp. 146, 155 (1950); Franklin D. Scott, *op. cit.*, pp. 113-15 (1950).

364. Female factory workers are entitled to a daily cash benefit of six to seven kroner from four to eight weeks. All expectant mothers with incomes below the limit for membership in the health clubs receive gratis a half liter of milk a day for six months before childbirth and a liter a day for six months after childbirth. Henning Friis, *op. cit.*, p. 161 (1950).

365. For the total sick-club and public expenditure in 1942, see *Social Denmark*, p. 50 (1947).

366. See B. N. Armstrong, *The Health Insurance Doctor: His Role in England, Denmark and France* (1939).

367. *Social Denmark*, p. 46 (1947).

368. Henning Friis, *op. cit.*, p. 158 (1950). American critics of the Scandinavian systems say "in contravention of plain fact, that they exemplify the deterioration of medical science when it gets into public hands," Bryn J. Hovde, *op. cit.*, p. 341 (1948).

369. *Social Denmark*, p. 1, (1947).

370. *Ibid.*, pp. 55-70 (1947). The principal causes of disability are set forth for the period from 1933 to 1942. *Ibid.*, p. 61 (1947).

371. *Ibid.*, pp. 416-48 (1947); Ben Arneson, *op. cit.*, p. 259 (1949); Henning Friis, *op. cit.*, Chapter VI on Housing by Charles Abrams (1950).

372. Henning Friis, *op. cit.*, p. 178 (1950).
373. *Social Denmark*, pp. 72-74 (1947).
374. Bryn J. Hovde, *op. cit.*, p. 664 (1948).
375. *Social Denmark*, p. 237 (1947).
376. *Ibid.*, pp. 237-41 (1947); Ben A. Arneson, p. 272 (1949).

377. Speech by Henrik de Kaufmann reported in *Nordisk Tidende*, August 3, 1950.

378. Franklin D. Scott, *op. cit.*, p. 6 (1950). The languages separated in the Viking Period (800-1100). The Danes were "a long time considered the main people" and for several centuries played the most important part. Paul Sinding, *op. cit.*, p. 27 (1858).

379. Ebbe Hertzberg, *op. cit.*, pp. 564-65 (1912); Gunnar Leistikow in Henning Friis, *op. cit.*, pp. 307-24 (1950); H. Munch-Petersen, "Main Features of Scandinavian Law," 43 *L. Q. Rev.* 366 (1937); T. Leivestad, *op. cit.*, p. 101 (1938); Bugge, 26 *Tidskrift for Retvidenskab* 80 (1914); Lester B. Orfield, "Uniform Scandinavian Laws," 38 *A.B.A.J.* 773 (1952).

380. Under the Scandinavian Pauper Convention of 1928, Scandinavian nationals acquire the right to public assistance (general relief) on certain conditions if they have lived in Denmark for ten years. *Social Denmark* p. 120 (1947).

381. H. Holm-Nielsen, "The Scandinavian Conventions on Bankruptcy and Arrangements Outside Bankruptcy," 18 *J. Comp. Leg. & Int. L.* 262-65 (1936).

382. Paul Sinding, *op. cit.*, pp. 159, 170, 224 (1858).

383. But the regulations provided expressly that "we are not following Roman law in these kingdoms, but have our own laws."

384. Bryn J. Hovde, *op. cit.*, p. 124 (1948).

385. Ebbe Hertzberg, *op. cit.*, p. 563, (1912). Previously lower court judges had been laymen; and higher judges nobles trained in Roman and canon law.

386. H. Munch-Petersen, "The System of Legal Education in Denmark," *J. of Pub. Teachers of Law* 31-32 (1928); *Vejledning for Juridiske Studerende*, prepared by the University of Copenhagen Law School.

387. In the Scandinavian states the case method is used only as supplementary to lectures. H. Munch-Petersen, "The Social Aspect of Procedure from a European Point of View," 11 *Minn. L. Rev.* 624, 633 (1927).

388. For a criticism of law office study as over against theoretical studies see *Ibid.*, pp. 631-33 (1927).

389. *Facts about Denmark*, p. 30 (1949).

390. On the Danish bar see *Den lille Salmonsen*, X (Sagfrer).

391. Axel Teisen, "The Danish Judicial Code," 65 *U. Pa. L. Rev.* 543, 547, 551-54 (1917).

392. *Ibid.*, pp. 543, 554-55 (1917).

393. Bryn J. Hovde, *op. cit.*, p. 374 (1948). The great physicist, Hans Örsted, liked his fellow Danes for their "kind and calm, active, well-poised character equally far from the two extreme vices—arrogance and humility," John Danstrup, *op. cit.*, p. 113 (1949).

394. John Danstrup, *op. cit.*, p. 58 (1949). See also Paul Sinding, *op. cit.*, pp. 243-44 (1858).

395. Bryn J. Hovde, *op. cit.*, p. 92 (1948). See Andreas Höjer, *Idea Jurisconsulti Danici* (1736) translated by Sommer under the title, *Forestilling paa en Dansk Jurist* (1937).

396. Ludvig Holberg, *Introduktion til Natur-og Folkeretten* (1716 and 1793). See John Danstrup, *op. cit.*, p. 77 (1949); Paul Sinding, *op. cit.*, pp. 339-41 (1858); Karen Larsen, *op. cit.*, pp. 339-41 (1948).

397. J. B. Dons, *Forelaesninger Over den danske og norske Lov* (1781).

398. L. Norregaard, *Natur—og Folkeret* (1776) and *Forelaesninger* (1797).

399. J. F. W. Schlegel, *Naturrettens Frste Grundsaetninger* (1805) and *Juridisk Retsencyklopaedi* (1825).

400. For references to other leaders in Danish philosophy of law see Ebbe Hertzberg, *op. cit.*, pp. 570-73 (1912).

401. Bryn J. Hovde, *op. cit.*, p. 144 (1948).

402. John Danstrup, *op. cit.*, p. 83 (1949).

403. Ebbe Hertzberg, *op. cit.*, p. 572 (1912).

404. John Danstrup, *op. cit.*, p. 92 (1949). Viewing him as the greatest Scandinavian jurist, see Axel Teisen, "Power to Declare Legislation Unconstitutional in Denmark," 10 *A. B. A. J.* 792 (1924).

405. Anders Örsted, *Eunomia, Samling af Afhandlinger, Henhörende Til Moralfilosofien, Statfilosofien og Den Dansk-Norske Lovkyndighed* (1815-1822).

406. Bryn J. Hovde, *op. cit.*, pp. 362-64, 371 (1948).

407. *Ibid.*, pp. 362-63, 698 (1948).

408. Holberg took a similar position. *Ibid.*, p. 698 (1948).

409. *Ibid.*, pp. 357-60, 372 (1948).

410. *Ibid.*, p. 370 (1948). See Anders Örsted, "Over graendserne mellom theorie og prakois i saedelaeren," *Eunomia*, I, 94-145 (1815).

411. Jerome Hall, Book Review of Alf Ross, "Towards a Realistic Jurisprudence" 63 *Harv. L. Rev.* 18 (1949).

412. Alf Ross, *A Textbook of International Law*, reviewed 43 *Am. J. Int. L.* 197 (1949), 10 *Camb. L. J.* 305 (1949), 26 *Can. B. Rev.* 1150 (1948), 44 *Ill. L. Rev.* 416 (1949).

413. Hal Koch and Alf Ross, *Nordisk Demokrati* (1949).

414. Paul Sinding, *op. cit.*, p. 215 (1858).

415. John Danstrup, *op. cit.*, pp. 30, 60 (1949).

416. On the literature of Danish legal history see Ebbe Hertzberg, *op. cit.*, pp. 574-76 (1912).

417. Christian Stubaeus, *De Lege Et Legatoribus Danorum* (1716-1719).

418. Ludvig Holberg, *Danmarks og Norges Geistlige og Verldslige State* (1762). See also Erik Solem, *Holberg som Jurist* (Oslo, 1947).

419. Peder Kofod-Ancher, *Dansk Lovhistorie* (1769-1776).

420. J. F. W. Schlegel, *Om de gamle danske Retssaedvaner og Autonomi* (1828).

421. J. L. A. Kolderup-Rosenvinge, *Grundrids af den danske Lovhistorie* (3rd ed., 1860).

422. J. E. Larsen, *Forelaesninger over den danske Retshistorie* (1861); and *Samlede Skrifter* (1857-1861).

423. Christian L. E. Steman, *Danske Retshistorie indtil Christian den Femtes Lov* (1871).

424. Konrad Von Maurer, *Udsigt Over de Norgermanske Retskilders Historie* (1878).

425. H. Matzen, *Forelaesninger over den danske Retshistorie* (1896).

426. S. Wiskinge, *Vor Forfatnings Historie* (1928).

427. Paul J. Jorgensen, *Dansk Retshistorie Retskildernes af Forfatningsrettens Historie indtil sidste Halvdel af den 17 Aarhundrede.*

CHAPTER II

ICELANDIC LAW

B ECAUSE of its connection with Norway from its first settlement in 874 up to 1814 and because of its connection with Denmark from 1380 to 1944 Iceland is of peculiar interest to all Scandinavians.[1] As Arnold J. Toynbee has so beautifully phrased it, "the finest flowering of an oversea Scandinavian polity was the republic of Iceland, founded on the apparently unpromising soil of an Arctic island, five hundred miles away from the nearest Scandinavian *point d'appui* in the Faroe Islands."[2] The same author states that "it was in Iceland, and not in Norway, Sweden or Denmark, that the abortive Scandinavian Civilization achieved its greatest triumphs in literature and in politics."[3]

Iceland is of no less interest to the United States. Many Icelanders have settled in the United States during the past century. Our troops were stationed in Iceland during World War II and even a half a year before the United States entered the war. In May 1951 American troops were again stationed in Iceland.

International Relations

An Icelandic scholar has said of Iceland: "No other nation possesses so full and detailed records of its beginnings."[4] According to one tradition the discoverer of Iceland was Nadd-Odd, a Norwegian outlaw who had settled in the Faroes about 850.[5] In 860 when he was sailing to Norway, storms carried him to Iceland where he found no people. From 870 to 930 between 15,000 and 20,000 settlers from Norway came to Iceland. Economic conditions perhaps were to some extent a cause. Many came who were unwilling to accept the unification of Norway under the first king of all Norway, Harald the Fairhaired (872-930).[6] Two chief sources afford a complete and reliable account of the settlement: the *Islandingabok*, (The Book of the Icelanders) written by Ari Thorgilson about 1130[7] and the *Landnamabok* (The Book of Land-Taking).[8] Ingolv Arnarson, a chieftain from western Norway, led the first settlement which was made on the future site of Reykjavik, capital of Iceland. Most settlers came from the Norwegian counties of Hordaland and Rogaland. Some settlers came from the Shetland Islands, Orkneys, Hebrides, Scotland, Ireland, and England, but the Celtic strain was perhaps small[9] and Iceland became thoroughly Norwegian in institutions and language. In 986 Icelanders led by Eirik the Red discovered and occupied Greenland.[10] In 1000 Eirik's son, Leif, discovered America.[11]

There was no king nor even jarl in Iceland as there was no need for cooperative preparation for war. But there were chieftains, or *godar*, who headed what in fact were small states, or *godord*.[12] An unusually strong feeling of family and clan was developed. But the need for a common law was soon felt. An Icelander by the name of Ulvljot was sent to study the laws of Norway, select such parts as were suited to Iceland, and compile a code. After a period of three years he returned with a code based on the Gulathing Law, the law of southwestern Norway, from which most of the Icelanders had come.[13] These laws were adopted in 930 at the first meeting of the national assembly called the Althing. The Althing held annual meetings. In 964 the number of chieftains was fixed at thirty-nine. The chieftains dominated the Althing, so that there was no democracy as we understand it. Often they stretched the law to suit their personal aims. Yet the central government was not strong enough to enforce the law, as the power of the family in fact was the strongest. But the Althing is frequently referred to as the oldest parliamentary body in the world.[14]

Legally, Iceland was independent. However, in some cases the king of Norway was recognized as having a position of influence if not authority. While Iceland was not incorporated into the areas controlled by the Norwegian king until 1262, close connections were maintained prior to that date.[15] At a time when Norwegian literature was meager Iceland made incomparable contributions to the preservation and writing of the history of Norway in sagas and scaldic verse.[16] While in Norway the language became Danish, Iceland preserved the Old Norse tongue.[17] Icelanders found greater economic opportunities in Norway. They retained their citizenship in Norway.[18] The Norwegian Gulathing Law dating from about 935 took account of Iceland's relation to Norway. Icelanders were to have the same rights to recovery in tort as the highest Norwegian class, that is to say, the landholders just above the class of the common freemen, while they were in Norway on their trading journeys, while all other aliens were to have merely the rights of the common freemen.[19] In turn, the Icelandic law conferred a privileged position not only to Norwegians but also to Danes and Swedes. Such rights were accorded to "heirs of the Danish tongue" and "men from the three kings' realms, where our language is spoken."[20]

Olaf Tryggvason, King of Norway from 995 to 1000, sought to introduce Christianity into Norway and to the islands settled by the Norwegians including Iceland.[21] Njall's Saga tells the story of how the Althing in 1000 made Christianity the official religion, yet permitted freedom of private worship, exposure of new-born infants and the eating of horse-flesh. The whole North including Iceland was at first within the archbishopric of Hamburg established in 831 and later in 864 combined with Bremen.[22] In 1104 an archbishopric for the Scandinavian countries was established at Lund in Skåne, then a part of Denmark.[23] Iceland received its first bishop in 1056, Isleif at Skalholt.[24] In 1152 the archbishopric of Trondheim was established, thus separating Norway from the archbishopric of Lund which had previously comprised all the Scandinavian states. The new archbishop had ten bishoprics under him, including two in Iceland, though Iceland was not legally a part of Norway.[25] The Icelandic church in contrast to the Norwegian, was so independent as to excite the displeasure of both the Pope and the King of Norway. Celibacy of the clergy as not at once introduced and bishops were chosen by the Althing. In the thirteenth century the Icelandic chieftains refused to submit to the claims of the archbishop of Norway that the Icelandic bishop have jurisdiction over their clergy, thus giving King Haakon the Old some reasons to intervene until finally in 1262 Iceland became legally a part of Norway.[26]

King Harald the Fairhaired (872-930) appears to have regarded Iceland as a quasi-Norwegian dependency, but failed to bring it under his dominion. The Icelanders invited Harald to arbitrate the size of landholdings in Iceland, and also agreed to pay the *landaurer* tax for unrestricted intercourse with Norway.[27] King Harald Bluetooth (950-985) of Denmark was interested in Iceland, but took no warlike steps to acquire it although he acquired an overlordship in Norway. From 930 to 995 the Norwegian king made no attempt to exert direct influence over Iceland.[28] King Olaf Trygvasson (995-1000) instigated Christianity in Iceland and perhaps wished to accompany it with political control as he had done in the Orkneys and the Faroe Islands.[29] King Olaf the Saint (1016-1028) secured a final purging of all heathen customs in Iceland and provided bishops. In 1022 he made an agreement with the Icelandic chiefs known as the "Institutions and Law Which King Olaf gave the Icelanders" providing for reciprocal interests in the two countries, and in 1024 he invited the Althing to recognize him as ruler but without success.[30] An Icelandic chieftain, Loptr Saemundarsen, brought to Iceland from Norway as his bride a daughter of King Magnus II (1066-1069).[31] Icelandic contacts with foreign nations were made through its scalds the best of whom went to Norway. Civil wars in Norway from 1130 to 1217 meant that Norway could pay but little attention to colonial policy. In 1152 Iceland came under the Norwegian archbishopric. In 1163 an Icelandic chieftain and bishop attended the coronation of the Norwegian king. In 1178 the archbishop in consecrating an Icelandic bishop so maneuvered as to impress on him that Iceland should be regarded as a mere dependency of Norway.[32] Snorri Sturlason upon retiring as law speaker for Iceland spent the years from 1218 to 1220 at the Norwegian court. Duke Skule planned a military expedition to subjugate Iceland, following a dispute, but Snorri induced him to give it up.[33] Snorri made a secret agreement with the king and duke to bring Iceland under Norway in a peaceful manner, but he did not attempt to carry it out. He was the first Icelander to be made a Norwegian baron since 1030. He did carry out an agreement to protect Norwegian merchants in Iceland. About 1235 an Icelandic chieftain, Sturla Sighvatsson, promised the Norwegian king to subjugate Iceland for Norway; in turn Sturla was to be made jarl.[34] About 1250 both countries abolished trial by ordeal.[35]

While there was close religious, cultural, racial, and economic ties between Iceland and Norway, Iceland remained politically independent with much success until the middle of the twelfth century.[36] At that date the balance of power between the chieftains was broken. Disorders arose from their rivalry. The want of a central executive was more and more felt. Shipping fell off, and there was an undue concentration on agriculture. Repeatedly, Norwegian help was asked for and given. Jarl Skule, who was very powerful in Norway prior to 1240, was the first to take steps leading to a political union. But prior to consummation of the union, there was a long period of civil war in Iceland from 1200 to 1262, called the Sturlunga Age, because of the prominence of a family bearing that name.[37] In 1241 King Haakon induced the leader of one faction to kill Snorri Sturlason who had supported Jarl Skule, the great rival of Haakon, Skule himself being killed about the same time. In 1258 Haakon made this leader Gissur Thorvaldsson the first jarl of Iceland even though Iceland had not yet recognized his overlordship. When Gissur died in 1268 no jarl was chosen as the title had proved unpopular. Instead the king appointed two royal magistrates with the title of *Valdsmadr,* one for the western and the other for the eastern districts.[38]

In 1262 there was a voluntary agreement under which Iceland recognized the Norwegian king and agreed to pay taxes and fines in return for a guarantee of trade and the maintenance of Icelandic law. Thus Iceland, which had been an independent republic for four centuries, became a part of the domains of the King of Norway. The Norwegian king had been strongly supported by the Norwegian archbishop who desired to strengthen his hold over the nationalistic church of Iceland.[39] The absence of a central government and the alienability of the *godord* eventually had produced disorder. Iceland could not go on indefinitely with no central executive, no system of taxation, no machinery for enforcement of judgments, no police, and no machinery for carrying on international relations. Haakon the Old thus found it easy to win over Iceland through bribes and threats, drawing Icelanders to his court, sending commissions all over Iceland, and influencing the few chieftains who controlled the Althing.

In 1319 the male line of Norwegian kings ended and Magnus, a son of the last king's daughter, married to a Swedish duke, became king of both Norway and Sweden. After reiterating their former demands for fulfillment of the union agreement of 1262, the Icelanders swore allegiance to the new king in 1320 and the king seems to have complied with their demands.[40] The union between Norway and Sweden lasted until 1371. When in 1355 King Magnus was deposed and replaced by his son Haakon as king of Norway, Magnus' wife, Queen Blanche, retained Iceland as her Norwegian dowry.[41]

In 1380 Norway came into a union with Denmark lasting until 1814, and Sweden which possessed Finland came into this union in 1397, remaining in it with some intermissions until 1523. Queen Margaret (1388-1405) was unpopular in Iceland because she sought increased taxes.[42] The Norwegian influence was not immediately lost. But gradually Danes were selected as higher officials and bishops, and Danish commercial and administrative policy came to control.[43] Although Sweden was a member of the Kalmar Union, she exercised no power over Iceland.

In 1302 the Norwegian king made a regulation that only Norwegian merchants might trade in Iceland.[44] English and German trade with Iceland had flourished up to this time. By 1340 much codfish was exported to Norway. From 1350 to 1400 fewer ships came to Iceland. Laws of 1382, 1383 and 1389 laid down tariffs on imports from Iceland. The large trade carried on by the merchants of Bergen, Norway with Iceland was largely destroyed by the ravages of the Victual brothers who burned Bergen in 1393 and 1428.[45] After a lapse of a century English trade with Iceland was resumed in the fifteenth century.[46] King Eirik of the United Scandinavian realms protested in vain in 1413, 1415, and 1431, and for a time the English exercised almost complete control over Icelandic trade. In 1433 the English king finally issued an order prohibiting English trade with Iceland. A war from 1469 to 1474 between Denmark-Norway and England did not seriously interfere with trade between Iceland and England. A treaty with England in 1490 gave the English the privilege of free trade in Iceland for seven years. German trade with Iceland commenced in 1430, the first German merchants coming from Lübeck and Danzig, then later from Hamburg and Bremen.[47] King Hans (1483-1513) had signed a convention with the Norwegian and Swedish councils that he would forbid Hanseatic trade with Iceland, and sought to limit such trade by admitting English and Dutch trade. In 1513 an ordinance forbade Hanseatic trade, but it was ineffectual, and during the reign of Frederick I (1524-1533) German and English merchants actually took part in the deliberations of the Althing.

Icelandic contacts of importance with outsiders occurred in the sixteenth century. There were disputes with English fishermen, and the Icelanders appealed to Copenhagen for help.[48] The Danish government forbade the English to fish in Icelandic waters. The English fishermen appealed to their king, Henry VIII. But he was preoccupied with the Reformation Parliament (1529-1536). The Icelanders were resisting the Reformation. Henry VIII offered to buy Iceland, thus acquiring fishing territory and relieving Denmark of a rebellious country. But the purchase never came off, and was not again considered.

From the middle of the sixteenth century Icelandic trade became increasingly Danish.[49] In 1547 King Christian III granted Iceland to the Mayor of Copenhagen for a certain yearly tax. About 1560 Danish merchants began to trade with Iceland. In 1572 all Icelandic harbors were closed to Hamburg and German trade was soon weakened, and finally ceased in the reign of Christian IV (1588-1648). In 1602 the king granted the Icelandic trade as a monopoly to three Danish cities: Copenhagen, Malmo, and Helsingor.[50] Negotiations by Hamburg for the lease of the island in 1645 and 1675 were unsuccessful. In 1662 a new Danish company was organized which received a twenty-year monopoly of Icelandic trade. Up to 1786 trade was conducted either by merchant companies or by the Danish government.[51] Finally in 1786 it was made free to all citizens of Denmark and Norway, although some restrictions on trade continued until 1854.[52]

From 1662 to 1814 the relation of Iceland to Denmark was very close, as an absolute monarchy then prevailed.[53] Laws were made by the king, administration was placed in Danish hands, and the Supreme Court of Denmark became the highest court for Iceland. The Danes kept close control over trade and government. In 1809 Americans commenced a small trade there, and gained a special license in 1815.[54]

About the year 1800 Napoleon imposed his Continental system on Denmark. England retaliated with a naval blockade, thus shutting off grain supplies from Iceland.[55] As the Danish fleet had been captured, no help could be expected from Denmark. England out of humanitarian motives adopted in 1810 an Order of Council declaring Iceland a noncombatant and food supplies were thus permitted to enter.

When the union between Norway and Denmark was severed in 1814 it would seem that Iceland should have continued in union with Norway rather than Denmark since the original union agreement was with Norway and, furthermore, since the Icelanders were overwhelmingly of Norwegian descent.[56] There is no evidence that the wishes of the Icelanders themselves were consulted. The preliminaries to the Treaty of Kiel referred to Iceland as having "never belonged to Norway." One writer has concluded that the separation from Norway arose out of the haste in drafting the Treaty of Kiel.[57]

Following the separation of Norway from Denmark and its union with Sweden, Denmark demanded fulfillment of a clause in the Treaty of Kiel for reimbursement for a fair share of the Danish-Norwegian debt. The Quintuple Alliance backed the Danish claim in 1818. Karl Johan, the king of Sweden and Norway, advanced a claim for the return of Iceland, which under the Treaty of Kiel had been retained by Denmark.[58] But the Norwegians were too timid to press the matter.

The meaning of the treaty of 1262 now became an issue. The Icelanders contended that it simply united Iceland and Norway under one king. The Danes asserted that a real union had occurred and that Iceland had been incorporated into Norway and therefore now had the same status in relation to Denmark.[59] When the Danish king set up consultative chambers in Denmark the Icelanders claimed equal rights.[60] The Danish king complied by summoning a commission of Icelandic officials to make proposals and later they re-established the Althing as a consultative assembly, chosen largely by the Icelanders, which first met in 1845.

In 1849 Denmark adopted a new Constitution and wished to apply it to Iceland. The Icelanders objected and cited the old treaty of union with Norway of 1262. This very nearly resulted in civil war which was averted through the efforts of Jon Sigurdsson (1811-1879), probably the greatest statesman Iceland has produced.[61] But in 1874 on the thousandth anniversary of the Norwegian settlement of Iceland, a new constitution was granted to Iceland, based on a Danish law of 1871.[62] The Althing was divided into two houses and given full legislative powers as to local matters. The king of Denmark was to appoint a resident governor who should lay the bills passed by the Althing before the king for his sanction. Iceland did not have to contribute to support the defense forces or the civil list, and had the power of local taxation, but no voice in foreign affairs. The Althing had also lost its power as the final appellate court. The Danish Minister of Justice was the key Danish official at Copenhagen, and the king vetoed many bills upon his advice as well as that of the governor. In 1904 an Icelandic ministry responsible to the Althing was established in Iceland itself. In 1913 nationalism was encouraged when Iceland secured a distinct flag of its own.

During the American Civil War period and shortly thereafter Secretary of State Seward was anxious that the United States buy Iceland and Greenland from Denmark.[63]

From 1870 to 1900 some 15,000 Icelanders emigrated to America, chiefly to Canada and the United States.[64] The main settlements were in Alberta, Manitoba, Ontario, Saskatchewan, Minnesota, North Dakota, South Dakota, Utah and Wisconsin. There are now about 40,000 such persons.

Under the Act of Union of November 30, 1918, Iceland was recognized as a sovereign state united with Denmark in the person of its ruler.[65] Among joint affairs were coinage and the supreme court, but these were almost immediately taken over by Iceland as the treaty permitted. But there remained in the joint category the rights of citizens of the one country in the other, Icelandic foreign affairs were handled by Denmark, and Denmark undertook to protect fishing in Icelandic waters. At the end of 1940 the states could demand a revision of the treaty. If no revision were made within three years of demand, each state could decide that the treaty had lapsed. The Act of Union offers an instance of "self-neutralization" which could have political but not legal consequences.[66]

Since 1918 Iceland has been a sovereign state. While Denmark was invited to accede to the Covenant of the League of Nations and did accede, Iceland was not so invited and did not accede.[67] Though Denmark joined the League sanctions against Italy when Italy invaded Ethiopia, Iceland concluded a trade treaty with Italy. Iceland became a party to the Paris Pact for the Renunciation of War of 1928.[68] It belongs to the Postal Union and a number of other international organizations.[69] On November 19, 1946, it was admitted to the United Nations.[70] As such it is a party to the Statute of the International Justice, but up to 1950 it had not become subject to its obligatory jurisdiction.[71]

The United States recognized Iceland through the conclusion of bilateral treaties with it.[72] In a letter of December 1933 the State Department stated that up to that time it had "not been found feasible" to send a resident representative to Iceland from the United States.[73] From 1946 to 1948 W. Trimble was in charge of the American legation in Reykjavik. In 1948 the United States sent a new envoy, Richard P. Butrick.[74]

By exchange of notes signed in 1922 the United States and Iceland provided for relief from double income tax on shipping profits.[75] They concluded an arbitration treaty on May 15, 1930. On January 16, 1932, there was an exchange of notes as to reciprocal recognition of load-line certificates.

Following the German occupation of Denmark on April 9, 1940, the Althing the next day appointed a regent, though it simply suspended instead of terminating the union with Denmark.[76] On May 10, 1940, British troops landed in Iceland. On May 17, 1941, the Althing passed joint resolutions indicating that Iceland would not renew the union with Denmark. On July 7, 1941, an agreement between the United States and Iceland provided for withdrawal of American troops at the close of the war. An executive agreement of July 1, 1941, provided that the United States would undertake to defend Iceland.[77] At a referendum on May 24, 1944, only 370 votes opposed severance from Denmark and 1,042 a republic. On June 17, 1944, the new Constitution went into effect and Iceland became an independent republic.

Before World War II Icelandic imports were chiefly from Denmark and Great Britain and her exports to Spain, Norway, Sweden, and Portugal.[78] But in 1946 and 1947 Soviet Russia was second only to Great Britain in purchases from Iceland. The purchases of Russia dropped off sharply in 1948 when American assistance under ERP was given.[79] From 1944 to 1946 two members of the Icelandic cabinet were communists.[80] In the June 1946 election three of the seventeen members of the Upper Chamber and seven of the thirty-five members of the Lower Chamber were communists. In the election of October 1949 the total number of communists in the Althing dropped from ten to nine.[81] In November 1950 the election of delegates to the biennial congress of the Icelandic Labor Federation resulted in a crushing defeat to the communists, and they also lost control of the Reykjavik Labor Council.[82]

In recent years some thirty nations have made claims to jurisdiction over submarine areas lying beyond the traditional limits of their territorial waters. In an action in 1948 directed solely to fisheries, Iceland has asserted the right to take conservation measures within the limits of the continental shelf.[83] In the spring of 1950 it declared a four-mile protected area off the north coast of Iceland.[84]

In June 1948 the International Civil Aviation Organization Conference on Air Navigation Services in Iceland was held at Geneva, Switzerland. The task of the conference was to reach agreement on the technical details of the air navigation services in Iceland for North Atlantic air navigation, and to agree upon the proportion which contributing states should pay to Iceland, and the terms under which Iceland would undertake to supply these services.[85] In September 1948 Iceland made an agreement with the Council of this body.

In 1949 Iceland signed the North Atlantic Treaty. The Foreign Minister for Iceland stated, on such signing, that although "we are quite unable to defend ourselves from any foreign armed attack . . . we also want to make it crystal clear that we belong to this free community of free nations which now is being fervently founded."[86] He added that

Icelanders "would all prefer to lose our lives rather than lose our freedom."

James Reston of the *New York Times* has pointed out that "even to protect the ocean approaches to the United States, it is necessary to have bases in such places as Iceland, Greenland and the Azores, which do not belong to us."[87] In turn, Iceland needs our aid. Asking with what country Iceland should ally herself, an English historian has concluded: "Her history of a thousand years, her respect for individual freedom of action, inherited from her Norwegian parentage, all point the way to the democracy of the West."[88] It has been contended that Iceland would come under the protection of the Monroe Doctrine.[89]

On May 7, 1951, a first contingent of two hundred American soldiers landed in Iceland at its invitation.[90] Their activities will center on the two main airports. The Icelandic government first consulted and obtained the approval of 43 out of the 52 members of the Althing, the other nine being communists.[91] Iceland retains control of the number of troops to be there. A treaty was signed on May 5, 1951, authorizing such troops in furtherence of the North Atlantic Treaty to which Iceland is a party.

Icelandic Law Before 1262

Those Icelanders learned in the ancient law of custom and pre-eminent in that respect were given the title of "lawmen."[92] They were instructors, private counsellors, and consulted at the *things*, thus in effect serving as judges in litigated cases. They retained a semi-official character for three centuries in both Norway and Iceland after the emigration and settlement of Iceland. An official custodian of the law about 930 was provided for when the first attempt was made to establish a legal system. The "Law-Saga Man," now made the custodian, was required to recite the existing rules of law before the annual meeting of the Althing.[93] In the course of every three years the entire body of the law would be recited. The "Law-Saga Man" or law speaker to some extent superseded the lawmen, but on certain occasions he was required to consult five or more of the lawmen. The principal reason for establishing the office was to eliminate confusion resulting from variances between the Icelandic system and that brought from Norway. It seems possible that the system of public recital of the law was copied from an earlier similar system in Sweden.[94] The *logretta* or law-making assembly had the function of approving or disapproving the public recital of the law by the law speaker. Where there were disputes as to interpreting and applying the legal rules this body determined and announced its will. The Icelandic law speaker was so emphatically viewed as the custodian of the law that the famous Njall Saga attributes to one of them the statement that he did not believe that any other person of his generation knew the rule of law for a certain case. Even after law texts and codes had been written, the lawmen exercised a supplementary authority.

The law speaker was the sole national official of the republic. He recited the law. He presided over the *logretta*. He answered questions as to the law. He was paid annually one-half of the fines imposed at the Althing and a certain amount of woolen cloth. He was one of the chief lawyers of his day. But in reality he was neither a judge nor a magistrate, nor a legislator. He gave no judgments, nor could he enforce judgments nor punish offenders. He did not open the Althing nor maintain order at its sessions. In effect he was the "living voice of the law."[95]

The Althing differed from legislative bodies in other countries. It was not a primary assembly. That is to say it was not attended by the people as a whole like a New England town meeting. It was not a representative assembly in the sense that it was selected by popular vote to represent the people. Nor was it a king's council, such as existed in Denmark, Norway, and Sweden.

For legislative purposes the Althing acted through a group of 144 men called the *logretta*.[96] Of these only one-third, the 39 *godar* and their nine nominees, could vote. These nine nominees were elected by the *godar* of the south, west, and east quarters in order to give them the same number in the *logretta* as the north quarter had. Each of these 48 appointed two assessors to advise him. When Christianity was introduced in 1000 the two bishops were added to the *logretta*. The law speaker presided over this body.

When the legal system was organized in Iceland in 930 the Althing received very broad authority. It was both the general legislative and the highest judicial body.[97] As has been seen this body was dominated by an inner circle, corresponding to the Norwegian *lagretten* or "law-right," which was made up of the Icelandic chieftains (*Godar*), the law-saga man, and the two bishops (after Christianity was introduced). In 965 four courts were set up to try cases in the four divisions of the country.[98] A fifth tribunal was set up in 1004 for special cases. The Althing was the final court of appeal. Each of the four divisions had three local courts (*thing-lag*). These local courts were presided over by local chiefs. But in form the people adopted the determinations of the local court. Each peasant chose to which chief's circle he would belong, as the *thing-lag* was more a union than it was a district.

Much of the early law of Iceland was customary law, preserved by the law speaker and the lawmen, and amended by the Althing.[99] A very technical judicial procedure grew up in part because form and substance were not as yet sharply distinguished and because both laymen and officials were conservative.

Schools of law seem to have flourished in the eleventh century.[100] They were conducted by sages such as Brennu Njall[101] and Skapti Thorodsson.[102] Discussions of the law are to be found in the sagas and ancient law books compiled about 1150 out of materials going back to the eleventh and even the tenth centuries.[103] The Icelandic scholars "made the classic digests of Scandinavian mythology, genealogy and law."[104]

Iceland was the first of the Scandinavian countries to establish a written law text or code. In 1117 the Althing appointed a commission to prepare a written collection of the prevailing rules and to prepare desirable changes in them.[105] The members of the committee were experts on the law of the time. Their text was adopted and ratified in 1118 and was called the *Haflida-Skra*[106] after the chairman of the commission, the chieftain Haflide Maarson. The text is in fact declaratory of the customary law rather than an official statutory code. The opinions of the lawmen as auxiliary authorities were recognized where consistent with its provisions. The text contains a number of contradictions between the various codes. It dealt with all the temporal affairs of the country, but its scope is not precisely known, as the original does not exist. Between 1122 and 1133 an ecclesiastical code known as the *Kristenret* was prepared by Bishops Thorlak and Ketil. Numerous texts based on these two collections appeared during the next century and a half. Chief among them still preserved are the "King-book" and the *Stadarholsbok* written between 1260 and 1270. These law texts are now commonly designated as the Icelandic *Gragas*.[107] A few decades later the Norwegians followed the Icelandic example and reduced their laws to writing.

Copies of the Icelandic *Gragas* were first published in 1829 by the Arnamagneam Foundation in Copenhagen. It consists of ordinances of the Althing, decisions and declarations of the law, speeches, ecclesiastical regulations, formulas of legal procedure and legal transactions, and memoranda of legal questions.[108]

An Icelandic professor of law has concluded that the *Gragas* was a "richly developed and remarkable law certainly on a Germanic basis but still different in many respects."[109] It was the "result of a long development, though it is seldom possible to follow the separate phases of such development." An American professor of law of Icelandic descent has pointed out that "no study of the customary law of Scandinavia can be regarded as even measurably complete until the oldest source of Scandinavian law, the Icelandic *Gragas*, has been translated into English. In that volume appears the customary law of ancient Scandinavia uncontaminated by the decretal amendments of monarchs who collectively concentrated in themselves all the powers which theretofore had belonged to and been exercised by the people."[110]

Norwegian Influence on Icelandic Law After 1262

The year 1262 is of tremendous significance in Icelandic history because it was in that year that Iceland, formerly an independent republic, first came under a foreign king.[111] This change obviously had permanent effects on the subsequent legal history of Iceland.

The wording of the agreement was so significant for almost seven hundred years that it deserves recording. The *logretta*, on behalf of the people, took the oath of allegiance and made the following agreement with the king of Norway, known as the "*Gamli satt-mali, 1262*":

"This is the agreement of the people of northern and southern Iceland, that we grant King Haakon and Magnus under oath land, thanes, and eternal taxes, twenty *alnar* for every man who pays the tax of *thingfararkaup*. These taxes are to be collected by the *heppstjorar*, brought to the ship, and delivered to the royal officials, after which there is to be no responsibility for them. In consideration hereof the king is to let us enjoy peace and the Icelandic laws. Six ships are to sail from Norway to Iceland every summer during the next two years. From that time forth this matter shall be arranged in such a way as the king and our best men shall deem most serviceable for the country. Any inheritance which falls to Icelanders in Norway is to be given them, however long it may remain due, so soon as the rightful heirs, or their legal representatives, appear to claim it. The *landaurar* tax is to be abolished. Icelanders are to have in Norway the most extensive rights which they have ever enjoyed there, and which have been promised them in your letters. You (King Haakon) are also to maintain peace for us, as God may give you strength to do so. The jarl's authority we will acknowledge so long as he keeps faith with you and peace with us. This agreement we and our descendants will keep in good faith so long as you also faithfully keep it, but we consider ourselves released from all obligations, if in the opinion of the best men, it shall be broken. To this end I place my hand on the Holy Bible, and call God to witness that I grant King Haakon and Magnus under oath land, thanes and eternal taxes according to the conditions here named, and as the written agreement bears testimony. May God so be merciful to me as I keep this oath, unmerciful if I do not."[112]

It does not appear that any change in the legal order was made at the meeting of the Althing in 1262 when Iceland submitted to the king of Norway. Among the conditions which the Icelanders imposed before submission was that the king should guarantee "peace and the

Icelandic laws." Possibly the people believed at the time that their old law, the *Gragas*, would continue in force and that the king had promised not to alter the law of the land.[113] But it is likely, as even Icelandic authorities such as Professor Larusson concede, that the people must have realized that the new factor of royal power and a foreign power must lead to changes in the law of Iceland.[114] They could anticipate that the king in his dealings with Iceland would apply law, but a law not necessarily identical with the law before 1262. They could also expect that the law as it developed would take account of local conditions in Iceland and not simply those of Norway.

Whatever may be the correct interpretation of the agreement of 1262, it is clear that during the ensuing decades substantial changes in the law were made. The initiative in making these changes came from the king. Moreover, Norwegians were appointed as lawmen and as *syslumenn*[115] or magistrates. At this particular time the royal power in Norway was stronger than it ever had been before the prolonged civil war which had gone on since King Sigurd Jerusalemfarer's death in 1130 ended with Jarl Skule Baardson's fall in 1240 with a complete victory for the descendants of King Sverri. The victory was one of royal power over the nobility. This inevitably meant that henceforth the king would play a larger role in law development. King Haakon the Old (1217-1263) had begun such work in the latter part of his reign. But the bulk of the work was done by his son, King Magnus (1263-1280). Magnus was one of the most remarkable and industrious lawmakers of the Scandinavian countries, as evidenced by his surname *Lawmender*. Magnus was successful in creating a unified and central legal system in Norway long before this occurred in Denmark and Sweden.[116] His law revision in Norway proceeded in two stages. The first in 1267 to 1269 was work on the old Norwegian provincial laws. Archbishop Jon the Red of Norway protested against any revision of the church law by the king and the Frostathing upheld the archbishop.[117] The second period was a development of the general national law from 1271 to 1274.[118] King Magnus had two codes drafted for Iceland.

The earlier code was sent to Iceland in 1271 for submission to the Althing.[119] Sturla Thordsson, an Icelander, had assisted the king in drafting it. The Althing was not in a very receptive mood. The Code was considered section by section in three long sessions. During the first year of consideration one of its books, that on *thing* organization and procedure, and two of the chapters of the book on inheritance were accepted. But it was not fully accepted until 1273, and then only because the Icelandic chieftains who were close to the king intervened. According to Professor Larusson it is not at all clear what had caused the opposition to acceptance of the book. It was given the name *Jarnsida,* or "Ironside," probably from its binding. It exists even to this day in the handwriting of that time. But the handwriting is not complete. Three or four pages seem to be missing. This gap is not very important, hence we can gain a clear conception of its form and contents. The gaps may be reasonably filled by examining the context. The old law was now supplanted. The old chieftainships disappeared, being thought inconsistent with royal power. There gradually arose a group of men of substance and prominence who loyally supported the government. Under the "Ironside" code two lawmen were to govern the country and the *logretta* was limited to judicial functions. The characteristic features of the Althing were abolished: the four district courts, the *fimtardomr* or appellate court, and the office of law speaker. The *thing* system was reorganized to correspond to the Norwegian system. The *voldsmadr* or royal magistrate was to choose a certain number of men from each *thing* district, 140 in all, to constitute the *thing.* From these the lawman was to select three from each *thing* district, in all 36, to sit in the *logretta.* As has been seen, a lawman, supplanted the law speaker as in Norway. After 1277 there were two lawmen. Judicial authority was to be in the *logretta.* Legislative authority was to be in the Althing and the king conjointly. Either might take the initiative in legislation. In practice the *thing* now became mainly a judicial tribunal as it had in Norway. There was no longer a recitation of the laws at meetings of the Althing. The Althing lost its popular character as its members now consisted of chosen representatives, and its size was soon reduced.

The "Ironside" represents the relatively hasty and crude efforts in the early part of the reign of King Magnus. On the one hand it combined provisions of the Norwegian law not suitable for Iceland. On the other hand it omitted several essential rules of the prior Icelandic law. Consequently, it added confusion and disorder to the law of Iceland. But fortunately a new national code had come into force in Norway about 1275. Use could now be made of the experience gained in the drafting of that code.

The second code was sent to Iceland in the summer of 1280, and was called the *Jonsbok* after Jon Einarsson, the lawman, who brought it back to Iceland and who most likely was one of its chief compilers.[120] It was presented for approval to the Althing in 1281, and approval with reservations was obtained. The saga of Bishop Arni Thorkaksson[121] describes its passage by the Althing. Three groups, clergy, nobles and peasants, gave their views about the book, and the saga sets forth the views of the priests and peasants. The criticisms of the clergy generally came to this: the law of the church is the best security against the temporal power. The opposition of the clergy was simply one part of the battle then going on in Norway between the archbishops in Trondheim and the regency of leading nobles, which then exercised the royal power in Norway.[122] The objections of the peasants were not of a unified character but went to individual details in the book, chiefly as to the rules of property law. It is notable that no one proposed to go back to the Law of the *Gragas*. The debate became rather heated. But the upshot was that the book was taken as law except for a few chapters.[123] One can determine to some extent from the handwriting to the *Jonsbok* which these chapters were. Provisions in the Code peculiar to Iceland are "in the law of descent, those regarding support of the destitute; in the law of land-leases, those regarding separation rights; and provisions in reference to marine law and taxation."[124] The number of members of the Althing was reduced to eighty-four.[125] There was established the title of *syslumadr* for the royal district magistrates. Iceland was divided into districts administered by the *syslumenn*.

The provisions of the *Jonsbok* as to taxes were very moderate.[126] Only one half of the whole sum was to be paid to the king. The other half was to be kept in Iceland for the payment of the usual taxes.

The criminal law underwent great changes.[127] Violation of the law was no longer a mere private matter to be settled by the criminal defendant and his victim, but as a crime for which the defendant must answer to the government. Banishment for serious crimes was retained. But fines payable to the king were instituted in many cases. There was to be capital punishment as to murder, robbery, rape, counterfeiting, forgery, and seduction.[128]

Early under the new procedure the practice grew up of summoning persons to Norway for trial there.[129] Norwegians were appointed as lawmen and *syslumenn*. At the debate in 1281 on the adoption of the *Jonsbok* the chieftains made a specific demand that only Icelanders be appointed to the higher offices. The Council of Regency in the reign of King Eirik Magnuson (1280-1299) granted this condition, but no specific provision was incorporated into the Icelandic laws.[130] When Eirik's brother, Haakon, succeeded him as king in 1299 the Icelanders protested again, and did not pledge their allegiance until 1303. In 1302 it was decreed that only Norwegians could trade with Iceland.

As has been seen, within two decades of the union with Norway two new codes were adopted in Iceland. The *Gragas* no longer prevailed as law. What then were the sources of the new law? The "Ironside," in the opinion of Professor Larusson, was manifestly based on a Norwegian code, copies of which no longer exist, resembling the Gulathing Law of 1267 or the Frostathing Law of 1269.[131] This code was to a large extent a compilation of the older Gulathing and Frostathing laws. But the Norwegian code was not the sole source of the "Ironside." Its authors had also made use of the *Gragas*. Professor Larusson points out that in 24 out of the 141 chapters appear rules arising out of the earlier Icelandic law, and possibly the missing gaps in the law had the same origin. But the Norwegian materials constitute the greater part of the book, and this was clear to the Icelanders of that time. Contemporaneous writings refer to the Ironside as the "Norwegian Code," and the contents of the book as "Norwegian law."

With respect to the development of the *Jonsbok* one must proceed more cautiously. The chief source was the national law of King Magnus Lawmender. Much of it is taken from that law virtually unchanged. To a very large extent it follows that law as to divisions into books and chapters. Thus the *Jonsbok* contains one book on the law of warfare, as in Magnus' law. But it contains two books on maritime law not found in Magnus' law, and a short book on the duty of citizens to the king. It is significant that the *Gragas* is much more frequently used as a source here than it is in the "Ironside." Professor Larusson points out that it was the direct source of 105 of the book's 251 chapters. It is the indirect source of various other parts, as the *Jonsbok* adopted certain rules from the "Ironside" and the national law of Magnus, which in turn came from the *Gragas*. Consequently, when the *Jonsbok* was accepted as law, much of the old law still remained in force.

Some students have concluded that the acceptance of the two codes should have created full legal unity between Norway and Iceland. An Icelandic law professor of today has rejected this conclusion.[132] First and foremost, as he points out, the method of procedure of the king in presenting both laws to the Althing and asking their consent shows that he fully recognized Iceland as a separate law-making jurisdiction, which had its own law. A comparison of the *Jonsbok* with the national law of Magnus shows distinctly the special position which Iceland occupied among the areas under the king. King Magnus sought through the development of his national law for a complete legal unity in Norway. All Norway was to have one law, instead of each subdivision having its own separate law. But formally, he proceeded on the basis of the prior local divisions.[133] He never developed a code for the whole nation without each district receiving its own code. In the Gulathing district it was called the Gulathing Law; in the Frostathing district, the Frostathing Law. Unity was attained by having all these laws similar in content. A chapter in the book as to procedure of the *thing* was different as to each district. This was proper as at that time each district had its individual peculiarities as to procedure. The same situation prevailed as to the code which the king sent to the Faroe Islands. It was identical in all respects with the Norwegian Code, and legal unity was secured. On the other hand, the *Jonsbok* was not identical with the national law of Norway. It departs from the Norwegian in a multitude of details and the departures are so extensive that it appears that the same code is not involved and that here there is no legal unity. It must be conceded, however, says Professor Larusson, that the adoption of the two codes brought in a comprehensive reception of Norwegian law, and as to some topics, such as criminal law and *thing* procedure, a nearly complete reception.

The "Ironside" prevailed only from eight to ten years.[134] But the *Jonsbok* was for many generations the chief source of law in Iceland. The opposition to the *Jonsbok* soon disappeared, not so much from diminution of suspicion of the royal power as from the fact that the peasants did not feel inclined to criticize what they felt was their own code.

For several centuries the *Jonsbok* was the most widely read book in Iceland. Absalon Pedersen Beyer, the Norwegian humanist who died in 1574[135] states that in the middle of the sixteenth century it was the custom in Iceland for young men to memorize the codes despite their substantial size,—boys learned to read with the help of the codes, and it is known that as late as about 1670 Paul Vidalin, subsequently a well known lawman, thus learned to read. Printing came in between 1530 and 1578.[136] But there still exists more than 100 handwritten manuscripts of the law written before 1578. In the sixteenth and seventeenth centuries many began to find certain parts of the law difficult to understand. Consequently, Iceland's first legal literature arose, almost all of it concerning the *Jonsbok*. This literature consisted mostly of explanations of its rules. There is a considerable amount of literature of this kind, the authors being lawmen, provincial judges, clergymen and farmers. Very few of these writings were printed, but there are quite a few handwritten manuscripts, indicative of the popular interest. In the seventeenth century there were proposals to revise the *Jonsbok*. The chief proponent was Gisli Hakonarson, who induced one of the ablest lawyers in the country, provincial judge Thorsteinn Magnusson, to ascertain which of the rules needed revision as well as the method of revision. The study of Magnusson still exists in handwritten form, as well as his proposal for a new *thing* procedure. But nothing came of his work. The lawman, Paul Vidalin,[137] who died in 1727, prepared a notable draft for a code, but the Danish government withheld its consent.[138]

It is a remarkable fact that the *Jonsbok* to some extent is still law in Iceland. It is true that several individual rules have been repealed, and many others have become so obsolete as not to be regarded in force. But Professor Larusson points out that in the most recent volume of the Icelandic laws in force in 1945 there appear parts of 56 chapters of the *Jonsbok* which contained a total of 251 chapters. Some of these provisions involve leasing, wreck and salvage, marking of cattle, and injuries to cattle. English and American lawyers may deem it strange that laws so ancient should still prevail, yet many of these provisions are even older than the *Jonsbok*, as they were taken from the *Gragas*. It is therefore fair to say that some of the law of the earlier free state of Iceland still prevails as law today in Iceland.

During the period of reception of the "Ironside" and the *Jonsbok* there was also a change in the law of the church.[139] In 1275 there was accepted by the Althing except as to one minor chapter a new "Christian law" or church law developed by Bishop Arni at Skalholt.[140] It was the understanding that it was later to be ratified by the King and the archbishop of Norway. Its reception involved the repeal of the old church law drafted by bishops Thorlak and Ketil in the twelfth century. The proposed new church code, calling for elimination of private ownership of churches and for greater powers in the clergy, was not acceptable to the Icelanders. It resembled in many respects the Norwegian church law drafted by Archbishop Jon of Norway at about the same time.[141] Part of the older church law prepared by Thorlak and Ketil was retained. In 1354 the Norwegian king by royal letter in substance made Archbishop Jon's law the law for Iceland.[142]

After this great period of change in the law of Iceland there followed a long period of stability which lasted until the sixteenth century. Neither the *Jonsbok* nor the national law of King Magnus contained any provisions as to the authority to make laws. In Norway the consequence was that the authority of the law *things* to make laws fell away, and only the king made laws. When the king established laws, they were called *rettarbot* or law reforms or supplements. From 1294 to 1314 the King established three law reforms for Iceland.[143] They constituted a kind of supplement to the *Jonsbok* and to some extent the reason for their reception was to correct the defects and gaps which the Icelanders had found in the *Jonsbok* and which they had criticized in the debate in the Althing in 1281 over the *Jonsbok*. In 1313 the king addressed a letter to the Icelandic people criticizing them because no Althing had met for nine years. In 1314 he issued a new supplement to the Icelandic code providing against bringing Icelanders to Norway for trial except when the lawmen and *syslumenn* were unable to try the case.[144] The demand for new taxes was dropped. But nothing was stated about appointment of

Icelanders to office, nor was any assurance given that six ships would be sent to Iceland each year.

But on the whole, the king made but few changes in the Icelandic law during this period. In fact, says Professor Larusson, one can count the number of such changes on one's fingers, and even these few were without great significance. This seems to indicate that the king was not much interested in Icelandic law development.[145] The same may be said about his representatives in the country. Apparently they were chiefly interested in collecting increased taxes.[146] But few indications can be found that they concerned themselves with problems of lawmaking. In 1354 the king farmed out taxes to the royal governor.[147]

About the year 1300 it became customary that people incorporate the king's law reforms in their handwritten lawbooks, and many did not carefully discriminate between Icelandic law reforms and various Norwegian law reforms which had never come into force in Iceland. The consequence was that both were treated as prevailing and decisions were based on them. But at times objections were made as to the application of these Norwegian law reforms to Iceland. In a great inheritance case at the end of the fifteenth century one party based his demand on a Norwegian law reform of May 2, 1313. But this view was rejected in the judgment of the lawman and later by the Althing. No attempts were made later to enforce this particular law reform in Iceland. By similar use of Norwegian law reforms additional Norwegian law was introduced into Iceland, but only on a small scale as the law reforms were few and unimportant. The method was a dubious one. Conceivably it arose out of the conception that laws decreed by the king should automatically prevail in all the domains over which he ruled.

As has been seen, the Norwegian law *things* lost their authority to make laws.[148] But, according to Professor Larusson, this did not happen to the Althing. The Icelanders asserted that the Althing had the power to make laws, both in conjunction with the king and separately.[149] The conception arose that the king's law proposals prevailed only on the condition that the Althing consented to them. For example, the Althing annulled some of the royal decrees, and modified some of them. Perhaps now and then some royal proposals were not laid before the Althing and yet were accepted by the people as law, but from the seventeenth century forward the conception was that the king could not prescribe laws for the country without the consent of the Althing.

The Althing made laws independently and without the king's joint action. But often this legislation was of a rather special nature. Some of the determinations were not designated as laws, but were judgments and were drawn up in the form of judgments. Before such a judgment could be pronounced it was not necessary that there be a specific law suit between specific persons, but rather a question of a general nature about it, as whether this or that scope shall be given to a law. The court gave its determination in the matter, and the rule thereby enunciated was subsequently followed. The judgment was referred to as prevailing law, and later judgments were based on it. The judgment was thus a proposition of a full law-creating character. The Althing was not the only body which handed down such general judgments. They were also often handed down by the *thing* of the *herred* or local area. When they were concerned, as they often were, with purely local matters, such judgments were considered as binding for the *herred*, even though the consent of the Althing had not been obtained. But often such judgments concerned other than local issues and were concluded with a direction to seek the approval of the Althing. Yet examples are to be found of such judgments of the local *thing* treated as if they were laws binding throughout the country. Even today copies exist of many such judgments of a general nature. Nearly all these judgments make references to equivocal or unintelligible rules in the *Jonsbok* or gaps in such rules. In this manner the *Jonsbok* was developed on a national basis. The custom of rendering such judgments of a general nature appears to have arisen shortly after the date when the *Jonsbok* was introduced and it continued until near the end of the seventeenth century. Even during the first decades of the absolute monarchy in Denmark and Norway beginning in 1661 several such judgments were rendered.

Danish Influence on Icelandic Law

A. THE PROTESTANT REFORMATION

The Protestant reformation occurred in Iceland in the middle of the sixteenth century.[150] One consequence was greatly to enhance the royal power.[151] The king gained control of the church and its authority and possessions. He took over the possession of the monasteries, and became the greatest land owner of the country.[152] His sources of revenue were thus powerfully enhanced, and a short time later he acquired great business interests, as a business monopoly was established. The relation of the king to Iceland was henceforth much closer. The Icelanders became completely dependent on the Danish government and promised never to carry resistence so far as to employ the sword against the Danish king. King Christian III's church decrees of September 2, 1541, replaced the "Christian law" of Bishop Arni. In 1607 a new church code for Iceland was drafted by Norwegian churchmen upon a formal request of the king, who now became the highest authority in all church affairs.[153] The Protestant bishops had no authority as to tithes, and many cases formerly under church jurisdiction were now transferred to the secular courts. After the Reformation only Icelanders were appointed as bishops.

Just as the political union between Iceland and Norway had paved the way for Norwegian influence on Icelandic law, it could rightly be anticipated that Danish influences would ultimately prevail when Norway's status with respect to Denmark was greatly diminished.[154] The weakening of the Norwegian influence was based on several factors. Norway had been more reluctant than Denmark in accepting the Protestant Reformation. Norway had given continued support to Christian II (1513-1524) who was deposed by his uncle, Frederick I. The Danish nobles were anxious to acquire estates in Norway when the old nobility had died out. About 1536 the Norwegian Council of State disappeared, the only national office left being that of Chancellor, and Norway was virtually incorporated into Denmark.[155] Out of funds appropriated during the Reformation the University of Copenhagen strengthened its law school. Inevitably, changes would eventually occur in the legal development of Iceland which was now in much closer relation to Denmark.

New rules concerning marriage were set forth in Frederick II's decree of June 2, 1587, and mention should also be made of the so-called Great Judgment (*Storidomr*) of July 2, 1564.[156] It was a law creating judgment of the Althing, but one taken on the initiative of the king's Danish representative, and sanctioned by the king on April 13, 1565. The *Storidomr* dealt with the crimes of debauchery, incest, concubinage and adultery, and provided for capital punishment or very severe punishments. Male offenders were hanged, and female, drowned. One half of their property was forfeited to the king, and one half was turned over to needy relatives. As to adultery, capital punishment could be inflicted only for the third offense and there was no forfeiture. Royal decrees of 1576, 1578, and 1594 somewhat mitigated the penalties. The *Storidomr* remained in force until 1838.

These, in the opinion of Professor Larusson, are the most significant and thoroughgoing decrees which were made by the king for Iceland from the Reformation up to the first decade of the eighteenth century. During this period the king made a good many statutes and wrote many open letters which were to prevail in Iceland, but these involved no significant changes in law. They dealt with isolated details, particularly with matters concerning the church and business. Final appeals lay to the king and his council, who continued to act as a court of last resort until 1661, when the Supreme Court of Denmark was established. The privilege of sanctuary, under which criminals could not be seized in churches, was abolished in 1587. By a law of 1596 the eating of horse meat was forbidden. Thieves were to be hanged, flogged or branded. Minor offenses were to be punished by the pillory, flogging, or heavy fines. From 1625 to 1690 there were about thirty prosecutions for witch-craft though it does not appear that the Danish law had been introduced in Iceland.[157]

B. ABSOLUTE MONARCHY

In 1662 the Icelanders swore allegiance to Frederick III as absolute monarch.[158] The king thus received unlimited power to make laws for Iceland. Changes in the highest administration occurred from 1683 to 1688. Copenhagen thus became the seat of law making power for the country as well as of its highest administration, and it was always Danes who exercised such power. The Supreme Court of Denmark then became the highest court in the Icelandic system. It is obvious that all this would greatly affect the development of Icelandic law.

For more than twenty years after the introduction of absolutism Icelandic administration remained unchanged. The administrative colleges and government departments in Denmark now gradually assumed the functions of government for Iceland. Iceland became little more than a Danish province. In 1683 *a landfoged* was appointed to receive the taxes and revenues after collection by the *syslumenn*.[159] The next year a *stiptbefalingsmadr* was appointed to conduct the general administration and adjudicate church cases and two years later an *amtmand*.[160] Since the *stiptbefalingsmadr* did not reside in Iceland, the royal government confined itself pretty much to the collection of taxes.

As a result of the vast increase in royal power the role of the Althing both as to legislation and administration steadily declined until 1800, when it was abolished and replaced by a Supreme Court.[161]

By the sixteenth century the system of landownership in Iceland had made economic and social progress difficult. Much land had been converted into crown estates and church lands, which the people had to cultivate as tenants. Out of 4,187 farms only 2,116 were privately owned.[162]

The first census taken in Iceland occurred in 1703 when the population was 50,358, compared with 141,042 in 1949.[163]

During this period of the sixteenth and seventeenth centuries there went on a development such as had occurred in the fourteenth and fifteenth centuries. Just as the earlier judges had brought in Norwegian law reforms in their handwritten law books and adjudicated in accordance with them, so says Professor Larusson, the Icelandic judges now began to base their judgments on Danish laws, which had never been enacted specially for Iceland. This development had already begun in the last decades of the sixteenth century.[164] But it had not become noticeably striking until the last year of the seventeenth century when the setting up of absolute monarchy had occurred. But it would still be accurate to say that the law of the *Jonsbok* had prevailed during this period. As a writer has said, "Since the introduction of absolutism in Denmark in 1660 Iceland had been regarded as an integral part of the Danish kingdom, governed by royal Danish officials, and often according to Danish laws, though it had retained its old code, the *Jonsbok*, which was still in force."[165]

In the ninth decade of the seventeenth century many important changes occurred in the Danish and Norwegian law when King Christian V decreed new codes of law, the Danish in 1683 and the Norwegian in 1688. Neither of these two codes was designed to prevail in Iceland, and the king simultaneously recognized that Iceland was a separate area for law making.[166] But like Magnus Lawmender, the king desired that there be law revision in all his countries, and in 1688 the king wrote to the two lawmen of Iceland and invited them to summon men learned in the law to draft a code for Iceland. At the same time the bishops were commanded to draft a new church law to be incorporated into the code. The code was to be drafted as much as possible like the Norwegian code "in order that a conformity and likeness between the Norwegian and the Icelandic law, to the greatest extent possible may hereafter be observed," as the matter is expressed in the royal letter. A draft of an Icelandic code was then made, but for reasons unknown to us the king refused to approve it. Nothing further was done until 1719 when a new group was set up to carry on the work. But the king delayed about approving its work. It was, however, anticipated that eventually the king would approve. But the king now began to apply a new method of law making. In a letter of instruction to Governor Nils Fuhrmann of May 30, 1718, he directed that the Governor should have "due discretion with the law, that it is properly administered, and that the Norwegian law should be followed as to the conduct of formalities and judicial proceedings."[167] A similar direction was given to Governor Peter Raben, in an instruction of March 25, 1720. As a consequence after 1720 the Icelanders began to apply the Norwegian rules of procedure. This direction of the king was repeated in a rescript of May 2, 1732. It is there stated, that until the new code comes into effect, the people and the servants of the law should apply the old code in all matters and the so-called law reforms, and the royal statutes which had been sent to the country, "except as concerns formalities and court procedure. As to them the Norwegian code shall continue to be applied."

The rules of procedure in the *Jonsbok* had in many respects become obsolete at this time and changes were needed. But this method of authorizing all rules in the Norwegian laws about "formalities and the mode of court procedure," without more exact specification of which provisions they were, and without consideration whether such rules were suitable for local Icelandic conditions, produced great doubts as to some situations, even though they were arguably concerned with "formalities and the mode of court procedure." The confusion was enhanced by the fact that the Norwegian law was never proclaimed in Iceland, and that no legal translation of it was ever made.

This authorization of the Norwegian rules of court procedure was undertaken as an interim measure. The new code was awaited sooner or later. But with the passage of time it became clear that it was not to be a mere interim measure. Preparation of a new code went on during the entire eighteenth century and even into the first decade of the nineteenth. But the code never emerged. The king was unwilling to approve any of the projects which were advanced. Norwegian law continued for a long interval to be the basis for Icelandic court procedure. Even today, says Professor Larusson, a small part of such Norwegian law prevails in Iceland.

After this authorization of the Norwegian court procedure there was a period of stability. Governor Fuhrmann inquired according to which laws one should adjudicate as to issues on which there were no rules in the *Jonsbok*, law reforms or statutes sent to Iceland. At the same time he intimated that in such cases it was the usage to follow the Norwegian law. He furthermore inquired to what extent the older laws should be absolutely applied with respect to several newly created types of crimes which under his view the law was very poorly suited for. In a rescript of February 19, 1734, the king replied to his questions as follows: That when certain details in a case required decisions for which the code (*Jonsbok*) lacked determinations, then the servants of the law should rather adjudicate with the guidance of the legal commandments, which had been issued in the country; that is to say, ordinances, decrees and statutes, "and in judgments consult the Norwegian law only when it is suitable, because if the Norwegian law should be used at random and equally with the Icelandic, this would give rise to confusion since some would apply the Icelandic and some the Norwegian law."[168] As to questions about crimes the older Icelandic laws should also prevail, except that "as to homicide and theft cases, with respect to the difference between Icelandic and the law of the present time, the Norwegian law should be followed until the new Icelandic law . . . has been completed and has been most graciously approved by us."

Here again reference to the Norwegian law was authorized as to the above mentioned situations without any narrower specifications, and doubts could arise as to what law gave way and what law prevailed. This authorization, like the former, was to prevail only temporarily, though in fact it prevailed a long time.

In summary, there are broad indications in the rescript that the older Icelandic law should be followed and respect accorded it; while the Norwegian law is given a very limited scope. The servants of the law must "consult" it in judgments when it is suitable. But as things went, most of them interpreted it as permitting the use of the entire Norwegian law as a subsidiary source of law, and it began to be applied, says Professor Larusson, even as to issues other than "formalities and the mode of legal procedure" or "homicide and theft cases," at random and equally with Icelandic law and thereby produced the "confusion" which the rescript sought to prevent.

Authorization of Denmark-Norwegian law on a broad scale for various types of legal situations continued. In 1769 the fifth book, second chapter of the Norwegian Code with respect to "Inheritance, Hereditary Succession and Division of Inherited Property" was authorized. In 1831 there was authorized the Danish law as to Majority and Administration of the Property of Infants; and in 1833 the Danish rules and later statutes as to judicial advertisements and publications. The upshot was that with some exceptions the entire Danish criminal law was introduced into Iceland under a statute of January 24, 1838, without close analysis of what was suitable for Iceland although the Danish criminal law was highly controversial. In this last case the authorization was no mere temporary measure. By this time it had become clear that a separate Icelandic code could not be hoped for. Instead, the aim was that of securing legal uniformity between Iceland and Denmark. This comes to light from language in the introduction to the statute of January 24, 1838, in which it is stated that it "would be very proper for our beloved and loyal subjects in Iceland completely to participate in the law and justice generally prevailing in our kingdom Denmark."[169]

In addition to the wholesale authorization of Danish-Norwegian law just described, there was a multitude of isolated edicts, statutes, and rescripts. Some of them had been prepared only for Iceland, but others were prepared for Denmark and then sent to Iceland, although some of them were not suitable for Iceland. Some of the law which the authorities and judges applied had neither been prepared for Iceland nor proclaimed in Iceland, but it had become the custom during the sixteenth century that the edicts which the king sent to Iceland should be proclaimed at the Althing. This usage created the greatest confusion, and it may be said that during the eighteenth century there were very few who understood what really prevailed as law for Iceland. The *Jonsbok* more and more ceased to prevail both because its rules had lost their force and because consequently people had ceased to settle their legal rights according to such rules. The Danish-Norwegian law supplanted it. For a second time there occurred a comprehensive reception of foreign law in Iceland.

In connection with such reception it should not be forgotten, says Professor Larusson, that two other factors contributed towards it. One was the power of the Danish Supreme Court to pass on Icelandic cases; the other was the fact that Icelanders studied law at the University of Copenhagen. In 1736 the first Icelander took his law examination at the University of Copenhagen.[170] From that date to 1908 all students of law from Iceland studied there. These students returned to Iceland with the theoretical knowledge which they had acquired during their period of study, and obviously Danish law was their chief topic of study. It was quite natural that when later they were called upon to deal with details which were not definitely fixed in the law, they fell back on the knowledge thus acquired and sought their solution in decisions of the Danish courts.[171]

The uncertainty as to which law prevailed was not the only noteworthy matter during this period. Most of the Icelandic laws were written in Danish, a language not understood by a large part of the inhabitants. In isolated cases the government accompanied the Danish text with an Icelandic translation. There are also several instances in which the king signed an Icelandic law text along side with a Danish. But much the larger part of the prevailing laws existed still only in a language which most of those subject to the laws did not understand. It was not before 1859 that it was settled by law that the king should sign two law texts, one Danish and one Icelandic.[172] Finally in 1891 it was determined that there should be only one text and that in Icelandic.[173]

This uncertainty which has been described above, the great doubt which prevailed as to which laws governed, naturally created much insecurity and inconsistency in adjudication and administration. It was therefore extremely necessary to seek to solve this maze through a critical approach. The work was undertaken and carried out by Magnus Stephensen.[174] He was not only the people's foremost promoter of culture of his day, but also one of the ablest jurists produced by Iceland. In his writings on legal topics, among them his doctoral dissertation *"Commentatio de legisbus quae jus Islandicum hodiernum effeciant"*[175] and in his work as a judge for almost half a century, as lawman (1789-1800) and chief justice and associate justice in the supreme court (1800-1833) he examined the question of what law prevailed with great sagacity and precision. Following his example other judges began to display more discrimination, and when he died in 1833 much of this uncertainty had been overcome. An Icelandic draft of a new code of March 29, 1826, was rejected by the Danish government.[176]

As has been seen the Althing lost its legislative power about the year 1700. During the next century it served purely as a judicial tribunal. The *logrettumenn* were now reduced to twenty, of whom ten should meet yearly at the Althing, but only eight should sit in the *logretta*.[177] In 1777 this number was further reduced to five. Thereafter but little attention was paid to the Althing, and law suits were taken directly to the king. In 1798 the Althing assembled for the last time at Thingvellir, where it had met for 868 years. All later sessions were held at Reykjavik, which then became the capital. On July 11, 1800, the Althing was permanently dissolved by royal order.[178] In its place there was set up a new court, the *landsyfirrettr*, consisting of a chief justice and two associate justices, to exercise the judicial powers formerly vested in the Althing. Forty-five years later the Althing was reconstituted to serve as a consultative assembly by a Danish decree of 1843. Its size was small, twenty members chosen by people who were landowners and six appointed by the king.[179]

C. CONSTITUTIONAL GOVERNMENT IN DENMARK

In 1848 the Danish king declared that he would henceforth act as a constitutional monarch and a new Danish Constitution became effective in June 1849. Governmental officials and the collegial departments in Copenhagen, particularly the Chancery and the *Rentekammer* had previously assumed the responsibility for the handling of Icelandic affairs both as to law making and administration. The Chancery controlled judicial affairs and the *Rentekammer* supervised administrative and commercial affairs, and both were under the king.[180] They took the initiative as to innovations in the law and they prepared all new laws. This system prevailed during the entire period of absolute monarchy from 1662 until 1849, when the Danish Constitution was adopted. Previous to 1662 the litigant might apply directly to the king, thereafter he had to proceed through these officials. In 1849 the various Danish ministers took over the conduct of such Icelandic affairs as necessarily involved their departments. This continued to be the situation until 1874 when Iceland got its first constitution and authority to pass laws for purely local Icelandic matters. As a matter of strict law the Danish king remained supreme in Iceland after 1849 even though he did not so remain in Denmark, as the Danish constitution did not apply to Iceland.[181] The Danish jurist J. E. Larsen argued in 1855 that Iceland was an integral part of Denmark.[182] Jon Sigurdsson wrote a book in reply refuting such contention.[183] The Danish Rigsdag proceeded to enact regulations regarding

Icelandic trade, and debated the Icelandic budget without consulting the Althing.[184]

D. THE ICELANDIC CONSTITUTION OF 1874

Beginning in 1874 Icelandic affairs were placed under the Danish Ministry of Justice until 1904.[185] A governor or *landshofdingi* was appointed to reside in Iceland to represent the king. The Althing was divided into two houses with 24 members in the lower house and 12 in the upper. The people elected 30 members and the crown appointed six members.[186] In 1904 a separate Icelandic ministry was established in Iceland itself. The offices of the *landshofdingi* and the two *amtmenn* were abolished.

From 1849 the Danish ministers who now conducted Icelandic affairs continued, as had the collegial government departments, to take the initiative in Icelandic law development. In the opinion of Professor Larusson law development between 1849 and 1874 was relatively slight. An inheritance law was enacted in 1850 and a general criminal code in 1869. Both laws were translations of Danish laws with some slight changes. Icelandic trade was made free to all nations in 1854. Freedom of the press was established in 1855. The ownership of all wrecks thrown ashore, which had been taken away by a royal ordinance of 1595, was restored to the Icelanders. During this period the Icelanders sought a legislature free from Danish control, independence for Icelandic officials, and abolition of the right of the Supreme Court of Denmark to render decisions in purely Icelandic cases.[187]

From 1875 to 1903 when the Danish Minister of Justice participated in the handling of Icelandic affairs and the Althing had gotten authority at biennial sessions to make laws for the separate local matters, many important laws were initiated by the government and adopted for Iceland.[188] Some of them were uniform Scandinavian laws, such as the Law of Exchange of 1882, the Company Law of 1903 and the Sale of Goods Law of the same year. Other laws were translations of Danish laws with slight changes, such as the law concerning distribution of inheritance of 1878, that concerning seizure for debt of 1885, that concerning executive measures of 1887, that concerning distribution of bankrupt estates of 1894, and that concerning the economic relations of husband and wife of 1900. Many other laws of less significance were enacted during this period, sometimes at the initiative of the government and sometimes following proposal by members of the Althing. In 1882 a law gave widows and other unmarried women over 25 and in independent circumstances a right to vote in local and church affairs.[189] A law of 1884 required a landowner not making use of his land to make it available to others. Professor Larusson concludes that on the whole the legal development of this period was such as to bring it in closer accord with the Danish law.

The election law of 1877 divided Iceland into nineteen election districts, eleven of which elected two representatives each and eight elected one each.[190] Suffrage was confined to males twenty-five years or more in age who paid taxes. Office could be held only by voters thirty years or over who had settled in the European part of the Danish realm for five years.

There was considerable legal writing and research in the nineteenth century.[191] Jon Sigurdsson together with Oddgeir Stephenson carried on a comprehensive and significant assembly of the laws governing Iceland. Sigurdsson published the first volume of *Diplomatorium Islandicum*. Vilhjalmur Finsen published a critical study of the *Gragas*. Beginning in 1874 and concluding in 1910 the German scholar Konrad Maurer published comprehensive studies of Icelandic law and legal history prior to 1262.

Icelandic Law Since 1904

Under the constitutional change of October 3, 1903, Iceland got its own minister, later increased to several ministers, who was to be responsible to the Althing.[192] The minister was to reside at Reykjavik and speak and write in the Icelandic language. This was the beginning of Parliamentary government in Iceland.[193] The highest administrative power was now located in Iceland in the hands of Icelanders. Obviously they would have a more intimate knowledge of the condition of the country and greater interest in its affairs than Danish ministers could have. It would have been strange if this great change did not result in a comprehensive legal development. This expectation was amply realized. Of the law now in force in Iceland about ninety per cent has been enacted since 1904.[194]

Up to 1904 apparently the Danes had assumed that Iceland was an integral part of the Danish kingdom.[195] But the Icelanders had never admitted this and asserted that the 1262 agreement with Norway established only a confederate union. Questions arose as to Icelandic commerce and a separate flag, just as such questions arose out of the union between Norway and Sweden from 1814 to 1905. The separation of Norway from Sweden in 1905 encouraged the Icelanders to seek a similar separation from Denmark. In 1907 a commission of seven Icelanders and thirteen Danes was appointed to draft a new law defining Iceland's position in the Union. In the election of 1908, at which time the Australian system of secret ballot was first used, the draft prepared by the commission was defeated, the vote being 3,475 in favor and 4,671 opposed. The draft was thought not to go far enough in making Iceland independent. In 1909 a law for the prohibition of the sale of liquor was enacted. This was one of the earliest laws of any nation on that subject. In 1913 the king sanctioned a separate flag for Iceland. In 1915 the king sanctioned constitutional amendments passed by the Althing in 1913 and 1914 providing for an Icelandic ministry in Reykjavik responsible to the Althing, the number of cabinet members to be fixed by law. The Althing was to have forty members, subject to change by law. Thirty-four members were to be chosen by separate constituencies for terms of six years, and six at large for terms of twelve years. The upper branch of the Althing was to consist of the latter six together with eight elected by the thirty-four from their own number. Only half the total membership was to be elected at each election. Persons twenty-five years in age, including women, could vote for the district representative, and persons thirty-five for the representatives at large. The Althing was to meet biennially. In 1915 women received the franchise. In 1917 the size of the cabinet was fixed at three.

The extensive legal development during this period cannot be explained only from the fact that the country had been given the power to initiate laws. The principal cause was the tremendous change which had occurred in social and economic matters since 1904.[196] When the Althing got the law making powers for Iceland's separate affairs in 1874, it was substantially correct to say, as does Professor Larusson, that Iceland was a society of peasants living almost as in the Middle Ages. The country was homogeneous and not cosmopolitan in character. People could manage without many of the rules which seem indispensable in a modern society as the circumstances productive of such a society were not present. It followed that the legal development was of a limited character. During the period of thirty years prior to 1904 this slowly began to change. Since 1904 the changes have been more rapid and on such an extensive scale that a complete revolution has occurred in nearly all areas of national activity. There are but few examples of a society which has undergone similar thoroughgoing changes in so short a period of scarcely fifty years.

These social and economic changes imposed a great burden on the law makers. A legal framework around the new society had to be created. On many occasions the rules of law had to be developed from the very beginning as to topics on which there had been no prior law. In other cases old rules of law required reexamination and revision.[197] The latter work produced some unequal results, but did at least display the determination of the country to establish a new order subject to law.

Among various things which have promoted an independent development of Icelandic law, and will continue to prompt it, is the fact that the highest court in the Icelandic system now is a local court. In the Danish-Icelandic Union of 1918 it was provided that the Supreme Court of Denmark should be the court of last resort in the Icelandic system until Iceland should decide to establish a supreme court sitting in Iceland. Such a decision was made in the following year, and the new Supreme Court of Iceland began its work in 1920.

Uniform Scandinavian Laws

In the preparation of the new Icelandic laws obviously models from other nations have often been sought. In addition to the Law of Exchanges of 1882 and the Company Law of 1903 the following such laws have been adopted by Iceland: maritime law, the law as to the rights of seamen, the sale of goods, contracts, the new laws as to checks, all without essential changes.[198] The rules of family law have been developed in close connection with the law of the other Scandinavian nations.[199] But aside from these laws, the old method of simply translating foreign laws for adoption in Iceland is used very rarely. But almost all the foreign models which have been followed have come from the Scandinavian nations. In 1919 a reciprocity convention between Denmark, Norway and Sweden as to industrial accident insurance was signed; reciprocity was extended to Iceland in 1927.[200] In 1937 all these countries and Finland concluded a new convention that extended the principles to cases in which the injured worker was not a resident of the country where he was injured. In 1926 Denmark and Norway signed a health insurance convention enabling members of an approved health insurance society in one country to be transferred to a similar society in the other irrespective of age or health. In 1939 Iceland signed a similar convention with Denmark. This convention was revised in 1948 to make it harmonize with the new Icelandic national insurance law. It seems likely that Iceland will make similar agreements with Norway and Sweden.

An Icelander has pointed out that whatever the problem of Icelandic law may be, Iceland wishes to profit from the drafting of uniform Scandinavian laws, even though Iceland has not taken as extensive a part in such work as the other Scandinavian nations.[201] After World War II Iceland was invited to participate in such work, but because so few persons could be found to undertake it and those who could most usefully participate were busy with other matters, it was impossible for Iceland to accept the invitation. Nevertheless the Icelanders wish to follow such developments and appreciate having the opportunity to do so.[202] Moreover the Icelanders feel as one of the Scandinavian nations and that "they are closer to them than any other people in culture and views of life."[203] Icelandic law is most closely related to the Scandinavian law. It is to the Scandinavian law that the Icelanders are likely to turn for models, even as to topics not covered in the uniform laws.[204] "Icelandic law has always been Scandinavian law, and we desire that it continue to be Scandinavian in the future."[205]

Iceland participated in the fourth Scandinavian Conference on Criminal Law held at Helsinki, Finland in February 1950, the topics of discussion being youthful criminals with special reference to work-schools and greater unity as to criminal statistics.[206] Iceland invited the fifth conference to meet in Iceland. Iceland participated in 1949 and 1950 in Scandinavian conferences on aircraft.[207] The four Scandinavian foreign ministers held their annual fall meeting for the first time in Iceland in 1950.[208]

The Constitution of 1944

Civil Liberties. Article 1 of the Constitution of June 17, 1944, provides that "Iceland is a republic with a constitutional government."[209] Articles 63 and 64 provide for freedom of religion. Article 62 provides that the "Evangelical Lutheran Church shall be the state church and as such shall be supported and protected by the State."[210] Under Article 65 an arrested person "shall be brought before a judge without undue delay, and if not released at once, the judge shall, within twenty-four hours, give a reasoned ruling as to whether he shall be detained." Under Article 66 the "home shall be inviolate. Houses may not be searched, nor any letters or documents be detained and examined, except by judicial warrant or a special provision of law."

Under Article 67 the "right of private property is inviolate." Article 69 provides for "individual freedom of employment." Article 70 provides for public support of persons unable to support themselves. Article 71 provides for education out of public funds for children of persons unable to pay such costs. Article 72 guarantees freedom of the press.[211] Article 74 guarantees freedom of assembly.

The President. Under Article 2 the executive power "is exercised by the President and other governmental authorities." Under Article 3 he is "elected by the people." Under Article 4 he must be at least 35 years of age. Under Article 5 he is elected by "a direct secret ballot, and a plurality is sufficient." He must previously have been proposed by from 1,500 to 3,000 persons. Under Article 6 he serves for four years. Under Article 8 if the office becomes vacant, the presidential power is exercised by the Prime Minister, the speaker of the United Althing and the Chief Justice of the Supreme Court, and a majority of them prevails. Under

Article 11 he ceases to hold office if this is approved by a plebiscite held after a three-fourths vote of the United Althing. Article 13 provides that the "President exercises his authority through his ministers." Under Article 15 the "President appoints the cabinet and accepts ministerial resignations." Under Article 19 the "Presidential signature countersigned by a minister validates a legislative measure or an act of government." Under Article 20 he appoints governmental officials. Under Article 21 he "concludes treaties with other states. Except with the consent of the Althing, he may not make such agreements if they entail renouncement of or servitude on territory or territorial waters or if they imply constitutional changes." Under Article 22 he "shall summon the Althing every year and determine when the session shall close." He may summon special sessions. Under Article 24 he "may dissolve the Althing" thus bringing about a new election within two calendar months after dissolution. Under Article 25 he may submit bills to the Althing. Under Article 26 a bill passed by the Althing becomes law after his approval; if he disapproves, it still becomes law, but is submitted to a plebiscite which may reject the law. Under Article 28 in the "event of extreme urgency" he may issue provisional laws between sessions of the Althing. But such laws must not violate the Constitution, and must be submitted to the Althing when it reopens; if the Althing does not approve they become invalid. Under Article 29 he "grants pardon and amnesty."

The Ministers and the Cabinet. Under Article 13 the "President exercises his authority through his ministers. The cabinet has its seat in Reykjavik." Under Article 14 the "cabinet is responsible for all acts of the government. The responsibility of ministers is established by law." Under Article 15 the "President appoints the cabinet and accepts ministerial resignations. He determines the number of ministers and assigns their duties." The new cabinet which took office on December 6, 1949, consisting of members of the Conservative party, known in Iceland as the Independence party, is made up of five persons: Olafur Thors, Prime Minister and Minister of Social Affairs; Bjarni Benediksson, Minister of Justice and of Foreign Affairs; Bjorn Olafson, Minister of Finance and of Commerce; Johann Th. Josefsson, Minister of Fisheries, of Industry, and of Aviation; and Jon Palmason, Minister of Agriculture and of Commerce.[212] But in actual practice it is the parliamentary majority which governs the process.[213] It is not required that ministers be members of the Althing. Under Article 51 ministers "have the right to attend meetings of the Althing and are entitled to take part in the debates as often as they may desire, subject to parliamentary procedure; but they have a right to vote only if they are at the same time elected members of the Althing." They may introduce bills. Under Article 17 cabinet meetings shall be held in order "to discuss new legislative proposals and important political measures. Furthermore, Cabinet meetings shall be held when one of the ministers so desires." Under Article 18 the "minister who desires to propose a measure shall, as a rule, submit it the President."

Amendment of the Constitution. Article 19 provides: "Proposals, whether amendatory or supplementary to this Constitution, may be introduced at regular as well as extraordinary sessions of the Althing. If the proposal is passed by both houses, the Althing shall be dissolved immediately and a general election be held. If both houses pass the resolution without amendments, it shall be ratified by the President of the Republic and come into force as a constitutional act.

"If the Althing passes an amendment to the status of the church affairs, according to Article 62, it shall be submitted to a plebiscite by secret ballot for acceptance or rejection."
Under Article 81 the Constitution of 1944 became effective as follows:
"This constitutional act comes into force when the Althing so resolves, provided that the act has been passed in a secret ballot by the majority of votes in the country."

The Althing. Under Article 2 of the Constitution the legislative power is jointly vested in the Althing and the President. Under Article 31 the members of the Althing "shall be elected for a term of four years." Under Article 33 all persons both men and women 21 years or more of age, if citizens of Iceland domiciled there for five years, may vote; voters must be "of unblemished character and financially responsible." Under Article 34 every qualified voter is "eligible for the Althing." Judges not holding administrative offices are not eligible; thus members of the Supreme Court are not eligible. Under Article 31 the Althing consists of fifty-two members. They are chosen in three ways. There is direct election by 21 districts or towns of one member each. Twenty members are chosen from a party list by proportional representation. Finally there are up to eleven compensatory seats to make up the balance between the parties, so that each party has seats in proportion to its popular vote. This scheme represents two purposes: to maintain representation from local constituencies and to represent all the parties according to their voting strength. Under article 32 the Althing is divided into a lower house and an upper house, although members are elected to the whole Althing as a single body as the Storthing is in Norway. The entire Althing after its election chooses one-third of its members to serve in the Upper House and the other two-thirds to serve in the Lower House. Under Article 42 finance "bills and supplementary finance bills shall be introduced in the

United Althing and passed in three readings." As to most other matters the two Houses sit separately.

As has been seen under Article 31 members of the Althing are "elected for a period of four years." But under Article 34 the "President may dissolve the Althing" and bring on new elections within two calendar months thereafter. Where the Althing approves any change in the Constitution, Article 79 requires an immediate dissolution of the Althing. The Constitution is silent as to prolonging the life of the Althing, although this was done in 1941.

Under Article 49 "No member may be arrested for debt during a session of the Althing, without the permission of the House of which he is a member, nor may be placed under restraint or an action brought against him unless he is found in *flagrante delicto*. No member may be made responsible outside the Althing for statements made by him in the Althing, except with the permission of the House concerned." The records show that such permission has been granted once.

Article 48 expresses a philosophy as to the function of legislators in providing: "Members of the Althing are bound solely by their conviction and not by any orders from their constituents."

Under Article 38 each house may "introduce and pass bills and proposals for resolutions. Each House individually or unitedly may send addresses to the President." Under Article 39 each house "may appoint committees of its members in order to investigate important matters of public interest. The House may grant authority to such committees to demand reports, oral or written, from government officials or private individuals." Under Article 44 "No bill, with the exception of the finance and the supplementary finance bill may be passed without three readings in each House." Under Article 45 if a bill is changed in one of the Houses it goes back to the other, and if no agreement is reached "both Houses shall meet in a conclave, and the matter is settled by one reading by the United Althing." After the first reading of a bill, it is the custom to refer it to a committee. There are eight committees in each House, and three for the United Althing. Under Article 26 if the "Althing has passed a bill, it should be submitted to the President for approval not later than two weeks after it has been passed, and upon such approval shall be enforced as law."

With respect to temporary or emergency laws, Article 28 provides: "In the event of extreme urgency, the President may issue provisional laws in the interval between sessions of the Althing. Such laws must not, however, be contrary to the Constitution, and they shall always be submitted to the Althing as soon as it reopens.

"If the Althing does not approve a provisional law, it shall become invalid.

"A provisional budget may not be issued if the Althing has passed the budget for the fiscal year."

A single type of law requires a national vote. Under Article 79 "If the Althing passes an amendment to the status of Church affairs, according to Article 62, it shall be submitted to a plebiscite by secret ballot for acceptance or rejection." Prior to the 1944 Constitution there was an advisory vote on the prohibition of import of alcohol in 1908, compulsory national service in 1916, and the repeal of the prohibition law in 1933.

Under Article 42 a "finance bill for the coming fiscal year containing an estimate of the revenue and expenditures of the State shall be submitted to the Althing immediately on reassembling for a regular session." Furthermore such bills "shall be introduced in the United Althing and passed in three readings." Article 44 provides that as to financial bills there need be no separate readings in each House. Under Article 43 the United Althing is to elect three salaried auditors to audit annually "the national revenue and expenditure accounts to ascertain whether the entire revenue has been included and whether any unauthorized disbursements have been made."

The Courts. Article 2 of the Constitution provides: "The judicial power is exercised by the judiciary." Article 59 provides: "The organization of the judiciary cannot be established except by law." The Althing thus has much discretion as to court organization. Perhaps the only limitation is contained in Article 14 providing: "The Althing may impeach ministers for the discharge of their official duties. The court of impeachment has jurisdiction in such matters." Thus far this court has never been made use of.

Article 61 provides: "Judges shall in the performance of their official functions be guided solely by the law. Judges who do not also hold administrative offices cannot be discharged from office except by a judicial ruling, nor may they be transferred to another office against their will except in the event of reorganization of the judiciary. A judge who has reached the age of sixty-five may, however, be asked to resign from office without reduction of salary." It is the judges of the highest appellate court who are thus protected as they do not hold administrative offices.

The court of last resort is called the *Haestirettur* or the Supreme Court.[214] There are five members at present. Almost all cases are appealable to this court.[215] The judges of the lower courts are the *syslumenn* in the rural areas and the *baejarfogetur* in the towns. There are twenty-one such judges. They have both civil and criminal jurisdiction. Their judicial work is the smaller part of their work. Most of their time is spent in the collection of taxes and duties, control of the police, and direction of local government. At the capital there are three district judges: one for criminal cases, one for ordinary civil cases, and one who carries out distraints, ejectments, bankruptcy proceedings, and probating of estates. All judges are appointed by the Minister of Justice for an indefinite period. Normally they must retire at 65, but the government may permit them to sit until they are 70 if their health continues good.

In the above cases there is always at least one judge who is a lawyer. There are also a number of special courts where the members are not necessarily all lawyers. Such courts are the maritime and commercial court and the boundaries court. As to these courts two persons are appointed to give judgment along with the regular district judge. In 1938 the *felagsdomur* or court of labor disputes was established with five members. It passes on the interpretation of agreements between employer and employees, the legality of strikes and lockouts, and so on. No appeal lies from its judgments. On the other hand as to ordinary cases both parties may take an appeal from the district court to the Supreme Court.

Legal Education

It seems likely that the future of Icelandic law will be substantially influenced by the fact that Icelandic lawyers now receive their training in Iceland instead of in other nations, as previously was the case. When the University of Copenhagen commenced to offer courses in law,[216] Icelanders went there to study. But when the movement for Icelandic independence commenced after 1830, proposals were made that law study should be made available in Iceland itself. When the first Althing for advisory purposes met in about 1845 Jon Sigurdsson, the great leader in the movement for Icelandic independence, proposed a plan for the founding of a school which among other things would offer legal studies.[217] But no action was taken on his proposal. A theological seminary was founded in 1847. In 1855 the Althing consented to a petition to the king for the establishment of a law school. Similar petitions were presented by all the subsequent sessions up to 1873, but without result. A medical college was founded in 1876. The Althing which then acquired law making, and not simply advisory power, from 1879 to 1903 ten times passed a law for establishing a law school, but the king declined to ratify. It was thought that the costs of maintaining such a school would be a burden on the country and that competent professors could not be secured.[218] The proposal, which was repeated in 1903, was not pressed until the new Icelandic minister had been selected, and it was the second of the laws which were presented by such minister to the king for approval. The law school opened in the fall of 1908. When the University of Iceland was founded in 1911, the law school became a part thereof.[219] The first graduates took their graduation examinations in the spring of 1912. Nearly all the lawyers now practicing in Iceland had their schooling there.

As of 1914 the law school had three professors. An act of 1914 made these professors extraordinary assessors of the appellate court to be called in order of appointment to fill out the court in cases of incapacity of ordinary assessors.[220] In 1915 Einar Arnorson, who had taught in the law school from its beginning in 1908, became Minister for Iceland, that is to say, the prime minister.[221] He had written several books in the relation of Iceland to Norway and Denmark and challenged the view of the great Danish authority on Danish Constitutional Law that Denmark had wide authority to control Icelandic affairs.

The law and political science faculty at the University in Reykjavik in 1950 consisted of five professors, two of them teaching socio-economic subjects.[222] There are also two lecturers on legal subjects. The professors of law are: Olafur Larusson, born in 1885, appointed in 1919 (Contracts, Damages, Obligations, Property, Admiralty, Corporations, and Legal History), Olafur Johanneson, born in 1913, appointed in 1948 (Civil and Criminal Procedure, Constitutional Law, Administrative Law), Armann Snaevarr, born in 1919, appointed in 1948 (Jurisprudence, Law of Persons, Family Law, Inheritance Law and Criminal Law). The lecturers are: Theodor B. Lindahl, born in 1898 (Legal Problems) and Hans G. Andersen, born in 1919 (International Law, Conflict of Laws). The distribution of subjects is determined by the faculty. The dean for 1949 to 1950 is Professor Johanneson. The average law student spends five years at the University. There are no tuition fees.

NOTES—CHAPTER II—ICELANDIC LAW

1. For an interesting novel of the fourteenth century period as to the relations between the three countries see Sigrid Undset, *The Master of Hestviken* (1934); and of the seventeenth century, Victor Hugo, *Hans of Iceland* (1891).

2. *A Study of History*, p. 107 (1947).

3. *Ibid.*, p. 146 (1947).

4. Jon Stefansson, *Denmark and Sweden With Iceland and Finland*, p. 154 (1917).

5. Knut Gjerset, *History of Iceland*, pp. 8-10 (1925). Irish monks are said to have reached Iceland in 790. William Langer, *An Encyclopedia of World History*, p. 170 (1948). See also Kristjan Eldjarn, "Romans in Iceland," 39 *Am. Scand. Rev.* 123 (1951).

6. Knut Gjerset, *op. cit.*, pp. 10-29 (1925). Harald's actions "were the chief causes of the colonization of Iceland." Bjorn Thordarson, *Iceland Past and Present*, p. 9 (1945).

7. This book surveys the political and ecclesiastical history, the founding of the

Althing, the early courts and the discovery of Greenland. Knut Gjerset, *op. cit.*, pp. 138-39 (1925).

8. Henry Goddard Leach, formerly editor of the American-Scandinavian Review, on a visit to Iceland in 1950 discovered that half of its inhabitants kept records of their descent back to ninth century Norway and that most of the other half could trace back their descent if they took the trouble.

9. A former prime minister estimates that from twelve to sixteen per cent came from the British Isles and Ireland, but even these were in turn of Norwegian descent with some foreign intermarriage. Bjorn Thordarson, *op. cit.*, p. 5 (1945).

10. Knut Gjerset, *op. cit.*, pp. 93-100 (1925).

11. *Ibid.*, pp. 110-16 (1925).

12. *Ibid.*, pp. 29-33 (1925). On the history of Iceland prior to its union with Norway in 1262 see the chapter on "Primitive Iceland" in James Bryce, *Studies in History and Jurisprudence*, I, 312-58 (1901).

13. Karen Larsen, *A History of Norway*, pp. 57-58 (1948); Knut Gjerset, *op. cit.*, p. 33 (1925). Bryce concludes that it was a reduction to writing of existing Norse customs which had not been reduced to writing in Norway. James Bryce, *op. cit.*, I, 312, 341 (1901).

14. Ben A. Arneson, *The Democratic Monarchies of Scandinavia*, p. 30 (2nd ed., 1949); Franklin D. Scott, *The United States and Scandinavia*, p. 47 (1950); S. M. Toyne, *The Scandinavians in History*, p. 304 (1948); William Langer, *op. cit.*, p. 170 (1948).

15. In "all essential features Norwegian life and customs were more carefully reproduced and successfully perpetuated in Iceland than in any other Norse colony." Knut Gjerset, *op. cit.*, p. 80 (1925).

16. Snorri Sturlason (1178-1241) wrote the *Heimskringla*, the first history of the Norwegian kings up to 1177. It is the greatest of the sagas. The Poetic Edda was also written in Iceland between 1150 and 1250. Konrad Maurer states: "The father of the old Scandinavian history writing was Ari Frodi, who died in 1148. Then came all also born in Iceland Odd Snorrason and Gunnlaug Leifsson, the prior Styrmer Karason and the abbot Karl Jonsson, and lastly Eirik Oddson, Snorri Sturlason and Sturla Thordsson. In the twelfth and thirteenth centuries these men were active not only as to the history of Iceland but also as to that of the Norwegian kings." Baedeker's *Schweden und Norwegen*, p. LIX (4th ed. 1888). The reasons for the lack of writing in Norway were that the Norwegian church adhered closely to its strictly clerical duties and the use of Latin; and that civil war raged in Norway. Knut Gjerset, *op. cit.*, p. 131 (1925).

17. Knut Gjerset, *op. cit.*, p. 256 (1925). The present Icelandic is similar to that of 1350, whereas the other Scandinavian, English and Germanic language later underwent great changes. For the best and most recent book on modern Icelandic see Stefan Einarsson, *Icelandic* (1949) published by the Johns Hopkins Press. As to the Old Norse language see E. V. Gordon, *An Introduction to Old Norse* (1927). For the only cultural history of the language see Halldor Hermansson, *Modern Icelandic, an Essay* (1919).

18. Karen Larsen, *op. cit.*, pp. 58, 84 (1948).

19. Laurence M. Larson, *The Earliest Norwegian Laws*, pp. 144-45 (1935). See also Knut Gjerset, *A History of the Norwegian People*, I, 434-35 (1927); Bryce, *op. cit.*, pp. 312, 344 (1901).

20. Henning Friis, *Scandinavia Between East and West*, p. 309 (1950).

21. Karen Larsen, *op. cit.*, p. 96 (1948); Thomas Carlyle, *The Early Kings of Norway*, pp. 66-67 (1875); Knut Gjerset, *History of Iceland*, pp. 48-70 (1925). According to Toynbee the conversion of Iceland brought on "the end of the Icelandic culture." Arnold Toynbee, *op. cit.*, p. 159 (1947). For a recent novel on this period see Henry Myers, *The Utmost Island* (1951).

22. Karen Larsen, *op. cit.*, pp. 102-03 (1948).

23. *Ibid.*, p. 123 (1948).

24. Tithing was introduced in 1096. Jon Stefansson, *op. cit.*, p. 159 (1917). In 1123 a church code was prepared by Bishops Thorlak and Ketil. Knut Gjerset, *op. cit.*, p. 68 (1925).

25. Knut Gjerset, *op. cit.*, pp. 158-60 (1925); Karen Larsen, *op. cit.*, pp. 134, 169 (1948).

26. S. M. Toyne, *op. cit.*, p. 305 (1948).

27. Knut Gjerset, *op. cit.*, p. 168 (1925).

28. *Ibid.*, p. 53 (1925).

29. *Ibid.*, pp. 62, 64, 168 (1925).

30. *Ibid.*, pp. 168-69 (1925).

31. P. Schweitzer, *Island Land Und Leute*, p. 28 (1890).

32. Knut Gjerset, *op. cit.*, pp. 160-62 (1925).

33. *Ibid.*, pp. 170-72 (1925).

34. *Ibid.*, p. 177 (1925).

35. *Ibid.*, p. 194 (1925).

36. Karen Larsen, *op. cit.*, p. 169 (1948).

37. Hjalmar H. Boyesen, *A History of Norway*, pp. 433-44 (1900); Knut Gjerset, *op. cit.*, pp. 173-202 (1925).

38. Knut Gjerset, *op. cit.*, pp. 212-13 (1925).

39. Bjorn Thordarson, *op. cit.*, p. 11 (1945). In 1238 two Norwegians were consecrated bishops of Iceland. About 1240 the archbishop made a regulation that Icelandic bishops should be chosen by the archbishop and the cathedral chapter at Trondheim. Knut Gjerset, *op. cit.*, p. 183 (1925). It was also asserted that the idea of a republic was less in conformity with true religion than a monarchy.

40. Knut Gjerset, *op. cit.*, p. 236 (1925).

41. Knut Gjerset, *History of the Norwegian People*, II, 15 (1927).

42. Knut Gjerset, *History of Iceland*, p. 246 (1925).

43. *Ibid.*, p. 257 (1925). The Danish influence became much greater after the Protestant Reformation and especially after the absolute monarchy set up in 1660.

44. *Ibid.*, pp. 229, 243 (1925).

45. *Ibid.*, pp. 257-58 (1925).

46. *Ibid.*, pp. 258-66 (1925).

47. *Ibid.*, pp. 272-77 (1925).

48. S. M. Toyne, *op. cit.*, p. 306 (1948).

49. Knut Gjerset, *op. cit.*, pp. 276-77 (1925).

50. *Ibid.*, pp. 276, 330-31 (1925). "In justice to the Danish government it must be said, then, that this way of dealing with Icelandic commerce did not differ from the general policy pursued by other nations at this time." *Ibid.*, p. 330 (1925).

51. *Ibid.*, pp. 335-45 (1925).

52. *Ibid.*, pp. 363-64 (1925).

53. *Ibid.*, pp. 332-34 (1925).

54. *Ibid.*, pp. 359-60 (1925); Austin H. Clark, *Iceland and Greenland*, p. 29 (1943).

55. S. M. Toyne, *op. cit.*, pp. 307-08 (1948); Knut Gjerset, *op. cit.*, pp. 350-61 (1925).

56. James Bryce, *op. cit.*, I, 312, 357 (1901).

57. Knut Gjerset, *History of the Norwegian People*, II, 415 (1927).

58. Karen Larsen, *op. cit.*, p. 409 (1948); S. M. Toyne, *op. cit.*, p. 281 (1948).

59. Bjorn Thordarson, *op. cit.*, p. 12 (1945).

60. Knut Gjerset, *History of Iceland*, pp. 372-75 (1925); Baldwin Einarsson, *Om de Danske Provincial Staender med Specielt Hensyn paa Island* (1832).

61. Knut Gjerset, *op. cit.*, pp. 376-86 (1925); S. M. Toyne, *op. cit.*, p. 308 (1948).

62. Knut Gjerset, *op. cit.*, pp. 406-12 (1925).

63. Hans Weigert, "Iceland, Greenland and the United States," *Foreign Affairs*, p. 112 (Oct. 1944).

64. Knut Gjerset, *op. cit.*, pp. 458-71 (1925); Bjorn Thordarson, *op. cit.*, p. 7 (1945). See also J. G. Holme, *Icelanders in the United States* (1921).

65. Bjorn Thordarson, *op. cit.*, pp. 14-16 (1945); Knut Gjerset, *op. cit.*, pp. 447-51 (1925). The treaty is set out in Manley O. Hudson, *Cases on International Law*, p. 37 (3rd ed., 1951). See also Charles C. Hyde, *International Law*, I, sec. 31, pp. 125-26 (2d ed., 1945); Green Hackworth, *Digest of International Law*, I, 59, 213 (1940). The act of union was adopted by the Danish Rigsdag and the Althing, and then approved by a popular vote in Iceland; 12,040 favoring and 897 opposing. Some writers regarded the union as a real rather than a personal union. Oppenheim, *International Law*, I, 158 n. 2 (5th ed. by Lauterpacht, 1937).

66. Charles C. Hyde, *op. cit.*, I, sec. 29, p. 110, n. 2 (1945); Green Hackworth, *op. cit.*, I, 66, 74 (1940).

67. Manley O. Hudson, *op. cit.*, p. 18 (3rd ed., 1951).

68. Manley O. Hudson, *Cases on International Law*, p. 24 (2nd ed., 1936).

69. See the list of memberships of specialized agencies in Louis B. Sohn, *Cases and Materials on World Law*, pp. 175-78 (1950).

70. *Ibid.*, p. 174 (1950). It was not an original member.

71. Manley O. Hudson, "The Twenty-Ninth Year of the World Court," 45 *Am. J. Int. L.* 1, 32 (Jan. 1951). Denmark, Norway and Sweden are all subject to such jurisdiction.

72. Green Hackworth, *op. cit.*, I, 167, 213 (1940); Charles C. Hyde, *op. cit.*, I, 150 (2d ed., 1945).

73. Green Hackworth, *op. cit.*, I, 213 (1940).

74. "The Quarter's History—Iceland," 36 *Am. Scand. Rev.*, 243, 244 (Sept. 1948).

75. Green Hackworth, *op. cit.*, I, 213 (1940).

76. Charles C. Hyde, *op. cit.*, I, 125 (2d ed., 1945). The legality of the separation is asserted by Sveinbjorn Johnson, "Iceland and the Americas," 26 *A.B.A.J.* 506 (1940).

77. Charles C. Hyde, *op. cit.*, II, 1415 (2d ed., 1945); Green Hackworth, *op. cit.*, V, 460-62 (1943).

78. Hans Weigert, *op. cit.*, p. 113 (Oct. 1944).

79. Franklin D. Scott, *op. cit.*, pp. 196, 200 (1950); "The Quarter's History—Iceland," 37 *Am. Scand. Rev.* 51 (Nov. 1949).

80. Franklin D. Scott, *op. cit.*, p. 289 (1950).

81. *Ibid.*, p. 323 (1950).

82. "The Quarter's History—Iceland," 39 *Am. Scand. Rev.* 55 (March 1951).

83. Law No. 44 of April 5, 1948. See Richard Young, "The Legal Status of Sub-Marine Area Beneath the High Seas," 45 *Am. J. Int. L.* 225 (April 1951).

84. "The Quarter's History—Iceland," 38 *Am. Scand. Rev.* 267, 269 (Sept. 1950). Iceland has urged that the International Law Commission give priority to the "regime of territorial waters," 44 *Am. J. Int. L.* 527, 533 (1950).

85. Paul A. Smith, "ICAO Conference on Air Navigation Services in Iceland," *Dept. State Bull.* 164 (Feb. 6, 1949).

86. *New York Times*, p. 32, col. 3, May 9, 1951.

87. *Ibid.*, April 22, 1951. See also Bjorn Thordarson, *op. cit.*, pp. 39-44 (1945).

88. S. M. Toyne, *op. cit.*, p. 310 (1948).

89. Gudmundur Grimson, "Iceland and the Americas," 26 *A.B.A.J.* 505, 506 (1940).

90. *New York Times*, p. 13, May 8, 1951.

91. At the October 1949 election to the Althing the Conservatives won 19 seats, the Progressives 17, the Communists 9, and the Social Democrats 7. The five members of the cabinet are all Conservatives. Franklin D. Scott, *op. cit.*, pp. 322-23 (1950). For the history of the political parties since 1903 see Knut Gjerset, *op. cit.*, pp. 420, 429-30, 434-35, 446 (1925). Asgeir Asgeirsson, elected President in 1952, is a Social Democrat.

92. Ebbe Hertzberg in A *General Survey of Continental Legal History*, p. 535 (1912). On Icelandic law prior to 1262 there are full accounts by Konrad Maurer, *Island von Seiner Entdeckung bis zum Untergange des Freistaats* (1874). His later revised views may be found in *Vorlesungen über altnordische Rechtsgeschichte*, IV and V (1909-1910).

93. He was elected by a unanimous vote of the *logretta*. Knut Gjerset, *op. cit.*, p. 42 (1925).

94. Ebbe Hertzberg, *op. cit.*, p. 537, n. 1 (1912).

95. James Bryce, *op. cit.*, I, 312, 327 (1901). For full discussion see Konrad Maurer, *Vorlesungen über altnordische Rechtsgeschichte*, IV, 263-80; V, 455-60 (1909-1910).

96. Jon Stefansson, *op. cit.*, pp. 154-56 (1917).

97. Ebbe Hertzberg, *op. cit.*, p. 541 (1912). See also Knut Gjerset, *op. cit.*, pp. 23-48 (1925); James Bryce, *op. cit.*, I, 312, 323-33 (1901); Konrad Maurer, *op. cit.*, IV, 325-402 (1909).

98. On the organization, jurisdiction and procedure of the Icelandic courts prior to 1262, see Konrad Maurer, *op. cit.*, V, 289-820 (1910).

99. James Bryce, *op. cit.*, I, 312, 337 (1901).

100. *Ibid.*, I, 312, 341 (1901).

101. Knut Gjerset, *op. cit.*, pp. 52, 59-60, 145-48 (1925).

102. *Ibid.*, p. 64 (1925).

103. Konrad Maurer, *Island von seiner erster Entdeckung bis zum Untergange des Freistaats*, pp. 464-66 (1874).

104. Arnold J. Toynbee, *op. cit.*, pp. 159-60 (1947).

105. Thomas Carlyle refers to the law as the Icelandic *Gragas, The Early Kings of Norway*, p. 168 (1875). It was at least a part of the *Gragas*. Knut Gjerset, *op. cit.*, p. 68 (1925). It is said that the "writing down of laws began in 1117." Bjorn Thordarson, *op. cit.*, p. 31 (1945).

106. *Skra* is the Icelandic word for scroll, thus indicating that this law was in writing.

107. As to the source of the name *Gragas*, Thomas Carlyle surmises with respect to the Norwegian *Gragas* of 1037 that it may have come from the gray color of the parchment or that it merely denotes antiquity, the witty expression for a man growing old having then been that he was now "becoming a gray goose." Carlyle, *op. cit.*, 168 (1875). He calls the Icelandic *Gragas* the more famous of the two. See also James Bryce, *op. cit.*, I, 312, 342 (1901). Bryce ascribes the name to the binding of the book. He concludes that the name was first applied to the early Frostathing law of Norway, and was applied to the Icelandic law for the first time in the seventeenth century. See also Konrad Maurer, *op. cit.*, pp. 464-66 (1874).

108. James Bryce, *op. cit.*, I, 312, 342 (1901).

109. Olafur Larusson, "Den islandska rättens utveckling sedan år 1262," 35 *Svensk Juristtidning* 241, 248 (1950).

110. Sveinbjorn Johnson, Book Review, 24 *Geo. L. J.* 223, 225 (1935). See also Sigurd B. Seversen, Book Review, 21 *Iowa L. Rev.* 821, 822 (1936).

111. For an excellent discussion of Icelandic law since 1262 see Olafur Larusson, *op. cit.*, 241-59 (1950).

112. Knut Gjerset, *op. cit.*, pp. 206-07 (1925). For a full discussion see Konrad Maurer, *op. cit.*, 470-80 (1874).

113. "There was some grumbling when Magnus, contrary to the agreement, promulgated a code for Iceland, which though recognizing peculiar Icelandic conditions, was not unlike the Norwegian." Karen Larsen, *op. cit.*, p. 170 (1948).

114. The Icelandic system "had not sufficed to secure the reign of law against the oppression of oligarchic powers, nor did it accord with the new principle of monarchy." Ebbe Hertzberg, *op. cit.*, p. 553 (1912). See also Hjalmar H. Boyesen, *op. cit.*, pp. 443-44 (1900).

115. These officials were royal officials in charge of the king's business in a *sysla* or

county. Laurence M. Larson, *op. cit.*, p. 425 (1935). See also Stefan Einarsson, *op. cit.*, p. 464 (1949).

116. In 1319 the Norwegians "were presumably the best situated nation in Europe with respect to legal organization and obedience to law." Ebbe Hertzberg, *op. cit.*, p. 552 (1912).

117. Karen Larsen, *op. cit.*, p. 167 (1948).

118. *Ibid.*, p. 164 (1948).

119. Knut Gjerset, *op. cit.*, pp. 213-15 (1925); Jon Stefansson, *op. cit.*, p. 161 (1917).

120. Ebbe Hertzberg, *op. cit.*, p. 553 (1912). The *Jonsbok* is said to have been in force in Greenland from 1281. Austin H. Clark, *Iceland and Greenland*, p. 20 (1943). It may be found in *Norges Gamle Love*, I (1846).

121. On the career of this bishop see Knut Gjerset, *op. cit.*, pp. 217-25 (1925).

122. Karen Larsen, *op. cit.*, pp. 159, 166 (1948); Knut Gjerset, *op. cit.*, p. 221 (1925).

123. The clerical opposition was offset when the royal commissioner pointed to the excessive burden of the tithes paid to the church. Knut Gjerset, *op. cit.*, p. 221 (1925).

124. Ebbe Hertzberg, *op. cit.*, p. 553 (1912).

125. Knut Gjerset, *op. cit.*, p. 215 (1925).

126. *Ibid.*, p. 208 (1925).

127. *Ibid.*, pp. 215-16 (1925).

128. Capital punishment was not used as a penalty prior to 1262. James Bryce, *op. cit.*, I, 312, 344 (1901). For discussion of the criminal law prior to 1262 see Konrad Maurer, *op. cit.*, V, 3-286 (1910).

129. Knut Gjerset, *op. cit.*, pp. 220, 221, 227, 230, 232 (1925).

130. Knut Gjerset, *op. cit.*, p. 228 (1925).

131. This law is said to be the civil law of the Gulathing Law of 1267 of Norway, as it contains provisions clearly intended for Norway with such changes as were deemed necessary for Iceland. Ebbe Hertzberg, *op. cit.*, 550 (1912). The same writer also calls it a "compilation of regulations from the earlier laws of the Gula- and Frosta-things, and was presumably a copy of the Gulathing code adopted in 1267." *Ibid.*, p. 553 (1912).

132. Olafur Larusson, *op. cit.*, pp. 244-45 (1950).

133. Ebbe Hertzberg, *op. cit.*, p. 551 (1912).

134. Jon Stefansson, *op. cit.*, p. 161 (1917). The "Ironside" may be found in *Norges Gamle Love*, I (1846).

135. Concerning him see Karen Larsen, *op. cit.*, pp. 251, 270, 274 (1948); Knut Gjerset, *A History of the Norwegian People*, II, 160-62 (1927).

136. Knut Gjerset, *History of Iceland*, p. 309 (1925). Following this, Arngrim Jonsson (1568-1648) rescued the old Icelandic writings, wrote a history of Iceland, and made Latin translations for European readers. S. M. Toyne, *op. cit.*, p. 306 (1948). Later Arni Magnusson, who died in 1730, brought the whole collection of manuscripts, old and new to Copenhagen. Jon Stefansson, *op. cit.*, p. 164 (1917). At the present time there is some agitation for the return of the manuscripts to Iceland. "The Quarter's History—Iceland," 39 *Am. Scand. Rev.* 55-56 (March 1951).

137. He also served on a commission which examined the operation of the laws on trade. Knut Gjerset, *op. cit.*, p. 338 (1925).

138. Ebbe Hertzberg, *op. cit.*, p. 567 (1912).

139. Knut Gjerset, *op. cit.*, pp. 217-20 (1925); Konrad Maurer, *op. cit.*, II, 109-110 (1908).

140. The "Ironside" contained no church law in the earlier sense of the word, as the church objected to including ecclesiastical regulations in a general code. But it did include civil affairs even though they rested on religious principles. Ebbe Hertzberg, *op. cit.*, p. 550 (1912).

141. Karen Larsen, op. cit., pp. 165-66 (1948); Knut Gjerset, op. cit., p. 218 (1925).

142. Knut Gjerset, op. cit., p. 238 (1925).

143. Ebbe Hertzberg, op. cit., p. 553 (1912).

144. Knut Gjerset, op. cit., p. 233 (1925).

145. The trade with the Norwegian islands which had been a royal monopoly since the thirteenth century was not kept up and fewer ships than had been promised went to Iceland. Karen Larsen, op. cit., p. 233 (1948).

146. As of about 1350 the royal officials were: two lawmen, several *syslumenn* as administrative officials for larger districts, and a royal governor called *hirdstjorar*. Knut Gjerset, op. cit., p. 239 (1925).

147. Knut Gjerset, op. cit., pp. 247-48 (1925).

148. Ebbe Hertzberg, op. cit., p. 542 (1912).

149. Bjorn Thordarson, op. cit., pp. 11-12 (1945). But the Althing existed in a modified form chiefly as a court of law with judges selected by the royal officials. King Haakon Magnusson (1299-1319) "took energetic measures to maintain the efficiency of the Althing as a supreme judicial tribunal." Knut Gjerset, op. cit., p. 234 (1925).

150. Unlike the situation in Denmark and Norway, the Catholic party in Iceland resisted vigorously, the Catholic bishop Jon Arason being executed in 1550. Knut Gjerset, op. cit., pp. 280-317 (1925). A Jon Arason Festival in his honor was held four hundred years later in Iceland where he is regarded as a national hero. "The Quarter's History—Iceland," 39 Am. Scand. Rev. 55, 56 (March 1951).

151. Bjorn Thordarson, op. cit., p. 12 (1945).

152. While the original intent had been to use the income to build schools, this intent was not carried out. Knut Gjerset, op. cit., p. 302 (1925).

153. Knut Gjerset, op. cit., pp. 305-06 (1925).

154. Danish rule over Norway did not at first result in much change, as the "easy way was followed and the Icelanders were left much to their own devices." S. M. Toyne, op. cit., p. 306 (1948). See also Bjorn Thordarson, op. cit., pp. 11-12 (1945).

155. During the interregnum in Norway from 1533 to 1536 the Icelanders were reluctant to accept the claims of Christian III (1536-1559) who became king of Denmark in 1534. Knut Gjerset, op. cit., pp. 285-86 (1925).

156. Ibid., p. 303 (1925).

157. Ibid., pp. 316-17 (1925).

158. Ibid., 331-32 (1925). The Icelanders demanded that their old laws be preserved to them, and the governor seems to have acceded.

159. Knut Gjerset, A History of the Norwegian People, I, 237-38 (1927); Knut Gjerset, op. cit., p. 234 (1925).

160. In 1770 Iceland was divided into two and in 1787 into three amter. Knut Gjerset, op. cit., pp. 334-35 (1925).

161. Bjorn Thordarson, op. cit., p. 12 (1945).

162. Knut Gjerset, op. cit., pp. 323-29 (1925).

163. "The Quarter's History—Iceland," 38 Am. Scand. Rev. 375, 378 (Dec. 1950); 39 Am. Scand. Rev. 55, 56 (March 1951). Of the present population, 54,707 live in Reykjavik; 84,835 live in the capital and other cities; 15,291 in villages; and 41,626 in rural areas.

164. King Christian IV (1588-1648) founded the Icelandic Company so that Denmark might profit by the trade formerly going to England and the Hanseatic League. Paul Sinding, History of Scandinavia, p. 266 (1858). The Norwegian Code of 1602 was not applied to Iceland. Knut Gjerset, History of the Norwegian People, I, 192, 268 (1927).

165. Knut Gjerset, History of Iceland, pp. 377-78 (1925).

166. Hence the following statement by Gunnar Leistikow in Henning Friis, Scandinavia Between East and West, pp. 312-13 (1950) seems too sweeping: "The

so-called 'Norwegian Law of Christian the Fifth' was to a great extent an adaptation of the corresponding 'Danish Law of Christian the Fifth.' Iceland was at that time a Norwegian dependency, and the Norwegian code was therefore in force in that country also."

167. Olafur Larusson, *op. cit.*, p. 251 (1950).

168. *Ibid.*, p. 252 (1950).

169. *Ibid.*, p. 253 (1950).

170. As to general university education following the Protestant Reformation Icelanders usually studied at the University of Copenhagen or in Germany. The University of Copenhagen was founded in 1479, but its law school did not become very active until the Reformation. Knut Gjerset, *op. cit.*, pp. 278, 308 (1925). Norway did not have a university until 1811 so attendance in a Norwegian law school was precluded.

171. Knut Gjerset, *op. cit.*, p. 366 (1925). Jon Eriksson translated into Icelandic Holberg's *Dannemarks og Norges Geistlige og Verdslige Stat* (Copenhagen, 1762), containing a rather full account of the legal history of Denmark and Norway.

172. Knut Gjerset, *op. cit.*, p. 399 (1925).

173. The Danish-Norwegian Government "never made any attempt to interfere" with the Icelandic language itself. Bjorn Thordarson, *op. cit.*, p. 8 (1945).

174. Knut Gjerset, *op. cit.*, pp. 345-53, 357-61 (1925).

175. This volume, published in 1819, is cited as a standard treatise on Icelandic legal philosophy by Ebbe Hertzberg, *op. cit.*, p. 573 (1912).

176. *Ibid.*, p. 567 (1912).

177. Knut Gjerset, *op. cit.*, p. 346 (1925).

178. The dissolution was suggested by the great Icelandic jurist Magnus Stephenson who thought the Althing useless and out of date. Knut Gjerset, *op. cit.*, p. 349 (1925).

179. *Ibid.*, pp. 374-75, 377 (1925).

180. *Ibid.*, p. 335 (1925).

181. Bjorn Thordarson, *op. cit.*, p. 13 (1945). The Danish Constitutions of 1849, 1855 and 1866 were not expressly made applicable to Iceland. Knut Gjerset, *op. cit.*, pp. 384, 398, 405 (1925).

182. *Om Islands hidtilvaerende Statsretlige Stilling.*

183. *Om Islands Statsretlige Stilling.*

184. Knut Gjerset, *op. cit.*, p. 398 (1925).

185. As to the Danish law of 1871 and the Icelandic Constitution of 1874, see Knut Gjerset, *op. cit.*, pp. 406-12 (1925).

186. Jon Stefansson, *op. cit.*, p. 166 (1917).

187. Knut Gjerset, *op. cit.*, pp. 376-408 (1925).

188. However, more than fifty bills passed by the Althing were vetoed by the King on the advice of the Danish Minister of Justice. Jon Stefansson, *op. cit.*, p. 167 (1917).

189. P. Schweitzer, *Island Land und Leute*, p. 68.

190. Knut Gjerset, *op. cit.*, p. 412 (1925).

191. P. Schweitzer, *op. cit.*, p. 151; Knut Gjerset, *op. cit.*, pp. 375-77 (1925); Ebbe Hertzberg, *op. cit.*, pp. 573, 576 (1912).

192. As to the steps leading up to this see Knut Gjerset, *op. cit.*, pp. 425-30 (1925).

193. Bjorn Thordarson, *op. cit.*, pp. 13-14 (1945); Jon Stefansson, *op. cit.*, pp. 428-30 (1917). The Althing was to meet every other year for eight weeks and to consist of party members of whom thirty-four were chosen by the people, and six by the king. While selected as a single chamber it was to split itself into two sections—the upper of fourteen and the lower of twenty-six members.

194. Olafur Larusson, *op. cit.*, p. 256 (1950).

195. For discussion of Icelandic affairs from 1904 to 1918, see Knut Gjerset, *op. cit.*, pp. 430-49 (1925).

196. For a description of such changes see Bjorn Thordarson, *op. cit.*, pp. 16-29, 39-44; Knut Gjerset, *op. cit.*, pp. 453-58 (1925). One may gain valuable insights from the following Icelandic novels which have been translated into English: Gudmundur Kamban, *The Virgin of Skalholt* (Little Brown & Co.: 1935); Gunnar Gunnarsson, *Ships in the Sky* and *The Night and the Dream* (The Bobbs-Merrill Co.: 1938); Kristmann Gudmundsson, *Morning of Life* (Doubleday Doran Co.: 1936); Halldor Laxness, *Salka Valka* (Houghton-Mifflin Co.: 1936) and *Independent People* (Alfred A. Knopf: 1946).

197. A large part of such law was customary law. Ebbe Hertzberg, *op. cit.*, p. 568 (1912).

198. H. Munch-Petersen, "Main Features of Scandinavian Law," 43 L. Q. Rev. 366, 367-69 (1927).

199. Sigrid Beckman, "Vinding Kruse: En Nordisk Lovbog," 35 *Svensk Juristtidning* 879, 888 (1950).

200. Henning Friis, *op. cit.*, p. 314 (1950).

201. Olafur Larusson, *op. cit.*, p. 259 (1950). The Scandinavian Conference of Lawyers as of 1948 had 458 members from Denmark, 394 from Finland, 346 from Sweden, 214 from Norway, and 40 from Iceland. See "Adertonde Nordiska Jurist-Motet," 33 *Svensk Juristtidning* 611 (1948).

202. Iceland was represented for the first time in social security legislation in 1948. Henning Friis, *op. cit.*, p. 313 (1950).

203. Danish is still taught in Icelandic schools. The Icelanders are 98 per cent Lutheran as are the Danes and Swedes; the Norwegians being 97 per cent and the Finns 96 per cent. More books are published in Iceland per capita than any other country, one for each 466 persons, while the number in Denmark is 1,106; in Norway 1,588; in Sweden 2,309; in Great Britain 3,205; and in the United States 12,497. Bjorn Thordarson, *op. cit.*, p. 34 (1945).

204. But doubting the feasibility and wisdom of a single comprehensive Scandinavian code see Thordur Eyjolfsson, "Vinding Kruse: En Nordisk Lovbog," 35 *Svensk Juristtidning* 883 (1950). The Icelandic Law of Majority does not follow the Danish-Norwegian-Swedish Law of 1922-1927. *Ibid.*, p. 886 (1950).

205. Olafur Larusson, *op. cit.*, p. 259 (1950).

206. 35 *Svensk Juristtidning* 306, 399 (1950); *Nordisk Tidsskrift for Kriminalvidenskab* 260 (1950).

207. 35 *Svensk Juristtidning* 1000 (1950).

208. "The Quarter's History—Iceland," 38 *Am. Scand. Rev.* 375 (Dec. 1950).

209. The Constitution is set forth in Amos J. Peaslee, *Constitutions of Nations*, II, 171-78 (1950).

210. Of the Icelanders 98 per cent are Lutherans. Under Icelandic law ministers are elected by popular vote in the various parsonages. "The Quarter's History—Iceland," 38 *Am. Scand. Rev.* 166, 167 (June 1950).

211. A majority of the Supreme Court therefore found invalid a statute providing that no one might publish old Icelandic texts except by permission of the Government. Gunnar Thoroddsen, in Amos J. Peaslee, *op. cit.*, II, 179, 187 (1950).

212. Franklin D. Scott, *op. cit.*, p. 322 (1950). The communists lost out in their attempt to block the Atlantic Pact and Iceland's cooperation with the nations opposed to Russia. "The Quarter's History—Iceland," 38 *Am. Scand. Rev.* 64 (March 1950).

213. Gunnar Thoroddsen, in Amos J. Peaslee, *op. cit.*, II, 182 (1950).

214. *Ibid.*, p. 186 (1950).

215. For a discussion of decisions of the Supreme Court of Iceland in 1949 see Arni Tryggvason, "Nagra Rattsfall Fran Islands Hogsta Domstol Ar 1949," 35 *Svensk Juristtidning* 950-57 (1950).

216. Paul Sinding, *op. cit.*, 159, 170, 224 (1858).

217. Knut Gjerset, *op. cit.*, p. 366 (1925).

218. "The Danish government had long regarded Iceland as a province which was to be connected as closely as possible with the realm. All efforts to provide home train-

ing for students of law was therefore opposed as this would lessen Danish influence over Icelandic officials." Knut Gjerset, *op. cit.*, pp. 366-67 (1925).

219. *Ibid.*, p. 424 (1925). See Alexander Johanneson, "The University of Iceland," 38 *Am. Scand. Rev.* 349 (Dec. 1950).

220. Axel Teisen, "Iceland. Legislation," 2 A.B.A.J. 267 (1916).

221. Knut Gjerset, *op. cit.*, 443-46 (1925).

222. 35 *Svensk Juristtidning* 388 (1950).

CHAPTER III

NORWEGIAN LAW

WHEN the Dutch settled in New York commencing in 1621 there were among them Norwegians who had been living in the Netherlands for one or more generations. The first group immigration from Norway occurred in 1825 when a number settled in New York. In 1836 a second group settled in Illinois. Thereafter Wisconsin was the goal of most settlers until 1850. From 1820 to the present time more than 800,000 have come to the United States.[1] Of a total of 924,688 Norwegians in the United States in 1940, 662,600 were native-born and 262,088 were foreign-born. Of the foreign-born, 52,025 were in Minnesota; 37,169 in New York; 23,211 in Wisconsin, and 21,637 in North Dakota. Many also live in South Dakota, Washington, Iowa and Illinois. In proportion to her population, Norway has sent more emigrants to the United States than any other Scandinavian state, and more than any European state except Ireland. The assimilation rate through naturalization has been high, namely, 75.2 per cent compared with 64.6 per cent for all foreign-born.

International Relations

Until the middle of the eighth century the Norwegians had played no part in the world's history.[2] It was the Viking attacks which made them known to the world at a time even before there was a single united Norwegian kingdom.[3] The first recorded Norwegian raid on England occurred at Lindisfarne in 793. The Faroes were raided about the same time. The Viking attacks on Ireland, Scotland, the Orkneys and the Shetlands, the Hebrides and Man, were almost entirely Norwegian. The attacks on France and the Netherlands were due to both Norwegians and Danes with the latter probably predominating.

"Sea power, sea law, the part of navigation as developed later in Northern waters by the ships of England and of the Hanseatic League, all go back to the Norse tradition. It was a goodly heritage."[4]

The unification of Norway into one kingdom was carried out by the Yngling family, which is said to be descended from the Swedish kings at Uppsala.[5] Halfdan Svarte, by his death in 860, ruled over the largest and best organized kingdom of Norway, including nearly all of southeastern Norway. His son Harald Fairhair (872-930) unified the entire kingdom.[6] The Swedish king occupied the territory between the

Glommen and the Göta Rivers, but Harald recovered the territory, which today is Bohuslän in Sweden. Between 872 and 892 the decisive battle for unification was won at Hafrsfjord near Stavanger. Harald defeated the aristocracy which had substantial help from the Viking colonies in the West, particularly Ireland. Many dissatisfied with the new unity went to Helsingland, Härjedalen and Jämtland, which had first been settled by people from the Trondheim area.[7] Others settled in Iceland, the Faroe Islands, the Orkneys, the Shetlands, the Hebrides, and the Viking colonies in the West. Because of attacks made by them, Harald in turn attacked and subdued the Hebrides and the Isle of Man, and the Shetlands and the Orkneys were annexed to Norway.[8] The Orkneys early gained control over northern Scotland. Following his expedition Harald became a friend of Aethelstan, the English king, made a treaty with him, promising not to support the Vikings in Northumbria, and sent his son Haakon (934-961) to be reared by him in England.[9] Although Iceland was independent, relations with Norway were close.[10] Harald not only had unified Norway, but had established a colonial empire, not as yet including Jämtland, the Hebrides and Greenland. Finnmark paid a yearly tribute.[11] Harald banished a Norwegian noble Rolf for ravaging within Norway; subsequently Rolf went to Northern France where in 911 he became Duke of Normandy and ancestor of William the Conqueror.[12] During Harald's reign there were Norwegian kings ruling in Dublin, Ireland.[13] The Dublin dynasty also became rulers of the kingdom of York in England. These rulers sometimes cooperated with Danish chieftains and sometimes fought against them. From 890 to 920 many Norwegian Vikings settled in Cumberland. Many also settled in Westmoreland, Northumbria, Chester and Anglesey in Wales. For two centuries they retained the Norse language and laws. They brought in concepts of personal liberty which resulted in the dying out of slavery earlier than in other parts of England.

Prior to the reign of King Harald the Danes seemed to have exercised some control over the southern part of Norway close to Denmark.[14] The Danish king Gorm, after unifying Denmark, pressed a claim to Vestfold in Norway.[15] Harald married a Danish princess, Ragnhild, daughter of King Eirik of Jutland, but the Danish claim was not given up. His own mother Ragnhild was a niece of Queen Thyra, wife of the first Danish king, Gorm the Old. His son Eirik Blood-Axe (930-934) married a Danish princess Gunhild, daughter of King Gorm. Eirik was soon forced to leave Norway, and eventually went to England where he became King of York. He was supplanted in Norway by his younger half-brother Haakon who had been reared at the court of the King of England. Haakon exercised but little control over the Norwegian dependencies. From 950 there were independent kings of Man and the Isles. His personal rule was largely limited to southwestern Norway, other parts of Norway enjoying a higher degree of local autonomy. As the sons of Eirik had taken refuge with King Gorm in Denmark he was forced to develop both an army and navy. The people of Jämtland invited Haakon to rule over that area.[16] Jämtland, though not fully integrated, remained Norwegian until 1028. Haakon brought priests from England in a vain attempt to introduce Christianity. In 961 with Danish support Eirik's son Harald Graypelt succeeded to the throne of Norway. In actual fact he ruled over only southwestern Norway, other parts being largely autonomous. When he killed Jarl Sigurd, the latter's son Haakon Jarl fled to Denmark. Having lived in and been baptized in England, Harald made a vain attempt to introduce Christianity. About 965 King Harald Graypelt made an expedition to Bjarmeland and fought the Permians on the Dvina. From that time all of Finland and the Kola peninsula were under Norwegian rule.[17] The Norwegian boundaries now extended to the White Sea.

King Harald Bluetooth of Denmark (950-985), most powerful Scandinavian ruler of his time, regarded Norway as a legitimate field for conquest.[18] Vestfold had long been a Danish province, yet his nephew, the Norwegian king, assumed control, over this area. A son of an older brother of the Danish king claimed a share in the Danish kingdom. Haakon Jarl persuaded the Danish king to seize Norway to turn it over to this claimant as a tributary kingdom. The Norwegian king was enticed to Denmark and killed by this claimant. Haakon Jarl then persuaded the Danish king that this claimant would be a dangerous rival, and attacked and killed the claimant. The Danish king now sailed for Norway with a fleet of 700 ships and was hailed as over-king of Norway. The Danish king ruled Viken through his own jarls, the Uplands remained autonomous, and Haakon Jarl held the Trondheim area and Haalogaland as his own and the rest of Norway as jarl under the Danish king. Norway was no longer a united kingdom even under Danish overlordship. But the Danish king was too far away to exercise real control.

In 974 Haakon Jarl helped the Danish king at the battle of Danevirke in Denmark against the German Emperor Otto II. Haakon then quarreled with the Danish king who invaded Norway and took possession of Viken. The new Danish king Svein renewed the attempt to subdue Norway. In 986 Haakon defeated the Jomsvikings at Jörundfjord near Aalesund. This victory assured the independence of Norway. A new competitor for the throne, Olaf Tryggvason, was now emerging.[19] He was reared in the court of Grand Duke Vladamir of Russia. He fought as a Viking in the Baltic. In 994 he joined King Svein of Denmark in attacking London. But he soon became a Christian and promised never to wage war on England and returned to Norway in 995 to become king and to Christianize Norway along Anglo-Saxon lines.[20] The Danish officials in southern Norway were driven out.

In 995 King Olaf Tryggvason forced the earl of the Orkneys to acknowledge his overlordship.[21] The earldom had been a Norwegian dependency since Harald Fairhair but the Norwegian suzerainty was not always firmly maintained until about 1015. The Shetland Islands were united with Norway in 995.[22] Olaf secured the introduction of Christianity in the Faroe Islands and Greenland. The Faroe Islands had become a Norwegian dependency, but little control had been exercised by Haakon Jarl. Olaf reestablished Norwegian authority over all its colonial dependencies. But Denmark wished to recover Viken and Sweden Bohuslän. The sons of Haakon Jarl formed marital connections with the daughters of the Danish and Swedish kings. Olaf first sought Swedish help by establishing marital connections but finally married the sister of the Danish king. But he was attacked by Denmark, Sweden, the sons of Haakon Jarl, and the jarl of Jomsburg and defeated in 1000. Norway was now divided among the victors.[23] The Danish king got Viken but Bohuslän went to Sweden. The Swedish king acquired seven *fylker* in Western Norway but gave them as a fief to Svein Jarl, a son of Haakon Jarl, married to his sister. Eirik Jarl, another son of Haakon Jarl, became independent sovereign over the coast region from Finnmark to Lindesnes and received other areas as a fief from the Danish king, his father-in-law. The Uplands became autonomous, and the island possessions drifted away. In the year 1000 the Norwegians discovered America, but established no colonies there. In 1014 at the Battle of Clontarf Norwegian power in Ireland was broken.[24]

In 1015 Eirik Jarl had gone to England to assist King Canute, who was now paying but little attention to Norway. Saint Olaf, a great-great-grandson of Harald Fairhair, now successfully invaded Norway.[25] He had previously been in personal touch with European life and ideas in Friesland, Holland, Normandy and England. In 1016 Olaf defeated Svein Jarl, who fled to Sweden and died on an expedition to Russia. At this time the Swedish king sent tax collectors into the Trondheim area and held Jämtland and Bohuslän, which he had seized. Bohuslän was soon regained. There were hostilities between Norway and Sweden but when in 1018 Canute became king of Denmark, fear of aggression by him resulted in the Peace of Konghelle in 1019. The marriage of the King of Norway to a daughter of the Swedish King was recognized, and Norway retained Jämtland.[26] The independence of Norway was recognized and boundaries were fixed. Olaf brought in bishops from England and

Normandy and achieved the Christianization of Norway. To avoid English dominance under the aggressive Canute, Olaf arranged to have the Norwegian Church under the supervision of the Archbishop of Bremen. Olaf regained the Orkney and Shetland Islands. The Faroes paid no taxes but accepted the king's code of church laws. Olaf negotiated an arrangement with Iceland in 1022, called "The Institutions and Laws which King Olaf gave the Icelanders," which lasted until 1262 when Iceland was united with Norway. Olaf bore down on the nobles who then went to Canute for aid. About 1026 Olaf allied himself with the king of Sweden, his brother-in-law, against Canute, but Canute defeated them near Skåne. Olaf had now lost support in northern and western Norway from the principal nobles. In 1028 Canute was recognized as king of Norway,[27] and Olaf fled to Kiev where his brother-in-law Jaroslaf was ruler. In 1030 Olaf returned, but his Norwegian, Swedish and Varangian army was beaten at Stiklestad and Olaf was killed. Canute's son Svein was now made viceroy of Norway, but his English mother was the real ruler. The rigorous Danish rule and the introduction of Danish law made Svein so unpopular that he left Norway. Olaf's son Magnus returned from Russia and was proclaimed king in 1035.

In 1035 Canute died and there was rivalry between his son Hardeknut, King of Denmark and Hardeknut's half-brother Harald Harefoot, King of England. It was therefore desirable for Hardeknut to end the hostilities between Norway and Denmark. A treaty of peace at Brennöerne was concluded in 1038.[28] Hardeknut recognized the independence of Norway, and an agreement was made that if one king died without an heir the other should inherit his kingdom. The independent national status of Norway was now clear from the Swedish treaty of 1019 and the Danish of 1038. The Norwegian colonial possessions fell away during the Danish rule from 1028 to 1034. In 1035 Norwegian sovereignty was restored over the Faroes. But full control of the Orkneys was not gained until 1066. In 1042 on the death of Hardeknut, Magnus was willingly received as king of Denmark under the agreement of 1038. For the first time the king of Norway was indisputably the mightiest Scandinavian king. From the time of Magnus the unity and independence of Norway remained comparatively undisturbed. Magnus arranged for the marriage of his sister Ulvhild to Ordulf, son of the Duke of Saxony, thus gaining a powerful friend. Magnus also claimed the English throne under the 1038 agreement. In 1046 the English expected a Norwegian invasion, but Svein of Denmark was in conflict with Magnus, who therefore did not undertake an invasion. In 1043 Magnus, aided by Ordulf of Saxony, defeated the Wends. He destroyed Jomsburg, the seat of ravaging Vikings.

In 1042 Harald the Hard, a half-brother of Saint Olaf, who had been a Varangian and fought over almost all of Europe, became co-king, the joint sovereignty being apparently limited to Norway.[29] For a brief prior time Harald had allied himself with Svein. In 1047 Magnus died after willing Denmark to Svein. But Harald claimed Denmark and fought without success for seventeen years to conquer it. Harald was also at war with Sweden for a long time.[30] While the Danish king allied himself with the German Emperor and the Archbishop of Bremen, Harald continued his friendship with the Saxon dukes, and refused to have Norwegian bishops consecrated by the Archbishop of Bremen, for which he was reprimanded by the Pope. Harald maintained the independence of the Norwegian church. To better his defensive position against Denmark he built the city of Oslo. Peace was finally made with Denmark in 1064. In 1066 when the English king died Harald claimed the throne on the basis of the 1038 treaty of Brennöerne between Hardeknut and Magnus. He invaded England with 250 ships and 20,000 men and was killed at the battle of Stamford Bridge.[31]

Harald maintained a firm supremacy over the Norwegian colonial possessions. When Magnus died, the Earl of Orkney and Shetland Islands seems to have submitted to him, so that he could better support Macbeth. Macbeth, King of Scotland from 1040 to 1057, ruled largely under the influence of the Earl of the Orkneys.[32] His successor Malcolm was the son-in-law of the earl, and his wife was a granddaughter of Finn Arneson of Norway. In 1064 the Norse colonies in Caithness and Sutherland passed permanently to the Scotch king. Harald maintained close relations with Iceland though the Icelanders did not formally acknowledge that they were subject to him. An Icelandic chieftain married a daughter of Magnus II (1066-1069). Annual voyages were made to Greenland.

Norway was much weakened by the loss of the great army sent to England. The Danish king claimed overlordship over Norway, but negotiations resulted in a treaty of peace in 1068.[33] Internal strife in Denmark and Sweden produced a period of peace under Olaf the Peaceful (1066-1093). When King Canute of Denmark (1080-1086) solicited his aid for an attack on England, Olaf refused to join but placed sixty warships at his disposal. But the expedition never came off so that renewed hostilities with England were averted. As relations with Denmark were friendly and Denmark was a part of the archdiocese of Bremen, Olaf upheld the authority of the archbishop, and maintained close relations with such popes as Gregory VII (1073-1085). But celibacy of priests was not as yet introduced into Norway, and the clergy remained subject to the king who exercised firm control in ecclesiastical affairs. When Pope

Gregory VII asserted his supremacy over the German Emperor, the archbishop of Bremen supported the Emperor while the Danish king supported the Pope. This finally led to the separation of the Scandinavian countries from Bremen, and the creation in 1104 of a new archbishopric at Lund in Skåne. Commerce, particularly with England, was facilitated by the founding of the city of Bergen about 1075. Bergen soon became, together with Wisby, one of the greatest centers of Northern trade.

King Magnus Bareleg (1093-1103) brought under closer control the border districts on the Göta River. While he did not aspire to the English throne nor the conquest of Iceland, he did wish to reduce the colonial possessions to full submission. He fought the Swedes to acquire Dalsland. In 1101 a peace meeting was held at Konghelle of all three Scandinavian kings with the Danish king serving as mediator, the first meeting of its kind. Each king retained the possessions his predecessors had held. Magnus was to marry Margaret, daughter of the Swedish king. As this marriage was without issue Dalsland reverted to Sweden in 1103. After the peace of Konghelle, Magnus reestablished his sovereignty over the Norwegian colonial possessions after invading the Orkneys, Hebrides and the Isle of Man.[34] About 1098 he aided the Welsh against the English. In 1102 he went to Ireland where he was killed. He succeeded in attaching the colonies more closely to Norway and his system and organization there endured for 150 years. Commercial intercourse with England was greatly stimulated. He was regarded as such a threat that an alliance was formed between the Irish king and King Henry I of England.

From 1103 to 1130, when the civil wars broke out, Norway had a period of peace.[35] In 1102 the Norwegian baron, Skofte Agmundsson, organized the first Norwegian Crusade to the Holy Land. In 1107, King Sigurd Jerusalemfarer sailed with 10,000 warriors from Bergen, undertook a crusade, and was absent for four years. About 1110 Jämtland was reunited with Norway.[36] It had been seized by Sweden in the time of Saint Olaf. In ecclesiastical affairs it was always a part of the diocese of Uppsala. Härjedalen, which is often mentioned together with Jämtland, seems always to have been a Norwegian province and belonged to the Trondheim diocese. "Neither the Gregorian program nor the Canon law made itself felt to any large extent in Norway before the twelfth century."[37] Several Benedictine monasteries were established during this century. Tithing was introduced. In 1123 the Norwegian king led a crusade into the Swedish province of Småland where paganism still existed.

In 1130 a series of civil wars commenced which lasted until 1241. The power of the nobles was growing. Many of those involved sought Danish or Swedish assistance. Harald Gilchrist came from Ireland claiming to be a son of Magnus Barefoot and entitled to the throne. In 1134 he received substantial aid from the Danish king. In 1135 the Wends attacked the city of Konghelle. The Norwegian hold on the Orkneys and the Shetlands was strengthened. In 1137 Magnus the Blind, an ousted king of Norway, son of Sigurd Jerusalemfarer, secured assistance from Jarl Karl Sunnesson, of Vestergötland in Sweden. The jarl's invasion of Norway was defeated. Magnus now secured Danish aid which was so ineffectual that the Danish king Erik Emune was assassinated upon his return to Denmark. The succeeding Danish king now gave aid to another claimant Sigurd Slembe. In 1139 Sigurd Slembe and Magnus the Blind joined forces in Denmark, but were defeated by the opposing Norwegian forces near Bohuslän, after the Danish auxiliary forces sailed away. This terminated the first period of the civil wars.

In 1152 Norway became a separate archdiocese with headquarters at Trondheim. The English Cardinal Nicholas Brakespeare, later Pope Adrian IV, sent a papal legate to establish archbishoprics in Norway and Sweden. There were to be five bishoprics in Norway and six in the Norwegian colonies. Iceland had two. The Hebrides and the Isle of Man together constituted the bishopric of Sodor and Man.[38] The Orkneys, the Faroes, and Greenland each had one. Following 1152 the aristocracy and the church were firmly leagued against the crown.[39] In 1152 a group of 2,000 Norwegians commenced a crusade to the Holy Land.[40] In 1153 King Eystein II made the last predatory expedition to England.

The civil wars commencing in 1130 weakened the Norwegian control of its colonies.[41] The Orkney earls still did homage to Norway, but exercised almost unrestrained authority. In 1158 there was a permanent partition of the Kingdom of Man and the Hebrides. At this time King Gudröd of Man obtained confirmation of his title from King Ingi of Norway. In 1193 a band of rebels against King Sverri assembled in the Orkneys. Sverri thereupon separated the Shetlands permanently from the Orkney earldom and joined them to the kingdom of Norway.[42]

A second period of civil war commenced about 1155. King Ingi Hunchback carried on negotiations with the Danish King.[43] A rival king, Haakon the Broadshouldered, sought refuge in Sweden. Upon the death of King Ingi in 1161, Erling Skakke secured the election of his son Magnus Erlingsson as king, Magnus being a descendant of Sigurd Jerusalemfarer through his mother. Erling went to Denmark and sought the promise of Danish aid in return for a cession of Viken. In 1163 the first coronation in Norway occurred, and Magnus surrendered up great power to the Church. A great chieftain and a bishop from Iceland attended the coronation. Archbishop Eystein Erlendsson exercised great authority and commenced the building of the "magnificent Trondheim cathedral, the grandest structure ever built in the Scandinavian North."[44] Erling was evasive about his promise to Denmark, so King Valdemar the Great of Denmark made an expedition to Norway in 1165. Later Erling assisted a plot against Valdemar and invaded Denmark. Valdemar in turn attacked Norway. Peace was made in 1170 at Ringsted. Viken was given to Valdemar, who in return made Erling a jarl and gave him Viken as a fief under the Danish crown. This was the first alienation of Norwegian territory since the year 1000. Erling now sought to exterminate the family of Harald Gilchrist. He thus incurred Swedish hostility as the Swedish jarl Birger Brosa was married to Harald's daughter Bergitta.

In 1177 Sverri, claiming to be a grandson of Harald Gilchrist, became a rival king of Norway. Before doing so he visited Birger Brosa and his aunt, and also visited his sister, married to a Swedish leader in Vermeland.[45] The Swedish king had previously aided another grandson of Harald Gilchrist.

In 1180 Sverri succeeded in forcing King Magnus to flee to Denmark and the archbishop to England. The aristocracy which opposed Sverri sought aid from the Danish king who gave it since Sverri represented a strong national government and an independent Norway. In 1184 Sverri defeated Magnus who had returned with substantial Danish aid. Magnus and the flower of the Norwegian aristocracy were killed. From 1190 to 1192 a joint crusade to the Holy Land was organized in Norway and Denmark. In 1194 Sverri was excommunicated by the Pope. The Norwegian archbishop and Bishop Nicolas Arnesson of Oslo were now in Denmark and organized the Baglers as a group of aristocrats and supporters of the church to defeat the king. "No bloodier civil war had ever been fought in Norway."[46] In 1198 Pope Innocent III, who had forced submission by the Kings of Aragon, Poland, Portugal and England, placed Norway under interdict and declared Sverri excommunicated and deposed. He also sent letters to the Kings of Denmark and Sweden asking them to overthrow Sverri. Sverri now published his "Speech against the Bishops", setting forth the divine right of kings over or against the church.[47] The Norwegian people reacted favorably to Sverri. The Danish king did not attack although he had lost control over Viken. Sverker, the Swedish king, remained friendly. Sverri was married to a daughter of King Eirik, the Saint of Sweden. Sverri's daughter married Sverker's son. Jarl Birger Brosa remained friendly, and Sverri made the jarl's son Philip jarl of the Uplands and Viken. Sverri had an alliance with England which gave him aid in 1201.[48]

Following the death of Sverri in 1202, the Norwegian archbishop revoked the interdict without awaiting the permission of the Pope. In 1204 King Valdemar Victorious of Denmark came to Norway with a fleet of 360 ships, and the Bagler chiefs did homage to him as their overlord.[49] Norwegian independence might have been endangered, but Valdemar's wars in other countries so absorbed his attention that he took no steps to maintain his supremacy over any part of Norway. Civil war ended in 1208 when the Norwegian king gave Viken to the Bagler leader, Philip Simonsson, who now married Sverri's daughter. Friendly relations were now established with Denmark. The Orkneys, Man and the Hebrides were now again forced to submit to Norwegian sovereignty. Another crusade to Palestine took place, and still another was about to commence in 1217 with royal assistance when the king died. Eric V (1208-1216), King of Sweden, who drove out King Sverker, received Norwegian support, while Sverker in turn obtained Danish support, but did not recover his throne.

In 1217 Haakon the Old became king. In 1223 his rival Skule Jarl went to Denmark to receive the aid of Valdemar Victorious in making him king of southern Norway with Valdemar as overlord.[50] But Valdemar had been captured by one of his own vassals, hence Skule could get no Danish aid. In the same year Skule was given the northern districts to rule over with the thought that he would find less opportunity to secure Danish aid. As the Danes sought an overlordship over Norway and supported the Guelfs, Haakon sought closer relations with the Ghibelline Emperor Frederick II of Germany.[51] Frederick sent ambassadors to Norway. Friendly relations with Henry III of England were maintained, and Norway's first commercial treaty was made with England in 1217. England's first commercial treaties were with Norway. In 1227 Haakon secured the disbanding of a rebel group, the Ribbungs, who had been receiving Swedish help. Skule was prepared to give aid to Valdemar Victorious who had now regained his liberty, but Haakon dissuaded him. In 1240 Skule was defeated and slain, thus ending the period of civil wars. Haakon was able to be crowned in 1247 because Pope Innocent IV, in his struggle with Emperor Frederick, needed friends.[52] During the period between 1219 and 1231, Norwegian sovereignty over the Hebrides and the Isle of Man was maintained despite Scottish intervention.[53] Haakon strengthened the Norwegian fleet "until Norway ranked all nations as a naval power."[54] Because of such strength and Haakon's reputation, the European powers sought to gain his friendship. He remained a friend of both Pope and Emperor, despite the struggle between them. Haakon rejected an offer by the Pope to become Emperor. He rejected an offer from the French to command the French fleet on a crusade. Haakon hesitated to leave Norway because of the great

Tartar invasions in Russia, Poland, Hungary and Germany. Many fugitive Russians were permitted to settle in Finnmark. In 1251 peace was made with Russia and the boundaries of Finland and Karelia were fixed.

At first Haakon's relations with Sweden and Denmark were not friendly. Haakon effected a reconciliation with Sweden and Crown Prince Haakon, his son, married the daughter of Birger Jarl. From 1268 to 1273 the boundaries with Sweden were marked, lasting until 1600. In 1256 Haakon sailed for Copenhagen with so strong a fleet that Denmark made peace on Haakon's terms without a fight. In 1261 Magnus, Haakon's surviving son, married the daughter of the Danish king. Relations with England were very friendly. The King of Castile sought Haakon's friendship, Haakon's daughter Christine married the son of the King of Castile and the two countries formed an alliance. But Haakon was to give no aid against England, Denmark or Sweden. Haakon's other daughter Cecilie was married in 1241 to a nephew of the Bagler leader Philip Simonsson, *lendermann* Gregorius Andresson of Stavrheim in Nordfjord who died in 1246.[55] In 1248 Cecilie married King Harald of the Hebrides and Man, but the couple were drowned the same year in a storm on their return from Norway.[56] In 1261 the King of Scotland vainly sought to induce Norway to cede the Hebrides to him. In 1263 Haakon made an expedition with 160 ships and 20,000 men to the British Isles to assert his supremacy over the Norwegian dependencies and to overthrow the Scotch king.[57] He encountered many difficulties and died in the Orkneys.

In 1261 Greenland became a Norwegian dependency or crown colony.[58] The Black Death in 1349 and Hanseatic control over Bergen finally cut off all contacts. The last Norwegian voyage to Greenland occurred in 1406. In 1262 Iceland also became a Norwegian dependency by voluntary agreement.[59]

The 1263 expedition showed the difficulty of defending the Hebrides against the Scotch. In 1266 King Magnus sold the Hebrides and the Isle of Man to Scotland by the Treaty of Perth.[60] Scotland paid a substantial purchase sum and agreed to make small annual payments to keep up some pretense of Norwegian sovereignty, but the payments soon ceased. It took some time before the ceded possessions submitted. The governmental and legal institutions of the Isle of Man today are largely a continuation of the Norwegian system.[61] From the date of the loss of the Hebrides "we note the beginning of the Hanseatic influence, the decay of national commerce, and the entering of Norway into the continental political system."[62] During the thirteenth century the Hanseatic League acquired control of all trade from Russia to England. The first trading privileges were granted to Lübeck about 1230. In 1250 after armed conflict, a general trade treaty was made with that city which was then the chief Baltic city. The Hanseatic hold on Bergen continued for three centuries.

During the reign of Magnus Lawmender the Papacy was at the zenith of its power. Except during the reign of Magnus Erlingsson (1162-1184) the Norwegian church was national in character and the king legislated for it. But Archbishop Jon Raude challenged the power of the king and Magnus Lawmender gave in to him.[63] In 1277 the Concordat of Tonsberg was subscribed to by the king and archbishop without asking the sanction of the Pope, who had objected to the Concordat of 1273 at Bergen, although the king had yielded on almost every point. Under Magnus, Norwegian commerce reached its greatest volume until modern times.[64] Commerce was carried on not only with the Norwegian colonies, but also with England and Flanders and other countries in the North Sea and with Wisby in Gotland and other towns on the Baltic coast. As the Danish king had failed to pay the dowry of his daughter married to Magnus, the Norwegian fleet attacked in Skåne in 1274. The attack was defeated but Norwegian attacks continued over a period of four decades. Magnus declined to intervene in a dispute between the King of Sweden and the latter's brother.

During the reign of Eirik Priesthater (1280-1299)[65] the relations of church and state became very strained. The archbishop excommunicated the king and many of his regents who then drove the archbishop into exile in Sweden. Strained relations with Denmark continued. The Danish king sought to gain the support of Lübeck and Hamburg by granting privileges in Skåne. The German merchants in Norway became more unpopular, and the laws restricting them were strictly enforced. Efforts were made to strengthen the ties with England and Scotland. King Eirik married a Scottish princess. In 1285 the Swedish king negotiated a treaty of peace between Norway and the Hanseatic League which had successfully blockaded Norway after Norwegian attacks on German shipping. Norway had to pay an indemnity and the German merchants gained a strong foothold which soon greatly injured Norwegian trade. In 1289 the assassin of the Danish king, Erik Klipping received refuge in Norway, and war broke out between the two countries. In 1290 Princess Margaret of Norway died on her way to become ruler of Scotland. The English king, Edward I, had given aid to Norway on the basis that Margaret should marry his son. King Eirik of Norway laid claim to Scotland upon the death of the princess, but King Edward rejected his claim. Relations with England now became unfriendly and Eirik married a sister of the later King Robert Bruce of Scotland, a rival of Edward. In 1294 the German merchants secured new privileges when the king was unable to pay the indemnity due to them. In 1295 France agreed to pay a large yearly sum to Norway in return for military assistance against England. As the war between England and France stopped, Norway never had to perform under this treaty. Before 1300 the Hanseatic merchants had secured their most important privileges in Norway.

King Haakon (1299-1319) was the last male member of the royal line. His reign marks the close of the older period in both external and internal affairs.[66] Norway ceased to be a maritime nation. The bonds of several centuries with England were severed. The king declined to grant privileges to English merchants such as the Germans had. The treaty of Perth with Scotland was renewed in 1312, but Norway derived no benefits. In 1302 Haakon's daughter became engaged to Eirik, brother of the Swedish king. In 1304, Haakon granted Konghelle in fief to Eirik. But Eirik was treacherous and Haakon demanded the return of Konghelle. Eirik refused and war broke out between Norway and Sweden in 1308. Eirik invaded Norway, captured Oslo and attacked Jämtland. In 1309 Norway made peace and a treaty of alliance with Denmark at Copenhagen. Denmark ceded Halland to Norway in perpetuity.[67] In 1310 the rebellious dukes who ruled Sweden made peace at Helsingborg with Haakon and agreed to cede to him northern Halland, Konghelle, Hunelacks, and Varberg. In 1312 Haakon's daughter married Eirik, and a son was born to them in 1316, thus securing an heir apparent to the Norwegian throne. Three years later this child Magnus succeeded to the throne on Haakon's death. The King of Sweden was then in exile for having murdered his two brothers, hence the leading Swedish nobles elected Magnus king of Sweden. Norway now lacked the economic foundations for independence. "In her need for grain, and in her dependence upon the Hanseatic towns of the Baltic, may be seen the most important premise for the decline of Norway in the latter part of the Middle Ages."[68]

The mother of Magnus and seven members of the Swedish royal council met to form a union between Sweden and Norway.[69] This was the first union between the two countries. They had nothing in common except the king, who was to spend an equal time in each kingdom. The Norwegian Council of State and the mother of the queen served as regents. In Sweden the Swedish Royal Council and the mother of the queen served as regents for Sweden. Knut Porse, a Danish noble and friend of the king's mother, misused the seal of the kingdom in foreign affairs and began a war on Denmark. In 1323 a council of magnates chose Erling Vidkunsson regent of Norway, a position he held until 1330. Relations with Denmark and England were strained because of acts of Knut Porse. Because of border disputes in Finnmark, the Russians and Karelians invaded Haalogaland in 1323. Three years later peace was made at Novgorod for a ten year period. Envoys sent to England came to a friendly understanding with Edward II in 1325. In 1332, King Magnus acquired Skåne and Blekinge and in 1340 Halland. But this involved Magnus in very great expense, without any great benefit to Norway as distinct from Sweden. Magnus paid but little attention to Norway and disregarded the Norwegian Council of State. A group of Norwegians now demanded the dissolution of the union and that Haakon, younger son of Magnus, born in 1340, be made king of Norway. Magnus yielded and a royal decree at Varberg in 1343 provided that Haakon become king of Norway upon reaching his majority, that his older brother rule over only Sweden and Skåne, and that the kingdoms be separated in 1355. Until 1355 Magnus was to serve as regent. In 1344 Haakon was elected king of Norway and the royal seal was returned to Norway and given to the chancellor. While Magnus continued as regent administration in fact was by the chancellor and the Council. But foreign affairs were conducted by Magnus. In 1342 Norway and Sweden became involved in war with Valdemar Atterdag of Denmark, who had the help of the Hanseatic cities. In the peace treaty of 1343 Valdemar sold large areas to Magnus, involving Magnus in great expense. Magnus borrowed money from the Hanseatic cities, and in turn had to give further trading privileges to them. In 1349 the Black Death resulted in the loss of a third of the population of Norway. It was reduced from 300,000 to 200,000.

In 1355 Haakon became king. But Magnus retained Vestfold and Skienssyssel and his queen kept Ranafylke, Borgarsyssel and Iceland as her Norwegian dowry. These districts were to revert to Norway on the death of the couple. Norway's rights under the Act of Varberg of 1343 were thus ignored. In 1361 Haakon imprisoned his father, and in 1362 Haakon was made joint king of Sweden with his father. In 1363 the three Scandinavian kings made peace. Haakon married Valdemar's daughter Margaret who two months later became heir to the Danish throne.[70] In 1364 Haakon and Magnus were formally deposed as kings of Sweden, being succeeded by Albrecht of Mecklenburg. The Swedes had been offended by the concessions made to Denmark. A small army led by Norwegian nobles was defeated in 1365. In 1370 Denmark was defeated by the Hanseatic League, leaving Haakon free to invade Sweden in 1371 and liberate his father. Magnus died in 1373 and Haakon then took over the western Swedish provinces and the Norwegian districts which his father and mother had been allowed to retain. In 1375 when Valdemar died Haakon's son Olaf was elected king of Denmark and Margaret acted as regent, as Haakon always remained in Norway. Valdemar had promised the throne to a grandson by his older daughter, Albrecht of

Mecklenburg, but the Danes preferred Olaf when Albrecht assumed the royal title without being elected. Hostilities between Norway and Sweden continued until Haakon's death in 1380.

On Haakon's death his son Olaf, already king of Denmark, became king of Norway. A dynastic union between Norway and Denmark was now established which lasted until 1814.[71] Margaret acted as regent of Norway only when in Norway. In her absence a Norwegian regent assisted by the Norwegian Chancellor administered Norwegian affairs. In 1387 King Olaf died and Margaret succeeded by election as ruling queen, while Eirik of Pomerania, a son of her sister's daughter was chosen heir to the Norwegian throne by the Council at Oslo. In 1389, upon the request of the Swedish nobles Margaret became ruler of Sweden. She continued to live in Denmark. She left many high Norwegian offices vacant and appointed Danes to the highest positions in the Church. In 1393 and 1395 a league of professional buccaneers known as the Victual Brothers, encouraged at first by the Hanseatic cities of Rostock and Wismar sacked and burned Bergen. In 1395 Margaret made peace with Rostock and Wismar. In 1397 the Kalmar union between Denmark, Norway and Sweden was formed.[72] While in Norway the kingship had been hereditary, it was now made elective. No central government, aside from the king, was provided for. The duties of each member of the union were not fully spelled out. There was no constitution and no limitation on the sovereign, hence an ambitious ruler might exercise great powers. During the last fifteen years of her reign (1397-1512) Margaret visited Norway only twice. When the Norwegian regent died no successor was appointed for several years. The office of chancellor was left vacant for some time when the chancellor died. The Norwegian Council seldom met, and many foreign officials ruled from Denmark.

From 1416 to 1435 King Eirik[73] was at war with Holstein and the Hanseatic League. The Hanseatic League cut off all trade with the North. In 1428 and 1429 pirates sacked and burned Bergen. The wars were of little benefit to Norway. While some attention was paid to the Norwegian colonies, trade with them was slowing down. In 1410 the last ship came from Greenland to Norway. From about 1432 to 1530 the Hanseatic cities enjoyed their greatest prosperity and power in Norway.[74] In 1413 Eirik protested to King Henry V of England against the operation of foreign merchants in the Norwegian colonies, and made a similar complaint in 1431. In 1432 Eirik made a treaty with England under which England agreed to pay for the damages done by such trade. Eirik, like Margaret, ruled Norway from Denmark. Several foreigners were made Norwegian Councillors. The Council always met in Denmark and the Councillors from Norway seldom attended; the Danish members were always in the majority. Eirik's popularity was small but Philippa, his English queen, daughter of Henry IV, aided him until her death in 1430. In 1434 the Norwegian Council declined to join the Swedish Council in renouncing allegiance to the king. The Norwegians thus lost their last opportunity to secure their independence. In 1435 several Norwegian councillors were present at a council in Stockholm when Eirik gave various assurances. In 1436 a revolt against the king occurred in Norway, as a result of which a council was summoned to negotiate with the rebels. Their demand that Danish lords and *fogeds* or sheriffs be expelled was granted. But the revolt was a local rather than a national affair. Norway, unlike Sweden, had no aristocracy to lead it. An unsuccessful Norwegian revolt occurred in 1438. Eirik remained king longest in Norway. In 1439 Eirik was formally deposed in Sweden and Denmark. Christopher of Bavaria became king in Denmark in 1440, in Sweden in 1441, and in Norway in 1442.

Under Christopher of Bavaria (1442-1448) separate administration of each kingdom was emphasized.[75] The king never visited Norway after his coronation. Administration was carried on by the Norwegian Council which now exercised its greatest authority since 1397. Revolts against the *fogeds* occurred in southeastern Norway. Efforts to restrain the authority of the Hanseatic League over Norwegian commerce were unsuccessful. In 1444 King Henry VI of England repeated his prohibition of English trade in the Norwegian colonies.

Christopher, like Eirik, left no descendants. The Danes now elected Christian of Oldenburg as king of Denmark.[76] In the preceding reigns the Danish Council had selected the candidates for the throne. The Swedes elected Karl Knutsson, a Swede, as king of Sweden. Some Norwegians favored Sigurd Jonsson, the regent and a descendant of Haakon V, but most were ready to follow Denmark or Sweden. The Norwegian Council was divided into a Swedish and a Danish party. The Norwegian archbishop Aslak Bolt met with the Swedish party in Bohuslän and chose the Swedish king. The Council later rescinded the action and a treaty of 1450 provided that Sweden surrender Norway to the Danish king. In 1449 a treaty between Christian and Henry VI of England made the trade with Iceland free on certain conditions in 1490. While the new act of union, drawn up at Bergen in 1450, emphasized the equality of Norway and Denmark, the king resided in Denmark and was surrounded by Danish councillors. He visited Norway only four times in a reign of thirty-one years. He ignored the Norwegian Council and sought to impose his personal choice as archbishop of Norway though the chapter had already elected a Norwegian. The Danish chancellor kept the seal of the Norwegian kingdom and the Norwegian chancellor became a mere judicial officer. The office of *drotsete* or regent, the highest in Norway, was virtually abolished. Since the king needed Hanseatic support in his wars against Sweden, he upheld Hanseatic authority in Norway.

In 1468 and 1469 the Orkney and Shetland Islands were mortgaged without consultation with the Norwegian Council, by King Christian I, to the king of Scotland as security for the dowry his daughter Margaret was to receive upon her marriage to the Scottish king.[77]A right to redeem was claimed until the seventeenth century. Use of the Norwegian language did not disappear until the eighteenth century. As late as 1903 an Orkney farmer insisted that Saint Olaf's law applied to some fisheries in dispute, and the English authorities made inquiries to a professor of law at the University of Oslo.[78]

Upon the death of Christian I in 1481 there was an interregnum of two years in Norway. The Norwegian Council repudiated its recognition given as early as 1458 to Christian's son Hans. Norway was ruled by the Council under the Norwegian Archbishop. Many Norwegians desired a union with Sweden rather than Denmark. The Norwegian councillors issued a letter complaining of the mortgaging of the Orkney and Shetland Islands, the outrages committed by the Hanseatic merchants in Bergen in 1455 without any effort by the Danish king to punish the guilty parties, the privileges granted to the German merchants, the numerous wars, the sending of revenues out of Norway and the extensive grant of fiefs and privileges to foreigners. The Swedish Council gave evasive answers, as many favored the continuation of the Kalmar Union. Hence the Norwegian Council joined the Danish Council in electing Hans in 1483.[79] The king signed a charter promising to correct many of the evils previously mentioned; the Norwegian Council was to meet once every two years and the king agreed to sanction and enforce all its decrees. Hostilities broke out between England and Norway and Denmark because English merchants continued to trade with Iceland, although trade with the Norwegian colonies was a crown monopoly. In 1490 a treaty was made with England making trade with Iceland free for seven years. Hans like Christian did not live up to the terms of his charter. But there was no nationalistic movement as one group favored Denmark and the other Sweden. About 1500 a revolt led by Knut Alfsson of the Swedish party was put down. In 1501 Prince Christian was sent as viceroy to Norway. In 1508 another revolt led by Herlog Hudfat in eastern Norway was crushed. Following a war with the Hanseatic cities, a favorable peace was made in 1512, and the Hanseatic naval supremacy in the North was lost. A powerful navy was established by Hans.

Upon the death of King Hans in 1513 the Norwegian councillors were summoned to Copenhagen. They complained that the king had acted as if the kingships were hereditary instead of elective and that the Orkneys and Shetlands had not been redeemed, and sought to safeguard Norwegian autonomy and equality with Denmark. But Christian II[80] ignored the demands of the Norwegian Council, yet was receptive to the demands of the Danish Council. Christian complained to King Henry VIII of England of English interference with Icelandic trade. In 1515 the treaty of 1490 with England was renewed. The Protestant Reformation made some headway in Denmark, but came more slowly to Norway. Christian II, anxious to acquire property secularized two Norwegian monasteries. Christian's war on Sweden resulted in use of Norwegian soldiers and increased taxes. Sweden revolted in 1521 and Gustaf Vasa became king in 1523. In 1523 the Danish Council renounced their allegiance to Christian II and chose his uncle Frederick I as king. The Norwegians took no part in the uprising against Christian II, as he was well liked there. But Denmark and Sweden would doubtless have prevented Norwegian separation from the Union. Gustaf Vasa occupied Bohuslän, but in 1524 through the mediation of the Hanseatic League it was restored to Norway.

Frederick I sent over various Danish nobles to influence the Norwegians in his favor. In 1524 the Norwegian Council chose him as king.[81] The King signed a charter guaranteeing rights demanded by the Council. But the kingdom was controlled by the Council under the leadership of Vincens Lunge, a Danish noble who had married a daughter of Lady Inger of Austraat, the leading Norwegian figure of her day and the subject of one of Ibsen's plays. Another Norwegian leader was the archbishop. The king had in mind incorporating Norway into the Danish kingdom but the Norwegian Council fought for autonomy. The first Lutheran preacher came to Norway in 1526 and Lunge supported him. The Archbishop now looked to Christian II who returned to Norway in 1531, but Christian was beaten and imprisoned.

Upon Frederick's death in 1533 another interregnum ensued. The Danes chose his son Christian III[82] in 1534. Lunge and a few Norwegian councillors proceeding irregularly elected Christian III. The archbishop favored a son-in-law of Christian II. In 1535 there were uprisings resulting in the killing of Lunge and the virtual destruction of the Council. The archbishop now led an uprising against Christian III but without success. Thus the Norwegian opportunity for independence was lost. In 1536 the king boldly asserted his intention to make Norway a mere province of Denmark. The Danish Council resolved that Norway should cease to exist as an independent kingdom. The Norwegian Council disappeared, the only national office remaining was that of chancellor, and the Norwegian dependencies such as Iceland and Greenland were brought directly under the crown. Christian III became king of Norway without a regular election as had occurred in the past. The Norwegian people were not informed of the provision in the charter given to the Danish Council contemplating a dependent status for Norway. Norway continued to be styled a kingdom and retained its old laws. In 1547 Norway received its own chancellor again. Administration of Norway continued separate from that of Denmark. The Danish flag became the official flag of both kingdoms. The Danish church ordinance of 1537 established by the Protestant Reformation became the temporary constitution of the Norwegian state church. By 1555 the secularization of the monasteries was completed. Protestantism came in slowly as it was suddenly imposed by royal edict. The Norwegian law codes were translated into Danish, and many Danes were appointed judges in Norway. Norwegian jurisprudence lost its high position. Many Norwegians held high positions in the navy. The king encouraged the development of mining. By a treaty of 1544 unobstructed trade with Holland was assured. In 1559 the Hanseatic hold on Bergen was finally broken. The king never visited Norway and neglected the country.

Under the next king, FrederickII[83] (1559-1588), the Seven Years' War with Sweden occurred from 1563 to 1570. The Swedish king hoped to take Norway, while Frederick II hoped to become king of Sweden. The Swedes hoped that the Norwegians would revolt, but the Norwegians lacked the means. The navy was largely recruited in Norway. The Swedes captured Jämtland and Härjedalen and occupied them throughout the war. The Swedish king was accepted as sovereign in Trondelag, Møre and Romsdal. But rough treatment soon ended the sentiment in favor of Sweden and created long-lasting ill-feeling. In 1567 attacks were made on southeastern Norway. Thereafter the war was fought chiefly on Swedish soil. When peace was made in 1570 Jämtland and Härjedalen were restored to Norway. Jämtland, once a part of the diocese of Uppsala, was now joined to the diocese of Trondheim. In 1572 the office of *statholder* or viceroy of Norway was created. In 1588 the *statholder* was placed in command of Norwegian military forces. While it was the theory that complaints would now be made only to the *statholder*, the Norwegians adhered to the earlier practice of application to the king. From 1568 councils of magnates were held regularly to pass on administrative questions and serve as a higher court.

The population of Norway increased from 300,000 in 1500 to 400,000 in 1600. The Danish population was twice as great, as much of southern Sweden was then Danish. Bergen was the largest city of the Scandinavian countries. Germans, Danes, Englishmen, Scotchmen and Hollanders constituted a rather sizeable addition to the native element. About 1512 gypsies first entered Norway, but they were outlawed in 1536. A heavy export of lumber to Holland and England developed during the latter half of the sixteenth century. This had political consequences as it produced a Norwegian middle class.

Under Christian IV[84] (1588-1648) the Council ruled during his minority up to 1597. Norwegian and Danish ships and crews had been hired to join Spain's Invincible Armada. Upon a remonstrance by the English ambassador the ships were not permitted to join. Christian was greatly interested in Norway and visited it twenty-six times. In 1599 he made a voyage to the North Cape so as to be able to regulate commerce there and to protect Finnmark from Russia and Finland. As in Sweden so in Norway the Jesuits sought converts to Catholicism. In 1604 the Norwegian bishops called this to the king's attention. In 1624 the Jesuits were banished from Norway, and the death penalty was imposed for returning to the country. Following the victories of Gustavus Adolphus there was less fear of Catholicism. Christian IV even allowed Catholic worship in a few specified places but only for foreigners. Jesuits and monks were still forbidden to live in Norway, as were also Jews. Catholicism was never strong after this time in Norway. In 1605 ships were sent to Greenland. In 1636 the king organized the Greenland Company to trade with Greenland, but most of the Greenland trade was English and Dutch. In 1619 a company was formed to trade with Iceland. The Danish-Norwegian fleet was so strengthened that it became by far the most powerful in the Baltic Sea.

Charles IX, who became king of Sweden in 1599, at once assumed a very aggressive attitude towards Christian IV, who had befriended the ousted Swedish king Sigismund. The Swedish aggressions in Finnmark, which had caused trouble in the previous reign, became more pronounced. Charles IX collected taxes and granted trading privileges in Norwegian areas. In 1611 Christian finally forced the Council to declare war on Sweden, with the object of not only protecting Norway against encroachment but also regaining Sweden. Swedish troops, largely foreign mercenaries from Scotland and Holland, invaded Norway. Attacks were made on Jämtland and Härjedalen and Romsdal and Gudbrandsdal. By the Treaty of Knäred, Sweden under British pressure renounced her claims to Finnmark. In 1614 Christian issued an order that a small Norwegian militia of 2,100 men be established, but the plan was soon abandoned. In 1608 the Protestant Union had sought Christian's aid, but Christian was more concerned with his relations with Sweden. The Union again turned to Christian and on a promise of English aid Christian invaded Germany. But his efforts were unsuccessful and he made peace in 1629 although Sweden was ready to become his ally. At the time the opposing forces offered Sweden a partition of Denmark-Norway, Norway to go to Sweden and Denmark to the Emperor. In 1628 Christian began the reorganization of the Norwegian Army so that foreign mercenaries were no longer necessary. In 1642 the new *statholder* Hannibal Sehested began a period of reform. He sought the advice of the Norwegian Estates. Unfortunately, his work was interrupted by a new war with Sweden. Sweden, assisted by Holland, attacked Denmark in 1643, and occupied it. The Norwegians were opposed to attacking Sweden. Attacks were made on Sweden from Jämtland, but the Swedes occupied Jämtland and attacked Osterdalen. The Norwegians regained Jämtland and held it until the end of the war. They also entered Dalsland. But after the loss of his fleet Christian made peace at Brømsebro in 1645. The Norwegian provinces of Jämtland and Härjedalen were now ceded to Sweden. While the districts of Indre and Saerna were not mentioned in the treaty, they were retained by Sweden as being a part of Härjedalen. This was the first time that Norway surrendered land to a victorious foe. The Norwegian *statholder* now adopted a policy of giving Norway a sufficient military and administrative economy so that it could be an active ally of Denmark. Norwegian revenues were to be retained in Norway. But the Danish Council and nobility opposed this new policy and it soon ended.

When Frederick III[85] (1648-1670) became king the Danish nobles sought to secure a charter reviving the provision in the Danish charter of Christian III in 1536 that Norway constituted a mere province of Denmark. But the charter became a purely Danish document and did not mention Norway. The Norwegian national spirit had been reawakened. While the Norwegian Council had disappeared, it was supplanted by the meetings of the Norwegian Estates. The Danish chancellor stated that the Norwegian Estates were not summoned to take part in the election of the king, as haste was necessary. Jens Bjelke, the Norwegian chancellor, replied that Norway accepted Frederick on the basis of hereditary, rather than elective, right to the throne. The king and the Norwegian *statholder* supported this view. In 1656 the Norwegian merchant class petitioned the king that officers in the Norwegian army be Norwegian and that Norway receive a chamber of commerce, a superior court, and a university. The king was anxious to regain the Swedish provinces lost in 1645. When Sweden became involved in war with Poland, the king with but little preparation or deliberation declared war on Sweden. The Norwegian army was very successful. It regained Jämtland and Härjedalen under the leadership of Jørgen Bjelke, the ablest Norwegian officer. Attacks were also made from Bohuslän, but the Norwegian army failed to effect a junction with the Danish army. In the northern areas the Norwegians destroyed the Swedish silver mines at Nasafjäll and Silbojocki. But the Danish armies were badly beaten. By the Peace of Roskilde in 1658 mediated by England, Bohuslän and the Trondheim area were ceded to Sweden, and the Norwegians had to evacuate Jämtland and Härjedalen. All these areas except Trondheim have been Swedish ever since. Both in 1645 and 1658 Norway suffered from Danish foreign policy. The 1658 treaty provision as to the Trondheim area was very vague, and Sweden claimed that it included Romsdal, Nordland, and Finnmark. Sweden declared war, but the other powers feared that Sweden would gain absolute control in the North. A Dutch fleet defeated the Swedish fleet, and Brandenburg and Poland attacked Sweden. The Swedish king planned to take possession of all Norway. Two thousand Norwegians from the Trondheim area were impressed into Swedish service; 1,400 of them were sent to Livonia and very few ever came back. The Swedish king issued a manifesto to the Norwegians to leave Denmark and join Sweden. But the Norwegians resented the Swedish methods, captured Trondheim and successfully defended Halden. England, France and Holland were interested in preserving the independence of Denmark-Norway and induced the acceptance of the Peace of Copenhagen in 1660. The Trondheim area was restored to Norway. There has been no change since in the common border of Norway and Sweden. Sweden at this time had a population considerably greater than Denmark as a result of her gains from 1645 to 1660. The seventeenth century was a period of great emigration from Norway. Many went to Holland and from Holland to America. Others went to England, and a few to Russia.

In 1661 the king became absolute monarch of Norway and Denmark. The Norwegian Estates signed the draft of a new fundamental law, which was a counterpart to the Danish act. Hereditary kingship was now established. The Danish nobility no longer ruled Norway. Both kingdoms were equal under the king. This system was the law until 1814 for Norway. In reality, rule was by administrative colleges. A supreme court or *Høiesteret* was set up to serve as a court of final jurisdiction for Norway, the Faroe Islands, Iceland, and Denmark. Previously the councils of magnates had acted as higher courts. But the new court was purely Danish and met always in Denmark. The office of Norwegian *statholder* continued. He watched relations with Sweden and supervised national defense. The Norwegian local area now became an *amt* instead of a *len*. Norway was divided into four *stiftsamter*, which in turn were divided into thirteen *amter*. The officials were appointed by the king and not the heads of the *amter*. The *stiftsamter* were Akershus, Christiansand, Trondheim and Bergenhus. The head of the first was the *statholder*, of the second the *vice-statholder,* of the third the Chancellor, and of the fourth the Vice-Chancellor. Mayors and city councilors were appointed by the king. By 1669 the work of registering and valuing all property and taking a census was completed by a commission of fifty appointed by the king. Ulrik Gyldenløve urged the creation of a Norwegian superior court and revision of the Code of Christian IV. Accordingly the *Overhofret* was established with an appeal possible to the Supreme Court in Denmark, and revision of the Code was directed.

In 1666 an alliance was formed with Holland. As a consequence war broke out with England which was terminated by the Peace of Breda in 1667. The next king, Frederick III[86] (1670-1699), under the new constitutional system succeeded as hereditary king and did not have to accept any charter. He set up a new type of nobility, but in Norway this group never became numerous. From 1675 to 1679 the Scanian War was fought by Denmark to regain its lost Swedish provinces. Norway had never been better prepared for war, its army numbering 12,000. The Norwegians called this war the Gyldenløve War as Gyldenløve was *statholder* and commander-in-chief. The war was fought partly in Germany and partly in Skåne and along the Norwegian border. The Norwegian troops occupied Bohuslän. The Norwegian army was now increased to 17,000 men. Jämtland was successfully invaded, but no attempt was made to take permanent possession of this old Norwegian province. The fleet which was largely Norwegian had great successes. Due to French interference to support her ally Sweden, the Peace at Lund in 1679 restored the status quo. A ten-year defensive alliance with Sweden was formed. During Christian's reign the army and navy were greatly strengthened, and new forts were erected. But Norway received no university nor central administration nor capital city nor bank.[87] The war of the great powers commencing in 1689 was injurious to Norwegian shipping. In 1691 the Scandinavian countries agreed upon the first armed neutrality.[88]

When Frederick IV[89] (1699-1730) became king, Gyldenløve retired as *statholder,* and no new *statholder* was appointed. A *vice-statholder* was placed in temporary charge. Gustav W. Wedel, a German by birth, became commander-in-chief of the Norwegian army which now numbered 21,000 men. In 1699 the king formed an alliance with Poland, Russia and Saxony against Sweden. The Norwegian army was mobilized and four regiments sent to Denmark. Peace was made at Travendal in 1700 without much loss or gain to either side. The system of Norwegian administration underwent a change. A commission of one military and four civil members was set up to assist the *vice-statholder* and perform the duties previously performed by the *statholder.* The military member was a German officer. Three of the civil members were Norwegians. But no real improvement in the military or civil service occurred. In 1701 when the War of the Spanish Succession began, both sides sought the support of the king. The king avoided participation though he opposed France. For a yearly subsidy he supplied England with 20,000 mercenaries, of whom 6,000 were Norwegians. Christian V had followed the same practice of supplying mercenaries to obtain revenue. In 1709 war with Sweden was resumed after the Russians had beaten Sweden at Poltova. The Norwegian army was mobilized to invade the Swedish border districts, but it had been so neglected that it was wholly ineffectual. A new *statholder*, V. F. V. Løvendal, was now appointed, who made a successful attack on Bohuslän in 1711. In 1715 Charles XII of Sweden returned to Sweden and planned to seize Norway. In 1716 the invasion began and Oslo was occupied. The Norwegian naval hero, Peter Tordenskjold, defeated the Swedish fleet, and the Swedes withdrew from Norway. In 1718 Sweden again invaded Norway, but the Swedish king was killed near Fredrikshald. In 1719 a Norwegian army invaded Bohuslän, and Tordenskjold captured Marstrand. At the solicitation of England peace was made with Sweden at Fredriksborg in 1720. The Swedish areas captured by the Norwegians were returned to Sweden. Sweden's age of imperial greatness was now over and the strained relations which had existed between Norway and Sweden were slackened. Following the war the system of government by commission was abolished and that of *statholder* was restored.

Christian VI[90] (1730-1746) restored the old system of administrative colleges and abolished the office of *statholder* for Norway. In 1734 a three-year alliance was concluded with England, but no wars were fought during his reign. In 1742 a treaty with France was made, under which France supplied a large yearly subsidy. For a brief time it looked as if Sweden would be united with Denmark-Norway through the selection of the king's son as king of Sweden, but the selection was opposed successfully by Russia. Norwegian trade fell off through strict regulations. Norway could import grain only from Denmark.

Frederick V[91] (1746-1766) made a treaty with Sweden resulting in elimination of frictions with that country. Moreover, the boundary dispute between Norway and Sweden was settled. Norway retained Kautokeino and Karasjok in Finnmark, and a commission was established to survey and mark the boundary line. Neutrality was maintained during the Seven Years' War from 1756 to 1763. There were 13,500 Norwegian soldiers stationed in Holland to defend Slesvig-Holstein. The neutrality permitted the development of a large commerce. In 1760 the Norwegian nationalistic sentiment was enhanced by the formation of the Scientific

Society of Trondheim. Agitation for a Norwegian university appeared. The first newspaper was established in 1763, but strict censorship prevailed. Higher taxes produced riots in 1765 known as the Stril War. It was the first mass movement of peasants against officials.[92]

The skillful policies of Minister of Foreign Affairs Johan Bernstorff who became minister in 1751 continued into the reign of Christian VII[93] (1766-1808), but Bernstorff was dismissed in 1770. In 1771 Struensee became minister and virtually absolute ruler. The Norwegians were at first indifferent, but objected to the dismissal of the popular *statholder*, Jakob Benzon. The Norwegians now requested a university, a bank, abolition of the extra tax levied in 1762, and revocation of the laws prohibiting the import of grains from countries other than Denmark. Struensee seems to have been sympathetic but remained in power only until 1772. The succeeding government of Ove Guldberg while promoting Danish national feeling discouraged Norwegian national feeling. In 1772 the Swedish king established absolutism in Sweden, and planned to gain possession of Norway. In 1773 Denmark-Norway allied herself with Russia against Sweden but war did not ensue as Russia was then fighting Turkey. In 1780 Denmark-Norway joined an Armed Neutrality aimed largely at England, but also made a special treaty with England. The arrangement soon disintegrated. Norwegian shipping expanded greatly during the war. In 1783 Denmark-Norway recognized the independence of the United States and made a commercial treaty with her. In 1784 the Crown Prince became a member of the Council and regent and gained dominance in the government, as the king was mentally incompetent. Many reforms were now instituted. Ole Colbjørnsen, a Norwegian, became one of the chief advisers of the king. In 1786 the Lofthus Rising of peasants occurred in southwestern Norway.[94] In 1788 Sweden attacked Russia, and Denmark, as required by the alliance of 1773, invaded Sweden. A Norwegian army of 12,000 invaded Bohuslän, but as England and Prussia threatened to intervene, the Norwegian army was withdrawn and peace was made in 1788. Following the war the Swedish king conducted negotiations with a few Norwegians who wished to separate from Denmark. While Sweden was hostile to the French Revolution until 1792, Denmark-Norway remained neutral.[95] When the Swedish king was assassinated, relations with Sweden became more friendly and a treaty of alliance was made in 1794. A Pan-Scandinavian movement emerged fostered principally in Denmark. The Swedes recognized the French Republic in 1795 and Denmark-Norway did so in 1796. In 1800 Denmark-Norway again joined the League of Armed Neutrality with Sweden, Russia and Prussia. The English government regarded this as hostile to England and bombarded Copenhagen in 1801, and seized the American and Asiatic colonies. Russia now withdrew from the alliance. France and Russia called upon Denmark-Norway to close her ports to England and join the Continental System. The English without investigation assumed that Denmark-Norway was a party to the arrangement between Russia and France, and ordered Denmark-Norway to turn over its fleet to England, and bombarded Copenhagen in 1807. The Danish-Norwegian fleet was destroyed, and Denmark-Norway made a treaty of alliance with France and Russia. England declared war and captured about 1,500 ships, but in turn lost 2,000 merchant vessels to the Norwegians and Danes.

The war with England was ruinous to Norwegian trade. In 1808 the new king, Frederick VI[96] (1808-1814), declared war on Sweden after Russia had occupied Finland. Since communications with Denmark were interrupted, a special government for Norway headed by the commanding general in southern Norway was established, known as the Government Commission for Norway. A superior court known as *Overkriminalretten*, to meet at Oslo, was created in 1807, to serve as the highest appellate court in criminal cases. The Swedes attacked Norway in 1808 but the Norwegians more than held their own. They had no desire to fight an offensive war at a time when Russia was seizing Finland. In 1809 peace was made with Sweden at Jönköping, leaving the countries in the status quo. War with England continued, but Norwegian trade with England was permitted. In 1811 the University of Oslo was authorized, and it opened in 1813. Proposals to elect the Danish king as Crown Prince of Sweden failed. The Danish king did not wish a constitution limiting the king. In 1810 the French general Bernadotte was elected Crown Prince. In 1812 when Napoleon seized Swedish Pomerania, Sweden and Russia became allies. Russia promised to help Sweden acquire Norway in turn for Swedish troops against Napoleon in Germany. England and Prussia also backed Sweden's claims to Norway. In 1813 the king sent his heir apparent, Christian Frederick, to Norway to counteract Swedish influence. The Swedes defeated the Danes in Holstein and threatened Jutland. On January 14, 1814, under the Treaty of Kiel, Norway was ceded to Sweden. The Norwegian possessions were not ceded to Sweden. One writer concludes: "Denmark had in 1814, by clever diplomacy, kept for herself the Atlantic possessions of Norway."[97] Another writer, however, states: "Because of the haste with which the treaty was drawn up, the Norwegian possessions, Iceland, Greenland, and the Faroe Islands, were not included in the cession."[98]

The dissolution of the union with Denmark did not mean that the Norwegians wished to enter a union with Sweden. The Norwegians selected the Danish Christian Frederick as king of Norway.[99] He sum-

moned an assembly of notables to Eidsvold, who chose him as regent
ad interim. A general constituent assembly was to be summoned to meet
at Eidsvold, a constitution would then be drafted and a king elected.
Sweden at first assumed that Norway had been clearly acquired and
appointed Count Von Essen as governor-general. Christian Frederick
created a royal council or cabinet. A special envoy was sent to England,
but England supported Sweden. When the Constitution was drafted a
large minority group favored union with Sweden, but the nationalist
group led by Christian Magnus Falsen won out. The Constitution was
adopted on May 17, 1814, and Christian Frederick was elected king on
the same date. On June 30, 1814, the envoys of Austria, Russia, England
and Prussia demanded that the Treaty of Kiel be enforced. The Swedish
king already had 40,000 soldiers to support him, as against 27,000 for
Norway. Sweden occupied part of Norway. An armistice was signed on
August 14, 1814, at Moss. Christian Frederick abdicated and returned
to Denmark. On November 4, 1814, the Norwegian Storthing ratified
a union agreement with Sweden and the king of Sweden was elected
king. A committee of the Swedish Rigsdag prepared an Act of Union,
which was ratified by the Norwegian and Swedish parliaments in 1815.
This act, like the Norwegian Constitution, recognized the union as rest-
ing on the free consent of the Norwegian people instead of on the Treaty
of Kiel; and recognized the equality of the two kingdoms. The Act gave
no superiority to Sweden as to foreign affairs.

A Swedish field marshal was appointed *statholder* for Norway to
exercise the highest administrative authority for the king. A ministry was
set up of nine members of whom two served on the Swedish branch. The
ministry exercised only the limited powers involving their own departments. The first regular Storthing met in 1815. As yet the peasant members of the Storthing had small influence compared with the official
classes in the Storthing. The Lagthing or second chamber of the Storthing contained only officials. The first Bernadotte Karl XIV[100] (1818-
1844) supposed he could secure amendments to the Norwegian Constitution destroying the sovereignty of the people and subjecting them to
Swedish supremacy. Norway had no flag. The diplomatic and consular
service was entirely Swedish. The name of Sweden preceded that of
Norway on public documents. A bill abolishing the Norwegian nobility
became law after being passed three times though the king objected
and did not give his royal sanction. Thus the principle became established that the king's veto was only suspensive. In 1818 the king demanded a return of the Faroes, Iceland and Greenland from Denmark
to Norway, but the matter was not pressed. When the powers backed
Denmark's claim that Norway pay a share of the state debt of Denmark-

Norway, the Storthing finally agreed to pay in 1821. The king proposed that the Norwegian Constitution be amended to give the king an absolute veto, the right to dissolve the Storthing, the right to appoint the presidents of the Storthing, the right to remove all officers except judges, and the right to create a new hereditary nobility. The Storthing rejected the proposals. The king objected to celebration of the Norwegian national holiday, the Seventeenth of May, and the Storthing in 1828 passed a resolution carrying out his wish. From 1830 on, the Storthing assumed a less defensive attitude.[101] In 1833 the peasant group secured control of the Storthing, and a great peasant leader, Johan Gabriel Ueland, emerged. In 1834 the Norwegian ministry made certain requests of the king. In response a royal resolution provided that the Norwegian minister of state in Stockholm should be present when Norwegian diplomatic affairs, or diplomatic affairs of interest to both countries, were considered by the Cabinet Council for Foreign Affairs. In 1836 it was provided that Norwegian consuls be appointed with the advice of the Swedish-Norwegian ministry. But the Swedish minister of state always presided and the Swedish members were in the majority. Moreover, the Norwegian minister was not present when Swedish affairs were considered. In 1836 a Norwegian, Wedel-Jarlsberg, was appointed *statholder*. In 1838 a royal decree provided that the Norwegian merchant flag should be used in all waters. In 1840 another Norwegian, Severin Løvenskiold, was appointed *statholder*. Relations with Sweden were better as the king was now more conciliatory while the Norwegian ministry became more conservative.

The next king, Oscar I[102] (1844-1859), made a number of concessions to Norway at the beginning of his reign. In all Norwegian documents the name of Norway was to precede that of Sweden. Norway received her own man-of-war flag. But a union sign was to be inserted on all Norwegian and Swedish flags. In 1848 Marcus Thrane advocated socialistic ideas for adoption in Norway, but he was persecuted and ultimately went to the United States.[103] The Revolution of 1848 in France frightened many Norwegians who now came to regard the union with Sweden as very desirable. With the consent of the Norwegian ministry a committee drafted a new Act of Union in 1844, but it was rejected by both countries. The draft contemplated extensive political amalgamation. Efforts were made to create a joint army. Commissions were appointed to draft new laws regulating trade and tariffs between the two countries, and for carrying into execution in one kingdom decrees rendered in the courts of the other. Conservative Norwegians favored this policy, but the Storthing rejected it.

During the decade from 1850 to 1860 there was friction in connection with the frontier problems along the Russian-Swedish-Norwegian border. Because of Russia's aggressive attitude a treaty was concluded at Stockholm on November 21, 1855 between England and France on the one hand and the united kingdoms of Sweden and Norway on the other hand. England and France agreed to give protection against Russian attack. When Denmark fought its first war with Prussia, the king stationed Norwegian and Swedish troops in northern Slesvig after the 1849 armistice and kept them there until peace was signed in 1850. In 1857 he offered Denmark an alliance to defend the Eider as her southern border.

In 1859 under a new king, Karl XV[104] (1859-1872), the Storthing passed a bill abolishing the office of *statholder*. The office had not been filled when Løvenskjold resigned in 1855. The Swedish Rigsdag now became very critical of the right of the Norwegian people to amend their constitution, and sought revision of the Act of Union. In 1865 a constitutional committee of seven Norwegian and seven Swedish members was established to revise the Act of Union. In 1871 the Storthing refused to agree to the proposed revision of the Union. Neither the Norwegian ministry nor the Storthing favored going to war to help Denmark in its war with Prussia and Austria in 1864, as England, France and Russia were not willing to cooperate. In 1869 the Liberal party was formed. Its leader, Johan Sverdrup, advocated a parliamentary system and supreme power in the Storthing. In 1871 when Norway first seriously attempted to take over Spitzbergen, Russia filed a protest.

King Oscar II[105] (1872-1905) favored a better understanding between Norway and Sweden. In 1873 he sanctioned a bill abolishing the office of *statholder* which had not been filled since 1855. A minister of state for Norway to head the Norwegian ministry was substituted. Frederick Stang, leader of the Norwegian ministry, was appointed to the new office. Until 1905 the Norwegian ministry consisted of two branches: that at Oslo first headed by the *statholder* and then since 1873 by the Norwegian minister of state, and that at Stockholm, consisting of a minister of state and two other ministers. Following the election of 1880 the Storthing for the third time passed a bill providing that the ministry could participate in the deliberations of the Storthing. For the third time it was vetoed by the king. The Storthing then adopted a resolution that the proposal be declared law without the king's sanction. The Constitution clearly provided that an ordinary bill enacted three times became law, but it was silent as to constitutional amendments. The king claimed an absolute veto power as to constitutional amendments. He was supported by the Conservative party and all but one member of the University of Oslo law faculty.[106] The Storthing ignored the veto and in 1883 impeached the ministry. From 1884 Norway had responsible parliamentary government, while Sweden had to wait until 1917. The ministry was headed by Johan Sverdrup, leader of the Liberal party.

Prior to 1885 the Cabinet Council for Foreign Affairs dealing with diplomatic matters affecting both countries consisted of the Swedish minister of state and one other Swedish cabinet member, together with the Norwegian minister of state in Stockholm. In 1885 the Rigsdag provided that Sweden have three members and Norway only one, and that diplomatic affairs be reported by the Swedish minister of foreign affairs instead of by the king. In 1891 a new ministry was formed by Johannes Steen, leader of the Pure Liberal party. The party advocated Norwegian control of Norwegian foreign affairs. In 1891 the office of viceroy of Norway, which could be held by the king's son, was abolished by the Storthing. The party leaders, aware that the Conservative party and Sweden opposed a foreign minister for Norway, now sought simply a separate Norwegian consular service. Norway's commerce was then twice as large as Sweden's. In 1892 the Storthing passed a bill for a separate consular service, but the king declined to sanction the bill and the Steen ministry retired. In 1893 the Storthing reduced the budget for the king and crown prince after the king had vetoed a bill removing the union sign from the Norwegian flag. The Riksdag doubled the Swedish war budget, and the minister of foreign affairs was replaced by a minister not friendly to Norway. In 1895 the Norwegian parties commenced to adopt similar policies as to foreign affairs, and the Storthing by a vote of 90 to 24 adopted a motion favoring negotiations with Sweden. The ministry appointed a committee of seven to negotiate with a similar Swedish committee. The cession committee reported to the Storthing in 1898 but both the Norwegian and Swedish groups had split and four plans were presented. In the same year the Storthing passed for the third time a bill for the removal of the union sign from the flag. The king vetoed, but the law was promulgated. From 1898 to 1902 the consular question was not reopened. In 1902 the Swedish minister of foreign affairs proposed a joint committee to investigate separate consular services. The committee thought such services feasible, and in 1903 the two governments reached a preliminary agreement. The Storthing ratified the agreement as did the joint ministry and the king. In 1904 the Storthing passed a bill organizing a Norwegian consular service. The Swedish minister of state delayed his examination of the law, and then demanded that the Swedish minister of foreign affairs be made joint foreign minister and that the Cabinet Council for Foreign Affairs be given the power to dismiss Norwegian consuls. The Norwegian ministers rejected the Swedish demands. A new ministry representing all parties was now formed by Christian Michelsen. Some slight concessions were now offered by Sweden, but

Norway refused to renew negotiations until a separate consular service was established. In May 1905 the Storthing unanimously passed such a bill, to be effective April 1, 1906. Ignoring the advice of the Norwegian members of the joint ministry the king vetoed the bill. On June 7, 1905, the Storthing unanimously dissolved the union.[107] A popular plebiscite resulted in an almost unanimous vote for dissolution. In September the two countries negotiated the dissolution.

By the agreement of dissolution at Carlstad in 1905, no decision was arrived at as to the November 21, 1855 treaty of guaranty by England and France, except that Norway and Sweden should give notice that their partnership in treaty rights and obligations had ended. A neutral belt on each side of the southern boundary was established. There was to be compulsory arbitration of disputes between the two except as to vital interests; and whether a vital interest was involved was made subject to arbitration. A popular plebiscite favored a monarchy, only a fifth of the votes opposing, and Prince Charles of Denmark was chosen king by the Storthing.

On November 2, 1907, a declaration was made in Oslo by the Norwegian Foreign Minister and the French and English ambassadors abrogating the November 21, 1855 agreement as to those three governments. On the same day a treaty guaranteeing the integrity of Norway was signed in Oslo on behalf of Norway, Germany, Great Britain, France, and Russia. It displaced the 1855 treaty. This treaty has been said to be one of integrity rather than of neutrality, as Norway wished to maintain her freedom of action.[108] The treaty was to run for ten years. From 1905 to 1914 relations between Norway and Sweden were somewhat suspicious because of the events leading up to the dissolution of the union. In 1909 a tribunal of the Permanent Court of Arbitration delimited the boundaries between Norway and Sweden, including water boundaries.[109] Relations with Denmark, which had long sympathized with Norway, were good.

Norway remained neutral during World War I.[110] In August 1914 the governments of Norway and Sweden agreed that under no circumstances would the two countries fight each other. Denmark soon joined in this policy. Before the end of the war the Norwegian Society for a League of Nations was founded which in 1919 drew up a list of principles regarded as the most democratic and adequate of any formulated. On March 4, 1920, the Storthing voted 100 to 20 in favor of joining the League of Nations.[111] Almost the only opposition to the League came from the Labor party, which changed its position in 1934 shortly before coming into power. Norway's first delegate was Fridtjof Nansen. F. P. Walters, Deputy Secretary-General of the League of Nations, in his recent *History of the League of Nations* refers to Nansen as "the noblest citizen of post-war Europe."

Among other leading Norwegian delegates to the League were John L. Mowinckel, a Norwegian prime minister; Christian Lange who was for 22 years general secretary of the Interparliamentary Union; Kristine Bonnevie, who served on the Committee of Intellectual Cooperation; and Carl J. Hambro, who as president of the Assembly, presided at the closing session of the League. Norway supported the Permanent Court of International Justice and accepted its compulsory jurisdiction.[112] At the general election of 1921 F. W. N. Beichmann of Norway was elected a deputy judge of the Permanent Court. Born in 1859 he had been a judge and president of the Court of Appeal at Trondheim, and had played a prominent part in international conferences on the unification of law and in various international arbitrations.[113] He served from 1922 to 1930 and was present at as many sessions as some of the judges.

Norway was represented at the Peace Conference by Wedel Jarlsberg. Through his efforts Norway won recognition of her sovereignty over Spitzbergen by a treaty of February 9, 1920.[114] Soviet Russia recognized Norway's sovereignty in 1924 and formally adhered to the treaty in 1933. Norway took formal possession on August 14, 1925. In 1927 she occupied Bouvet Island and in 1929 Jan Mayen Island in the Arctic. Jan Mayen was incorporated into the kingdom. Bouvet and Peter I's Islands were declared dependencies. In addition, Norway claimed part of the Antarctic continent. In 1933 the Permanent Court of International Justice confirmed Denmark's sovereignty over all of Greenland after a dispute of a decade.[115]

Norway, like Denmark and Sweden, sought to improve the League of Nations. The Covenant was silent as to measures for conciliation. Membership in the League was not universal. The Council had too much power and the Assembly too little. Arbitration and disarmament were still in the future. The great powers exercised too much influence. The use of sanctions might involve the small states in war. Norway was particularly critical of political Scandinavianism, and no meeting of the Scandinavian states was held from 1920 until 1932. Foreign policy was largely within the framework of the League of Nations. In 1924 Norway concluded bilateral agreements with Denmark, Finland, and Sweden, establishing permanent conciliation commissions for all disputes not coming under the Permanent Court. In 1925-1926 Norway provided by treaties for the peaceful settlement of any dispute that might arise with the other Scandinavian states. All political disputes that had not been solved by conciliation were to be referred to a specially created tribunal. Norway ceased to support the use of economic sanctions by the League when the Assembly abolished sanctions against Italy in its dispute with Ethiopia. Absolute neutrality now became Norway's policy.

In 1939 Norway rejected Hitler's offer of a nonaggression pact after President Roosevelt had asked Hitler what his intentions towards Norway were. The judgment of the Nuremberg tribunal reveals that Raeder and Rosenberg began to plot the invasion of Norway as early as October 3, 1939.[116] When Russia attacked Finland in November 1939, Norway like Denmark declared neutrality. Norway declined a request from England and France for permission to send troops across Norway to Finland. In April 1940 Germany invaded Norway and occupied it for five years. Norway held out for 63 days, a longer period than that of any other continental states. Poland had lasted 29 days, France 39, Belgium 19, and Holland 4. Norway maintained an exile government in London, and was thus, unlike Denmark, able to conduct a foreign policy during the war.

Two incidents involving important issues of international law occurred before Norway was invaded. In the *City of Flint* case Norway followed the rule of international law that a captor of a neutral prize may not take the vessel into the port of another neutral state and there sequestrate it pending the decision of a prize court.[117] In the *Altmark* case there was involved the right of innocent passage of belligerent vessels through neutral territorial waters.[118]

In 1944 Russia approached Norway about a revision of the Spitzbergen treaty.[119] Russia wished an arrangement for joint Norwegian-Russian defenses. In April 1945 the Norwegian government stated that it was prepared to sign a preliminary joint declaration expressing its willingness to negotiate about military use of the islands. But a declaration was never signed. When the Russians again sought action in 1947 the Norwegian government took the position that the approval of all the signatories of the 1920 treaty was necessary. During the war Quisling laid claim to Greenland. After the war a supplementary clause was inserted in the East Greenland Treaty stipulating that in spite of Danish sovereignty over Greenland, Danish decisions about Greenland were to be preceded by consultations with Norway.[120]

On November 14, 1945, the Storthing unanimously ratified the Charter of the United Nations. On February 2, 1946, Trygve Lie of Norway took the oath of office as the first Secretary-General of the United Nations. Norway is a party to the Statute of the International Court of Justice, and has accepted its compulsory jurisdiction. Helge Klaestad of Norway was elected to the new court for a term to end in 1952, and was then re-elected for a nine-year term. Born in 1885 Judge Klaestad served as president of the Anglo-German Mixed Arbitral Tribunal from 1925 to

1931 and as a member of the Supreme Court of Norway from 1931 to 1946.[121] Edvard Hambro of Norway is Registrar of the Court.

Like the other Scandinavian states Norway favored strengthening the Assembly of the United Nations and in 1947 voted for the creation of the interim committee known as the "little assembly." Retention of the veto is favored as it is regarded as symptomatic of the political situation rather than the cause of it. After two years of membership on the Economic and Social Council, Norway was elected to the Security Council in 1949. In January 1949 Sweden offered Norway and Denmark a ten-year military alliance. But Norway thought such protection not adequate and proposed that the three powers seek a unilateral United States guarantee, and that if such guarantee was obtained, the three powers should enter into immediate military conversations to make it effective. But the proposal was not acceptable to Sweden. On March 3, 1949, the Storthing voted 110 to 11 to participate in discussions about the Atlantic Pact. Following Norway, Denmark became receptive. On March 29, 1949, the Storthing voted 130 to 13 to adhere to the pact. When the pact was signed in Washington April 4 Norway became an original signatory. In March 1950 Foreign Minister Lange stated that while Norway was interested in the movement for a larger entity in Europe, because of her geographic position and economic interests, she had developed ties with Great Britain and the United States that were stronger than her ties with the Continent.[122] Great Britain should be included in the cooperation. Collaboration with other Scandinavian states is also important.

On December 18, 1951, the International Court of Justice rendered a decision in favor of Norway in the Fisheries Case between Great Britain and Norway. The Court held that the method employed in delimiting the fisheries zone by Norway in 1935 was not contrary to international law and that the actual base lines fixed in application of this method were proper.[123]

The Lagthings *and Lesser* Things

The most ancient Norwegian political unit was the *bygd* or settlement or parish.[124] Some sort of judicial agency was needed to settle disputes. At an unknown time there arose the *thing*, a gathering like the old English moot. The *bydgething* was mainly a political body. Customary law grew out of its actions. Later to protect themselves from robbers several settlements united in forming a district or shire, generally called a *herred* and sometimes a *fylke*. This group also had a *thing*, known as the *herredthing* or *fylkesthing*. At the date Norway became a united kingdom there were about thirty such units in existence. Gradually as local isolation was broken down by war and trade, these units became consolidated into *lags* or "laws" or jurisdictions. Each *lag* had a central *thing*.[125] The word *lag* was used to designate both the law and the district to which the law applied. Three *lagthings* were formed in the ninth century. First came the Eidsivathing, consisting of Hedemark, Romerike and Hadaland, meeting at the south end of Lake Mjösen, not very far north from the present Oslo.[126] Next came the Gulathing consisting of Hordaland, Sogn, and the Fjords, which met at the mouth of the Sognefjord a little north of Bergen.[127] It must have been organized before 930 because at that date it furnished the model for the law of Iceland. About the same time there was organized the Eyrathing for the eight *fylker* surrounding the Trondheim Fjord. It met every June near the mouth of the Nid River close to Trondheim. It resembled the Swedish *landthing* more closely than did the other Norwegian *lagthings*.

The *lagthings* introduced essential changes in the ancient law of custom by making official enactments. Their legislative and judicial functions were delegated to a committee of thirty-six members, chosen from those most influential and learned in the law by the chieftains, known as the *logretta*. The function of legislation and that of adjudication were intimately connected. This is seen in the Case of Sigurd Ranesson[128] in which a question arose as to the proper interpretation of the law as to certain facts. The judicial proceeding was abruptly halted and a legislative debate took place as to what the rule of law ought to be. A law was enacted and the judicial proceeding then resumed.

This was the system which prevailed when Norway became united into a single state. Further development occurred at the instance of the kings, especially the introduction of the principle of representation in the establishment of diets or *diaeter*. This assured the regular convening of the *lagthings* despite the hardships of the long journeys.[129] During the reign of Haakon (934-961) the eight *fylker* of the Trondheim area together with Naumdale, Nordmøre and Romsdal were incorporated into the Frostathinglag, which met near Trondheim.[130] At the same time Rogaland and Agder and still later South Möre were incorporated into the Gulathinglag. Under Olaf (1015-1030) Gudbrandsdal was added to the Eidsivathing, and the Borgarthing was established in Sarpsborg, southeast of Oslo.[131] No more *lags* and *things* were established; though some *fylker* remained unattached, they did not build up legal systems of their own, but copied from their neighbors.

The lawmaking power exercised by the *lagthing* theoretically rested solely in the people. Kings and officials were considered bound by their proceedings. But the people seem not to have been as sovereign in Norway as they were in Sweden.[132] From the moment Norway became a united state the kings took the lead in initiating legislation. That the *lagthing* no longer retained its full powers is shown by the fact that in 1046 an important statute was enacted by a gathering of chiefs; in 1164 a violent change in the law of succession to the throne was made and other laws were revised at a meeting of temporal and religious dignitaries. Similar assemblages were held later but they obtained no independent title or powers. Under the leadership of the kings, they proposed statutes which were subsequently formally enacted by the *lagthings*.

Beginning in the thirteenth century the judging agency at the *lagthing* was the *logretta* consisting of three or more twelves of chosen men.[133] But at the lower levels of the parish and the *fylke* judicial authority still remained in the general populace; however, the lawmen played important roles.

The Lawmen

Among most primitive races the custodian of the law was the priest. But this was not true among the Scandinavians.[134] Knowledge of the law was open to all, including those of humble birth. Persons pre-eminent in their knowledge of the customary law were accorded the title of lawmen. They served as instructors and as practitioners. They were also consulted at the meetings of the *thing*. Thus in effect they acted as judges in litigated cases. They retained this semi-official character in Norway and Iceland for about three centuries after 870.

Until the twelfth century the Norwegian lawmen appeared at the general and local *things* collectively and in rather sizeable groups. They would declare the legal rules applicable to a given case and construe its effects in specific situations. It is not clear whether or not they constituted a class with exclusive privileges.[135] Lawmen are not mentioned in the Gulathing law and the references in the Frostathing law were probably later interpolations.[136] There were also public law-recitals, chiefly as to affairs before the *things*, but no persons specially trained in law were elected for this purpose. Legal administration developed more slowly in Norway than in Sweden until the reign of King Sverri (1177-1202).[137] Certain lawmen were now made royal officials. Their functions now became more definite. The lawman was now recognized as the presiding officer of the provincial assembly. He could act in a judicial capacity at least to a limited extent without regard to the older powers of the *lagthing*. At first there was no fixed number. Each jurisdiction probably had more than one lawman, so that each lawman could serve in his part of the province. In the fourteenth century the old jurisdictions were divided and new *things* were created. From 1632 to 1719 there were nine or ten jurisdictions instead of the historic four. The people were at first reluctant to acknowledge the authority of their lawmen. King Haakon IV (1217-1263) complained that their decisions were not recognized as binding. Although the judicial system was thoroughly reformed between 1250 and 1300 the judgment of the lawman was not made directly self-executory. It is not clear to what extent popular acquiescence was given to the public recitals of law and the judgments rendered in litigated cases by the lawmen. In the Case of Sigurd Ranesson, about 1115, the unanimous declaration of the lawmen in a judicial proceeding was adopted and followed.

The Chancellery and the Council

From the time of the civil wars (1130-1240) it became the custom for a member of the clergy attached to the court to serve as chancellor.[138] In the thirteenth century there developed a chancellery with a number of clerks to attend to documents and correspondence. The chancellor needed a good deal of legal learning, and kept a record of all important governmental events. He was the keeper of the king's seal, and became the king's chief official.

King Haakon the Good (934-961) surrounded himself with a sort of council of wise men.[139] The council developed side by side with the chancellery.[140] Its membership was somewhat shifting, but was composed of aristocrats both clerical and lay. Magnus' Court Law provided that barons were next after duke and jarl to be the king's advisers and could sit on the Council. There were from ten to fifteen barons who were not connected with the local government. When Haakon V abolished the title of baron in 1308, it was largely to make the council a royal rather than an aristocratic institution.[141] Haakon V chose a few prominent men to act as his council. In the early part of the fourteenth century the council grew rapidly in power as it acted as a regency during the minority of the kings.[142] The king was expected to act only with the advice of the council. The Council continued to exist until 1536.

The Early Law Texts

Iceland in 1118 was the first Scandinavian state to adopt a written code. Within a few decades Norway followed her example.[143] The Case of Sigurd Ranesson indicates that in the early part of the twelfth century there was no consultation of any written texts. But in the latter half of the century during the struggles between the kings who desired hereditary succession and the church which desired electoral succession, written laws were invoked by both parties. The church cited the revised law texts, which were asserted to be an agreement between Archbishop Eystein and the king whom he crowned, Magnus Erlingson (1162-1184). The advocates of hereditary succession quoted earlier texts of the traditional law, which must have appeared between 1100 and 1150. An ecclesiastical law-text of the Borgarthing is ascribed to the period between 1140 and 1152; one of the Eidsivathing is ascribed to the period between 1152 and 1162. These had likely been preceded by others. The earliest written texts not confined to ecclesiastical law are the Gulathing and the Frosta- thing Laws.[144] The most satisfactory text of the former that has come down to us dates from about 1150.[145] The Frostathing Law was in exist- ence in 1190 in Trondheim, under the title of *Gragas*,[146] and King Sverri then cited it. It contained what were known as Saint Olaf's Laws. A thirteenth-century manuscript of it, the Codex Resenianus, has come down to us. Between 1164 and 1180 there appeared the "Goldfeather" by Archbishop Eystein covering the laws of the church. The text of the *Bjarkö-ret*, covering borough and mercantile law, goes back to the thir- teenth century.

These written collections of laws were regarded as law-texts or *retsböker*, lacking the official authority of the more modern codes. The ecclesiastical regulations in the Borgarthing Law conclude: "The law of the church is now written and presented such as we remember it; wherein it be lacking, let the bishop amend therein." In fact, even in revising and amending the early manuscripts in later periods, the characteristics of mere textbooks were retained. For example, Chapter 314 of the revised Gulathing Law provides: "We have now written down the laws govern- ing the coast defense but we do not know whether the statement is right or wrong. But even though it be wrong, we shall keep the legal arrange- ments as to the levy that we had of old and which Atli recited before the men at Gula."[147] This is an express admission that the written text was not perfect. Moreover, it should be noted that the conflicting law- texts were not viewed or referred to as official authorities at the national assembly in 1223 in Bergen when the lawmen were consulted as to the proper construction of Saint Olaf's Law as to the succession to the throne. But gradually the revised texts were treated as authoritative. As of 1244 the ecclesiastical provisions of the Frostathing Law seem to have been enacted as law in the strict sense.

The National Codes

By the middle of the thirteenth century there had developed a strong hereditary monarchy. The king implicitly believed that he exercised divine authority. One of the most significant and beneficial results was the legal reform occurring during the reign of Magnus Lawmender (1263-1280).[148] The reform was the adoption of a common code for the entire state. Haakon the Old (1217-1263), after the end of the wars over the throne, had undertaken to revise the existing system. In 1240 he made an agreement with the archbishop to introduce an ecclesiastical code for the entire kingdom. His plans were carried out by his son, whose name is a recognition of his contribution. The desirability of a uniform law instead of the laws of the four *lags* had long been realized. The new ecclesiastical laws of the Gulathing and the Borgarthing were referred to as the "Church Law of King Magnus." The movement to secure uniformity as to church law must have been accompanied by a movement to secure elimination of conflicts in other fields. The king would not have to face obstruction from the church as to the temporal fields. During 1267 and 1268 Magnus promulgated codes, of which the portions covering temporal matters have not been preserved. The principal work of common codification seems to have been done in these years. Subsequently they were completed and put into actual operation throughout Norway. The subjects covered by the first consolidation probably were personal security, descent, and barter and sale. But the allodium and land-title laws of the *lags* were not included. It seems probable that we still possess the temporal law of the Gulathing book of 1267 by way of the code enacted in Iceland, known as *Jarnsida* or "Ironside." The latter contains provisions obviously intended for Norway with such changes as were thought necessary for Iceland.

The "Ironside" is unique in the history of law reform in that it contains no church law in the earlier sense of that term. Under the title of "An Act in Regard to Christianity" it contains only a series of general provisions concerning civil matters. Ecclesiastical regulations were also excluded from the Land and Village Law. The church was unwilling to acknowledge the propriety of including the Law of God among the general statutes which were to have authority through traditional popular acquiescence. In 1269 when the Frostathing authorized the king to revise its code, as he had done for the Gulathing, his authority was limited "to revise the Book of the Frostathing, as he deemed best, in all matters concerning the temporal law and the government of the king." This restriction is ascribed to Archbishop Jon Raude, who subsequently undertook to draft a law of the church, his purpose being to establish the independent power of the church to make its rules. But the king ultimately retained in this work the same provisions as had been included in the codes of 1267 and 1268, that is to say, provisions relating to civil affairs, even though based on religious principles. The "Ironside" is the first instance in which this alternative was adopted. Later on the king was reluctant to yield to the demands of the church, and insisted on dealing with several questions of a religious character.

The Frostathing Law was completed in 1274. In his introduction the king announced that this law surpassed the laws of the other localities both as to substance and clarity. It provided for the constitutional hereditary succession of the throne as agreed upon in 1260: legitimate birth, primogeniture, and single kingship. The blood-feud and the principle of collecting damages for homicide from others than the killer and of distributing them among others than the nearest heir of the victim were abolished. Daughters might inherit, although only half as much as sons. In 1271 and 1273 two councils of the kingdom at Bergen adopted these and other rules, for formal ratification by the *lagthings*. This procedure made necessary a revision of the king's earlier codes. The Frostathing Law had incorporated rules for the allodium and tenantry of land for the entire kingdom. But in form, the earlier system was maintained, in that each of the four *lagthings* preserved its individual laws, the statutes being respectively known as the Laws of the Gulathing, Frostathing, Eidsivathing, and the Borgarthing. It was the king's aim to make the Frostathing Law "a law book which would go over all Norway." The Gulathing adopted it in 1275 and the Eidsivathing and Borgarthing in 1276. The king himself journeyed to the *things* to procure ratification. In 1277 a new code of municipal laws was published. In the same year the *lendermaend* were given the foreign title of barons and a new nobility was developed under Magnus' Court Law or *Hirdskraa*.[149]

Authentic details as to the work of preparing this national code are lacking. It seems not unlikely that the drafters were Audun Hugleiksson[150] of Hegranes, the king's Marshal, executed in 1302, and the Chancellor Thore Haakonson of Smaalenene. Both were made barons after the preparation of the codes. The former was called the "wisest man in the land-law," and the latter "well versed in the ecclesiastical law."

The National Code of Magnus Lawmender is largely a consolidation of the laws of the Frostathing and the Gulathing with provisions concerning land tenure taken from the laws of the other two *lagthings*. A considerable number of changes were made in the former law by incorporating resolutions of the councils of the kingdom. There were also added a series of principles of a theological character and statements as to the purposes of the law. The chief aim was to harmonize its details with the basic legal principles of Norway. Like the old laws it contained ten parts. First were the rules of procedure for the *thing* or *thingfarerbolken*. Then came such regulations of the church as were preserved from the earlier church law. Next was the *Mandhelgebolk* covering crimes against the person; the *Arvebolken* or the law of inheritance; the law of land tenure, allodium, and tenantry; the law merchant; the law of theft; and last of all the proclamations of Haakon and Magnus for establishing and extending the authority of the code. The text of the

Code is unlike that of the earlier law-texts which adopted the concise oral form of expression. It is like the Latin court style of the Middle Ages, containing much superfluous verbiage. "Its great merit is that, in a period when over all Christendom there was a general separation and localizing of laws, Norway was able to introduce an almost complete and common system, which embraced its colonies and operated through a well-combined series of institutions and legal principles."[151] The Code though much amended constituted the formal basic law for four centuries. Thus it probably corresponded with the needs of the people. While the Land Law of Magnus contains deficiencies in contents, order, and phraseology, much the same defects appear in similar codes of a later period in other nations. Moreover, the Land Law was very speedily drafted. In 1319 the Norwegians "were presumably the best situated nation in Europe with respect to legal organization and obedience to law."[152] When in 1340-1350 Magnus Eriksson, king of Norway and Sweden, proceeded to codify Swedish law, "his immediate motive was undoubtedly the great difference between the orderly and uniform conditions obtaining in Norway and the insecurity and lawlessness in Sweden."[153]

In the reign of Christian III (1536-1559) the Norwegian codes were translated into Danish, and many Danes served as judges.[154] It became customary to appeal from the *lagthings* to the king, who with his council acted as an appellate court. Members of the council were sent to Norway to hold court with the royal *lensherrer* and lawmen in order to hear complaints against *lensherrer* or lords and *fogeder* or sheriffs. This undermined Norwegian law. Lawmaking was confined to issuance of charters and granting of trade privileges to the Hanseatic merchants. The Danish judges were often ignorant of both substantive and procedural law. Interest in the older law diminished.

During the reign of Christian IV (1588-1648) the old codes were no longer understood by the lawmen and the officials. There had never been a revision of the Code of Magnus Lawmender. Many new laws had been passed without being incorporated into the Code. In 1602 Christian ordered the Norwegian lawmen to prepare a new code to be printed and put in use for Norway.[155] The new code, known as the Code of Christian IV, was submitted to the king in 1604. After he had caused it to be read before an assembly of nobles and lawmen in Bergen, it was formally authorized and printed. It was largely a translation of the laws of Magnus. It was also introduced into the Faroe Islands, but not into Iceland. The church laws were not embodied in the Code, but the king had a new church ordinance prepared, which was proclaimed at a council in Stavanger.

The Code of Christian IV was not long satisfactory. Hannibal Sehested, *statholder* in 1642, and Jens Bjelke, chancellor in 1648, considered the preparation of a new code. Ulrik Gyldenløve, *statholder* in 1664 and a natural son of the king, urged revision of the Code. After an absolute monarchy was set up for Denmark and Norway in 1661, Gyldenløve received in 1666 a general command from the king to the lawmen for revision of the Norwegian law.[156] No progress was made until the 1680 draft of the new Danish code appeared. The Danish commission, together with some Norwegian lawmen, was then directed to do the work. On March 2, 1682, a new order was issued to a commission of Norwegians to secure uniformity in the laws of the two kingdoms so far as possible. Christian Stockfleth, the Norwegian chancellor, later envoy to Sweden and a member of the Supreme Court (died in 1704), and the leading Norwegian judge, submitted a draft the same year.[157] His draft was a worthy one, but it departed from the new Danish Code more than had been contemplated. Not only did it eliminate provisions unsuitable for Norway, but it sought to revise the Danish law. Hence on January 23, 1683, a new drafting body was commissioned, consisting entirely of Danes, including the chief author of the Danish Code, Rasmus Vinding. In substance they restored the original provisions irrespective of their suitability for Norway. But they admitted their unfamiliarity with conditions peculiar to Norway, and a commission of Norwegians was convened at Oslo on October 11, 1684, to revise the draft contemporaneously. By a harmonization of these various drafts the codification was completed in July 1687. King Christian V's Norwegian Law was then on April 16, 1688 proclaimed as the law of Norway to go into effect on September 29, 1688. It was printed in Copenhagen by Caspar Schöller and a handwritten copy is preserved in the library of the University of Oslo. It differs from the Danish Code principally as to courts and rural matters. In Denmark the royal appointee or *foged* served both as executive and judge. In Norway these offices were separated. Corresponding to the Danish *land* judge, Norway retained the lawman. In towns the lowest judge was the *byfoged*. From him an appeal lay to the councillor (*raad*) or burgomaster, and then to the lawman or *lagthing*.[158] From the latter appeal lay to an intermediate appellate court or *overhofret*.[159] In turn appeal lay to the Supreme Court or *Høiesteret*, thus making four appeals possible.

The intent of the Code was to supersede the prior legislation, either abolishing it or absorbing it.[160] The preamble declared "all former laws, ordinances and rules, as far as the same are not herein included" to be repealed. But the Code omitted a mass of social and political provisions, impliedly referring these to the special laws in force. The Code declared to be beyond its scope "laws which by reason of altering circumstances of the times will have to be changed." To this class was thought to belong special ordinances as to trades, commerce, forestry, harbors, weights and measures, the post, and the practice of medicine, and the special privileges of persons, corporations, and communities. Also excluded were military affairs, the revenue system, and the State administration. A considerable number of ecclesiastical regulations were preserved in the Code. The adoption of the Code was immediately followed by a mass of new regulations issued by the king who had absolute power. The Code was put into effect in the Faroe Islands in 1688, but only a part of it was adopted for Iceland.

Customary Law

Norwegian law is different from that of the major European states in that it is not codified. It is different from that of England and the United States in that it has no fully developed case-law. Custom has been and still is a major source of Norwegian law.[161] The Code of 1688 repealed most of the earlier law and is the basis of Norwegian statutory law today. Subsequent important changes in Norwegian law up to 1884 occurred more by custom and case-law than by legislation. Even in the nineteenth century the views of the historical school prevailed and only a few statutes in the field of private law were enacted. But since 1884, when the Liberal party came into power, the amount of legislation has increased constantly and rapidly. Much of such legislation was social legislation, and did not involve private law. But the adoption of uniform Scandinavian statutes has resulted in a large mass of legislation in the field of private law.

The situation at present is as follows. The Norwegian statute book, *Norges lover 1682-1948*, published in 1950 is chronological in order and not systematic, and starts with the Code of 1688. But much of the 1688 Code has been repealed and most of the remaining parts cover minor matters. Of the statutes and ordinances between 1688 and 1814 almost nothing remains in force. Beginning in 1814 there was a slowly increasing number of fragmentary codifications and other statutes. Since 1880 the number of statutes has grown rapidly as have uniform Scandinavian laws. But codification is far from complete. Customary law has had a great influence on judicial procedure, constitutional law, and private law. It still plays an important role as to torts, transport by land, unincorporated associations, agriculture, and registration of land. In the customary law are to be found the rules of statutory interpretation and the rules as to the application of judicial precedents. It is thus at the basis of the Norwegian legal system.

The earliest law of Norway was customary law.[162] The introduction of written statutory law largely displaced such law. Nevertheless, it continued to occupy an important place in the law. The Norwegian Code occasionally referred to such customary law. Later legislation recognized it as being in force. In Norway, more than in Denmark and Sweden, the tendency "is to assign it an important place both in theory and in practice."[163] Today its chief domain is that of business and occupations. It operates in the form of customs of merchants and local usages which are implied in contracts. The jurists of the eighteenth century ascribed its authority to the approval, express or implied, of the legislator. The fact that statutes have replaced much of the early law is not a justification for denying to the other original sources their character of rules directly effective. The makers of the early codes had an exaggerated belief that all details could be covered by statutes. Later writers agree in attributing to the customary law the character of a supplementary source for legal decisions.

A great advantage of customary law is that it is flexible and capable of growth. It involves a continuous process. No legislative body is required. Changes in the law are made gradually. At the same time it has some disadvantages. It is not laid down by an impartial outsider, but is developed from the activities of those to whom it applies. It may develop too slowly. A custom may become obsolete. It is less stable and definite than precedent and statute. Sweeping social reforms can be attained only by legislation. But Norwegian jurists and lawyers prefer customary law at least in the field of private law.

When is a principle recognized as customary law? Professor Knoph concludes that there must be a firm custom and usage which has been practiced over a long period in the belief that one is legally bound to follow it.[164] Thus Norwegian customary law is like Continental customary law. A custom need not be just or rational any more than a statute. Customs are usages. The most important usages are those of merchants, but there are also usages of artisans, farmers, seamen, lawyers, fishermen and others.

There has been some uncertainty as to conflicts between an old statute and a later rule of custom. One writer has concluded that in "Norwegian judicial law the dominant view is that such a custom is contrary to law."[165] Yet it is an historical fact that considerable parts of the Norwegian codes have been amended by customary law. In practice customary law has even amended the Constitution. Norwegian courts pass on constitutionality of statutes though the Constitution does not expressly so provide. Parliamentary government was introduced in 1884 solely by custom as the language of the 1814 Constitution seems contrary.

A leading Norwegian writer has concluded as of 1890 that the "mere lack of observance in practice of a statute ('desuetudo') is under no circumstances a ground for rejecting its validity."[166] At the same time he points out that the answer is to some extent dependent upon the relative importance of the intent of the legislator and the actual conditions which prevail in the legal system. For example, there are several old Norwegian laws never formally repealed which would no longer be regarded as in effect.[167]

While Norwegian law admits the doctrine of desuetude, it has been said that "it is in most respects more like our own system than like the continental systems."[168] Although the criteria for a custom that will prevail against a statute are the same as those used in Roman law, the principle is accepted that a statute can be in desuetude as to some applications, and not as to others. For example, a 1735 statute forbade all private gatherings and public entertainments on Sundays. In 1915 the proprietor of an international exposition kept his amusement concessions open on Whitsunday, and was fined. The court held that while the prohibition of private gatherings had become obsolete because of the universal practice of the people and while the licensing of public entertainments under municipal regulation had displaced the ban on public entertainments, it was nevertheless still unusual to hold such entertainments on the major church holidays, so that the fine was proper.[169]

Norwegian law being largely customary is very elastic. The distinction between written law and unwritten law is vague. Statutes may be abrogated or altered by custom. The distinction between legal and non-legal customs is not easy to ascertain, there being no fixed rule as to age or universality. The authority of judicial precedents and legal theory is in conflict. But reasonable stability does exist. Custom does not often alter the law. Statutes are not often seriously altered by custom. Change by custom is at a very slow pace. The Norwegians are satisfied with less stability than the English system involves. Resort to customary law together with the frequent use of lay judges must make for highly individualized justice in Norway.

Case Law

The orthodox theory as to sources of law in Norway is that there are only two: customs and legislation.[170] But judicial precedents and legal writings are said to contribute to the rise of customary law, though they are not as in France a prerequisite to its growth. The Norwegian Supreme Court is not bound to follow its own precedents though of course it usually follows them.[171] Even a lower court may ignore a Supreme Court precedent, and is most likely to do so when it thinks that the precedent will be overruled by the Supreme Court. No official reports of judgments are printed in Norway. Since 1836 the bar association has published the leading Supreme Court decisions, setting forth the conclusions and votes of all the judges. Because of the steady increase in the number of decisions the law reports for each year now constitutes a volume of about 1,500 pages. Lower court decisions have to some extent been reported for several years in "Rettens Gang," the publication of which was taken over by the bar association on July 1, 1949. The reports are frequently cited by both the bench and the bar. Judicial precedents have played important roles in developing the law of judicial procedure and the law of surnames. The statute of 1923 codified the judge-made law as to surnames.

The weight given to precedents in Norway has changed from time to time. In 1273 King Magnus Lawmender ordered that important decisions be written down, partly with a thought to future similar cases. An ordinance of 1308 prescribed that the judgments of the lawmen be written "lest the judgments and decisions be forgotten." But these reforms were soon overlooked. Following the union with Denmark in 1380 the judges engaged in a wholesale reception of Danish law. A prohibition against the citation of precedents by lawyers was in effect from 1690 to 1771. By 1700 a firm practice, even though believed to be incorrect, was followed. By 1800 the Supreme Court seldom overruled its own precedents.

Following the separation from Denmark the Norwegian Supreme Court at first felt free to overrule its own decisions. By 1850 several Supreme Court judges were attracted to the English approach. But by 1900 the Court again became skeptical as to the absolutely binding effect of precedents. In 1902 the Court expressly overruled one of its own decisions. As of 1938 a Norwegian writer felt that the "authority of precedents has been declining."[172] This was thought to be due to the increasing number of cases and the sitting of the court in two divisions. But by a statute of 1926 if three or more judges of a division think that a case must be decided so as to conflict with a prior Supreme Court decision, the whole Court must then sit. But this procedure has been seldom used.

Less weight is given to a precedent thought not to be just. Less weight is also given when the court was closely divided or when the full court did not sit. Single precedents carry less weight than a line of decisions. A very old precedent carries less weight. Yet a recent precedent carries less weight than one several years old as there has been no long reliance on it. The chief factor in behalf of a precedent is popular reliance as the emergence of customary law is then involved. This is especially true as to the law of contracts, but less true as to gifts, wills, torts and criminal law. But where a criminal law precedent has *favored* an accused, the courts are likely to follow it. No sharp distinction is drawn between *obiter dicta* and the *ratio decidendi*.

Legal Writings As a Source of Law

Another source of law or of customary law is the writings of the jurists.[173] But legal theory is not as authoritative as judicial precedents. Nevertheless, since the code is incomplete and the case law largely undeveloped, practitioners make extensive use of textbooks. Counsel in law suits often obtain *responsa* from the most learned jurists, especially from the professors at the University of Oslo. A Danish law professor has pointed out that "one of the peculiarities which the Scandinavian countries—Norway and Denmark in particular—share with Germany is that the *Theory of Law* has played so great a role in making and developing our law. This work does not confine itself, as do many British and American textbooks, to giving merely a well-arranged, systematic array of precedents and the legal conclusions appertaining thereto, but in many cases adds quite exhaustive advice upon the line to be taken in cases where positive legislation fails. These scientific rulings have often formed the basic foundation of subsequent codifications."[174]

The Constitution

Article 1 of the Constitution provides that the "form of government is a limited and hereditary monarchy."[175] Under Article 49 legislative power is exercised "through the Storthing, which consists of two divisions, a Lagthing and an Odelsthing." Under Articles 50, 54, 57, and 58 the 150 members of the Storthing are elected directly by universal suffrage, specified numbers for each *fylke* and town, for a period of four years. Two-thirds of the representatives are to come from the country and one-third from the towns. At the first ordinary meeting of the Storthing after an election, it selects one-fourth of its members to form the Lagthing and the others to form the Odelsthing.

Under Article 3 the "Executive power is vested in the king." Under Article 6 the crown is hereditary in the male line. Under Articles 5 and 12 provision is made for a council of state of at least eight members whose ministers are responsible. Under Articles 62 and 74 the ministers may not attend the Storthing as representatives as long as they are members of the council, but may take part in the proceedings without a right to vote. Under Article 88 provision is made for a Supreme Court to consist of a president and at least four other members. Under Article 83 the Storthing may demand its opinion on questions of law.

Under Article 96: "No one may be convicted except according to law, or be punished except according to judicial sentence. Examination by torture must not take place." Article 99 provides: "No one may be arrested and committed to prison except in the cases determined by law and in the manner prescribed by the laws." Article 97 provides: "No law may be given retroactive effect." Freedom of speech and of the press is provided for in Article 100: "There shall be liberty of the press. No person may be punished for any writing, whatever its contents may be, which he has caused to be printed or published, unless he wilfully and manifestly has either himself shown or incited others to disobedience to the laws, contempt of religion or morality or the constitutional authorities, or resistance to their orders, or has advanced false and defamatory accusations against any other person. Everyone shall be free to speak his mind freely on the administration of the State or on any other subject whatsoever." Under Article 102 domiciliary visitations may not be made except in criminal cases. Article 104 abolishes forfeiture of land and goods. Under Article 105 there may be no expropriation without compensation. Article 108 provides: "No earldoms, baronies, majorats, or perpetuities may be created in the future." Article 2 provides: "The Evangelical-Lutheran religion shall remain the public religion of the State. The inhabitants professing it shall be bound to bring up their children in the same. Jesuits shall not be tolerated."

Provision is made in Article 112, the last article in the Constitution, for amendments thereof. A proposed amendment must be submitted to the first or second ordinary Storthing after a new election, and be published in print. But only the first or second ordinary Storthing after the next election following shall have power to decide whether the proposed amendment be adopted. Two-thirds of the Storthing must agree to the alteration. A limitation on the substantive content of the amendment is expressly provided. It "must never be inconsistent with the principles of this Constitution, but must only bear on such modifications of particular provisions as do not change the spirit of this Constitution."[176] When an amendment has been thus adopted it shall be signed by the President and Secretary of the Storthing and sent to the king for public notification in print. An amendment does not require the approval of the king.

The Storthing

General councils, other than the small royal councils, were assembled at various times to settle important questions of general interest. The scope of the power of the *herrèmøte* was not defined.[177] It is not known who were regarded as constituent members. Apparently they were assembled in an advisory capacity. But the advice was given very great weight, and the king would scarcely venture to oppose the council which acted on behalf of the whole people. Its consent was necessary to alter the written laws of the kingdom. Hence when in 1273 a change in the law of royal succession was proposed by the king its consent was required. It was regarded as settled that the king could promulgate no measure which the council refused to sanction. Out of these meetings a parliament might have developed as in other countries. But it never became an established regular institution in Norway. In 1344 when the Norwegians gave their allegiance to Haakon VI representatives of the cities and rural districts appeared as separate classes with the nobles and bishops.[178] This seemed like an incipient estates-general of four estates. The first complete estates-general truly national in scope met in Oslo in 1591 when the Norwegians gave allegiance to Christian IV.[179] Because Christian IV needed money he called the estates together. But the estates failed to present a united front, and the meetings strengthened the royal rather than the popular power. In 1661 the estates accepted the absolute power of the king, and were never again convened.[180]

The Storthing dates from the adoption of the Constitution in 1814.[181] Article 49 provides: "The people exercise legislative power through the Storthing, which consists of two divisions, a Lagthing and an Odelsthing." Legislation is its most important function. The introduction of the parliamentary system in 1884 of course modified the methods of legislation. Through its power to grant money under Article 75 the Storthing can intervene directly in other matters. It has the most authority of any branch of the government.

Under the original constitution the size of the Storthing depended upon the number of persons entitled to vote. In 1859 the Constitution fixed the number at 111. In 1919 an amendment fixed the present number of 150. Article 57, paragraph 2, of the Norwegian Constitution provides: "The number of representatives of the country districts and the number of representatives of the towns shall always be in the proportion of two to one." This provision is unduly favorable to the rural areas. After the election of 1949 Prime Minister Einar Gerhardson promised to take up the matter of reform at the first opportunity. The national executive committee of the Labor party has recently come forth with a permanent and satisfactory solution.[182] The Constitutional provision would be repealed. The nation would be divided into twenty, and eventually twenty-two, election districts in which the cities vote together with the rural areas in the *fylker* in which they are located. As a result of the new proposals the Labor party would lose six of its seats. Under the present Article 58 there are eleven urban constituencies, each electing from three to seven members. Each of the eighteen *fylker* constitutes an election district, each electing from three to eight members. The cities and towns are not included in such districts. In 1919 a system of proportional representation was introduced. The mandates in the various constituencies are allotted on the basis of the d'Hont system. The statutes provide for party nominating conventions in each election district to select candidates. The law thus makes the political parties the basis of the whole election system. The election is based on lists of candidates, which must be handed in to the district election control committee in advance and be accepted by it. The election to the Storthing only decides how many from each list are to be elected. Alternates are elected.

Originally only three groups could vote: government officials and employees, farmers, and those who were citizens by virtue of practicing some trade or craft in a town. Universal male suffrage was introduced in 1898; and women suffrage in 1913. Originally the voter under Article 50 had to be 25 years old. In 1920 this was reduced to 23 and in 1946 to 21. The voter must have lived in Norway for five years and be living there. Norway has the most liberal Scandinavian law permitting absent voting.

Under an amendment of 1938 to Article 54 the electoral period is four years. Prior thereto the period had been three years. The last election was held in 1949. The king has no power to dissolve the Storthing before the conclusion of the electoral period. Prior to 1948 a member had to be thirty years old. Under the present Article 61 he may be 21 years and must have resided in the country for ten years and must be entitled to vote in his constituency. But a member of the ministry or a past member thereof may be elected even though he is not entitled to vote in the constituency.

Since 1884 cabinet ministers have had the right under Article 62 to sit in the Storthing and take part in debates, but without the right to vote. Their alternates take their places. They may be excluded from secret sessions, though this rarely occurs. The members of the ministry need not have been members of the Storthing though the prime minister always has been. Under Article 65 members of the Storthing are entitled to traveling expenses and medical expenses and to a salary fixed by law. From January 1, 1948, the law provides that he receive 11,000 kroner per session, plus 60 kroner a day for attendance exceeding six months. Under Article 66 members of the Storthing are not subject to arrest "unless caught in public crimes." They are not responsible outside the Storthing for opinions they express in the Storthing.

Prior to 1870 the Storthing met only once every three years and then only for a month. Under Article 68 they now meet annually on the first weekday after January 10. Before the War sessions usually lasted for six months. Now they last the entire year with two months for summer holidays. Under Article 69 the king may summon extra sessions.

The Storthing is elected as a whole. Under Article 73 when it has been constituted, one-fourth of its members are chosen by the Storthing to serve in the Lagthing while the others constitute the Odelsthing. This partition lasts throughout the electoral period.

Most of the powers and functions of the Storthing are set forth in Article 75. Only the Storthing can grant citizenship. Agreements with foreign powers are not binding without the sanction of the Storthing. It controls finances and state loans require its consent. Its sanction is necessary as to various military matters. It may summon any citizen to appear for questioning in matters of national concern. Under Article 48 it chooses a new king if the male line of the royal family has become extinct and no successor to the throne has been elected.

Under the practice in force only formal laws, that is to say, laws which determine the legal position of the private citizen in relation to his fellow citizens or to the state, are dealt with in the two divisions. The Odelsthing also exercises constitutional control and prosecuting authority at the instigation of the Protocol Committee. Apart from the specific functions that fall to the two divisions, all resolutions are passed as measures by the Storthing in plenary session and are not given the form of law. This is true as to constitutional amendments, budget and financial matters, questions of organization and political questions. Of these functions the most important are appropriating and taxing. Resolutions as to taxes, budgets, customs and duties are valid for only one year. Any person may submit applications and suggestions to the Storthing. A bill involving formal law must be framed in legal form and introduced in the Odelsthing by a member of the Odelsthing or of the cabinet. Normally bills and budget proposals are submitted by the government in the form of a government sponsored bill. Private bills must be submitted before the end of February and government bills before the end of March.

Under the rules of procedure the president and vice-president of the entire Storthing and of its two sections constitute the Council of Presidents.[183] The president of the entire Storthing serves as chairman of this six-person group. After a certain date no bill, including even government bills, may be introduced if the council unanimously opposes. There is also something like a steering committee made up of this council and the chairman of the fifteen standing committees. A group of five auditors is chosen by the Storthing under Article 75 to examine the accounts of the state at the end of each fiscal year. This is a most effective device to secure legislative supervision over administration.[184]

The members of the Storthing are allotted to fifteen standing committees and may serve on only one such committee at a time. They are selected by an election committee of 37 members chosen by the Storthing on the basis of geographical areas and party strength, and serve for the electoral period. The committee chairmen are chosen by the respective committees for a one-year term. The committees are: Administration, Finance and Customs, Health, Justice, Church and School, Local Affairs, Agriculture, Military Affairs, Post, Marine and Shipping, Forestry and Water Power, Social Affairs, University and Professional Affairs, Foreign Affairs and Constitutional Amendments, and Highways and Railroads. The Committee on Administration deals with appropriations for the ministry and the royal family. The Committee on Local Affairs deals with matters of local government and amendments to the Storthing rules of procedure. In addition the Storthing has a credentials committee, a protocol committee serving as a steering committee, and a committee provided for in Article 75 of the Constitution from the Odelsthing to deal with matters calling for secrecy, such as diplomatic and military affairs. Special committees may be appointed to deal with special matters. Party representation in committees is on a proportional basis. Members of both houses serve on the standing committees. Committees do not necessarily correspond to definite ministries or departments. All important matters receive committee attention. Most of the work of the Storthing and its two divisions is done in committee.

Under Article 84 the meetings of the Storthing are open to the public, and its proceedings are published except where a majority vote decides to the contrary. Members of the Storthing are summoned to its meetings by notices specifying the business of the day posted at least 24 hours in advance. The findings of the committees are printed and distributed to members, but may not be included in the order papers until at least two days after distribution. Under Article 73 at least one-half of the members must be present to constitute a quorum. As to constitutional amendments at least two-thirds of the members must be present. It has become a rule that members must vote.

Article 76 of the Constitution provides: "Every bill shall first be introduced in the Odelsthing, either by one of its own members, or by the government through a member of the council of state. If a bill is passed, it is sent to the Lagthing, which either approves or disapproves it, and in the latter case sends it back with comments appended. These are taken into consideration by the Odelsthing, which either drops the bill or again sends it to the Lagthing, with or without alteration. When a bill from the Odelsthing has twice been laid before the Lagthing and has been a second time rejected by it, the whole Storthing shall meet in a joint sitting, and the bill is then disposed of by a majority of two-thirds of the votes. Between each of these deliberations there shall be an interval of at least three days." In general the Storthing decides its own rules of procedure. In February 1949 a question time each Wednesday from one to two P.M. was instituted.

Legislative procedure in the entire Storthing and in its two divisions is much the same. Bills may be introduced by the government and by private members. Following introduction bills are usually referred to a committee, though the rules of procedure do not require this. The chamber involved may conclude to pass or reject a bill at once unless the president or one-fifth of the members present object. Neither the Constitution nor the rules of procedure require three separate readings. In order that amendments to bills receive proper consideration the rules of procedure require that if the Odelsthing passes a bill with amendments which were not before the committee, the committee shall be heard at the subsequent discussion in the Lagthing. A standing vote is the usual method but a roll call is necessary if the president or one-fifth of the members demand it. A secret ballot is never used except in cases of election of the president.

With respect to the budget the Storthing sits as one body. A special procedure is followed as to this important function of the Storthing. The state budget or "Yellow Book" is submitted to the Storthing supplemented by an oral statement on the budget by the Minister of Finance. The Finance and Customs Committee make their first report on the budget (Stage One). The Storthing discusses this report in the finance debate. The special committees report their findings on the individual items. The Finance and Customs Committee embody these findings in a joint report to the Storthing called the "Gray Book," thus reaching the second stage. The budgets are debated by the Storthing. The Finance and Customs Committee then put their budget proposals before the House for final debate, the third stage. It is only then that it can be said that the budget as a whole, and the budget items which have already been provisionally agreed upon, has been passed. The budget is dealt with almost entirely by one committee, that on Finance and Customs. Norway has gone further in such centralization than Denmark and Sweden.

Under Articles 77-79 the king exercises only a suspensive veto. If a bill has been passed by the Odelsthing and the Lagthing, or by the Storthing, it becomes law without the royal assent, if it is passed in unchanged form by two properly constituted Storthings assembled after two consecutive elections, and with at least two ordinary sessions of the Storthing intervening, and provided no contrary legislation has been passed in the period between the first and last passage of the bill. While the veto power was occasionally exercised during the union with Sweden, since 1905 it has fallen into disuse. The royal assent is not required for constitutional amendments.

Under Article 17 the king, acting through the Cabinet, "may issue and repeal regulations concerning commerce, customs, trade and industry, and police." But such regulations must not conflict with the Constitution or statutes. They operate provisionally until the next Storthing. Norway uses the device less than Denmark though more than Sweden.

Under Article 86 charges of official misconduct against members of the Cabinet, the Supreme Court, and the Storthing for criminal offenses committed in their official capacity may be filed by the Odelsthing. Trial is by the high court of the realm or *Riksretten*, consisting of the Supreme Court together with the Lagthing.

As in Denmark and Sweden, the members of the legislative body are mostly farmers, small businessmen and public officials. There are many newspapermen but few lawyers. Re-election is common. There is virtually no lobbying.

Since 1935 the Labor party has been in power in Norway though it has had a majority rather than a plurality in the Storthing only since 1945.[185] The Norwegian Labor party has long had the reputation of being one of the most radical European socialist parties. "Between 1921 and 1923 it enjoyed the dubious distinction of affiliation with the Comintern, and not until 1927 did it cease to advocate 'dictatorship of the proletariat.' "[186] Yet the party is less dogmatic than the British about nationalization as an end. Since 1945 government regulation rather than ownership has been the order of the day. One causative factor was the much closer collaboration of all Norwegian parties during World War II. Another factor was that long before the War much of the Norwegian economy had been under government ownership. The laws of 1909 had provided for the reversion of the waterfalls. The production of gas and the generation of electric power were long municipal functions. The state owned the railroad, telephone and telegraph systems. Bus lines had been nationalized in part, and coastal shipping closely controlled through government subsidies. Most motion-picture theaters were municipally owned. The most important factor is the belief of Norwegian workers that much social reform is possible without government ownership. There has been no agitation to nationalize the merchant marine, comparable in Norway to steel in Great Britain. The 1945 platform of the Labor party promised merely to investigate the desirability of socializing the banking and insurance systems and to nationalize large forests when in the general interest. The Labor party favors a mixed economy not only because of its practicality and efficiency but also because it is most compatible with civil liberties and democratic principles. While in 1945 the Communists elected eleven members of the Storthing, in 1949 they elected none. The Labor party increased its representation from 76 to 85, out of a total of 150 seats. The Conservatives now hold 23 seats, the Liberals 21, the Agrarians 12, and the Christian People's party eight.

The Courts

Articles 86-91 of the Constitution deal with courts. Only two courts are mentioned: the *Riksretten* or high court of the realm and the *Høiesteretten* or Supreme Court. As seen in connection with the discussion of the Storthing, the former is a court only in a broad sense. It tries impeachments of members of the Cabinet, Supreme Court, and Storthing. It may impose capital punishment. Under Article 20 its sentence is not subject to the pardoning power of the king in Council except that exemption from capital punishment may be granted. The pardoning power extends to all sentences of all other courts.

Article 88 provides: "The Supreme Court of Justice shall pronounce judgment in the last instance. The right to bring an action in the Supreme Court of Justice may, however, be limited as determined by law." Thus there is no constitutional right to appeal in all cases. Under Article 90 its judgments "may not in any case be appealed against." Under Article 91 no one may be appointed to the Court until he reaches 30.

The Constitution of 1814 established the principle of separation of powers, thus paving the way for judicial review. In Norway, unlike Sweden, the king is not the foundation of justice. Since 1818 the courts have had the right and the duty to determine the question whether an administrative act was lawful. The Norwegian judges have attained greater powers than any other Scandinavian judges. In 1827 a Norwegian professor complained that the judges "are considered, God knows why, as the patron saints of the idolized Constitution."[187] With the coming of parliamentary government in the 1880's many Norwegians felt that they needed protection against an "accidental" majority of the Storthing and the Supreme Court began to adjudicate on the principle that it could determine the constitutionality of legislation. Professor Fredrik Stang had doubted the power in 1833. Professor Thorkel H. Aschehoug took a different view half a century later. Since the decade from 1890 to 1900 there is a series of supreme court decisions predicated on the basis that the courts may pass on constitutionality of laws. The Storthing joined in this view when in 1926 it passed a law that the Supreme Court can only decide in full session that a law violates the Constitution. A principle of customary law in constitutional law seems to be involved. But in practice the power is exercised only with great caution.[188] The power developed with the establishment of parliamentary government. As the king could no longer veto, the Supreme Court must keep the Storthing within constitutional bounds. With respect to private law the Supreme Court has to some extent developed new legal principles not based on positive law. Gaps in the law have been filled in by the Court. Best known is the Court's breaking away from the old rule of tort law that liability must always be based on fault. High standards of good faith are required of mortgagees. Abuse of legal rights has been checked. Bona fide purchasers from agents are given full protection against principals. The Court has taken a reserved attitude with respect to social development of the law, preferring to leave this to the Storthing. For example, unlike the Danish Supreme Court, the Norwegian Court has been reluctant to sustain the validity of boycotts in certain cases.

Under the Constitution of 1814 the Court could not sit with less than seven judges. The first court had seven judges. In the decade from 1920 to 1930 it increased to twenty-three, but from 1884 to 1939 not all were named as permanent judges. Later the reduction of cases litigated brought it down to eighteen members in 1940. Mention should be made of another group of non-permanent judges, namely, officials in other positions who were named for a year at a time, and who could sit only when called by the chief justice and their other duties permitted it. From 1818 until 1842 they could be called only because of the sickness or disability of a regular member. Since 1842 they could be called because of congestion of cases. At first few such judges were called but by 1938 the number was considerable. The constitutional basis for this was very dubious and their use not altogether satisfactory.

In 1938 Article 88 of the Constitution reduced the minimum size of the court from seven to five. In 1939 the statute was revised so that five judges might sit as a court. At the same time the possibility of using temporary judges was abolished. Since that time only permanent judges can sit and they are removable only by a judgment of the *Riksretten*. The court sits at Oslo. At present it sits in two divisions of five judges each. If three or more judges think that a case must be decided so as to conflict with a prior Supreme Court determination, or that a statute violates the Constitution then the entire court passes on the issue. The court may do the same as to other questions of a particularly doubtful character.

For more than two generations the Supreme Court could review both the law and the facts in all cases. But when the jury law of 1887 was passed the Court could no longer review the facts in criminal cases. Under the 1915 code of civil procedure appeal to the Supreme Court lay only as to errors of procedure or application of law. But this rule never became the practice. The Supreme Court can review the facts as well as the law as to all cases accepted by the appeals committee consisting of three judges. But the appeals committee may reject the appeal when it finds that it was of great significance that the lower court had opportunities to hear the parties and witnesses, not possible in the Supreme Court. Witnesses may not be heard by the Supreme Court, and the Supreme Court is in no position to make an examination of its own. It is due to Justice Ferdinand Schjelderup that the 1915 law did not come into effect.

The procedure of the court has always envisaged oral argument before the court. The 1818 statute permitted written procedure in certain exceptional cases. Because of congestion this group of cases was expanded in 1891. Such expansion was intended to be temporary but continued for fifty years. Since January 1941 written procedure may be used only when both parties wish it and the appeal concerns only procedure or application of law.

According to the 1818 statute the Supreme Court was to give its votes in secret and to give no reasons for its judgments. The judgments would contain only the conclusions of the court. In 1863 the Storthing required a public voting though the Court had long been opposed. Today all Norwegians agree that the public oral voting and assigning of reasons has done more than anything else to create respect for the court. The natural consequence of the new system should have been official reporters of the decisions. Yet the old system continued long after 1863. The clerks, who were not stenographers, did the best they could to record the decisions in their records, but the reporters were never controlled by the judges and were often ill prepared to undertake the work. The *Norsk Retstidende*, the Norwegian legal publication, to be sure, took stenographic reports of the decisions in matters of legal interest, but it acted in a purely private capacity. It was not until 1929 that the Supreme Court got its own official reporter; the decisions are now taken down by a secretary with stenographic training and are submitted to the judges for correction. From 1836 to 1929 there are available the reports of the *Norsk Retstidende* as to the more important cases.

Judges must be Norwegians and graduates in law of a Norwegian university. Judges in all courts are appointed by the King in Council for a life term.[189] Under Article 22, like other appointed officials they may be retired at the age provided for by law. Seventy is the usual retirement age. Judges of courts other than the Supreme Court must be at least 25 years old. The rules governing the composition, competence and geographical jurisdiction of the courts in civil cases as well as the rules governing court procedure in such cases are laid down in two laws of August 13, 1915.[190] The leading characteristics of the procedure are that it should be oral and that the evidence should be submitted directly to the court which is to deliver judgment.

Since 1795 civil cases must have undergone conciliation before they could be commenced in the regular courts. Conciliation tribunals were set up in the market towns of Norway in 1795 pursuant to a royal edict. A law of 1797 provided for such tribunals in the rural districts. In 1824 the Storthing passed a new conciliation law containing several improvements over the Danish law. Though amended it is still the basic law in effect today.[191] Judges and lawyers may not serve on the commissions. The commissions each had two members elected by popular vote. By an amendment of 1869 dealing with claims not exceeding 500 kroner there were added to the commission's regular duties of mediation certain powers to enter judgments on default and to act as arbitrators in certain cases. The awards of the commissions were made reviewable by the lower courts. An 1880 amendment related to locus in quo cases, primarily boundary and land disputes. The commission could adjourn their hearings to the place involved and seek to conclude a conciliation agreement. If that failed, either party could ask the commission to decide the case by its award.

In practice the commissions dispose of many more cases than they refer to the courts for litigation. Moreover, of the cases which the commissions are obliged to refer to the courts, not more than a third are actually entered in court. Even after the cases are actually in court the judges are enjoined to attempt conciliation when the circumstances seem propitious. As in Denmark conciliation has been more successful in the rural districts. In the cities the hearings of the commissioners are made as short as possible. Judicial mediation has been but little used. It is most frequently used in disputes between employer and employees. It is rarely used in the maritime and commercial courts. A parliamentary committee headed by Bernhard Getz proposed its abolition. But the new judicature act of 1915 increased its authority. The size was increased from two to three members. The members are appointed by the county or town council for four-year terms. The courts may mediate at any stage of a proceeding. Hence lay conciliation and judicial conciliation operate side by side. If mediation fails, the commission may proceed to try the case and enter judgment when the parties so request in real estate disputes involving not more than 1,000 kroner, in personal property cases involving not more than 250 kroner, and in other cases within its jurisdiction if the commission approves. In money claims not exceeding 1,000 kroner the commission can enter judgment if the defendant appears and admits the debt or fails to appear and is defaulted. The Norwegians seem to be as much attached to conciliation as Americans are to the system of trial by jury.[192]

The ordinary courts of first instance in civil cases[193] are district and town courts (*Herredsrettene* and *Byrettene*). In Oslo, Bergen, Trondheim, and Stavanger there is a *byrett*, consisting of a presiding judge and a number of associate judges, varying from twenty in Oslo to two in Stavanger. In about twelve of the other larger cities there is a *byfogd*, who is a combination of constable and notary public. The remainder of Norway is divided into between eighty and ninety districts each of which has a local magistrate or *sorenskriver* paid 15,000 kroner a year. These courts deal with all cases which either cannot be decided by the conciliation tribunals or which have been referred to them from the latter. They also serve as courts of appeal as to decisions by the conciliation tribunals delivered in their judicial capacity. These judges are professional judges appointed by the king. The judge acts alone or with the assistance of two lay judges[194] chosen by ballot for the particular case. In some cases, such as those involving shipping and real estate, lay judges are required. In other cases they take part if a litigant requests or the judge deems it desirable. On the request of one of the litigants it may be decided that the court be composed of three professional judges if the case is especially important and difficult and if the case is not of the kind legally requiring lay judges. It is the duty of these courts to supervise and carry out the public registration of all deeds relating to real property, to deal with inheritance and bankruptcy matters, and to act as notary publics.

Norway has intermediate appellate courts which bear the name of *Lagmannsrettene*. Prior to July 1, 1936, there were three superior courts with civil jurisdiction and three *Lagmannsrettene* with criminal jurisdiction. Since that time the superior courts have been supplemented by five *Lagmannsrettene*: the Eidsivathing at Oslo, the Agder at Skien, the Gulathing at Bergen, the Frostathing at Trondheim, and the Hålogaland at Tromsø. Each court consists of three professional judges. If requested by a litigant, lay judges may be called to take part in the hearing and decision, the number being fixed at four unless the parties agree on two. The court may decide on its own motion, even though there be no request, to call two lay judges if their assistance is considered desirable. The professional judge senior in appointment serves as president or

Lagmann of the court. The other two professional judges are either permanently attached to the court or are *herred* and town court judges who have been called to serve in the trial of one or more particular cases.

A decision of the courts of first instance may, on certain conditions laid down by law, be appealed by either party to the *Lagmannsrett*. The decision of the latter court may in turn be appealed to the Supreme Court. As a rule the right to appeal depends upon the economic values involved. A case involving less than 1,000 kroner cannot be taken to the *Lagmannsrett* unless special leave is granted. A case involving less than 5,000 kroner cannot be taken to the Supreme Court unless special leave is obtained. But this limit does not apply if the case involves real estate, family matters or other matters of a non-economic character. But the Supreme Court may refuse to admit the appeal for hearing if the judgment is dependent on factual evidence or other circumstances of a specific nature which the *Lagmannsrett* is more qualified to adjudicate.

In 1947 the conciliation tribunals dealt with 12,501 civil cases.[195] In 4,232 cases decided by judgment the tribunal acted as a court proper. In 3,600 cases judgment was delivered against litigants who failed to appear before the tribunal. The *herred* and town courts dealt with 18,215 cases; judgment was delivered in 6,341 cases, the others being settled by mediation, withdrawal, etc. The *Lagmannsrettene* had 1,751 cases, of which 663 were settled by judgment or otherwise. The Supreme Court had 473 cases, of which 131 were decided.

The criminal courts[196] consist of: the Examining and Summary Courts or *Forhørsrettene*, the courts of first instance, the *Lagmannsrettene* and the Supreme Court. In the examining and summary courts the cases are dealt with by a professional judge only. The functions of these courts are special functions of the courts of first instance. Hence the judge is always the local judge of the courts of first instance. The main object of the examining court is to assist the prosecution to obtain in a fair manner evidence which will assist in deciding whether an accused person should be committed for trial. But if the accused has confessed to the crime charged, the judge may proceed summarily and pronounce sentence. When the case has been referred to the court of first instance, it is usually tried by the professional judge with the assistance of two lay judges chosen by ballot for each case from a panel prepared by the local authorities. The lay judges pass not only on guilt but also on the penalty along with the professional judge. The courts of first instance have jurisdiction to try all criminal cases in which the penalty does not exceed five years' imprisonment.

When the penalty exceeds five years the case is tried by the *Lagmannsrett*, which then acts as a court of first instance. The *Lagsmanns-*

rett also has jurisdiction to hear appeals from the regular lower courts, but such appeals are subject to leave being granted by the Appeals Committee of the Supreme Court. When acting as a trial court in criminal cases the *Lagmannsrett* is assisted by a jury of ten on which women as well as men may serve. Juries are used only in this court and only in criminal cases. They are chosen from a panel prepared for a three-year period by a committee selected by the local authorities. It is for the jury to decide after the summing up by the president of the court, whether the accused is guilty or not. That is the sole function of the jury. It requires the votes of seven of the ten jurors to convict. If four or more members favor acquittal, the jury verdict must be acquittal, and there is no mistrial. Certain crimes are tried without a jury: treason, war crimes, offenses against the price, rationing, and supply regulations. In such cases the court consists of three professional and four lay judges, and five votes are required to convict.

The Supreme Court decides criminal cases in the last instance. It may order a new trial because of newly discovered evidence, errors in procedure, or errors in the lower court's understanding of the law. But appeal does not lie on the ground that the evidence relating to guilt has been wrongly adjudged by the lower court. It has the power to change the penalty imposed by the lower court.

Norway also has a number of special courts which have jurisdiction over matters such as labor, fisheries, and military conduct.[197] In 1933 a law was passed providing for a Civil Service Court to settle disputes between members of the civil service and the government. As in Denmark there is no separate system of administrative courts.

Local Government

By about 1250 there had grown up in the trade centers rules and regulations governing business intercourse known as the *Bjarköret*.[198] When the trade centers developed into towns and cities, this law became a code of municipal laws distinct from the other laws of Norway. After revising the general code Magnus Lawmender published a new code of laws in 1277 based on the laws of Bergen, the largest city.[199] The cities now received their own *lagthing* and lawman, whereas previously the general *lagthings* had exercised jurisdiction over them.

When absolutism was established in 1661 mayors and councilmen became royal officials appointed by the king.[200] The localities lost their autonomy. But gradually more authority was left to the local leaders, particularly in the cities. The modernization and democraticization of local government did not occur until the nineteenth century. Norway took the lead among the Scandinavian countries.[201] The Constitution of 1814 provided that local government should be regulated by law. Attempts to secure action failed in 1821, 1830, 1833, and 1836. A special session in 1837 passed a law and the king signed it. The law established the same franchise for local as for national affairs. The smallest units of local government were made identical with the parishes in the local districts and with the corporations in the towns. Each unit elected a council, called since 1863 a *herredstyre*, out of which one-fourth were selected by the rest as an executive committee. The executive committee or *formannskap* acted together with the centrally appointed magistrate. The province or *amt* became a *fylke*. Each *fylke* had a *fylkesthing*, consisting of the chairman of the *herredstyrer*. This system became a model for Denmark and Sweden. The laws of 1837 remained in effect until 1922.[202]

The largest local government area is the *fylke*. There are twenty such areas, eighteen for the rural areas and two for Oslo and Bergen. The chief executive is the *fylkesmann*, who is appointed by the cabinet on recommendation of the minister of justice and serves as the highest national representative. He is usually a lawyer and chosen from the lower courts. His basic salary is now 20,000 kroner, and usually an official residence is furnished. The *fylkething* selects its own chairman or *ordförer* and committees, and the *fylkesmann* cannot be chosen as chairman, though he serves as chairman of its executive committee. It meets for one regular session each year. Its chief functions are education and public highways. The executive committee meets on call of the *fylkesmann* or of two of its members.

There are 680 *herreder* or rural districts in Norway. Such a *herred* consists of one or more *sogner* or ecclesiastical districts. There are now 1,019 ecclesiastical districts. The government of a *herred* consists of the *ordförer* or chairman, the *herredstyret* or district council and the *formannskapet* or executive committee. The chairman is chosen by the district council, usually presides over the executive committee, and is legal and official head of the district. He represents the district in the *fylkesthing*. The district council varies in size from 12 to 48, except when the population is over 25,000, when it may be as high as 64. It is elected for a four-year term, and elects one-fourth of its members to serve on the executive committee. The district council exercises the legislative power including taxation and appropriation. The executive committee is the chief administrative agency. The national cabinet and *fylkesmann* have wide supervisory powers. The *fylkesmann* has a suspensive veto over many types of ordinances. The Association of Norwegian Rural Districts was founded in 1923 with the objects of "protecting the mutual interests of rural districts, of promoting cooperation between them and of disseminating knowledge of municipal matters."

Norway is divided into 66 urban municipalities. Besides the two city *fylker* there are 44 *kjöpstäder* or province towns and 20 *ladesteder* or small seaports. Their government differs from that of the rural municipalities in the following respects: (1) no supervision by the *fylkesmann*, though there is by the central government; (2) a more complicated system of administrative agencies; (3) the greater power of the executive committee; and (4) the office of *raadmann* in addition to that of *ordförer*. The *raadmann* or mayor is elected by the council as is the *ordförer* or chairman. The *raadmann* plays a large role in preparing the budget, and supervises financial administration. He may take part in the proceedings of the council and the executive committee but has no vote. He is paid a salary by the council. The council is elected for a four-year term by the list system of proportional representation. It varies in size from 20 to 84. It elects one-fourth of its members to serve as an executive committee. It has general legislative power including control over finances. No salaries are paid to members of the council or executive committee. The chief functions of the town and cities involve education, poor relief, health and hospitals, street maintenance, and operation of numerous publicly owned utilities. The Association of Norwegian Towns, founded in 1903, meets every third year to discuss questions of mutual interest.

There is public ownership of water, gas and electric utilities, and streetcar systems in almost all municipalities. In 1939, 116 out of 320 motion-picture theaters were municipally owned. A 1933 statute permits municipalities securing consent of the minister of justice to go into voluntary bankruptcy. In recent years, *fylker*, towns, and rural districts have cooperated as to larger enterprises, such as hospitals, insane asylums and electric power.

Religion

From the introduction of Christianity in 1000 to 1150 the Norwegian Church was strongly influenced by England. The Christian Church in Norway "never had courts of its own, at least not in the continental sense."[203] But the bishop's bailiff attended the meetings of the *thing* to prosecute offenders against the law of the church. Saint Olaf (1015-1028) seems to have given law as well as organization to the church.[204] There was further church legislation under Olaf the Peaceful (1066-1093). The latter legislation was importantly amended by Magnus Erlingsson in 1164 when he bought the crown from Archbishop Eystein.

Eystein was not entirely satisfied with the Concordat of 1164 and secured a revision known as the Goldfeather. Eystein aimed to bring the law of the Norwegian Church into closer agreement with the canon law which had been codified in Gratian's Decretum of about 1140. In the early days bishops were appointed by the king. The early church law was made a part of the old Norwegian law through action of the *things* which were often very independent.

In the reign of King Sverri (1177-1202) there was a severe clash between church and state which culminated in the bloodiest and most bitter civil war ever waged in Norway. King Magnus Lawmender undertook to draft a new church law, but encountered the protests of the archbishop who was learned in both Norwegian and canon law. The upshot was the Concordat of Tonsberg of 1277 defining the power of the church. The archbishop then completed the church law which was sanctioned by the king and approved by the bishops. These two documents continued to operate until the Protestant Reformation.

The Lutheran Reformation, introduced in 1537, marked the beginning of German influence which has predominated up to recent times. In 1624 Jesuits were forbidden to enter Norway under pain of death. After the victories of Gustavus Adolphus Catholics were permitted to hold services at specified places, but there could be such services only for aliens. Jews were not permitted to enter Norway. About 1730 a Sabbath ordinance made failure to attend church punishable by fine or pillory. A Sunday Ordinance Act of 1735 was found to be valid in part as late as 1915. A Conventicle Act of 1741 prohibited unauthorized non-churchly religious meetings. In 1736 the rite of confirmation of young people prior to their first communion was established. A vagrancy act of 1754 was later invoked against itinerant lay preachers.

Between 1804 and 1813 proceedings under the Conventicle Act of 1741 were brought against Hans Nielsen Hauge, leader of a Protestant religious movement outside the established church.[205] But after 1814 the authorities seldom interfered with the Haugean movement. Two factors produced tolerance: to secure national unity the bureaucracy catered to the peasants; and the upper classes came to accept Haugean ideas. In 1842 the Conventicle Act was repealed. The Methodists gained many converts in the decade from 1850 to 1860. Mormonism made less headway than in Denmark and Sweden. The first Catholic congregation was established in 1853 in Oslo. Catholicism spread slowly into the larger cities; in 1930 there were 2,827 Catholics. The Constitution in Article 2 provides: "Jesuits shall not be tolerated." There is a strong movement to repeal this provision. As in Denmark and Sweden, Catholics have virtually unrestricted rights to exercise their religion. The population is

97 per cent Lutheran and the largest Protestant element outside the State church are the 19,142 members of the Lutheran free congregations. The State church has eight dioceses, 700 clergymen and 1,030 congregations. The salaries and old age pensions of its clergy are fixed by law, and the clergy are financially independent of their own congregations. The cost to the nation is 20 million kroner a year or about seven kroner per member. The State church is supervised by the Ministry of Ecclesiastical Affairs and Education.

As early as 1788 the government of Denmark-Norway placed native Jews on almost the same plane of civic equality as other citizens. But the Norwegian Constitution of 1814 forbade the admission of Jews into Norway. In 1839 Henrik Wergeland, the great Norwegian writer, began the movement to repeal the constitutional bar.[206] Between 1814 and 1839 very few Jews sought to enter Norway. When Norway arranged a loan in 1822 through the Danish-Jewish banker Hambro, Hambro was not permitted to enter Norway to carrry on the negotiations. Every Storthing from 1842 to 1851 considered the repeal which was advocated by the ministry. At first the peasants opposed repeal on religious grounds, but finally adopted a humanitarian position. The urban members at first favored repeal but ultimately opposed it because of fears of business rivalry. In 1851 repeal was effectuated. In 1930 there were 1,359 Jews in Norway.

A government proposal favored by the clergy to place the State church under a synod in which the clergy would predominate was defeated about a century ago by the peasant group in the Storthing as they feared that if such a synod should begin by giving advice to the lawmakers it would finally displace them. The peasant group wanted parish councils, elected by universal suffrage, and with power to check upon the pastor. They did not secure this. While there was much wrangling about ecclesiastical affairs, the laity was far more successful than the clergy.[207] But since 1885 there has been a strong movement to give the State Church greater independence.[208] In 1920 a law was passed providing for parish councils. In 1933 a diocesan council was established for each diocese. The church now has a limited right to settle internal affairs and to express its wishes when new bishops and clergymen are appointed. By an order in Council of 1945 a commission was set up to consider legislation for settling the position of the church. The report of the commission seems to favor a legally constituted Church Council and greater freedom of the church to settle its internal affairs. The outstanding courage and leadership of the church during the war doubtless contributed to this attitude.

Education

By 1720 the elementary education of pauper children in the towns had come to be recognized as a public obligation.[209] In 1739 all young persons were required to learn to read. There was but niggardly support of the schools preparing for the universities. The 1739 decree was widely criticized and soon modified to leave it to the judgment of the parishes when and how schools should be established. Hence no national system of elementary education was established for another century. The rite of confirmation was introduced in 1736, and proved a great stimulant to education as ability to read religious texts was a prerequisite. By a law of 1809 the schools preparing for the universities were required to give more attention to the vernacular ·and to utilitarian subjects. In 1811 Norway got its own university at Oslo. The first teachers' college was established in 1824; by 1837 there were eight.

In 1837 a rural school law was enacted. The schools received support from the sale of public ecclesiastical lands, but had to compete with the university and the urban preparatory schools. In 1848 a law required every town to maintain a common school, and attendance was compulsory from seven to the age of confirmation. After long agitation the Storthing passed an epoch-making law on rural elementary schools in 1860. Rural school districts were set up of rather large size so that good school boards might be selected and financial burdens equalized. The common schools were divided into lower and upper. In order to provide enough schools in the lower division, each district was to be subdivided into circuits small enough for its children to walk to school. Each school district was obligated to maintain at least one institution, comparable to a high school, to which only boys fifteen years or older were admitted. Provision was made for qualified teachers and trained school inspectors in each district. Instruction was to have secular as well as religious content. Thus Norway's elementary school system was fully and permanently established by 1865. In 1831 Anton Schweigaard began agitation for the teaching of practical subjects in the preparatory schools. A commission headed by Hartvig Nissen prepared the law of June 17, 1869, which began the coordination of the preparatory school with the elementary system, set up the Intermediate School (*Middelskolen*) with only minor emphasis on Latin for ages nine to fifteen, to be followed by three years in either the *Latingymnasium* or in the *Realgymnasium*. The first Norwegian folk school was established in 1864.[210] Theologians like Christopher Bruun, Herman Anker, and Ole Arneson sponsored the movement. They have become a part of the regular school system. As early as

1902 the Storthing approved a plan to modernize the library system. Study circles have grown popular during the past generation.

Today the elementary school course lasts seven years and all must attend.[211] In 1946 a bill was passed permitting each municipality to adopt an eighth obligatory school-year. An act concerning technical schools came into force in 1945. These schools are designed to give practical instruction and theoretical knowledge as a supplement to the training received in employment. The Act of 1935 established two kinds of higher education: *realskoler* and *gymnas*; that is to say, secondary schools and colleges. The *realskole* provides a more advanced general education. The terms may be two, three, and four years. The education thus acquired may serve as a basis for further specialized training. The *gymnasium* provides a higher general education and prepares for the university. The terms may be four, five, and six years. There are nine teacher training colleges, and the two universities of Oslo and Bergen. The Ministry of Ecclesiastical Affairs and Education supervises education.

Agriculture

Land was of such importance that much of the early law is that of land-ownership and inheritance.[212] Individual ownership was the rule, as only an owner could make the land yield. Under the "odal" law each owner held as the representative of a family, thus assuring family continuance of ownership. In case of sale the land must first be offered to relatives. If sold outside the family it could under certain conditions be redeemed. *The King's Mirror*, written about 1250 by an anonymous author, treats the *bønder* or farmers not only as an independent and highly respected class, but as a separate estate equal in rank to the nobility and the clergy. This is notable as elsewhere in Europe the agricultural classes had sunk into serfdom.[213]

Frederick I (1524-1533) granted the Danish nobles a very sweeping jurisdiction over the peasants. But in Norway the nobles never had such powers.[214] In the first place, the "odal" law guaranteed a large group of free peasants who owned their farms. In the second place, the more numerous tenants were protected by the Norwegian laws. The amount of rent was fixed by law. The old Norwegian nobility had almost died out. At the time of the Reformation 10,000 farms were owned by the peasants and 20,000 were operated by tenants. Following the Reformation the crown acquired one-fourth of the taxable lands in Norway. The Danish officials in Norway sought to introduce the Danish system as to these lands and as to the tenants on their own estates. But the Norwegian peasants put up a sturdy and successful resistance. Christian IV (1588-1648) increased taxes very extensively, with the result that the peasants became the weakest of the four estates. But their freedom and spirit remained. In the latter half of the seventeenth century the independence of the peasants was endangered by the increasing practice of wealthy burghers to buy lands. Over two-thirds of the peasants were now renters. The Crown owned a third of the lands, but paid off its creditors with lands. The purchasers from the Crown were harsh landlords who tried to apply Danish ideas. The Norwegian *statholder* Gyldenløve saw that the policy was unwise.

Statutes of 1684 and 1685 provided for a low maximum land rent. Subsequently there were imposed upon proprietors who personally used more than one manor or *gaard* double taxes for such extra holdings.[215] This had the effect of lessening the number of landlords. An act of May 6, 1754, allotted to those desiring it on payment of rent an acreage in the eastern parts of the highlands for cultivation and settlement, not only on public domains but also on private estates. This act was repealed in 1760, but that on double taxation survived until 1827. By 1765 the Norwegian rural population had been almost entirely freed of its former obligations to buy and sell in certain towns. The period from 1680 to 1700 presented opportunities in industry and trade while farm products ceased to rise in value. This resulted in a movement which by 1750 had increased the proportions of owners to tenants from 1:3 to 2:1. Royal decrees were issued in 1764 and 1769 permitting subdivision of family farms, but had little effect. The great agricultural reforms in Norway occurred after 1800.[216]

By 1814 only the ecclesiastical properties remained in the hands of the public. In 1821 their sale was permitted. In 1827 the regulations governing sales were liberalized so that in a few decades most of the public land became private property. By 1850 the movement to consolidate small holdings had become strong. Agriculture was altered from a communal to an individual basis. In 1860 the peasants were relieved of the burden of posting, and fixed livery stations were established along all roads. In 1837 the Storthing abolished the land tax on peasants. Norway preceded both Denmark and Sweden in protecting the peasant against inequitable taxation. A society to promote the welfare of agriculture was established in 1829, but the government did not set up a ministry for agriculture until 1900.[217] Public agronomists were first appointed in 1855.

The problem of the cotters or *husmaend* has been solved by emigration. This group owned small plots of land, but earned most of their living by working for the owners of the larger farms. It declined from one-quarter of the population in 1845 to three per cent in 1920.[218] Today 92 per cent of all farmers own their farms, and the remaining eight per cent hold their farms on lease. Only three per cent of Norway is tillable, and nine-tenths of the farms are less than 25 acres in size. In the 1930's the Storthing set up a Loan Bank for Farmers to adjust debts.[219] When the mortgage became higher than the actual value of the farm through deflation, the Bank could adjust the mortgage. It could then grant new small loans to help the farmer get back on his feet. There has been important legislation as to producers' cooperatives.[220] By an act of 1928 a state grain corporation was established to buy all the home-grown grain offered for sale by growers.

Criminal Law

The earliest criminal law was but little concerned with public order and was almost entirely concerned with the victim's injury.[221] From 900 to 1100 the Sagas tell of numerous acts of violence, mayhem, and murder. In the last case the relatives of the slain could wreak blood vengeance. Account was taken of provocation, passion, and the subsequent conduct of the killer. Under the early Gulathing law-text the slayer could tender reparation after three years. The introduction of Christianity resulted in the placing of limitations upon private vengeance. Restitution by way of cattle or cloth, instead of money, continued from the days of paganism. Dueling was abolished in 1012.

In the twelfth century there was virtually no machinery for the apprehension of criminals. The victim or his heir had to find the wrongdoer and bring him before the local *thing*.[222] The actual hearing did not normally occur at the initial *thing*. When possible the testimony of witnesses was heard. If the facts were not known and the defendant persisted in his denial of guilt, he might clear himself with oaths and oath helpers.[223] Appeal to the ordeal was not often used.[224] Murderers might be fined or, in heinous cases, outlawed temporarily or even permanently with loss of property. Capital punishment was not often used. Mutilation was more common. Petty thieves were flogged. Secret crimes, such as theft, were regarded as particularly odious, and could involve the forfeiture of both life and property. The above system continued without radical change up to the sixteenth century.[225] Almost the only changes were increases in the penalties for certain crimes and non-enforcement of some of the earlier provisions. Legislation during the first half of the sixteenth century tended to stress public order rather than private redress.[226] The Laws of Christian II provided a death penalty for all cases of deliberate homicide. Witchcraft trials and executions were numerous in the latter part of the sixteenth century and the opening of the seventeenth.[227] The last trial occurred in 1737.

While the Code of 1688 had abolished capital punishment for gross and repeated thefts, it was restored on March 4, 1690.[228] Barbaric penalties continued until 1772 when under Minister Struensee, the death penalty for theft was abolished, and likewise torture. In 1789 the government, whose legal expert was Christian Colbjörnsen, enunciated two important principles: punishment should be as mild as is consistent with public safety, hence the penalty for theft should be lessened; and its purpose should be redemption of the offender.

Article 94 of the Constitution provides: "The first, or if this is not possible, the second ordinary Storthing, shall make provision for the publication of a new general civil and criminal code." But numerous obstacles hampered codification, such as the pressing problems of the moment. Scientific investigation of the theories of punishment for crime led to a series of modern codes of substantive criminal law in 1815 and 1842.[229] In 1815 all penalties involving torture or mutilation were abolished. State Councilor Christian Krogh was appointed to prepare a new code. Upon his death a new commission was appointed with Jörgen H. Vogt serving as its president and Winter-Hjelm playing an important part. The draft and commentary of this commission appeared in 1832-1835. The Storthing approved the draft in 1839, and the king approved the code on August 20, 1842. This code, which was the first systematic codification of Norwegian criminal law was largely based upon the revised Hanoverian Code but also influenced by the French Code Penal.[230] In 1867 the police system of Oslo was reorganized and the state undertook to pay all the costs above 20,000 kroner per year. Norway thus moved in the direction of centralizing its urban police.

Because of the increase in crime a commission on penal institutions was established by the Norwegian government in 1837. Its leading member was Professor Frederik Holst (1791-1871), a physician. For the first time criminals were classified according to age, and first-time offenders were distinguished from recidivists.[231] Previously servitude was the most severe penalty for all serious offenses. According to a decree of July 12, 1799, all those undergoing servitude were placed in irons, and only a physician could make an exception. The work of the commission was completed in 1841. It proposed seven prisons to contain 2,100 prisoners. This was not adopted, but in 1842 the ministry proposed a prison to be built in Oslo. A law was passed in 1848, and the first prisoner was received in 1851. The Philadelphia system was followed. At first the prisoners were kept alone day and night, but today some prisoners work together during the day. The prison system today is governed by the Prison Act of December 12, 1903, with subsequent amendments. This law also contains provisions relating to release on probation.

In January 1885 a general revision of the criminal law was again undertaken. The State Council, with Bernhard Getz as its head, was commissioned to prepare a draft.[232] A draft was first published in 1887, which went into effect on January 1, 1902, and remained in effect half a century. It was widely reviewed in the journals of criminal law. It contained no death penalty, nor short periods of imprisonment, and provided for indeterminate sentences for dangerous offenders likely to become recidivists. Important changes in the law of 1902 became effective July 1, 1951, following the work of commissions set up in 1934 and 1947.[233] The Commission of 1934 was authorized to deal with crimes against property, while that of 1947 dealt with crimes against the person. Norwegian theories of punishment in chronological order are represented by the views of Anders S. Örsted, Anton Schweigaard, Bernhard Getz, and Francis Hagerup.

There is no juvenile court in Norway. Under the law of 1896 concerning the treatment of neglected children, largely drawn up by Bernhard Getz, Norway was the first Scandinavian state to abolish court procedure for juvenile delinquents. Each municipality is required to have a child welfare board or so-called Watch Committee to deal with children.[234] This body can place children under the age of eighteen in reliable and decent families, or put them in school, or in service, or in a home, according to a plan approved by the king, or in special schools or institutions.

Following changes in the substantive criminal law came a new criminal procedure. Inquisitorial process, instead of the accusatory system, was more effectively established on July 24, 1827, and March 17, 1866.[235] The Code of Criminal Procedure of July 1, 1887, came into operation on January 1, 1890.[236] Its chief innovation was the introduction of the jury. Witness fees were introduced, as were penal orders.[237] A statute of July 1, 1887, provided for indemnity to persons wrongfully prosecuted.[238]

The power to commence criminal proceedings is vested in the Public Prosecuting Authority or *Påtalemyndigheten*.[239] Its agencies are the commissioners of police, the States attorneys or advocates and the Director of Public Prosecutions or *Riksadvokaten*. Prosecuting attorneys are chosen by the Department of Police and Justice. Free legal advice is offered to criminal defendants irrespective of financial status.[240] Public defenders are drawn by the court, usually in a certain order, from a panel of lawyers appointed by the Department of Police and Justice. But if the accused wants a certain lawyer that lawyer will usually be appointed.

In October 1941 and January 1942 provision was made for the use of the death penalty which had been abolished in 1875.[241] In July 1945 the Storthing re-enacted this change. Thus when Quisling was given the death penalty, its application was not retroactive. By September 1949 thirty-eight persons had been executed for treason and war crimes. The trial of Quisling in 1945 attracted world-wide attention. The writers agree that he was given a fair criminal prosecution.[242] Following 1945 there were numerous prosecutions for treason and related offenses.[243] General von Falkenhorst, commander-in-chief of the German armed forces in Norway from 1940 to 1944, was tried in 1946 by a military court on which one Norwegian sat.[244]

Under the Police Act of 1936 it is a duty of the national government to provide police.[245] Since January 1, 1937, the national government has paid all police expenses, although the municipalities refund much of such expenses. There are 56 police districts each headed by a commissioner of police or *politimester* assisted by deputy commissioners or *politifullmektiger*, who are law graduates appointed by the king. In the more important districts the commissioner is assisted by chief constables and police adjutants or *politiinspektører*. In the country districts there are subdivisions headed by a sheriff or *lensmann*.

Civil Procedure

In litigation involving title to property or infraction of property rights, the procedure of early Norwegian law resembled criminal procedure, but was much more elaborate.[246] No action could be brought against one except in his own home. First the defendant was given a "home summons" directing him to be at home. Then the plaintiff and his witnesses would go to the home and summon the defendant to appear at court. The court would first hear the witnesses to the various forms of summons. If satisfied that the case was legally brought, the trial on the merits would then go on. The witnesses would be persons who had been invited to hear the terms of a transaction and to watch its consummation. As written records were not at first easily available, the records had to be made in the minds of men. Purchases were made in the presence of others. Neighbors were invited to hear the terms of a betrothal or of a legal separation. The duties of the court ended on decision. If the plaintiff won, it was the plaintiff's own affair to secure execution of the judgment. If resistance was feared, the aid of the *thingmen* could be asked. The provincial jurisdictions failed to develop executive or administrative institutions.

Under the laws of Magnus Lawmender of 1274 civil cases could be brought before the *fylkesthing*, the parish *thing*, or submitted to the lawman.[247] From his decision an appeal lay to the *lagthing*, which could only lay the matter before the king. The *fylkesthinger* were assembled and presided over by the *sysselmaend*, who appointed the judges and executed the decrees of the court. The *sysselmaend* were royal officials who collected the taxes, served as chief administrator, military commander, and chief police officer.[248]

During the period of union between Norway and Denmark prior to 1814 the civil procedures of the two nations closely resembled each other.[249] In the development of such law the Romano-canonical influence operated at an earlier time than it did in Sweden to overcome the formalism of the older law. But the persistence of this influence, particularly through the German common-law system, produced in the eighteenth century a procedure in Norway and Denmark that was almost entirely written.[250] In the first stages of the transformed procedure there was distinct legislative recognition of the right of the judge to call in the party for interrogation. But with the change to the written form this feature virtually disappeared. Thus at the beginning of the present century there were no means of party-examination for the ascertainment of facts in either country.

While commissions began work on new criminal and civil codes soon after the Constitution of 1814 the codification of civil procedure remained unfinished as of 1890.[251] The adoption of the modern Scandinavian codes was characterized by great deliberateness. The Norwegian Code of 1915 was not permitted to go into effect until 1927, the Danish Code of 1916 became effective in 1919, and the Swedish code of 1942 in 1948.[252]

While in Denmark the court of general civil jurisdiction is collegial, consisting of three judges, in Norway the proceedings are heard before a single judge, assisted in certain cases by two lay assessors or doomsmen.[253] The Norwegian Code, like the Danish Code, embodies the idea of orality, as against written procedure. It was strongly influenced in that direction by the Austrian *Zivilprozessordnung* of 1895.[254] Similarly, following the Austrian Code, Norway, Denmark and Sweden make use of a preparatory proceeding which is determinative of the mode, whether oral or written, in which the exchange of allegation shall be conducted.[255] The Norwegian Code definitely recognizes the right of the court to call a witness on its own motion.[256] The decisory oath has been abolished in Norway, Denmark and Sweden.[257] Likewise, witness examination has been substantially transferred to the hands of the parties, with a recognition of the right of cross-examination in all three countries.[258] The Norwegian Code discourages arguments of law and facts in the pleadings (sec. 122).[259] Judicial aid is provided for as to pleading. Section 331 of the Code provides: "The President of the court by questioning or other communications with the parties must see that their declarations are as clear and complete as possible." The effect of a failure to deny is left to the court, as it is in Denmark (sec. 184).

The Norwegian code has taken substantial steps to provide means of party-examination for the ascertainment of facts.[260] The examination is not a separate episode of the case. No distinction is taken between examination for proof purposes and examination for clarification of the issues. Statements of fact favorable to the opposite party obtained this way are not classed as technical proof, but rather as substitutes for proof.[261] It is for the court to determine whether the case will best be prepared by exchange of preparatory pleadings or by personal appearance of the parties. Personal appearance at this stage may also be required by the court even though there have been written pleadings (sec. 317). At such personal appearance, as well as where there is personal appearance at the hearing-in-chief, resort may be had to the examination (secs. 113, 320). The examination is largely left to the court's own initiative, thus differing from the Danish code. Probably the interested party may move the court to this end during the preparatory stage. Express recognition of this right to ask for personal appearance of the adversary apparently is confined to the case of such an appearance at the hearing-in-chief (sec. 320).

As respects examinations at any time the party must answer the questions put to him by the court concerning the circumstances of the case (sec. 111). At the preparatory stage time may be given him for investigation unless there is lack of good faith. But at the hearing-in-chief he must normally answer at once (sec. 112). He is to answer personally and without taking advice, but is allowed a limited use of written memoranda to refresh his recollection (sec. 113). The examination is not under oath, but where an answer is given at the hearing-in-chief or is to be used at that hearing, it is to be followed by affirmation "upon honor and conscience." But the affirmation will not be received if in the view of the court the answer is not credible (sec. 114). The judicial discretion determines the admissive effect of recalcitrancy (sec. 184). While witnesses are examined by the parties (sec. 212), examination of the party is by the court, with the right in his counsel and the opposite party to request postponement of further questions (sec. 113). As under Danish law, securing facts by means of the examination is not conditioned upon the absence of other proof. Indeed, the chief significance of the summons for personal appearance is that it compels admissions and thus reduces or eliminates the need for proof.

Social Legislation

Mrs. Florence Harriman, Minister to Norway from the United States from 1937 to 1940, has stated: "When I was first appointed to Norway, the first thing Justice Brandeis said to me, and he said it in a voice of smiling envy, was, 'Those Scandinavian countries are twenty-five years ahead of us all.' "[262] In 1949 the Norwegian government published a white paper[263] in which it set forth an elaborate social security plan which if carried out will place Norway on a par with Denmark and Sweden in social welfare.

Free trade and freedom of occupation. Norway enjoyed the benefits of the liberal tariff law of 1797. Professor Anton Schweigaard became a powerful proponent of free trade. From 1842 Norway had free trade.[264] Freedom of occupation was proposed by the Storthing in 1827, but the king did not sanction until 1839.[265] Internal trade was freed in 1842, with revisions in 1857 and 1866.[266]

Women. The publication of Camilla Collett's *Amtmandens dötre* in 1855 inaugurated the women's movement in Norway. While the Norwegian code had provided that daughters inherit equally with sons, the law was not put into effect until July 31, 1854.[267] Unmarried women were authorized to earn their living in any trade or craft by laws of 1842 and 1866. The age of majority for both males and females was reduced from 25 to 21 years by an act of March 27, 1869. Women were given the same right as men to employment in the common schools in 1869. As early as 1804 girls were admitted to the *realskole* at Trondheim. After 1825 they could attend university lecture courses but without any privilege to take examinations.

By 1890 most occupations were open to women, and married women had the same rights as unmarried. In 1882 entrance examinations to the university were opened to women. In 1884 university degrees and professional examinations were opened to them. In 1901 women having a certain income were given the right to vote in local elections. In 1907 the right was extended to national elections. In 1910 they gained equal suffrage in local government and in 1913 this was extended to national elections. Norway was thus the first country to confer the vote on women. In 1938 positions in the clergy, diplomatic and consular service, the cabinet and the armed forces were open to women.

Illegitimacy. Concerning the Norwegian illegitimacy laws Minister Harriman has stated: "I was interested in the Norwegian laws regarding illegitimate children. They are, I believe, the most advanced in the world. The child born out of wedlock shares equally with the legitimate children in all matters of inheritance, irrespective of the wishes and will of the father, his wife and his lawful children. Illegitimacy is no social drawback to any honorable career in society, for the child; but the same cannot yet be said for the child's mother. A father, by law, must support an illegitimate child until he is sixteen and in some degree its mother also."[268]

Insanity. Prior to 1848 Norwegian localities placed the insane in private families with the purpose of preventing their starving or causing injury. They were often chained or locked in a cage. In 1822 Frederik Holst criticized the Oslo asylum. A commission reported in 1825, but lack of money prevented action. Dr. Herman Wedel Major's suggestions resulted in the law of August 17, 1848, "the most expertly drawn and humane law on insanity that had been adopted in any country."[269] Partial insanity is a ground for reduction of criminal penalties.[270]

Labor. The modern trade union movement in Norway goes back to about 1875.[271] A central labor federation, the Norwegian Federation of Labor, was formed about 1900. Almost every worker belongs to a union affiliated with the Federation. The Norwegian movement was the last of the Scandinavian and did not attain stability until the decade from 1930 to 1940. The Norwegian and Swedish federations unlike the Danish are federations of industrial unions. The highest legislative authority is the congress which meets every three years. Between congress sessions important matters are submitted to the representative council convened at least once a year. There is an executive board of about a dozen members. The Federation is a highly centralized organization, in contrast to the Danish. It has broad power over the national unions which are required to submit their economic demands to the executive board of the Federation for approval. Federation representatives participate in the negotiation of all important collective agreements that are national in scope or concern more than one union. The Federation under its constitution may assume leadership of a dispute that is likely to affect the interests of more than one affiliate and may order sympathetic strikes. While in the United States acceptance of contract terms by union negotiators is tantamount to union ratification, in Norway a secret ballot on proposed agreements is taken. Compact minorities may thus reject in case of majority apathy. Legislation giving greater powers to negotiators was repealed one year after its adoption. But the executive committees of national unions may require new balloting if they regard participation as too low. Collective affiliation of local trade unions provides the Labor party with about 45 per cent of its membership; and many trade union members are enrolled individually. There is statutory machinery for coordinating the policies of the trade unions and the Labor party.

Norway has a central federated association of employers. With it are affiliated industrial employer associations and individual employers who cannot be grouped within an appropriate association. All the larger manufacturing establishments are within the association. The highest legislative body is a general assembly elected by the members. In turn it selects a central board and a small executive committee of eight members. The association normally represents the side of the employer in collective bargaining over national agreements. An individual employer may not make an agreement with his workers differing from the general agreement unless the association consents. Since World War I the association has unreservedly accepted employee organization and collective bargaining.

Government regulation of labor relations is more complete in Norway than in Denmark and Sweden. There is a well developed system of government mediation. There is a state mediator at Oslo, and several subordinate mediators in the field. Mediation proceedings are conducted by a single mediator. The most important cases are handled by the state mediator. Both parties must attend mediation proceedings and postpone direct economic action for a maximum period of one week at the request of the mediator. The mediator may submit a "mediation proposal," which both sides must submit to their constituents. The proposal is not binding but is usually accepted. If mediation fails, the parties may resort to their economic weapons. But Norway adopted compulsory government arbitration during the years 1916-1920, 1922-1923, 1927-1929, and 1945-1949. No strike or lockout may take place over disputed interpretations of collective agreements. Such disputes, if not settled by grievance machinery, must be brought to special tripartite labor courts for final adjudication. The Norwegian Labor Court was established in 1915. A special Boycott Court was established in 1933 to administer a statute that set forth the conditions under which a boycott was permissible in labor disputes. The Boycott Act was repealed in 1947, as Norwegian labor opposed it.

There were direct negotiations between the central organizations of labor and management in Norway since 1900. But the bargaining rules were found in collective agreements restricted to particular unions or in statutes. In 1935 an agreement was finally made between the two groups. Under the agreement there is mutual recognition of the right to organize for collective bargaining; regulations governing the appointment and functions of shop stewards; grievance and disputes procedure; procedure for referenda on proposed agreements; and rules for the imposition of sympathetic work stoppages.

As in Sweden but unlike Denmark, the closed shop is not unlawful in Norway, but it is virtually non-existent. Since 1907 the attitude of the organized Norwegian employers has been like that of the Swedish. No member is allowed to include a union-security clause in a collective contract. But the absence of the clause has had no ill effects on the unions. In many large industries there are no unorganized workers.[272]

Child Labor. In 1875 an extensive study of child labor was made by

Jacob Neumann Mohn.[273] In 1892 a factory law forbade the employment of children under twelve; children from twelve to fourteen could work no more than six hours and those from fourteen to eighteen no more than ten hours. Recent legislation defines children as persons under fifteen.[274] Children may not work in industry generally, but excepted are office work, educational work, theaters, restaurants, forestry and traveling sales work. Thus the law is less strict than in Denmark and Sweden where the age limit is fourteen and fewer exceptions are permitted. Children from fifteen to eighteen are defined as youths. No youth may engage in tasks which are strenuous or unsafe or dangerous to health, nor work in steam boilers nor within machinery where caution is necessary. A physician's certificate that a youth is physically capable is required. School attendance must not be interfered with. Decisions as to whether children or youths may be employed are made by the Ministry of Social Affairs.

Workmen's Compensation. The first workmen's compensation law was passed in 1894.[275] Seamen were included in 1911 and fishermen in 1925. Woodsmen and forestry workers are covered; but not domestic servants. Only agricultural workers who use machinery are covered. The National Insurance Bureau administers the law, and acts as insurer and as custodian of the insurance fund. In case of injury all medical and hospital expenses are paid, as well as a daily cash allowance as in the health insurance scheme. A person totally disabled receives a life annuity of 60 per cent of his annual wage. If the worker dies the widow and other dependents receive an annuity. Occupational disease is not covered, but all workers are required to carry health insurance. Norway has no separate system of disability pensions, such as in Denmark and Sweden. But an allowance of the same amount as the old age pension may be given to helpless invalids.

Unemployment Insurance. In 1915 Norway passed an unemployment insurance act much like that of Denmark in that it supported the unemployment insurance clubs of the unions.[276] But it failed to attract the interest of the workers and a new act in 1938 introduced compulsory insurance for all wage earners in industry, trade and shipping. The act was amended and broadened in 1946. Insurance is now compulsory for the same group that must carry health insurance. The premiums are paid one-half by the employer and one-half by the worker. The national and municipal governments also contribute. The daily allowance is like that in health insurance. Cash benefits are paid for not more than fifteen weeks in a year. The worker must have been employed for at least 45 weeks in the preceding four years. Benefits are not paid to those unreasonably declining employment or to strikers. If the worker has to move to obtain a new job, his removal expenses are paid. He is given financial assistance in learning another trade. His health insurance premiums are paid for him by the unemployment insurance organization during the period of no employment.

Unemployment insurance might not be adequate in the case of a long and severe depression. Norway, like Denmark and Sweden, prefers to solve the problem by work relief rather than by cash relief, though some cash relief is given. From 1920 to 1934 an average of 15 million kroner per year was spent on public works.[277] The system has been less comprehensive than the Swedish and more than the Danish. National works, such as road building, reclamation, and improvement of harbors and waterways, is one device. A second is work initiated by the locality but subsidized by the state. A third is local projects to which the national government does not contribute. A fourth is private projects such as reclamation or drainage subsidized by public funds.

Old Age Pensions. Norway was later than Denmark and Sweden in providing for old age pensions.[278] A noncontributing pension system was set up in 1936. The pension is fixed by the local governments. The minimum annual pension to persons without income is 1,620 kroner for a single person and 2,640 for a married couple in Oslo; 840 and 1,260 in the urban areas; and 720 and 1,080 in the rural areas. Marital status and private income are taken into account. Other income up to one-third of the basic pension may be received without reduction. The pensioner may own a home worth up to 6,000 kroner without reduction. Larger pensions are paid to pensioners supporting minors. Pensioners must be seventy or older. Whether a married couple receives a pension depends on the husband's age. The costs are met in part by general taxation and in part by a special income tax of one per cent on persons receiving an income of 1,000 kroner or more. The municipalities pay part of the costs. Pensions similar in amounts are paid to the blind and the disabled.

Health Insurance. A compulsory health insurance act for workers was passed in 1909.[279] The national program was administered by the National Insurance Bureau. The present system is based upon a 1930 statute providing for compulsory insurance for members from fifteen to seventy years whose income is below the amount fixed by the cabinet. The present regulations cover workers whose income does not exceed 9,000 kroner and all seamen and fishermen. About 80 per cent of the population are members of the health insurance societies. Sixty per cent of the costs come from the workers, ten from his employer, twenty from the national treasury and ten from the municipality. Two-thirds of the costs of local medical attention and the full cost of hospital service are paid, as well as a daily allowance for time lost not exceeding six months. The daily allowance is up to six kroner according to the income of the member.

There are supplements of .67 kroner for family supporters and for each child. The total daily allowance must not exceed nine kroner or 90 per cent of daily earnings. Maternity aid is given. Provision is made for voluntary membership of persons not gainfully employed or those whose income is above the income limit. Wives and children under sixteen of covered workers are also covered.

By 1750 Norway like Denmark had a system of public physicians with well established duties.[280] They were to engage in actual medical practice and not merely statistical and supervisory work. They were to receive fixed salaries and live in the communities which they served. They were to give aid to the poor without charge; from others they might take fees at fixed rates. From time to time more physicians were appointed as the demand arose and the means were found. Under the provincial physicians there were district physicians. Local boards of health were set up. Between 1780 and 1800 several public hospitals were established. By 1865 Norway had one of the best systems of public health administration. Dentistry developed very slowly. By 1870 Norway had only 21 dentists. Norway required vaccination against smallpox in 1810, but enforcement was lax. Hospitalization and medicine could be had after 1788 for venereal diseases, which by 1844 were largely stamped out. In 1847 scientific study of leprosy was commenced. The number of lepers declined from 2,858 in 1856 to 107 in 1925. Between 1720 and 1865 there had developed a "system of public health administration so extensive as to justify the appellation of state medicine."[281] That is to say, the drug trade was closely controlled, public hospitals existed and pyramidal structures of public physicians and midwives had been erected.

Today the general hospital system is administered by the local authorities. The central government administers mental hospitals. Privately supported hospitals have only about ten per cent of all hospital beds. Each *fylke* has a central hospital. The hospital staff doctors receive a fixed salary and give their entire working day to hospital work. Physicians in private practice do not continue to treat patients who are hospitalized. Hospital treatment is free to all members of the health insurance societies.

As has been seen the health insurance societies provide free medical attention. The doctors are paid directly by the patients as in Sweden and the health insurance system refunds a fixed amount per consultation to the members. The refund corresponds to about two-thirds of the doctor's bill. A new proposed plan would adopt the Danish system of having the insurance system pay the total fee of the doctor. The Norwegian system permits a patient to select a new doctor for each new case of illness. In recent years many Norwegians have come to prefer the Danish family doctor system. Norway has 2,481 licensed physicians or one doctor for 1,200 inhabitants and they are evenly distributed throughout the country. There are 400 district physicians and each *fylke* has a medical officer. Today free hospitalization and free medical attention are unquestioned in Norway.

The health insurance system pays a daily allowance corresponding to sickness benefits to all expectant mothers for a period of twelve weeks. Abortion is legal only for purely medical reasons, the law being stricter than in Denmark and Sweden. Free midwife services are provided under the health insurance scheme. Maternity and pediatric centers give pregnant women free examinations. School doctors and nurses are provided and regular medical examinations are held. If a child needs medical treatment, he is referred to his family doctor. The school doctor gives an annual tuberculosis examination to all pupils and teachers. Free school meals are often provided.

In June 1949 a dental care bill was submitted to the Storthing providing free dental attention to all children between six and eighteen.[282] The Association of Norwegian Dentists, most of whom are in private practice, thought the bill should cover children from the age of three. Dental districts would be established corresponding roughly with the medical districts. Each district would have at least one district dentist to provide free care. The law was enacted on July 28, 1949. In 1946 Norway had 1,476 dentists.

General Assistance. Until September 20, 1845, poor relief in Norway was governed by a decree of December 2, 1741.[283] In 1755 it was ordered that beggars be placed in workhouses. In 1843 the city of Oslo provided salaries for poor relief administrators. In 1845 a new poor law was adopted, modeled on the English law. A definite term of residence was made a prerequisite for poor relief in any community. Poor relief was to be administered by the newly established system of local government. The act of 1845 was replaced by that of 1863 which in turn was replaced by that of 1900 which is still in force.[284] With the growth of social insurance, relief has become supplementary in character. The recipient need not be a Norwegian nor reside in Norway. It is a prerequisite, however, that his spouse, children or parents be unable to aid him. If these fail to support, aid is given. In principle each municipality cares for its residents. The resident's qualification is acquired by two years' consecutive residence without receiving relief aid. If the applicant lives in another district, he may still receive aid but the district of his residence must then reimburse for two-thirds of the amount. If a person has no residence qualification, the State reimburses in full.

While poor relief seems to be a national problem, it is largely left to local authorities.[285] Each municipality elects a board of guardians responsible for the distribution of the allocations granted by the town or district council for poor relief. Such relief amounts annually to 50 million kroner and is usually the largest item in the municipal social budget.

Family Allowances. Under the act of October 24, 1946 family allowances are made for children under sixteen.[286] Each child other than the first is to receive 180 kroner a year. Widows and unmarried or divorced mothers receive the allowance even for the first child. Although abolished in Sweden, tax rebates for children are still permitted in Norway. For example, in the case of a family of three children with an income of 7,000 kroner, the tax reduction is about 165 kroner per child in Oslo. A recent study made under the auspices of the United Nations shows that while France gives fifteen types of aids to families, Norway and Sweden give ten, Denmark seven and the United States four.[287]

Housing. In 1838 Hans Linstow, builder of the Royal Palace in Oslo, advocated decent housing for workers in Oslo.[288] The Thrane labor movement between 1848 and 1851 advocated public housing. Partly to deflate the Thrane movement and partly to remove a cause of the cholera epidemic of 1850, a group of public spirited citizens built Oslo's first low-cost housing unit in 1851. The city of Oslo began to build houses as early as 1896 and by 1911 had a separate housing bureau. Oslo has gone further than any other city in the world, 90 per cent of its people living in houses owned by the city or by cooperatives which receive governmental subsidies. In 1921 the city built 889 dwellings while private enterprise with municipal assistance built only 162. But by 1936 private enterprise was doing the entire work again. Following World War II state aid again became essential. The cooperatives rather than the stock corporations are absorbing the investments of the people. Overcrowding has been worse in Norway than in Denmark and Sweden for the past two decades, so that much of the national budget goes towards housing. Prefabricated housing whether of wood or of concrete has proved expensive and gotten no further than in America.

Before World War II there was only one cooperative building society in Norway. Since that time they have expanded rapidly and formed a national union. More than ten per cent of current home construction is now done by these societies. Full attention has been paid to planning and house design. A central planning bureau has been set up to help the local communities with their plans. Local wishes are scrupulously respected, and decisions are made only after consultation with the mayor, municipal engineer and local planning authority. Prior to World War II a dearth of mortgages and high interest rates retarded construction of housing. In 1946 a housing bank was established. The capital was supplied by state and local authorities, supplemented by local subscriptions. Mortgage loans are made up to 75 per cent of estimated value on houses built for profit, and up to 95 per cent in other cases. Cooperatives can borrow 90 per cent of value and owner occupants of one- to four-family houses 85 per cent. By 1943, 350 homes for old people were erected throughout Norway. Pension aid extended in 1936 assisted in paying the low rent. There is provision of some small cottages with gardens for the use of couples. The program is administered from Oslo by designated representatives of the city, the church, and the taxpayer. Cities are increasing their land holdings both within and without their city limits. Oslo owns a suburb twice its own area.

Temperance. As early as 1728 distilling was forbidden in the rural districts of Norway upon the representations of Bishop Deichman.[289] The period from 1810 to 1830 was probably the most drunken one in Norway. In 1816 the Storthing restored the right to distill brandy for the peasant's own use though he could not sell it unless he paid a tax. The first temperance society was founded in 1836, and the movement attained its climax about 1850. A law of 1837 raised the fee for licenses and discouraged small establishments. Laws enacted in 1845 limited production to large distilleries, and drastically regulated the retail trade. In the rural districts no licenses might be issued without the consent of the district councils. Municipal governments might fix a maximum number of licenses. The per capita consumption of hard liquor declined from 16.2 liters in 1833 to 4.49 liters in 1865. By 1869 the trade in brandy had practically ceased in the rural districts. Prohibition was tried from 1921 to 1927 and then abandoned by a popular vote. There is now a system of state monopoly for the manufacture and sale of spirits and wines and local option for local sales.[290] Under an act of 1932 sobriety boards have been set up in each municipality to look after drunkards and help their dependents.[291]

Uniform Scandinavian Laws

Norway has participated actively in the movement for uniform Scandinavian laws. She was a party to the Scandinavian monetary convention of 1872 under which coins and notes of each country were legal tender in Norway, Denmark, and Sweden. She adopted the Bank Draft Act of 1880.[292] The main Scandinavian uniform laws are the Navigation Act of 1892, Purchase and Selling of 1905-1907, Contracts of 1918, and family law of 1918-1927.[293]

Norway has been interested in uniform acts on social security since 1907. The objective has been reciprocity so that nationals of one Scandinavian country living in another could receive the same benefits as that state's own citizens. Reciprocity was first extended to industrial accident insurance. A reciprocity convention between Norway, Denmark and Sweden was signed in 1919. Reciprocity was extended to Finland in 1923 and to Iceland in 1927. In 1937 all five states concluded a new convention applying also to cases in which the incapacitated worker was not a resident of the state of injury. Up to 1950 old age pensions and disability insurance had not been coordinated. In 1926 Norway and Denmark signed a health insurance convention enabling members of an approved health insurance society in one state to be transferred to a similar society in the other. In 1948 Norway concluded a convention with Sweden along similar lines. In Norway resident foreigners are eligible for membership in unemployment insurance societies on the same conditions as citizens. Full reciprocity as to unemployment insurance has not been obtained because of differences in local legislation. Norway has been preparing arrangements to permit transference of members from the societies of one country to those of another. Denmark and Sweden had done so earlier in 1946. Norway has been more reluctant than Denmark and Sweden as to ratification of a convention on exchange of labor.

Shortly after World War I the Scandinavian Wholesale Society was organized as chief purchaser for the national cooperative societies of Norway, Denmark, Finland and Sweden with its central office in Copenhagen. On November 8, 1950, the transport ministers of Norway, Denmark and Sweden reached full agreement on merging the three Scandinavian airlines into a joint consortium. Thus these countries may compete more effectively in the international air transport field.

A commission of negotiators from the Scandinavian states have concluded that the time is not ripe for the establishment of a Scandinavian Customs Union.[294] A provisional report issued in January 1950 stressed the absence of a working basis. Norwegian representatives pointed out that capital deterioration during the war and post-war concentration on export industries have placed Norway's domestic consumer industries in a very exposed position.

Recently there has been a movement for a Scandinavian Passport Union. Hand baggage would be made free from tax and toll. Money restrictions at the border would be abolished and confined to control through the banks. These proposals would be achieved through conventions rather than through legislation. Finland would perhaps not participate at first. Only Scandinavian citizens would come within the scope of the system.

First the Danes and subsequently the Swedes have proposed the establishment of a Scandinavian Parliamentary Council for the five

Scandinavian states. The Scandinavian Interparliamentary Union at Stockholm recently named a five-nation committee to report on the proposals. Former Prime Minister Hans Hedtoft of Denmark stated that the Strasbourg Council of Europe had shown that there should be a closer liaison between the parliaments and ministers of the various European countries. Finland has rejected the proposal because of fear of Russia. Denmark, Iceland, and Sweden have unequivocally favored the proposal. The minority parties in Norway are opposed, but most of the Labor party favors it.[295] The committee appointed in August 1951 at Stockholm proposed a council to prepare, coordinate and advise on legislation and procedure in matters of common interest, but no super-parliament would be established. The Council would among other things obtain equal facilities for Scandinavians traveling or working in each other's countries. Norway, Denmark, and Sweden would each have sixteen delegates and Iceland five. All political parties would be represented. The premier and foreign minister would attend. Annual sessions would be held, rotating among the capitals, and a permanent secretariat would be established in each capital. Subject to parliamentary approval the first session would be held in 1952. On March 16, 1952, the Scandinavian foreign ministers, meeting at Copenhagen, favored a council. On May 7, 1952, the Danish foreign minister submitted a bill to the Rigsdag to establish a permanent Scandinavian parliamentary council.

The Bar

The bar has developed under official sanction since a decree of August 29, 1735.[296] After her separation from Denmark, Norway adopted additional statutes on August 12, 1848 and September 28, 1857. At the present time there is no officially recognized or authorized bar association as in Denmark and Sweden.[297] Admission to the bar is administered by the Ministry of Justice. There are certain prerequisites such as age, character, and juridical qualifications. Before a lawyer may appear before a *lagmannsrett* he must have had two years of experience in the practice. The lawyers practicing before the Supreme Court are a class separate from those permitted to practice in the lowest courts. All lawyers are subject to discipline through fines or deprivation of license to practice. Improper conduct is a basis on which the Ministry of Justice may deprive a lawyer of his license, but an appeal lies to the Supreme Court. The bar association is known as the Norwegian lawyers' association *(Den Norske Sakførerforening)*. It has about 1,300 members, including almost every lawyer in the country. Its directorship may rebuke or fine a lawyer up to 500 kroner; or expel him from the association for three years with a possible restoration earlier if the directors are unanimous.

Legal Education

As Norway had no university until 1809 Norwegians had to go abroad for university training.[298] In the thirteenth and fourteenth centuries they went to Paris, Orleans, Prague and Bologna; and later to Oxford, Cambridge, Louvain, Leyden, Cologne, and Leipzig. When the University of Rostock was founded in 1418, many Norwegians attended because of the extensive Hanseatic trade with Norway. Although the University of Copenhagen was founded in 1479 many still went to Rostock. After the Reformation many attended the University of Wittenberg. Finally in the seventeenth century royal decrees made it difficult to attend foreign universities, and Norwegians now went to Copenhagen.[299]

The law school of the University of Oslo consists of thirteen professors, eight teaching courses in law and five in socio-economic subjects.[300] Except for the professor teaching insurance law, those professors teaching courses in law are designated as professors of jurisprudence. The division of subjects is determined by the faculty. Frede Castberg, appointed in 1928, teaches constitutional law, administrative law, and international law. Th. Grundt, appointed in 1930, teaches insurance law. Carl J. Arnholm, appointed in 1933, teaches the law of agreements, the law of mortgages, the law of persons, family law, and inheritance law. Kristen Anderson, appointed in 1939, teaches the law of special obligations, the law of damages, and labor law. Knut Robberstad, appointed in 1941, teaches legal history, property, and the law as to protection of intangible rights. Per Augdahl, appointed in 1941, teaches legal bibliography, the general law of obligations, corporations and civil procedure. Johan Andenaes, appointed in 1945, teaches criminal law and criminal procedure. Sjur Braekhus, appointed in 1948, teaches admiralty law. Professor Arnholm was chosen dean for the period 1950-1952. There are unfilled a professorship and an instructorship. The study of law lasts five years and leads to the degree of *Candidatus juris*.[301] The study of economics also extends over five years and leads to the degree of *Candidatus oeconomiae*.

Jurisprudence and Legal Philosophy

It was the medieval conception that the ecclesiastical system of rights founded on the Mosaic Law and the biblical canons should be acknowledged as directly and universally in force as being the "Laws of God." The legislator must keep such laws in mind when formulating the law. The Protestant Reformation did not completely end this attitude. The Norwegian Code of Christian V contains references to the Decalogue and the "Law of God."[302] Later, Roman law became a source, it being taught at the University of Copenhagen as early as 1539. But the regulations of the University made it clear that "we are not following Roman law in these kingdoms, but have our own laws."

Ludvig Holberg (1684-1754), a native of Bergen and the first completely modern philosopher of the Scandinavian states, presented a system of natural law similar to that of Pufendorff and Thomasius in a leading treatise.[303] That part of the treatise on property rights is largely founded on Roman law and the whole treatise is pervaded by Christian teachings. J. B. Dons[304] and L. Norregaard[305] sought to bring the principal truths of natural law into actual operation. Norregaard, a disciple of Christian Wolff, the German advocate of natural law, concluded that "the law of Nature is the sole subsidiary law, to which the Danish and Norwegian jurist must turn for the decision of anything left doubtful in the laws." If positive law and natural law conflicted, natural law prevailed. He stressed the kinship between natural law and Roman law and urged jurists to consult the latter as a guide to the former. Systematic works on the nature of law were written by L. L. Kongslev[306] and F. T. Hurtigkarl.[307]

The abandonment of natural law as basic in the development of positive law, for Norway as well as for Denmark, was to a large extent effected by the Danish jurist Anders S. Örsted (1778-1860).[308] He interpreted natural law as largely embodying the general concepts which had developed within the field of law, particularly in customary law.[309] Örsted laid the foundation for both Danish and Norwegian law. He forced the change from a speculative to a realistic basis. "In Danish-Norwegian jurisprudence no one stands higher than he nor even equal with him."[310] Norwegian legal philosophy is close to that of other Scandinavian states, but closest to the Danish.

Prior to 1850 Norway had almost no professional philosophers.[311] At the University of Oslo, Niels Treschow (1751-1833), its first rector and professor of philosophy, allied himself rather closely to Wolff's theory of natural law, but he subjected this theory to a further eclectic criticism.[312] In 1833 the older Frederik Stang published a treatise in the vein of Savigny.[313]

The transition to an empirical and historical point of view was made by Professor Anton Martin Schweigaard.[314] Schweigaard is the first great name in Norwegian jurisprudence among native Norwegians, ranking second only to Örsted in his influence on Norwegian law.[315] With Örsted's help he developed a historical view of Norwegian law similar to Savigny's. He made foundational studies in procedure. But he adopted an analytic-descriptive method and was too preoccupied with the particular. A third great figure was Francis Hagerup (1853-1921). Contrary to

Schweigaard he advocated a following of general principles in a constructive fashion. He relied heavily on German and Roman law concepts in his broad scholarship. Frederik Stang (1867-1941) was outstanding in the economic branches of the law, and sought closer contacts between theory and practical business life.[316] Outstanding in the field of constitutional law were the older Frederik Stang, Thorkel Aschehoug,[317] and Bredo Morgenstierne. Bernhard Getz is the leading figure in criminal law, and was notable in court procedure. L. M. B. Aubert was famous in both legal history and philosophy.[318] Ebbe Hertzberg played a similar role. Hallager, Platou, Scheel and Gjelsvik made contributions in the economic branches of the law. Recent leaders are Ragnar Knoph[319] and Frede Castberg.[320]

Ragnar Knoph has made a useful study of classification of Norwegian law.[321] The two broadest classes are public law and private law. Under public law he would place constitutional law, procedure, and criminal law. Under private law he would place: *personretten* governing the rights of individuals as persons such as minors and insane; *familieretten* governing family rights such as marriage, divorce, illegitimacy and adoption; *formueretten* governing numerous important economic rights; *tingsretten* governing rights of property such as possession and joint property; *fordringsretten* governing bills and notes and sales; *aandsretten* governing various intangible rights such as patents, art, names, and photography; *panteretten* governing mortgages and creditor's rights; *sammenslutningenes rett* governing rights of association; *arveretten* governing rights of inheritance; and *skadebot* and *straff* governing torts and crimes.

Legal History

Norwegian legal history may best be studied by breaking it down into four fixed periods.[322] The first period ends in 1274 at which time the national laws of King Magnus Lawmender came into effect. The second period ends in 1688 when King Christian V's Norwegian law became effective. The third period ends in 1814 when Norway was separated from Denmark. The fourth period is that since 1814 and commences with the Norwegian Constitution.

One of the first fairly complete accounts of the early legal history of Norway was by Holberg.[323] Konrad Maurer of Munich, born in 1823, wrote numerous treatises concerning the ancient law of Norway.[324] He marks the transition to a critical and systematic approach. Ludwig M. B. Aubert made several significant contributions,[325] as did Frederik Peter Brandt;[326] Peter Andreas Munch[327] and Rudolf Keyser[328] produced notable works. Professor Ebbe C. H. Hertzberg is one of the leading writers on northern legal sources.[329] An important writer at the end of the nineteenth century was Absalon Taranger.[330] Thorkel Aschehoug has written a history of the constitutional status of Norway up to 1814.[331] The leading American writer has been Professor Laurence M. Larson of the University of Illinois.[332]

NOTES—CHAPTER III—NORWEGIAN LAW

1. *The Immigration and Naturalization Systems of the United States*. Report of the Committee on the Judiciary pursuant to Sen. Res. 137, Sen. Rep. No. 1515, 81st Cong., 2d Sess. 118-120 (1950). See also Karen Larsen, *A History of Norway*, pp. 431, 467 (1948); Leola Nelson Bergmann, *Americans from Norway* (1950).

2. Hjalmar H. Boyesen, *A History of Norway*, p. 25 (1900).

3. Allen Mawer, *The Vikings* (1913); T. D. Kendrick, *A History of the Vikings* (1930); Karen Larsen, *A History of Norway*, pp. 35-63 (1948).

4. James Westfall Thompson, *An Economic and Social History of the Middle Ages*, p. 283 (1928).

5. Knut Gjerset, *History of the Norwegian People*, I, 118 (1927); Snorre Sturlason, *Heimskringla*, pp. 7-43 (Everyman's Library, 1930).

6. Knut Gjerset, op. cit., I, 120-60. But the period of consolidation continued until 1030. Johan Schreiner in *The Norway Year Book*, p. 53 (1950).

7. As early as 700 a small group of Norwegians had settled in Jämtland. Konrad Maurer, *Vorlesungen Über Altnordische Rechts Geschichte*, I, 7, 34 (1907).

8. A short time later the Faroes are spoken of as a Norwegian dependency. Knut Gjerset, op. cit., I, 137 (1927).

9. *Ibid.*, I, 130 (1927).

10. *Ibid.*, p. 141 (1927).

11. *Ibid.*, pp. 142-45 (1927).

12. *Ibid.*, pp. 145-53 (1927).

13. *Ibid.*, pp. 153-59 (1927).

14. Karen Larsen, op. cit., p. 81 (1948); Knut Gjerset, op. cit., I, 171 (1927).

15. Gorm, the first king of all Denmark, is said to have been the son of a Norwegian chief, Hardeknud. E. C. Otte, *Norway, Sweden and Denmark*, p. 20 (1928).

16. Knut Gjerset, op. cit., I, 166 (1927). After Haakon's death the ties of Jämtland to Norway were very weak. It has been asserted that it was not lost until the time of Saint Olaf. Karen Larsen, op. cit., p. 115 (1948).

17. Knut Gjerset, op. cit., I, 145, 169 (1927).

18. *Ibid.*, p. 171 (1927).

19. *Ibid.*, pp. 174-97 (1927).

20. Absalon Taranger, *Den Angelsaksiske Kirkes, Indflydelse Paa Den Norske*. Oslo, 1890.

21. Knut Gjerset, op. cit., I, 131, 179 (1927). The earl had taken possession of Caithness, Sutherland, Ross, Moray and Argyle in Scotland.

22. *Ibid.*, p. 136 (1927).

23. *Ibid.*, pp. 196-97, 243-44 (1927).

24. *Ibid.*, pp. 223-29 (1927).

25. *Ibid.*, pp. 250-52 (1927).

26. Hjalmar H. Boyesen, *History of Norway*, pp. 197-98 (1900).

27. For Canute's career see Laurence M. Larson, *Canute the Great* (1912).

28. Knut Gjerset, op. cit., I, 270 (1927).

29. *Ibid.*, p. 279 (1927).

30. Hjalmar H. Boyesen, op. cit., pp. 267-68 (1900).

31. Knut Gjerset, op. cit., I, 287-94 (1927); Hope Muntz, *The Golden Warrior*, pp. 197-267 (1950).

32. Knut Gjerset, op. cit., I, 237, 286 (1927).

33. *Ibid.*, p. 294 (1927).

34. *Ibid.*, pp. 231, 238, 306 (1927).
35. *Ibid.*, p. 312 (1927).
36. *Ibid.*, pp. 320-21 (1927).
37. Karen Larsen, *A History of Norway*, p. 122 (1948).
38. Knut Gjerset, *op. cit.*, I, 231, 348 (1927).
39. *Ibid.*, p. 338 (1927).
40. *Ibid.*, pp. 355-58 (1927).
41. *Ibid.*, p. 374 (1927).
42. *Ibid.*, pp. 239, 396 (1927).
43. *Ibid.*, p. 360 (1927).
44. *Ibid.*, p. 365 (1927).
45. *Ibid.*, pp. 375-86 (1927).
46. *Ibid.*, p. 397 (1927).
47. *Ibid.*, pp. 399-404 (1927).
48. *Ibid.*, p. 408 (1927).
49. *Ibid.*, p. 409 (1927).
50. *Ibid.*, p. 414 (1927). Haakon is the subject of Henrik Ibsen's play *The Pretenders*.
51. *Ibid.*, p. 416 (1927).
52. *Ibid.*, p. 420 (1927).
53. *Ibid.*, pp. 424-26 (1927).
54. *Ibid.*, p. 430 (1927).
55. Among their descendents was Erling Vidkunsson, regent of Norway from 1323 to 1330. Øverland, *Det Norske Folks Liv Og Historie*, III, 744-45, 823.
56. T. D. Kendrick, *op. cit.*, p. 317 (1930).
57. Knut Gjerset, *op. cit.*, I, 438-43 (1927).
58. *Ibid.*, p. 201 (1927).
59. *Ibid.*, pp. 434-38 (1927).
60. Karen Larsen, *op. cit.*, p. 171 (1948); Knut Gjerset, *op. cit.*, I, 442-43 (1927).
61. Knut Gjerset, *op. cit.*, I, 233-34 (1927).
62. Peter A. Munch, *Det Norske Folks Historie*, II, 529. See John A. Gade, *The Hanseatic Control of Norwegian Commerce During the Late Middle Ages* (1951).
63. Knut Gjerset, *op. cit.*, I, 457-58 (1927).
64. *Ibid.*, pp. 467-73 (1927).
65. *Ibid.*, pp. 473-83 (1927).
66. *Ibid.*, pp. 483-92 (1927).
67. Paul Sinding, *History of Scandinavia*, p. 124 (1858).
68. Johan Schreiner in *The Norway Year Book*, p. 54 (1950).
69. Knut Gjerset, *op. cit.*, II, 4 (1927). For a valuable historical note on the period from 1319 to 1335 see Sigrid Undset, *Kristin Lavransdatter*, pp. 1060-62 (1939).
70. "The Norwegians were solidly behind an alliance with the conqueror of the Hansa." Fletcher Pratt, *The Third King*, p. 258 (1950).
71. Knut Gjerset, *op. cit.*, II, 30 (1927).
72. *Ibid.*, pp. 36-43 (1927).
73. *Ibid.*, pp. 43-64 (1927).
74. *Ibid.*, p. 36 (1927).
75. *Ibid.*, pp. 64-66 (1927).
76. *Ibid.*, pp. 66-67 (1927).
77. *Ibid.*, pp. 132, 136; II, 73-74 (1927). Payments due from Scotland under the Treaty of Perth as to the Hebrides were annulled.
78. *Ibid.*, I, 134 (1927).
79. *Ibid.*, II, 77-89 (1927).
80. *Ibid.*, pp. 103-19 (1927).
81. *Ibid.*, pp. 115-27 (1927).

82. *Ibid.*, pp. 127-48 (1927).

83. *Ibid.*, pp. 148-83 (1927).

84. *Ibid.*, pp. 183-215 (1927).

85. *Ibid.*, pp. 216-47 (1927).

86. *Ibid.*, pp. 247-300 (1927).

87. The complaints of the Norwegians against Danish rule are set forth by a contemporary poet. Petter Dass, *Nordlands Trompet*, pp. 49-56 (Oslo, 1927, ed. by Didrik A. Seip).

88. On neutrality policy from 1600 to 1814 see Franklin D. Scott, *The United States and Scandinavia*, pp. 205-11 (1950).

89. Knut Gjerset, *op. cit.*, II, 300-28 (1927).

90. *Ibid.*, pp. 328-43 (1927).

91. *Ibid.*, pp. 343-49 (1927).

92. Bryn J. Hovde, *The Scandinavian Countries, 1720-1865*, pp. 195-96 (1948).

93. Knut Gjerset, *op. cit.*, II, 349-89 (1927). In 1769 the first census was taken. The population was about 700,000. Karen Larsen, *op. cit.*, p. 327 (1948).

94. Bryn J. Hovde, *op. cit.*, pp. 199-202 (1948).

95. As to the attitude of the Norwegian people see Bryn J. Hovde, *ibid.*, pp. 219-20 (1948).

96. Knut Gjerset, *op. cit.*, II, 389-416 (1927).

97. Franklin D. Scott, *The United States and Scandinavia*, p. 38 (1950).

98. Knut Gjerset, *op. cit.*, II, 415 (1927).

99. *Ibid.*, pp. 417-44 (1927).

100. *Ibid.*, pp. 450-89 (1927).

101. On the position of the Storthing between 1815 and 1830 see Bryn J. Hovde, *op. cit.*, pp. 510-18 (1948). From 1830 to 1865 see *Ibid.*, pp. 555-67 (1948).

102. Knut Gjerset, *op. cit.*, II, 489-522 (1927).

103. Bryn J. Hovde, *op. cit.*, pp. 636-41 (1948).

104. Knut Gjerset, *op. cit.*, II, 522-34 (1927).

105. *Ibid.*, pp. 534-85 (1927).

106. For citation of the literature on this question see Knut Gjerset, *op. cit.*, II,. 536-37 (1927).

107. For the Swedish viewpoint see K. Nordlund, *The Swedish-Norwegian Union Crisis*. Upssala. (1905).

108. Bredo Morgenstierne, "Norway's Integrity and Neutrality." 31 *L. Q. Rev.* 389, 391 (1915).

109. The Grisbadarna Case, Scott, *Hague Court Reports*, pp. 122, 487; 4 *Am. J. Int. L.* 226 (1910).

110. Karen Larsen, *op. cit.*, pp. 505-11 (1948).

111. S. Shepard Jones, *The Scandinavian States and the League of Nations*, pp. 70-76 (1939).

112. Francis Hagerup was on the advisory committee of ten jurists which prepared plans for the Court. S. Shepard Jones, *op. cit.*, pp. 173-79 (1939).

113. Manley O. Hudson, *The Permanent Court of International Justice*, pp. 242, 250 (1934). See P. I. Paulsen, "Frederik Valdemar Nikolai Beichmann," 51 *Tidsskrift for Rettsvitenskap* 221-23 (1939).

114. On Spitzbergen, Jan Mayen, and the Antarctic Possessions see Anders K. Orvin's discussion in *The Norway Year Book*, pp. 20-31 (1950).

115. L. Preuss, "Dispute Between Denmark and Norway over the Sovereignty of East Greenland," 26 *Am. J. Int. L.* 469 (1932); Charles Cheney Hyde, "The Case Concerning the Legal Status of Eastern Greenland," 27 *Am. J. Int. L.* 732 (1933).

116. The judgment is set forth in 20 *Temp. L. Q.* 168, 198-202 (1946).

117. Charles Cheney Hyde, "The City of Flint," 34 *Am. J. Int. L.* 89 (1940); Note, 19 *Neb. L. Bull.* 45 (1940); Florence J. Harriman, *Mission to the North*, pp. 229-45 (1941).

118. Edwin M. Borchard, "Was Norway Delinquent in the Case of the Altmark?"

34 *Am. J. Int. L.* 289 (1940); Note 21 *Neb. L. Rev.* 190 (1942); Halvdan Koht, *Norway: Neutral and Invaded,* pp. 37-41 (1941).
119. Henning Friis, *Scandinavia Between East and West,* p. 281 (1950).
120. *Ibid.,* p. 290 (1950).
121. Manley O. Hudson, "The New Bench of the World Court," 32 *A.B.A.J.* 140, 142 (1946).
122. "The Quarter's History—Norway," 38 *Am. Scand. Rev.* 269 (1950).
123. I.C.J. Reports, 1951, pp. 116-206. See D. H. N. Johnson, "The Anglo-Norwegian Fisheries Case," 1 *Int. and Comparative L. Q.* 145 (1952).
124. Laurence M. Larson, *The Earliest Norwegian Laws,* p. 4 (1935); Karen Larsen, *op. cit.,* p. 30 (1948); Knut Gjerset, *op. cit.,* I, 111-14 (1927). The three classes of *things* are described in Sigrid Undset, *Kristin Lavransdatter,* p. 1062 (1939).
125. Laurence M. Larson, *op. cit.,* pp. 6-7 (1935); Karen Larsen, *op. cit.,* p. 79 (1948).
126. *The Older Eidsivatinglov* (Oslo, 1914); Laurence M. Larson, *op. cit.,* pp. 6-7, 11 (1935). Only the laws concerning the church survive.
127. The Older Law of the Gulathing is set forth in Laurence M. Larson, *op. cit.,* pp. 35-210 (1935). As to its date of origin see A. Taranger, "Alting og Lagting" in *Historisk Tidsskrift,* XXXIX, 137-38 (1930, No. 3). For description of its operation see Laurence M. Larson, *op. cit.,* pp. 7-9 (1935).
128. Gustav Storm, *Sigurd Rannesöns Proces* (Oslo, 1877); Knut Gjerset, *op. cit.,* I, 326-33 (1927).
129. The *lagthings* are said to have become in a measure representative bodies in the reign of Haakon the Good (934-961). Knut Gjerset, *op. cit.,* I, 165 (1927).
130. The older law of the Frostathing is set forth in Laurence M. Larson, *op. cit.,* pp. 213-405 (1935). For description of its operation see *ibid.,* pp. 9-11 (1935).
131. *The Older Borgartinglov* (Oslo, 1914). Only the law concerning the church survives. For discussion of governmental and legal reforms under Olaf see Knut Gjerset, *op. cit.,* I, 256-60 (1927).
132. Ebbe Hertzberg in *A General Survey of Continental Legal History,* pp. 531, 541-42 (1912). Compare Franklin D. Scott, *op. cit.,* p. 48 (1950): "The kings in Sweden and Denmark gradually took over the administration of justice, but in Norway the *things* persisted."
133. Engelmann, *A History of Continental Civil Procedure,* p. 203 (1927); Ebbe C. H. Hertzberg, *Grundtraekkene I Den Aeldste Norske Proces,* pp. 114, 116, 170, 177 (Oslo, 1874); Knut Gjerset, *op. cit.,* I, 114 (1927).
134. Ebbe Hertzberg in *A General Survey of Continental Legal History,* pp. 531, 534 (1912).
135. *Ibid.,* p. 537 (1912); Ebbe Hertzberg, *Grundtraekkene I Den Aeldste Norske Proces,* pp. 156-77 (1874).
136. Absalon Taranger, *Trondheimens Forfatningshistorie,* p. 28. For references in the Frostathing law see Laurence M. Larson, *op. cit.,* pp. 213, 215, and 218 (1935).
137. Laurence M. Larson, *op. cit.,* p. 24 (1935). In the thirteenth century the lawmen got jurisdiction outside of the *thing* and a casting vote in the *logretta* where its members disagreed. Engelmann, *op. cit.,* p. 203 (1927). See also Knut Gjerset, *op. cit.,* I, 388-90 (1927).
138. Karen Larsen, *op. cit.,* p. 162 (1948).
139. Knut Gjerset, *op. cit.,* I, 165 (1927).
140. Karen Larsen, *op. cit.,* p. 163 (1948).
141. The title of "baron" existed only from 1277 to 1308 the older title being *lendermann.* The *lendermann* was a high feudal dignitary who held a fief under the crown in return for certain services in war and peace fixed in each separate case. Neither the title nor the fief was hereditary. Knut Gjerset, *op. cit.,* I, 387-88 (1927); Karen Larsen, *op. cit.,* pp. 119, 162 (1948).
142. Knut Gjerset, *op. cit.,* II, 4 (1927).
143. Ebbe Hertzberg in *A General Survey of Continental Legal History,* pp. 531,

543-45 (1912); Hertzberg, Vor Aeldste Lovtexters Oprindelige Nedskrivelsetid, Historiske Afhandlinger Tilegnede Professor Dr. J. E. Sars, Oslo, 1905; Knut Gjerset, op. cit., I, 354-55 (1927).

144. "It seems that the establishment of the original text of these Norwegian codes has presented a much simpler problem than has been the case with the text of many of the national sources of English law." Henry L. McClintock, Book Review, 20 Minn. L. Rev. 700, 701 (1936).

Holdsworth has pointed out that these laws help us to understand the early law of northern England and that "they present a more instructive period of tribal society and ideas than many codes earlier in date. They are less influenced by the ideas drawn from Roman and ecclesiastical law, which, even in the sixth and seventh centuries were reshaping the old tribal ideas of nations settled in less remote parts of Europe." 2 Holdsworth, History of English Law, p. 33 (1922).

"Norway has an unusually large treasure of old laws extant, which furnish the richest sources we possess for the study of the whole civilization of the age." Karen Larsen, op. cit., p. 118 (1948).

145. Laurence M. Larson, op. cit., pp. 26-31 (1935).

146. Bryce, Studies in History and Jurisprudence, I, 312, 342 (1901); Ebbe Hertzberg in A General Survey of Continental Legal History, pp. 531, 544 (1912). Thomas Carlyle refers to a code of King Magnus of 1037 as the Gragas. The Early Kings of Norway, p. 168 (1875). To the same effect see Snorre Sturlason, Heimskringla, p. 141 (Everyman's Library, 1930).

147. Laurence M. Larson, op. cit., p. 200 (1935).

148. Ebbe Hertzberg, op. cit., pp. 549-52 (1912); Knut Gjerset, op. cit., I, 456-67 (1927).

149. Karen Larsen, op. cit., pp. 161-62 (1948).

150. As to his career see Knut Gjerset, op. cit., I, 473-76, 481-82 (1927); Gustav Storm, "Audun Hestakorn og St. Margrete paa Nordnaes," Historisk Tidsskrift, 2nd Ser., IV, 209 et seq.

151. Ebbe Hertzberg, op. cit., p. 552 (1912).

152. Ibid., p. 552 (1912).

153. Ibid., p. 554 (1912).

154. Knut Gjerset, op. cit., II, 142-43 (1927). The Old Norse Language lingered on towards 1600 in legal procedure. A. Sommerfelt in The Norway Year Book, pp. 47-48 (1950).

155. Kong Christian Den Fjerdes Lovbog Af 1604, edited by Hallager and Brandt, Oslo, 1855; Knut Gjerset, op. cit., II, 192 (1927).

156. Ebbe Hertzberg, op. cit., pp. 559-60 (1912); Knut Gjerset, op. cit., II, 236, 267-68 (1927); N. Prebensen and H. Smith, Forarbeiderne Til Kong Christian Den Femtes Norske Lov.

157. Other Norwegian commission members were Jens Toller Rosenheim, Lauritz Christenson, and Jens Alexandersson Hoffener. Hoffener was secretary and the main author of the draft. Absalon Taranger, Utsikt Over Den Norske Retts Historie, pp. 78-79 (1935).

158. The office of lawman and the lagthings were abolished by a law of August 11, 1797. Ebbe Hertzberg, op. cit., p. 564 (1912).

159. The Overhofret was abolished in 1797, but a Stiftsoverret was established.

160. Ebbe Hertzberg, op. cit., p. 562 (1912).

161. Trygve Leivestad, "Custom as a Type of Law in Norway," 54 L. Q. Rev. 95, 266 (1938).

162. Ebbe Hertzberg, op. cit., pp. 533-34 (1912).

163. Ibid., p. 568 (1912).

164. Ragnar Knoph, Oversikt Over Norges Rett, pp. 15-16 (1948). See also Trygve Leivestad, op. cit., 106-07 (1938).

165. Ebbe Hertzberg, op. cit., p. 569 (1912).

166. Ibid., p. 569 (1912).

167. A doctrine of desuetude is stated by Leivestad, *op. cit.*, pp. 107, 279 (1938).

168. Note, "Judicial Abrogation of the Obsolete Statute: A Comparative Study," 64 *Harv. L. Rev.* 1181, 1186 (1951).

169. (1915) *Norsk Retstidende* 81.

170. Trygve Leivestad, *op. cit.*, pp. 110, 269, 272 (1938).

171. On the status of precedents see Leivestad, *op. cit.*, pp. 110-15, 266-70 (1938); Ebbe Hertzberg, *op. cit.*, pp. 569-70 (1912).

172. Leivestad, *op. cit.*, p. 114 (1938).

173. *Ibid.*, pp. 266, 270-72 (1938).

174. H. Munch-Petersen, "Main Features of Scandinavian Law," 43 *L. Q. Rev.* 366 (1927).

175. For a description of the preparation and adoption of the Constitution see Knut Gjerset, *op. cit.*, II, 423-32 (1927). For a socio-economic approach see Bryn J. Hovde, *op. cit.*, pp. 221-28 (1948).

176. It has been asserted that this provision has been violated several times both formally and informally and that the question is one for the Storthing and not the courts. Trygve Leivestad, *op. cit.*, pp. 266, 278 (1938).

177. Knut Gjerset, *op. cit.*, I, 459 (1927); Karen Larsen, *op. cit.*, 163 (1948); T. H. Aschehoug, *Statsforfatningen I Norge Og Danmark Indtil 1814*, p. 140 (1886).

178. Karen Larsen, *op. cit.*, p. 194 (1948).

179. *Ibid.*, p. 253 (1948).

180. *Ibid.*, p. 289 (1948).

181. See Gunnar Hoff in *The Norwegian Year Book*, pp. 64-71 (1950); Ben A. Arneson, *The Democratic Monarchies of Scandinavia*, pp. 77-79, 92-99 (2d ed. 1949).

182. *Nordisk Tidende*, March 13, 1952.

183. As to legislative procedure in Norway see *Stortingets Forretningsorden*. For reports of the debates and proceedings of the Storthing see *Stortingstidende*.

184. Ben A. Arneson, *op. cit.*, pp. 132-33 (2d ed., 1949).

185. In 1945 the majority was only by one vote; in 1949 by ten votes.

186. Walter Galenson, "Nationalization of Industry in Great Britain and Norway," 36 *Am. Scand. Rev.* 234 (1948).

187. Paal Berg, C. J., "Norges Høyesterett," 26 *Svensk Juristtidning* 3, 6 (February 1941).

188. Ben A. Arneson, *op. cit.*, pp. 160-62 (2d ed., 1949); Trygve Leivestad, *op. cit.*, pp. 266, 275-77 (1938).

189. Though Norway has had a Labor government since 1935 there is complete satisfaction with this system. Evan Haynes, *The Selection and Tenure of Judges*, pp. 182-83 (1944).

190. See J. Aars Rynning, "The Legal System," in the *Norway Year Book*, pp. 135-39 (1950).

191. Reginald Heber Smith, "Conciliation Procedure in the Administration of Justice in Norway," *Monthly Labor Review*, June 1926; Nicolay Grevstad, "Norway's Conciliation Tribunals," 2 *J. Am. Jud. Soc.* 5 (1918). The Minneapolis Conciliation Court is based on the Norwegian system. William R. Vance, 1 *Minn. L. Rev.* 107 (1917) and 2 *J. Am. Jud. Soc.* 16 (1918). The Norwegian system is discussed in 68 *Atlantic Monthly* 401 (July 1891) and 72 *Atlantic Monthly* 671 (Nov. 1893).

192. J. Aars Rynning, *The Norway Year Book*, pp. 135 and 138 (1950).

193. As to the position of aliens with regard to suits in Norwegian courts see *ibid.*, pp. 138-39 (1950).

194. "Except for the fact that the legal profession rather disfavors the use of lay judges, the Scandinavian courts as a whole seem to be held in high esteem." Evan Haynes, *op. cit.*, p. 183 (1944).

195. J. Aars Rynning, *op. cit.*, p. 138 (1950).

196. See *The Norway Year Book*, pp. 140-42 (1950).

197. Ben A. Arneson, *op. cit.*, pp. 150, 166 (2d ed. 1949).

198. *A General Survey of Continental Legal History*, pp. 544, 738 (1912); Knut

Gjerset, op. cit., I, 5 (1927). The law may be found in Norges Gamle Love, I, Part III.

199. Knut Gjerset, op. cit., I, 464-66 (1927); T. H. Aschehoug, De Norske Communers Retsforfatning för 1837.

200. Knut Gjerset, op. cit., II, 234 (1927).

201. Bryn J. Hovde, op. cit., pp. 567-69 (1948).

202. For a description of the present system see A. Engh and K. M. Nordanger, Kommunalkunnskap, 2 Vols., Oslo, 1947; Ben A. Arneson, op. cit., pp. 190-99 (2d ed., 1949); The Norway Year Book, pp. 75-80 (1950).

203. Laurence M. Larson, op. cit., p. 20 (1935); A. C. Bang, Udsigt Over Den Norsk Kirkes Historie Under Katholicismen (Oslo, 1887).

204. Knut Gjerset, op. cit., I, 256 (1927). See Konrad Von Maurer, Vorlesungen Über Altnordische Rechtsgeschichte, II (1908).

205. Bryn J. Hovde, op. cit., pp. 315-19, 556-57 (1948).

206. Ibid., pp. 562, 696-97 (1948).

207. Ibid., p. 346 (1948).

208. Egil Brekke, "The Church," in The Norway Year Book, p. 153 (1950).

209. On education between 1720 and 1865 see Bryn J. Hovde, op. cit., pp. 589-616 (1948).

210. See Per G. Stensland, "Adult Education" in Henning Friis, op. cit., pp. 225-53 (1950).

211. Einar Boyesen, "Educational System" in The Norway Year Book, pp. 157-164 (1950).

212. Franklin D. Scott, op. cit., pp. 48, 58 (1950).

213. Knut Gjerset, op. cit., I, 449 (1927).

214. Knut Gjerset, op. cit., II, 186-92 (1927); Bryn J. Hovde, op. cit., p. 61 (1948); Halvdan Koht, Norsk Bondereising (Oslo, 1926).

215. Ebbe Hertzberg, op. cit., pp. 565-66 (1912); Knut Gjerset, op. cit., II, 278-81 (1927).

216. As to such reforms see Bryn J. Hovde, op. cit., pp. 276-302 (1948); as to the situation prior to 1800 see ibid., pp. 59-88 (1948).

217. On agriculture today see The Norway Year Book, pp. 290-98 (1950).

218. Franklin D. Scott, op. cit., p. 73 (1950); Simon Skappel, Om Husmandsvaesenet I Norge (Oslo, 1922); Bryn J. Hovde, op. cit., pp. 617-25, 642-43, 660-61 (1948).

219. Franklin D. Scott, op. cit., p. 105 (1950).

220. Ben A. Arneson, op. cit., pp. 266-69 (2d ed., 1949); The Norway Year Book, pp. 295-97 (1950).

221. Von Bar, A History of Continental Criminal Law, pp. 119-41 (1916), based largely on Stemann, Den Danske Retshistorie Indtil Kristian V's Love (Copenhagen 1871).

222. Laurence M. Larson, op. cit., p. 15 (1935).

223. Laurence M. Larson, "Witnesses and Oath Helpers in Old Norwegian Law," in Haskins Anniversary Essays, pp. 144-52 (1929).

224. The best known form consisted of holding or walking on red-hot irons. This mode of trial was abolished in 1247. Knut Gjerset, op. cit., I, 115, 423 (1927).

225. As to changes made under Magnus Lawmender see ibid., 460-62 (1927).

226. Von Bar, op. cit., pp. 291-97 (1916).

227. Knut Gjerset, op. cit., II, 175-76 (1927).

228. Ebbe Hertzberg, op. cit., p. 563 (1912).

229. Ibid., pp. 563, 567 (1912); Von Bar, op. cit., p. 368 (1916).

230. Bryn J. Hovde, op. cit., p. 704 (1948); Anton Schweigaard, Commentar Over Den Norske Criminallov (Oslo, 1844-1846).

231. Sigurd Grieg, "Botsfengslet 100 år," Nordisk Tidende, July 5, 1951, p. 3. As to prison legislation from 1770 see Bryn J. Hovde, op. cit., pp. 699-705 (1948).

232. Franz von Liszt has influenced the Norwegian criminal law more than any

foreigner except Anders S. Örsted of Denmark. Johannes Andenaes, "Franz von Liszt og Straffelovsreform i Norge," 36 *Svensk Juristtidning* 167 (1951).

233. Ole F. Harbek, "Endringer i den norske straffelov," 37 *Svensk Juristtigning* 66-71 (1952).

234. *The Norway Year Book*, p. 200 (1950). Sweden followed in 1902 and Denmark in 1905. *Social Denmark*, pp. 137, 155 (1947).

235. Ebbe Hertzberg, *op. cit.*, pp. 563-64 (1912).

236. Esmein, *A History of Continental Criminal Procedure*, p. 593 (1913). It has been translated into Italian and accompanied with an introduction on the history of criminal procedure in Norway. Brusa, *Codice Di Procedure Penale Norvegese* (Turin, 1900).

237. Under the system of penal orders a judge may convict the accused without hearing him and without prior proceedings as to certain lesser crimes if the defendant desires. The penal orders are issued by the public prosecutor. It permits the defendant to avoid public trial. Esmein, *op. cit.*, 605-06 (1913); *The Norway Year Book*, p. 143 (1950).

238. Edwin M. Borchard, *Convicting the Innocent*, pp. 385-401 (1932). It is translated in Sen. Doc. 974, 62d Cong., 3rd Sess., p. 25.

239. *The Norway Year Book*, p. 141 (1950).

240. Eric F. Schweinburg, "Legal Assistance Abroad," 17 *U. Chi. L. Rev.* 270, 291.

241. Terje Wold, "The 1942 Enactment for the Defence of the Norwegian State," 20 *Can. Bar Rev.* 505 (1942).

242. A. Hemming Sjöberg, *Domen Over Quisling*, Stockholm 1946; Benjamin Vogt, "Quisling: Menneske og Forbryter," 32 *Svensk Juristtidning* 161-76 (1947); Henrik Bergh, "Quisling," 32 *ibid.*, 359-63; Johannes Andanaes reviewing Sjöberg's book, 32 *ibid.*, 450-55; Birger Ekeberg, Erik Solem, 34 *ibid.*, 561-66 (1949).

243. J. Aars Rynning in *The Norway Year Book*, pp. 144-48 (1950); Johan Lyng, *Forraederiets Epoke* (Oslo, 1948).

244. *War Crimes Trials*, VI, *The Trial of Von Falkenhorst* (1949), reviewed by Lester B. Orfield, 23 *Temp. L. Q.*, 442 (1950).

245. *The Norway Year Book*, p. 143 (1950).

246. Laurence M. Larson, *op. cit.*, p. 18 (1935); Konrad Von Maurer, "Altnorwegiches Gerichtswesen," *Vorlesungen über Altnordische Rechtsgeschichte*, Vol. I, Part 2 (1907).

247. Knut Gjerset, *op. cit.*, I, 463 (1927); Sigrid Undset, *Kristin Lavransdatter*, pp. 1062-63 (1939).

248. Sigrid Undset, *op. cit.*, pp. 1053, 1063 (1939).

249. Robert W. Millar, "The Mechanism of Fact-Discovery: A Study in Comparative Civil Procedure," 32 *Ill. L. Rev.* 424, 432 (1937).

250. Hagerup, *Forelaesninger over den Norske Civilproces*, I, 103 (2d ed., 1903); Munch-Petersen, *Den Danske Retspleje*, I, 25 (2d ed., 1923).

251. Ebbe Hertzberg, *op. cit.*, p. 567 (1912).

252. Robert W. Millar in *David Dudley Field Centenary Essays*, pp. 120, 121, 137 (1949).

253. Except in the cities a single judge is also used in Sweden and Finland. Robert W. Millar, *op. cit.*, pp. 120, 121-22 (1949).

254. *Ibid.*, pp. 120, 123 (1949).

255. *Ibid.*, p. 128 (1949).

256. *Ibid.*, p. 130 (1949), citing *Lov Om Rettergangsmaaten for Tvistemaal*, sections 190-212.

257. *Ibid.*, p. 131 (1949).

258. *Ibid.*, p. 139 (1949).

259. As to pleading see Robert W. Millar, "Some Comparative Aspects of Civil Pleading Under Anglo-American and Continental Systems," 12 *A.B.A.J.* 401 (1926).

260. The Norwegian and Danish systems are described by Robert W. Millar, "The

Mechanism of Fact-Discovery: A Study in Comparative Civil Procedure," 32 *Ill. L. Rev.* 424, 432-35 (1937).

261. Skeie, *Den Norske Civil Proces,* II, 390 (1931).

262. Florence J. Harriman, *Mission to the North,* p. 142 (1941). On social legislation in Norway see "Social Welfare" in Henning Friis, *op. cit.,* pp. 139-68 (1950); Ben A. Arneson, *op. cit.,* pp. 218-78 (2d ed., 1949); Ottar Lund, "Social Legislation" in *The Norway Year Book,* pp. 187-202 (1950).

263. Joint Committee on International Social Policy, *New Universal Social Security Plan for Norway* (Oslo, 1949).

264. Bryn J. Hovde, *op. cit.,* pp. 230-34 (1948). On industry and trade between 1720 and 1830 see *ibid.,* pp. 15-58 (1948).

265. *Ibid.,* p. 239 (1948).

266. *Ibid.,* p. 240 (1948).

267. Ebbe Hertzberg, *op. cit.,* p. 565 (1912). This law was largely the work of Professor John Collett, husband of Camilla Collett. Bryn J. Hovde, *op. cit.,* pp. 686-88 (1948).

268. Florence J. Harriman, *Mission to the North,* p. 146 (1941). See also L. Magnusson, "Norwegian Laws of Illegitimacy," *U. S. Children's Bureau, Leg. Ser. No. 1,* Pub. No. 31 (1918); Robbins and Deak, "The Familial Property Rights of Illegitimate Children," 30 *Col. L. Rev.* 308, 325 (1930); Note, 16 *Col. L. Rev.* 698 (1916).

269. Bryn J. Hovde, *op. cit.,* p. 698 (1948).

270. Henry Weihofen, *Insanity as a Defense in Criminal Law,* p. 99 (1933).

271. For the history of the movement see Walter Galenson, *Labor in Norway* (1949); Galenson, "The Labor Movement and Industrial Relations" in Henning Friis, *op. cit.,* pp. 113-38 (1950).

272. Walter Galenson, *Labor in Norway,* pp. 205-07 (1949).

273. Karen Larsen, *op. cit.,* pp. 464-66 (1948).

274. Ben A. Arneson, *op. cit.,* pp. 218-19 (2d ed., 1949).

275. *Ibid.,* pp. 220-21 (2d ed., 1949); *The Norway Year Book,* pp. 189-91 (1950).

276. *Ibid.,* pp. 225-26 (2d ed., 1949); *The Norway Year Book,* pp. 191-93 (1950).

277. *Ibid.,* p. 238 (2d ed., 1949).

278. *Ibid.,* pp. 242-43 (1949); *The Norway Year Book,* pp. 193-94 (1950).

279. *Ibid.,* pp. 247-50 (1949); *The Norway Year Book,* pp. 188-89 (1950).

280. On public health in Norway prior to 1865 see Bryn J. Hovde, *op. cit.,* pp. 573-88 (1948).

281. *Ibid.,* p. 588 (1948). On the present system see "Public Health Administration" in *The Norway Year Book,* pp. 184-87 (1950).

282. "The Quarter's History—Norway," 37 *Am. Scand. Rev.* 266, 267 (1949).

283. Bryn J. Hovde, *op. cit.,* p. 641 (1948).

284. Ottar Lund in *The Norway Year Book,* p. 197 (1950).

285. *The Norway Year Book,* p. 79 (1950).

286. *Ibid.,* pp. 194-95 (1950).

287. *New York Times,* May 18, 1952.

288. See Charles Abrams, "Housing," in Henning Friis, *op. cit.,* pp. 169-98 (1950).

289. Upon the temperance movement in Norway see Bryn J. Hovde, *op. cit.,* pp. 662-79 (1948).

290. Ben A. Arneson, *op. cit.,* pp. 272-75 (2d ed., 1949).

291. *The Norway Year Book,* p. 201 (1950).

292. In 1932 new legislation was enacted in Norway as to checks and bills of exchange.

293. Ragnar Knoph, *Oversikt Over Norges Rett,* p. 14 (1948).

294. "The Quarter's History—Norway," 38 *Am. Scand. Rev.* 168, 170 (1950).

295. *New York Times,* December 24, 1951, p. 3.

296. Ebbe Hertzberg, *op. cit.*, p. 564 (1912).

297. Holger Wiklund, "Advokatersamfundet efter processreformen," 35 *Svensk Juristtidning* 812, 815-17 (1950).

298. Knut Gjerset, *op. cit.*, II, 89-90 (1927); *Oslo the Capital of Norway*, p. 78 (1950).

299. For a description of early law study at Copenhagen see Ragner Knoph, "Et 200—års jubileum," 50 *Tidsskrift for Rettvitenskap* 321-37 (1938).

300. 35 *Svensk Juristtidning* 223 (1950).

301. Einar Molland, "The University and Academic Life," in *Oslo the Capital of Norway*, pp. 113, 130 (1950).

302. Ebbe Hertzberg, *op. cit.*, p. 570 (1912).

303. *Introduktion til Natur-Og Folkeretten* (Copenhagen 1716 and 1763). See Erik Solem, "Holberg som jurist," 59 *Tidsskrift for Rettsvitenskap* 381-433, 525-56 (1946).

304. *Forelaesninger over den Danske og Norske Lov* (Copenhagen, 1781).

305. *Natur-og Folkeret* (Copenhagen, 1776) and *Forelaesninger* (Copenhagen, 1797).

306. *Den Danske og Norske Private Rets Første Grunde* (Copenhagen, 1792).

307. *Den Danske og Norske Rets Første Grunde* (Copenhagen, 1820).

308. Ebbe Hertzberg, *op. cit.*, pp. 572-73 (1912).

309. *Eunomia, Samling af Afhandlinger, Henhörende til Moralfilosofien, Stats-Filosofien og den Danske-Norske Lovkyndighed* (Copenhagen, 1815-1822).

310. Ragnar Knoph, *Oversikt over Norges Rett*, p. 21 (1948).

311. Bryn J. Hovde, *op. cit.*, p. 353 (1948).

312. *Lovgivningsprincipper* (Oslo, 1821-1823).

313. *Fremstilling av Norges Konstitutionelle Ret* (Oslo, 1833).

314. "Betragninger over Retvidenskabens Naervaerende Tilstand i Tyskland," in *Dansk Juridisk Tidskrift* (1834); "De la philosophie allemande," in *La France Litteraire* (17th Vol., 1835).

315. Ragnar Knoph, *Oversikt over Norges Rett*, p. 21 (1948).

316. See articles on Stang in 55 *Tidsskrift for Rettsvitenskap*, 1-57 (1942).

317. *Indledning til den Norske Retsvidenskab* (Oslo, 1845); *Norges Offentlige Ret: Den Nuvaerende Statsforfatning* (Oslo, 1875-1885).

318. *De Norske Retskilder og Deres Anvendelse* (Oslo, 1877).

319. *Rettslige Standarder, Saerlig Grunnlovens, #97.* (Oslo, 1939.)

320. *Rettsfilosofiske Grunnsporsmal* (Oslo, 1939). See the review by Ivar Strahl, "Idealism och Realism i Rättsvetenskapen," 26 *Svensk Juristtidning* 302-30 (1941).

321. *Oversikt over Norges Rett* (1948).

322. Absalon Taranger, *Utsikt Over Den Norske Retts Historie*, p. 16 (1935).

323. *Danmarks og Norges Geistlige og Verldslige Stat* (Copenhagen, 1762).

324. *Die Bekehrung des Norwegischen Stammes Zum Christentum* (Munich, 1855-1856); *Die Eingangsformel der Altnordischen Rechts—Und Gesetzbücher* (Munich, 1886); *Die Enstehungszeit der Älteren Frostutingslog* (Munich, 1875); *Die Entstehungszeit der Älteren Gulatingslog* (Munich, 1872); *Udsigt over de Nordgermanske Retskilders Historie* (Oslo, 1878); *Vorlesungen über Altnordische Rechtsgeschichte* (Leipzig, 1907-1910).

325. *Grundbögernes Historie i Norge, Danmark, og Tildels i Tyskland* (Oslo, 1892); *Kontraktpantets Historiske Udvidling Isaer i Dansk og Norsk Ret* (Oslo, 1872); *De Norske Retskilder og Deres Anvendelse* (Oslo, 1877).

326. *Forelaesninger over den Norske Retshistorie* (Oslo, 1880-1883); *Om Foreløbige Retsmidler i den Gamle Norske Rettergang* (Oslo, 1862); "Nordmaendenes gamle strafferet," in *Norsk Historisk Tidsskrift*, Ser. I, Vol. IV (1877) 327-391; Ser. II, Vol. IV (1884) 20-113.

327. *Det Norske Folks Historie*, 4 Vols. (Oslo, 1852-1863).

328. *Norges Stats—Og Retsforfatning i Middelalderen* (Oslo, 1867). See also *Norges Gamle Love Indtil 1387*, 5 vols. (Oslo, 1846-1895), edited by Keyser, Munch, Gustav Storm and Ebbe Hertzberg.

329. "De Nordiske Retskilder," in *Nordisk Retsencylopaedi* (Copenhagen, 1890), with an English translation in *A General Survey of Continental Legal History*, pp. 531-76 (1912). See also *Grundtraekkene i den Aeldste Norske Proces* (Oslo, 1874); *Norges Gamle Love*, V, *Glossarium* (Oslo, 1895).

330. *Udsigt over den Norske Retshistorie* (Oslo, 1898); "De norske folkelovsböker för 1263," in *Tidsskrift for Retvidenskab*, XXXIX, 183-211, XLI, 1-68; "The Meaning of the Words Odal and Skeyting in the Old Laws of Norway," in *Essays in Legal History*, edited by Vinogradov (London, 1913).

331. *Statsforfatningen i Norge og Danmark Indtil 1814* (1886).

332. *The King's Mirror* (translation) (New York, 1917); *The Earliest Norwegian Laws* (New York, 1935); "Witnesses and Oath Helpers in Old Norwegian Law," in *Haskins Anniversary Essays* (Boston, 1929).

CHAPTER IV

SWEDISH LAW

Swedish immigration to the United States dates back to 1638 at which time New Sweden on the Delaware River was founded. But in 1655 New Sweden was taken over by the Holland Dutch. For the next two centuries Swedish immigration was slight. Between 1820 and 1948 over 1,200,000 Swedes came to the United States.[1] The leading decade was in the 1880's, when 391,776 arrived. The second largest number, 249,534, entered between 1901 and 1910. The annual quota for Swedes is 3,314, but in the fiscal year 1948 only 2,022 emigrants were admitted. Of the 1,301,390 Swedes in the United States in 1940, 856,320 were native-born while 445,070 were foreign-born. Of the foreign-born Swedes 79,348 were in Illinois, 67,161 in Minnesota, 34,899 in California, 26,899 in Washington, and 10,096 in the South. 77.8 per cent were in the North, 19.9 per cent in the West, and 2.3 per cent in the South. By 1940, 77.1 per cent of the foreign-born Swedes had become naturalized American citizens, as compared with 64.6 per cent of all foreign-born. The attraction of the United States for the Swedes is indicated by the fact that 98 per cent of all Swedish emigrants went to the United States, compared with 96 per cent of Norwegians and 88 per cent of Danes.[2] In absolute numbers three times as many Swedes have come in comparison with Danes, and one and one-half times as many as Norwegians.

International Relations

Tacitus mentions the Swedes in the first century.[3] Ptolemy mentions the Goths, as well as Scandinavia, named after Skåne in southern Sweden, in the second century. Procopius, a Greek historian of the sixth century, stated that there were thirteen tribes living in Scandinavia, of whom the Götar were the most numerous.[4] The most ancient of the small kingdoms consisting of several tribes was that of Svithiod consisting of Uppland as the main province and also of Västmanland and Södermanland. The most famous of the ancient Scandinavian temples was located at Uppsala, capital of this kingdom. The other important kingdom was that of the Goths, consisting of the main province of Västergötland and also of Östergötland. The *Thing* of the former province retained until medieval times the name of "Thing of all the Goths."

On the basis of Tacitus' writings one writer states: "From this it may be concluded that the nucleus of the present Swedish state existed about two thousand years ago, thus giving to Sweden the distinction of being the oldest among the present European states."[5] On the other hand, Sigrid Undset, the great Danish-Norwegian writer, has asserted that Denmark was the first European country to be integrated into one kingdom, with Norway second in 872.[6] A leading American historian has called the Swedish king, Erik Victorious (980-995), the "founder of the Northern Kingdom."[7] Perhaps no certain answer may be given.

Early in the fourth century the tribe of Heruls living north of Skåne made a raid on the Roman Empire.[8] Later after being forced out by the Goths to the north of them and the Danes to the south of them they set up a kingdom in Hungary. When the original dynasty died out in the sixth century, they sent to Sweden for another king. The Heruls were the ruling class in Hungary and came to be known as Magyars. They were a a menace to the Empire and to the Austrians for centuries.

The famous poem, Beowulf, dating from about 700, mentions Denmark as an existing kingdom, but speaks of the two different states of the Götar and the Svear. It has been concluded that the Swedish kingdom may be dated back to the union of these two states at some time prior to 836.[9] Speaking of the period about 600 A.D. one writer has pointed out that while the "Danes were at this time the most renowned people in the North," the "Swedes rivaled them in warlike achievements as well as in wealth and power. The Swedish kings waged war with the Danes, and made expeditions into Esthonia, and other regions east of the Baltic. Their royal family was the oldest in the North, and their kingdom, Svithiod, had risen into prominence before that of the Danes."[10] During the sixth and seventh centuries there was a long struggle between the Swedes and the Goths, the upshot of which was the defeat of the latter.[11] A medieval law states: "Through the union of the land of the Suiones with the land of the Goths in heathen time, the kingdom of Sweden was established."

As of about 800 what is now Sweden was divided up as follows: The Danes had possession of Halland in the west, Skåne in the south, and Blekinge in the east.[12] They thus controlled Öresund and Kattegat. The Swedes in the north had conquered the Goths, who now lived between the Swedes and the Danes. What is now the northern part of Sweden was very thinly populated. The boundary with Norway was ill-defined. Norway possessed or laid claim to Härjedalen and Jämtland, and many Norwegians settled in Helsingland. The Norwegians early claimed Värmland and occupied Bohuslän or Viken. The Danes claimed Bohuslän too, at various times, and the Norwegians at certain periods recognized their claims. Bohuslän may therefore be looked upon as the meeting-point of the three Scandinavian nations. About 870 when Harald the

Fairhaired was unifying Norway, the Swedish king, Erik Eimundsson, invaded those areas but Harald was successful in recovering them.[13] In general, Lake Vänern and the Göta River were the boundaries between Sweden and Norway.

In the ninth century the Eastern Vikings from Sweden penetrated Finland, Courland, Carelia and Esthonia.[14] In 862 they founded Novgorod and in 900 Kiev. The Swedes, referred to as "Russ," gave Russia its name and founded a dynasty in 900 by merging the two kingdoms, which lasted until 1578.[15] Close relations continued until the death of Jaroslav in 1054.[16] Thus the Swedes had founded dynasties in Hungary and Russia before the Danes and Norwegians became finally established in England.

The wars with Denmark and Norway and the naval expeditions against the Baltic-Finnish peoples of this last period seem not to have led to any permanent conquests. But Gotland, then a center of Northern commerce, agreed to pay tribute to the Swedish king.[17]

There is a tradition that a Swede named Gardar Svavarsson discovered Iceland between 860 and 870.[18] However, it was mainly Norwegians who settled in Iceland. When the Duchy of Normandy was founded in 911 while most of the settlers were Danes and Norwegians there were also many Swedes from what is now the southern part of Sweden.[19] While it is common to think of the Viking raids in England as being Norwegian and Danish there can be little doubt that many such Vikings came from Bohuslän, Blekinge, and Skåne, now Swedish but formerly Norwegian and Danish.[20] Many Swedes served as mercenary soldiers under Danish and Norwegian leaders.

Jämtland was first settled by people from the Trondheim area of Norway. The people invited Haakon the Good of Norway (934-961) to rule over the area.[21] Jämtland recognized the Norwegian king from 934 to about 1028.[22] It was reunited to Norway without bloodshed by King Eystein (1103-1122), but as to ecclesiastical matters it continued to belong to the Uppsala diocese.[23] Härjedalen was also Norwegian, and this was true in ecclesiastical matters as well.

The first Swedish king to be frequently and prominently mentioned in international affairs was King Erik (980-995).[24] He defeated a Danish fleet of 1,200 ships supporting his nephew and is said to have seized all Denmark while Sweyn, the Danish king, was attacking Finland.[25] His son, Olaf Skött-Konung (995-1022), made peace with Sweyn, who married Olaf's widowed mother, Sigrid. The two kings then joined the sons of an earlier Norwegian king in defeating Olaf Tryggvason, king of Norway, in the year 1000.[26] They then held Norway jointly until 1015. The Swedish king secured Bohuslän and seven western counties, but gave them in fief with his other Norwegian acquisitions to the brother of the Norwegian king.[27] Before King Canute of Denmark invaded England in 1015 he was careful to secure the approval and support of the Swedish king, thus precluding any attack on Denmark in his absence.[28] In 1019 the kings of Sweden and Norway met and drew up the Peace of Konghelle; the marriage of the king of Norway to a daughter of the Swedish king was recognized, and Norway retained Jämtland.[29] About 1026 Norway allied itself with Sweden and attacked Denmark.[30] Canute, who conquered Norway in 1028, also claimed the Swedish throne and conceivably might have invaded Sweden but for his premature death. Sweden gave aid to Norway in 1028, but no longer dared to ally itself against Canute. Consequently a Scandinavian union was not established until more than three centuries later.

Between 1042 and 1047 there was conflict between Denmark and Norway. Sweyn, claimant to the Danish throne, was defeated by King Magnus of Norway and obliged to take refuge in Sweden.[31] Harald the Hard of Norway (1047-1066) was almost constantly at war with Sweden.[32] About 1063 the Swedish king granted Vermland to a Norwegian jarl under the Danish king.[33] About 1060 the old royal family of Sweden died out and troubled times commenced for Sweden largely due to conflicts over religion, the Goths having been Christianized while the Swedes reverted to paganism. This conflict continued for a century, as did the conflict between rival dynasties. The date of 1060 is a "landmark between the ancient and the medieval history of Sweden."[34] At this time only the church was strongly organized. Magnus Bareleg (1093-1103) of Norway claimed the Swedish province of Dalsland and waged war with Sweden.

In 1101 a peace meeting was arranged at Konghelle, with King Erik of Denmark participating as mediator.[35] Present also were Magnus of Norway and Inge of Sweden (1080-1110). This was the first peace treaty of three Scandinavian kings. Norway retained the land east of the Folden Fjord to the Göta River, much of which today belongs to Sweden. To seal the peace Magnus married Inge's daughter Margaret. As the marriage was without issue Dalsland again became a part of Sweden in 1103. About 1110 Jämtland was reunited with Norway though it is not clear why Sweden submitted without bloodshed.[36]

In 1123 King Sigurd of Norway led a crusade into Småland where paganism still lingered.[37] Magnus, the Blind, ousted king of Norway, secured help from a Swedish jarl in 1137.[38] A Swedish crusade in Finland occurred in 1157. In 1164 the Swedes fought the Russians. By 1200 the Swedish settlements in Finland were becoming permanent in character.

This was the first real expansion of Sweden. During the reign of Canute Ericsson (1167-1196) Sweden enjoyed peace for almost three decades.[39] As the east Baltic had become infested with Esthonian and Carelian pirates, Stockholm was built in 1187, and the capital was transferred there from Uppsala. During this period the Hanseatic League with headquarters at Lübeck came to dominate the Baltic. It virtually took over Gotland, and established the city of Visby. A commercial treaty was negotiated by Sweden with Henry the Lion of Saxony, resulting in an influx of Germans into Sweden. There was some fighting in Livonia and Esthonia. Denmark had designs on this territory, hence bad feeling arose between Sweden and Denmark.[40] When about 1170 King Magnus Erlingsson of Norway sought to extirpate the family of King Harald Gille, he incurred Swedish hostility, as Jarl Birger Brosa was married to the daughter of Gille.[41] King Sverri of Norway (1177-1202) strengthened his position by marrying Margaret, daughter of the Swedish king, Eric the Saint (1150-1160). Although the Pope placed Sverri under interdict Sweden still supported him.[42] Norway sought Swedish help to counterbalance the constant Danish threat throughout the eleventh, twelfth, and thirteenth centuries.[43]

In 1208 King Sverker was driven into exile by Eric V (1208-1216), the son of Canute, who received support from Norway. Sverker appealed to the Pope and got a papal letter to the Swedish bishops. Two years later Sverker returned at the head of a Danish army but fell in battle.

In 1249 Jarl Birger Magnusson at the exhortation of the Pope subdued the Tavastian tribes in Finland, but Russia prevented the conquest of eastern Finland.[44] From this time until 1809 Sweden controlled most of Finland. An attack on the mouth of the Neva was beaten off by the Russian Grand Duke Alexander Nevsky in 1240. These wars were the most important of early Swedish medieval foreign policies. The wars with Denmark and Norway were minor, and resulted in no boundary changes. These countries often supported pretenders to the Swedish throne. Jarl Birger often acted as mediator between Norway and Sweden. Relations with Norway under the great King Haakon the Old (1217-1263) were especially friendly, Birger's daughter marrying the heir to the Norwegian throne.[45] Relations with Denmark were difficult because of chaos in the Danish government. The rulers of the three countries met in 1254 to seek the solution of irritations between them, and in 1256 a treaty between Denmark and Sweden was formally ratified. Sweden sought friendly relations with the other Scandinavian nations in large part because of the menace of German control of trade in the Baltic. About 1260 Norway made a treaty of alliance with Castile in Spain, but it was expressly provided that Norway need not give aid against Sweden. Jarl Birger considered the possibility of Scandinavian cooperation and even thought of bringing England into his political plans.

A minor conflict with the Hanseatic city of Lübeck in 1251 resulted in diplomatic discussions and the ratification of a former trade agreement with certain amendments. One amendment provided that any person from Lübeck settling in Sweden should obey Swedish law and be called Swedish.[46] From this time many Germans settled in Swedish cities, and foreign trade increased. A similar treaty was made with Hamburg, and Swedish representatives were sent to England to negotiate a commercial treaty. Beginning in the thirteenth century Swedish international contacts turned eastward and southward, and German influences replaced English.[47]

About 1275 King Erik Glipping of Denmark intervened in a dispute between King Magnus Ladulås (1275-1290) of Sweden and Valdemar, the brother of Magnus.[48] King Magnus Lawmender of Norway (1263-1280) declined to intervene.[49] In 1285 the Swedish king negotiated, as umpire, a treaty between Norway and the Hanseatic League.[50] Magnus Ladulås incurred the enmity of the Hanseatic League when in 1285 he succeeded in gaining authority over Gotland.[51] From 1275 to 1279 relations with Denmark were poor because of Danish intervention against Magnus and for Valdemar. Thereafter Magnus maintained good relations with both Denmark and Norway. To make Sweden strong as against Denmark Magnus created a cavalry through setting up a new class of knight. A royal ordinance provided that in every town one of the two burgomasters and half the aldermen should be Germans.

Torgils, Regent of Sweden (1290-1298), built a fortress at Viborg. He became involved in a war with Russia lasting from 1293 to 1300, and conquered Carelia.[52] The border between Sweden and Russia remained the same throughout the Middle Ages. In 1303 Birger, the oldest son of Magnus Ladulås, became king, but war soon arose between him and his brothers, Eric and Valdemar. King Birger married a sister of King Eric Maendved of Denmark who in turn married Birger's sister. His brother Eric married Ingeborg, the oldest daughter of King Haakon of Norway, who supported Eric's claims.[53] King Birger relied on Danish help. In 1309 following a long war between Denmark and Norway, Denmark ceded Halland to Norway.[54] In 1309 Eric led an attack on Jämtland despite his engagement to the daughter of the Norwegian king.[55] In 1310 the kings of Denmark and Norway arranged a treaty splitting Sweden into three parts as between the brothers. Birger had his brothers murdered, and was then driven into exile in Denmark.

In 1319 Magnus, the only son of Eric, was elected king of Sweden, and the same year succeeded his grandfather, King Haakon, as king of Norway. The Councils of the two kingdoms ruled their respective countries until 1332 and the personal union continued until 1371.[56] Denmark was at its lowest ebb at this time. In 1319 the Danish king mortgaged Halland to Knud Porse and in 1326 ceded it to him.[57] The northern part of Halland, which was mortgaged to Norway during the reign of Christopher II of Denmark (1320-1332), was later taken by a Holstein duke, and then returned to Denmark about 1365.[58] In 1332 Sweden bought Skåne and Blekinge, and in 1340 Halland. Thus all the southern part of present Sweden was brought under Swedish control, one-third of Denmark having been made over to Sweden in perpetuity. Unfortunately, the price was so high as to wreck the Swedish finances. Norway did not profit by the arrangement. Hence a joint session of the State Councils of Norway and Sweden in 1343 decided on the election of Haakon, the younger son of Magnus, as king of Norway on his coming of age in 1355, with Eric, the older son, to be king of Sweden.[59] Magnus was to remain as regent of Norway until Haakon came of age. About 1356 Erik revolted against his father who kept his throne only through the help of King Valdemar Atterdag of Denmark.[60] In 1355 Haakon became king of Norway, but Magnus kept two areas in Norway and his wife Blanche kept two other areas together with Iceland as her Norwegian dowry.[61] In 1355 the Pope excommunicated Magnus for his failure to pay his debts to the church from which he had borrowed large sums. Though Erik was king from 1356 to 1359, on his death Magnus continued to rule as king of Sweden, and Norway did not object.[62] In 1360 Denmark regained Skåne, Blekinge and south Halland by cession from Sweden without any adequate return, thus taking away a source of large revenues from the herring fisheries.[63] In 1362 Denmark conquered Gotland. This made Magnus extremely unpopular and was opposed by King Haakon of Norway, who was made joint king of Sweden with his father in 1362.[64] In 1363 the three Scandinavian kings made peace and Magnus ceded to Denmark the provinces sought by Denmark. King Haakon was to marry Valdemar's daughter Margaret. This was unpopular in Sweden among the nobles who offered the throne to Albrecht, son of the Duke of Mecklenburg, and a nephew of Magnus, in 1364, after formal deposition of Magnus and Haakon.[65] In 1365 Albrecht defeated Magnus and Haakon in a war. Denmark then occupied North Halland and Gotland. In 1370 Denmark was forced to make a humiliating treaty of peace with the Hanseatic League, which with Sweden had attacked it.[66] This left Haakon of Norway free to invade Sweden in 1371.[67] For several years Norway and Sweden had been technically at war as Sweden had imprisoned Haakon's father Magnus. Haakon liberated Magnus, but recognized Albrecht as king of Sweden. Upon the death of Magnus in 1373 Haakon took over the western Swedish provinces which Magnus had been allowed to retain.[68] Hostilities between Norway and Sweden continued until the death of Haakon in 1380. Haakon often chose Swedes as his chief officials, and the Swedish influence was strong in Norway.

Early in the reign of Magnus, the Russian wars had been ended in 1323 by the first treaty between Sweden and Russia at Nöteberg.[69] Western Carelia and Sanalaks were ceded to Sweden. But Sweden did not profit much, while the Teutonic knights came into possession of Livonia and Esthonia. The Lapps recognized Swedish suzerainty. Magnus started a second war with Russia in 1336 which lasted twelve years.

The German influence in the cities was strong under Magnus. By the charters conferred by Magnus half the burgomasters and city counsellors were required to be German.[70] This was finally abolished in 1471. In 1360, as has been seen, Magnus and Haakon formed an alliance against Denmark with the Hanseatic League. In 1361 a new charter was granted permitting unrestricted trade in both kingdoms. Thus the League secured final control over all trade.[71]

Upon the death of King Valdemar of Denmark in 1375 his daughter Margaret, now Queen of Norway, secured the election of her son Olaf as king of Denmark. Five years later he succeeded his father, Haakon, as king of Norway. As Olaf was a minor his mother acted as regent. In 1385 Margaret proclaimed Olaf as king of Sweden, as the last of the Swedish royal line, but in 1387 Olaf died. In 1389 the Swedish nobles asked Margaret to become ruler of Sweden. They had objected to the exercise of autocratic powers by Albrecht and his favoritism toward his German followers.[72]

Margaret was now queen of Sweden, Denmark and Norway, together with Iceland which belonged to Norway, and Finland which belonged to Sweden. This was the first union of all Scandinavian states. The period from 1389 to 1521 has been called the Age of Union. Margaret was the "first great ruling queen in European history."[73] In 1397 Denmark, Norway and Sweden agreed that her great-nephew through her sister Ingeborg, Eric of Pomerania, should be her successor. But Sweden reserved the right of election, thus making a permanent union more difficult. The queen resided in Denmark.

The Scandinavian Union lasted until 1521.[74] But whenever the Danish king attempted to exercise real authority in Sweden, he was able to do so only for limited intervals. The kingdom was now the largest in Europe. About half of its population lived in Denmark, the population of Denmark being 750,000, of Sweden 450,000 and of Norway 250,000. England and France sought the assistance of Margaret. Eric, her heir, married a sister of Henry V of England. But England secured no assistance against France.[75] Blekinge, Halland and Skåne remained Danish through the mediation of the Hansa towns.[76] Sea and army power were rather weak during the reign of Margaret. The Hanseatic cities of Rostock and Wismar dominated the North Sea.[77] In 1392 Margaret had to obtain two English ships to fight the depredations of the Victualers, German pirates. At great cost German soldiers were hired for land warfare. In 1398 the Teutonic Knights captured Gotland, and the Hanseatic League controlled Visby. In 1408 Gotland was restored to Sweden. Margaret appointed bailiffs to administer in Sweden, but as nearly all of them were Danish much hostility was aroused.[78] The Royal Council always met in Denmark. From 1416 to 1435 King Eric was at war with Holstein and the Hanseatic League.[79]

Eventually the Swedes under the leadership of Engelbrecht Engelbrechtson revolted against the Danes, in effect destroying or seriously weakening the union. The basis for the Swedish Riksdag or parliament was laid when he summoned an assembly of nobles, clergy, burghers and peasants to Arboga in 1435.[80] The first similar assembly in England had met in 1265. The Swedish parliament is the first of the Scandinavian parliaments, the Norwegian being established in 1814 and the Danish in 1849. The Riksdag continued to be an assembly of four estates until 1866. The immediate purpose of its calling was to free Sweden from Denmark. It concluded to separate the Swedish government from the Danish. King Eric had failed to summon the *Riksrad* or Council of the Kingdom and the two highest offices of Swedish administration—Chancellor and Lord High Constable—were left vacant. Eric was dethroned as king of Sweden in 1436 after violating his agreement of 1435 with the Swedes, and as king of Denmark and Norway in 1439. Karl Knutsson, a Swede, supported by the nobles, was elected Protector, and then regent from 1438 to 1440.[81] Early in the revolt the Norwegians and the Norwegian Council were appealed to to join, but rejected the appeal thus losing the best opportunity Norway ever had to secure independence.[82] The Swedish movement was successful because it had an ambitious aristocracy with large landholdings while Norway's aristocracy had died out and Norway had much less arable land.[83]

Another relative of Margaret, Christopher of Bavaria, now became king of Denmark in 1440 until his death in 1448. He was crowned king in Sweden in 1441 and in Norway in 1442.[84] There were now two distinct parties in Sweden: the Unionists, favoring a titular king of Scandinavia with no administrative power in Sweden; and the Separatists, who wished to set up a distinct national Swedish government. When Christopher died, Karl Knutsson was elected king of Sweden in 1448.

He was also elected king of Norway in October 1449, but Norway was given up to Denmark in 1450.[85] Gotland fell into Danish hands. The Treaty of Bergen of 1450 deprived Knutsson of all Norway, and sealed a pact of permanent union between Denmark and Norway not broken until 1814. In 1451 Denmark attacked Värmland in Sweden from the Norwegian side. An armistice was signed in 1453, but war was renewed in 1455. In 1457, Christian I, king of Denmark since 1448 and of Norway since 1450, was placed on the Swedish throne. Karl Knutsson had been driven out of Sweden by a revolt largely inspired by the church. In 1463 a revolt broke out in Sweden against the Danish king, also led by the church, when he tried to levy an extra tax for an expedition against Russia. In 1464 a Danish army was unsuccessful in Sweden. Karl Knutsson again served as king of Sweden from 1467 to 1470.

Knutsson was succeeded by his nephew, Sten Sture the Elder, who ruled as regent, rather than as king, from 1470 to 1503. The Danes were defeated at Brunkeberg in 1471. The Danish king maintained his claim to Sweden, but his authority was very shadowy. When Christian died in 1481 there was an interregnum of two years in Norway. The Norwegians sought in vain to secure joint action by Sweden and Norway in the coming election for king.[86] The Norwegians therefore joined with the Danes in electing Hans, the son of Christian, while the Swedes took no part in the election.

For the first time Russia became a dangerous foe. But Sweden in the war from 1455 to 1497 successfully repelled her.[87] At the same time the Danes attacked Sweden, and in 1497 King Hans, supported by Svante Sture, leader of the Unionist party, was finally elected king of Sweden after entering Stockholm. The defeat of the Danish army by the peasants in Ditmarschen, Holstein, gave the Swedes an opportunity. In 1502 Svante Sture united with Bishop Hemming Gadh, a Separatist leader, in driving out the Danes, and served as regent from 1503 to 1512. The peace of 1509 between Denmark and Sweden recognized the Swedish regency, but the Danish king was to receive an annual tribute unless he or his son was elected king of Sweden. In 1510 the Swedes secured the assistance of the Hanseatic League. Then there was war with Denmark from 1510 to 1512. Svante Sture was succeeded as regent by Sten Sture the Younger (1512-1520). In 1517 the Riksdag with Sture's authority deposed the Danish supported Gustav Trolle, Archbishop of Uppsala.[88] The deposition was a direct challenge to papal authority as well as to Denmark. It thus paved the way for the Protestant Reformation in Sweden and for Swedish independence from Denmark. The Pope placed Sweden under interdict. Christian II, the Danish king, entered Stockholm and was proclaimed as hereditary king at a Riksdag in October

1520. The Stockholm "Blood-Bath" now occurred, and two bishops, thirteen royal counsellors and many others were executed. The Swedes now rose in revolt, led by Gustavus Vasa, a nephew of Stan Sture the Younger. Gustavus was elected regent in 1521 and king in 1523.[89] The cities of Lübeck and Danzig gave him assistance. The deposition of Christian II in Denmark in 1523 and in Norway in 1524 made the revolt easier. The Swedes now secured independence, which they have ever since maintained. Gustavus renewed old plans for a Swedish-Norwegian union and occupied the Bohuslän area of Norway. In 1524 through the mediation of the Hanseatic League, Bohuslän was restored to Norway, and Blekinge and Gotland to Denmark.[90] Gustavus now allied himself with the new Danish king against the deposed Christian II.

Gustavus Vasa has been called the "creator of Modern Sweden."[91] During the period from 1533 to 1537 Gustavus Vasa (1523-1560) saw his opportunity to destroy the supremacy of the Hanseatic and Lübeck naval forces.[92] He joined his brother-in-law, Christian III of Denmark, and completely destroyed the naval power of Lübeck. For two centuries previously Lübeck had dominated. After a dispute over Gotland the Swedes and Danes renewed their alliance in 1541 for a fifty-year term, but by 1560 the relations became strained. An alliance was made with France for the first time in 1542.[93] Gustavus built up a strong standing army and a modernized navy, making use of the funds gained from the Reformation. In 1556 Russia attacked Finland; in 1557 a forty-year truce was concluded, the frontiers to be regulated according to the treaty of 1323. When the Russians took Narva in 1558 and Danish bases were established at Ösel, it was obvious that a clash would soon come with the new rival in the Baltic, namely, Sweden.[94] The Swedes occupied North Esthonia and Reval in 1561, and Denmark at once allied herself with Russia.

From 1563 to 1570 Sweden and Denmark fought a war very costly to both of them.[95] Russia sought to conquer Livonia and came near Baltic territory claimed by Denmark. The Danish aim was to control the Baltic and eventually to reconquer Sweden. Eric XIV (1560-1568) entered the struggle to make Sweden instead of Denmark the leading Scandinavian power, to establish Swedish hegemony in the Baltic, to prevent his brother John from setting up a kingdom under the aegis of Poland, and to block the Russian path to the Baltic. Eric defeated John and came to terms with Russia. Sweden and Denmark then fought it out alone. Sweden occupied much of Norway.[96] This was the first partly successful aggressive war against Denmark, and the first triumph in the Baltic. Under the Treaty of Peace of 1570 Sweden had to pay Denmark 150,000 riksdalers for the return of Älvsborg, the only Swedish port on the North Sea, and leave the Sound and its dues in Danish hands. The Norwegian provinces of Jämtland and Härjedalen which the Swedes had occupied during the war and which had previously belonged to the diocese of Uppsala were now joined with the diocese of Trondheim. But Sweden gained Esthonia. Denmark retained Skåne and Gotland, and had maintained her hegemony in the North. The Emperor and the Elector of Saxony had intervened to end the war. This period began an antagonism for a century between Sweden and Poland, and a Russian movement westward. Russia soon captured the Danish bases in the Baltic near Russia.

After peace with Denmark in 1570 Sweden carried on a war with Russia in Livonia and Esthonia.[97] King John (1569-1592) was the first Swedish king to have a truly European policy.[98] He carried on negotiations with the Emperor, Spain, the Pope, Poland, England, and Russia. Attempts from 1576 to 1580 to make an alliance of Sweden, Spain and the Emperor on behalf of the Counter-Reformation failed. In 1578 Sweden allied itself with Poland against Russia and secured the lost provinces of Esthonia and Livonia. In 1583 a truce permitted Sweden to retain her conquests. In 1587 Sigismund, heir to the Swedish throne, was elected king of Poland. Finland was raised to a grand duchy of Sweden. In 1592 Sigismund also became king of Sweden (1592-1599), a personal union between Sweden and Poland thus being established. But in reality Sweden was ruled by the regent, his uncle, who in 1599 was made king of Sweden. By the Peace of Teusina with Russia in 1595 Sweden acquired all of Esthonia with Narva. In 1600 Sweden began a war with Poland by invading Livonia, but from 1601 to 1605 the Poles were victorious. In 1610 Sweden proposed a Protestant alliance against Poland and Spain, but the proposal was rejected by England, France, and Holland. In 1611 a Swedish general compelled the Russian city of Novgorod to promise to support the Swedish king's son, Charles Philip, for Czar of Russia.

Because the Swedish king had assumed the title of "King of the Lapps in Nordland" and levied taxes in Finmark, thus encroaching on Norway, the Danish king, despite the opposition of the State Council, declared war on Sweden and fought the Kalmar War of 1611 to 1613.[99] Denmark hoped to reestablish the union of the three kingdoms. She feared Swedish expansion in Esthonia and Livonia. By the treaty of Knäred, Sweden under British pressure renounced her claims to Finmark and Lapland. Älvsborg was to be redeemed by Sweden for one million riksdalers and was to be held by Denmark with seven counties of Västergötland as security. But Sweden was exempted from tolls in the Sound. For the last time Denmark upheld her hegemony in the North. During the war Swedish troops, largely foreign mercenaries, invaded Norway. The Danish navy was still the stronger, but the Swedish infantry was far superior.[100] Sweden had become the political and military equal of Denmark. The harsh treaty resulted in closer relations between Sweden and the Netherlands.

When Sweden fought Poland she tried to prohibit all commerce with Riga. This injured Danish commerce, and Denmark soon went to war with Sweden. Denmark then forbade all shipping into Swedish ports. Lübeck and the Netherlands objected to this and agreed to defend their commerce. In 1614 Sweden joined this agreement, but it never came into force. If it had it would perhaps have been the first "armed neutrality" in modern times.[101]

In 1613 a Romanov was elected Czar of Russia before the Swedish czar-elect arrived in Russia. Sweden now carried on an extensive war in Russia.[102] At the request of Russia, King James I of England mediated and peace was concluded in 1617 at Stolbova. Russia ceded Eastern Carelia and Ingria to Sweden. Nöteberg on the Neva, key to Finland, became Swedish. Russia renounced her claims to Esthonia and Livonia. Russia was thus excluded from the Baltic and Sweden was secured against Poland.

In 1621 war with Poland was resumed and Riga, capital of Livonia, was captured. In 1625 Dorpat was taken and the Poles were completely expelled from Livonia. In 1626 Sweden attacked West Prussia, which then belonged to Poland, and by 1629 the whole province was taken.[103] Through the mediation of England and France a six-years' truce with Poland was arranged.

In 1617 Sweden sought in vain to interest England in a Protestant alliance. Similarly in 1624 negotiations with England fell through. In 1628 Sweden was prepared to ally herself with Denmark in the Thirty Years' War to defend the Baltic and the Protestant cause against the Emperor. The Danish king had taken part as leader of the Protestant forces since 1625 but without great success. On behalf of the Emperor, Wallenstein offered to partition Denmark-Norway so that Sweden would receive Norway and the Emperor Denmark. Denmark made peace with the Emperor in 1629. At the request of the Protestant princes of Germany Gustavus led an army into Germany. Sweden was then in a very strong position. Finland, Ingria, Esthonia and Livonia belonged to her and Courland was under her influence. If Sweden acquired Pomerania and Prussia, the Baltic would become a Swedish lake. For two years Gustavus took part in the Thirty Years' War, and raised Sweden to the proudest position she ever occupied in history.[104] In September, 1631, in a battle fought near Leipzig, the turning point of the Thirty Years' War occurred for the Protestants. Without his intervention Protestantism might have been crushed. By December, 1631 he commanded one hundred thousand men, only one-fifth of whom were Swedes. By May 1632 his conquests extended as far south as the Alps. He was killed at the Battle of Lützen in 1632. A German inscription at Breitenfeld stated: "He saved religious liberty for the world." He had aimed to be a Protestant Emperor of a Baltic Empire with Sweden as its center.

In 1638 a Swedish colony was founded in Delaware.[105] In 1644 the colony received a constitution. A court of justice was set up in 1643.[106] In 1655 the Dutch conquered Delaware and Swedish colonial efforts ceased in North America. Today the former Swedish colony forms part of Delaware, New Jersey, and Pennsylvania, including the city of Philadelphia. The first president under the Articles of Confederation of the Continental Congress was John Hanson, a descendent of one of these Swedes.[107]

The war on behalf of Protestantism continued after the death of Gustavus Adolphus under the leadership of Chancellor Axel Oxenstierna.[108] After a war commencing in 1621 Sweden had acquired Livonia and four Prussian ports from Poland. In 1635 Sweden made a 26-year truce with Poland but she was forced to yield the Prussian cities with their huge customs revenues. Sweden had allied herself with France in 1631, and therefore acquired French subsidies. From this time Sweden maintained close relations with France up to the time of Napoleon.

In 1643 Sweden, aided by the Netherlands, commenced a successful war against Denmark.[109] By the Peace of Brömsebro, Denmark ceded to Sweden Gotland and Ösel, mortgaged Halland for thirty years as security for exemptions of Sound dues, and also ceded the Norwegian provinces of Jämtland and Härjedalen, though the war from the Norwegian border had been waged successfully by the Norwegians.[110] Sweden was also exempted from the Danish Sound dues.

The Thirty Years' War was terminated in 1648 by the Peace of Westphalia under which Sweden gained the bishoprics of Bremen and Verden, part of Pomerania with Stettin, and the islands of Rügen, Usedom and Wallin, the city of Wismar and a war indemnity of five million riksdalers.[111] Full civil and religious liberty was given to all German Protestants. Sweden was to hold her German possessions as fiefs of the German Empire, and Sweden could vote on their behalf in the German diet. Sweden and France were to be joint guarantors of the peace. Sweden now held the mouths of the three greatest rivers in northern Germany: the Oder, the Elbe, and the Weser. She had reached the greatest territorial extent which she ever had.[112]

In 1653 Cromwell sought an alliance with Sweden against Denmark and the Netherlands.[113] In 1655 Sweden attacked and occupied Poland, which still claimed the Swedish crown, and compelled the Elector of Brandenburg to become a Swedish ally. The Swedish aim was to gain control of the southern Baltic. When Russia attacked Sweden the Elector seized East Prussia, thus laying the foundation of the kingdom of Prussia. The Netherlands, jealous of her commerce, were now on bad terms with Sweden. Sweden desired a personal union with Poland, and the conquest of Denmark-Norway. In 1657 Denmark declared war on Sweden.[114] But by the Peace of Roskilde in 1658, mediated by England, Denmark had to cede Blekinge, Halland, Skåne, and Bornholm, and the Norwegian provinces of Bohuslän and Trondheim. All but Bornholm and Trondheim have been Swedish ever since. Today one-fourth of the population of Sweden live in Blekinge, Halland, and Skåne. In January 1658 Cromwell in a speech to Parliament asserted that only Sweden could save Protestantism. In 1658 Sweden again invaded Denmark which she thought too intimate with the Netherlands.[115] The Netherlands aided Denmark. An English fleet entered the Baltic to watch the Dutch, and to enforce an armed mediation. By the Peace of Copenhagen in 1660 Denmark regained Bornholm, and Norway Trondheim from Sweden. Sweden retained Skåne permanently because a balance of power was wanted by western Europe in the Sound.[116] There has been no change in such borders since. In 1660 the Peace of Oliva was concluded with Poland after a sixty-years' war of succession between the Protestant and the Catholic branches of the House of Vasa. Poland ceded Livonia to Sweden, and gave up all claim to the Swedish throne. Brandenberg gained East Prussia permanently. But West Pomerania, and Bremen and Verden remained Swedish. In 1661 the Peace of Karedis ended the war which restored Russian conquests in Esthonia and Livonia. In 1660 the population of Sweden was 2½ million to 1½ million in Denmark. When in 1665 England fought the Netherlands, Sweden made a defensive alliance with England.[117] In 1668 Sweden made an alliance with England and the Netherlands against France, but the alliance was destroyed in two years when England deserted it.

In 1672 Sweden became the ally of France in the wars against the Netherlands, Great Britain, and Brandenburg. Sweden was no longer leader of the Protestant nations but virtually a satellite of France. In 1675 the Swedish army was defeated by the Elector of Brandenburg at Fehrbellin. At the Peace of St. Germain in 1679 Sweden was saved from the loss of Pomerania through the intervention of the French. From 1675 to 1679 the Scanian war was fought by Denmark to regain its lost provinces in Sweden, but due to French interference the Peace of Lund restored the status quo as of the date when the war began.[118] A ten-year

defensive alliance between Sweden and Denmark was formed.[119] Foreign
policy now turned toward support of the Netherlands and England
against France. A treaty was made with the Netherlands in 1681. In 1691
the Scandinavian kingdoms formed an alliance in defense of neutral
trade.[120] It was the first active armed neutrality. They insisted on freedom of navigation, retaliation, joint convoys, and joint action if war
developed. Denmark was persuaded to modify her demands within three
months, but the treaty was reinstated in 1693.

 In 1699 Denmark, Poland, Saxony and Russia formed an alliance
against Sweden which led to the great Northern War.[121] These countries
were opposed to Swedish supremacy in the Baltic. The Danes had lost
their strength in the Baltic and the initiative had passed to Sweden.
Sweden was aided by England and the Netherlands and the Duke of
Gottorp, long an enemy of Denmark. Denmark made peace at Travendal
in 1700 and agreed not to join the enemies of Sweden. In 1702 Sweden
deposed the Elector of Saxony from the Polish throne. By the treaty of
Altronstädt in 1706 the Elector acknowledged the deposition. In 1709
Peter the Great of Russia defeated the Swedes at Poltava. According to
Creasy this was one of the fifteen decisive battles of world history. As
stated in the *New York Times* of July 1, 1951, it "started the Slavs on
the road of conquest, whose end we do not yet see."

In 1714 a league between England, Hanover, Prussia, Saxony, Denmark, and Russia was formed to dismember Sweden. By the Peace of
Stockholm in 1719 Sweden for one million dollars ceded Bremen and
Verden, which had been conquered by the Danes, to England-Hanover.
Sweden also ceded the larger part of Swedish Pomerania for two million
dollars to Prussia. By the Peace of Frederiksborg in 1720 Denmark retroceded all her conquests for 600,000 riksdalers, but Sweden paid indemnity
and gave up her alliance with Holstein-Gottorp, acquiesced in the incorporation of the ducal port of Slesvig, and gave up her exemption from
Sound dues.[122] England gave Sweden no material aid against Russia,[123]
and by the Peace of Nystad, Sweden ceded to Russia her Baltic provinces
Ingria, Livonia, and Esthonia, and Ösel. She also ceded southeastern
Carelia with Viborg, but the rest of Finland was retroceded to Sweden,
and Russia paid Sweden two million dollars. Thus to a considerable
extent Sweden lost her role as a great power. For twenty years a policy
of peace then prevailed. Withdrawal from French connections and
better relations with England and Russia were sought. But in 1741
Sweden declared war on Russia, and Finland was conquered by Russia.[124]
But Russia was opposed to the election of a Danish prince as heir to the
Swedish throne, and consented to restore Finland to Sweden on condition that the Duke of Gottorp, a cousin of the Russian ruler, be selected

as heir.[125] By the Treaty of Abo in 1743 Finland was restored to Sweden. In 1745 a Swedish attempt to form a West Indian Company failed.[126] In 1746 Russia formed an alliance with Denmark to encircle Sweden, an alliance continued with some intermissions until 1809.[127] About 1750 a boundary dispute with Norway was settled, Norway retaining Kautokeino and Karasjok.[128] From 1757 to 1762 Sweden took part in the Seven Years' War in the orbit of France.[129] Entrance was largely due to the Swedish nobility. The war was fought in Pomerania to recover Stettin without advantage to Sweden. Sweden, Austria, Russia, and France were opposed to Prussia and England. In 1764 diplomatic relations with England were resumed after a long period of severance. During the early part of the Seven Years' War Sweden occasionally cooperated with Denmark. France induced them to reestablish an armed neutrality.[130] Sweden contended that "free ships made free goods." But this clause was omitted from the Treaty as Denmark wished to maintain freedom of action for herself. But the next year France induced Sweden to enter the war and Swedish collaboration with Denmark then ceased. During the middle of the eighteenth century Sweden opened her ports to captors of both sides. Neutrality was thought of as impartiality alone. In fact, the policy favored the French as against the British, as the French and Scandinavian ports were bases for attacking British commerce and bringing in British prizes. On the other hand, the British could not capture French ships, as the French did not use these routes for commerce.

At this time the Scandinavian nations conducted a large trade with the Far East. They began to entertain a fear of American competition in their iron and other trade. As one Swedish statesman wrote during the American Revolution: "What future may this greatest field of Swedish commerce expect if the English colonies win their independence and they, in peace and with liberty's stimulus, carry all such undertakings to the height to which their country with so much advantages seems to entice them."[131]

In 1769 Russia and Denmark allied themselves to support the ineffectual system of Swedish government as against the Swedish king. In 1772 the Swedish king by a coup d'etat established the supremacy of the king. In 1773 the alliance of Russia and Denmark was renewed, but no hostilities ensued as Russia was at war with Turkey. Russia sought to bribe many Swedish nobles. From this time forward Sweden was anxious to acquire Norway.[132]

Great Britain was the chief customer for Swedish goods, hence Sweden was reluctant to offend her. In 1780 Sweden joined an Armed Neutrality with Denmark and Russia, though it soon disintegrated.[133]

The principles of the Armed Neutrality were four: (1) Neutral vessels may navigate freely port to port and on coasts of the powers at war. (2) Property of belligerents on neutral vessels except contraband is to be free. (3) Contraband is that which is so listed in treaties of Sweden and Russia with Great Britain. (4) For a blockade to be recognized it must be effective. In 1780 the American Congress passed a resolution agreeing to the principles of the Armed Neutrality. On February 5, 1783, Sweden recognized American independence twenty days before Denmark-Norway did so. The first American Treaty with Sweden, April 3, 1783, incorporated the principle of "free ships free goods." In 1788, while Russia was at war with Turkey, Sweden on a pretext attacked Russia, and Denmark, as required by her alliance with Russia, invaded Sweden.[134] Through British and Prussian intervention the Danish troops evacuated Sweden, and Sweden gave up no territory or indemnity. England and Prussia feared Russian expansion. Peace was made with Russia in 1790 at Varälä, restoring the status quo on the understanding that Russia would abstain from further interference in the internal affairs of Sweden. During the prior century there had been wholesale bribery of members of the Riksdag by both Russia and France. From this time on Russian meddling ceased.

When the French revolution broke out Sweden proposed to intervene with Russia and Austria in favor of the French king. A treaty with Russia to that effect was made in 1791. The Swedish king was assassinated in 1792 before he could carry out the plan. During the regency of Duke Charles (1792-1796) the French Republic was recognized in 1795 and friendly terms were maintained. Relations with Denmark-Norway were now good, and they became allies in 1794 and 1800.[135] In 1794 and 1800 Sweden joined the League of Armed Neutrality of the North to patrol the seas to protect their merchantmen against being searched by the British.[136] In 1801 the British fleet bombarded Copenhagen and was about to proceed to attack Sweden, but Sweden reached an agreement with the British.

In 1804 Sweden joined the coalition against Napoleon and 13,000 Swedish troops were maintained in Pomerania.[137] In 1807 the French seized Pomerania and Stralsund. France and Russia called on Sweden to close her ports to England and join the Continental System. In 1808 Russia invaded Finland without a declaration of war. Denmark declared war on Sweden, as Denmark after the bombardment of Copenhagen by the British fleet in 1807 became an ally of Napoleon.[138] By the Peace of 1809 at Frederikshamn, Sweden signed the hardest peace in her history, giving up more than a third of her territory: Finland, the Aland Islands, and part of Västerbotten and Swedish Lapland.[139] The Peace of Jönköping of the same year with Denmark left the parties in the status quo. The Danish military leader, later chosen Crown Prince of Sweden, had so conducted the war as not to permit Russia to overwhelm Sweden.[140] In 1810 peace was made with France. Pomerania was restored to Sweden on condition that she join the Continental System and close her ports to England. In 1810 a French general, Bernadotte, was elected Crown Prince of Sweden as the Swedish king had no heir, and the heir-elect had died. Proposals to elect the king of Denmark failed.

Sweden continued to import British goods in spite of the Continental System. Napoleon compelled Sweden to declare war on England, but no hostilities occurred and Sweden gradually moved toward alliance with England. Sweden gave up the hope of regaining Finland and now sought to acquire Norway.[141] When France occupied Swedish Pomerania in 1811 Sweden made a secret treaty with Russia under which Russia guaranteed the acquisition of Norway in return for thirty thousand Swedish troops against Napoleon in Germany. After Napoleon's retreat from Russia, England and Prussia also promised aid in the acquisition of Norway on condition that Sweden first assist in overthrowing Napoleon. Sweden sent troops to Germany in 1813, and soon invaded Denmark. By the Peace of Kiel in 1814 Denmark ceded Norway to Sweden while Denmark received Swedish Pomerania. By the Treaty of Paris, Guadeloupe, which England had given to Sweden, was returned to France, England then making a money payment to Sweden. Norway disputed the right of the Danish king to renounce Norway to Sweden, and adopted a constitution on May 17, 1814, and elected a Danish prince as king.[142] But the guaranteeing powers—Russia, Britain, Austria and Prussia—demanded fulfillment of the Treaty of Kiel, and Sweden occupied part of Norway. Only Austria supported Denmark. The Norwegians agreed to the union in October 1814 and the Act of Union was passed in 1815.[143]

At the Congress of Vienna, in 1815, Swedish Pomerania was ceded to Prussia, while Denmark received the Duchy of Lauenburg.[144] For the first time in almost six centuries Sweden had no possessions on the other side of the Baltic. Sweden has not been at war since 1814. She was the only Scandinavian nation to enjoy such good fortune.

In 1783 and again in 1845 the Swedish government wished to sell the island of St. Bartholomew to the United States.[145] But the United States adhered to the policy as expressed by James Buchanan "that the acquisition of distant insular possessions for colonial dependencies has never been deemed desirable or expedient by the United States."[146]

A policy of reconciliation with Russia resulted in the Treaty of 1826 at St. Petersburg under which the districts previously occupied in common by Russians and Norwegians were partitioned between the two countries.[147] This checked Russian expansion westward. When British relations with Russia were strained in 1833 to 1834 Sweden issued a declaration of neutrality.[148] In 1840 the Swedish king was ready to join Great Britain and Russia in a war against France, but his advisers forced him to modify his position and Denmark refused cooperation. The next Swedish king was opposed to German aggression and secured an armistice in the German war against Denmark in 1848 to 1849.[149] In 1851 when Russia sought to acquire fishing rights for the Russian Lapps in Norway he declined to permit it. But the Crimean War soon commenced and prevented Russia from attacking Sweden. Sweden declared her neutrality as did Denmark. Naval vessels of both Great Britain and Russia entered Swedish ports, though the right was more helpful to Britain than to Russia. In 1855 Sweden concluded the November Treaty with France and England under which these powers agreed to assist Sweden and Norway in the event of Russian aggression. In the Treaty of 1856 Russia agreed not to fortify the Åland Islands near Stockholm. When Denmark was attacked by Germany in 1864 Sweden remained neutral, as none of the Great Powers stood ready to help Denmark.[150] Sweden declined to help France in the Franco-Prussian War of 1870, particularly when Russia remained neutral.[151]

Friction between Norway and Sweden arose over a number of issues.[152] The Norwegian parliament abolished the privileges of the nobility and celebrated the Norwegian day of independence against the king's wishes. The Norwegians were reluctant to pay their share of the Danish National Debt as provided in the Treaty of Kiel. The king sought to amend the constitution to increase his powers. The Norwegians objected to a Swedish viceroy and from 1836 the post was always held by a Norwegian. None was appointed after 1859 and the position was abolished in 1873 and a prime minister residing in Norway was established. The Norwegians desired their own national flag. The Swedes after some decades took steps in that direction. The Norwegian parliament in 1880 asserted that a constitutional amendment permitting members of the cabinet to participate in its debates could not be vetoed by the Swedish king after its passage three times.[153] The king asserted that he had an absolute veto, a view supported by the Conservative party in Norway and by all but one member of the law faculty of the University of Oslo. The Storthing ignored the king's veto and impeached the cabinet. From 1884 on, Norway had responsible parliamentary government, while Sweden did not get it until 1917. Norway was long dissatisfied because the foreign minister for the joint kingdom was always Swedish.[154] Several joint commissions in 1844, 1871 and 1895 were appointed to revise the Act of Union. Sweden finally offered to let the foreign minister be either Swedish or Norwegian. But as Norway now had the largest commerical fleet next to England she demanded a separate consular service. The king vetoed a Norwegian law setting up such a service. The Storthing now declared him out of office as king of Norway. A plebiscite supported the Storthing by a vote of 362,980 to 182. The Karlstad Treaty of 1905 provided for severance of the Union.[155] A narrow strip on both sides of the border was neutralized and the rights of nomad Lapps to reindeer pasturage on both sides of the borders were protected. Disagreements arising out of the treaty were to be submitted to the Hague Court of Arbitration. The frontiers between Norway and Sweden, between the United States and Canada, and the boundaries of Switzerland, are the outstanding examples of effective neutralization.

Sweden has been fortunate in remaining at peace since 1814. Mr. Justice Jackson has pointed out that "the Swedes are so incorrigibly independent that of all Europe they alone live in a land never occupied by a conqueror."[156] In 1912 the Scandinavian states issued joint regulations on neutrality. When World War I broke out each Scandinavian government issued independent declarations of neutrality but employed similar phraseology.[157] In August 1914 Norway and Sweden issued supplementary declarations that the two countries would under no circumstances attack each other. This was done on the suggestion of the Swedish foreign minister in view of the separation of 1905. On the initiative of King Gustav V the kings of the three Scandinavian states met in Malmö in December 1914. The Scandinavian foreign ministers held several joint meetings and have met three or more times a year since that time. The war increased Scandinavian cooperation and stimulated governmental power and activity as over and against private enterprise. Finland, which had been a part of Sweden for six centuries prior to 1809, became independent of Russia.

The Swedes were the most reluctant of the Scandinavians to join the League of Nations. The Danish parliament joined by a unanimous vote, the Norwegians by a vote of 100 to 20, and the Swedish by a vote in the lower chamber of the Riksdag of 152 to 67 and in the upper chamber of 86 to 47 on March 3, 1920.[158] From 1923 to 1926 Sweden was a member of the Council of the League and played a leading role.[159] In 1917, ninety-five percent of the people in the Åland Islands following the Communist revolution in Russia voted to join Sweden. Sweden reluctantly accepted the decision of the League of Nations assigning them to Finland with the proviso that they may be demilitarized.[160] In 1923

Sweden rejected a defensive alliance with Finland although the Swedish foreign minister had advocated it. From 1920 to 1932 there was no meeting of the Scandinavian foreign ministers.

Sweden, like the other Scandinavian states, advocated the principle of universality of membership in the League of Nations. The Swedes therefore favored the admission of both Germany and Russia. They sought to strengthen the position of the Assembly in relation to the Council. They advocated arbitration and disarmament but opposed the creation of international security by a system of guarantees. They early accepted the compulsory jurisdiction of the Permanent Court of International Justice. In 1924 Sweden, Denmark, Finland, and Norway concluded bilateral agreements establishing permanent conciliation commissions for the solution of disputes not dealt with by the World Court. They favored the provisions of the Geneva Protocol of 1924 calling for disarmament, compulsory arbitration and compulsory jurisdiction of the World Court, but opposed its security provisions calling for sanctions possibly through military assistance. But they did not have to make a decision, as Britain rejected the protocol and it was taken off the agenda of the League. In 1925 and 1926 Sweden, Denmark and Norway concluded conventions with each other and with Finland calling for peaceful settlement of any dispute that might arise. All political disputes that were not solved by conciliation were to be referred to a specially created arbitral tribunal. In 1928 Sweden signed the Paris Pact outlawing war.

After Italy invaded Ethiopia in October 1935 the League appointed a special committee to prepare sanctions procedures. The Scandinavian states at once accepted the economic sanctions recommended. In 1936 the Assembly of the League came out for abolition of the sanctions against Italy. From that time the Scandinavian states returned to a policy of absolute neutrality. They had always opposed compulsory military sanctions.

In 1938 all five Scandinavian states signed a set of neutrality rules revising those of 1912.[161] Military plane flights over the air territory of the northern states were forbidden. Esthonia, Latvia, and Lithuania sought in vain for a Baltic military pact. Finland was anxious to come into close contact with Sweden, but all that came of it was an abortive plan for joint fortification of the Åland Islands.[162] In 1939 Sweden like Norway declined a non-aggression pact offered by Hitler.

On the outbreak of World War II Sweden like the other Scandinavian states declared neutrality.[163] When Russia attacked Finland in November 1939, Denmark and Norway declared neutrality but Sweden explicitly did not declare neutrality and so informed Russia in a note.

When sanctions were proposed in the Assembly of the League of Nations Sweden refused to take a stand on the proposal. But over $100,-000,000 in gifts and loans were sent by the Swedish government and people to Finland. War materials were supplied and 12,000 Swedes volunteered to fight for Finland. While Britain and France were eager to send troops across Norway and Sweden to assist Finland, both countries declined to permit passage in February 1940. Possibly, if the Finns had requested such passage Britain and France would have demanded it. But no request was made by the Finns who made peace in March 1940. Finland now asked Sweden and Norway for a defensive alliance and both expressed willingness. But no agreement was arrived at when there came a Russian warning and the attack on Norway and Denmark. When the latter attack came in April 1940 Sweden could do nothing as she had sent her military equipment and money to Finland. Sweden was therefore in no position to do for Norway what she had done for Finland, and if she had, no doubt Germany would have attacked Sweden.[164] Germany demanded of Sweden that she remain neutral and that she refrain from military mobilization. Sweden replied that she would remain neutral, but undertook mobilization.

Sweden forbade the transportation of war material for Norway. She refused to let Germany smuggle munitions through Sweden. Unquestionably, her sympathies lay with Norway and Denmark. The attack on these two countries ended whatever sympathies the Swedes might have previously entertained for Germany. After the withdrawal of the Norwegian government to London and the conquest of Holland, Belgium and France, Sweden permitted German transit through Sweden to Norway for the German forces of occupation. But she leased half of her merchant marine to the Allies. When Germany attacked Russia in 1941 Sweden under German and Finnish pressure permitted the Germans to send one division through Sweden to Finland. This was treated as aid to the Finns and not to be repeated as its was admitted to be a departure from neutrality.

Sweden did many things for her neighbor. During the time before Norway was conquered she permitted export of 24,000 steel helmets, 850 compasses, 4,500 maps, 46,000 pounds of clothing, 770,000 pounds of food stuffs, and much hospital material. Many prefabricated houses and much food for children were sent to Norway. Many Norwegians found a haven as refugees. Many Norwegian youths studied in Swedish schools, and trained in a police force to take over in Northern Norway. Fifteen thousand Danes, including 6,000 Danish Jews, received refuge in Sweden. There were 35,000 refugees from the Baltic states and 70,000 Finnish children. Count Folke Bernadotte secured the release of 19,000 Danes and Norwegians from German prison camps in the spring of 1945. In July 1943 Sweden notified Germany that military transit to and from Norway must cease. This removed the greatest strain in Sweden's relations with Norway. Sweden also stopped all exports of ball bearings and iron ore to Germany.

In the Swedish elections of September 1944, the Communists raised their vote from 100,000 to 300,000 and their seats in the Riksdag from three to fifteen.[165] In the election of 1948 their number of seats was reduced from fifteen to eight.[166] In 1948 Sweden made a trade agreement with Russia, providing Russia with a credit of $278,000,000.[167] The United States protested on the ground that trade with other countries would be disrupted. It was feared that Sweden would also be entangled politically. But the total trade contemplated over a six-year period was only 15 per cent of Sweden's export, and merely filled the gap left by the loss of trade with Germany. Moreover, the agreement merely granted credit, and left the contracting for goods to individual transactions between Russia and Swedish industries. While pressure was brought by the Swedish government on some industries to sell to Russia, by the end of 1948 the total contracts made exhausted only one-third of the available credit. This was slightly increased in 1949.

While Denmark and Norway were charter members of the United Nations, Sweden was admitted on November 19, 1946, as one of the first three non-charter members.[168] The Riksdag unanimously favored such membership. Recently a Swede has been elected a member of the Economic and Social Council of the United Nations. Sweden is subjected to the compulsory jurisdiction of the International Court of Justice under Article 36 of the Statute. It had also accepted the optional clause as to the Permanent Court of Justice. In 1949 Sweden joined the Council of Europe. But unlike Denmark and Norway she did not join the Atlantic Pact.[169]

In January 1949 Sweden offered Denmark and Norway a ten-year military alliance, to be regarded as a regional agreement under Article 52 of the United Nations Charter. But each country was required to pledge itself not to enter any military alliance with other states. Norway, however, felt that she must have aid from the west and Denmark was unable to find a compromise solution. Sweden thus clings to her neutrality up to the present moment. Many Swedes contend that if war does not come but there is a long period of cold war, then such cold war will be pulled into Scandinavia, and Russia may invoke its mutual armistice treaty with Finland and thus in effect occupy Finland.[170] Were Sweden to join the Atlantic Pact, immediate Russian occupation of Finland might occur.

In October 1950 Sweden and Finland engaged in a diplomatic exchange of views as to the autonomy of the Aland Islands.[171] Apparently Finland under direct orders from Russia was proposing to deprive them of their guarantees given by the defunct League of Nations. The new Finnish statute deleted a section incorporating the League guarantee.

In February 1951 the Swedish government explained why it abstained from voting on the American resolution as to sanctions against China. It doubted that sanctions against China would be practical and effective and feared that such measures might develop into something quite different from what was intended.[172] The Swedish government was reluctant to blockade Russia and its satellites as to strategic materials, because of Sweden's traditional neutrality and because of its credit and barter agreement with Russia and its trade treaties with Russian satellites.[173]

Swedish lawyers played an important role in the Mixed Courts of Egypt which existed from 1876 to October 15, 1949.[174] The eleven Swedish judges were: Magnus Armfelt, 1876-1884 and 1887-1892; Carl Petersén, 1884-1886; Conrad Cederkrantz, 1895-1901; Carl Otto Montan, 1901-1913; Patrick Adlercreutz, 1907-1917; Erik Sjöberg, 1913-1918; Henrie Nordenskjöld, 1917-1925; Emil Sandström, 1918-1926; Pehr Cederschiöld, 1925-1926; Torsten Salén, 1926-1949; and Hugo Wikström, 1926-1947. The last to sit was Torsten Salén; he served the longest of any Swedish judge; namely, 23 years, and was the only one to serve as a judge of the Mixed Court of Appeals. It is significant that Nubar Pascha, the instigator of the court, had originally proposed that all its judges be taken from the Scandinavian states.

The work of the Committee of Jurists who drafted plans for the Permanent Court of International Justice was assisted by Åke Hammarskjöld as the chief member of its expert secretariat.[175] In 1930 Hammarskjöld came near to election as a judge of the court, as on the tenth ballot in the Assembly he received a majority of votes, but the Council chose another.[176] In 1922 he was elected the first Registrar of the Court for a seven-year period and in 1929 reelected for a like term.[177] As Professor Hudson states: "Owing partly to his previous experience in connection with the drafting of the Court's statute and owing to the continuity of his service, his work has been of inestimable value to the Court."[178]

In 1936 he was elected a member of the Court, but died within nine months of his election.[179] In 1937, of 27 nominating national groups, four nominated Alfred E. F. Sandström and three Östen Undén of Sweden.

On November 3, 1948, through the same procedure as was employed in electing judges of the International Court of Justice, A. E. F. Sandström of Sweden was elected one of the fifteen members of the International Law Commission created by the General Assembly.[180] In a report to the Commission he concluded that an international judicial organ for international criminal jurisdiction was not desirable.[181] At the 1950 meeting in Geneva, Switzerland, he was elected First Vice-Chairman of the Commission.[182]

In April 1953, Dag Hammerskjöld of Sweden was elected Secretary-General of the United Nations.

Custom, Case-Law and Codes

Prehistoric Swedish law at first took the form of custom.[183] The early law grew up "in undisturbed isolation," thus exhibiting "a unique instance of law almost solely self-developed."[184] But specially enacted and positive law early appeared. While among many primitive races the custodian of knowledge of the law was the priest, this was not true in the Scandinavian nations. Knowledge of the law could be acquired by any one so inclined. Persons learned in the customary law, and pre-eminent in this respect, were called lawmen. They served as private counsellors, instructors, and in effect as judges as they were consulted by the local assembly known as the *thing*. The Swedish lawman, unlike the Norwegian and Icelandic, early acquired the powers of an elected public official.[185] His district was a *land*, and he was elected by the farmers. He administered justice, presided at the *thing*, and gave advice as to the law applicable to cases as they arose. He also had political and administrative duties. The system arose largely to preserve local independence as against close central rule. This is shown by the language of the most ancient Swedish law books still in existence: "Yeoman-born shall lawman be; to this let every yeoman see." The lawmen from various districts combined themselves under chieftains. This fact had considerable influence on the development of the nation which had gone a long way by the eleventh century. The lawman delivered a regular public address (*Lag-saga*) containing the law of the land. Though eventually having no time to give private instruction, he indirectly achieved this end in such public address. Preserved even to this day are the names of several lawmen who formulated law-sagas: Lum, whose laws-sagas were known as the "Laws of Lum," and Vig Spa, after whom was named "Vigers Flokker."

The evidence is uncertain as to the degree of popular acquiescence given to the public recitals of law and the decisions rendered in litigated cases by the lawmen.[186] According to Snorre, where there was a variance between the laws of different *lands* or between the lawmen, the laws of Uppland and the lawman representing Tiundaland were determinative. But as each *land* retained judicial power over its local affairs, it would seem that this rule applied only to political affairs. There was no system of appeal or other recourse against a lawman who abused his position.

The smallest community unit among the Goths was known as the *Härad* and among the Svears as the *Hundred*.[187] The judicial and legislative assembly of a *Härad* was called a *Härad-thing*, and that of a hundred a *Hundred-thing*. In turn, a group of these units combined to form a *Land*. The *Land* had a *Land-thing* with legislative and judicial powers. In southern Sweden the most important *thing* was known as the "Thing of all the Goths." This area later contained six Lands: Westergötland, Ostergötland, Värmland, Småland, and the islands of Öland and Gotland. In Svea-land in central Sweden there were five Lands: Uppland, Södermannland, Westmannland, Helsingland, and Nerike.

The legislative or law-making power exercised by the Swedish *land-thing* rested in the populace alone.[188] Kings and officials had to conform to their proceedings. This was more true in Sweden than in Denmark and Norway. The early Swedish king had more dignity than power. His influence on development of the law was slight. He could promulgate decrees as to military affairs and his own retinue. The Swedish chieftains like the king were not able to strip the *land-things* of their power to adopt or reject acts proposed by the king.

Laws were the subjects of the earliest writings in Sweden. The oldest law-text is the *Vestgöta-lag* from the early part of the thirteenth century.[189] It is still in existence, as is a revision in 1300. In 1296 King Birger Magnusson approved a code, which he had directed a committee to write for Uppland, at the request of the lawmen in Tiundaland. Similar law-books were prepared for Östergotland, Öland, Södermannland, Westmannland, and Helsingland, the latter covering Swedish settlements in Finland.[190] Some of those books were expressly given the title of *Lag-saga*. There were also municipal codes for Stockholm and two other cities entitled *Biaerköa raetter* or market laws.

Birger Jarl, regent of Sweden about 1250, attempted to draft laws for the entire kingdom and to set up a sovereign monarchy. The scope of Birger Jarl's proposals is of interest.[191] His aim was to establish peace and order, security of the home, the *thing*, women, and the church. The king swore to preserve these, and was empowered to issue decrees to secure them. Breaches of the decrees were made punishable by outlawing and forfeiture of all personal property. Servitude for debt,[192] and trial by ordeal were abolished. Daughters were given the right to inherit. Private vengeance was forbidden. Inns were set up so that travelers would not enter private homes. Provision was made for service in the cavalry; the nobility thus got its start. The highest state offices now became the Chancellor, the Marshal and the Drost. Something like typical European feudalism was introduced. The power of the barons was checked.

King Magnus Ladulås (1275-1290)[193] proclaimed: "What we ordain in writing shall be frequently announced to all men, that they may observe our commands and avoid what we forbid." The *land-things*, however, received this order as something which they had discretion to adopt or reject. There developed also at this time as a fixed institution the *Riksråd* or Council of the Kingdom. Like the Norwegian kings, Magnus Ladulås abolished the popular election of judges, and appointed the lawman and other district officials himself. Magnus extended the powers of the clergy. Numerous town charters were granted. The Statute of Alsnö in 1279 exempted from taxation all who rendered military service on horseback. This had the double effect of creating a strong cavalry and fostering a powerful nobility.

Centralization and unification of the Swedish legal systems came later than the Danish and Norwegian largely due to the independent development of the Swedish *land* and *things*.[194] Sweden and Norway formed their first union under one king, Magnus Eriksson, in the fourteenth century. In the decade from 1340 to 1350, Magnus commenced this task in Sweden. He was doubtless influenced by the tremendous differences between the good order of Norway and the lawlessness of of Sweden. He began with a series of decrees modifying the prior law. Serfdom was abolished, and changes were made in the jury system, the law of evidence, and the king's peace. The next step was the drafting of a code. In 1347 the king summoned to Örebro a commission of three lawmen, Ulf Ambjörnson of Småland, Algot Bengtson of Westergötland, and Thorgeir of Värmland, "*ad corrigendum reformandum, et ad unam concordantiam et conventiam leges singulorum legisferatum regni Sveciae redigendum.*" The work of drafting had by that time progressed so far that it was then submitted to a much larger committee of revision. No bishops appear to have been present, but there were nobles and others of the highest discretion and understanding. The work was done between 1347 and 1352.[195]

The Land Law was based on the laws of Uppland and Ostgöta. The Law of the church was not made a part of the Code as it was in Norway. The prelates of the church resisted such incorporation, as they felt it would permit the king and laymen to participate in making ecclesiastical law. Consequently, the old church regulations were retained by each *land*. It was only gradually that the church Law of Uppland became in practice law throughout Sweden. The security of the person was dealt with in six divisions: breaches of the king's peace, felonies, homicide with intent, homicide without intent, injuries to the person with intent, and injuries without intent. There were other titles dealing with marriage, indentures, land-titles, buildings, the law merchant, and theft. The Code was distinctly superior to former works in arrangement and compilation. It expressly declared that "in the future no laws should be given to the common people without their aye and good will." It took a half century to secure its adoption by all the *lands*, some of which even then retained many local laws and customs.

A decree of King Erik of Pomerania in 1413 largely displaced the *things* of the *härad* and the *land*. This decree instituted the royal *Räfste-things*, which held two annual sessions.[196] These courts were made up of judges appointed by the king. They sat with the lawman as a royal appellate court for the *land-things*. In the reign of Christopher of Bavaria the Land-Law of 1442 provided for an annual session of such court to be held either by the king, or by a lawman or bishop or another appointed by the king. There had already been established lower courts for each *härad*, with intermediate courts of appeal or *rättare-thing*. But this system did not come into actual use. The public did not realize that the new courts embodied the royal judicial authority. Hence litigants came directly to the king, who usually acted through the Council of the kingdom. The new courts thus gradually ceased to exist.

Another defect was that the lawmen, being also chieftains, held seats in the National Council and delegated their judicial work to inferior subordinates. A similar abuse developed as to the *härad* courts when King Johan III in 1569 ennobled their presiding chiefs. The above defects were perceived by King Gustavus Adolphus II, when he ascended the throne. In 1614 he organized a court of final appeals called *Svea Hoffrätt*. He issued a decree that lower judges perform their judicial functions in person at regular sessions. The ancient *land-things* now disappeared. An order of 1615 provided for appeals from the *Hoffrätt* to the king and the Council of State. In 1623 another *Hoffrätt* was established at Åbo and in 1634 in Jönköping. In 1684 the Svea *Hoffrätt* was ordered to refer doubtful questions to the king. From 1617 to 1634 the legislative functions of the old *land-things* were also taken from them. They were turned over to the National Assembly made up of nobility, clergy, freeholders, and burghers. Subsequently the *Rådstugurätt* was made the main trial court of the cities, and the *Hoffrätt* the sole intermediate appellate court.[197]

The King of Denmark ruled as an absolute monarch over Denmark from 1661 to 1848 and over Norway from 1661 to 1814. The Swedish

Riksdags of 1660, 1682, and 1693 conferred somewhat more limited powers on the king. Thus the Swedish people have "never passed through an entire reign during which the right of the representatives of the people to take part in legislation has been abolished in form or in fact."[198]

But the great increase in the power of Charles XI, who died in 1697, stimulated codification. Acting in compliance with his wishes the Riksdag in 1686 requested codification, and he immediately appointed a commission of twelve members.[199] Its first chairman, Count Erik Lindsköld, had already prepared a draft resembling the Danish Code of 1683. His draft was adhered to as to its essentials. When he died in 1690 he was succeeded by Count Niels Gyldenstolpe, who died in 1709. The third chairman was Count Gustav Cronhjelm who finished the work and was the chief figure in it. The long delay before completion was due to the fact that care was used to obtain suggestions from numerous judges, magistrates, and learned jurists, as well as the wars of Charles XII. It was laid before representatives of the nation in 1723. Following their comments a new commission was formed whose revised plan was in substance adopted by the Riksdags of 1731 and 1734. It was ratified by the king in 1736 and became effective that year with the official title of *Sveriges Rikes Lag.*

The code consists of nine parts: Marriage, Inheritance, Land Tenure, Buildings, Commerce and Market Towns, Crimes, Punishments, Executions, and Court Practice. Its editorial form is owed largely to Cronhjelm and also to Karl Lundius of the University of Uppsala, who prepared a new draft of the entire code except two parts.

It was the intent that the new code either abolish or absorb the prior law. But the code omitted many provisions important in social and political life, thus arguably referring these to the special laws that were in force. The boundary between the general law and the special laws hinged on their immutability or subjection to changes. The Swedish code omitted ordinances found to be subject to change according to circumstances; that is to say, "economic and political regulations." Such regulations were those governing trades, commerce, forestry, harbors, weights and measures, the mails, and practice of medicine. The revenue system, state administration, and military affairs were excluded. A general church system, adopted in 1686, was included. If the subject was treated in principle or substantially in the code a general statute rather than a special one was involved. The question is not so important today, as there is now much less special legislation. Shortly after the adoption of the code, legislation of an interpretational character was passed. The new statutes were entitled *Förklaringar* or Explanations. A proposed code governing political affairs failed of adoption.

The great commission which prepared the Code of 1734 continued its development until 1811, when a new commission undertook to prepare another code of civil law.[200] Its chief member was Jan Gabriel Richert (1784-1864). A draft submitted to the Riksdag in 1815 was not acted upon. In 1840 the Riksdag organized a commission under the leadership of Richert to "prepare the law." Since that date the commission has become a permanent institution, and has played an important role in law improvement. Sweden, more than Denmark and Norway, has made great use of consultations with the official and social organizations affected by proposed laws.

Although custom was to a large extent displaced by written statutes, it long continued important in Sweden, especially during the legal confusion in Sweden from the fourteenth to the sixteenth century.[201] The "Rules for Judges" in the Swedish code expressly provided that "in whatsoever matters there be no written law, the reasonable custom is to be applied as law in judgments." Its chief area in modern law is that of business, where it operates in the form of customs of merchants and local usages, which are implied in contracts, even though not contemplated by all the parties. There is less resort to custom in Sweden than there is in Denmark and Norway.[202]

During the past century uncertainty arose as to conflicts between an old statute and a later customary rule. The statutes of Sweden now expressly limit the application of customary law to cases which are not covered by written law, hence the older statute represents the law.

Sweden is less attached to the doctrine of stare decisis than are Denmark and Norway.[203] Both in theory and practice it asserts the freedom of each court to follow its own conception of law and justice. However, a Swedish act of 1876 directed the Supreme Court to refer the case to the entire court whenever the majority in either of its two branches should overrule a previous line of decisions.

The King

The unification of Sweden into one kingdom began to be effective about the year 800.[204] The kingship became elective about 1060. Birger Jarl, father of two kings, who lived in the thirteenth century, sought successfully to increase the prestige of the *thing* or local assembly. During the reign of Magnus Ladulås (1266-1290) the king occasionally consulted the clergy and the nobility at meetings. Two other estates, the burghers and the free peasants, had already emerged. In 1359 the burghers were summoned for the first time to sit in the National Assembly by King Magnus Ericsson. This Assembly provided by law that the kingship should be elective. The first Assembly to include the free peasants with the other three estates was called in 1435 by Engelbrekt, a leader against the Danes. This had much to do with the fact that the Swedish peasants never became serfs. The Rigsdag as established in 1435 has continued up to the present time.[205] It consisted of four estates until 1866. It has played an important part in Swedish government for five centuries in sharp contrast to the much shorter periods of legislative assemblies in Denmark and Norway. In 1523 the Riksdag elected Gustavus Vasa as king and terminated the Kalmar Union. In 1527 it declared that the king rather than the Pope was the Swedish sovereign, and eventually it formally declared the nation to be Protestant. In 1544 it made the kingship hereditary instead of elective. The Riksdag was strengthened during the reign of the greatest Swedish king, Gustavus Adolphus (1611-1632).

In 1617 he enacted regulations for procedure in the Riksdag at a time when the only other European country having a parliamentary procedure was England.[206] The king addressed the four assembled estates. He appointed a noble to be the spokesman for the nobility while the Swedish primate was the spokesman for the three lower estates. Each estate debated separately the royal bills laid before it. But the reply of each was handed to the king in joint session. If the estates differed with the king, they met together with the king to adjust matters. If the estates differed with each other, the king was free to accept the opinion he liked best. The king determined the frequency of sessions. He often joined with the lower estates against the nobles. Up to 1682 there was a limited monarchy.

The first period of absolutism was from 1682 to 1719. During a period of regency the nobility abused its powers. This facilitated the king's joining forces with the other three estates against the nobility. The wide powers of the nobility were thus forever ended. In 1682, King Charles XI persuaded the Riksdag to confer all legislative power on the king.[207] His son, Charles XII, a brilliant military leader, was killed in 1718 in battle and left no heirs. The Riksdag then reasserted its earlier powers.

The Riksdag was predominant from 1719 to 1772.[208] A new constitution adopted in 1719 gave the king but little power. The king was to be subject to a council of seventeen and the council in turn was subject to the Riksdag. The three estates other than the peasants were predominant. Political parties were established. Only in England was there similar parliamentary government. In 1734 a new general code of laws was adopted. The committee system was developed in the Riksdag. By the Press Ordinance of 1766 Sweden became the first country after England to establish freedom of the press by legislation.[209]

There was a second era of absolutism from 1772 to 1809.[210] Gustavus

III proposed a new constitution restoring the royal power and the Riksdag unanimously adopted it. Legislative power was now in the king and the Riksdag. But the king's Council now became responsible to him alone. Religious toleration and freedom of the press were provided. But a second coup d'etat in 1789 made the king absolute. The king was given the power to fix the size of his council, and he exercised such power by completely abolishing it. The French Revolution and Swedish military reverses resulted in the deposition of Gustavus IV in 1809.

Following the deposition the Riksdag adopted a new constitution on June 5, 1809,[211] which, still in force today, is one of the oldest written constitutions in the world, that of Norway being adopted in 1814 and of Denmark in 1849. The French general, Jean Bernadotte, was chosen as Crown Prince, and ascended the throne in 1818. The Bernadotte family still reigns, the present king, Gustav VI, commencing his reign in 1950.

The Constitution

Sweden is governed by a written constitution adopted in 1809,[212] with several amendments, and the Organic Law of the Riksdag, adopted June 22, 1866. Next to the American it is the oldest written constitution. Article 1 of the Constitution declares that Sweden is an hereditary monarchy. It repeals the previous constitution of 1772 and certain fundamental laws such as the Act of Union and Act of Settlement of 1789, and the Riksdag Law of 1617. Today the Swedish constitution may be said to consist of four parts: (1) the Constitution of 1809, (2) the law of succession to the throne of 1810, (3) the law of the freedom of the press of 1812, and (4) the laws reorganizing the Riksdag enacted in 1866.

The Constitution does not expressly state the source of sovereign power. It was, however, promulgated by the "undersigned estates, counts, barons, bishops, nobles, clergy, burghers, and common peasants," and was confirmed by the king.

Comprehensive provisions are made for the protection of the rights of the people.[213] The king shall not deprive or allow anyone to be deprived of life, honor, personal liberty, or well-being without legal trial and sentence. No one is to be deprived of real or personal property without due trial and judgment in accordance with the provisions of Swedish law. The peace of any person in his home is not to be disturbed. No person may be banished from one place to another. Everyone is to be protected in the free exercise of his religion, provided that he does not thereby disturb public order or occasion general offense. Persons are to be tried only by the courts having proper jurisdiction. Under Article 86 freedom of the press is to be preserved.[214] The "ancient privileges, advantages, rights, and liberties of the estates of the kingdom shall remain in force." Sweden is the most aristocratic of the Scandinavian countries, having 900 titled families compared with 220 in Denmark and none in Norway other than the royal family.[215] Special privileges given them have been abolished with their consent.

Executive power is vested in the king under Article 1 of the Constitution. There is to be a council of state composed of the heads of departments of administration and not less than three councilors without portfolio. All government business except that relating to matters of military command must be decided by the king in council of state.[216] In actual practice power is in the hands of the council, which acts as a cabinet and is responsible to the majority in the Riksdag.

The judicial power, which belongs to the king, is vested in not less than twelve judges appointed by the king who form the Supreme Court.[217] The Supreme Court is the final court of appeal and passes on the interpretation of laws.[218] Three of its members together with one legal member of the supreme administrative court form the king's law council, which gives its opinion on proposals of law or statutes referred to it by the king.[219]

The Swedish Constitution may be amended by a majority vote of the two houses of the Riksdag acting separately in an ordinary session, followed by another similar vote in an ordinary session following the next popular election for the lower house.[220] The approval of the king is required, but in practice he rarely uses his veto power. Amendments go into effect on the reading of an open letter from the king read in each chamber simultaneously.

The Riksdag

Legislative power, according to the Constitution, is to be exercised by the Riksdag, a bicameral body. The composition is determined by the Riksdag Law. There is to be a foreign affairs committee of sixteen members with which the king must consult "concerning the relations of the kingdom with foreign powers."

The 150 members of the upper chamber are elected by the provincial councils for a term of eight years. The lower chamber consists of 230 members elected for four years by direct universal suffrage.

The Riksdag was reorganized in 1866.[221] A bicameral assembly replaced the four estates which had served since 1435. The nobility and the clergy were no longer to have separate chambers. There were age and property qualifications for membership in both houses, with lower qualifications for the lower house, the Second Chamber. About forty years later the qualifications were lowered still further and the differences between qualifications for the upper and lower chamber were diminished.

Swedish political parties date from 1866 when the Riksdag became bicameral. Since 1912 there have been three political groupings ranging from right to left as follows: (1) the Conservatives, (2) the Liberals, including the Agrarians, and (3) the Social Democrats. The Conservative party is a direct descendant of the first modern political party in Sweden, *Lantmanna partiet* (the Agricultural party), formed about 1867. The Liberals date from about 1895. The Social Democrats were organized in 1889. The left wing of the Social Democrats seceded in 1919 to form the Left Socialist party. In 1922 after the Left Socialists had joined the Third International some of them returned to the Social Democratic party. The right wing of the Communists joined the Social Democrats in 1926. The Social Democrats have had a plurality in the lower chamber since 1914 and in the upper since 1920. They have had an absolute majority in the lower chamber only from 1940 to 1944. They have had an absolute majority in the upper chamber since 1941. The Communist party came into existence in 1921. In 1948 they elected nine members to the lower chamber compared with fifteen in 1944. In the county and municipal elections of September 17, 1950, they got less than five per cent of the vote, compared with 11.2 per cent in 1946 and 6.3 per cent in 1948.[222] Membership dropped from 60,000 in 1946 to 33,000 in 1950, a loss of 45 per cent compared with a loss of 65 per cent in Denmark and Norway.

The present Social Democratic party resembles the labor parties of Denmark and Norway. It is much less similar to the Socialist parties of France, Italy and Germany. As stated in a leading history of Sweden: "Swedish socialism, like that of England, has been characterized less by theoretical speculations in the German style than by common sense and a strong realistic bent."[223]

Hans Hedtoft, Prime Minister of Denmark in 1950, has summarized the development of parliamentary government in Scandinavia as follows: "While Parliamentarism first became a tradition of government in Denmark in 1901, and in Sweden even as late as 1917, in Norway it dates back to 1884."[224] The persistent and active opposition of the Conservative party and the king to parliamentarism did not end until 1917.

The members of the upper house are elected for an eight-year term, one-eighth being elected each year, by electoral colleges. The nation is divided into 19 election districts which in turn are combined into eight groups, one group electing its representatives each year. The electoral colleges are proportionately elected by the list system of proportional representation by voters aged 21 or over. The electoral college uses a system of proportional representation in making its choice for members of the Riksdag. The seats are redistributed among the nineteen districts every ten years on the basis of population.

With respect to elections to the lower chamber Sweden is divided into 28 election districts. Usually a county constitutes such a district. There is a redistribution of seats before each four-year term. Since 1945 the voting age has been twenty-one. A system of proportional representation is used.

Universal male suffrage was introduced in 1909 for elections to the lower house and in 1918 for the upper house. Women were given the right to vote in 1921.

What in other nations is designated as the upper chamber is called in Sweden the First Chamber.[225] The other chamber is known as the Second Chamber. The First Chamber contains 150 members and the Second 230. Generally speaking, the two chambers are equal as to legislative powers. However, as to matters in the fields of taxation and public finance on which there is disagreement a joint vote is taken, hence the Second Chamber is the more powerful. Any person may be elected to the Second Chamber who can vote in the district. A member of the First Chamber need not live in the district he represents, but must be at least 35 years old and entitled to vote in the municipal elections. Women may be elected to either chamber. Members of both chambers receive the same salary and traveling expenses. They enjoy freedom from arrest and freedom of expression in debate.

The regular session of the Riksdag commences in January of each year. The cabinet may call special sessions. At the opening each chamber elects a speaker and two vice-speakers.

It is a peculiarity of the Swedish committee system that they are provided for in the Constitution. The complete list of the eight standing committees are there set forth.[226] They are: (1) Foreign Affairs, (2) Constitution, (3) Appropriations, (4) Ways and Means, (5) Banks, (6) Private Law, (7) Social Legislation, and (8) Agriculture. No bill can be passed by either chamber until acted upon by the proper committee. The eight standing committees are all joint committees of the two chambers. Thus there is simultaneous study by both chambers and the advantages of a unicameral legislature are enjoyed in part. Members of the ministry are excluded from committee meetings. Efforts to change this have been unsuccessful although there are many severe Swedish critics. There are at least sixteen members on a joint committee, with one-half from each chamber. They are selected by proportional representation and for the duration of the regular session.

Under Article 54 of the Constitution the members of the Committee on Foreign Affairs shall also be members of an Advisory Committee to confer with the king concerning foreign affairs. Conference with the committee must take place before all matters of major importance are decided.

The Riksdag and each chamber may select special committees to assist the regular standing committees. But not very much is left for them to deal with. Special sessions may select only such joint standing committees as are necessary to handle the specific purposes for which the special session is called.

In Sweden a government committee normally works on a bill prior to its introduction in the Riksdag.[227] This system is more than two centuries old in Sweden. At first such committees had a purely fact-finding objective, but this has been combined with a more political one. The committees are appointed by the government at the request of the Riksdag or on its own initiative. Representatives of political parties may be appointed as well as experts on the subject. Finished reports are sent to various private groups and public authorities for criticism before the cabinet decides whether it approves the proposal.

Bills may be introduced by the ministry, by a standing committee, or by any member of either chamber. Each bill is turned over to the appropriate joint committee. When the joint committee is ready to report, the bill may be taken up in both houses at the same time. There is no requirement of three separate readings of bills. There is virtually no time limit on the ensuing debate in the chambers, yet little filibustering occurs. Since 1925 secret voting has been abolished. The vote is by acclamation. On demand there may be a standing vote and a roll call. Where there is a tie vote, the decision is made by lot.

Except as to appropriations or revenues the chambers must vote separately. If the chambers disagree as to appropriations or revenues, the issue is determined by a majority of the total vote of both chambers. The joint vote is not used often and does not always result in a victory for the larger chamber. The annual budget is handled by the Committees on Appropriations, Ways and Means, and Banks.

An ordinary tax bill does not require the king's signature, as Article 57 of the Constitution provides that the Riksdag alone shall levy taxes. All other bills require the royal sanction, but the king acts only through his ministers. The veto has thus become virtually obsolete. The last one occurred in 1912 and only upon the advice of the ministry.

The entire statutory law of Sweden is published in annually revised editions in a single volume, called *Sveriges Rikes Lag,* of about 3,000 pages.[228] As of 1938 it sold for about $5.25. It is available in all Swedish bookshops.

The king, acting through the ministry, has wide ordinance powers, particularly as to the administration of the social services. Such powers embrace a large field of administrative orders relating to the supervision of the governmental agencies. Under the Constitution the king may ask the Riksdag to share the ordinance powers with him, and it has become the practice to bring matters of general interest directly to the Riksdag. Sweden uses the device of provisional laws less than Denmark and Norway.

Each Riksdag appoints two officials to supervise the general administration of the laws. Under Article 96 of the Constitution, at each regular session there is chosen a procurator for judicial affairs and a procurator for military affairs. They act as representatives of the Riksdag. They are to hear complaints about maladministration and to bring charges of official misconduct. The former official may scrutinize the work of the courts. Thus a close liaison between the Riksdag and the administration and judicial organizations may be maintained. Under Article 21 of the Constitution there is set up the King's Law Council, consisting of three members of the Supreme Court and one judge from the Supreme Administrative Court. The Law Council is to give its opinion on proposals for the enactment, annulment, amendment or elucidation of the laws or statutes referred to them by the king.

There is almost no lobbying in Sweden. Most members of the Riksdag are small farmers, small businessmen and public officials. Reelection is common.

The ministry or cabinet is selected from the controlling party or coalition of parties, and may come from either chamber. It may include administrators without parliamentary experience. A minister may attend sessions of both chambers, but vote only in his own chamber. There is a right of interpellation. The answers are often delayed, and do not involve a possibility of fall of the cabinet. It initiates virtually all important bills. The ministry may not participate in committee deliberations. An effort to change the rule in the 1930's failed. The standing joint committee on Constitution of the Riksdag may scrutinize the acts of the ministers and bring charges of illegal misconduct.[229]

The Courts

The Swedish Constitution has some rather detailed provisions as to the organization and functions of three courts: the Supreme Court (*Högsta Domstolen*), the court of last resort in the regular judicial hierarchy;[230] the Supreme Administrative Court (*Regeringsrätten*), the court of last resort as to administrative problems;[231] and the Court of Impeachment (*Riksrätten*).[232] The other courts are governed by statute.

Prior to 1948 these statutes consisted largely of the Law of 1734 and amendments. Legislation effective in 1948 substantially changed the procedure but not the organization of the courts.

Sweden has an independent court system.[233] Neither the executive nor the Riksdag may interfere with them except where the Constitution or statutes permit. A power of judicial review over statutes is not exercised in Sweden, hence theoretically the independence of the courts could be destroyed. But the Riksdag has been careful not to interfere. Under Article 21 of the Constitution a Law Council consisting of three judges of the Supreme Court and one judge of the Supreme Administrative Court, serve as an advisory body as to important bills, and its opinion is transmitted to the Riksdag. The Riksdag need not but does give due respect to such opinions. But if a proposed bill is passed by the Riksdag it may not then be reviewed for violating the Constitution.

Under Article 96 of the Constitution the procurator for judicial affairs acts as the agent of the Riksdag in continuous scrutiny of the judicial branch. While he has no power of direction over the courts, any report he makes to the Riksdag is likely to be followed by prompt action by the Riksdag. He is also vested under Article 101 with the power of bringing charges against the members of the Supreme Court and the Supreme Administrative Court. The charges are to be heard by the Court of Impeachment provided for in Article 102. No cases of this nature have ever been brought so that the Court of Impeachment is not important.

Under Article 103 the Riksdag shall every fourth year appoint a commission to determine whether the members of the Supreme Court and the Supreme Administrative Court should be retained or removed even though they have not demonstrably committed impeachable offenses. If the commission votes for removal the king is to remove upon report by the Riksdag of its decision. This procedure seems also to have fallen into disuse. Thus on the whole the courts are free from interference.

Swedish judges are appointed by the king, acting through the cabinet, and serve until they reach sixty-five.[234] They are removed only after a proper judicial hearing.

Up to 1909 the regular Swedish courts had jurisdiction over cases of administrative law. In 1909 the Supreme Administrative Court was set up. It hears appeals from decisions of the administrative agencies both national and local. Under Article 18 it is to have at least seven members. In 1948 there were ten members. It is to include persons who have held administrative posts. At least two-thirds of its members must have the qualifications prescribed by law for judges. They are paid 22,500 kronor per year.

The courts for ordinary cases whether civil or criminal consist of the Supreme Court, six courts of appeal (*Hövrätterna*), and the courts of first instance. In the cities and larger towns the lower courts are known as *radhusrätterna*, city hall courts or borough courts. In the rural areas and smaller towns the lower courts are designated as *häradrätterna* or district courts.

The Supreme Court was established in 1789.[235] Prior to 1789 the King's Council, corresponding to the modern ministry, acted as the court of last resort. Under Article 17 of the Constitution there must be at least twelve members on the court. The court now consists of twenty-four judges, acting in three sections.[236] In ordinary cases from five to seven judges must participate, according to Article 22(1). In some cases the entire court sits *en banc*. Members are paid 22,500 kronor per year, as are judges of the Supreme Administrative Court. The presiding judge is appointed by the king.

The Supreme Court has final jurisdiction over cases appealed from the military courts. In such cases three persons of high military rank must be added to the court. Certain church matters such as neglect of duty by bishops go to the court, although cases involving ecclesiastical administrative law go to the Supreme Administrative Court.

The six courts of appeal are (1) the Svea Court in Stockholm set up in 1614; (2) the Göta Court in Jonköping set up in 1634; (3) the Court for Skåne and Blekinge in Malmö set up in 1820; (4) the Court for Upper Norrland in Umeå set up in 1936; (5) the Court for Western Sweden in Gothenburg set up in 1948; and (6) the Court for Lower Norrland in Sundsvall set up in 1948.[237] There are eight divisions in the Stockholm Court, three in those at Jonköping, Malmö and Gothenburg, and two in those at Sundsvall and Umeå. The divisions specialize as to types of cases. The Svea court has two rather unusual divisions. One of the divisions is made up of three regular judges and two military members. It hears appeals from courtmartial. Another division is made up of four regular judges and one expert on water rights. It hears appeals on water rights from four lower water rights courts. In these lower water rights courts only the presiding judge is a jurist; four are not lawyers, two of them being engineers. The six courts of appeals have supervisory authority over the lower courts in their districts.

There are about 125 district courts. Each district court has a single judge who holds court in the subdivisions of his district.[238] He does not hold court alone. He is assisted by a committee (*nämd*) of eighteen citizens who are elected for six-year terms.[239] These assistants, together with the judge, pass on questions of law and evidence. If the assistants disagree, the judge decides. At least seven and not over twelve must be present in each case and a unanimous vote may overrule the judge. In some very simple cases only three assistants are required. The positions of assistants are regarded as very honorable and are unpaid. What we regard as a jury is not used in Sweden except in cases involving freedom of the press.

About fifty larger cities and towns are outside of the jurisdiction of the district courts, and have instead borough courts (*magistraten*). The burgomaster (*borgmästaren*) is the presiding judge. He must have legal training. The other judges are trained lawyers. The size of the borough court depends on the size of the city. In criminal cases, where the sentence may be ten or more years in prison, the court consists of one judge and from seven to twelve laymen. In Stockholm there are twenty-four judges in addition to the burgomaster, and the court acts in sections. Experts are sometimes called in to join the courts. In some large cities there are police courts for petty offenses.

Each of the three levels of the Swedish courts has both civil and criminal jurisdiction. In the district courts the unanimous vote of the lay assistants may overrule the judge. In the borough courts in civil cases a majority vote of the judges decides, and if the vote is evenly divided, the presiding judge has the casting vote. The same is true as to criminal cases where no lay assistants are used; but in criminal cases where lay assistants are used a unanimous vote of the lay assistants may overrule the judge. Where no lay assistant is used, the decision in criminal cases is by a majority vote of the judges. If the vote is evenly divided the milder sentence will prevail. In the upper courts decision is by majority vote. Normally a proceeding commences in a district or borough court. Their jurisdiction covers all cases irrespective of the amounts at issue.

All cases, whether civil or criminal, may be appealed to a Court of Appeal. New evidence may then be admitted. But appeals from a Court of Appeal to the Supreme Court lie in civil cases only when the amount is 1,500 kronor or more and in criminal cases only when the penalty goes beyond a fine. Under a law effective in 1948 the Supreme Court need not hear all such cases. It may now refuse to hear any appeal unless the decision involved is of special importance in securing unified interpretation of the law or unless the court feels after a preliminary review that the verdict of the lower court appears to need further examination. Prior to 1948 the procedure in the appellate courts was written. Under the new law oral procedure is used in the lower as well as the higher courts. There is a very limited original jurisdiction in the appellate courts. Typically such original jurisdiction involves charges of malfeasance in office against certain officials including judges.

There are a number of special courts. The water rights courts have already been mentioned. The Labor Court (*Arbetsdomstolen*) is made up of a president and seven associates. Most of its members are specialists in labor and industry.

There are three notable features of the Swedish courts. The jury is not used at all except in cases involving freedom of the press. There is no judicial review of the constitutionality of statutes. Sweden has set up a separate administrative court system. In all three respects Sweden resembles Anglo-American law less than Denmark and Norway.

Local Government Law

From the outset there have been local assemblies in Sweden which acted on matters of local interest.[240] The *härad* goes back to this time. The *socken* or parish was among the early local units of importance. When Christianity was introduced the parish became the local ecclesiastical unit. By 1550 the parish assembly exercised certain powers. But it did not officially receive broader powers until about 1700. It dealt with poor relief, schools, and public health. The *härad* eventually became a judicial district, making place for the parish as to other matters. By 1600 the towns had considerable local government under the mayor and his councilors aided by the "elder citizens."

Following the adoption of the 1809 Constitution there was passed in 1817 the first general local government law. Church affairs were separated. They were placed in the hands of the church council (*kyrkordet*) while other matters were placed in the hands of the general assembly of taxpayers. In 1843 a statute provided for a parish committee (*sockenmämden*) to act as an administrative agency in nonecclesiastical matters. In 1862 a statute reorganized the parish. It also gave the *län* its first elected council. The *län* (county or province) had existed since 1634. Town government was altered. The assembly of citizens (*kommunalstämman*) continued to operate as the chief legislative agency of the parish. But there was set up an elective group of deputies to serve as the local administrative agency replacing the parish committee. The 1862 law is still the main basis for local government, though partially modified by a 1930 statute. In 1918 universal municipal suffrage was established for persons over twenty-one. All who may vote in the parliamentary elections, may vote in municipal elections.

Sweden, aside from Stockholm, is divided into 24 *län* or counties. These *län* are divided into 2,323 parishes or *landskommuner*, 64 small towns or *köpingar*, and 124 cities or *städer*. There are 2,552 ecclesiastical parishes. These parishes exercise very full self government as to church matters. They also serve as local school districts. But more and more the schools are supervised by nonecclesiastical officials. As has been seen, the *härad* serves as a judicial district. The Department of the Interior of the national government closely supervises local administration including police administration.

The county council or *landsthing* governs the *län*. The council was first set up in 1862. Prior to 1862 the local *things* had practically disappeared during the unification of the kingdom and the growth of the Riksdag. Under the 1862 statute legislative and administrative machinery was set up. In addition to regional duties there is supervision of the parish and city governments. The historic *län*, now called *landskap*, still exists but merely as a geographic and historic area. There are 28 such areas.

The *län* is headed by a governor or *landshövding* appointed by the national government. He represents the national government and is chief executive for the local government. Under the government are the chief county clerk or *lands sekretararen*, who is responsible for public health, poor relief, police, and elections; and the chief accountant or *lands kamreren*, who is responsible for county financial administration. There is also a bailiff or *landsfogden* in charge of the police. For police administration there is set up below the county the bailiwick or *fögderi*. There are 119 bailiwicks in Sweden. The bailiwick in turn is divided into local police districts or *landsfiskaler*, of which there are 406.

Each *län*, except Kalmar, has one *landsthing* whose size is never less than twenty. Its members are elected for a four-year term by proportional representation. It has a regular annual meeting in September. Special sessions may be called by the king through the governor or by three-fourths of the *landsthing*. The special session is confined to the items included in the call. It selects its own chairman for a one-year term. A quorum requires at least two-thirds of the members. It has an administrative committee to cooperate with the governor. The council may pass ordinances and adopt a budget. Measures may be proposed not only by its members but also by the governor. Some legislation requires approval by the central government. Some requires approval by the governor. The validity of its ordinances may be challenged. It acts as an electoral college for electing members of the First Chamber of the Riksdag.

The *landskommun* or parish has jurisdiction as to poor relief, public health, child welfare, alcoholic liquors, old age pensions, unemployment and local policing. In many parishes it controls the schools. It levies taxes, appropriates money, and superintends all elections. Every parish having more than 700 inhabitants has a parish council or *kommunalfullmäktige*. Where there is no parish council the voters' assembly or *kommunalstämma* meets three times a year. In other parishes it holds no regular sessions. Under 1947 legislation the smaller parishes are being merged so that each will have at least 2,000 members. Members of the council are elected for four-year terms by proportional representation. They vary in size from 15 to 40 members. They meet regularly three times a year, and elect a chairman for a one-year term. The chairman may take part in council meetings, but has no vote. Many of its measures require approval by the central government, and some must be approved by the governor of the *län*. The parish council must have a parish executive committee (*kommunalnämnden*) to serve as the chief executive agency. It is made up of from 5 to 11 members and elected for a four-year term. The committee has jurisdiction over the public properties and supervises other parish administrative committees, and prepares the parish budget.

There are a number of densely populated areas in the rural parishes, not large enough to be set up as cities or towns. The Swedish law permits the setting up of a special municipal district with the consent of the governor of the *län*. It remains a part of the rural parish, yet may handle problems not parish-wide in character. These hybrid areas are called *municipalsamhällen* or urban communities. They are 235 in number.

There are 64 *köpingar* or small towns. They resemble the rural parishes but also deal with city planning and housing and other municipal functions. They are set up by royal orders; that is to say, by the central administration.

Including Stockholm there are 125 cities or *städer* in Sweden. Many statutes applicable to the rural parishes also apply to them. All of them except Stockholm are under the jurisdiction of the *län*. Population is not the sole basis for classification as a city, as a few have only 1,000 population each. They have jurisdiction over public health, housing, and policing, and maintain the streets. Often there is municipal ownership of water, gas, and electric plats and street railways. Some cities operate slaughter houses, market places, and laundries. A town meeting or *allmän rådstuga* is held only on special call and is not much employed. The city council or *stadsfullmäktige* varies in size from 15 to 60 members. They serve for four years. The council elects a chairman and vice-chairman for a term of one year. They meet monthly except in the summer. The mayor may attend but not vote. Important measures require a two-thirds vote. Some measures require the approval of the national government.

The mayor or *borgmästare* is appointed by the national government from a list of three names selected by popular vote. As he presides over the borough court or *magistrat* he must have legal training. He serves for an indefinite term. The two or more associate judges or *rådmän* are chosen by the city council, and usually have legal training. The *magistrat* also has responsibility for public administration. They collect taxes due to the national government. One of its members often serves as chief of police.

Every city must have a board of finance or *drätselkammaren*, chosen by the city council. In most cities it is the chief administrative agency. It is responsible for the collection of local taxes. It corresponds to the executive committee of the rural parish. In many cities there are also other administrative agencies such as a fire board, school board, and poor relief board.

While Stockholm is governed much like other Swedish cities there are some differences. The *överståthallåre* or governor general is appointed by the central government. He has broad supervisory power as to taxation and police administration. He may veto certain measures passed by the City Council, and participates in its meetings without, however, a vote. The *Magistrat* of Stockholm consists of the burgomaster and twenty *rådmän*, and serves largely as a court. The City Council has one hundred members chosen by proportional representation. Its important actions must be approved by the central government. It selects each year a chairman or *ordförande*. The chief executive agency of the city is the City Board or *Stadskollegiet*. It consists of nine members chosen for a one-year term by the City Council from its own membership. It sits with the Chairman of the City Council and eight aldermen or *borgerråd* chosen by the City Council, but only members of the City Board may vote. The eight aldermen are the chairmen of the agencies working under the City Board.

All Swedish municipalities may levy taxes. Local taxes are of two kinds: property and income. Each municipality prepares an annual registry of residents. For administration of the poor laws or *fattigvård* each local area is a poor law district with a poor board chosen by the local council. The municipality also looks after the welfare of children, and gives aid and advice to mothers through a child welfare commission. Each area is also an old age pension district with an old age pension board in charge. Each area also has an unemployment committee to act as an employment agency and aid the workless. Each area administers the law as to the use of intoxicants through a temperance commission or *nykterhitsnämd*. Health laws are administered, and each city must set up a health commission or *hälsovårdsnämd*. The aims are pure water supply, pure food, and sanitary house conditions. Each *län* has a physician who supervises the health work in the *län*; above them are regional physicians. Hospitals are maintained, both general and special. Other municipal factors are fire protection, police protection, city planning, and education. There is close supervision of the local areas by the national government. Local finances are closely scrutinized. Many local ordinances may be vetoed by the governor of the *län*. Local administrative actions may be appealed to the Supreme Administrative Court.

Religion

In 830 Ansgar, a German who had been expelled from Denmark, started a mission in Sweden but his missionaries were compelled to flee. It was not until the beginning of the twelfth century that two English missionaries and a Swede started an enduring movement. The early Swedish church was English in organization and outlook. Sweden remained pagan for almost two centuries longer than Denmark and a century longer than Norway.[241] Olaf Sköt-Konung, king from 995-1022, was baptized at about the year 1000 A.D., but this had little consequence, and his son, given the Christian name Jacob (1022-1050), was compelled by the assembly at Uppsala to change his name to the heathen name Anund. Prior to 1160 the Christian kings of Sweden were supported chiefly by the Götar, while the Svear set up a rival king and restored paganism. Erik the Saint (1156-1160) restored Christianity, and is the royal saint of Sweden. Like Norway, Sweden was at first a part of the see of Bremen and Hamburg. In 1103 an archbishopric to include Sweden was established at Lund in Skåne, then Danish. Peter's pence was levied in 1152. In 1164 an archbishopric was established at Uppsala for Sweden alone. Monasteries were now established. The king granted jurisdiction to the bishops over the clergy in 1200, and the clergy were no longer subject to the regular secular courts. The church was given jurisdiction over laymen in ecclesiastical matters. Tithes were collected. In 1248 a church council summoned by the papal legate completed the organization of the Swedish church.[242] Celibacy was introduced. Bishops were to be selected by the chapters set up in 1250, and were enjoined to study canonical law. During the reign of Magnus Ladulås (1275-1290) the privileges of the church were less than those in Norway. Ecclesiastical legislation was in the hands of the state. The king was arbiter in cases of episcopal encroachment over the peasants. Parishes or private patrons could appoint to benefices.

During the period of Union, prior to 1520, the rights of the church were more recognized in word than in deed. The ecclesiastical jurisdiction was not preserved in its full extent. The right to choose bishops and abbots and the property and tax exception privileges of the church were not always respected. The church was more imperilled from within than from without. It lost strength due to its becoming worldly and through its loss of influence over the common people.[243] Its position was weaker in Sweden than in Norway. The Swedish nobility grew stronger and formed alliances with the clergy.[244]

As in England the Reformation came from the king rather than from the masses of the people. Under Gustavus Vasa (1523-1560) Sweden felt itself menaced by the Danish connection with the hierarchy.[245] Sweden was the first country of Western Europe to break away from Rome. The first step in the Reformation in Sweden was political. Vasa insisted on two major principles: The superfluous wealth of the Church must be used for the benefit of the State and prelates must not be appointed who would interfere with Swedish State affairs. Sequestration of the monasteries commenced in 1526. At a meeting in 1527 at Vesterås the Reformation was placed into effect. The king became the head of the Church and the Church properties were taken over by the State. The ordinances of the Synod of Örebro in 1529 made the church services Protestant. Another meeting in 1544 completed the Reformation. Under Johan III (1568-1592) and his son, deposed in 1599, steps were taken towards a return to Catholicism.[246] Johan wished Rome to accept the following conditions: that the Swedish clergy be exempted from celibacy; that the laity at Holy Communion be permitted to partake of both elements; and that the worship of saints should cease. But the conditions were unacceptable and the negotiations broke down. In 1593 the Angsburg Confession was accepted anew by a synod at Uppsala.[247] Persons living in Sweden who belonged to another faith were forbidden to hold services, although Charles IX (1599-1611) was friendly to Calvinism. Under Gustavus Adolphus (1611-1632) there was harsh treatment of Catholics because many of them favored Sigismund of Poland who had abdicated the Swedish throne.[248] Calvinistic Walloons were permitted to enter Sweden though other Lutheran countries were not so tolerant.[249] Queen Christina (1632-1654) on her abdication became a Catholic, but this had no effect on Sweden. The Church Ordinance of 1686 greatly restricted the previously relatively independent position of the clergy.[250]

In 1706 the Swedish government forbade conventicles.[251] At the same time that Sweden was enacting its famous code of 1734, its ecclesiastical law was revised.[252] In 1726 an Edict of permanent character was passed for the punishment of persons taking part in private religious meetings or conventicles. This law was aimed at the Pietist movement. There was more persecution in Sweden than in Denmark and Norway, largely due to the fact that the Swedish clergy constituted one chamber of the Riksdag.

By a law of 1719 all religions were tolerated in Sweden except those of Jews, Mohammedans, and pagans.[253] But dissenters, except foreign ministers and their servants, were prohibited from meeting publicly for worship. Non-attendance or tardiness at church services was made punishable.

In 1781 Christian noncomformists were granted freedom of worship. In 1782 Jews were allowed to settle down in the larger cities and to practice their own religion.[254] But severe restrictions on their political and social life continued. The Swedes were perhaps as much activated by a desire to attract capital as by zeal for religious toleration.[255]

The Norwegian Constitution of 1814 expressly forbade the entrance of Jews into Norway. In 1815 the Swedish Riksdag expressed the desire that similar action be taken in Sweden.[256] A violent debate by way of pamphleteering arose. The Swedish king deplored the strength of Swedish anti-Semitism. No legislation against Jews was adopted, however, and they continued to reside in the towns to which they had been admitted in the eighteenth century. In 1838 the Swedish government granted Jews something close to complete equality. It did not yield to the riots partially of an anti-Semitic character which occurred a short time later. In almost each session of the Riksdag there were proposals to permit Jews to live anywhere in Sweden and to conduct worship freely. Conservatives opposed such proposals as they were against the increase of religious liberty. Liberals, such as Professor Johan Henrik Thomander of Lund, a member of the Chamber of the Clergy, pointed out that this attitude was opposed to the modern spirit and that no danger from freedom of worship would result as the Jews did not proselyte. In 1854 a law in that spirit was promulgated.

In the 1840's the Conventicle Act was invoked against a dissenter from Lutheranism, Eric Janson, who taught that the true Christian is not only absolved from the penalties for sin but also from sin itself. In 1846 his followers began the first mass emigration from Sweden. In 1848 the first Baptist congregation was organized in Sweden. Following a riot in 1850 the Baptist leader was exiled.[257] In 1859 the Conventicle Act was repealed.[258] Penalties for deserting the State Church, and exile for joining heretical faiths were discontinued. Members of other faiths now could organize their own congregations and enjoy complete religious freedom.

Prior to 1866 the clergy constituted one of the four chambers of the Riksdag. During the period of its existence it was second in importance only to the chamber of the nobility. But this is said to have made the Swedish clergy prior to 1866 more worldly than the Danish or Norwegian.[259] In Denmark and Norway the Parliaments passed considerable legislation closely regulating the authority of the clergy. On the other hand, in Sweden a synod was established to be in charge of the development of ecclesiastical affairs.[260]

More than 99 per cent of the population of Sweden is Lutheran.[261] There are 6,500 Roman Catholics and 6,500 Jews. Under Article 16 of the Constitution the king "shall not constrain or allow to be constrained the conscience of any person, but shall protect everyone in the free exercise of his religion, provided he does not thereby disturb public order or occasion general offense." Only the king and certain officials must belong to the State Church. But while a person is free to belong to another church, "the records of his birth and his movements are kept by the parish priest, and when he wants a liquor ration book he obtains it as a resident in a parish."[262]

Article 2 of the Norwegian Constitution provides: "Jesuits shall not be tolerated." There is a strong movement in Norway to repeal this provision, many pointing out that there is no similar restriction as to communists.[263] There is no similar provision in Sweden. But the Roman Catholic Church was not permitted to establish religious houses such as monasteries and convents.[264] At the same time Swedish Catholics had their own churches and priesthood and worshiped without hindrance. While Lutheranism is taught in schools, parents have the right to withhold their children from such classes.

A new Swedish Dissenter Law was passed on May 19, 1951, almost forty years after the subject was first broached in the Riksdag. Nominally, religious freedom had been part of the Swedish Constitution since 1809, but some vestiges of the State Church rule still remained. Every Swedish citizen born into the State Church as a result of his parents' affiliation was required, if he wished to renounce his membership, to make a formal statement of his new affiliation. The new law provides for unconditional acceptance of renouncement. One of the major new provisions is the permission for religious orders to found monasteries and convents. Another important change is the right for priests and ministers of churches other than the State Church to officiate at marriage ceremonies with full legal recognition of the contract without a complementary civil ceremony.

Education

The Protestant Reformation helped increase literacy among the common people in Sweden as knowledge of the Bible and the basic Lutheran texts was expected of all.[265] But elementary instruction was not regarded as a public function. Hence it was the Swedish Church Law of 1686 which required every young person to learn to read. By

1720 the elementary education of pauper children and their training in some craft was recognized as a public function. In 1723 the Riksdag, this time from no pietistic motive, passed a statute repeating the requirement of 1686 that every child be taught to read either at home or in schools at the expense of the parish. But no satisfactory system to enforce the law was established, hence it became a dead letter. The rite of confirmation was decreed for Denmark and Norway in 1736. Agitation for its establishment in Sweden began the same year, though it was not officially established until 1811.[266] Confirmation necessarily involved an ability to read religious texts, hence it had educational as well as religious aspects.

The chamber of the clergy in the Riksdag frequently discussed education. In 1768 the provincial governors were required to report the state of affairs, and made reports in 1771. The Educational Commission of 1745 reported in 1760, but its recommendations were too far-reaching to obtain support. Another commission of 1788 had no better luck. In 1801 a Directory of Education was established. It prepared the School Regulations of 1807, but these regulations affected only the Learned Schools and were not progressive in character. The Revolution of 1809 cut short the work of the Directory. In 1828 to 1829 the peasants' chamber of the Riksdag debated over education. Many were aware of the advantages of education, but feared the costs thereof and subjection to the clergy. In 1834 the peasants' chamber voted to establish a proper school in each parish. For a time a "mutual" system of instruction, introduced in 1819 and continuing until 1865, was widely used. It was inexpensive as one teacher could supervise many groups in which the older children taught the younger. However, thoroughness was sacrificed. The first teachers' college was established in 1830 in Sweden, in 1791 in Denmark and in 1824 in Norway.

During 1834 and 1835 every chamber of the Riksdag requested that the government initiate some action toward a national system of education. In 1840, following the interest of Crown Prince Oscar, the government brought in a bill which the Riksdag after amendment adopted. In 1842 the government promulgated the law creating the national elementary school system. Denmark had adopted such a law in 1814 and Norway in 1827. Each parish must maintain at least one school with at least one teacher whose minimum salary was fixed. The parish was both to administer and support it. In 1849 all preparatory schools were united with two courses, the classical and the practical; a final reorganization occurred in 1871. Following parliamentary reorganization in 1866, folk schools were established in Sweden.[267] They had previously been set up in Denmark in 1844. In 1833 the first public library bill was presented in the Riksdag. Until the later 1870's Sweden's secondary schools were devoted to scholastic studies or to training for public services and their students came almost altogether from professional families or the well-to-do. Municipal secondary schools were not authorized until 1904. The first tax support of public libraries came in 1912 from American impulses.[268] Beginning in 1902 study circles were set up as an important avenue of adult education.[269] In 1947 a law was passed granting state support, matching local funds, to all accredited circles.[270] Local supervisory boards and central study circle associations must approve the leaders and the textbooks used. The circles must be either foundation circles in elementary and skill subjects, education circles in social, civic, and cultural subjects, or youth circles. The number of hours per session and sessions per semester is prescribed. The minimum number of circle members in foundation and education circles is specified. The difference between the American and Swedish systems is that while public support in the United States is tied to public institutions, in Sweden it is given to voluntary popular movements.

On May 24, 1950, the Riksdag voted unanimously to change the compulsory education period in Sweden from eight years to nine, and to establish a unified elementary and early secondary school system.[271] The system is not expected to become operative for at least a decade. The various existing schools would be absorbed and recast into one form. The eighth and ninth grades would then correspond to the junior high schools of the United States. In the last two years vocational training would be included in the curriculum and attempts made to train pupils for local jobs. Those having sufficient mental ability to go on would then be promoted to the Gymnasia. The Gymnasia are either technical high schools or the classical schools. English would be taught to all children from the fifth grade up and French taken up at a later period.

Agriculture

The development of the status of the peasant prior to 1523 was on the whole favorable to him.[272] In Norway the peasant remained free as to his person, and retained his rights to his property; and if he worked on the lands of another he was not in serfdom. This was the opposite of the Danish development. A movement similar to the Danish had commenced in Sweden. But Swedish law early confined his forced labor for the landlord to eight days. Serfdom is said to have been abolished in 1335.[273] In 1403 the peasant was also required to do eight days' service for the king. Since the national movement beginning in 1435 required the aid of the peasant, care was taken not to oppress him unduly.

By a law of 1396 it was enacted that no more land subject to taxation could be bought by the nobles and thus made tax-exempt.[274] Consequently, at the end of the medieval period only ten per cent of the land was owned by the nobles. One-eighth of the estates of the nation were then held by the Church.

From 1632 to 1660 much of Swedish land came into the hands of the nobles. But from 1660 to 1697 they were forced to return much of their land to the Crown and to freehold, and individual ownership became much more usual.[275] This was the result of the sale of crown lands, either directly into freehold, or indirectly into freehold through land speculators. Until 1700 there was little subdivision of individual farms. Population had increased but slowly and there was a strong social tradition toward conserving the unity of the family holdings as the social position depended on the family's keeping its landed property. There developed a customary system of inheritance, in effect amounting to entail although it was not always the oldest son who inherited. The national revenue depended largely on a fixed assessment in kind from each farm, hence the legislation aimed to preserve its taxpaying power. If the area of the farm were reduced it would be more difficult to collect the tax. This continued as the policy until 1757.

As of 1700 the position of the peasants in the Swedish lowlands was little better than that of the German serfs.[276] This was true also in most of Denmark but only to a slight extent in Norway. Tenure for a term of years at the end of which the owner might or might not renew the lease was common. Charles XII (1697-1718) needed money to wage his wars, and allowed crown tenants to purchase their holdings. It was not until about 1800 with the growth of the grain trade that economic conditions warranted the tenant's exchanging crown tenantry for taxable freehold as the latter was encumbered with almost as many services and dues as ordinary tenancy. The commonalty continued to pay a land tax from which the nobility were exempt though the nobility no longer performed valuable military and civic functions. The nobility were also exempt from the special taxes made necessary by the wars of the seventeenth and eighteenth centuries. Taxes were paid largely in produce. No changes were made in the eighteenth century in the old rule that the peasants must labor on the estates of the nobility. Tithes were still collected in the sheaf rather than in money. Work on roads was required. There was a duty to keep horses and drivers ready to transport passengers and goods. In 1686 decrees were promulgated limiting the number of grown children and servants that a peasant might keep on his farm. These restrictions were finally removed in 1747 to encourage the growth of population.

By the Enclosure Act of 1747 every part owner in the Swedish villages was allowed to exchange his numerous small, scattered holdings for one large single piece of property.[277] Thus a more rational system of agriculture became possible. Internal trade in agricultural products was freed from restrictions and customs for part of Sweden in 1775 and for all of it in 1780 by royal decrees. Between 1740 and 1770 Swedish public opinion was coming to demand consolidation of strips into single or very few holdings, division of the commons, break-up of the village system, the end of communal cultivation, and the regulation by law of the compulsory labor obligations of the tenant to his lord preparatory to their redemption or total abolition.[278] There was no improvement of the standard of living of Swedish peasants between 1720 and 1800, but if anything a reduction because of enhanced consumption of spirits and increase in population.[279] It should be noted, however, that from 1435 on, the peasants were represented in a separate chamber of the Riksdag. But in comparison with the other three chambers it seems to have been the weakest.[280]

In 1803 the Swedish government issued a decree authorizing any villager in Skåne to demand the complete consolidation of his property.[281] In 1807 this was extended to all but Dalarne and Norrland. By 1865 the communal routine and the strip system had virtually disappeared. Under the older law one might graze his cattle upon anyone's stubble. In 1857 the Swedish law imposed upon the owners of the cattle responsibility for the damage they might do on another's property.[282] It was not until 1878 that Swedish law relieved the peasant of his posting obligation, a system under which peasants along the highways were compelled to haul passengers and goods for a fixed fee from private individuals and for no compensation from public officials.[283] In 1869 tithes were commuted into cash payments. Simplification of rural taxes came slower in Sweden than in Norway and Denmark, being finally achieved in 1853.[284] Equalization as against the nobility was arrived at in 1892.

There is a strong movement to encourage numerous small farm holdings, occupied and operated by the owner.[285] A state supported home ownership loan fund has for many years furnished long-term loans at low rates of interest. This has been done through local cooperative societies or the municipalities. Central administration is in the hands of the Home Ownership Board in the Department of Agriculture. The government furnishes loans for buying lands and erecting buildings. It also makes loans for improvements. Extremely important legislation was enacted in 1947. The government is given priority rights to buy farms offered for sale after certain relatives and tenants are given an opportunity to buy. The government is given the right to expropriate land and forests from large private estates. The government may sell lands so acquired to individual owners. Generous loans are made available to such purchasers.

Criminal Law

From 900 to 1100 kin vengeance existed as to murder, and the acceptance of a money satisfaction was thought to be dishonorable except in certain limited situations.[286] Private fines might be arranged for murder and other violent felonies. The introduction of Christianity resulted in limitations on private vengeance. Church mulcts might be collected under the church law of Skåne.[287]

The provincial codes of the fourteenth century largely retained concepts of private vengeance.[288] Certain heinous offenses were not finable, but necessarily involved outlawry or some other public punishment.[289] Outlawry involved forfeiture. Under the earlier Swedish code the forfeiture extended both to real and personal property. The later codes limited it to personal property. Up to the sixteenth century the provincial codes show that the penal law was still considered as chiefly private in character, both as to the specific crimes, the penalties imposed, and the mode of prosecution.[290] For most crimes reparation might be made by fines to the victim and to the ruler. If the fine was not paid there might be outlawry.

In the seventeenth century the dominant principles of the Swedish-Finnish penal code were as follows: (1) the *lex talionis* is the highest justice according to the Law of God; (2) the legislator should endeavor to frighten prospective criminals by the most severe penalties; and (3) the legislator shall seek to appease the Diety by the most severe penalties.[291] The Mosaic law was thus treated as the law of the land. Gustavus Adolphus prescribed death for the killing of a stag or a swan. A severe Sabbath Law was enacted in 1665, and a law on infanticide in 1684. Witches were burned at this time. The Penal Code of Christina (1632-1654) ameliorated the law, as did the important Code of 1734. Prosecutions for witchcraft were abolished in 1778.[292]

Gustavus III had studied Beccaria's *Crimes and Punishments*.[293] Under the Code of 1734 sixty-eight offenses carried the death penalty, which in some cases might take the form of breaking on the wheel or be accompanied by public exposure on the wheel or by the cutting off of the offender's right hand.[294] In 1772 Gustavus abolished the use of torture. He intended this as the first step in a broad revision of the criminal law, which was to include abolition of capital punishment for all crimes except treason and parricide. But his proposal was strongly opposed, hence the law of 1779 was much less sweeping. The yearly average of executions fell from 26.8 to 10.8.[295]

Fredrika Bremer and Crown Prince Oscar, king from 1844 to 1859, became greatly interested in prison reform as it developed in the United States.[296] Oscar studied the Philadelphia system of single cells and the Auburn system of common-work, and published in 1840 a book concerning the American experiments. The book influenced the development of new types of prisons and penal methods in Sweden. Early in the twentieth century American experience with the indeterminate sentence, honor system, and parole were closely scrutinized and Judge Harold Solomon made an extensive study tour in the United States.[297]

In 1809 the Riksdag appointed a commission headed by Professor Holmhernsson to prepare a complete codification of both private law and criminal law.[298] The criminal code was assigned to Professor Rabenius, who with some of his colleagues resigned when a majority of the commission concluded that a wholly new draft on the foundation of science and foreign legislation should be worked out. The 1815 draft was prepared by Staaff, Richert, and Alfzelius, and submitted to the Riksdag. The commission did not resume the preparation of the criminal code until 1826, when it worked with a similar Norwegian commission. A revision, based on the Bavarian, Hanoverian, and Austrian codes, was ready in 1832. This revision was criticized by Boethius, Rabenius, Grubbe, Atterborn, Holmhernsson, and Cederschiold. A new commission published a revised draft in 1839. In 1844 the commission, which had been enlarged to include Schlyter, Bergfalk, and Richert, published its draft and commentary. This draft recognized only one type of punishment, imprisonment, and was not accepted by the Riksdag. During the next two decades there was piecemeal reform: the death penalty was abolished, as was whipping and church penance. In 1862 a new draft code was presented, which went into effect in 1864. In 1923 a new draft for a criminal code was presented by a commission headed by John Thyrén.[299] A commission has been working on modernization of Swedish criminal law during the past decade. Thorsten Sellin, an American sociologist, served as a consultant from 1946 to 1947.[300]

There is no Juvenile Court in Sweden.[301] The Scandinavian countries, starting with Norway in 1896, then Sweden in 1902, have followed a different pattern. Juvenile delinquency is not a crime. The legal age of responsibility has been raised to fifteen.[302] Child Welfare Boards have been set up to deal with delinquent children and with children in need of guardianship or protection from moral, educational or material neglect. The boards also deal with offenders between fifteen and eighteen, and in some cases up to twenty-one, who are referred to the boards before or after trial. The Public Prosecutor in many cases obtains the opinion of the Board before deciding whether to prosecute in such cases. The board is appointed for a two-year period by the municipal council. Every village, town and city has a board. Each board has at least five members. It must include one woman, one member of the local Poor Relief Committee, a local clergyman and a teacher, and a doctor and a lawyer if available. The chairman in the larger cities receives a salary, but does not work full time. The appointments to the boards have been comparatively free from partisan considerations. The boards when meeting proceed as committees rather than as judicial tribunals. Most cases are dealt with on the basis of information supplied by social workers. In difficult cases there is a personal interview. The boards are required to employ every method of persuasion, supervision at home, change of employment, or placing in a foster home, before sending a child to a Welfare School. The Welfare Schools contain only 1,100 persons, a clear indication that children are not lightly taken away from their homes. Both parents and children may insist on access to the board, hence there is no want of due process. When an erring child is seized, he is placed in the custody of the board. The board's officers must be informed at once and the child may not be interrogated except in the presence of a board officer. The child must be taken at once to the board officer and never to the police station. The initiative is taken by the board officers. A great value of the system is that it has focussed official and public interest on the social and educational problems connected with the treatment of young offenders. In 1945 a commission found child care too decentralized in Sweden. Legislation was then adopted providing for consolidation to become effectual in 1951.

While Sweden has a population of almost seven million, in 1949 there were only two life prisoners, and only 2,180 persons in prison, of whom 154 were women.[303] Capital punishment was abolished in 1921. There are 34 larger prisons in Sweden and 178 prisons exclusively for the detention of persons awaiting trial. Under the law of 1864 persons arrested for minor crimes are not to be detained in the same place as those arrested for major crimes, nor with those serving a prison sentence.[304] It is the Swedish view that a good prison system depends relatively little on buildings as compared with a well-trained personnel of a high, ethical level holding humanitarian views. Longer terms of imprisonment commence with solitary confinement. Adequate provision is made for work, education, and recreation. Since 1906 something like probation has been employed by way of suspension of execution of sentence.[305]

In general, penalties in Sweden are light. As has been seen, capital punishment was abolished in 1921. There is a statutory limit of ten years on prison terms except life sentences, sentences to preventive detention of defective delinquents, and sentences of recidivists. The overwhelming majority of sentences involve fines.[306] Equality between rich and poor defendants has been secured since 1931 by a system of day-fines, based on the income of the defendant. Fines may be paid in installments. Very few are sent to jail for failure to pay fines since the law of 1939. Only if the defendant fails to pay because of deliberate neglect or stubborn refusal is a prison term imposed for nonpayment, and even then the judge may suspend execution of such sentence. In 1946 only 286 persons went to prison for failure to pay a fine. Since 1945 an indeterminate sentence may be imposed on defective delinquents or habitual criminals. Swedish prisons are small in size, the largest having only 300 prisoners. Classification of prisoners is facilitated by such smallness and by the fact that a presentence investigation is now required before a defendant can be sentenced to six months or longer, placed on probation, given a suspended sentence or sentenced to a reformatory.

Every person serving six months or more must be released on parole.[307] He may apply for parole if he has finished two-thirds of his term. But if he is not granted it, he must be so released when he has served five-sixths of his term. If the prison term is less than one year, he must remain on parole for six months. If the time is a year or more, the parole period is at least a year. Thus unlike the American system every prisoner is subjected to parole supervision, whereas American prisoners serving the maximum term go out free from supervision.

During the nineteenth century, particularly in 1866, though the accusatory system of the 1734 Code was retained, inquisitorial process was to some extent provided for.[308] In 1886 provision was made for indemnity to persons punished through mistake.[309] Witness fees were also introduced.

The new code of civil procedure effective in 1948 laying down new rules of pleading, practice and evidence has been accompanied by changes in criminal procedure.[310] It has moved, though somewhat uncertainly, in the direction of the accusatorial rather than the inquisitorial principle.[311] Sweden has not yet gone as far as England in restricting newspaper discussion of criminal proceedings so as to insure a fair trial.[312] Under the new code the preparatory proceeding in criminal cases is the preliminary investigation. It can be concluded without prosecution and a hearing-in-chief.[313] Prosecution need not follow the apprehension of one reasonably suspected. In some cases there will be no indictment. In other cases there may be a proposal for a direct fine (*straffäreläggarde*) instead of prosecution. At the hearing-in-chief the prosecutor is to state his case. The defendant is then requested to state whether he admits or denies. The prosecutor is then to substantiate the charge. The injured party, that is to say, the victim of the crime, is then heard. The defendant is then to give a coherent account of the case and to state what he wishes to say as to the statements of the prosecutor and the complainant (*mälsägarden*). The prosecutor and the complainant may then question the defendant upon first having obtained permission of the court. Counsel for the defendant may then put questions. When the examination of the complainant or the defendant is carried on, written records of what he said previously before the prosecutor or the police may not be recited unless his statements during the examination differ from his previous statements or unless he remains silent during examination.

Civil Procedure

A distinct civil procedure, not blended with the criminal, developed in the latter half of the thirteenth century.[314] The proceedings were public and oral. At first only the judgment was reduced to writing. The principle of immediacy prevailed. That is to say, the court dealt directly with parties and witnesses and not through an intermediate agency. Usually the parties conducted their cases in person. Suits were commenced by summons. There might be judgment by default where a defendant without lawful excuse failed to appear. A jury or *nämnd* was used as an agency of proof. The chief species of proof under the older Swedish law were (a) witness-proof, (b) the party-oath, and (c) proof by the *nämnd*.[315] The first two might be combined with the oath of oath-helpers. In some cases circumstantial evidence might be used.

The jury or *nämnd* consisted of twelve persons.[316] Half were selected by one side and half by the other. They passed only on questions of fact. Seven jurors could render a verdict. A new jury was at first chosen for each case, but eventually became a standing body. Proof by the *nämnd* took place in the more important civil and criminal cases.

Judgment was rendered by the judge alone, and had to be without unnecessary delay.[317] Appeal to a higher court or to the king seems to have existed from early times.[318] A settled form of appeal, the *vad*, involved the deposit of money or movables by the appellant. It was concerned chiefly with questions of law. The parties to the appeal were the losing party as against the judge. Appeal by *vad* might lie from a verdict of the *nämnd*. In addition, the king might set aside fraudulent and excessive judgments.

During the first part of the period from 1500 to 1734 the chief changes were designed to improve the mode of exercise of royal jurisdiction, while the second period involved improvement in procedure itself.[319] The former involved the establishment of royal appellate courts or *Hofrätter* and the judicial section of the State Council or *Justitiere-*

visionen.[320] About the time of the Protestant Reformation the *nämnd* participated in the decisions of questions of law as well as of fact.[321] It now became a standing body.

To what extent did Roman ideas of civil procedure affect the Swedish law? Professor Robert W. Millar has stated: "As for Sweden, her remote situation defers even longer than in the case of Germany any acceptance of the Italian principles. But here, too, they begin to make themselves felt in the 1500's, coming by way of the made-over German procedure, and end by producing radical change, though by no means to the same extent as in Germany. The resultant system is given its final form in the Code of 1734."[322] The Code of Civil Procedure of Napoleon of 1806 did not affect the Swedish law.

The most pronounced change in procedure was in the doctrines of proof. The influence of foreign law affected it, and to a lesser degree other phases of procedure.[323] The city courts, particularly those of Stockholm, were affected by the common law procedure of Germany. The mandatory and preclusive rules of the German procedure, however, came in as mere directory canons. The old distaste for representation by counsel continued, thus making for informal procedure. The older principle of orality gave way only in part to documentation, and Swedish procedure assumed the fixed status of an oral proceeding based upon a written record.[324] There did not develop as in Germany, Denmark, and Norway a predominance of documentation and an ultimate suppression of orality. There was emphasis at first on the duty of the judge to interrogate the parties. By certain seventeenth century legislation the judges were required to endeavor to effect a voluntary settlement between the parties in cases where both parties appeared.[325] The Procedural Rules of 1615 permitted the parties to employ authorized representatives in the *Hof-rätt*. An ordinance of 1661, adopted by the magistracy of Stockholm, provided for the admission of lawyers to practice in that court, upon their obtaining the magistracy's approval, by the production of "good testimony."

The Code of Procedure or *Rättegångsbalk* adopted in 1734 was very largely a compilation and revision of the rules of procedure which had been worked out by legislation, theory, and practice.[326] The Code in full and consistent manner regulated the system of proof and appellate procedure, the appointment of substitute judges, the relation of the *nämnd* to the judge, and forensic representation. The chief subsequent changes have been concerned with organization and jurisdiction of the courts.

An ordinance of 1830 abolished the oral summons in civil cases.[327] An Ordinance of 1855 modified the evidentiary effect which under the

1734 Code was unconditionally attached to sworn account books. This effect was entirely abolished in 1868 as to cases other than those between merchants. An Ordinance of 1849 removed the requirement that one taking an appeal to the *Hofrätt* must satisfy the judgment appealed from as a condition of prosecuting his appeal. The principle of publicity for hearings in the lower courts was provided for by an enactment of 1881.

A projected revision of 1884 drafted by an official commission failed of acceptance.[328] During the ensuing four decades only piecemeal change occurred. An 1886 law imposed a duty of furnishing security for costs upon a foreign plaintiff suing a Swedish defendant, in the absence of a contrary treaty stipulation. Women were given the right to act as representatives of parties in the conduct of cases in 1897. Three laws of 1899 regulated certain international aspects of civil procedure: one dealt with execution of foreign judgments, one with depositions of witnesses taken in foreign courts, and one with the rendering of judicial assistance to foreign courts. A 1915 law decreased the burden of the Supreme Court as to review of decisions of the *Hofrätt* by requiring that the amount involved be 1,500 kronor or more. Aid to indigent litigants was given by a 1919 law, which enabled such persons to be exempted from payment of certain costs. A law of 1915 laid down distinctive rules for matrimonial cases, later incorporated in the new National Code of 1920. A 1917 law deals with procedure in cases involving legitimate birth, adoption and illegitimate children.

In 1915 a special one-man commission, Johannes Hellner, began work on a project to modernize civil procedure and judicial organization.[329] He was soon appointed Minister of Foreign Affairs and was succeeded by Herman Falk. In 1919 the commission was enlarged with Falk as chairman together with Karl Schlyter, Henrik Almstrand and Professor Thore Engströmer. Falk soon died and was succeeded as chairman by Hjalmar Westring. Nils von Steyern was made secretary. Schlyter became a member of the Cabinet and early ceased to take part, and Almstrand died in 1925. Westring died in 1926 just as the commission was ready to submit a report. The work was continued by Engströmer and Von Steyern and Tryggve Liljestrand as secretary. At one stage there was talk of including criminal procedure, but this was soon given up. A draft was submitted to the courts, law school faculties, judges' conferences, the bar and to a number of officials and societies. In 1931 the Riksdag accepted the general principles proposed in the draft despite some argument that a mere revision would be sufficient. Prior to 1932 much of the work of preparation was done in the Department of Justice. In 1932 Nathaniel Gärde became chairman with Engströmer and Per Santesson as associate members. In 1934 Tore Strandberg was made a member. A final draft was ready in 1938. With some changes after having received the approval of a conference of judges as well as of the bar, it was adopted by the Riksdag in 1942. For various reasons it was not placed into effect immediately. Certain technical changes were needed and were presented in 1944. Santesson and later Strandberg left the commission and were succeeded by Erik Söderlund and Sven Strömberg as secretary. The only member serving from the beginning of the Collegial Commission was Professor Engströmer.[330]

The new Swedish code of civil procedure went into effect on January 1, 1948.[331] The decisory oath is discontinued, as it had previously been in Denmark and Norway.[332] Under the prior law a party was entitled to request his adversary to assert or deny under oath a determinative fact of the case. The opponent then had to take the oath or tender it back to the proponent. The taking of the oath or its refusal was decisive of the case. While the Swedish law does not, like the Anglo-American law, make a party a competent and compellable witness, there may be an oral examination of the party in open court. Such examination is not merely a subsidiary means of proof, but is rather an independent means of proof.[333] This is emphasized by the provision that in the absence of special reason to the contrary, the examination shall be held before the hearing of witness-proof touching its subject-matter. As in Denmark and Norway, there has been a substantial transfer of witness-examination to the hands of the parties accompanied by recognition of the right of cross-examination.

The new Swedish code divides civil proceedings into two stages: preparatory and trial. At the preparatory proceeding the parties file informal pleadings and offer of proof. They then appear before a single judge to clarify the issues, and for other purposes inherent in the nature of a pre-trial hearing. The trial itself is concentrated into "one day in court" before the full bench, much as in Anglo-American practice. And like the Anglo-American procedure, the new Swedish procedure is largely oral.

The theories back of the preparatory proceeding are: (1) to enable the case to be ended at the hearing-in-chief; and (2) to make possible the decision of certain matters during a preparatory proceeding without a hearing-in-chief. Some cases in which procedural obstacles arise may be ended at the preparatory proceeding. In some cases the court may take up the case and adjudicate it during the preliminary proceeding. Where one party defaults, or the case is settled, or a disputed claim is admitted or given up, a judgment may be reached at this stage. In some cases where the case is clear or the parties agree, the two stages may be held together. The preparatory proceeding may be conducted by as few as a single judge. The same judge may, though need not, serve at the hearing-in-chief.

At the preliminary proceeding the judge is to acquaint himself with the position of the parties as to claims, objections, and alleged facts. He is to prepare the evidence so that it can be coherently produced at the hearing-in-chief, thus avoiding delay. The object is not to establish grounds for the judgment, as the finished materials have not yet been obtained. The preliminary hearing is intended to determine the position of the parties and their means of defense and attack. Before the preliminary hearing can occur there must be an application for a summons. The hearing is oral. Immediately following the hearing the judge is to fix the time for the hearing-in-chief. When the plaintiff makes his application for a summons, he should specify the facts on which he founds his claim, the claim advanced by the plaintiff, the written proofs cited by the plaintiff, and the circumstances necessitating the authority of the court if this is not already evident. The summons and application are then sent by mail to the defendant through the court. At the preliminary hearing the defendant gives his reply. In his reply the defendant states the objections he wishes to make as to procedural obstacles, his admission to, or denial of, plaintiff's claim, the grounds for his denial of plaintiff's claim, and the particulars of the written proofs quoted by the defendant. Both parties are to announce all the further evidence they wish to cite, and to state what it is they wish to prove by every separate piece of evidence.

At the hearing-in-chief the plaintiff is at the outset to state his claim, and the defendant is to indicate whether he admits or contests the claim. Both parties are to give an account of their cases and to refute the other. When plaintiff and defendant have been heard the evidence is produced. After the evidence has been produced both parties have the right to state what they deem necessary with regard to their claims.

The old rule still prevails that the witness may be interrogated by the court.[334] But the new rules provide that ordinarily the court is to leave cross-examination of witnesses to the attorneys. It is also provided that as a rule there shall be only one trial. But this appears to be merely a directory provision. If this provision is liked by the Swedish judges, then chopping up of trials into a number of successive interrogations of witnesses, which is so common on the Continent, will become the exception rather than the rule.

The most important new rules of evidence may be summarized as follows: Free estimation of evidence is established, whereas this was not true under the 1734 Code.[335] It is provided broadly: "The court shall after conscientious consideration of all the facts decide what is proved in the case." Under this provision the court is to consider every fact that in any way may influence the convictions of the court, such as the behavior of the party during the trial. No evidence need be given of facts that are generally known. Parties are heard, but not as witnesses. Hence their testimony is estimated like anything else occurring before the court. Children under fifteen and persons of unsound mind may be heard as witnesses only by leave of court. The following are exceptions to the general rule that everyone has a duty to give evidence: (a) persons closely related to a party need not give evidence at all; (b) civil servants may not be heard as to facts covered by their duty of secrecy; (c) confidential communications to lawyers, physicians, and clergymen are privileged, but the client may waive; (d) trade secrecies are privileged unless there is a particular reason to disclose; and (e) the witness need not say anything that would disclose that he or someone close to him has committed a crime. Perhaps the most important rule is that witnesses are to be examined by the court, but by leave of court examination may be left to the parties. In general, a witness should be asked to tell his story without interruption. Then later he may be questioned. A witness may use written notes to support his memory. Leading questions may be used only when there are special reasons for doing so. As a rule, a witness may not listen to a case before he is heard.

Under the present Swedish law as to courts of first instance there is a virtually unlimited right to appeal.[336] But as to appeal from the Courts of Appeal to the Supreme Court appeal is only by leave. Leave may be given to secure uniform interpretation of the laws and when decisions are important beyond the cases in question. In all civil cases except where the value of what the appellant has lost in the Court of Appeal is less than 1,500 kronor, leave to appeal may be granted if there is reason to alter the judgment of the Court of Appeal, or if with regard to the circumstances of the case there is reason to have it tried. Swedish cases are not decided by laymen, save as to libel or other infringements of the press law. In fact, judgments are based on the written record, hence appellate courts can easily weigh the evidence. It should be remembered that many courts of first instance have unlimited jurisdiction—about 175 in all.

As in England the successful party to a suit has the right to recover all legal expenses. The court estimates the costs. Litigation is much cheaper in Sweden than it is in England. Swedish appeals have been inexpensive, costing from $50 to $75, an amount less than the costs below.

In 1944 there were 3,123 civil actions involving more than 1,500 kronor tried and determined in the first instance courts. But few of these were automobile accident cases. At the same time there were

1,193 cases in the Courts of Appeal and 156 in the Supreme Court. As to civil actions where the amount involved could not be estimated, there were 14,369 cases in the lower courts, of which 5,340 involved divorce and 7,129 separation. There were 683 in the Courts of Appeal and 241 in the Supreme Court. In suits involving business about one-third of the cases tried by the lower courts were brought up to the Courts of Appeal for review.

Social Legislation

Sweden like Denmark and Norway has adopted a huge mass of social legislation. As Mr. Justice Jackson has stated Swedes do "not believe in or encourage great disparities in wealth or worldly goods."[337]

Slavery. As early as 1779 an anti-slavery society was founded in Sweden. In 1813 Sweden prohibited the slave trade and gave support at the Congress of Vienna in 1814 to 1815 to efforts to end it by international agreement.[338]

Women. Advocates of women's rights began to appear in Sweden in the eighteenth century. Olov Dalin, Johan Fischerström, and Christopher Polhem defended the right of women to equality of education, work, and political activity.[339] Hedvig Nordenflycht (1718-1763) wrote a *Defense of Woman* in reply to Rousseau. In 1839 C. L. Almquist, the Swedish novelist, in his book, *Det gar an*, or, *It will do*, implied that the economic mastery of man in marriage is fatal to love. The great feminist leader was Fredrika Bremer, who visited the United States in 1849, and met Lucretia Mott, Lucy Stone, and Margaret Fuller. In 1856 her novel *Hertha* was published. Her work was continued by Sophie Adlersparre and Rosalie Olivencrona.

In 1825 a draft of the reformed Swedish civil code, largely due to the efforts of J. G. Richert, made women independent of guardianship at the age of twenty-five.[340] The two lower chambers supported this proposal, but it failed when the nobility and the clergy rejected it. Daughters were given the right to share equally with sons as to inheritance in 1845.[341] Unmarried women were classified as minors along with children and insane persons as late as 1854. In the 1856-1858 session of the Riksdag steps were taken in the direction of making them independent. Their rights were further extended in 1863 and 1884. The age of majority for both males and females was reduced to twenty-one in 1884.

Proposals to admit women to occupations outside the home were made in the eighteenth century, but the guilds stood in the way. In 1809 the Riksdag voted to extend freedom of occupation to unmarried women and widows, if they employed male laborers. But the law did not receive

enforcement. In 1864 the Swedish law established the right of the unmarried woman to earn her living in any trade or craft.[342] In 1859 a royal
circular permitted properly qualified women to teach in Sweden and
teachers' colleges for women were set up. In 1862 women were given the
right to vote in local elections with the same property qualifications as
men. When the reform of the national representation in the Riksdag
occurred in 1865, women obtained the same indirect franchise for members of the upper house as men. Women were given the full right to vote
in 1921. Thus they obtained the right to vote directly for the members of
the lower house or the Second Chamber. As of 1951 the new Minister
of Church and Education in the Swedish cabinet is a woman, Hildur
Nygren. She is the second woman to serve in the Swedish cabinet, the
first having been Karin Kock, Minister of Civilian Supply.

An employer may not dismiss a woman because of her betrothal or
marriage.[343] Women who have worked for their employer for a year or
more may not be dismissed because of pregnancy and childbirth, but
may obtain leave of absence up to six months. Neither Denmark nor
Norway has such a law. The Swedish theory is that it is morally wrong
to subject pregnant women to fear of dismissal.

Marriage and Divorce. The present Swedish law of marriage and
divorce was enacted on June 11, 1920, effective January 1, 1921.[344] It
appears at the beginning of the Swedish statute book. It consists of sixteen chapters regulating marriage, the rights and duties of husband and
wife, and divorce. The minimum age for marriage is twenty-one for men
and eighteen for women. The permission of the king is required for
marriage below such ages. Parental consent is needed as to women under
twenty-one. If there is a prior marriage it must have been ended by
divorce unless the other spouse has died. Other obstacles to marriage
are mental illness and feeble-mindedness. Certain types of epilepsy and
infectious venereal disease preclude marriage unless the king grants permission. The marriage may not take place until at least three weeks have
elapsed after the announcement of intention to marry. The twofold
purpose is to give the parties a chance for further reflection and to prevent illegal marriages.

Prior to 1921 a husband was in effect the legal guardian of his wife,
as he was recognized as her representative in legal affairs, and he was the
one to decide domestic questions such as residence and education of
children. Under the new law both husband and wife are equal in legal
and domestic issues. Consequently, the two together make the decisions
as to residence, standard of living, and other domestic matters. But the
law is silent regarding what happens if the parties disagree. Both parties
must support the family, and a failure may result in a court order.

In 1938 marriage loans were introduced in order to encourage early establishment of families and prevent abuse of installment buying.[345] The interest rate is four per cent, repayment is required within five years, and no more than 2,000 kronor may be loaned. One-fourth of newly married couples resort to such loans.

Prior to divorce there is mediation by clergymen. Divorce may be granted at the request of either party after one year of separation. Grounds for immediate divorce are: actual separation for three years, desertion for two years, bigamy, infidelity, infection with a venereal disease, severe ill-treatment, criminal punishment and mental illness. The American divorce rate is three times as high as the Swedish, but the Swedish is twice as high as the English. Of the Scandinavian nations Denmark has the highest divorce rate, Sweden is second, Finland third, and Norway fourth.

Labor. Both employers and workers are strongly organized in Sweden.[346] The chief organization of employers is the Federation of Swedish Employers or *Svenska Arbetsgivareföreningen*, which includes the employers of about 60 per cent of all organized Swedish workers. There are separate employers' organizations as to agriculture, lumbering, and shipping. The largest labor organization is the Federation of Trade Unions or *Landsorganisationen* with 1,200,000 members. About 240,000 belong to the Central Organization of Salaried Employees, and 165,000 to a rural federation.

Cases arising under existing collective agreements are heard by the Labor Court or *Arbetsdomstolen* consisting of six members and a chairman as in Denmark and Norway. The chairman and two associates represent the public, two represent labor and two industry. Delay is avoided by prompt decisions after brief hearings, and there is no appeal. More than 75 per cent of all industrial workers are covered by collective agreements. The Labor Court has no jurisdiction over matters not covered in the collective agreements nor over disputes as to the renewal of such agreements. Such cases are dealt with by mediation. The mediation agency cannot make a decision or enforce its suggestions. To offer assistance in mediation Sweden is divided into seven districts. Each district is in charge of a conciliator or *forlikningsmann* appointed by the central government and supervised by the Social Board in the Department of Social Affairs. No strike or lockout may be commenced without notifying the conciliator. Both parties must appear before him. In 1938 an agreement between labor and employers was drawn up at Saltsjöbaden establishing informal systems of negotiations between labor and management and setting up machinery for arbitrating disagreements not covered by collective contracts. But the right to strike or lockout was not renounced. This agreement with subsequent additions has reduced strikes to a minimum.

Swedish workers will get three weeks' vacation with full pay each year under a law recently adopted.[347] The law extends the legal vacation from twelve working days, which had been in effect since 1938, to fifteen working days. After 1953 the vacations will be increased to eighteen working days.

Workmen's Compensation. An act of 1901 required Swedish industrial employers to carry liability insurance to cover accidents to workers. The scope of workmen's compensation was so broadened by the Industrial Accident Act of 1916, as amended, and the Occupational Disease Act of 1929, as to make the Swedish system as good as that of any other country.[348] Every person working for another for pay is covered. Apprentices and students at certain trade schools are covered, as are domestic servants. Every employer is required to take out liability insurance with the National Institute of Insurance or *Riksförsäkringsanstalten,* or with a mutual liability insurance company approved by it. Many kinds of occupational disease are covered in addition to accidents.

An injured employee is entitled to receive all medical treatment and necessary artificial appliances. In case of a convalescent period of incapacity, he is entitled to a daily cash allowance, based on his wage scale and the degree of incapacitation.[349] A permanently disabled worker who is severely disabled is given an annuity. No annuity is paid if the disability is rated at ten per cent or less. If the worker dies, funeral benefits are paid, and his dependents receive certain annuities. The survivors of one dying from an occupational disease receive benefits only if the death occurs within two years of the appearance of the disease. Administration is in the hands of the National Institute of Insurance. Its decisions may be appealed without cost to the Insurance Council or *Försäkringsradet.* This body resembles a workmen's compensation court and consists of ten members, two of whom represent the employers and two the workers. It has final jurisdiction.

Unemployment Insurance. Legislation enacted in 1934 established a system of state-subsidized unemployment insurance.[350] It is administered by the Social Board or *Socialstyrelsen,* and is based upon the unemployment funds which have long been set up by the trade unions. Approved unemployment benefit societies receive public grants. The system is on a voluntary basis, and trade unions may elect to come under the law. Membership in a society is limited to wage earners who are in the paid employ of another for at least seven months of the year. The unemployed worker must report periodically to a public employment office to be eligible. Financing is through payments by members and by state subsidies. The employer does not contribute. Daily benefits are paid to workers out of work for longer than a short waiting period. The daily amounts vary from two to seven kronor, but never greater than four-fifths of the prevailing local wage.[351] The payments may continue from 90 to 156 days, as determined by the society. No benefits are paid to those unemployed as the result of a labor dispute, or to one unreasonably refusing to accept other employment. Official agencies are studying the advisability of a compulsory system as many regard the present system as inadequate.

In 1934 there was also established a nationwide system of labor exchanges with local offices in all parts of the nation. City councils are required to provide labor exchange offices. All private employment offices were gradually discontinued by 1950. In 1947 the exchanges were placed under a new central agency, the Labor Market Board. Moving expenses are given to workers who have to transfer to another locality. Training courses to prepare workers for new trades are conducted.

General Assistance. Poor relief dates back to the time of the introduction of Christianity in Sweden.[352] In 1763 a decree was issued giving to poor relief the external organization which in large part continues up to the present time.

In 1837 a committee of the Riksdag was established to study the problem of general assistance or relief.[353] The committee was uncertain whether assistance should be centralized or left to the localities. But it felt that workhouses and begging were not the ways out. From 1840 many unemployed were assigned to draining marshes, building highways, and later railroads. In 1847 a statute set up a plan of cooperation between the state, the county, and the locality. The arrangement of details was left almost altogether to the parish councils. The lesser peasantry were dissatisfied as they would now have to contribute for the paupers produced by the crofters on the large estates.

The poor relief system was very defective until the decade of the 1920's. In 1918 the Riksdag passed a new poor law which, slightly modified, continues up to the present. There had been a tendency to give too much thought to social insurance and not enough to poor relief. In 1937 a committee was appointed to revise the poor law.

Poor relief is given according to the circumstances of the individual case.[354] Need must be shown. Investigation occurs to determine the need, form and scope of the aid. Often poor relief is complementary to other forms of social aid, as in the case of inadequate old age pension. Poor relief is left up to the localities both as to organization and costs. There are at least 2,500 localities. Each locality has a poor relief board, elected by popular vote. The chairman of the board is the executive officer and represents the board. In small localities the chairman takes care of everything. In middle-sized localities, all members of the board are active. In large localities, one or more salaried public assistance workers is hired. The county supervises the boards, assisted by poor relief consultants. The central authority is the Royal Social Board, assisted by the state inspector of poor relief and child care.

In some cases the poor relief board is required to give aid, while in others it has discretion. Aid is required when the needy person is under sixteen, or cannot earn a living on account of old age, sickness, or other incapacity. On the other hand, the board has discretion with respect to unemployed persons. Other forms of aid are often given to this class, but if it is not, poor relief will be given. The amount of relief depends on what is regarded by the locality involved as necessary for subsistence. The boards may in some cases receive reimbursement from relatives. There is no duty to support as between brothers and sisters or grandparents and grandchildren.

Aid may be given to the indigent in his home or in an institution. The former is considered first, and is given unless it would be abused or the indigent requires institutional care. Formerly board for the needy with other persons was provided, but today this is exceptional. If home aid is not suitable, care is given in an institution belonging to the locality, the county or the state. Many persons are placed in "old-age homes" which have replaced the older almshouses. Asocial individuals may be transferred from the "old-age home" to a workhouse. There are provisions for transfer to hospitals, sanatoriums, or insane asylums.

As to which locality must support, the present rule is that a person has his legal residence in the locality where he was registered for tax purposes during the year prior to his application for relief. Where the recipient is maintained in a public hospital the locality is reimbursed by the state or the county. As of 1935 poor relief was costing Sweden about 90 million kronor a year, of which the localities paid 74 millions, the counties 11 to 12 millions, and the central government from two to three millions. About two million kronor are repaid by recipients. About 8.6 per cent of the population were receiving relief. Out of 537,000 receiving relief, about 443,000 received it in their homes, while 84,000 were hospitalized, and 44,000 were in "old-age homes."

If an applicant is denied relief or denied as much as he seeks, he may appeal to the county administration which may order the locality to grant the obligatory type of relief. In disputes between private persons and localities, or between different localities, the decision of the county council may be appealed to the Audit Court in Stockholm, and in certain cases to other authorities.

Work Relief. In general, Sweden, like Denmark and Norway, has favored work relief in preference to direct or cash relief.[355] From 1918 to 1939 a public works program was established to provide work for the unemployed. Since that time it has not played so significant a role. Sweden appears to have given work relief a more searching test for a larger interval than any other country. The Swedish works program was placed in the hands of the National Employment Commission or *Statens Arbetslöshetskommissionen* in 1914 to study the problem. But most of the details of administration were left to the local areas. The municipality took the first step, but its project had to be approved by the commission. The central government contributed very substantially both for labor costs and material. The most important projects were road building, forestry services, stadium construction, and laying out of athletic fields, bridge building, inland waterways, harbors and canals, water supply, and drainage systems. Since 1933 the wages paid have been based on the wage rate in the open market. Labor camps for unemployed youths have been set up. The program envisages the possible subsidization of private enterprise in fields such as housing.

Child and Family Welfare. The first child welfare legislation was enacted in 1902. The existing system is based on the Child Welfare Act of 1924 with amendments, including one in 1934 which increased the age from 18 to 21.[356] Child welfare activity is directed by the child welfare committee of the municipality. This committee is made up of a member of the poor relief board, a clergyman, a teacher, and at least two other persons interested in child welfare. There must be at least one woman on the committee. Often there is a physician. The main activities are of two kinds. In the first place, the committee takes charge of children for protective upbringing. Orphans and adopted children are supervised. In the second place, public care is given to needy sick and helpless children under sixteen. The Royal Social Board gives national supervision.

Under the Child Care and Youth Protection Act of 1945 the local committees were given very broad functions as to child and youth care. The county council is made responsible for all children's homes, including day care for preschool children when the mother is employed. Under a new plan effective in 1947 all children in elementary and high schools may take advantage of school meals irrespective of family income. The localities are responsible for such programs but may request state subsidies.

Since 1948 there has been a subsidy of 260 kronor per year for each child under sixteen, regardless of income.[357] Ultimately the money value of the grants and services will amount to 600 kronor per child per annum for a family with two children of school age.[358] This is about half the cost of raising children in a working-class family. Rent subsidies are furnished to large families. Free vacation trips are given to certain children under fourteen. Since 1946 Swedish children whose parents have only a certain income are entitled to one free return ticket a year for a vacation of at least four weeks.[359] The children in 90 per cent of Swedish families are thus included. Housewives having at least two children and only a certain income may be given similar vacation trips.

Under legislation enacted since 1937 state aid of health in connection with child welfare is confined to preventive medicine, and is not comparable to the English system of socialized medicine.[360] All prospective mothers are entitled to free prophylactic treatment, examination, and advice as to prenatal care. It is resorted to by more than two-thirds of such mothers. All infants are entitled to free examination and preventive treatment, and more than 85 per cent receive it. Both mother and infant may obtain medicines and vitamins. The state supplies subventions for equipment and also pays part of the salaries of nurses and physicians, the locality also paying part. Dental clinics have also been set up, but the individual child pays $1.25 per year if he is the first child in the family, ninety cents if the second, and sixty cents if the third. When such clinics exist almost all the children in the area make use of them.

In 1938 the acts of 1910 and 1911 prohibiting the exhibition and advertising of contraceptives were repealed on the recommendation of the Population Commission established in 1938.[361] Birth control is now not only permitted but considered desirable.

Prevention of increase of the mentally inadequate is accomplished by sterilization as the most effective solution.[362] The new Swedish sterilization law has been operative since July 1, 1941. While largely voluntary in character, no consent need be obtained from those mentally incompetent to give it. If feeble-minded persons are not sterilized prior to their discharge from an institution, the reason for it must be stated. In practice the number of sterilizations of the feeble-minded has been equal to the number of feeble-minded children born each year.

Swedish law permits abortion for medical reasons, as in cases of heredity involving insanity or imbecility, or where there is danger to the life or health of the mother because of exhaustion, chronic malnutrition, attempted suicide, or other acts indicative of despair.[363] Abortion is also permitted if the child was conceived as a result of rape. Several centers financed largely by the central government have been set up by the counties to offer free advice and aid to women seeking to have their pregnancies interrupted.

With respect to illegitimate children, the father is required to contribute to the mother both before and after her confinement. Since 1933 a man denying paternity has been given the right to a blood test. As a consequence, about 15 per cent of such men have been freed. A special guardian is appointed by the local child welfare committee for an illegitimate child. He does not take the place of the parents, but looks after the establishment of the child's parentage and its general welfare until the child reaches eighteen.

No child under fourteen may be employed except on a farm or as a domestic.[364] But in certain non-industrial employment the age limit is thirteen. No one under eighteen may be employed in dangerous or unhealthful work, or if medical examination shows him unfit for the work; this also is the rule as to certain work on ships. With some exceptions, no one under eighteen may be employed until he has completed elementary school.

Old Age and Disability Insurance. Old age pensions and disability are connected together in the same system.[365] Compulsory old-age and disability insurance applying to the population in general has existed since 1914. But until recently the payments were so small that local poor relief had to supplement them. The National Pension Act of 1935, as amended by the Act of 1937, provided a more comprehensive system, which operated until 1948. All able-bodied persons from 18 to 65 had to pay into the National Pensions Fund at least six kronor a year. The Swedish system thus differed from the Danish and Norwegian. The Danish and Norwegian met the payments through taxation instead of through contributions.

The Pension Act of 1946 effective in 1948 involved a great increase in the amount of annual pension and the substitution of an additional income tax. Citizens reaching the age of 67 will receive a basic pension of 1,000 kronor a year or 1,600 kronor for a married couple, regardless of income.[366] To the basic pension may be added special housing and dependency allowances, varying with the cost of living in different areas.[367] There is also provision for disability pensions, adjusted according to the other income of the recipient.[368] Widows' pensions are provided as well as special pensions for the blind and the disabled. The system is supported by a special income tax of one per cent. Such tax may range from six to one hundred kronor a year. Three-fourths of the costs will have to come from the national treasury, about ten per cent from the special income tax, about ten per cent from the municipalities, and about five per cent from the old age pension fund. Additional old age annuities may be obtained through a voluntary system operated by the government. Administration of the pension system is by the Royal Pensions Board (*Pensionstyrelsen*).

Health Insurance. Up to 1951 the Swedish sickness insurance system has been that of subsidization of private sick benefit societies or *sjukkassor.*[369] Since 1891 these societies have been subjected to more and more state supervision. At the same time they have received subsidies from both the national and local governments. A law of 1931 provided that there should be only one subsidized local society in each municipality. Besides the local societies there were central societies operating over larger areas and responsible for group protection for prolonged and more serious illnesses. The law provided that every member of a local society must also be a member of a central society. The societies paid benefits of two kinds: medical treatment and daily cash allowances during illness. All costs of hospitalization were paid. Unlike the Danish and Norwegian systems, the Swedish system up to 1951 was voluntary.

There was increasing agitation for a compulsory system and in 1946 a law was passed adopting the compulsory system effective in 1950. Hospitalization and health insurance are handled separately under the new law. Every Swedish citizen is to receive free hospitalization in publicly owned and operated hospitals. Almost all hospitals are owned and operated by the government. Basic medicines are furnished free, and other medicines at reduced rates. The costs will be paid for out of public revenues.

Since 1950 health insurance has been compulsory for all Swedes over sixteen. The benefits included are: three-fourths of the necessary reasonable medical fees, the cost of transportation to the doctor, and per diem compensation during illness. The patient may choose his doctor. The regular daily allowance is 3½ kronor.[370] It may not be received for more than 730 consecutive days. The old societies will continue to function, but the managing officials will be responsible to the municipalities where they are located. Premiums will be collected as taxes. The costs are subsidized further out of the public treasury.

Maternity cases are included, and there are special benefits. Upon the birth of a child the mother is paid a lump sum.[371] There are proposals to amend the maternity aid system so as to include every Swedish woman, to provide for dental care, and a daily cash allowance for from three to six months. Working women would receive larger daily allowances and for longer periods than women not gainfully employed.

The national supervision of the system is in the Royal Pensions Board. Public health is in the hands of the Royal Medical Board or *Medicinalstyrelsen.* Under it is the public physician assigned to each *län.* The *län* administers public health laws and cares for the sick.[372] Each *län* has a head physician in charge of other government-employed doctors in the *län.* There are about 500 such doctors in Sweden. They are paid a salary and handle almost all rural cases not requiring a specialist. Consultation is free or for a very low fee. The counties also employ more than 1,000 nurses and about the same number of midwives. The cities also employ physicians for local medical care and sanitary problems. The counties, with aid from the nation, are beginning to set up dental clinics to furnish dental services at low cost. There is now a shortage of physicians and dentists. Recently a special investigation committee of public officials has recommended that medical care be completely nationalized within the next two decades or earlier.

Housing. Housing credit systems have existed in Sweden for more than three decades.[373] Loans and even grants were available to builders. In 1930 the National Building Loan Office or *Svenska Bostadskreditkassen* was established, and generous loans were made to stimulate private building. This program was connected with the effort to relieve unemployment. At first the program involved mostly middle-class persons. But in 1935 a lending program was instituted to stimulate low-cost housing. Between 1935 and 1946 one-third of all Swedish families with three or more children were assisted. Housing for the aged was given special attention. The government has worked closely with the cooperative housing organizations. Forty-five per cent of all apartments for low-income families have been built by the largest cooperative housing organization, the National Association of Tenants Savings and Building Societies. By 1910 about one-eighth of the dwellings in Stockholm were owned by the city or by cooperatives. In 1936 Stockholm bought more than 20,000 acres of land, all less than ten miles from the center of the city, for suburban housing projects for the working classes. According to a survey by the Swedish Board of Housing, 32 housing units per 1,000 inhabitants have been erected in Sweden during the four years just prior to 1950, compared to 24 in New Zealand, 21 in Canada, 19 in the United States of America, 17 in England, and 16 in Australia.[374] In 1949 a group of United States Senators went to Sweden and Denmark and returned with the feeling that much could be learned from the Scandinavian approach to housing for the middle-income group.[375] Noteworthy are their housing cooperatives, planning and house design, housing of the elderly, aid to large families, and land policies.

Liquor Control. The Swedish system of limited consumption of liquors has attracted attention all over the world.[376] Under the law a spirituous liquor is any liquor not derived from malt or wine with an alcoholic content of more than 2.25 per cent by volume. Wine is defined as fermented plant juice above the same limit. The sale of all malted beverages containing alcohol above 3.2 per cent by weight is prohibited.

Beer between 1.8 and 3.2 per cent is sold under fixed government regulations.

Liquor control is under the direction of the National Control Board or *Kontrollstyrelsen* under the Ministry of Finance. Wholesale trade is handled by a limited dividend corporation. No Swedish producer of intoxicants may sell his products to other than this corporation. The retail trade is handled by several limited dividend companies. There is such a company in almost every city. Application for a charter is made to the governor of the county, who in turn submits it to the local council, thus in effect securing local option. A company receiving a charter obtains a complete monopoly of the retail trade.

The most notable feature of the Swedish system, called the Bratt System after its proponent, is the control exercised over the individual purchases. A person may not purchase unless he is registered and has a pass book, in which each purchase is recorded. The amount purchasable is determined by the charter of the company and the local temperance board appointed by the local council. No one may buy more than three liters of spirits per month. The original limit had been four liters. The monthly allotment varies with age, sex, and domestic status. Liquor is not available in eating places except with purchase of food. The results of the legislation have been striking.[377] There has been a reduced per capita consumption of intoxicants, the number of arrests for drunkenness has decreased. There has been a particularly great decrease of drunkenness among persons under twenty. Fewer patients are now admitted to the hospitals for alcoholics. There are fewer deaths due to alcoholism. The number of crimes of violence has dropped sharply.

Tariffs and Freedom of Occupation. The principles of mercantilism continued to be influential in Sweden longer than in Denmark and Norway.[378] In 1816 the new tariff law contained hundreds of import prohibitions and more than fifty export prohibitions. In 1824 these were reduced by half. In 1823 the Riksdag gave the government power to alter the schedules, and a number of changes were made. In 1853 there was a majority in the Riksdag favoring moderate freedom of trade. The peasants no longer were offered a reduction in rates, and the old industrial and crofts groups had disintegrated as a result of freedom of occupation and internal trade.[379] Moreover, Sweden enjoyed great prosperity at the time. Its union with Norway resulted in pressure to keep up with the advanced Norwegian free-trade principle. While the bar-iron industry still desired protection, the new textile industry sought low rates on foodstuffs and raw materials. Consequently, the tariff law of 1857 greatly reduced rates, but still kept several protective features. In 1865 a treaty was negotiated with France limiting the legislative power of the Riksdag for several years.

Uniform Scandinavian Laws

Until about a thousand years ago all Scandinavians used a single language sometimes referred to as the Danish tongue. The law code of the Swedish province of Västergötland about 1200 required a higher *wergild* for the killing of a Dane or Norwegian than for that of an Englishman or a German.[380] Finland was a part of Sweden for the six centuries prior to 1809. There was a personal union between Sweden and Norway from 1319 to 1371. Sweden was a member of the Scandinavian Union with Denmark and Norway from 1389 to 1521. As Finland then belonged to Sweden and Iceland belonged to Norway all five of the present Scandinavian states then had the same sovereign. From 1814 to 1905 there was a union between Sweden and Norway.

Scandinavian cooperation in adopting uniform laws has been signally successful.[381] A Swedish lawyer has concluded: "A like example of advanced cooperation in adoption of uniform laws among several independent states is not to be found anywhere else in the world."[382] Scandinavian Jurists Conventions have been held usually every third year for eighty years since the first was held at Copenhagen in 1872. The eighteenth conference, held after an interval of eleven years, met at Copenhagen in 1948.[383] There are also periodical joint sessions of the Scandinavian ministers of justice and the Scandinavian Inter-Parliamentary Union.

The Scandinavian Monetary Convention of 1872 which lasted until its disruption in 1914 by the First World War provided common names and common values for Scandinavian coinage.[384] The money of each state was legal tender in the others. The Bank Drafts Act of 1880 achieved better coordination of the laws governing bank drafts. An identical bill was passed in Sweden, Denmark and Norway after a joint committee of members of the three parliaments had agreed on the texts. Among important common codifications are the Navigation Act of 1892,[385] the Law of Purchase and Selling of 1905-1907, the Marriage Law of 1921-1925, and laws regulating trademarks, insurance, trade registers, bank checks, commercial agents, selling on the installment plan, promissory notes, property in various aspects, and air traffic. A law concerning corporations is being prepared. Some Scandinavian states have adopted common regulations as to minority and tutelage and certain aspects of legacy. Basic principles have been worked out as to juvenile delinquency, alcoholism, and abortion. Sweden and Denmark have nearly identical laws regarding citizenship. During World War I Sweden,

Denmark and Norway adopted identical regulations as to neutrality.

Social security has been a topic of inter-Scandinavian coordination. On the initiative of John May, the Swedish social security director, the social security agencies of Sweden, Denmark and Norway met in Copenhagen to discuss workmen's compensation in 1907. Since the First World War the ministers of labor and social affairs have met every two or three years to discuss social security. The objective has been to obtain reciprocity, so that nationals of one Scandinavian state living in another could receive the same benefits as that state's own citizens. There has been cooperation as to administrative problems and exchange of information and experience. Up to 1950 old age pensions and disability insurance had not been coordinated. Reciprocity was first extended to industrial accident insurance. Sweden signed a reciprocity convention with Denmark and Norway in 1919. In 1937 all five Scandinavian states including Finland and Iceland concluded a new convention to apply to cases in which the incapacitated worker was not a resident of the state of injury. In 1926 Denmark and Norway signed a health insurance convention, enabling members of an approved health insurance society in one state to be transferred to a similar society in the other regardless of age or health. Sweden could not join until the Swedish statutes were amended. The Swedish statutes were finally amended in 1939. Though the war made a convention with Denmark and Norway impossible, the Swedish societies accepted many Danish and Norwegian refugees as transferred members. In 1947 Sweden concluded a convention with Denmark and in 1948 with Norway.

Because of differences in local legislation there has been less reciprocity as to unemployment insurance. In Sweden, as distinguished from Denmark and Norway, resident foreigners are eligible for membership in unemployment insurance societies only if the foreigner is a citizen of a country which has a reciprocity convention with Sweden. Moreover, in Sweden unemployment insurance is voluntary, whereas in Norway it is compulsory. But a more important issue is transference of members of the societies from one country to those of the other. In 1946 representatives of Swedish and Danish societies met and developed a standard agreement permitting transference without loss of status. Most of the societies adopted the agreement. Consequently, most workers from one of the two states may receive benefits in the other, though they may have lived there a short time only. Similar arrangements are being made with Norway. ·

Following the Second World War Sweden and Denmark ratified a convention as to exchange of labor. The convention abolished the prior rule that foreigners could accept employment only with the consent of the authorities of the state. The convention provides for cooperation between the states' employment services and exchange of information as to employment. In 1928, 1937, and 1948, conferences as to workmen's safety were held, and a commission is now drafting joint regulations for safety devices for machinery and tools. A convention on bankruptcy became effective in 1935.[386] Under the Scandinavian Pauper Convention of 1928 Scandinavian nationals acquire the right to public assistance in any Scandinavian state on certain conditions when they have lived there for a certain period.[387]

By the convention of 1931 common rules of conflict of laws were adopted for all five Scandinavian nations.[388] The convention related to marriage, adoption, and guardianship. Previously in Denmark and Norway conflict of laws was based on domicile, whereas in Sweden and Finland it was based on nationality. As to inter-Scandinavian matters the result of the convention is to adopt the principle of domicile. A later convention of 1934 extended the principle of domicile to succession, wills and administration.

Uniform legislation is now being prepared which will make it possible to recover fines and execute short-term prison sentences imposed by the courts of one state in the other states. Following the Second World War there were special arrangements to prevent quislings from Denmark and Norway from obtaining refuge in another Scandinavian state. In civil cases judgments of one state may be executed in the other states. Sweden and Denmark concluded a convention to that effect in 1861, later adhered to by Norway.

A draft for new and uniform legislation concerning the citizenship of married women, worked out by delegates from Sweden, Denmark, and Norway, was submitted simultaneously to the parliaments of the three countries in 1950, effective January 1, 1951.[389] Marriage is not automatically to confer citizenship, but it must be applied for. A Swedish woman marrying a foreigner will be able to retain her Swedish citizenship even though she lives in her husband's country. Women who have lost their citizenship under the prior law may regain their status if a declaration is made within five years from the date of enactment. Children born in wedlock will have the father's nationality; otherwise, the mother's. If the father is stateless, they will have the mother's nationality.

In the 1890's the Riksdag was receptive towards the drawing up of a commercial code for Denmark, Norway, and Sweden. In 1899 Julius Lassen proposed a codification of the entire civil law in a Scandinavian private law code. Carl Lindhagen advocated this in the Riksdag but without success because of the breadth of the project. It was, however, willing that work be undertaken as to the law of obligations. In 1901

Sweden worked together with Denmark, and a short time later Norway also joined in.[390] The following subjects were dealt with: sale of goods, commercial agents, and promissory notes. After agreement of the governments of the three nations a new program of continued cooperation began. This program was divided into two parts. The first had to do with obligations, payment of debts, insurance, letters of credit, rents, security, and the statute of limitations. The second was a new field, that of family law. Marriage and guardianship were taken up. Subsequently, air law and the law of citizenship have been considered. Finland and Iceland since attaining independence have joined in the work.

Following the Second World War the Scandinavian countries were eager to resume work on uniform laws. The Swedes felt no special need for work on civil procedure except as to execution, as they had just drafted a new code. The same was true in regard to criminal law. Some revision of family law seemed in order. On the other hand, it was felt that there was a great need to codify the law of obligations and related subjects. Early in 1946 a meeting was held at Copenhagen of officials from Denmark, Norway, and Sweden, and it was apparent that all concurred in the scope of the work to be undertaken. In June 1946 a similar meeting was held at Stockholm. There was agreement that they should not consider common Scandinavian citizenship, as political considerations made this impossible. They could, however, deal with acquisition and loss of national citizenship. They should continue work on air law. Ten topics were deemed ripe for codification: (1) torts, especially where automobiles are involved; (2) responsibility of the state and locality for torts of its employees; (3) prescription; (4) revision of the law of sales; (5) creditors' rights; (6) bail with respect to proceedings in another Scandinavian country; (7) mortgage law; (8) separation agreements; (9) law of names; and (10) the law of citizenship, such as the effect of marriage and the effect of naturalization of a citizen in another country. A meeting was held in Oslo in November 1946 at which Finland and Iceland were invited to join in the work. It was decided that the first subject to be taken up should be purchases on credit, then the responsibility of the state and locality for acts of their servants. Other subjects to be taken up later are: prescription, revision of the law of sales, arbitration agreements, and the law of names. There was discussion of a stronger and more stable method of cooperative effort for codifying the uniform laws. This had been discussed in the Riksdag as far back as 1911 and 1912. At the eleventh conference of Scandinavian jurists in 1919 Professor Viggo Bentzon of the University of Copenhagen made such a proposal. The Swedish Minister of Justice, Eliel Löfgren, proposed that each of the Scandinavian Departments of Justice set up a bureau chief with the special duty of being a Scandinavian liaison official. At the 1946 Oslo meeting it was proposed that each nation appoint two or three persons to engage in codification. Sweden did so in 1947.

A recent book on Scandinavian cooperation in legal matters has proposed the establishment of a permanent commission consisting of jurists from the five Scandinavian nations with the duty to investigate the possibilities and carry on proposals for increased cooperation and greater unity in law development.[391]

In 1948 Professor Vinding Kruse of the University of Copenhagen published a book of 626 pages entitled, *A Scandinavian Law Code. Plan for a Common Law Code for Denmark, Finland, Iceland, Norway, and Sweden.*[392] The plan is divided into six parts: general, the rights of persons, family law, inheritance law, property law, and creditors' rights.

In connection with the movement for uniform laws it should be noted that after World War I there was organized the Scandinavian Wholesale Society, as chief purchaser for the national cooperative societies of Finland, Denmark, Norway and Sweden.[393] Its central office is located in Copenhagen.

The idea of a northern customs union has been discussed since 1863.[394] In 1948 a Joint Economic Commission began consultations. As of 1950 the commission conceded failure largely due to Norwegian fear of Swedish industrial competition. In December 1949 the British sought to integrate more closely the Scandinavian economies with the British. All the Scandinavian nations are in the Council of Europe.

Legal Education

At an early time Swedish students attended the University of Paris.[395] Later many preferred to go to Prague and Leipzig, and still later to Rostock and Greifswald. A suggestion for setting up a Swedish university in 1417 came to nothing.

The first Swedish, as well as the first Scandinavian, university was founded in 1477 at Uppsala by Archbishop Jakob Ulfsson.[396] But it lacked firm financial foundations until Gustavus Adolphus (1611-1632) turned over to it the Gustavian Estate consisting of more than three hundred farms.[397] Many Swedish law students attended German and Dutch universities, especially Leyden and Utrecht.[398] In 1668 after the acquisition of Skåne by Sweden from Denmark the University of Lund was founded. A law school was established at the University of Stockholm in the nineteenth century.

While the University of Uppsala was established in 1477, the law school was founded in 1620 and only one professor of law was employed until 1657.[399] Thereafter there were two chairs: Swedish law and Roman law. After the 1734 Code, interest in Roman law declined. Interest in Roman law was renewed in the nineteenth century when German law became very influential in Sweden. Today Roman law is not studied in the Swedish universities. In 1739 the Riksdag ordered that the professorship in Swedish law be abolished and one in economics be established in its place.[400]

The curricula of the Swedish law schools are more rigid and prescribed than those of the American.[401] The Swedish law schools were founded by the government. While the American law schools aim at developing practitioners, the Swedish aim chiefly at developing government employees. The period of study in the Swedish law schools is longer. The Swedish plan of study aims at an integrated and systematic unity. The various subjects complement each other, and follow in an order determined by their relation to each other. Swedish students commence with the periphery of the law before they take up the civil law and other central subjects. Swedish instruction is of scientific and theoretical character and does not aim so much as the American schools to fit the student for immediate practice. Swedish law professors are selected more for scholarly attainments and less for pedagogical ability and experience as practitioners. More emphasis is placed on study of statutes and less on study of cases.

The Bar

Sweden was the first of the Scandinavian nations to develop a sizable profession of the bar.[402] Owing to the efforts of King Gustavus Adolphus toward the promotion of the legal practice in the seventeenth century there has been a legal profession ever since that period.

No qualifications are required to appear as an attorney before the courts. Every citizen may act as his own attorney. A private association of attorneys founded in 1887 certifies that its members are legally trained. Since 1948 the association has been given recognition to the extent that no one may call himself an attorney unless he belongs to the association.[403] The bar had previously been subject to regulation in Denmark and Norway, though not in Finland. To be a lawyer, one must be a Swedish citizen, twenty-five years old, and have passed an examination on the law. Admission is in the hands of a governing committee of the bar with appeal to the Supreme Court. This committee is also in charge of disciplinary control of the bar, as is the case in other Scandinavian countries except Norway where it is in the hands of the courts.

The discipline may consist of reminder, cautioning, and exclusion. The Swedish and Danish bars are now officially recognized associations, but the Norwegian association is still private in character.

Legal Service for Low-Income Groups

Sweden has most generous provisions for providing low-income groups legal service both in litigated and nonlitigated matters.[404] The problem is dealt with in two ways: the Free Legal Proceedings Act of 1919 and the Public Institutes for Legal Assistance.

The Free Legal Proceedings Act of 1919 authorizes the courts to exempt a party from all the costs of litigation in both civil and criminal cases. This includes even the costs of serving process, of witness fees, and of executing judgments. Moreover the court may order that the cost of attorney's fees be paid by the State. Only Norway makes similar provision. The party is permitted to select his own attorney in such cases. The same free procedure applies to appeals, but if the appellant loses out the State will not pay his attorney's fees. The provision relieving litigants of costs and expenses is the more important as the bulk of litigation is handled by the Public Institutes for Legal Assistance. But in rural areas the provision for payment of attorney's fees is valuable as often no Public Institute for Legal Assistance is available. It should be noted that in about one-third of the cases conducted by the Public Institutes the litigants are not relieved of the costs and expenses of trial. Unlike most European laws the Swedish law does not require the court to make a preliminary inquiry into the substantive merits of the applicant's claim for relief.

The Public Institutes for Legal Assistance differ from the American legal aid societies in that they are governmental undertakings. Expenses are paid by the State and the municipalities. They are under the general jurisdiction of the Ministry of Justice. Each is managed by a board of directors, the chairman and vice-chairman being appointed by the governor of the county, and the other members by the municipalities. In turn, each board selects as its manager a trained lawyer, who, in turn, selects his legal staff. In 1938 five Swedish cities had such institutes. In the second place, unlike the American legal aid societies, the Swedish institutes are not limited to indigents. For example, in Stockholm apparently one-half the population might use them. Consequently, in contrast to our legal aid societies, the Swedish institutes have much larger and better paid staffs, handle more cases, are better financed, have larger incomes, have a much wider clientele including white collar workers, and handle a greater variety of legal problems. Although Stockholm and Milwaukee are alike in population, the Stockholm Institute handled about six times as many matters as the Legal Aid Society in Milwaukee, tried about 21 times as many law-suits, and settled about 20 times as many law-suits. The Swedish institutes represent plaintiffs predominantly, while the American legal aid societies represent defendants. American legal aid societies seldom handle appeals or serve outside areas, as the Swedish institutes do.

The Swedish institutes are based on two principles: (1) that the responsibility of providing the needy with legal service is a responsibility of the government; (2) the legal needs of people with very small means are as serious as the needs of indigents, and should be provided for at least in cities. The Swedish system combines care of the indigent with care of low-income groups all within one single system. Such combination has several advantages. It is less expensive. It results in greater variety of legal work, hence a better staff may be secured. There is no discrimination as between indigent and the near poor. There is brought into one office a concentrated attention on the techniques of handling, and on the laws and procedure in relation to all the small matters involving ordinary people. "More than any other country, Sweden gives recognition to the need for preventive legal services."[405]

Legal Philosophy

During the medieval period of European history the "Laws of God" as found in the Mosaic Law and the biblical canons were regarded as a part of the national law. The Protestant Reformation in Sweden did not entirely eliminate this attitude in Sweden.[406] King Charles IX in his publication of Christopher's National Code, directed the judges to be guided in imposing sentences for several grave offenses "by the Law of God, which is put forth in Holy Writ, and which shall hereafter be included herein." A tendency arose to invoke the Roman law as a source of law. Both the Roman and Swedish systems were taught at the University of Uppsala, according to John Loccennius, author of the first scholarly work on the Civil Law of Sweden.[407] Charles Rålamb[408] and David Nehrmann,[409] the chief writers of their day, nevertheless stressed the fact that the Swedish law was the sole basis of their treatises. Rålamb praised the excellence of Roman law and its value for purposes of comparison and enlightenment, and referred favorably to natural law. Nehrmann regarded natural law as the chief source of law, and opened the door to the use of Roman law in formulating general principles. But when he dealt with specific subjects he treated them independently of the Roman law, thus materially assisting in paving the way for a strictly

Swedish code when the Code of 1734 was prepared. Two great foreign jurists had an intimate connection with Sweden. Grotius (1583-1645) was Swedish ambassador at Paris from 1635 to 1645. Pufendorff (1632-1694) was a professor at the University of Lund and also royal historiographer. Both of them propounded doctrines of natural law. The adoption of the Code of 1734 stimulated some commentary on Swedish law.

The Swedish literature gave less prominence to natural law than did the Danish and Norwegian. Its chief advocate was Johan Holmhergsson.[410] On the other hand, critics of natural law had great influence on the attempts at codification resumed after 1811. A strongly idealistic spirit gained wide acceptance upon its introduction by C. J. Boström (1799-1866), the most widely known Swedish philosopher.[411] Other nineteenth-century writers were Schrevelius,[412] H. L. Rydin,[413] and Th. Rabenius.[414]

A distinguished student of Scandinavian history and culture has stated: "The Scandinavian countries have produced almost no philosophers of first rank. If the Swedish Boström and the Danish Kierkegaard be admitted to the great company, the list is exhausted."[415] Sweden was less affected by the Hegelian system than Denmark and Norway, as she was developing an independent, national, speculative philosophy of her own. As developed by Boström this philosophy was independent of science and psychology. Thought, or more precisely, personality alone has genuine reality. This system gave full respect to history and tradition, particularly in ideals and law. Boström was professor of practical philosophy at Uppsala from 1840 to 1866. He was influential until the twentieth century. He seems to have laid too much stress on the reality of spirit and the unreality of matter. Unlike two other Swedes, Benjamin Höjer (1767-1812) and Erik Geijer (1783-1847),[416] he refused to concede any evolution in the absolute. Since the finite represents imperfection, the sciences of the finite can make no contribution to philosophy. Boström's system is erected on an a priori basis. This of course excluded scientific psychology. This phase of his system was doubtless derived in part from Hegel, but his system was more flexible than that of Hegel.[417]

Professors Vilhelm Lundstedt of the University of Uppsala and Karl Olivecrona of the University of Lund are the outstanding followers of the Swedish philosopher, Axel Hägerstrom.[418] Their views are largely joined in by the well known Alf Ross of the University of Copenhagen Law School. They bear a close relation to American Legal Realism. They are disposed to reject conventional legal theory as fictitious. They have perhaps made a fetish of analyzing the realities of law "as fact." According to Professor Lundstedt, Karl Olivecrona "has no superior in the Scandinavian countries in the field of legal philosophy."[419]

Legal History

Scholarly and scientific writing on legal history began in Sweden before it did in Denmark and Norway.[420] It commenced with the publication of the earlier laws and the establishment of professorships of law at the University of Uppsala in the seventeenth century. One of those professors appointed by Gustavus Adolphus was Johan O. Stiernhöök (1596-1675) who wrote a classic on the origin of the Swedish law.[421] Karl Lundius concluded that the ancient laws came from Zamolxis, the liberated slave of Pythagoras.[422] Johan Locennius was one of the foremost early authorities on Germanic legal institutions.[423]

The transition to critical, systematic, and scientific legal history is represented by the work of C. J. Schlyter of the University of Lund.[424] Other notable writers of the nineteenth century are: Schrevelius,[425] S. D. R. K. Olivecrona,[426] Hans Järta,[427] Chr. Naumann,[428] and J. J. Nordstrom.[429] Wilhelm Uppström is the author of an invaluable history of Swedish civil procedure.[430] Ernst Kallenberg published from 1917 to 1939 a three thousand page study of Swedish civil procedure with much historical material.[431]

Professor J. E. Almquist published in 1946 a history of Swedish legal literature.[432] It contains biographical references to forty-five authors with discussion of their most important writings. Professor Lagerroth published in 1947 a comparative study of the development of Swedish law.[433]

NOTES—CHAPTER VI—SWEDISH LAW

1. *The Immigration and Naturalization Systems of the United States*, 1950 81st Cong., 2d Session, Senate Report No. 1515, p. 128. See also Adolph Benson and Naboth Hedin, *Americans from Sweden*.

2. Franklin D. Scott, *The United States and Scandinavia*, p. 70 (1950).

3. Ragnar Svanström and Carl Palmstierna, *A short History of Sweden* (1934); Carl Hallendorff and Adolf Schück, *History of Sweden*, p. 8 (1929); Andrew A. Stomberg, *A History of Sweden*, pp. 56, 63 (1931).

4. Carl Hallendorff and Adolf Schück, *op. cit.*, p. 11 (1929).

5. Andrew A. Stomberg, *op. cit.*, p. 65 (1931). "As an undivided whole, the Kingdom of Sweden is at least 1,200 years old, being one of the oldest in Europe." Maxwell Fraser, *In Praise of Sweden*, p. 10 (1939).

6. Sigrid Undset, *Sigurd and His Brave Companions*, p. V (1943).

7. William L. Langer, *An Encyclopedia of World History*, p. 203 (1948), See also listing of the Swedish kings in Gordon Young, *The Viking Lands* p. 154 (1949). It has been suggested that consolidation into one kingdom began about 800 A.D. Ben A. Arneson, *The Democratic Monarchies Of Scandinavia*, p. 40 (2d ed., 1949).

8. S. M. Toyne, *The Scandinavians in History*, p. 40 (1948); Carl Hallendorff and Adolf Schück, *op. cit.*, pp. 9-12 (1929); Andrew A. Stomberg, *op. cit.*, pp. 61-62 (1931).

9. William L. Langer, *op. cit.*, p. 203 (1948); Andrew A. Stomberg, *op. cit.*, pp. 65-76 (1931).

10. Knut Gjerset, History of the Norwegian People, I, 31 (1927). The first account of the old Yngling dynasty was given about 850 by the Norwegian scald Tjoddv of Hvin in Ynglingatal. There is a fuller account by the Icelander Snorre Sturlason in Heimskringla about four centuries later.

11. Ragnar Svanström and Carl Palmstierna, op. cit., pp. 9-10 (1934); Carl Hallendorff and Adolf Schück, op. cit., pp. 12-13 (1929).

12. Andrew A. Stomberg, op. cit., pp. 106-108 (1931); S. M. Toyne, op. cit., p. 21 (1948); Konrad von Maurer, "Zur Geschichte Schwedens und Norwegens," 4th ed. (1888) of Baedeker, Schweden und Norwegen, pp. LI at LII-LIII. See maps in Carl Hallendorff and Adolf Schück, op. cit., p. 32 (1929).

13. Knut Gjerset, op. cit., I, 120-21 (1927). Many Norwegians opposed to Harald's unification moved to Jämtland. Hjalmar H. Boyesen, History of Norway, pp. 57-58, 65 (1900).

14. Ragnar Svanström and Carl Palmstierna, op. cit., pp. 16-18 (1934); Andrew A. Stomberg, op. cit., pp. 93-105 (1931); W. L. R. T. Thomsen, The Relations Between Ancient Russia and Scandinavia and the Origin of the Russian State.

15. Pares, History of Russia.

16. Jaroslav was married to a daughter of the King of Sweden, and was a brother-in-law of King Olaf of Norway.

17. Carl Hallendorff and Adolf Schück, op. cit., p. 23 (1929).

18. Knut Gjerset, History of Iceland, pp. 8-10, (1925); Andrew A. Stomberg, op. cit., p. 89 (1931).

19. Ragnar Svanström and Carl Palmstierna, op. cit., p. 11 (1934).

20. Ragnar Svanström and Carl Palmstierna, op. cit., pp. 10-16 (1934); Andrew A. Stomberg, A History of Sweden, pp. 79-80, 90-93 (1931); "The Treasure of Sutton Hoo," Life, p. 82 (July 16, 1951).

21. Knut Gjerset, op. cit., I, 166 (1927).

22. Karen Larsen, A History of Norway p. 115 (1948); Hjalmar H. Boyesen, op. cit., pp. 194, 198 (1900).

23. Hjalmar H. Boyesen, op. cit., pp. 293, 300 (1900); Knut Gjerset, op. cit., I, 320-21 (1927).

24. For a complete list of the kings of Sweden see Carl Hallendorff and Adolf Schück, op. cit., pp. 437-38 (1929).

25. Carl Hallendorff and Adolf Schück, op. cit., pp. 22-23 (1929); Ragnar Svanström and Carl Palmstierna, op. cit., pp. 19-20 (1934); Paul Sinding, History of Scandinavia p. 60 (1858).

26. Andrew A. Stomberg, op. cit., pp. 139-40 (1931).

27. Knut Gjerset, op. cit., I, 194-97, 243-44 (1927).

28. Ragnar Svanström and Carl Palmstierna, op. cit., p. 13 (1934); Paul Sinding, op cit., p. 68 (1858).

29. Hjalmar H. Boyesen, op. cit., pp. 197-98 (1900); Knut Gjerset, op. cit., I, 252-54 (1927).

30. Ragnar Svanström and Carl Palmstierna, op. cit., p. 21 (1934); Knut Gjerset, op. cit., I, 261-62 (1927); Paul Sinding, op. cit., pp. 71-72 (1858).

31. Paul Sinding, op cit., p. 75 (1858).

32. Hjalmar H. Boyesen, op. cit., pp. 267-68 (1900).

33. Knut Gjerset, op. cit., I, 287 (1927).

34. Carl Hallendorff and Adolf Schück, op. cit., p. 29 (1929).

35. Karen Larsen, op. cit., p. 115 (1948); Hjalmar H. Boyesen, op. cit., p. 288 (1900); Knut Gjerset, op. cit., I, 305 (1927).

36. Knut Gjerset, op. cit., I, 320-21 (1927).

37. Hjalmar H. Boyesen, op. cit., p. 301 (1900).

38. Ibid., p. 312 (1900).

39. Carl Hallendorff and Adolf Schück, op. cit., p. 34 (1929).

40. Andrew A. Stomberg, op. cit., p. 146 (1931).

41. Knut Gjerset, op. cit., I, 368, 375 (1927).

42. *Ibid.*, I, 398, 404-05 (1927).
43. Karen Larsen, *op. cit.*, p. 143 (1948).
44. Carl Hallendorff and Adolf Schück, *op. cit.*, p. 40 (1929); Andrew A. Stomberg, *op. cit.*, pp. 148-49 (1931).
45. Karen Larsen, *op. cit.*, p. 172 (1948); Hjalmar H. Boyesen, *op. cit.*, pp. 412, 416 (1900); Knut Gjerset, *op. cit.*, I, 431 (1927).
46. Carl Hallendorff and Adolf Schück, *op. cit.*, pp. 50-51 (1929); Andrew A. Stomberg, *op. cit.*, pp. 150-52 (1931).
47. Ragnar Svanström and Carl Palmstierna, *op. cit.*, pp. 24-25, 28-29, 31-32 (1934).
48. Paul Sinding, *op. cit.*, pp. 119-20 (1858).
49. Hjalmar H. Boyesen, *op. cit.*, p. 449 (1900).
50. *Ibid.*, p. 455 (1900).
51. S. M. Toyne, *op. cit.*, pp. 57-58 (1948).
52. Carl Hallendorff and Adolf Schück, *op. cit.*, p. 55 (1929); Ragnar Svanström and Carl Palmstierna, *op. cit.*, pp. 34-35 (1934).
53. Karen Larsen, *op. cit.*, pp. 174-75 (1948).
54. Paul Sinding, *op. cit.*, pp. 123-24 (1858).
55. Hjalmar H. Boyesen, *op. cit.*, p. 459 (1900).
56. Knut Gjerset, *op. cit.*, II, 4-29 (1927); Ragnar Svanström and Carl Palmstierna, *op. cit.*, pp. 36-42 (1934); Carl Hallendorff and Adolf Schück, *op. cit.*, pp. 60-70 (1929); Andrew A. Stomberg *op. cit.*, pp. 155-77 (1931).
57. Fletcher Pratt, *The Third King*, p. 56 (1950).
58. *Ibid.*, p. 268 (1950).
59. Knut Gjerset, *op. cit.*, II, 7 (1927).
60. Fletcher Pratt, *op. cit.*, p. 203 (1950).
61. Knut Gjerset, *op. cit.*, II, 15 (1927).
62. *Ibid.*, *op. cit.*, II, 16-17 (1927).
63. Fletcher Pratt, *op. cit.*, pp. 228-32, 238-49 (1950).
64. Karen Larsen, *op. cit.*, pp. 195-96 (1948).
65. Knut Gjerset, *op. cit.*, II, 18 (1927). The interrelationships of the Scandinavian rulers from 1263 to 1533 may be seen in the table in William Langer, *op cit.*, p. 311 (1948).
66. Fletcher Pratt, *op. cit.*, pp. 273-83 (1950).
67. *Ibid.*, pp. 268-69 (1950).
68. Karen Larsen, *op. cit.*, pp. 196-97 (1948); Hjalmar H. Boyesen, *op. cit.*, pp. 464-65 (1900).
69. Carl Hallendorf and Adolf Schück, *op. cit.*, p. 169 (1931).
70. Andrew A. Stomberg, *op. cit.*, p. 169 (1931).
71. Knut Gjerset, *op. cit.*, II, 19 (1927).
72. Carl Hallendorf and Adolf Schück, *op. cit.*, pp. 70-73 (1929); Andrew A. Stomberg, *op. cit.*, pp. 164-68 (1931); Ragnar Svanström and Carl Palmstierna, *op. cit.*, pp. 42-45 (1934); Paul Sinding, *op. cit.*, pp. 143-46 (1858); Karen Larsen, *op. cit.*, pp. 208-10 (1948).
73. Knut Gjerset, *op. cit.*, II, 34 (1927).
74. On the Period of Union see Ragnar Svanström and Carl Palmstierna, *op. cit.*, pp. 45-73 (1934); Carl Hallendorff and Adolf Schück, *op. cit.*, pp. 74-109 (1929); Andrew A. Stomberg, *op. cit.*, pp. 178-237 (1931).
75. Ragnar Svanström and Carl Palmstierna, *op. cit.*, pp. 48-49 (1934).
76. S. M. Toyne, *op. cit.*, p. 80 (1948).
77. Knut Gjerset, *op. cit.*, II, 35-36 (1927).
78. Ragnar Svanström and Carl Palmstierna, *op cit.*, p. 48 (1934).
79. Knut Gjerset, *op. cit.*, II, 43-44 (1927).
80. Andrew A. Stomberg, *op. cit.*, pp. 185-88 (1931); Ragnar Svanström and Carl Palmstierna, *op. cit.*, pp. 52-56 (1934); Paul Sinding, *op. cit.*, pp. 155-58 (1858); S. M. Toyne, *op. cit.*, pp. 85-88 (1948).

81. Ragnar Svanström and Carl Palmstierna, *op. cit.*, pp. 56-58 (1934); Paul Sinding, *op. cit.*, pp. 156-60 (1858).

82. Knut Gjerset, *op. cit.*, II, 47-50 (1927).

83. J. E. Sars, *Udsigt over den Norske Historie*, III, 128 (Oslo, 1874-1877).

84. Paul Sinding, *op. cit.*, pp. 159-60 (1858).

85. Karen Larsen, *op. cit.*, p. 218 (1948); S. M. Toyne, *op. cit.*, p. 90 (1948); Paul Sinding, *op. cit.*, pp. 166-67 (1858); Knut Gjerset, *op. cit.*, II, 67-72 (1927); Carl Hallendorff and Adolf Schück, *op. cit.*, pp. 89-90 (1929); Andrew A. Stomberg, *op. cit.*, pp. 193-94 (1931).

86. Andrew A. Stomberg, *op. cit.*, p. 200 (1931); Knut Gjerset, *op. cit.*, II, 77-80 (1927); Karen Larsen, *op. cit.*, pp. 221-22 (1948).

87. Andrew A. Stomberg, *op. cit.*, p. 201 (1913); S. M. Toyne, *op. cit.*, pp. 90-91 (1948).

88. Ragnar Svanström and Carl Palmstierna, *op. cit.*, pp. 67-70 (1934); Andrew A. Stomberg, *op. cit.*, pp. 212-14 (1931).

89. On the career of Gustaf Vasa see Ragnar Svanström and Carl Palmstierna, *op. cit.*, pp. 71-89 (1934); Carl Hallendorff and Adolf Schück, *op. cit.*, pp. 110-63 (1929); Andrew A. Stomberg, *op. cit.*, pp. 223-84 (1931). For a complete listing of the house of Vasa (1523-1818) see William L. Langer, *op. cit.*, p. 470 (1948).

90. Carl Hallendorff and Adolf Schück, *op. cit.*, p. 121 (1929); Karen Larsen, *op. cit.*, p. 228 (1948); Jon Stefansson, *Denmark and Sweden with Iceland and Finland*, p. 204 (1917).

91. Carl Hallendorff and Adolf Schück, *op. cit.*, p. 119 (1929).

92. S. M. Toyne, *op. cit.*, pp. 109, 124, (1948); Ragnar Svanström and Carl Palmstierna, *op. cit.*, p. 88 (1934); Carl Hallendorff and Adolf Schück, *op. cit.*, pp. 144-46 (1931).

93. In 1557 England sought in vain to negotiate a commercial treaty with Sweden. Ragnar Svanström and Carl Palmstierna, *op. cit.*, p. 86 (1934).

94. John Danstrup, *History of Denmark*, pp. 54-55 (1949).

95. S. M. Toyne, *op. cit.*, pp. 111-13 (1948); Jon Stefansson, *op. cit.*, pp. 69-72 (1917); Karen Larsen, *op. cit.*, pp. 249-51 (1948); Ragnar Svanström and Carl Palmstierna, *op. cit.*, pp. 89-99 (1934); Carl Hallendorff and Adolf Schück, *op. cit.*, pp. 168-80 (1929); Andrew A. Stomberg, *op. cit.*, pp. 291-93, 297-98 (1931).

96. Knut Gjerset, *op. cit.*, II, 149-55 (1927).

97. Jon Stefansson, *op. cit.*, pp. 235-41 (1917); Carl Hallendorff and Adolf Schück, *op. cit.*, pp. 180-81 (1929).

98. Ragnar Svanström and Carl Palmstierna, *op. cit.*, p. 97 (1934).

99. Jon Stefansson, *op. cit.*, pp. 243-45 (1917); Karen Larsen, *op. cit.*, p. 283 (1948); Ragnar Svanström and Carl Palmstierna, *op. cit.*, pp. 112-13 (1934); Carl Hallendorff and Adolf Schück, *op. cit.*, pp. 212-15 (1929); Andrew A. Stomberg, *op. cit.*, pp. 322-23 (1931).

100. John Danstrup, *op. cit.*, pp. 56-57 (1949).

101. Franklin D. Scott, *op. cit.*, p. 205 (1950).

102. Jon Stefansson, *op. cit.*, pp. 245-46 (1917); Ragnar Svanström and Carl Palmstierna, *op. cit.*, pp. 113-14 (1934); Andrew A. Stomberg, *op. cit.*, pp. 331-32 (1931).

103. Ragnar Svanström and Carl Palmstierna, *op. cit.*, pp. 122-23, 125 (1934); Andrew A. Stomberg, *op. cit.*, pp. 347, 350 (1931).

104. Jon Stefansson, *op. cit.*, pp. 250-69 (1917); Ragnar Svanström and Carl Palmstierna, *op. cit.*, pp. 123-32 (1934); Carl Hallendorff and Adolf Schück, *op. cit.*, pp. 236-48 (1929); Andrew A. Stomberg, *op. cit.*, pp. 344-66 (1931).

105. Andrew A. Stomberg, *op. cit.*, pp. 378-80 (1931); Ragnar Svanström and Carl Palmstierna, *op. cit.*, p. 140 (1934); Carl Hallendorff and Adolf Schück, *op. cit.*, p. 229 (1929); Amandus Johnson, *The Swedish Settlements on the Delaware* (1911); Justice Robert H. Jackson, "Swedish Contributions to Our Law," 15 Pa. Bar Assn. Q. 122 (1944).

106. Justice Robert H. Jackson, *op. cit.,* p. 122 (1944).
107. Henning Friis, *Scandinavia Between East and West,* p. 326 (1950).
108. On the war between 1632 and 1648 see Ragnar Svanström and Carl Palmstierna, *op. cit.,* pp. 132-42 (1934); Carl Hallendorff and Adolf Schück, *op. cit.,* pp. 250-57 (1929); Andrew A. Stomberg, *op. cit.,* pp. 367-91 (1931). During the war Sweden issued general interdictions of commerce, military advantage being regarded as more important than trade. Franklin D. Scott, *op. cit.,* p. 206 (1950).
109. Jon Stefansson, *op. cit.,* pp. 77-79 (1917); Knut Gjerset, *op. cit.,* II, 209-13 (1927); John Danstrup, *op. cit.,* pp. 57-58 (1949); Carl Hallendorff and Adolf Schück, *op. cit.,* pp. 255-57 (1929); Andrew A. Stomberg, *op. cit.,* pp. 383-87 (1931).
110. Karen Larsen, *op. cit.,* pp. 284-85 (1948); Northwestern Dalarna also had belonged to Norway up to this time. Maxwell Fraser, *op. cit.,* p. 195 (1939).
111. Andrew A. Stomberg, *op. cit.,* pp. 387-89 (1931); Ragnar Svanström and Carl Palmstierna, *op. cit.,* pp. 141-42 (1934); Jon Stefansson, *op. cit.,* pp. 274-75 (1917); S. M. Toyne, *op. cit.,* pp. 174-75 (1948).
112. Andrew A. Stomberg, *op. cit.,* p. 427 and map (1931).
113. Ragnar Svanström and Carl Palmstierna, *op. cit.,* p. 142 (1934).
114. Jon Stefansson, *op. cit.,* pp. 277-80 (1917); Knut Gjerset, *op. cit.,* pp. 220-23 (1927); John Danstrop, *op. cit.,* pp. 64-66 (1949); Carl Hallendorff and Adolf Schück, *op. cit.,* pp. 261-63 (1929); Andrew A. Stomberg, *op. cit.,* pp. 411-19 (1931).
115. Andrew A. Stomberg, *op. cit.,* pp. 419-23 (1931); Ragnar Svanström and Carl Palmstierna, *op. cit.,* pp. 159-60 (1934); Knut Gjerset, *History of the Norwegian People,* II, 224-28 (1927); Jon Stefansson, *op. cit.,* pp. 278-82 (1917).
116. Carl Hallendorff and Adolf Schück, *op. cit.,* pp. 263-64 (1929); John Danstrup, *op. cit.,* p. 67 (1949). For a map of Sweden in 1660 see S. M. Toyne, *op. cit.,* p. 182 (1948).
117. Andrew A. Stomberg, *op. cit.,* p. 435 (1931); Ragnar Svanström and Carl Palmstierna, *op. cit.,* p. 163 (1934).
118. Carl Hallendorff and Adolf Schück, *op. cit.,* pp. 279-80 (1929); Andrew A. Stomberg, *op. cit.,* pp. 441-47 (1931); Jon Stefansson, *op. cit.,* pp. 283-84 (1917); Knut Gjerset, *op. cit.,* pp. 253-61 (1927); John Danstrup, *op. cit.,* p. 70 (1949). In 1660 Denmark claimed that Halland under the 1645 treaty was held by Sweden as a pledge for thirty years only. Sweden so conceded, but in 1675 it became Swedish and has remained so since. S. M. Toyne, *op. cit.,* p. 180, n. 1 (1948).
119. Karen Larsen, *op. cit.,* pp. 292-93 (1948); Ragnar Svanström and Carl Palmstierna, *op. cit.,* p. 171 (1934); Andrew A. Stomberg, *op. cit.,* pp. 447-48 (1931).
120. Franklin D. Scott, *op. cit.,* p. 206 (1950).
121. Jon Stefansson, *op. cit.,* pp. 287-97 (1917); Karen Larsen, *op. cit.,* pp. 295-97 (1948); Ragnar Svanström and Carl Palmstierna, *op. cit.,* pp. 176-77 (1934); Carl Hallendorff and Adolf Schück, *op. cit.,* pp. 295-96 (1929); Andrew A. Stomberg, *op. cit.,* pp. 479-85 (1931).
122. John Danstrup, *op. cit.,* p. 73 (2d ed., 1949); Carl Hallendorff and Adolf Schück, *op. cit.,* p. 316 (1929).
123. There was a breach between Sweden and England from 1718 to 1720. B. J. Hovde, *The Scandinavian Countries, 1720-1865,* p. 30 (1948).
124. Jon Stefansson, *op. cit.,* pp. 299-301 (1917); Ragnar Svanström and Carl Palmstierna, *op. cit.,* pp. 214-22 (1934); Carl Hallendorff and Adolf Schück, *op. cit.,* pp. 328-30 (1929); Andrew A. Stomberg, *op. cit.,* pp. 533-35 (1931).
125. For a table of the Swedish kings and royal family from 1751 to the present time see William L. Langer, *op. cit.,* p. 700 (1948). For a table of the Holstein Gottorp line and its connections with Russia, Denmark and Sweden see S. M. Toyne, *op. cit.,* p. 217 (1948).
126. B. J. Hovde, *op. cit.,* p. 38 (1948). But a successful East India Company was founded in 1731, lasting until 1813.

127. Ragnar Svanström and Carl Palmstierna, op. cit., p. 224 (1934).
128. Knut Gjerset, op. cit., II, 344 (1927).
129. Jon Stefansson, op. cit., pp. 302-03 (1917); Ragnar Svanström and Carl Palmstierna, op. cit., p. 242 (1934); Carl Hallendorff and Adolf Schück, op. cit., p. 333 (1929); Andrew A. Stomberg, op. cit., p. 538 (1931).
130. Franklin D. Scott, op. cit., pp. 206-07 (1950).
131. Dagboksanteckningar förda vid Gustof III's Hof af Friherre Gustof Johan Ehrensvärd, II, 115 (Stockholm, 1878).
132. Ragnar Svanström and Carl Palmstierna, op. cit., p. 272 (1934).
133. Franklin D. Scott, op. cit., pp. 208-09 (1950); Andrew A. Stomberg, op. cit., p. 578 (1931); Ragnar Svanström and Carl Palmstierna, op. cit., pp. 265-66 (1934); John Danstrup, op. cit., p. 83 (1949).
134. Jon Stefansson, op. cit., pp. 315-18 (1917); Knut Gjerset, op. cit., II, 369-70 (1927); Ragnar Svanström and Carl Palmstierna, op. cit., pp. 276-81 (1934); Carl Hallendorff and Adolf Schück, op. cit., pp. 349-54 (1929); Andrew A. Stomberg, op. cit., pp. 584-85 (1931).
135. John Danstrup, op. cit., pp. 83, 86 (2d ed., 1949); Ragnar Svanström and Carl Palmstierna, op. cit., pp. 296, 301 (1934); Andrew A. Stomberg, op. cit., pp. 593, 598 (1931).
136. Franklin D. Scott, op. cit., pp. 209-10 (1950). Sweden approached the United States about acceding to the 1794 agreement without success. The Scandinavian nations were protesting against British activity, while the United States fought a naval war with France in 1798.
137. Jon Stefansson, op. cit., pp. 321-27 (1917); Ragnar Svanström and Carl Palmstierna, op. cit., p. 303 (1934); Carl Hallendorff and Adolf Schück, op. cit., p. 358 (1929); Andrew A. Stomberg, op. cit., p. 599 (1931).
138. Knut Gjerset, op. cit., II, 390-98 (1927); Karen Larsen, op. cit., pp. 366-67 (1948); Andrew A. Stomberg, op. cit., p. 600 (1931).
139. Andrew A. Stomberg, op. cit., pp. 600-11 (1931).
140. Andrew A. Stomberg, op. cit., p. 606 (1931); Knut Gjerset, op. cit., II, 394-95 (1927).
141. Knut Gjerset, op. cit., II, 406-46 (1927); Andrew A. Stomberg, op. cit., pp. 609-15, 627-30 (1931); Franklin D. Scott, op. cit., p. 211 (1950); Carl T. Sörenson, Bernadotte I. Norden, Eller Norges Adskillelse Fra Danmark Og Forening Med Sverige. Copenhagen, 3 vols. (1902).
142. Knut Gjerset, op. cit., II, 417-46 (1927); Karen Larsen, op. cit., pp. 373-95 (1948); Andrew A. Stomberg, op. cit., pp. 630-32 (1931).
143. Professor Hudson states that the Union was perhaps a real, rather than a personal, union. By real union is meant an arrangement under which two or more states form a single unit for purposes of international intercourse, but not for all purposes, whereas there is a personal union when there is merely a common head of state. Hudson, Cases on International Law, pp. 37-38 (3rd ed., 1951).
144. Andrew A. Stomberg, op. cit., p. 632 (1931).
145. France transferred the island to Sweden in 1783. Andrew A. Stomberg, op. cit., p. 581 (1931).
146. Franklin D. Scott, op. cit., p. 78 (1950).
147. Ragnar Svanström and Carl Palmstierna, op. cit., pp. 335-36 (1934); Jon Stefansson, op. cit., p. 334 (1917).
148. Franklin D. Scott, op. cit., p. 212 (1950).
149. Carl Hallendorff and Adolf Schück, op. cit., p. 376 (1929); Andrew M. Stomberg, op. cit., pp. 695-700 (1931).
150. Andrew A. Stomberg, op. cit., pp. 700-03 (1931); Knut Gjerset, op. cit., II, 528-29 (1927); Laurence D. Steefel, The Schleswig-Holstein Question, pp. 22-28, 62-70, 150-71, 252-53 (1932).
151. Franklin D. Scott, op. cit., p. 214 (1950).
152. Jon Stefansson, op. cit., pp. 330-43 (1917); Knut Gjerset, op. cit., II, 450-85

(1927); Hjalmar H. Boyesen, *op. cit.*, pp. 516-53 (1900); Karen Larsen, *op. cit.*, pp. 396-495 (1948); Ragnar Svanström and Carl Palmstierna, *op. cit.*, pp. 344-49 (1934); Carl Hallendorff and Adolf Schück, *op. cit.*, pp. 381-82 (1929); S. M. Toyne, *op. cit.*, pp. 279-84 (1948); Andrew A. Stomberg, *op. cit.*, pp. 703-05, 746-53 (1931).
153. Knut Gjerset, *op. cit.*, II, 534-44 (1927); Andrew A. Stomberg, *op. cit.*, pp. 746-47 (1931).
154. Knut Gjerset, *op. cit.*, II, 559-81 (1927).
155. Knut Gjerset, *op. cit.*, II, 582-84 (1927); Andrew A. Stomberg, *op. cit.*, pp. 751-53 (1931). For an arbitration over boundaries in 1909 between Norway and Sweden see the Grisbadarna Case, Scott, *Hague Court Reports*, pp. 122, 487; Hudson, *Cases on International Law*, pp. 258-62 (3rd ed., 1951).
156. Jackson, *op. cit.*, p. 125 (1944).
157. On Sweden and World War I see Franklin D. Scott, *op. cit.*, pp. 215-24 (1950). For an excellent discussion of Swedish foreign policy from 1914 to the present time see Brita S. Ahman in Henning Friis, *op. cit.*, pp. 255-305 (1950).
158. Henning Friis, *op. cit.*, pp. 262-63 (1950).
159. Ragnar Svanström and Carl Palmstierna, *op. cit.*, pp. 390-96 (1934).
160. Ragnar Svanström and Carl Palmstierna, *op. cit.*, pp. 374-82 (1934); Andrew A. Stomberg, *op. cit.*, pp. 780-84 (1931); Franklin D. Scott, *The United States and Scandinavia*, pp. 225-28 (1950); Louis B. Sohn, *Cases on World Law*, pp. 87-120 (1950); Henning Friis, *op. cit.*, pp. 257-65 (1950).
161. Norman J. Padelford, "The New Scandinavian Neutrality Rules," 32 *Am. J. Int. L.* 789 (1938).
162. Henning Friis, *op. cit.*, pp. 276-77 (1950); Norman J. Padelford and K. Gösta A. Anderson, "The Aaland Islands Question," 33 *Am. J. Int. L.* 465 (1939).
163. On Sweden and World War II see Franklin D. Scott, *op. cit.*, pp. 231-84 (1950); Henning Friis, *op. cit.*, pp. 277-86 (1950).
164. But at this stage Russia warned Germany that she would regard a German attack on Sweden with disfavor. Henning Friis, *op. cit.*, p. 279 (1950).
165. Franklin D. Scott, *op. cit.*, pp. 269-70 (1950).
166. *Ibid.*, p. 290.
167. *Ibid.*, pp. 183, 291; Henning Friis, *op. cit.*, pp. 295-96 (1950).
168. Louis B. Sohn, *op. cit.*, p. 174 (1950); Henning Friis, *op. cit.*, pp. 291-92 (1950).
169. Franklin D. Scott, *op. cit.*, pp. 301-13 (1950); Henning Friis, *op. cit.*, pp. 299-305, 322-24 (1950).
170. Henning Friis, *op. cit.*, p. 305 (1950); Ernest O. Hauser, "The World's Happiest King," *Saturday Evening Post*, p. 23, August 26, 1951.
171. *New York Times*, November 1, 1951.
172. "The Quarter's History—Sweden," 39 *Am. Scand. Rev.* 148, 149 (June 1951).
173. *New York Times*, February 21, 1951.
174. Emil Sandström, "Upphörandet av de blandade domstolarna i Egypten," 35 *Svensk Juristtidning* 304-06 (1950).
175. Manley O. Hudson, *The Permanent Court of International Justice*, p. 108 (1934).
176. *Ibid.*, p. 246 (1934).
177. *Ibid.*, p. 292 (1934).
178. *Ibid.*, pp. 292-93 (1934).
179. Manley O. Hudson, "The Sixteenth Year of the Permanent Court of International Justice," 32 *Am. J. Int. L.* 1, 11 (1938).
180. "First Session of the International Law Commission," 43 *Am. J. Int. L.* 758 (1949).
181. "Second Session of the International Law Commission," 45 *Am. J. Int. L.* 148, 149 (1951).
182. 44 *Am. J. Int. L.*, Supp. 105, 106 (Oct. 1950).

183. Ebbe Hertzberg in *A General Survey of Continental Legal History*, p. 533 (1912).

184. *Ibid.*, p. xli (1912).

185. *Ibid.*, pp. 535-37 (1912). See also Engelmann, *A History of Continental Civil Procedure*, pp. 203-08, 834-35 (1927); Carl Hallendorff and Adolf Schück, *op. cit.*, pp. 36-37 (1929).

186. Ebbe Hertzberg, *op. cit.*, pp. 538-39 (1912).

187. *Ibid.*, p. 539 (1912). For a brief account of Swedish law and government prior to 1319 see Konrad von Maurer, *op. cit.*, pp. LXIILXIV (4th ed., 1888).

188. Ebbe Hertzberg, *op. cit.*, p. 541 (1912); Ragnar Svanström and Carl Palmstierna, *op. cit.*, pp. 23-24 (1934); Carl Hallendorff and Adolf Schück, *op. cit.*, pp. 24-25, 36-39 (1929). That the king early exercised judicial powers see Engelmann, *op. cit.*, pp. 204-10 (1927).

189. Ebbe Hertzberg, *op. cit.*, pp. 545-46 (1912); Carl Hallendorff and Adolf Schück, *op. cit.*, p. 37 (1929).

190. Ebbe Hertzberg, *op. cit.*, pp. 738-41 (1912). The Provincial Codes, City Codes and Codes of the Realm up to 1442 are listed by Engelmann, *op. cit.*, p. 204, n. 4 (1927).

191. Ragnar Svanström and Carl Palmstierna, *op. cit.*, pp. 29-30 (1934); Carl Hallendorff and Adolf Schück, *op. cit.*, pp. 48-55 (1929).

192. On slavery in Sweden see Andrew A. Stomberg, *op. cit.*, pp. 110-11, 158 (1931). "Serfs are unknown in Swedish history." Justice Robert H. Jackson, *op. cit.*, p. 125 (1944).

193. Ragnar Svanström and Carl Palmstierna, *op. cit.*, pp. 32-34 (1934); Carl Hallendorff and Adolf Schück, *op. cit.*, pp. 52-55 (1929); Andrew A. Stomberg, *op. cit.*, pp. 152-53 (1931).

194. Hertzberg, *op. cit.*, pp. 553-56 (1912).

195. Carl Hallendorff and Adolf Schück, *op. cit.*, pp. 64-66 (1929); Frederik Lagerroth, "Magnus Erikssons Landslag. Et 600 Årsminne," 32 *Svensk Juristtidning* 641 (1947). Professor Lagerroth calls this law Sweden's Magna Carta. *Ibid.*, 647 (1947).

196. Ebbe Hertzberg, *op. cit.*, pp. 555-56 (1912).

197. *Ibid.*, p. 564 (1912).

198. *Ibid.*, p. 561 (1912).

199. For general discussion of the 1734 Code see also Wilhelm Chydenius, "The Swedish Lawbook of 1734: An Early German Codification," 20 *L. Q. Rev.* 377 (1904); N. Gärde, "Lagrevisionen," 35 *Svensk Juristtidning*, 1-9 (1950).

200. Ebbe Hertzberg, *op. cit.*, p. 568 (1912).

201. *Ibid.*, p. 568 (1912).

202. See T. Leivestad, "Custom as a Type of Law in Norway," 54 *L. Q. Rev.* 95, 266; Note 64 *Harv. L. Rev.* 1181 (1951).

203. Ebbe Hertzberg, *op. cit.*, pp. 569-70 (1912).

204. Ben A. Arneson, *op. cit.*, p. 40 (1949).

205. "The Swedish Parliament is the fourth oldest in the world, with the English Parliament third, the Manx House of Keys second, and the Icelandic Alting first." Maxwell Fraser, *op. cit.*, p. 12 (1939).

206. Jon Stefansson, *op. cit.*, pp. 247-48 (1917); Andrew A. Stomberg, *A History of Sweden*, pp. 334-36 (1931).

207. Ragnar Svanström and Carl Palmstierna, *op. cit.*, pp. 167-71 (1934); Andrew A. Stomberg, *op. cit.*, pp. 459-72 (1931).

208. Ragnar Svanström and Carl Palmstierna, *op. cit.*, pp. 189-253 (1934); B. J. Hovde, *op. cit.*, pp. 180-91 (1948).

209. Ragnar Svanström and Carl Palmstierna, *op. cit.*, p. 247 (1934).

210. Ragnar Svanström and Carl Palmstierna, *op. cit.*, pp. 253-316 (1934); Andrew A. Stomberg, *op. cit.*, pp. 563-615 (1934); B. J. Hovde, *op. cit.*, pp. 189-93, 207-28 (1948).

211. Ragnar Svanström and Carl Palmstierna, *op. cit.*, pp. 316-20 (1934).

212. Hans Järta, a young lawyer, was one of the chief drafters. Andrew A. Stomberg, *op. cit.*, pp. 607-08 (1931). Because the international situation required quick formulation the Constitution was not greatly influenced by that of the United States. Henning Friis, *op. cit.*, p. 334 (1950); B. J. Hovde, *op. cit.*, pp. 214-19 (1948).

213. Arts. 16, 85, and 114.

214. Freedom of the press was first provided in 1766. The organic law of 1812 prevents all previous restraint upon the printed word. There is liability for damages or at criminal law for slanderous, blasphemous, or indecent publications. Jury trial by nine jurors is permitted, the only instance of jury trial in Sweden. It takes six jurors to convict.

215. Ben A. Arneson, *op. cit.*, p. 51 (2d ed., 1949).

216. Arts. 4, 5, 6, and 7.

217. Art. 17.

218. Arts. 18 and 19.

219. Art. 21

220. Arts. 81 and 82.

221. Carl Hallendorff and Adolf Schück, *op. cit.*, pp. 374-75 (1929); Andrew A. Stomberg, *op. cit.*, pp. 662-66 (1931); B. J. Hovde, *op. cit.*, pp. 522-38 (1948).

222. "The Quarter's History—Sweden," 38 *Am. Scand. Rev.* 382, 385 (1950).

223. Ragnar Svanström and Carl Palmstierna, *op. cit.*, p. 410 (1934).

224. Hans Hedtoft, "Centenary of the Danish Constitution," Danish Foreign Office Journal, No. 1, p. 1 (1949). See also Ragnar Svanström and Carl Palmstierna, *op. cit.*, pp. 412-21 (1934); R. C. Spencer, "Party Government and the Swedish Riksdag," 39 *Am. Pol. Sc. Rev.* 437, 445 (1945); Henning Friis, *op. cit.*, p. 4 (1950).

225. As to membership and organization of the Riksdag see Ben A. Arneson, *op. cit.*, pp. 99-104 (2d ed., 1949).

226. Art. 53.

227. Henning Friis, *op. cit.*, pp. 11-12 (1950).

228. Lloyd K. Garrison, "Legal Service for Low Income Groups in Sweden," 26 A. B. A. J. 292, 296, n. 58 (1940).

229. Arts. 105-07.

230. Arts. 17, 22 (1), 23, 24.

231. Arts. 18, 19, 22 (2), 23, 25, 26.

232. Arts. 101, 102.

233. See Ben A. Arneson, *op. cit.*, pp. 166-77 (1949). For the history of the Swedish Courts see Engelmann, *A History of Continental Civil Procedure*, pp. 203-10, 225-32, 834-43, 864-65, 868-69 (1927).

234. Arts. 17, 18, 28, 31 and 36.

235. Engelmann, *op. cit.*, pp. 843, 864-65, 868-71 (1927).

236. A constitutional amendment of 1909 abolished the right of the King to participate in the hearing and to have two votes in deciding the case. *Ibid.*, p. 868 (1927).

237. For the history of the courts of appeal see *ibid.* pp. 850-52, 858-63, 867-71 (1927).

238. In the cities a bench of judges sits. Robert W. Millar in David Dudley Field, *Centenary Essays*, pp. 121-22 (1949).

239. Owing to the historic Swedish influence the *nämnd* is also used in Finland. *Ibid.*, p. 122, n. 2 (1949).

240. For discussion of local government in Sweden see Ben A. Arneson, *op. cit.*, pp. 200-16 (2d ed., 1949); B. J. Hovde, *op. cit.*, pp. 571-72, 718-36 (1948); Per Edwin Skold, *Kommunalkunskap*; Skold-Vanner, *Sveriges Kommunallagar.*

241. S. M. Toyne, *op. cit.*, pp. 24-25, 44-50 (1948); Sinding, *History of Scandinavia*, p. 54 (1858); Ragnar Svanström and Carl Palmstierna, *op. cit.*, pp. 18-19, 21-28 (1934); Carl Hallendorff and Adolf Schück, *op. cit.*, pp. 26-29 (1929).

242. Carl Hallendorff and Adolf Schück, *op. cit.*, pp. 40-44 (1929).

243. However in 1378 the Order of St. Bridget which spread all over Europe was

founded in honor of a Swedish saint of the fourteenth century. Ragnar Svanström and Carl Palmstierna, op. cit., pp. 39-42 (1934).

244. King Magnus (1319-1365) who had great financial difficulties tried to abolish the privileges of the church especially as to tax exemptions. Ragnar Svanström and Carl Palmstierna, op. cit., pp. 38, 40 (1934). He was excommunicated in 1355 for failure to pay his debts.

245. Jon Stefansson, op. cit., pp. 205-18 (1917); Ragnar Svanström and Carl Palmstierna, op. cit., pp. 81-85 (1934); Carl Hallendorff and Adolf Schück, op. cit., pp. 127-40 (1929); Andrew A. Stomberg, op. cit., pp. 238-59 (1931).

246. Jon Stefansson, op. cit., pp. 234-41 (1917); Ragnar Svanström and Carl Palmstierna, op. cit., pp. 99-104 (1934); Carl Hallendorff and Adolf Schück, op. cit., pp. 181-87 (1929); Andrew A. Stomberg, op. cit., pp. 299-305 (1931).

247. Andrew A. Stomberg, op. cit., pp. 309-13 (1931).

248. Carl Hallendorff and Adolf Schück, op. cit., pp. 226-27 (1929).

249. Ibid., pp. 228-29 (1929).

250. B. J. Hovde, op. cit., p. 94 (1948).

251. Ibid., p. 98 (1948).

252. Ragnar Svanström and Carl Palmstierna, op. cit., p. 205 (1934).

253. Andrew A. Stomberg, op. cit., pp. 527-28 (1931).

254. Ragnar Svanström and Carl Palmstierna, op. cit., p. 271 (1934); Andrew A. Stomberg, op. cit., pp. 571-72 (1931).

255. B. J. Hovde, op. cit., p. 43 (1948).

256. Ibid., p. 696 (1948).

257. Ibid., pp. 325-26 (1948).

258. Ragnar Svanström and Carl Palmstierna, op. cit., pp. 401-02 (1934); Andrew A. Stomberg, op. cit., pp. 655 (1931); B. J. Hovde, op. cit., p. 660 (1948).

259. B. J. Hovde, op. cit., p. 332 (1948).

260. Ibid., p. 346 (1948).

261. Ben A. Arneson, op. cit., p. 5 (2d ed., 1949). For a discussion of the present status of the Lutheran Church in Sweden see Carl C. Rasmussen, What About Scandinavia? (1948).

262. Franklin D. Scott, op. cit., pp. 44-45 (1950).

263. Nordisk Tidende, March 22, 1951.

264. E. Ingleson, "The Church in Sweden," Catholic World, pp. 736-37 (March 1938); Hugh K. Wolf, "Scandinavian Catholicism," Catholic Digest, pp. 17-21 (April 1946).

265. For general discussion of education in Sweden see B. J. Hovde, op. cit., pp. 589-616 (1948); Per G. Stensland, "Adult Education," in Henning Friis, op. cit., pp. 225-53 (1950); Ragnar Lund, Swedish Adult Education (1930); Gunnar Hirdman, Adult Education in Sweden (1947).

266. B. J. Hovde, op. cit., pp. 592-93 (1948).

267. Henning Friis, op. cit., p. 228 (1950). Financial support from the government came earlier in Sweden than in Denmark, hence the Swedish schools had greater stability. Ibid., 236, 239; Ragnar Lund, "Adult Education in Sweden," 197 The Annals of the American Academy 232, 235-36 (May 1938).

268. Ibid., 232, 233-34 (1938).

269. Henning Friis, op. cit., pp. 244-52 (1950).

270. Ibid., p. 251 (1950).

271. "The Quarter's History—Sweden," 38 Am. Scand. Rev. 273-74 (Sept. 1950).

272. Konrad von Maurer, op. cit., p. LXIX (4th ed., 1888); Andrew A. Stomberg, op. cit., pp. 109-10 (1931).

273. Carl Hallendorff and Adolf Schück, op. cit., p. 45 (1929).

274. Andrew A. Stomberg, op. cit., pp. 206, 239 (1931).

275. B. J. Hovde, op. cit., p. 62 (1948).

276. Ibid., p. 61 (1948).

277. Ragnar Svanström and Carl Palmstierna, *op. cit.*, pp. 236, 300 (1934); Andrew A. Stomberg, *op. cit.*, pp. 545, 571 (1931); B. J. Hovde, *op. cit.*, pp. 64-65, 286-87 (1948).

278. For a valuable discussion of the status of the peasant from 1720 to 1865 see *Ibid.*, pp. 59-88, 276-302 (1948).

279. Wohlin, *Den Svenska Jordstyckningspolitiken*, pp. 707-13.

280. B. J. Hovde, *op. cit.*, p. 183 (1948).

281. *Ibid.*, p. 280; E. J. Schütz, *Om Skifte af Jord i Sverige*, p. 115 et. seq. (Stockholm, 1890).

282. B. J. Hovde, *op. cit.*, p. 282 (1948).

283. *Ibid.*, p. 284 (1948).

284. *Ibid.*, p. 285 (1948).

285. Ben A. Arneson, *op. cit.*, pp. 257-58 (2d ed., 1949); Ernst Michanek, *Socialboken*, pp. 269-71 (1949).

286. L. E. Stemann in Von Bar, *A History of Continental Criminal Law*, 120-21 (1916). The substantive criminal law up to 1500 is discussed at 119-41, but with chief emphasis on the Danish law. According to Wigmore there is no Swedish work on the subject. *Ibid.*, p. XXXII (1916).

287. *Ibid.*, p. 124 (1916).

288. *Ibid.*, p. 125 (1916).

289. *Ibid.*, p. 134 (1916).

290. *Ibid.*, p. 139 (1916).

291. J. L. A. Kolderup-Rosenvinge in Von Bar, *op. cit.*, pp. 295-96 (1916).

292. B. J. Hovde, *op. cit.*, p. 131 (1948).

293. Leon Radzinowicz, *A History of English Criminal Law*, pp. 287-90 (1948); K. D. Olivecrona, *De La Peine de Mort*, p. 59 (2d ed., 1893).

294. B. J. Hovde, *op. cit.*, pp. 699-701 (1948).

295. That Swedish laws were now relatively lenient see William Coxe, *Account of the Prisons and Hospitals in Russia, Sweden and Denmark*, pp. 31-32 (1781).

296. Franklin D. Scott, *op. cit.*, p. 81 (1950); B. J. Hovde, *op. cit.*, pp. 702-03 (1948). Modernization of the police system in Stockholm occurred in 1850. *Ibid.*, p. 722 (1948).

297. Thorsten Sellin, "Sweden's Substitute for the Juvenile Court," 261 *The Annals of the American Academy* 137, 147 (January 1949).

298. L. Von Thot in Von Bar, *op. cit.*, pp. 368-69 (1916); B. J. Hovde, *op. cit.*, pp. 704-05 (1948).

299. Axel Teisen, "Scandinavia: Legislation," 12 A. B. A. J. 268, 271 (1926).

300. Thorsten Sellin, *Recent Penal Legislation in Sweden*. Stockholm, 1947.

301. Cicely M. Craven, "The Child Welfare Boards in Sweden," 41 *J. Crim. L.* 344 (1950); Thorsten Sellin, "Sweden's Substitute for the Juvenile Court," *Annals of the American Academy of Political Science*, pp. 137-49 (June 1949); Thorsten Sellin, "The Treatment of Offenders in Sweden," *Federal Probation*, XII, No. 2, p. 14 (June 1948).

302. Under the 1734 Code children under seven were free from criminal responsibility. Children under fifteen were exempt from most of the penalties that could be administered to adults.

303. "The Quarter's History—Sweden," 37 Am. Scand. Rev. 383, 386 (1949). The American percentage of commitment to prison is seven times as great as that in Sweden. *Federal Probation*, XI, No. 4, p. 69 (October-December 1949).

304. Victor Almquist, "Scandinavian Prisons," 157 *Annals of the American Academy of Political Science* 197-98 (Sept. 1931).

305. Hardy Göransson, "Treatment of Criminals and other Asocial Individuals," 197 *The Annals of the American Academy* 120, 122-23 (May 1938).

306. Thorsten Sellin, "The Treatment of Offenders in Sweden," *Federal Probation*, XII, No. 2, p. 14 (1948).

307. *Ibid.*, p. 18 (1948).

308. Ebbe Hertzberg, op. cit., p. 563 (1912).

309. Sweden was the first Scandinavian nation to so provide, but her law is the most conservative of the Scandinavian. Edwin Borchard, Convicting The Innocent, pp. 385, 393-404 (1932).

310. Nils Dillén, Föreläsningar I Straffprocessrätt Enligt Den Nya Rattegangs-balken (1947); Karl Olivecrona, Straffprocessen. Kompendium, Lund, 1948.

311. Ernst Leda, "Den Tilltalade och den Nya Strafprocessen," 35 Svensk Juristtidning 635, 639 (1950).

312. Hugo Lindberg, "Brott och Publicitet," 35 Svensk Juristtidning 646 (1950).

313. Gunmar Lagergren, "The Preparatory Proceeding and the Hearing-in-Chief," 82 Ir. L. T. 165 (July 10, 1948).

314. On medieval civil procedure in Sweden see Engelmann, op. cit., pp. 203-38 (1927).

315. Ibid., p. 217 (1927).

316. Ibid., pp. 225-32 (1927).

317. Ibid., pp. 232-33 (1927).

318. Ibid., pp. 233-38 (1927).

319. Ibid., pp. 833-63 (1927).

320. On Justitierevisionen see ibid., pp. 834, 842-43, 864-65 (1927).

321. Ibid., pp. 836-38 (1927).

322. Engelmann, op. cit., p. xli (1927). See also pp. 840, 854-55. The first instance of a following of German civil procedure occurred in 1540.

323. Ibid., p. 843 (1927). See also Robert W. Millar, "The Mechanism of Fact-Discovery: A study in Comparative Civil Procedure, II," 32 Ill. L. Rev. 424, 431 (1937).

324. Robert W. Millar in David Dudley Field, Centenary Essays, p. 123 (1949).

325. Engelmann, op. cit., p. 847 (1927).

326. Ibid., p. 864 (1927). It was concluded in 1937 that the Code of 1734 "with interim amendment, today serves as the basic regulation of civil procedure, both in Sweden and Finland." Robert W. Millar, "The Mechanism of Fact-Discovery: A Study in Comparative Civil Procedure, II," 32 Ill. L. Rev. 424, 431 (1937).

327. Engelmann, op. cit., p. 866 (1927). Changes from 1734 to 1884 are discussed at 864-67.

328. Ibid., p. 868 (1927). The discussion is by Professor Thore Engströmer of the University of Uppsala. For a description of Swedish civil procedure as it existed in 1876 see "Administration of Justice in Sweden," 3 Cent. L. J. 564 (1876).

329. Nils Alexanderson, "Den Nya Rättegångsbalken," Svensk Juristtidning 1-5 (1948).

330. See "Thore Engströmer 70 Ar," 33 Svensk Juristtidning 161-64 (1948) for an account of his work.

331. Robert W. Millar in David Dudley Field, Centenary Essays pp. 121, 137 (1949). There are several excellent discussions in the festschrift in honor of Natanael Gärde in 35 Svensk Juristtidning 483-858 (1950), as well as in other issues of the Svensk Juristtidning. See also "A Few Points in the New Civil Procedure in Sweden," 82 Ir. L. T. 159-61 (July 3, 1948); Gunnar Lagergren, "The Preparatory Proceeding and the Hearing-in-Chief," 82 Ir. L. T. 165-67 (July 10, 1948).

332. Robert W. Millar in David Dudley Field, Centenary Essays, pp. 130-131 (1949), citing Processlagberedningens Förslag Till Rättegangsbalk, p. 410 (1938).

333. Ibid., pp. 131-32 (1949), citing Rättegangsbalk, Chap. 37, Chap. 43, sec. 8; Förslag, 409.

334. Rudolf B. Schlesinger, "Note on the New Swedish Code of Civil Procedure." Comparative Law Cases and Materials, p. 219 (1950).

335. "A Few Points on the New Civil Procedure in Sweden," 82 Ir. L. T. 159 (July 3, 1948).

336. Ibid., pp. 159, 160 (1948).

337. Jackson, op. cit., p. 126 (1944). For a handbook in Swedish of 285 pages on

social legislation in Sweden see Ernst Michanek, *Socialboken* (1949). It is obtainable through Bonniers, 605 Madison Ave., New York 21, N. Y., for $1.20.

338. B. J. Hovde, *op. cit.*, p. 695 (1948).

339. *Ibid.*, p. 684 (1948).

340. *Ibid.*, p. 687 (1948).

341. Ebbe Hertzberg, *op. cit.*, p. 565 (1912).

342. B. J. Hovde, *op. cit.*, pp. 688-89 (1948).

343. Henning Friis, *op. cit.*, p. 161 (1950).

344. Torgny Segerstedt and Philipp Weintraub, "Marriage and Divorce in Sweden," 272 *Annals of the American Academy of Political Science* 185 (November 1950).

345. Henning Friis, *op. cit.*, p. 160 (1950).

346. Ben A. Arneson, *op. cit.*, pp. 228-35 (2d ed., 1949). For discussion of the Swedish legislation concerning labor see Ernst Michanek, *op. cit.*, pp. 145-234 (1949).

347. *New York Times*, p. 24, July 13, 1951.

348. Ben A. Arneson, *op. cit.*, pp. 221-23 (2d ed., 1949); Tor Jerneman, "Social Insurance in Sweden," 197 *The Annals of the American Academy*, 80, 83-86 (1949); Ernst Michanek, *op. cit.*, pp. 35-41 (1949).

349. Daily allowances are calculated as about 70 per cent of his wage; the minimum 3.50 kronor and the maximum 14 kronor. There is a supplement for family supporters of 1.50 kronor per day. The disability annuity is 11/12 of the annual wage, the maximum annuity being 7,200 kronor. Henning Friis, *op. cit.*, p. 151 (1950).

350. Ben A. Arneson, *op. cit.*, pp. 226-28 (2d ed., 1949); Tor Jerneman, "Social Insurance in Sweden," 197 *The Annals of the American Academy* 80, 89-91 (1949); Ernst Michanek, *op. cit.*, pp. 42-47 (1949).

351. The size of the allowance depends on the size of the premium. There are supplements for family supporters of 1.25 kronor and for each child of one krone. Henning Friis, *op. cit.*, p. 150 (1950).

352. Karl J. Höjer, "The Care of the Indigent in Sweden," 197 *The Annals of the American Academy* 72 (May 1938).

353. Franklin D. Scott, *op. cit.*, p. 110 (1950); B. J. Hovde, *op. cit.*, pp. 630-34, 642 (1948).

354. As to the present Swedish law of general assistance see Ernst Michanek, *op. cit.*, pp. 51-55 (1949).

355. Ben A. Arneson, *op. cit.*, pp. 235-38 (2d ed., 1949); Gustav Möller, "The Unemployment Policy," 197 *The Annals of the American Academy* 47-71 (June 1938).

356. Ben A. Arneson, *op. cit.*, pp. 254-56 (2d ed., 1949); Franklin D. Scott, *op. cit.*, pp. 118-20 (1950); Otto R. Wangson, "Maternal and Child Welfare," 197 *The Annals of the American Academy* 93-103 (May 1938); Ernst Michanek, *op. cit.*, pp. 56-64 (1949).

357. As to the earlier systems of aid to dependent children known as "child allowances" see Tor Jerneman, "Social Insurance in Sweden," 197 *The Annals of the American Academy* 80, 88-89 (May 1938); Otto R. Wangson, "Maternal and Child Welfare," 197 *The Annals of the American Academy* 93, 95-96 (May 1938).

358. Henning Friis, *op. cit.*, pp. 160, 167 (1950).

359. *Ibid.*, pp. 165-66 (1950).

360. Franklin D. Scott, *op. cit.*, pp. 119-20 (1950).

361. Waldemar Kaempffert, "Science in Review," *New York Times*, May 20, 1951.

362. *Ibid.* (1951).

363. Henning Friis, *op. cit.*, pp. 162-63 (1950).

364. Ben A. Arneson, *op. cit.*, p. 219 (2d ed. 1949); Otto R. Wangson, "Maternal and Child Welfare," 197 *The Annals of the American Academy* 93, 102 (May 1938). As to legislation prior to 1865 see B. J. Hovde, *op. cit.*, pp. 644-45 (1948).

365. Ben A. Arneson, *op. cit.*, pp. 243-45 (2d ed., 1949); Tor Jerneman, "Social

Insurance in Sweden," 197 *The Annals of the American Academy* 80, 86-87 (May 1938); Ernst Michanek, *op. cit.*, pp. 19-28 (1949).

366. In Stockholm the total annual pension to persons without income is 2,230 kronor for single persons and 3,380 kronor for a married couple. In the cheapest communities it is 1,050 kronor for single persons and 1,680 kronor for a married couple. Henning Friis, *op. cit.*, p. 150 (1950).

367. Housing has been provided for both old age pensioners and old people with independent incomes. *Ibid.*, pp. 195-96 (1950).

368. In cases of total disability the amount is the same as for old age pensions. For other cases it is lower. *Ibid.*, p. 151 (1950).

369. Ben A. Arneson, *op. cit.*, pp. 250-53 (2d ed., 1949); Tor Jerneman, "Social Insurance in Sweden," 197 *The Annals of the American Academy* 80, 81-83 (May 1938); Ernst Michanek, *op. cit.*, pp. 28-34 (1949).

370. There is a daily allowance of 1.50 kronor for married women not gainfully employed, two kronor for pensioners, and 3.50 kronor for all other adult persons. There are supplements of two kronor for married beneficiaries and 0.50 kronor for each child. Henning Friis, *op. cit.*, p. 150 (1950).

371. All women who belong to an insurance plan receive 125 kronor. Women with low income not subscribing to an insurance plan receive 75 kronor. About 95 per cent of all mothers receive maternity grants. Henning Friis, *op. cit.*, p. 161 (1950).

372. Alex Höjer, "Public Health and Medical Care," 197 *The Annals of the American Academy* 104-19 (May 1938); B. J. Hovde, *op. cit.*, pp. 573-88 (1948); Ernst Michanek, *op. cit.*, pp. 235-64 (1949).

373. Ben A. Arneson, *op. cit.*, pp. 261-63 (2d ed., 1949); Franklin D. Scott, *op. cit.*, pp. 120-28 (1950); Alf Johansson, "Social Housing Policy in Sweden," 197 *The Annals of the American Academy* 160-70 (May 1938); Henning Friis, *op. cit.*, pp. 170-98 (1950); Ernst Michanek, *op. cit.*, pp. 103-44 (1949).

374. "The Quarter's History—Sweden," 38 *Am. Scand. Rev.* 69, 72 (1950).

375. Henning Friis, *op. cit.*, p. 172 (1950).

376. Ben A. Arneson, *op. cit.*, pp. 275-78 (2d ed., 1949); Franklin D. Scott, *op. cit.*, pp. 128-30 (1950); Olov Kinberg, "Temperance Legislation in Sweden," 163 *The Annals of the American Academy* 206-15 (Sept. 1932); Halfden Bengtsson, "The Temperance Movement and Temperance Legislation in Sweden," 197 *The Annals of the American Academy* 134-53 (May 1938). As to legislation prior to 1865 see B. J. Hovde, *op. cit.*, pp. 662-79 (1948).

377. Olov Kinberg, "Temperance Legislation in Sweden," 163 *The Annals of the American Academy* 206, 210-12 (Sept. 1932).

378. B. J. Hovde, *op. cit.*, pp. 234-35 (1948); Arthur Montgomery, *Svensk Traktatpolitik, 1816-1914.*

379. Freedom of occupation was legislated in 1846, whereas it occurred in Norway in 1839 and in Denmark in 1857. B. J. Hovde, *op. cit.*, p. 238 (1948). Internal trade was freed in Sweden in 1846 and 1864; in Norway in 1842, and in Denmark in 1856 and 1857. *Ibid.*, p. 240 (1948).

380. Henning Friis, *op. cit.*, p. 309 (1950).

381. A. Bugge, "The Scandinavian Uniform Laws," 26 *Tidskrift for Retvidenskab* 80 (1914); H. Munch-Petersen, "Main Features of Scandinavian Law," 43 *L. Q. Rev.* 366 (1927); Gunnar Leistikow in Henning Friis, *op. cit.*, pp. 307-24 (1950).

382. Herman Zetterberg, "Planlaggningen av det Nordiska Lagstiftningsarbetet," 32 *Svensk Juristtidning* 33 (1947).

383. For a resume of the meeting see "Adertonde Nordiska Juristmötet," 33 *Svensk Juristtidning* 611-20 (1948).

384. Henning Friis, *op. cit.*, p. 311 (1950); Franklin D. Scott, *op. cit.*, pp. 172, 223 (1950).

385. F. W. Raikes, "Maritime Laws in Sweden," 17 *L. Mag & Rev.* (4th Ser.) 235, 18 *Ibid.*, 33. To a considerable extent modern maritime law developed out of the Laws of Wisby in Gotland, Sweden, prevalent in the fourteenth century. Wigmore,

Panorama of the World's Legal Systems (1928); Manley O. Hudson, *Cases on International Law*, p. 371 n. 8. (3rd ed., 1951).

386. H. Holm-Nielsen, "The Scandinavian Convention on Bankruptcy and Arrangements Outside Bankruptcy," 18 *J. Comp. Leg. & Int. L.* 3rd ser., 262 (1936).

387. *Social Denmark*, p. 120 (1947).

388. Folke Schmidt, "Nationality and Domicile in Swedish Private International Law," 4 *Int. L. Q.* 39, 44 (1951).

389. "The Quarter's History—Sweden," 38 *Am. Scand. Rev.* 273, 276-77 (1950).

390. H. Munch-Petersen, "Main Features of Scandinavian Laws," 43 *L. Q. Rev.* 366 (1927).

391. Bernt Hjejle, *Nordisk Retsfaelleskab*. Copenhagen, 1946.

392. *En Nordisk Lovbog. Udkast Til En Faelles Borgerlig Lovbog for Danmark, Finland, Island, Norge Og Sverrig.* Copenhagen, 1948. This volume is the subject of discussions in 35 *Svensk Juristtidning* 321-37, 879-97 (1950).

393. Franklin D. Scott, *op. cit.*, p. 102 (1950); Henning Friis, *op. cit.*, p. 317 (1950).

394. Franklin D. Scott, *op. cit.*, pp. 172-73 (1950); Henning Friis, *op. cit.*, pp. 321-22 (1950).

395. Andrew A. Stomberg, *op. cit.*, pp. 198-99 (1931).

396. Ragnar Svanström and Carl Palmstierna, *op. cit.*, p. 62 (1934). The Danish charter was secured earlier, but the University of Copenhagen opened in 1479.

397. *Ibid.*, p. 120 (1934).

398. Carl Hallendorff and Adolf Schück, *op. cit.*, p. 217 (1929).

399. Nils B. Skavang, "History and Development of Scandinavian Law—Some Salient Traits," 6 *Seminar* 60, 66 (1948).

400. Andrew A. Stomberg, *op. cit.*, p. 552 (1931).

401. Folke Schmidt, "Amerikansk Juristubildning," 32 *Svensk Juristtidning* 411 (1947). The International Committee for Comparative Law has a 1951 project to study law teaching in Sweden and seven other countries. Note 45 *Am. J. Int. L.* 369 (1951).

402. Ebbe Hertzberg, *op. cit.*, p. 564 (1912); Sture Petrén, "Våra Första Advokáter," 32 *Svensk Juristtidning* 1 (1947).

403. Holger Wiklund, "Advokatsamfordet Efter Processareformen," 35 *Svensk Juristtidning* 812 (1950).

404. Lloyd K. Garrison, "Legal Service for Low Income Groups in Sweden," 26 *A. B. A. J.* 214, 293 (1940); Eric F. Schweinburg, "Legal Assistance Abroad," 17 *U. Chi. L. Rev.* 270, 289-91 (1950).

405. Eric F. Schweinburg, "Legal Assistance Abroad," 17 *U. Chi. L. Rev.* 270, 290 (1950).

406. Ebbe Hertzberg, *op. cit.*, p. 570 (1912).

407. *Synopis Juris Privati Ad Leges Accommodata* (Stockholm, 1653).

408. *Observationes Juris Practicae* (Stockholm, 1679).

409. *Indledning Till Den Svenska Jurisprudentiam Civilem* (Lund, 1729).

410. *De Fundamentis Et Adminiculis Jurisprudentiae Legislatoriae* (1788).

411. See H. Edfendt's edition of Boström's *Skrifter* (Uppsala, 1872) containing his works on legal problems: *Satser Om Lag Och Lagstiftning Grundlineer Till Philosophiska Statsläran*, and *Grundlineer Till Philosophiska Civil Rätten.*

412. *Lärobok I Sveriges Allmänna Civilratt* (Lund, 1872).

413. *Svensk Rigsdagen* (Stockholm, 1878).

414. *Handbok I Sveriges Gällande Förvaltningsratt* (Uppsala, 1873).

415. B. J. Hovde, *op. cit.*, p. 348 (1948).

416. Geijer visited Savigny in 1825 and adopted the views of the "historical school." B. J. Hovde, *op. cit.*, pp. 355, 371, 443-44, 464 (1948).

417. *Ibid.*, pp. 353-57, 365 (1948).

418. For citation to their writings see the bibliography. Much of their work has been translated into English.

419. Book Review, 35 *Svensk Juristtidning* 127, 129 (1950). For reviews and criticisms of his philosophy see 53 *Harv. L. Rev.* 507 (1940); 63 *Harv. L. Rev.* 181 (1949).

420. Ebbe Hertzberg, *op. cit.*, p. 574 (1912).

421. *De Jure Sveonum et Gotorum Vetusto Libri Duo* (Holmiae, 1672). He is called the "father of Swedish legal knowledge," Maxwell Fraser, *op. cit.*, p. 189 (1939).

422. *Zamolxis Primus Getarum Legislatur* (Uppsala, 1687).

423. Andrew A. Stomberg, *op. cit.*, p. 433 (1931).

424. *Sveriges Gamla Lagar; Cordus Juris Sveo Gothorum Antiqui* (Lund, 1827-1877, 13 vols.); *Juridiska Skrifter*. See B. J. Hovde, *op. cit.*, p. 465 (1948).

425. *Lagfarenhetens Tillstånd, Sverige Under Medeltiden* (1936).

426. *Anteckningar I Sveriges Rättshistoria* (1860).

427. *Svenska Lagfarenhetens Utbildning* (1838).

428. *Svenska Statsförfattningens Historiska Utveckling* (Stockholm, 1856).

429. *Svenska Samhallsförfatningens Historia* (Helsinki, 1840).

430. *Öfversigt af den Svenska processens historia* (Stockholm, 1884).

431. See the account of his career in "Ernst Kallenberg," 32 *Svensk Juristtidning* 721-25 (1947).

432. *Svensk Juridisk Litteraturhistoria* (Stockholm, 1946).

433. *Den Svenska Landslagens Författning i Historisk och Comparativ Belysning* (Lund, 1947).

Bibliography of Danish Law

A. REFERENCES IN ENGLISH

American Scandinavian Review. Four reviews of Danish affairs are published each year.

Armstrong, B. N. *The Health Insurance Doctor: His Role in England, Denmark and France* (1939).

Arneson, Ben A. *The Democratic Monarchies of Scandinavia.* 2nd ed.; New York: D. Van Nostrand, 1949. This contains an excellent study of Danish government.

"Aviation Arrangements Between the United States and Denmark," 5 *Journal Air Law* 472-77 (1934).

Bain, A. N. *Scandinavia.* Cambridge: 1905. A history from 1500 to 1900.

Birch, J. H. *Denmark in History.* London: J. Murray, 1938. This is out of print.

Borchard, E. M. "European Systems of State Indemnity for Errors of Criminal Justice," 3 *J. Crim. L.* 684-718 (1913).

Childs, Marquis W. *This is Democracy: Collective Bargaining in Scandinavia.* New Haven: 1938.

Chricton, A., and Wheaton, H. *Scandinavia, Ancient and Modern.* New York: 1841.

Constitution of Denmark. English translation published by the Rigsdag Bureau, Copenhagen. It also appears in Amos J. Peaslee, *Constitutions of Nations,* I, 644-53. Concord, N. H.: The Rumford Press, 1950.

Danstrup, John. *A History of Denmark.* Copenhagen: 1949. This is the only recent history of Denmark in English. It is only 195 pages in length.

DeMontmorency, J. E. G., "Danish Influence on English Law and Character," 40 *L. Q. Rev.* 324-43 (1950).

"Denmark's Antipolitical Union," 6 *Can. B. Rev.* 296-97 (1928).

Facts about Denmark. 5th ed.; Copenhagen: 1949.

Fogdill, Soren. *Danish-American Diplomacy.* Iowa City: 1922.

Foster, J. B. "Danish Office Employees and Vacation Laws," 2 *Comparative L. Ser.* 33-37 (Jan. 1939).

Friis, Henning. *Scandinavia between East and West.* Ithaca: Cornell University Press, 1950. This is an extremely fine symposium.

Gade, John A. *Christian IV, King of Denmark and Norway.* Boston: 1928.

Galenson, Walter. *The Danish System of Labor Relations.* Cambridge: Harvard University Press, 1952.

Givskov, Carl G. "The Danish 'Purge-Laws,'" 39 *J. Crim. L.* 447-60 (1948).

Goldmark, J., and Hollman, A. H. *Democracy in Denmark.* Washington: 1936.

Hertzberg, Ebbe, in *A General Survey of Continental Legal History.* 1912. Pp. 531-76.

Hill, Charles E. *Danish Sound Dues.* Durham, N. C.: 1926.

Hoffman, Willy. "The Danish Law against Disturbances of Radio Broadcasting," 3 Air L. Rev. 44-47 (1932).

Holm-Nielsen, H. "Law of Torts in Denmark," 15 J. Comp. Leg. & Int. L. (3rd ser.) 176-79 (1933).

———. "The Scandinavian Convention on Bankruptcy and Arrangements Outside Bankruptcy," 18 J. Comp. Leg. & Int. L. (3rd ser.) 262-65 (1936).

Hovde, Bryn J. *The Scandinavian Countries, 1720-1865*. Ithaca: Cornell University Press, 1948. The author was recently in Scandinavia to bring the study up to date.

Howe, F. C. *Denmark—The Cooperative Way*. New York: 1936.

———. *The Most Complete Agricultural Recovery in History*. Washington: 1934.

Jessel, Albert H. "Poor Man's Lawyer in Denmark," 7 L. Q. Rev. 176-83 (1891).

Jones, S. Shepard. *The Scandinavian States and the League of Nations*. Princeton: 1939.

Kalijarvi, T. "Scandinavian Claims to Jurisdiction over Territorial Waters," 26 Am. J. Int. L. 59-69 (1932).

Kampmann, E. "Prisons and Punishment in Denmark," 25 J. Crim. L. 115-17 (1934).

Kean, A. W. G. "Early Danish Criminal Law," 19 J. Comp. Leg. & Int. L. (3rd ser.) 253-59 (1937).

Kemble, H. S. "Refuge Camps—A Social Dilemma in Denmark," 111 Just. P. 624-26 (1947).

Kemp, F. "Danish Law Rules Relating to Bankruptcy and Composition," 5 J. Nat. Assoc. Ref. in Bank 103-06 (1931).

Koch, Hal. *Grundtvig*. Yellow Springs, Ohio: The Antioch Press, 1952.

Koht, Halvdan, "Scandinavian Kingdoms Until the End of the Thirteenth Century," 6 Cambridge Medieval History 382. New York: 1936.

Kruse, Vinding. *The Community of the Future*. New York: Philosophical Library, 1952. A blueprint for the society of tomorrow.

Kulsrud, C. J. "Seizure of the Danish Fleet, 1807," 32 Am. J. Int. L. 280-311 (1938).

Larsen, Jens. *Virgin Islands Story*. Philadelphia: Muhlenberg Press, 1950.

Larsen, Karen. *A History of Norway*. Princeton: 1948. This volume contains much Danish history.

Larson, Laurence M. *Canute the Great and the Rise of Danish Imperialism during the Viking Age*. New York: 1912.

Leach, Henry Goddard. *Angevin Britain and Scandinavia*. Cambridge: 1921.

Lester, R. A. and Christensen, C. L. "The Gold Parity Depression in Norway and Denmark, 1925-1928," 45 J. Pol. Econ. 433-65, 800-15.

Moss, John. "Public Assistance Administration in Scandinavia," 95 Just. P. 151, 168 (1931).

Munch-Petersen, H. "Main Features of Scandinavian Law," 43 L. Q. Rev. 366-77 (1927). The author was a professor of law at the University of Copenhagen and a member of the Maritime and Commercial Court of Copenhagen.

Munch-Petersen, H. "The Social Aspect of Procedure from a European Point of View," 11 Minn. L. Rev. 624-34 (1927).

————. "The System of Legal Education in Denmark," *J. Pub. T. of L.* 31-32 (1928).

————. "New Danish Constitution," 59 *Sol. J.* 551 (1915).

Ostenfeld, George H. "Danish Courts of Conciliation," 9 *A.B.A.J.* 747-48 (1923).

Padelford, N. J. "New Scandinavian Neutrality Rules," 32 *Am. J. Int. L.* 789-93 (1938).

Pearson, P. H. "Industrial Property Protection in Denmark," *Comp. Law Ser.* 7-12 (Jan. 1938).

Peel, R. V. "Local Government in Scandinavia," 25 *Nat. Munic. Rev.* 528-34 (1936).

Peterson, C. Stewart. *American-Scandinavian Diplomatic Relations, 1776-1876.* Baltimore: 1948.

Pratt, Fletcher. *The Third King.* New York: William Sloane Associates, Inc., 1950. This book deals with Valdemar Victorious and Valdemar Atterdag.

Preuss, L. "Disputes between Denmark and Norway on the Sovereignty of East Greenland," 26 *Am. J. Int. L.* 469-87 (1932).

Reid, W. S. "Place of Denmark in Scottish Foreign Policy, 1470-1540," 58 *J. Rev.* 183-200 (1946).

Ross, Alf. *A Textbook of International Law.* London: Longmans, Green and Co., 1947. The author is a professor of law at the University of Copenhagen.

————. *Towards a Realistic Jurisprudence.* Copenhagen: Einar Munks-gaard, 1946.

Satz, M. "Enemy Legislation and Judgments in Denmark," 31 *J. Comp. Leg. & Int. L.* (3rd ser.) 1-3 (1949).

"Scandinavian Law of Husband and Wife," 9 *J. Comp. Leg. & Int. L.* 263-64 (1927).

Scott, Franklin D. *The United States and Scandinavia.* Cambridge: Harvard University Press, 1950.

Sinding, Paul. *History of Scandinavia.* New York: Pudney & Russell, 1858. This is mainly a history of Denmark up to 1850. The author was a professor at the College of the City of New York.

Skavang, Nils B. "History and Development of Scandinavian Law—Some Salient Traits," 6 *Seminar* 60-71 (1948).

Smith, Reginald H. "The Danish Conciliation System," 11 *J. Am. Jud. Soc.* 85-93 (1927).

Social Denmark. Edited by *Socialt Tidskrift.* Copenhagen: 1947. This is the best survey in English of the social legislation of any Scandinavian state. It contains a valuable bibliography.

Sørensen, Max. "Federal States and International Protection of Human Rights," 46 *Am. J. Int. L.* 195-218 (1952).

Steefel, L. D. *The Schleswig-Holstein Question.* Cambridge: Harvard University Press, 1932. This is the best description in English of the events leading up to the loss of Schleswig-Holstein.

Steincke, K. K. "The Danish Social Reform Measures," *Int. Labor Rev.* 620-48 (1935). The author has been Minister of Justice and is one of the most prolific Danish writers.

Teisen, Axel. "Adverse Possession-Prescription," 2 A.B.A.J. 189-201. The
     author grew up in Denmark and practiced law in Philadelphia.
————. "Danish Judicial Code," 65 U. Pa. L. Rev. 543-70 (1917).
————. "How They Decide Cases on Appeal in Denmark," 76 Cent. L. J.
     185-86 (1913).
————. "Lawmaking Bodies of Denmark, Sweden and Norway," 23 Case
     and Comment 635 (1917).
————. "Power to Declare Legislation Unconstitutional in Denmark,"
     10 A.B.A.J. 792-94 (1924).
————. "Scandinavia. Bibliography of Comparative Law," 1 A.B.A.J. 160-62
     (1915); 2 A.B.A.J. 270-75 (1916).
————. "Seisin Gewere," 1 A.B.A.J. 76-91 (1915). A discussion of early
     Danish property law.
Toyne, S. M. The Scandinavians in History. London: Edward Arnold & Co.,
     1948.
Ussing, Henry. "The Scandinavian Law of Torts—Impact of Insurance on
     Tort Law," 1 Am. J. Comp. L. 359-72 (1952).
Warming, Jens. "The Taxation of Real Property in Denmark," 39 Pol. Sc. Q.
     414-31 (1924).
Westergaard, Waldemar. A History of Denmark. In preparation for the
     American-Scandinavian Foundation. The author is professor of history
     at the University of California at Los Angeles.
Wheaton, H. "Public Law of Denmark," 27 North American Review.

B.   REFERENCES IN DANISH

Andersen, Carl O. B. Statsomvaeltningen i 1660: Kritiske studier over kilder
     og tradition. Copenhagen: Levin and Munksgaard. A study of the
     absolute monarchy set up in 1660.
Andersen, Paul. Dansk statsforfatningsret. Copenhagen: Gyldendal, 1944. A
     treatise on Danish constitutional law.
Arup, Erik. Danmarks Historie. This history of Denmark is still under way.
Aschehoug, Thorkel. Statsforfatningen: Norge og Danmark indtil 1814. Oslo:
     1886. The constitution of Denmark and Norway until 1814.
Aubert, Ludvig M. B. Grundbogernes historie i Norge, Danmark og tildels
     i Tyskland. Oslo: 1892. A history of real property in Denmark, Nor-
     way, and Germany.
Bentzon, Viggo. Den danske Arveret. Copenhagen: 1931. Danish law of
     inheritance.
————. Familieretten. Copenhagen: 1924. Family law.
Berlin, Knud K. Den danske statsforfatningsret. Copenhagen: Nyt nordisk
     forlag, 1943. This is the standard treatise on Danish constitutional
     law.
Dahl, Frantz. Almindelig borgerlig straffelov. Copenhagen: 1914. Danish
     criminal law.
Danmarks Love, 1665-1949. Copenhagen: 1950. The laws of Denmark.
Engelstoft, P., and Wendt, F. W. Haandbog i Danmarks politiske historie.
     Copenhagen: 1934. A handbook of Danish political history.
Fabricius, Knud. Danmarks Historie for Folket. A popular history of Denmark
     by a professor at the University of Copenhagen.

Goos, C. *Den danske Strafes proces.* Copenhagen: 1880. Danish criminal procedure.

————. *Den danske Strafferet.* Copenhagen: 1875. The Danish criminal law.

————. *Forelaesninger over den almindelig Retslaere.* Copenhagen: 1885-1890. Lectures on the nature and sources of law.

Helveg, Ludvig N. *Den danske Kirkes Historie efter reformationen.* 2d ed.; Copenhagen: 1857-1883. A history of the Danish church after the Reformation.

Holberg. *Dansk Rigslovgivning.* Copenhagen: 1889.

————. *Kong Valdemar's Lov.* Copenhagen: 1886. The laws of King Valdemar.

Hurwitz, Stephen. *Den danske Strafferetspleje.* Danish criminal procedure.

————. *Tvistemaal.* Civil procedure.

Holck, Karl G. *Den danske Statsforfatningsret.* Copenhagen: F. Hegel, 1869. Danish constitutional law.

Ilsoe, Peter. *Norden's Historie.* This history of Scandinavia is used in Danish high schools.

Jensen, Adolph. *Danmarks Statsforfatningen efter Grundloven af 5 Juni, 1915.* The Danish Constitution of 1915.

Jensen, Hans. *De danske Staenderforsamlingens Historie, 1830-1848.* Copenhagen: J. H. Schultz, 1934.

Jorgensen, Paul J. *Dansk Retshistorie: Retskildernes af Forfatningsrettens Historie indtil sidste Halvdel af det 17 Aarhundrede.* Copenhagen: G. E. C. Gad, 1947. History of Danish law until 1650.

Koch, Hal and Ross, Alf. *Nordisk demokrati.* Copenhagen: 1949. This is the most comprehensive survey of Scandinavian democracy.

Kolderup-Rosenvinge, J. L. A. *Grundrids af den danske Retshistorie.* 3rd ed.; 1860. A ground-plan of Danish legal history.

————. *Samling af gamle danske Love.* Copenhagen: 1821, 1837. Collection of old Danish laws.

Krabbe, O. *Dansk Lovsamling.* Copenhagen: 1921.

Kruse, Vinding. *En nordisk Lovbog.* Copenhagen: 1948. A Scandinavian Law Code prepared for the five Scandinavian states. The author is one of the best-known Danish legal scholars.

————. *Retslaeren.* This volume deals with the use of customs and judicial decisions as bases for law.

Larsen, J. E. *Forelaesninger over den danske Retshistorie.* Copenhagen: 1861. Danish legal history.

Lassen, Julius. *Obligationsretten.* 2d ed.; Copenhagen: 1908. The law of obligations.

Lovtidende. Law journal. This is an official publication of the statute and session laws.

Matzen, H. *Den danske Statsforfatningsret.* Copenhagen: 1900-1909. Danish constitutional law.

————. *Forelaesninger over den danske Retshistorie.* Copenhagen: 1896. Lectures on Danish legal history.

Maurer, Konrad von. *Udsigt over de Nordgemanske Retskilders Historie.* Oslo: 1878. History of North German legal sources.

Moller, Jens. *Om Orla Lehmanns Del i Udkastet til Junigrundloven.* Copenhagen, *Historisk Tidsskrift,* 1927. This deals with the role of Lehmann in the drafting of the Constitution.

Munch, P. *Laerebog i samfundskab.* 13th ed.; Copenhagen: 1933. The outstanding treatise on government and politics in Denmark. The author is a former Minister of Foreign Affairs.

Munch-Petersen, H. *Den danske Retspleje.* 2d ed.; Copenhagen: 1923. Danish law of procedure.

Petersen, Arthur. *Grundloven, Forudsaetningen og Indhold.* Copenhagen: Danske Forlag, 1946. The Danish Constitution, its provisions and contents.

Petersen, N. M. *Danmarks Historie i Hedenhold.* The history of Denmark in ancient times.

———. *Den danske Litteraturs Historie fra Middal Alderen til 1800.* History of Danish literature up to 1800.

Rigsdagtidende. Parliamentary journal. This is published daily during the sessions and contains verbatim reports of proceedings in both houses.

Rosenkrantz, P. A. V. *Den danske regjering og rigsdage, 1903-1934.* Copenhagen. The Danish Cabinets and Parliaments from 1903 to 1934.

Schultz. *Danmarks Historie.* This is a six-volume history of Denmark.

Steenstrup, J. *Danmarks Riges Historie.* 6 vols. Copenhagen: 1897-1906. This is the standard general history of Denmark.

Thorsen, C. *Forsikringslaeren i Hovedtraek.* Copenhagen: 1914. Main principles of insurance law.

Torp, Carl. *Besiddelsen.* Copenhagen: 1884. The law of possession.

———. *Dansk Tingsret.* 2d ed.; Copenhagen: L. A. Grundtvig, 1905. Danish property law.

Ussing, Henry. *Erstatningsret.* Copenhagen: 1947. Law of Torts. The author is professor of law at the University of Copenhagen.

Wiskinge, S. *Vor Forfatningshistorie.* Copenhagen: 1928. A history of the Danish Constitution.

C.   REFERENCES IN GERMAN

Dreyer. *Beitrage zur Litteratur der nordischen Rechtsgelahrsamkeit.* Hamburg: 1794.

Goos and Hansen. *Das Staatsrecht des Königreichs Danemark.* Freiburg: 1889.

Hausen, Henrig. *Das offentliche Recht Danemarks 1914-1921. Jahrbuch des offentlichen Rechts.* Tübingen: 1922.

Kath, Werner. *Die geschichtliche Entwicklung und gegenwartige Gestalt des dänischen Regierungssystems, eine staatsrechtsvergleichende Studie.* Bonn: L. Rohrschedi, 1938.

Maurer, Konrad von. In Holtzendorff's *Encyclopäedie der Rechtswissenschaft.* 1889.

Michaelis. *Das dänische Strafrecht und der dänische Straff velzug. Blätter fur Gefängniskunde.* 1914.

Bibliography of Icelandic Law

A. REFERENCES IN ENGLISH

American Scandinavian Review. This review contains four reviews each year of Icelandic affairs.

Bjornson, Sveinn. *The Kingdom of Iceland. Some Remarks on its Constitutional and International Status.* Copenhagen: 1939. The author was President of Iceland until his death in 1952.

Briem, Helgi P. *Iceland and the Icelanders.* Princeton, N. J.: 1945. Published by the American-Scandinavian Foundation.

Bryce, James. "Primitive Iceland" in *Studies in History and Jurisprudence.* I, 312-58. London: 1901.

Chamberlain, William C. *The Economic Development of Iceland Through World War II.* New York: Columbia, 1947.

Clark, Austin H. *Iceland and Greenland.* 1943.

Clinton, George, Jr. "Icelandic Lawsuit of the Eleventh Century," 2 *Lincoln L. Rev.* 6-13 (October 1928).

Economic Cooperation Administration pamphlet *Country Studies on Denmark, Norway, Sweden and Iceland.* Washington: ECA, 1949.

Einarsson, Stefan. *History of Icelandic Prose Writers, 1800-1940.* Ithaca: Cornell University Press, 1948. The author is professor of Scandinavian philology at Johns Hopkins University.

———. *Icelandic.* Baltimore: The Johns Hopkins Press, 1949. This is the most complete grammar and all-around study of the Icelandic language.

Eldjarn, Kristjan. "Romans in Iceland," 39 *American Scandinavian Review* 123-26 (1951).

Gjerset, Knut. *History of Iceland.* New York: The Macmillan Company, 1925. This volume is out of print. It is the standard history of Iceland published in English. The author was a professor at Luther College, Decorah, Iowa.

———. *History of the Norwegian People.* New York: 1927. See especially I, 137-42, 189-94, 434-38; II, 14-15, 107, 139-42, 237-38, 415.

Grimson, G. "Iceland and Its Relation to the North American Continent," 5 *Lawyer* 15-18 (February 1952). The author is a state judge in a trial court of general jurisdiction in North Dakota.

Grimson, G., and Johnson, Sveinbjorn, "Iceland and the Americas. Present Status of the Northern Island in International Law. Discussion by two Distinguished Legal Scholars born in Iceland," 26 *A.B.A.J.* 505-09 (June 1940).

Heckscher, Eli; Keilhau, Wilhelm; Cohn, Einar; and Thorsteinsson, T. *Sweden, Norway, Denmark and Iceland in the World War.* New Haven: Yale, 1930.

Hermansson, Halldor. *Catalogue of Icelandic Collection bequeathed by Willard Fiske.* Ithaca: 1914 and 1927.

Hermansson, Halldor. *Modern Icelandic, an Essay.* Ithaca: 1919.

Hertzberg, Ebbe, in *A General Survey of Continental Legal History.* 1912. Pp. 531-76. The author was a leading Norwegian student of early Scandinavian law.

Holme, J. G. *Icelanders in the United States.* New York: 1921.

Johanneson, Alexander. "The University of Iceland," 38 *American Scandinavian Review* 349-54 (December 1950). The author is president of the University of Iceland.

Johnson, Skuli. *Iceland's Thousand Years.* Winnipeg: 1945.

Johnson, Sveinbjorn. *Pioneers of Freedom. An Account of the Icelanders and the Icelandic Free State, 874-1262.* Boston: 1930. The author was professor of law at the University of Illinois.

Larsen, Karen. *A History of Norway.* New York: Princeton, 1948. See especially pp. 55-58, 84, 96, 134, 169, 233, 326, 350, 409. The author was professor of history at Saint Olaf College, Northfield, Minnesota.

Mallet, P. H. *Northern Antiquities,* pp. 276-96. Percy translation 1847.

Munch-Petersen, H. "Main Features of Scandinavian Law," 43 *L. Q. Rev.* 366-77 (1927).

Peaslee, Amos. *Constitutions of Nations,* "Icelandic Constitution," II, 171-78 (1950).

Repp, Thorleifr Gudmandarson. *A Historical Treatise on Trial by Jury, Wager of Law and other Co-ordinate Forensic Institutions formerly in use in Scandinavia and in Iceland.* Edinburgh: 1832.

Rothery, Agnes. *Iceland, New World Outpost.* New York: Viking Press, 1948.

Smith, Paul A. "ICAO Conference on Air Navigation Service in Iceland," *Dept. State Bull.* 164-66 (February 6, 1949).

Stefansson, Jon. *Denmark and Sweden with Iceland and Finland.* New York: 1917. See pp. 153-68. The author was lecturer in Icelandic at King's College, London.

Teisen, Axel. "Scandinavia. Legislation and Bibliography of Law," 1 *A.B.A.J.* 160-62 (1915), 2 *A.B.A.J.* 267-75 (1916).

Thordarson, Bjorn. *Iceland Past and Present.* London: 1945. The author has been Prime Minister in Iceland.

Thoroddsen, Gunnar. "Comments on Constitution of Iceland" in Amos Peaslee, *Constitutions of Nations,* II, 179-87 (1950). The author was secretary of the commission drafting the 1944 constitution, is a member of the Althing, and a professor of government at the University of Iceland.

Thorsteinsson, Thorsteinn. *Iceland.* 3rd ed.; Reykjavik: 1936.

Weigert, Hans. "Iceland, Greenland and the United States" in *Foreign Affairs* 112-22 (Oct. 1944).

Zimmerman, J. L. "A Note on the Occupation of Iceland by American Forces," 62 *Pol. Sc. Q.* 103-06 (March 1947).

B. REFERENCES IN ICELANDIC

Nordal, Sigurd. *Islenzk Menning.* Reykjavik: 1942. There are two more volumes to be published. This is the best critical evaluation of Icelandic culture.

Sigurdson, Jon. *Diplomatorium Islandicum.* 1857-1876.

Sigurjonsson, Arnor. *Islandingasaga.* Akureryri: 1948. This is the most up-to-date history of Iceland.

C. REFERENCES IN DANISH

Arnason, Jon. *Historisk Indledning til den gamle og nye Islandske Raettergang.* 1762.

Arnorsson, Einar. "Den ny islandske lov av Besvangrelse og Afbrydelse af Svangerskab," *Nordisk Tidsskrift for Strafferet* 1-32 (1936).

Finsen, V. *Den islandske Fristats Institutioner.* Copenhagen: 1888.

―――. *Om de islandske love i Fristatstiden.* Copenhagen: 1873.

Gragas, *Islaendernes Lovbog i Fristatatens.* Translated into Danish by V. Finsen. 4 vols. Copenhagen: 1870.

D. REFERENCES IN SWEDISH

Larusson, Olafur. "Den islandska rättens utveckling sedan år 1262," 35 *Svensk Juristtidning* 241-59 (1950). The author is professor of law at the University of Iceland.

Tryggvason, Arni. "Nagra Rättsfall Fran Islands Högsta Domstol år 1949," 35 *Svensk Juristtidning* 950-57 (1950). The author is a member of the Supreme Court of Iceland.

E. REFERENCES IN GERMAN

Hermann, Paul. *Island, das Land und das Volk.* Leipzig and Berlin: 1914.

Kose, Olaf. *Islandkatalog der Universität—Bibliothek Kiel und der Universitäts und Stadtbibliothek Koln.* Kiel: 1931.

Maurer, Konrad von. *Die Entstehung des islandischen Staates und seiner Verfassung.* Munich: 1874. The author, born in 1823, was a professor at the University of Munich and a leading student of early Icelandic and Norwegian law.

―――. *Die Rechtsrichtung des alten islandischen Rechtes.* Munich: 1887.

―――. *Island von seiner ersten Entdeckung bis zum Untergange des Fristaates.* Munich: 1847.

―――. *Vorlesungen über altnordische Rechtsgeschichte.* Vols. 4 and 5. Munich: 1909-1910. These volumes represent Maurer's revised ideas concerning Iceland.

Schweitzer, Ph. *Island Land und Leute.* Leipzig and Berlin: about 1890.

F. REFERENCES IN FRENCH

Gregersen. *L'Islande, son statut à travers les ages.* Paris: 1937.

Bibliography of Norwegian Law

A. REFERENCES IN ENGLISH

American Foreign Law Association. *Bibliography for Scandinavia*. 1926. Prepared by Axel Teisen.

American Scandinavian Review. Four reviews of Norwegian affairs are published each year.

Arneson, Ben A. *The Democratic Monarchies of Scandinavia*, 2d ed.; New York: D. Van Nostrand, 1949. This is an excellent study of Norwegian government.

Ashmead, A. S. "Norwegian Leper Law and International Leper Law," 16 *Medical Legal Journal* 10 (1899).

"Aviation Arrangements between the United States and Norway," 5 *Journal Air Law* 134-40 (1934).

Borchard, E. M. "Was Norway Delinquent in the Case of the Altmark?" 34 *Am. J. Int. Law* 289-94 (1940).

Boyesen, Hjalmar H. *A History of Norway*. London: 1900. The author was a professor at Columbia University.

Brögger, Anton Wilhelm. *Ancient Emigrants, A History of Norse Settlements of Scotland*. Oxford: 1929.

Carlyle, Thomas. *The Early Kings of Norway*. London: 1875.

Child Welfare Committee, League of Nations. *Child Welfare Councils, Denmark, Norway, Sweden*. (Official No.: C. 8. M. 7. 1937, IV, I.)

Collinder, Björn. *The Lapps*. Princeton University Press, 1949.

Constitution of Norway. Oslo: 1937. Published by the Norwegian Ministry of Justice. See also Dodd, *Modern Constitutions*. Chicago: 1909. II, 123-43.

"Declaration by Norway, Denmark and Sweden Relative to the Establishment of Uniform Rules of Neutrality," 7 *Am. J. Int. L. Suppl.* 187-91 (1913).

Elviken, Andreas. "The Genesis of Norwegian Nationalism," 3 *Journal of Modern History* 365-91 (September 1931). The author was a professor of history at Temple University.

Evensen, Jens, "The Anglo-Norwegian Fisheries Case and its Legal Consequences," 46 *Am. J. Int. L.* 609-30 (1952).

Falnes, Oscar J. *National Romanticism in Norway*. New York: Columbia University Press, 1933.

Family and Child Welfare in Norway. Oslo: Joint Committee on International Social Policy, 1949.

Friis, Henning. *Scandinavia Between East and West*. Ithaca: Cornell University Press, 1950.

Gade, John A. *The Hanseatic Control of Norwegian Commerce During the Late Middle Ages*. Leiden, Holland: 1951.

Galenson, Walter. *Labor in Norway*. Cambridge: Harvard University Press, 1949. The author was Labor Attaché at the American Embassy in

Oslo in 1945 and 1946, and is a professor of economics at Harvard University.

Galenson, Walter. "Nationalization of Industry in Great Britain and Norway," 36 *Am. Scan. Rev.* 234-38 (Sept. 1948).

Gjerset, Knut. *The History of the Norwegian People.* New York: 1927. This volume is out of print. It is the earlier outstanding history in English. The author was a professor at Luther College, Decorah, Iowa.

Grevstad, Nicolay. "Norway's Conciliation Tribunals," 2 *J. Am. Jud. Soc.* 5-8 (1918).

Grimley, O. B. *The New Norway.* Oslo: 1937. A discussion of economic, political and social problems.

Haavind, T. "Bankruptcy Act of Norway," 5 *J. Nat. Assoc. Referees in Bankruptcy* 100-01, 115 (1931).

Hambro, Carl J. *I Saw It Happen in Norway.* New York: 1940. The author is president of the Storthing.

Hambro, Edvard. "Small States and a New League from the Viewpoint of Norway," 37 *Am. Pol. Sc. Rev.* 903-09 (1943). The author is the registrar of the International Court of Justice.

———. "Some Remarks about the Relation between Municipal Law and International Law in Norway," *Acta Scandinavia juris gentium,* 3-22, in *Nordisk Tidsskrift for International Ret.* (1949, Nos. 1 and 2).

Harris, Seymour E. *Economic Planning.* New York: 1949. The author is professor of economics at Harvard University.

Heckscher, E. F., Keilhau, William, and others. *Sweden, Norway, Denmark and Iceland in the World War.* New Haven: Yale University Press, 1930.

Hertzberg, Ebbe C. H. *A General Survey of Continental Legal History,* 531-76 (1912). The author was a professor at the University of Oslo.

Holm-Nielsen, H. "The Scandinavian Convention on Bankruptcy and Arrangements Outside Bankruptcy," 18 *J. Comp. Leg. & Int. L.* (3d ser.) 262-65 (1936).

Hovde, Bryn J. *Diplomatic Relations of the United States with Sweden and Norway, 1814-1905.* Iowa City: 1921.

———. *The Scandinavian Countries, 1720-1865; The Rise of the Middle Classes.* 2 vols. Boston: 1943. Reissued in 1948 by the Cornell University Press. The author is now bringing the study up to the present time.

Hyde, Charles Cheney. "The Case Concerning the Legal Status of Eastern Greenland," 27 *Am. J. Int. Law* 732-38 (1933). The author was a professor at Columbia University.

———. "The City of Flint," 34 *Am. J. Int. L.* 89-95 (1940).

"Integrity of Norway Guaranteed," 2 *Am. J. Int. L.* 176-78, 646-48 (1908).

Jensen, Arne Sigurd. *The Rural Schools of Norway.* Boston: 1928.

Johnson, Amanda. *Norway, Invasion and Occupation.* 1948.

Johnson, D. H. N. "The Anglo-Norwegian Fisheries Case," 1 *Int. and Comparative Law Quarterly* 145-80 (1952).

Jones, S. Shepard. *The Scandinavian States and the League of Nations.* New York: 1939.

Jorgenson, Theodore. *Norway's Relation to Scandinavian Unionism, 1815-1871.* Northfield, Minn.: 1935.

"Judicial Abrogation of the Obsolete Statute: A Comparative Study," 64 *Harv. L. Rev.* 1181 (1951).

Kalijarvi, T. "Scandinavian Claims to Jurisdiction over Territorial Waters," 26 *Am. J. Int. Law* 57-69 (1932).

Keilhau, Wilhelm. "Evolution of Labour Legislation in Norway," 1 *The Norseman* (July 1943).

———. *Norway in World History.* London: 1944.

Kendrick, Thomas D. *A History of the Vikings.* New York: 1930.

Klein, L. R. "Planned Economy in Norway," 38 *American Econ. Rev.* 795-814 (December 1948).

Koht, Halvdan. *Norway: Neutral and Invaded.* New York: 1941. The author was Foreign Minister of Norway and a leading historian.

———. "Scandinavian Kingdoms Until the End of the Thirteenth Century," in 6 *Cambridge Medieval History* 382. New York: 1936.

Koht, Halvdan and Skard, Sigmund. *The Voice of Norway.* New York: Columbia University Press, 1944.

Larsen, Karen. *A History of Norway.* Princeton University Press for the American-Scandinavian Foundation: 1948. The author was a professor at Saint Olaf College, Northfield, Minnesota.

Larson, Laurence M. *The Earliest Norwegian Laws.* New York: Columbia University Press, 1935. The author was a professor at the University of Illinois.

———. "Witnesses and Oath Helpers in Old Norwegian Law," in *Haskin's Anniversary Essays.* Boston: 1929.

Leach, Henry Goddard. *Angevin Britain and Scandinavia.* Cambridge: 1921. The author was editor of the *American Scandinavian Review.*

Lee-Smith, H. B. "The Parliamentary System in Norway," 5 *J. Comp. Leg. & Int. Law* (3rd ser.) 35 (1923).

Leivestad, Trygve. "Custom as a Type of Law in Norway," 58 *L. Q. Rev.* 95-115, 266-86 (1938).

Lindegren, Alina M. *Institutions of Higher Education in Norway.* U. S. Govt. Printing Office: 1934. (U. S. Office of Education, Bull. 1934, No. 2.)

Loftfield, Gabriel. *Secondary Education in Norway.* U. S. Govt. Printing Office: 1930. (U. S. Office of Education, Bull. No. 17.)

Mawer, Allen. *The Vikings.* Cambridge: 1930.

Morgenstierne, Bredo. "Norway's Integrity and Neutrality," 31 *L. Q. Rev.* 389-96 (1915). The author was rector and professor of law at the University of Oslo.

Moss, J. "Public Assistance Administration in Norway," 95 *Just. P.* 256-58 (April 18, 1931).

Munch-Petersen, H. "Main Features of Scandinavian Law," 43 *L. Q. Rev.* 366-77 (1927). The author was professor of law at the University of Copenhagen.

New Universal Social Security Plan for Norway. Joint Committee on International Social Policy. Oslo: 1949.

Nordskog, J. E. *Social Reform in Norway.* Los Angeles: University of Southern California Press, 1935.

"Norway: Legislation in Exile," 24 *J. Comp. Leg. & Int. Law* (3d ser.) 125-30 (1942).

Norwegian Social and Labour Legislation. Issued by the Norwegian Joint Committee on International Social Policy. Oslo: 1950. This covers child welfare, public health and social security, workmen's protection, employment, labor relations, housing, and seamen. Under social security are covered accident insurance, health insurance, unemployment insurance, old age pensions, pensions for seamen, and blind and crippled.

Norwegian Social Insurance Laws. Issued by the Joint Committee on International Social Policy. Oslo: 1949. This covers accident insurance for fishermen, industrial employees and seamen, sickness insurance, blind and crippled, old age pensions, and unemployment insurance.

Otte, Elise C. *Norway, Sweden and Denmark.* New York: 1936. This is Volume 16 of the *History of Nations.*

Oyen, E. "Commercial Arbitration in Norway," 3 *Arb. J.* (N.S.) 164-68 (Fall 1948).

Padelford, N. J. "New Scandinavian Neutrality Rules," 32 *Am. J. Int. Law* 789-93 (1938).

Peaslee, Amos J. *Constitutions of Nations,* II, "The Constitution of Norway," 675-88 (1950).

Peterson, C. Stewart. *American-Scandinavian Diplomatic Relations, 1776-1876* (1948). Distributed by the author. Box 611, Baltimore, Md.

Preuss, L. "Dispute between Denmark and Norway on the Sovereignty of East Greenland," 26 *Am. J. Int. Law* 469-87 (1932). The author is a professor at the University of Michigan.

Ratzlaff, C. J. *The Scandinavian Unemployment Relief Program.* Philadelphia: 1934.

Scott, Franklin D. "American Influences in Norway and Sweden," in 18 *Journal of Modern History* 37-47 (1946). The author is a professor at Northwestern University.

————. *The United States and Scandinavia.* Cambridge: Harvard University Press, 1950.

Scott, James Brown. "United States—Norway Arbitration Award" (with Text of Award), 17 *Am. J. Int. Law* 287-90, 362-99 (1923).

Skavang, Nils B. "History and Development of Scandinavian Law—Some Salient Traits," 6 *Seminar* 60-71 (1948). Published by Catholic University of America, Washington, D.C.

Smith, H. P. "Arbitration with Norway," 16 *Am. J. Int. Law* 81-84 (1922).

Smith, Reginald Heber. "Conciliation Procedure in the Administration of Justice in Norway," *Monthly Labor Review* (June 1926).

Social Insurance in Norway. Norwegian Joint Committee on International Social Policy. Oslo: 1949.

Sturlason, Snorre. *Heimskringla: The Norse King Sagas.* New York: 1930. History of Norway to 1177 by an Icelandic lawyer who lived from 1178 to 1241. The translation is by Samuel Laing. There is also a translation by Erling Monsen and A. H. Smith. Cambridge: 1932. It is the greatest of the sagas.

Sverrissaga. The Saga of King Sverri of Norway. London: 1899. Translated by John Sephton. This covers the period from 1177 to 1202.

Taranger, Absalon. "The Meaning of the Words Odal and Skeyting in the Old Laws of Norway," in Essays in Legal History, edited by Paul Vinogradov. London: 1913. The author was a professor at the University of Oslo.

Teisen, Axel. "Scandinavia. Bibliography of Comparative Law." 1 A.B.A.J. 160-62 (1915), 2 A.B.A.J. 270-75 (1916).

The Norway Yearbook. Oslo: 1950. Prepared by the Royal Norwegian Information Service.

Toyne, S. M. The Scandinavians in History. London: 1948.

Vigness, Paul G. Neutrality of Norway in the World War. Stanford University Press, 1932.

War Crimes Trials. Vol. VI. The Trial of Von Falkenhorst. London: 1949.

Wold, Terje. "The 1942 Enactment for the Defence of the Norwegian State," 20 Canadian Bar Rev. 505-09 (1942).

Young, Richard. "The Anglo-Norwegian Fisheries Case," 38 A.B.A.J. 243-45 (1952).

B. REFERENCES IN SCANDINAVIAN, PRINCIPALLY NORWEGIAN

Alten, E. Tvistemålsloven, 2d ed.; Oslo: 1940. Court procedure.

Andenaes, Johannes. "Norsk juridisk literatur 1946-1948," 34 Svensk Juristtidning 702-706 (1949). Legal literature in Norway after the war. The author is a professor of law at the University of Oslo.

————. Rättsuppgörelsen i Norge efter Andra Varldskriget. Stockholm: 1950. Legal development in Norway after the Second World War.

————. Statsforfatningen i Norge. Oslo: 1948. Norwegian constitutional law.

————. "Straffensformal," 58 Tidsskrift for Rettsvitenskap 481-99 (1946). The purpose of punishment.

————. Svek och Motstand under Norges Ockupationsår. Stockholm: 1950. Norwegian resistance during the German occupation.

Andersen, Kristen. Norsk kjøpsrett i hovedtraekk. Oslo: 1945. Law of sales. The author is a professor of law at the University of Oslo.

Andersen, J. E. Handbok i Norsk sinnsykerett. Oslo: 1950. Handbook on the law of insanity in Norway.

Arnholm, Carl J. Alminnelig avtalerett. Oslo: 1949. The general law of agreements. The author is dean and professor at the University of Oslo Law School.

————. Forelaesningen over Norsk personrett. Oslo: 1947. Lectures on Norwegian law of persons.

————. Laerebok i familierett. Oslo: 1945. Textbook on family law.

————. Panteretten. 2d ed.; Oslo: 1950. The law of mortgages.

Aschehoug, Thorkel H. De norske communers Retsforfatning för 1837. The legal status of Norwegian municipalities before 1837. The author was a professor of law at the University of Oslo.

Aschehoug, Thorkel. *Indledning til den norske retvidenskab.* Oslo: 1845. Introduction to Norwegian jurisprudence.
————. *Norges nuvaerende statsforfatning.* 1891-1893. The constitutional system as of 1891.
————. *Statsforfatningen i Norge og Danmark Indil 1814.* Oslo: 1886. The constitutional systems of Norway and Denmark up to 1814.
Aubert, Ludvig M. B. "Bevissystemets udvikling i den norske criminalproces indtil Christian V's lov." *Ugeblad for lovkyndighed,* Oslo: 1804. A study of proof and evidence in the period up to 1688. The author was professor of law at the University of Oslo.
————. *Grundbögernes historie: Norge, Danmark, og tildels i tyskland.* Oslo: 1892. History of real property law in Norway and Denmark.
————. *Kontraktpantets historiske udvikling isaer i dansk og norsk ret.* Oslo: 1872. Historical development of mortgages and other forms of pledges involving contracts.
————. *De norske retskilder og deres anvendelse.* Oslo: 1877. Sources of Norwegian legal history and their application.
Augdahl, Per. *Aksjeselskapet.* Oslo: 1946. The law of corporations. The author is professor of law at the University of Oslo.
————. *Laerebok i skifterett.* Oslo: 1946.
————. *Norsk Civilprocess.* Trondheim: 1947. Norwegian civil procedure.
Berg, Paal. *Arbeidsrett.* Oslo: 1930. Labor law. The author was a Chief Justice of the Supreme Court.
————. *For Godvilje og Rett.* Oslo: 1947. Discusses the function of judges, the Norwegian Supreme Court from 1815 to 1940, the concept of democracy, labor law, and the University of Oslo.
————. "Norges Høyesterett 1815-1940," 26 *Svensk Juristtidning* 3-16 (1941). The Norwegian Supreme Court from 1815-1940.
Bjornberg, Arne. *Parlamentarismens utveckling i Norge efter 1905.* Uppsala: 1939. Parliamentary development in Norway after 1905.
Braekhus, Sjur. *Meglerens rettslige stilling.* Oslo: 1947. The legal status of the mediator. The author is a professor of law at the University of Oslo.
Brandt, Frederik Peter. *Forelaesninger over den norske retshistorie.* 2 Vols. Oslo: 1880, 1883. Lectures in Norwegian legal history. The author was professor of law at the University of Oslo.
————. "Nordmaendenes gamle strafferet," in *Norsk historisk tidskrift,* Ser. I, Vol. IV (1877) 327-391; Ser. II, Vol. IV (1884) 20-113. Ancient Scandinavian criminal law.
————. *Om förelobige retsmidler i den gamle norske rettergang.* Oslo: 1862. Preliminary proceedings in old Norwegian legal procedure.
Bugge, N. Article on the Scandinavian Uniform Laws, 26 *Tidskrift for Rettsvidenskap* 80 (1914).
Castberg, Frede. *Folkerett.* Oslo: 1948. International law. The author is rector and professor of law at the University of Oslo.
————. *Norges statsforfatning.* 2d ed.; Oslo: 1947. The Norwegian Constitution.
————. *Norsk livssyn og samfunnsliv.* Oslo: 1949. Legal and ethical principles in Norwegian life.

Castberg, Frede. *Rettsfilosofiske grunnspörsmal.* Oslo: 1939. Basic problems of legal philosophy.

Decorah Posten. A newspaper published weekly in Decorah, Iowa. It is one of the two leading Norwegian-American newspapers.

Den norske sjöfarts historie fra de aeldste tider til vore daga, by Alexander Bugge, Fredrik Scheel, Roar Tank, Jacob S. Worm-Müller, et al. 3 vols., Oslo: 1923-25. History of Norwegian seafaring.

Det norske folks liv og historie gjennom tidene. 10 vols., Oslo: 1929-1935. Vol. 1, Haakon Shetelig. Vol. 2, Eduard Bull. Vol. 3, S. Hasund. Vols. 4-7, Sverre Steen. Vols. 8-10, Wilhelm Keilhau. A social and economic history of Norway.

Diplomatorium Norvegicum. Oslo: 1847. Materials on Norwegian diplomacy.

Dons, J. B. *Forelaesninger over den danske og norske lov.* Copenhagen: 1781.

Dons, Erik. *Norsk statsborgerrett.* Oslo: 1947. The law of citizenship in Norway.

Engh, A., and Nordanger, K. M. *Kommunalkunnskap.* 2 vols. Oslo: 1935. An account of the structure and functions of local government by persons who have served in the Storthing.

Getz, Bernard and Hagerup, Francis. *Lov on rettergangsmalen i straffesager.* Oslo 1890. Criminal procedure.

Gjelsvik, Nikolaus: *Innleiding i rettstudiet.* 3rd ed.; Oslo: 1939. This is one of the leading Norwegian books on introduction to the study of law. The author was a professor of law at the University of Oslo.

Gjerdrum, A. *Utsikt over den nye civil process.* Oslo: 1927. A survey of the new code of civil procedure.

Gragas, Islaendernes Lovbog i Fristatens Tid. Translated from the Icelandic into Danish by Vilhjalmar Finsen. 4 Vols. Copenhagen: 1870. The Gray Goose, the Icelandic law text before 1262.

Gulbransen and Hoffman, *Norsk juridisk ordbok.* Oslo: 1948. Norwegian legal dictionary.

Hagerup, Francis. *Civilprocessen paa grundlag av de nye love av 13 Aug., 1915, alminnelig fremstillet.* Oslo: 1915. A commentary on the Code of Civil Procedure of 1915. The author was a professor of law at the University of Oslo, and prime minister.

———. *Forelaesninger over den norske civilproces.* 2d ed., 1903. Lectures on Norwegian legal procedure.

———. *Udvalgte mindre juridiske afhandlinger.* Oslo: 1915. Selected minor legal essays.

Hambro, Edvard. *Norsk fremmedrett.* Oslo: 1950. The rights of aliens in Norway.

Hansson, Kristian. *Norsk Kirkerett.* Oslo: 1935. Norwegian church law.

Hertzberg, Ebbe C. H. "De Nordiske Retskilder" in *Nordisk Retsencyclopaedi.* Copenhagen: 1890. The sources of Scandinavian law. For an English translation see *A General Survey of Continental Legal History,* 531-576 (Boston, 1912). The author was a professor of law at the University of Oslo.

———. *Grundtraekkene i den aeldste norske proces.* Oslo: 1874. Outlines of the oldest Norwegian legal procedure.

———. *Norges gamle, love,* V, *glossarium.* Oslo: 1895. A glossary to the old Norwegian laws prepared with Gustav Storm.

Hertzberg, Ebbe C. H. "Vore aeldste Lovtexters oprindelige Nedskrivelsetid" in *Historiske Afhandlinger tilegnede Professor dr. J. E. Sars.* Oslo: 1905. The time at which the oldest laws were written.

Holberg, Ludvig. *Danmarks og Norges geistlige og verldslige stat.* Copenhagen: 1762.

————. *Introduktion til Natur og Folkeretten.* Copenhagen: 1716 and 1763. Introduction to natural law and international law.

Holmboe, C. Stub. *Foreldelse av Fordringer.* Oslo: 1946. Prescription and statutes of limitations. The author is a member of the Norwegian Supreme Court.

Hurtigkarl, F. T. *Den Danske og Norske Rets første Grunde.* Copenhagen: 1820. Basic principles of Danish and Norwegian Law.

Ipsen. "Den danske og Norske proces" in *Nordisk Retsencyclopaedi,* Vol. 4. Norwegian and Danish legal procedure.

Johnsen, Oscar Albert. *Norges bonder; utsyn over den norske bondestands historie.* Oslo: 1919. A history of the freemen of rural Norway.

Keyser, Rudolf. *Norges stats—og retsforfatning i middelalderen.* Oslo: 1867. The legal and constitutional system in Norway in the Middle Ages.

Knoph, Ragnar. *Aandsretten.* Oslo: 1936. Law as to protection of intangible right. The author was a professor in the University of Oslo Law School.

————. *Oversikt over Norges rett.* Oslo: 1948. A survey of Norwegian law. 3rd ed. by Sverre Grette.

————. *Rettslige Standarder, saerlig grunnlovens #97.* Oslo: 1939. Legal principles, particularly of retroactivity.

Koht, Halvdan. *Johan Sverdrup.* 4 vols. Oslo: 1918-1925.

————. *Vore høvdinger.* Trondheim: 1929. This volume contains short biographies of Norwegian leaders.

Kongslev, L. L. *Den danske og norske private Rets første Grunde.* Copenhagen: 1792. Basic principles of Danish and Norwegian private law.

Langfeldt, Gabriel. *Rettspsychiatri for Jurister og Leger.* Legal psychiatry for lawyers and physicians.

Larusson, Olafur. "Den islandska rättens utveckling sedan år 1262." 35 *Svensk Juristtidning* 241-59 (1950). The growth of Icelandic law after it became a part of Norway. The author is a professor of law at the University of Iceland.

Lindbraekke, Sjur. *Eiendomsrett og konkursbeslag.* Oslo: 1946. The right of possession and creditors' rights.

Lutken, Hans and Platou, Carl. *Lov om indgaaelse og opløsning av aegteskap av 31. Maj 1918.* Oslo: 1920. The 1918 statute on marriage and divorce.

Lyng, Johan. *Forraederiets epoke.* Oslo: 1948. The era of treason and the trials of Norwegian traitors.

Malmstrom, A. and Ujlaki, N. *The Law Literature of the Scandinavian States Edited in Foreign Languages.* A bibliography about to be published by the Institute of Comparative Law of the University of Uppsala.

Maurer, Konrad von. *Udsigt over de Nordgermanske retskilders historie.* Oslo: 1878. Survey of the sources of Scandinavian legal history.

Morgentierne, Bredo H. *Den norske stats forfatningsret.* 2 vols. Oslo: 1926-

1927. A standard authority on Norwegian constitutional law. The author was rector and professor of law at the University of Oslo.

Munch, Peter Andreas. Det norske folks historie. 4 vols. Oslo: 1852-1863. History of the Norwegian people. The author is one of the greatest Norwegian historians.

Naess, Axel T. Haandbok i Norske ret. Trondheim: 1913. A handbook of Norwegian Law.

Nielsen, Yngvar. Jens Bjelke til Østraat. A study of the Norwegian chancellor of 1648.

————. Lensgreve Johan Caspar Herman Wedel Jarlsberg. 3 vols. Oslo: 1901-1902.

Nordisk Tidende. A newspaper published weekly in Brooklyn, New York. It is the leading Norwegian newspaper published in the United States, and contains numerous references to Norwegian legislation and legal proceedings.

Norges forhold til Sverige under krigen, 1940-1945. 2 vols. Oslo: 1947-1948. Norway's relations with Sweden from 1940 to 1945.

Norges gamle love indtil 1387. Edited by Rudolf Keyser, Peter Munch, Gustav Storm, Ebbe Hertzberg and Absalon Taranger. 5 vols. Oslo: 1846-1895. The laws of Norway to 1387.

Norges historie. 2 vols. Oslo: 1938-1939. Vol. 1. Andreas Holmsen, vol. 2. Magnus Jensen. History of Norway.

Norges historie fremstillet for det Norske folk. 6 vols. Oslo: 1909-1917. Vol. 1, Alexander Bugge, vol. 2, Ebbe Hertzberg and Alexander Bugge, vol. 3, Absalon Taranger, vol. 4, Yngvar Nielsen, vol. 5, Oscar Albert Johnsen, vol. 6, J. E. Sars. History of Norway.

Norges lover 1682-1948. Oslo: Grondahl & Sons, 1950. 2,585 pages. This is the latest volume containing the law of Norway, the last prior edition dating from 1936. It was edited by the law faculty of the University of Oslo under T. Grundt of that faculty and a member of the Supreme Court, Einar Hansen.

Norges prokuratorer, sakførere og advokater. Oslo: 1940-1941. A publication about Norwegian lawyers by the Norwegian Bar Association.

Norsk forsikringsjuridisk forenings publikasjoner. 1940-1948. Numbers 1-20. Publications of the Norwegian insurance law association.

Norsk literaturhistorie. 5 vols. Oslo: 1923-1937. Vols. 1 and 3, Fredrik Paasche, vols. 2 and 4, Francis Bull, vol 5, A. H. Winsnes. History of Norwegian literature.

Norsk lovtidende. An official publication containing all session laws of the Storthing and important regulations and orders.

Oftedal, Christian S. Daglig liv i Norges Storting. Oslo: 1949. Daily life in the Storthing.

Örsted, Anders S. Eunomia, Samling of Afhandlinger, henhörende til Moral-filosofien, Statsfilosofien og den dansk—Norske Lovkyndighed. Copenhagen: 1815-1822. A philosophical study of Danish and Norwegian Law.

Östberg, Kristian. Norsk bonderet. Oslo: 1939. The law governing the farmer.

Övergaard, Jörgen. Norsk erstatningsrett. Oslo: 1951. Norwegian law of torts.

Petersen, Richard. Fengselsliv. Oslo: 1894. A book on prison life by the director of the Oslo prison from 1858 to 1892.

Platou, C. (editor). *Norsk statsborgersbok.* Oslo: 1929. Constitutional law and elementary private law, and national and local administration.
Platou, Oscar. *Forelaesninger over Norsk Sjöret.* 2d ed. by Jacob Aars. Oslo: 1929. Lectures on Norwegian admiralty law.
———. *Forelaesninger over retskildernes Theori.* Oslo: 1915. Lectures on the sources of law.
———. *Forelaesninger over udvalgte emner af privatrettens almindelige del.* Oslo: 1913-1914. Lectures on certain phases of the conflict of laws.
Prebensen, N. and Smith, H. *Forarbeiderne til Kong Christian den femtes Norske lov.* The drafting of Christian V's Norwegian Law.
Norsk Retstidende. This is a Norwegian legal periodical founded in 1836.
Röed, Ole Torlief. *Fra krigens folkerett.* Oslo: 1945. The law of Norway during the German occupation.
Salomonsen, Olaf. *Den Norske Straffesproceslov.* 2d ed.; Oslo: 1925. Norwegian criminal procedure.
Sars, Johan E. W. *Historisk indledning til grundloven.* 1887. Historical introduction to the Constitution. The author is one of the greatest Norwegian historians.
———. *Udsigt over den Norske historie.* 4 vols. Oslo: 1874-1877. General survey of Norwegian history.
Schjodt, Magne. *Norsk ekspropriasjonsrett.* Oslo: 1947. Norwegian law of expropriation.
Schweigaard, Anton Martin. "Betragtninger over Retvidenskabens Naervaerende Tilstand i Tyskland" in *Dansk Juridisk Tidsskrift.* 1834. Reflections on the status of jurisprudence in Germany.
———. *Den Norske proces,* 2 vols. Oslo: 1891. Norwegian court procedure.
Semmingsen, Ingrid. *Veien mot vest.* Oslo: 1941 and 1951. 2 vols. Emigration from Norway to the United States. This is the leading Norwegian book on this subject.
Sjöberg, A. Hemming. *Domen över Quisling.* Stockholm: 1946. The trial of Quisling.
Skeie, Jon. *Den Norske civil process.* 3 vols. Oslo: 1935. Norwegian civil procedure. The author was a professor of law at the University of Oslo.
———. *Den Norske straffe process.* 2 vols. Oslo: 1939. Norwegian criminal procedure.
———. *Strafferet.* 2 vols. Oslo: 1946-1947. The substantive criminal law.
Smedal, Gustav. *Patriotisme og Landssvik.* Oslo: 1950. Patriotism and treason.
Solem, Erik. "Den praktiske Gjemnomføring av den Norske process reformen," 25 *Svensk Juristtidning* 265-70 (1940). How the Norwegian Code of Civil Procedure was introduced to the bar.
———. *Forliksradene under den nye rettergang.* Oslo: 1927. Conciliation under the new code of civil procedure.
———. *Holberg som jurist.* Oslo: 1947. Holberg as a jurist.
———. *Lappiske rettstudier.* Oslo: 1933. Studies of Lappish law.
———. *Praktisk rettergang.* Oslo: 1927. Practical aspects of legal procedure.
———. *Straffesak mot Vikdun Abraham Lauritz Jonsson Quisling.* Oslo: 1946. The criminal proceeding against Quisling.

Stang, Emil. *Rettergangsmaten i Straffesaker.* Oslo: 1951. Criminal procedure.

Stang, Fredrik. *Fremstilling av Norges konstitutionelle ret.* Oslo: 1833. Norwegian constitutional law up to 1833.

Sterri, Martin. *Bondens Juridiske Formularbok.* Oslo: 1949. A law book on the rights of farmers.

Storm, Gustav. *Sigurd Rannessöns proces.* Oslo: 1877. A famous law suit of about 1115 in which the joint kings intervened.

Stortingets forretningsorden. Oslo: 1934. Rules of Procedure in the Storthing.

Stortingstidende. Parliamentary Journal. Reports of the debates and proceedings of the Storthing.

Stoylen. *Separasjon og skilsmesse.* Oslo: 1948. Separation and divorce.

Sund, Haakon. "Bernhard Getz," 60 *Tidsskrift for Rettsvitenskap* 4-19 (1950).

Sund, Harold. "Krigsforbryterne i Norge og oppgøret med dem," 59 *Tidsskrift for Rettsvitenskap* 1-29 (1946). War criminals in Norway and their disposition.

Taranger, Absalon. "Alting og lagthing" in *Historisk Tidsskrift,* XXXIX, 137-138 (1930, No. 3). The author was a professor of law at the University of Oslo.

———. "De norske folkelovböker för 1263" in *Tidsskrift for retvidenskap,* XXXIX, 183-211, XLI, 1-68. The Norwegian provincial law texts before 1263.

———. *Norsk familierett.* 2d ed.; Oslo: 1926. Norwegian family law.

———. *Udsigt over den norske retshistorie.* Oslo: 1898. A general survey of Norwegian legal history. There is a later edition in 1935 by Knut Robberstad of the law school of the University of Oslo.

Thomle, C. S. *Norsk Navnerett.* Oslo: 1931. The Norwegian law as to names.

Tidsskrift for Rettsvitenskap. The leading Norwegian law review. It has been edited by Fredrik Stang, Francis Hagerup and Ragnar Knoph. It was commenced in 1888.

Treschow, Niels. *Lovgivningsprincipper.* Oslo: 1821-1823. Principles of law development. The author was rector and professor of philosophy at the University of Oslo.

Vogt, Adler. *Bernhard Getz.* Oslo: 1950. A biography of a leading Norwegian authority on criminal law.

Vullum, Erik. *Kristian Magnus Falsen, Grundlovens fader.* Oslo: 1881. The father of the Constitution, Kristian Falsen.

Welle, Ivar. *Norges Kirkehistorie.* Oslo: 1949. A history of the Norwegian Church.

Winge, Paul. *Den norske sindssygeret historisk fremstillet.* Oslo: 1913. The law of insanity.

C. REFERENCES IN GERMAN

Aal and Gjelsvik. *Die Norwegisch Schwedische Union. Ihr Bestehen und ihre Lesung.* Breslau: 1912. The union between Norway and Sweden.

Amira, Karl von. *Das altnorwegische Vollstrechungsverfahren.* Munich: 1874.

———. "Zur Textgeschichte der Frostathingsbok" in *Germania,* XXXII, 129-164. Vienna: 1887. History of the Frostathing Law.

Aschehoug, Thorkel. *Staatsrecht der Vereinigten königreiche. Schweden und Norwegen.* 1886. The constitutional system of the united kingdom of Sweden and Norway.

Drolsum, Axel C. *Das Königreich Norwegen als souveraner Staat.* Berlin: 1905. The kingdom of Norway as a sovereign state.

Fleischmann, Max. *Das Staatsgrundesetz des Königreichs Norwegen nebst urkundlichen Beilagen uber die Union mit Schweden.* Breslau: 1912. The constitutional status of Norway during the union with Sweden.

Maurer, Konrad von. *Die Bekehrung des Norwegischen Stammes zum Christenthum,* 2 vols. Munich: 1855-1856. History of Norway up to its Christianization. The author is the leading German writer on Norwegian law.

————. "Die Eintheilung der älteren Frostathingslog" in *Norsk historisk tidsskrift,* Ser. II, vol. VI (1888) 203-35. The older Frostathing Law.

————. *Die Entstehungszeit der älteren Frostathingslog.* Munich: 1875. The older Frostathing Law.

————. *Die Entstehungszeit der älteren Gulathingslog.* Munich: 1872. The older Gulathing law.

————. *Vorlesungen über altnordische Rechtsgeschichte.* Leipzig: 1907-1910. Vols. I-III. Lectures on old Scandinavian legal history.

————. "Zur Geschichte Schwedens und Norwegens" in Baedeker's *Schweden und Norwegen.* pp. LI-LXXXVIII, 4th ed.; Leipzig: 1888. A concise résumé of Norwegian history.

Meissner, Rudolf. *Das Rechtbuch des Frostathings.* Weimar: 1939. The Frostathing Law.

————. *Das Rechtsbuch des Gulathings.* Weimar: 1935. The Gulathing Law.

————. *Landrecht des König Magnus Hakonarson.* Weimar: 1941. The Land Law of King Magnus Lawmender.

Morgenstierne, Bredo H. *Das Staatsrecht des Königreichs Norwegen.* Tübingen: 1911. The constitutional law of Norway.

Stuckart, Wilhelm, and Höhn, Reinhard. *Verfassungs, Verwalthungs und Wirt schaftsgesetze der Völker, Norwegen.* Darmstadt: 1942. The constitutional administrative and economic law of Norway.

D. REFERENCES IN FRENCH

Tenaille-Saligny. "Le Code Penal de Norwege," *Revue historique de droit francais et étranger.* May-June, 1862. The Penal Code of Norway in 1862.

E. REFERENCES IN ITALIAN

Astuti, Guido. *Le Constuzioni della Svezia e della Norvegia.* Firenzi: 1946. The constitutions of Sweden and Norway.

Brusa. *Codice di procedura penale Norvegese.* Turin: 1900. The Norwegian code of criminal procedure.

Bibliography of Swedish Law

A. REFERENCES IN ENGLISH

Adlercreutz, A. "Some Features of Swedish Collective Labor Law," 10 *Modern L. Rev.* 137-58 (April 1947).

"Administration of Justice in Sweden," 3 *Cent. L. J.* 564-66 (1876).

"A Few Points on the New Civil Procedure in Sweden," 82 *Ir. L. T.* 159-61 (July 3), 1948.

Ahnlund, Nils. *Gustaf Adolf the Great*. Princeton, N. J.: 1940.

"Air Navigation Agreements between the United States and Sweden," 5 *J. Air L.* 140-42 (January 1934).

Alfsen, F. A. M. "Arbitration in Sweden," 1 *Comparative L. Serv.* 281-84 (July 1938).

———. "Deduction of Reserve Funds from Taxable Income in Sweden," 1 *Comparative L. Ser.* 380-90 (Sept. 1938).

———. "The Swedish Share Company Law," 1 *Comparative L. Ser.* 529-65 (December 1938).

Almquist, Viktor. "Scandinavian Prisons," 157 *The Annals* 197-207 (September 1931).

American Scandinavian Review. There are quarterly accounts of major events in Sweden.

Anderson, Ingvar. *History of Sweden*. London: 1952.

———. *Introduction to Sweden*. Stockholm: Forum, 1949.

Anderson, Mary. "Social Progress in the United States and Sweden," 30 *Am. Scand. Rev.* 32-40 (March 1945).

Arneson, Ben A. *The Democratic Monarchies of Scandinavia*, 2d ed.; New York: D. Van Nostrand Co., Inc., 1949. This is an excellent study of Swedish government. The author is professor of political science at Ohio Wesleyan University.

Bagge, A. "Civil and Commercial Arbitration Law; Arbitration Procedure in Sweden," 1 *Arb. L. J.* 271-77 (July 1937). The author is a member of the Supreme Court of Sweden.

Bain, R. N. *Scandinavia*. Cambridge: 1905. This is a history of government and politics from 1513 to 1900.

Beckman, H. G. *Married Misery and Its Scandinavian Solution*. London: 1923. A reprint of Lord Buckmaster's articles and a digest of Scandinavian legislation.

Bellquist, E. C. "Five Hundredth Anniversary of the Swedish Riksdag," 29 *Am. Pol. Sc. Rev.* 857-65 (October 1935). The author is professor of political science at the University of California.

———. "Political and Economic Conditions in the Scandinavian Countries," XXIV *Foreign Policy Rep.* (May 1948).

———. *Some Recent Aspects of the Foreign Policy of Sweden*. Berkeley, California: 1929.

Bellquist, E. C. *The Development of Parliamentary Government in Sweden.* 1932.

Bengtsson, Halfdan. "The Temperance Movement and Temperance Legislation in Sweden," 197 *The Annals of the American Academy* 34-53 (1938).

Bogoslovsky, Christina. *Educational Crisis in Sweden in Light of American Experience.* New York: Columbia University Press, 1932.

Borgeson, F. C. *The Administration of Elementary and Secondary Education in Sweden.* New York: Columbia University Press, 1927.

Braatoy, Bjarne. *The New Sweden.* London and New York: Thos. Wilson & Sons, 1939.

Carlson, Knute Emil. *Relations of the United States with Sweden.* Allentown, Pa.: H. R. Haas, 1921.

Childs, M. W. *Sweden: The Middle Way.* New York: 1936. New and enlarged edition. New York: Penguin Books, 1948.

——. *This is Democracy: Collective Bargaining in Scandinavia.* New Haven: 1938.

Chricton, A., and Wheaton, H. *Scandinavia, Ancient and Modern,* New York: 1841.

Chydenius, Wilhelm. "Swedish Law Book of 1734: An Early Germanic Codification," 20 *L. Q. Rev.* 377-91 (1904).

Clark, Harrison. *Swedish Unemployment Policy.* Washington: Public Affairs Press, 1941.

Cole, Margaret and Smith, Charles. *Democratic Sweden.* London: G. Routlidge, 1938. Under auspices of New Fabian Research Bureau.

Constitution of Sweden. It appears in Peaslee, *Constitutions of Nations,* III, 96-117. Concord, N. H.: The Rumford Press, 1950.

Craven, Cicely, M. "The Child Welfare Boards of Sweden," 41 *J. Crim. L.* 344-45 (1950).

Dahlberg, G. "New Method in Crime Statistics Applied to the Population of Sweden," 39 *J. Crim. L.* 327-41 (Sept.-Oct. 1948).

Dickerson, C. E. "Business Taxes in Sweden," 1 *Comparative L. Ser.* 53-59, 2 *Comparative L. Ser.* 180-85 (Feb. 1938 and April 1939).

Eldh, Arvid. *Facts About Sweden.* Stockholm: 1948.

Engelmann, Arthur. *A History of Continental Civil Procedure,* pp. 203-38, 833-71 (1927). This is a translation of Uppström, *Öfversigt af den Svenska Processens Historia.* Stockholm: 1884.

Erlander, Tage. "Swedish Social Policy in Wartime," 47 *Int. Labour Rev.* 297-311. The author is prime minister of Sweden.

Fahlkrantz, Gustof E. "The Naemnd; or the Remnant of the Jury in Sweden," 22 *Am. L. Rev.* 837-52 (1888).

Fehr, M. N. "Bankruptcy Law and Practice in Sweden," 5 *J. Nat. Assoc. Referee in Bankruptcy* 102-03 (January 1931).

Friis, Henning. *Scandinavia Between East and West.* Ithaca: Cornell University Press, 1950. This is an up-to-date symposium on Sweden.

Garrison, L. K. "Legal Service for Low Income Groups in Sweden," 26 *A.B.A.J.* 215-20, 293-97 (March-April 1940).

Gille, Halvor. "Recent Developments in Swedish Population Policy," 2 *Population Studies* Nos. 1 and 2 (London 1948).

350 *The Growth of Scandinavian Law*

Göranson, Hardy. "Treatment of Criminals and Other Asocial Individuals,"
197 *The Annals* 120-33 (May 1938). The author was in 1936 Direc-
tor General of the Prison Board at Stockholm.
Graham, John. *Housing in Sweden*. Chapel Hill, N. C.: U. of N. C. Press,
1940.
Greene, W. E. "Survey of the Economic Defense Measures in Sweden," 2
Comparative L. Ser. 527-38 (November 1939).
Grimberg, C. *A History of Sweden*. Rock Island, Illinois: 1935.
Gullander, Ake. *Farmers' Cooperation in Sweden*. London: Crosby Lock-
wood & Co., 1948.
Hagander, J. "The Swedish Labor Court," 1 *Arb. L. J.* 411-14 (1937). The
author is vice-president of the Swedish Labor Court.
Hallendorff, Carl, and Schück, Adolf. *History of Sweden*. London: Cassell,
1929.
Hammarskjöld, Ake. "Sidelights on the Permanent Court of International
Justice," 25 *Mich. L. Rev.* 327-53 (1927). The author was first regis-
trar and then a member of the Permanent Court of International
Justice.
Heckscher, G. "Pluralist Democracy—the Swedish Experience," 15 *Soc.
Research*, 417-61 (December 1948). The author is a leading Swedish
economist.
Hedberg, Anders. *Consumers' Cooperation in Sweden*. Stockholm: Nordisk
Rotogravyr, 1948.
Hedin, Naboth. *Guide to Information about Sweden*, New York: American-
Swedish News Exchange, Inc., 1947. This is a very comprehensive
bibliography.
———. "Sweden: The Dilemma of a Neutral," XXIII *Foreign Policy
Rep.* 435-49 (April 1945).
Herlitz, Nils. *Sweden, A Modern Democracy on Ancient Foundations*.
Minneapolis: University of Minnesota, 1939.
Hertzberg, Ebbe, in *A General Survey of Continental Legal History*, pp. 531-
76 (1912). The author was a Norwegian legal scholar and government
official.
Hewins, Ralph. *Count Folke Bernadotte; His Life and Work*. Minneapolis:
T. S. Denison & Co., 1950.
Hinshaw, David. *Sweden, Champion of Peace*. New York: Putman, 1949.
The author interprets Swedish history as a struggle for peace.
Hohman, Helen F. *Old Age in Sweden*. Washington: Social Security Board,
1939.
Höjer, Axel. "Public Health and Medical Care," 197 *The Annals* 104-19
(May, 1938). The author has been Director General of the Medical
Board of Sweden.
Höjer, Karl. "The Care of the Indigent in Sweden," 197 *The Annals* 72-79
(May 1938). The author has been director of the Swedish Poor
Relief and Child Welfare Association, Stockholm.
———. *Social Welfare in Sweden*. Stockholm: Forum, 1949.
Holm-Nielsen, Henning. "Scandinavian Conventions on Bankruptcy and
Arrangements Outside Bankruptcy," 18 *J. Comp. Leg. & Int. L.*, 3rd
Ser., 262-65 (November 1936).

Hopper, Bruce. "Sweden: A Case Study in Neutrality," 33 *Foreign Affairs* 435-49 (April 1945).

Hovde, Bryn J. *Diplomatic Relations of the United States with Sweden and Norway, 1814-1905.* Iowa City: 1921.

————. *The Scandinavian Countries, 1720-1865,* 2 vols. Boston: 1943; reissued in 1948 by the Cornell University Press. This is an invaluable study of social, economic, and cultural problems. The author is now in the process of bringing the study up to the present time.

Jackson, Robert H. "Swedish Contributions to Our Law," 15 *Pa. Bar Assn. Q.* 122-27 (January 1944). The author is a member of the United States Supreme Court.

Jagerskiöld, S. "A Swedish Case on the Jurisdiction of States over Foreigners," 41 *Am. J. Int. L.* 909-11 (1941).

————. "Immunity of State-Owned Vessels in Swedish Judicial Practice During World War II," 42 *Am. J. Int. L.* 601-07 (July 1948). The author is a professor at the University of Uppsala.

Janson, F. E. "Minority Government in Sweden," 22 *Am. Pol. Sc. Rev.* 407-13 (May 1928).

Jerneman, Tor. "Social Insurance in Sweden," 197 *The Annals* 80-92 (May 1938). The author is an official of the Social Board of Sweden.

Joesten, Joachim. "Phases in Swedish Neutrality," 33 *Foreign Affairs* 324-29 (January 1945).

————. *Stalwart Sweden.* New York: 1943.

Johansson Alf. "Social Housing, Policy in Sweden," 197 *The Annals* 160-70 (May 1938). The author is a professor at the University of Stockholm.

Johnson, Amandus. *The Swedish Settlements on the Delaware, 1638-1664,* 2 vols. Philadelphia: University of Pennsylvania Press, 1911. Abridged edition in 1944.

Jones, S. Shepard. *The Scandinavian States and the League of Nations.* New York: 1939.

Kalijarvi, T. "Scandinavian Claims to Jurisdiction over Territorial Waters," 26 *Am. J. Int. L.* 57-69 (January 1932).

Kinberg, O. "Criminal Policy in Sweden During the Last Fifty Years," 24 *J. Crim. L.* 313-32 (May-June 1933). The author is a professor of psychiatry in Stockholm.

————. "Obligatory Psychiatric Examination of Certain Classes of Accused Persons," 2 *J. Crim. L.* 858-67 (March 1912).

————. "Temperance Legislation in Sweden," 163 *The Annals* 206-15 (September 1932).

Kitchin, S. B. "Suspended Sentences and the Probation System," 31 *So. Afr. L. J.* 10-18 (February 1914).

Lagergren, G. "The Preparatory Proceeding and the Hearing-in-Chief in Sweden," 82 *Ir. L. Times* 165-67 (July 10, 1948).

Lamming, N. *Sweden's Cooperative Enterprises.* Manchester, England: Holyoake Press, 1940.

Lindbom, Tage. *Sweden's Labor Program.*

Lundbergh, Holger. "Where There's No Will, There's a Way," *Survey Midmonthly* 125-26 (April 1940).

Lundstedt, Vilhelm. "Law and Justice: A Criticism of the Method of Justice" in *Interpretations of Modern Legal Philosophy: Essays in Honor of Roscoe Pound*, New York: 1947. Pp. 450-83. The author is professor of Civil and Roman Law at the University of Uppsala.

Lundstedt, Vilhelm. "Responsibility of Legal Science for the Fate of Man and Nations," 10 N. Y. U. L. Q. Rev. 326-40 (March 1933).

————. *Superstition or Reality in Action for Peace—A Criticism of Jurisprudence*. London: 1925.

————. "The Relation Between Law and Equity," 25 Tul. L. Rev. 59-69 (1950).

Maktos, J. "Arbitration Between the United States and Sweden relating to the Swedish Motor Ships 'Kronprins Gustaf Adolf' and 'Pacific'," 1 Geo. Wash. L. Rev. 105-08 (November 1932).

Möller, Gustav. "The Unemployment Policy," 197 The Annals 47-71 (May 1938). The author is a former Minister of Social Affairs for Sweden.

Moss, John. "Public Assistance Administration in Sweden," 95 Just. P. 240-41 (1931).

Munch-Petersen, H. "The Main Features of Scandinavian Law," 43 L. Q. Rev. 366-77 (1927). The author was professor of law at the University of Copenhagen.

————. "The Social Aspect of Procedure from a European Point of View," 11 Minn. L. Rev. 624-34 (1927).

Myrgaard, Arvid. "Sweden's Public Health System," 35 Am. Scand. Rev. 304-20 (December 1947).

Nial, Hakon. "Arbitration Law and Practice in Sweden," 1 Arb. L. J. n.s. 320-27 (Fall 1946). The author is a professor at the University of Stockholm.

Norgren, Paul H. "Collective Wage-Making in Sweden," 46 J. Pol. Econ. 788-801 (December 1938).

————. *The Swedish Collective Bargaining System*. Cambridge, Mass.: Harvard University Press, 1941.

Ohlin, B. "Social Problems and Policies in Sweden," 197 The Annals 1-249 (May 1938). This is a symposium on Swedish social and economic problems honoring the three hundredth anniversary of the Swedish settlement in Delaware.

————. "Tendencies in Swedish Economics," 35 J. Pol. Econ. 343-63 (June 1927).

Olivecrona, Karl. *Law as Fact*. London: Oxford University Press: 1939. Reviewed 53 Harv. L. Rev. 507 (1940) by Max Radin. The author is professor of law at the University of Lund.

————. "Law as Fact" in *Interpretations of Modern Legal Philosophy: Essays in Honor of Roscoe Pound*. New York: 1947. Pp. 542-57.

————. "Realism and Idealism: Some Reflections on the Cardinal Point in Philosophy." 26 N. Y. U. L. Rev. 120-31 (1951).

O'Neill, A. A. "United States-Sweden Arbitration, relating to Motorships 'Kronprins Gustaf Adolf' and 'Pacific'," 26 Am. J. Int. Law 720-34 (October 1932).

Oxholm, A. H. *The Small Housing Scheme of the City of Stockholm*. Washington: U. S. Dept. of Commerce, 1935.

Padelford, N. J. "New Scandinavian Neutrality Rules," 32 Am. J. Int. Law 789-93 (October 1938).

Padelford, N. J., and Anderssen, K. "The Aland Island Question," 33 *Am. J. Int. L.* 465-87 (1939).

Peel, Norman. "Local Government in Scandinavia," 25 *Nat. Mun. Rev.* 528-34 (September 1936).

Peel, Roy V. "Bibliography," 197 *The Annals* 243-49 (May 1938).

Peterson, C. Stewart. *American-Scandinavian Diplomatic Relations, 1776-1876* (1948). Distributed by the author, Box 611, Baltimore, Maryland.

"Probation in Sweden," 4 *J. Crim. L.* 599-601 (November 1913).

Raikes, F. W. "Maritime Laws in Sweden," 17 *L. Mag. & Rev.* (4th Ser.) 235-44; 18: 33-49 (London: 1892).

Ratzlaff, C. J. *The Scandinavian Unemployment Relief Program.* Philadelphia: University of Pennsylvania Press, 1934. The author was professor of economics at the University of Maryland at his death in March, 1951.

Robbins, J. J. "Jurisdiction of the Labor Court in Sweden," 35 *Ill. L. Rev.* 396-408 (1940).

———. *The Government of Labor Relations in Sweden.* Chapel Hill, N. C.: 1942.

Robbins, J. J. and Heckscher, G. "Collective Bargaining in Sweden," 24 *A.B.A.J.* 926-27, 933 (November 1938).

Royal Social Board. *Social Work and Legislation in Sweden.* Stockholm: 1938.

Sandelius, W. "Dictatorship and Irresponsible Particularism: A Study in the Government of Sweden," 49 *Pol. Sc. Q.* 347-71 (September 1934).

Schlesinger, Rudolf B. "Note on the New Swedish Code of Civil Procedure," in *Comparative Law Cases and Materials.* Brooklyn: 1950. P. 219.

Schmidt, F. and Heineman, H. "Enforcement of Collective Bargaining Agreements in Swedish Law," 14 *U. Chi. L. Rev.* 184-99 (Feb. 1947).

Schmidt, Folke. "Nationality and Domicile in Swedish Private International Law," 4 *Int. L. Q.* 39-52 (January 1951). The author is professor of law at the University of Stockholm.

Scott, Franklin D. *Bernadotte and the Fall of Napoleon.* Cambridge: Harvard University Press, 1935. The author is professor of history at Northwestern University.

———. *The History of Sweden.* Now in preparation.

———. *The United States and Scandinavia.* Cambridge: Harvard University Press, 1950.

Segerstedt, Torgny, and Weintraub, Philipp. "Marriage and Divorce in Sweden," 272 *The Annals* 185-94 (November 1950). The former author is professor of sociology at the University of Uppsala, the latter at Hunter College, New York.

Seidenfaden, Erik. "Scandinavia Charts a Course," XXVI *Foreign Affairs* 653-54 (July 1948).

Sellin, Thorsten. *Marriage and Divorce Legislation in Sweden.* Minneapolis: Augsburg Pub. Co., 1922. The author is professor of sociology at the University of Pennsylvania.

———. *Recent Penal Legislation in Sweden.* 1947.

———. "Sweden's Substitute for the Juvenile Court," 272 *The Annals* 137-49 (January 1949).

Sellin, Thorsten. "The Treatment of Offenders in Sweden," XII *Federal Probation* 14-18 (June 1948).

Silk, Leonard. *Sweden Plans for Better Housing*. Durham: Duke University Press (1948).

Sinding, Paul. *History of Scandinavia*. New York: 1858. The author, a Dane, was professor of history at College of the City of New York.

Skavang, N. B. "History and Development of Scandinavian Law—Some Salient Traits," 6 *Seminar* 60-71 (1948).

Spencer, R. C. "Party Government and the Swedish Riksdag," 39 *Am. Pol. Sc. Rev.* 437-58 (June 1945).

———. "Separation of Control and Lawmaking in Sweden," 55 *Pol. Sc. Q.* 217-30 (June 1940).

Stomberg, Andrew A. *A History of Sweden*. New York: Macmillan, 1931. The author was professor of Scandinavian literature at the University of Minnesota.

Svanström, Ragnar, and Palmstierna, Karl. *A Short History of Sweden*. Oxford: 1934.

"Swedish-American Double Tax Treaty," 2 *Comparative L. Ser.* 475-85 (October 1939).

The Swedish Institute. *Public Health and Medicine in Sweden*. Stockholm: Forum, 1949.

"The Tax Convention with Sweden," 18 *Taxes* 30-33 (January 1940).

Teisen, Axel. "Law-Making Bodies of Denmark, Sweden and Norway," 23 *Case and Comment*, 635 (1917).

———. "Legislation, Literature," 12 *A.B.A.J.* 268-72 (April 1926).

———. "Sweden. Legislation. Bibliography." 1 *A.B.A.J.* 160-62 (1915); 2 *A.B.A.J.* 268-75 (1916).

Thompson, Seymour. "Swedish Law Reform," 38 *Am. L. Rev.* 388-401 (1904).

Thompson, W. *The Control of Liquor in Sweden*. Berkeley: The University of California Press, 1935.

Thulstrup, Åke. "Swedish Parliamentarism," 10 *J. Comp. Leg. & Int. L.*, 3rd Ser., 314-17 (November, 1928).

Tingsten, H. *The Debate on the Foreign Policy of Sweden, 1918-1939*. Oxford University Press: 1949.

Towne, Arthur W. "Probation in Sweden," 4 *J. Crim. L.* 599-601 (November 1913).

Toyne, S. M. *The Scandinavians in History*. New York: Longmans, 1949.

Von Heidenstam, Werner. *The Swedes and their Chieftains*. New York: 1925.

Wallace, Ralph. "The True Story of Swedish Neutrality," *Readers Digest*, pp. 89-96 (September 1946).

Walton, "Scandinavian Law of Husband and Wife," 9 *J. Comp. Leg. & Int. L.* 3rd Ser., 263-64 (November 1927).

Wangson, Otto R. "Maternal and Child Welfare," 197 *The Annals* 93-103 (May 1938).

Wigforss, H. "Sweden and the Atlantic Pact," 3 *Int. Organ* 434-43 (August 1949).

Wurzel, H. "A Tax Agreement with Sweden," 17 *Taxes* 460-62, 495-97 (August 1939).

B. REFERENCES IN SWEDISH

Almquist, J. E. *Svensk juridisk litteraturhistoria.* Stockholm: 1946. The history of Swedish legal literature.

Beckman, Birger. *Svensk folkfrihet genom tiderna.* Stockholm: 1937. The freedom of the Swedish people through the ages.

Brusewitz, Axel Karl Adolf. *Studier öfver 1809 års författningskris. Den idepolitiska mottsättningen.* Uppsala: A—B. Akademiska Bokhandeln, 1917. A study of the drafting of the Swedish Constitution in 1809.

Dillén, Nils. *Foreläsningar i straffprocessrätt enligt den nya rattegangsbalken.* Stockholm: 1947. Lectures on the new Swedish criminal procedure.

Eden, N. *Den svenska rigsdagen under femhundra ar.* Stockholm: 1935. The Swedish Parliament through Five Hundred Years.

Edelöf, Per Olof. *Kompendium över civil-processen.* Uppsala: 1948.

Eriksson, Bernhard. *Folkpensionering och barnbidrag.* Stockholm: Tiden.

Fahlkrantz, G. E. *Rättfardighet i Rättskipning.* Stockholm. Righteousness in law development.

Handlingar Rörande Sveriges Politik under Andra Varldskriget. Stockholm: Norstedt, 1947-1948. These are four "white books" on Sweden's policy during World War II.

Hassler, Åke. *Den nya rattegangsbalker.* Stockholm: 1947. The new Swedish procedure.

Hedgren, Nils. *Lagarna om olycksfall i arbete.* Stockholm: Tiden. The law of workmen's compensation.

Herlitz, Nils. *Grunddragen av det svenska statsskickets historia.* Stockholm: P. A. Norstedt og söner, 1936. Outlines of History of the Swedish system of government.

Höjer, Karl J. *Samhället och barnen,* 2d ed.; Stockholm: 1946. This is a popular presentation of child welfare legislation.

Ingleson, Allan. *"Officielt." Domstolar. Departemet och verk.* Stockholm: 1947. A description of the organization and functions of the judicial and administrative agencies of Sweden.

Kallenberg. *Svenska civilprocessrät. 1917-1939.* Swedish civil procedure. The author was a professor at the University of Lund.

Karlgren, H. *Kortfattad lärobok i internationell privatratt.* Lund: 1945. A short textbook on conflict of laws.

Karlgren, I. *Skades Tåndsläran.* Lund: 1943. Law of torts.

Lagerroth, Fredrik. *"Magnus Erickssons Landslag. Et 600 Arsminne,"* 32 *Svensk Juristtidning* 641-57 (1947). An article in commemoration of the six hundredth anniversary of King Magnus' Swedish Code.

Leander, Gösta. *Handledning vid olycksfall och sjukdom.* Stockholm: Tiden. A guide to the Swedish law of workmen's compensation and health insurance.

Liljegren, Hildebrand and Silverstolpe. *Diplomatorimum Suecanum: 1826,* first and second series, 9 vols. A history of Swedish diplomacy.

Lundstedt, Vilhelm. *Grundlinjer i skadeståndsrätten,* 3 vols. Uppsala: 1935-1948. Principles of the law of torts.

———. *Kritik av straffrättens grundaskadningar.* Uppsala: 1920. A criticism of the criminal law.

Lundstedt, Vilhelm. *Obligationsbegreppet,* 2 vols. Uppsala: 1929-1930. The law of obligations.

──────. *Till fragan om rätten och samhället.* Svar till professor Thyren. Uppsala: 1921. Law and society.

Malmgren, Robert. *Sveriges grundlagar och tillhörande författninger, med forklaringor utgivna.* Stockholm: P. A. Norstedt og söner, 1947. This is the standard work on Swedish Constitutional Law.

Michanek, Ernst. *Socialboken.* Tiden: 1949. A short handbook of present-day social legislation in Sweden.

Nordisk Retsencylopaedi, Part I, "De Nordiske Retskilder" by Ebbe Hertzberg, Copenhagen, 1890. For an English translation see *A General Survey of Continental Legal History,* 533-576, 1912.

Olsson, J. *Sveriges kommunalstyrelse.* Stockholm: 1935. Swedish municipal administration.

Reuterskiold. *Foreläsninger i svensk stats—och förvaltningsrätt.* Uppsala and Stockholm: 1915. Lectures on Swedish constitutional and administrative law.

Schlyter, C. J. *Sveriges Gamla Lagar.* The old laws of Sweden.

Sköld-Vanner. *Sveriges kommunallagar.* Stockholm: Tiden. Swedish municipal law.

Strindberg, August. *Folkstaten; studier till en stundande forfättningsrevision.* Stockholm: Fram, 1910.

Sundberg, Holvar. *Kyrkorätt.* Uppsala: 1948. The law of the church.

Svensk författningssamling. The Swedish statute book. This is issued separately for each law, proclamation or order. At the end of the calendar year it is published as one volume.

Svensk Juristtidning. This is the leading Swedish law journal, is now in its 36th volume, and is published monthly.

Sveriges Förhållande till Danmark och Norge under Krigs åren. Stockholm: Norstedt. Sweden's relations with Denmark and Norway during World War II.

Sveriges Riksdag. 1931. This is a seventeen volume history of the Riksdag by 23 authors in commemoration of its 500th anniversary.

Sveriges rikes lag. The law of the Swedish kingdom. It is published annually at Stockholm.

Thulin, E. J. *Sveriges Riksdag. Sammanjämkning och gemensam votering.* Stockholm: 1935. This is a study of the adjustment of differences between the two chambers of the Swedish parliament and joint voting by the two chambers.

Thylin, Henning. *Våra skatter.* Stockholm: Tiden. Swedish taxes.

Thyren, Johan C. W. *Principerna for Strafflagsreform.* Lund: 1914. Principles which should govern a reform of the criminal code.

Tingsten, H. "Folkestyret i Norden" in *Nordisk gemenskap.* Stockholm: 1940. This is a comparative study of the Scandinavian governments.

──────. *Sveriges Riksdag. Utskottväsendet.* Stockholm: 1934. The committee system of the Riksdag.

Unden, Östen. *Om panträtt i ratligheder.* Lund: 1915. The pledging and mortgaging of interests. The author is now the Swedish foreign minister.

Uppström, Wilhelm. *Öfversigt af den svenska processens historia.* Stockholm: 1884. Translated into English in Engelmann, *A History of Continental Civil Procedure*, 203-38, 833-67 (1927).

Von Koch, Ragnar. *Samhällets barnevård*, 4th ed.; Stockholm: 1945. This is the best discussion of child welfare legislation.

C. REFERENCES IN GERMAN

Aal and Gjelsvik. *Die Norwegish-Schwedische Union, ihr Bestehen und ihr Lesung*. Breslau: 1912. The union of 1814 to 1905 between Sweden and Norway.

Aschehoug, T. H. *Das Staatsrecht der vereinigten Königreiche Schweden und Norwegen*. Freiburg: 1886. The constitutional law of the Swedish-Norwegian Union.

Fischler, "Neues Schwedisches Prozessrecht," 2 *Monatschrift für Deutsches Recht* 276 (1948). The new Swedish law of procedure.

Lundstedt, V. *Die Unwissenschaftlichkeit der Rechtswissenschaft 1932-1936*.

Maurer, Konrad von. "Zur Geschichte Schwedens und Norwegens" in Baedeker, *Schweden und Norwegen*, LI-LXXXVIII (4th ed., 1888). A concise resume of Swedish history.

Von Amira, Karl. *Altschwedishches Obligationsrecht*. The old Swedish law of obligations.

Wrede, *Das Zivilprozessrecht Schwedens und Finnlands*. 1924. The law of civil procedure of Sweden and Finland.

D. REFERENCES IN FRENCH

Fahlbech. *La Constitution Suédoise et le Parlementarisme Moderne*. The Swedish Constitution and modern parliamentarism.

Grasserie. *Les Codes Suédois de 1734*. 1895. The Swedish codes of 1734.

Hambro, Edvard. "Les Sanctions et l'Attitude Actuelle des États du Nord apres l'Assemblee de la Societe des Nations de 1938," 1 *Le Nord* 340-50 (1938). Sanctions and the attitude of the Scandinavian states after the meeting of the League of Nations in 1938.

Lundstedt, Vilhelm. *Le droit des gens, danger de mort pour les peuples*. Brussels: 1937. International law and the danger of the annihilation of the nations.

E. REFERENCES IN ITALIAN

Astuti, Guido. *Le Constituzioni della Svezia e della Norwegia*. Firenze: G. C. Sansoni, 1946. The constitutions of Sweden and Norway.

INDEX

www.ingramcontent.com/pod-product-compliance
Lightning Source LLC
Chambersburg PA
CBHW021428180326
41458CB00001B/180